EDITH SOMERVILLE

# EDITH SOMERVILLE

*A biography*

GIFFORD LEWIS

FOUR COURTS PRESS

Typeset in 10pt on 13.5pt Sabon by
Carrigboy Typesetting Services, County Cork for
FOUR COURTS PRESS LTD
7 Malpas Street, Dublin 8, Ireland
e-mail: *info@four-courts-press.ie*
and in North America for
FOUR COURTS PRESS
c/o ISBS, 920 N.E. 58th Avenue, Suite 300, Portland, OR 97213.

A catalogue record for this title is available
from the British Library.


ISBN 1–85182–863–X

Printed in Great Britain
by MPG Books, Bodmin, Cornwall.

# Contents

For
Katherine Coghill
Diana Somerville
Sylvia Gorges Townshend
Rose Marie Salter Townshend
with gratitude

# Illustrations

appearing after pages *150* and *310*

## FIGURES

*A general guide to the value of the pound from 1880 to 2005*

For 1880 to 1950 use a multiple of three.

For 1950 to 2005 use a multiple of twenty.

# Acknowledgments

Michael Adams; Bruce Arnold; Caroline Belgrave of Curtis Brown; Charles Benson, Keeper of Early Printed Books, TCD; Peter Cave Bigley; Professor Thomas Charles-Edwards; the late Canon Claude Chavasse; Judith Chavasse; the late Captain P.M.B. Chavasse; Professor John Cronin; Colonel John Darroch, Hon. Archivist, Royal Hampshire Regiment; Stephen Davies; Lady Coghill; Sir Patrick Coghill; the late Sir Patrick Coghill; the late Sir Toby Coghill; Tom Desmond, Manuscripts Reading Room, NLI; Rosemary ffolliott; Professor R.F. Foster; the late Colonel H.D. Gallwey; Faith Coghill Garson; Sir Brian Harrison; Cal Hyland; Aideen Ireland, Archivist, NAI; Noel Kissane; Brigitte Istim, Archivist, *Punch*; the late Mrs Katharine Coghill Johnston; Mary Kelly, Special Collections, QUB; the late Contessa Sylvia Lovera di Maria; Gerard Lyne, Keeper of Manuscripts, NLI; Philomena McKennedy; Bernard Meehan, Keeper of Manuscripts, TCD; Anne Oakman, QUB; Betty O'Brien; Lana O'Connor Pringle; James O'Donoghue, Lough Derg Yacht Club; Jean O'Hara, Alumni Office, TCD; Elisabeth Leedham-Green, late of Cambridge University Archives; Ian O'Neill; the late Billy O'Sullivan; the late John Peacock; Jennie Rathbun, Houghton Reading Room, Harvard College Library; Victoria Rea, Archivist, Royal Free Hampstead NHS Trust; Christopher Robson; Hilary Robinson; the late Rose Marie Salter Townshend; David Scrase, Keeper of Paintings, Drawings and Prints, Fitzwilliam Museum Cambridge. Julie Anne Stevens; P.J. Thwaites, Curator, Sandhurst Collection, RMC Sandhurst; Steven Tomlinson, Assistant Librarian, Bodleian Library, Oxford; Evan Salholm, Librarian, St Patrick's College, Drumcondra; the late Colonel and Mrs Brian Somerville; Christopher Somerville; the late Diana Somerville; the late Michael Somerville; Frances White, C.C.C. Oxford; Hardress Waller, Commodore, Lough Derg Yacht Club; Christina Weir; Kevin Yelverton; Mark Yelverton; Stratton Yelverton.

Among the above I would like to give especial thanks to Mary Kelly and Tom Desmond and their respective reprographics departments at QUB and the NLI, who, over a long period, provided enlargements of sections of manuscripts in order to provide, among others, a clear comparison of the hands of Herbert Greene, Hewitt Poole and Barry Yelverton. I am very grateful for the generosity of the Yelverton family, whose response shed much light in a dark area. Without the genealogical guidance of Rose Marie Salter Townshend the quest to identitfy the personalities and family connections of Castletownshend in the 1880s and 1890s, could never have succeeded. From 1978 I benefited greatly from her knowledge; I regret that she did not live to re-read the manuscript, that she annotated so thoroughly, in print. I am grateful also to Lady Coghill and Mrs Garson for reading various drafts of this book. It was edited by Elizabeth Mayes, and the transcriptions were checked by the author who is responsible for any errors therein. Baffled by the lack of clarity regarding the Coghill Archive, which he inherited from the late Sir Patrick, Sir Toby Coghill authorised the writing of this biography in 2000; I acknowledge with gratitude his permission to quote from the papers and works of Edith Somerville.

Quotations from the letters between Somerville and Ross in the NYPL are reproduced with the kind permission of the Henry W. and Albert A. Berg Collections, the New York Public Library, Astor, Lennox and Tilden Foundations, and the executor of the literary estate of Somerville and Ross. Letters of Bernard Shaw are quoted with the permission of The Trustees of the British Museum, The Governors and Guardians of the National Gallery of Ireland and the Royal Academy of Dramatic Art.

Material from the Coghill Archive that has been rediscovered by Lady Coghill since this biography was authorised in 2000 including the diaries of Hildegarde, Lady Coghill, financial and banking records of Somerville and Ross, copies of material subsequently given by Sir Patrick Coghill to Moira Somerville, and letters between the Coghill brothers, is quoted with the permission of the executors of the estate of Somerville and Ross.

# ABBREVIATIONS

| | |
|---|---|
| BLGI | *Burke's Landed Gentry of Ireland* |
| BTS | [Henry] Boyle Townshend Somerville |
| CFS | [Thomas] Cameron Fitzgerald Somerville |
| ECP | Ethel Coghill Penrose |
| E Œ S | Edith [Anna] Œnone Somerville |
| ES | Ethel Smyth |
| GL | [Davina] Gifford Lewis |
| HAC | [Elizabeth] Hildegarde Augusta Somerville, later Lady Coghill |
| IFAS | Irish Fine Arts Society |
| IMC | Irish Manuscripts Society |
| MPC | Marmaduke Nevill Patrick Somerville Coghill |
| QUB | Queen's University Belfast |
| TCD | Trinity College Dublin |
| VFM | Violet Florence Martin |
| WCH | West Carbery Hunt |
| WFL | Women's Franchise League |
| WSPU | Women's Social and Political Union |

# Introduction

BECAUSE ADMITTING TO an admiration for the writing of Somerville and Ross in some quarters in Ireland is like admitting to a secret vice, and because their reputation in England has gone adrift somewhere in the Irish Channel since the separation of Britain and Ireland, they have fallen into a deep-freeze between two cold shoulders. In her elegiac memoir of her family house, *Bowenscourt*, Elizabeth Bowen acknowledged the inevitability of such a violent closure of memory on the Irish 'Big House' and the class that lived in it: 'My family got their position and drew their power from a situation that shows an inherent wrong. In the grip of that situation England and Ireland turned to each other a closed, harsh, distorted face – a face that in each case their lovers would hardly know ...'[1] Though from a previous generation, Edith Somerville's memoirs of her own family home, published in *Irish Memories* and *Wheeltracks*, are as hauntingly well-written as Bowen's and as valuable on account of the coming destruction of the intricate world that revolved around that home.

Both Ireland and Britain, it seemed, were embarrassed to own Somerville and Ross; and they still inspire some of the violent feelings that Kipling arouses. In her life of Augustine Henry, Sheila Pim described any Irish person's reaction to Somerville and Ross's *Some Experiences of an Irish RM* as an unfailing index to that person's nationalism. Frozen distaste for this book, the comic tone of which was deliberately concocted and encouraged by the authors' literary agent as a money-spinner, has blighted appreciation of their more serious work. The notice given to them recently by Declan Kiberd in his *Irish Classics* may signal something of a thaw in their home country.[2] The two Irishwomen, who were cousins, wrote for their living – novels and short stories in a light tone about major social changes, sexual and political. Not only did they write about New Ireland coming into being: as New Women they wrote about a new kind of equal relationship between men and women. To Molly Keane, a devoted enthusiast of their writing, they were important as forerunners in her own field – both as writers and as great escapers from the cramping and rigid rules of life for the women of the Anglo-Irish gentry class. What Edith Somerville likened to being born 'in a cage' Molly Keane referred to as 'cruel limitations beyond our

I

sufferance today'.[3] The bars of their cages were locked in place by their parents. Molly Keane, who had suffered similarly, felt intense sympathy for Edith Somerville in her revolt against an overwhelming mother. But, in truth, during her revolt against the social conventions of her time in going abroad to study art in the 1880's, Somerville's father was a bigger obstacle.

A shared humour helped Somerville and Ross to break away into independence within their families. Their humour has two aspects intertwined: the one graphic and cartoon-like, the other subtle and verbal, giving us a kind of text in stereo. It is of the self-knowing variety that is able to laugh at itself. They laughed at the Irish and the English in themselves. Somerville was quite clearly influenced as a child by her grandfather's complete set of *Punch*, and she remained both entranced by its vigorous combination of graphic and verbal humour, and blinkered to its racism: 'a more intensive educator for the young than Mr Punch could hardly be found'.[4] Violet Martin employed a less visual and more subtle discursive humour. They enjoyed depositing an unknowing English character in the wilds of Ireland, as they did with the hapless Major Yeates, RM, of their bestselling series *Some Experiences of an Irish RM*; but it was a trick they often employed – for example, when 'The Captain' who travels to Robert Trinder deep in south-west Ireland to buy his 'grand filly' introduces himself:

> I am an Englishman. I say this without either truculence or vainglorying, rather with humility – a mere Englishman who submits his Plain Tale from the Western Hills with the conviction that the Celt who will read it will think him more mere than ever.[5]

This is the opening of 'A Grand Filly', later to appear in the collection of stories in *All on the Irish Shore* (1903). Written in 1896 and first published in the *Badminton Magazine*, it was, significantly, the story that persuaded their agent James Pinker to formulate the recipe for the RM series. It has a dig at Rudyard Kipling, who was one of their sincerest admirers, and a tone of self-deprecation that Somerville and Ross liked in their men. Their portraits of men are as interesting as their portraits of women. They were quite unconventional in their portrayal of sexual attraction and repulsion, both of which were the speciality of Somerville, who had at least two failed affairs and a faithful suitor who was sexually unappealing. A number of the novels have convincing romances, many of which run on the rocks. A persistent theme is cross-class sexual attraction, and in *The Big House of Inver* (1925) Somerville boldly wrote, after Violet Martin's death in 1915, on illegitimacy in the gentry class, a taboo subject only hinted at in their first novel *An Irish Cousin* (1889).[6] In this novel they also drew a woman suffragist, Miss Henrietta O'Neill, and what might today be described as a 'New Man' – Miss O'Neill's brother Nugent, who marries the heroine, Theo(dora). Intimate knowledge of the sympathetic type of new man came to the writers through Edith's favourite brother Boyle Somerville, and through her first cousin Egerton Coghill, who married Edith's only sister, Hildegarde.

Where they excelled as writers was in their portraiture of the half-sirs and the hunting and shooting fraternity, closely observed men in their natural sporting habitat where they themselves were becoming an endangered species. These were men who, with the help of their Army and Navy pay or pension and hardy womenfolk, were hanging on to the last of their Irish inheritance. The 'Troubles' of the 1920s saw many of them drift away to the West of England, having sold up as best they could. And by their creation of the character of Flurry Knox, Somerville and Ross gave us a man who, at the same Anglo-Irish interface, gives up Englishness in favour of Irishness. It is typical of their many-layered wordplay that they give this slippery and attractive man, detested by George Bernard Shaw, the surname of the arch-bigot, misogynist and Scottish reformer.[7] The Martins were Anglophile, but the Somervilles in Edith's generation were divided: she herself and her brothers Boyle, Cameron and Aylmer (the supposed model for Flurry), were all to show sympathy with Ireland rather than England.

By the time of Elizabeth Bowen's novel *The Last September*, set in 1922, its reader apprehends that the Big House world, beleaguered for some years, is about to be destroyed forever. Intensely sympathetic with their brothers' plight, Somerville and Ross in their novels and stories show us, live and in perfect detail, the last generation of the working system of the Big House in Ireland: it is still working in *The Real Charlotte* (1894), but dead and gone by *The Big House of Inver* (1925). Out of this sympathy with their brothers in spirit they never left home until they saw that it was ended. Violet Martin with her mother restored Ross House in County Galway and kept it running from Violet's twenty-sixth year in 1888 to her forty-fourth, when her mother died in 1906. Edith Somerville became mistress of Drishane House in County Cork for a fifty-year term of service on her mother's death in 1895. The size and quality of their output disguises the fact that, although they were indeed great escapers from their families in their literary work, their families always had first claim on their time and their achievements are all the greater for this.

For all their sympathy with certain types of men, the writers were eloquent in their revolt against a patriarchy which made use of them, but yet kept them powerless and by which they felt caged. They were both prominent in the Irish Women's Suffrage movement. Violet Martin, in particular, from a patrician Unionist background, as a child had the experience of being unwanted and not

valued as the eleventh daughter of a rather unlikeable father. One of her step-
sisters had been physically forced into a marriage that was financially
convenient to her father. To such women the Married Women's Property Act of
1882 was all-important and worth fighting for to the death; eventually Edith
Somerville was enabled to be both a property owner and a financial speculator.
Mrs Fawcett, the President of the National Union of Women's Suffrage Societies
(NUWSS), had also pursued reform after her personal experience of being
mugged: the mugger had been charged with the theft of her husband's property,
which had happened to be on her person at the time. Improvements in the legal
status of women, which took place over the half century from Somerville's birth
in 1858, were very slow in coming, and it was only when like-minded women
banded together that progress was made. When Edith Somerville was born, a
woman's only hope of promotion was to get married and have children; she and
her kind created an alternative. In the course of her long life, women suffragists,
and later suffragettes, fought long-drawn-out battles to gain the vote, education,
participation in public affairs and employment in the professions. In the year
before Edith's birth, Barbara Bodichon had founded the *Englishwoman's Journal*,
which set its sights on employment, pay and independent life for women. In the
suffrage movement from the first there were strong clusterings of sisters, mothers
and daughters, and aunts and nieces. The spearhead of the movement into
professions was formed by women medics like Dr Elizabeth Garrett Anderson,
who was the sister of Mrs Fawcett. Edith Somerville came to know and admire
many women doctors through her first cousin Violet Coghill, who qualified in
1900 at the London School of Medicine for Women.

   Some women gave up their whole lives to 'The Cause' of women's suffrage.
The ideal of comradeship was as powerful and important among these women
as among the men of the early Labour party. That political brotherhood of man
was fortified and complemented by the political sisterhood of women, a
proportion of whom we would now see as overtly lesbian (Dr Jex Blake and
Emily Faithfull, for example), and some of these were separatists. Because
lesbianism was then thought of as unnatural, this gave a great lever to the Anti-
Suffragists who assumed that the entire sisterhood of women wishing to vote
and control their own affairs was sexually unnatural. This was a misconception
that Mrs Pankhust and Mrs Fawcett were keen to dispel. To win the day, the
longest battle was not fought by separatists, but by those suffragists who fought
their corners within their families, and convinced their menfolk of their case.
Edith Somerville was not so strongly politicised as Violet Martin, but she was
among the first successful professional women journalists and novelists. She
belonged to the first generation of women who, having lived and worked
together, were able to make wills whereby they left their property to their

friends, putting them before any family ties. Though seemingly very alike, at the end Violet Martin put Edith Somerville before her family, but for Edith Somerville her family came first above all.

Violet Martin died before Edith Somerville, leaving all her copyrights, papers and her possessions to her writing partner.[8] She died in debt, unable to take in that she could no longer afford to give to charities; Edith Somerville paid off her debts. There seems little doubt that, of the two, Violet Martin was the more thoroughgoing feminist. Somerville's will, and her disposition of her capital before her death, shows that she remained in thrall to the menfolk of her family, and did everything in her power to preserve the male entail and the inheritance of Drishane lands for it. For all her apparent 'newness' and independence as a woman, at the close of her life Edith Somerville reverted to primitive conservative type and in an emergency delivered up her capital to her family.[9] This was a surprising volte-face in one whom we might have expected to fund by bequest a scholarship for a woman student of the Cork School of Art to study in Paris.

When she died in 1949, Edith Somerville had lived long enough to see young women become blasé about the suffrage battles of the past, and pass on to the question of sexual rather than political liberation. In her time she had seen the greatest suffrage leaders in action, and with avid interest had followed the dealings of the Liberal party with them. The writing partnership of Somerville and Ross flourished between 1889 and 1915. The year 1889 saw the establishment of both the Anti-Suffrage League and the Women's Franchise League, to which the writers belonged.[10] As professional women paying taxes and involved in local public affairs, they spent long years in watching and waiting for change. The General Election of 1880 had returned a majority of Liberal members who were in favour of women's suffrage; unfortunately, as Gladstone himself was an anti-suffragist there was no mention of women in the 1884 Reform Bill. But in 1883 a Corrupt Practices Bill had cleaned up many of the dirtier corners of electioneering, and for the first time women were allowed to participate in canvassing, as Somerville and Ross did. From this small foothold gained by voluntary women workers, the thin end of a very big wedge was driven. Edith Somerville acted as a voluntary political aide to her much-loved cousin 'Gendie' Townshend, Mrs Miller Mundy of The Castle, Castletownshend, who was deep in the affairs of the Primrose League, the Conservative women's union, whose 'Ladies' Grand Council' was founded in 1884.

Before the turn of the century, two Suffrage Bills had been presented; one came before Parliament in 1885 and was passed on its second reading; the other was defeated in 1892. The lack of progress was particularly frustrating for the British societies when women's suffrage was established in New Zealand in

1893 and in Southern Australia in 1894. A huge reorganisation of suffrage societies in Britain led to the foundation of the National Union of Women's Suffrage Societies in 1897, with the revered Mrs Fawcett as President. But, maddened with frustration at the lack of progress, militants under the Pankhursts with their Women's Social and Political Union [WSPU], founded in 1903, began a physical force campaign. It was not until Somerville and Ross attended the 1908 Hyde Park Suffrage Rally and heard Christabel Pankhurst and Mrs Pethick-Lawrence speak that they were converted to active participation in the movement.[11] They became President and Vice-President of the Cork branch of the Irish Women's Franchise League in 1909. They were suffragists and never suffragettes.

Physically their relationship was quite semi-detached, while both remained embedded in their huge families and fixated on their respective houses; a time and motion study of their working life together makes this surprisingly clear. Their lives were defined as daughters and sisters, and only very briefly, it seems, did either of them venture into the role of lovers of men. From 1888 until 1906 their career in letters owed much to the excellence of the Irish postal service, as it was not until 1906, when Martin's mother died, that both nomadic writers theoretically worked from the same address. Violet Martin spent a great deal of time living with her married sisters, particularly during the harvesting season, when her writing partner was otherwise occupied with the running of the farm she shared for almost four decades with her sister Hildegarde. Violet Martin was four years younger than Edith Somerville and four years older than Hildegarde, and with both she had a most harmonious relationship; they called her 'the third sister'.[12] They belonged to a society of like-minded independent women. When they travelled, it was usually in a group drawn from this society. Edith Somerville kept up her connections with her fellow painting students to the end of her life. Both writers were remarkably sociable and could talk to anyone anywhere on the social scale, if they so wished. Their family backgrounds, crucial to their development, could not have been more different, and between them they show the extraordinary variations that could be contained within that rag-bag term 'Anglo-Irish gentry' – a group that contained a large proportion of families that were in origin neither born English or born gentlemen.

Fuelled by heavy drinking, the violence of male behaviour in this society was shocking. The fate of Major Apollo Riggs (in *In Mr Knox's Country*), the over-flirtatious house-guest who is murdered and his body dropped down a well, which was then closed up, is not a fantastic invention. He had cast too loving an eye on his married hostess, and offended his host. When Edith was in her mid-teens, the young and widowed Jane de Burgh Townshend of the Castle was courted by two men, Arthur Cave of Schull and a rich incomer. In the woods, still called Cave's Wood in memory, the two men went shooting together. The incomer shot Arthur Cave in the head with his double-barrelled shotgun; Arthur took the first barrel of shot in his unprotected face, but such were his sportsman's quick reactions that he took the second barrel in his hands. His assailant fled abroad. Arthur Cave was not dead, but blinded. Jane married him and became the progenitrix of the Cave-Townshend family. Perhaps it was awareness of this potentially violent male nature that caused the women to communicate in such different ways between themselves and with their menfolk. We can observe this dualism in all three of those women whose lives were so bound up together, the Somerville sisters and Violet Martin, and at the end of Edith's life we see how this feminine yielding and indulgent behaviour towards favoured males allows her heir and godson to place his own comfortable misinterpretation on her words and actions. For such women, freely expressed desires, thoughts and feelings were mostly restricted to their own sex until they married. Spiritualism, much resorted to by the women of Castletownshend, offered a communicant the means both of experiencing power and fortifying the female position. Professor Lewis has given a convincing analysis, regarding female mediumship and ancestor cults, which relates to their peculiar social position and difficulties. He writes of women's 'possession cults' seeing them as 'thinly disguised protest movements directed against the dominant sex. They thus play a significant part in the sex-war in traditional societies where women lack more obvious and direct means of forwarding their aims. To a considerable extent they protect women from the exactions of men.'[13] Though Edith Somerville and her sister were open to spiritualism and used it, Violet Martin bolted from it in fear. She was unable to merge it with her Christian beliefs, as they did.

A full understanding of the relationship between the writers has been prevented by some unfortunate accidents in the dispersal and destruction of manuscripts, so that information on the first third of Somerville's life has been extremely scarce, and undue importance has been given to the views of her younger generation of relatives who have in some cases unwittingly misled biographical research.[14] In the closing decades of her life, some of them experienced her only as a grumpy old battleaxe and there has been difficulty in taking an unbiased view based on records from her early life. This can now be remedied. Though stronger physically, Somerville was not as independent a character as Martin Ross, for whom the more child-like and dependent Somerville eventually felt a reverence bordering on adulation. Before she met Violet Martin, we find Somerville dependent upon earlier idols, her grandfather, her Uncle Kendal and her cousin Constance Bushe. Her many relationships with young men do not seem serious in comparison, though it is clear from newly discovered evidence that one of them gave her a crippling wound. She came to associate sexual passion with burning and pain. In the romanticised *Irish Memories* of 1917 she claimed that when she met Violet Martin, who was to become her working partner in 1888, Violet was 'about twenty' and she herself four years older. In fact Violet Martin was twenty-four and Edith nearer thirty than twenty. What she contrives to paint out of existence is a period of intensive emotional and sexual turmoil in her life between 1878 and 1885. Her determination to hide this was quite extreme. Like many who have written about Somerville and Ross, Lillian Faderman, who devotes five pages to the 'romantic friendship', uses *Irish Memories* as if it were factual, taking from it those wrong ages at their meeting, wrongly assuming from it that 'after their third meeting they decided to collaborate as authors', and placing the men in their lives far out in the margins.[15] Rendering those men invisible and ineffectual is the natural outcome of the focus of Faderman's important work; but it is possible to make an examination of their lives in relation to men by using their papers with a more open mind, and by being aware that Somerville imported fiction into *Irish Memories*.

The more self-contained Martin was brought up among many sisters, but Edith grew up among many brothers, for whom her mother showed an open preference. Like her brothers, she trained herself to be strong, to hide pain and emotion. Her mother was outspokenly critical of her eldest daughter. From her adolescence Edith suffered from a crippling lack of confidence, well hidden behind bonhomie and a mocking, humorous attitude, that lead her to rely heavily on close companionship for assurance and comfort, and to become to her siblings a kind of honorary brother. In this, her experience was similar to hundreds of women who entered the women's suffrage movement with feelings of triumphant emancipation from what they saw as a top-heavy and false relationship between men and women, who were both trapped in the workings of the marriage market.

In her letters Edith Somerville presents many conflicting aspects, depending on her correspondent, so that the reader becomes baffled by a series of false fronts; but the series of letters to her sister and her brother Boyle are among the most intimate, and may be taken for solid ground. She was a snob, given to supercilious categorising from physical appearance, but how far this was an affected front we might guess from the vital importance of genealogical status in her society and from her knowledge that the Somerville family tree was fake. Her servants loved her and served her faithfully, appreciating her kindness and gentleness, but others could encounter only a prickly and defensive front. It is possible that she was, as her niece 'K' Coghill insisted, a shy person in brave disguise. With her brothers, she was brash but deferred to them. In the 1880s

she and Martin both referred to the charming and attractive Somerville
coachman as 'Tom' in their letters to one another, but when she referred to Tom
in letters to her brothers he was 'Connell'.

The surviving papers from the first third of her life, mislaid for some time,
show that Edith Somerville had personal experience of the marriage market, as
is, and has always been, clearly suggested by the romantic passages of Somerville
and Ross novels, which she alone wrote. She had two extreme emotional crises
in her life, one in 1880 and the other in 1915 at the death of her writing
partner. She pulled herself out of the first by working as an artist, with the help
of her cousin Egerton Coghill; and, unable to believe that she could have a
successful writing career on her own, she escaped from her second crisis by
communicating with her writing partner in spirit form. She incorporated into
the books written after Martin Ross's death material received by 'automatic'
trance writing (an inspirational source also used by Yeats);[16] she did use forces
that were within herself, but through lack of confidence she affected to believe
that they came from without. She was skilled at the manipulation of personalities,
facts and appearances, and could mimic not only voices, but also handwritings. It
is difficult to avoid the conclusion that, in continuing to write as the representative of two writers in one person, she carried this off as a knowing ventriloquist
in order to achieve her aim successfully. Her life passed in a series of holding
manoeuvres – losing ground as a member of the Anglo-Irish gentry class as it
folded, yet gaining ground as a woman in the first wave of professional
independents. She had two watchwords: 'Needs must' and 'If it'll do, it'll do'.
Out of what appears on the surface to have been a ramshackle career, dodging
from one expediency to the next, pinched and restricted all along by family
demands, there developed the superlative writing style of a string of evergreen
Irish classics.

Somerville and Ross have been enthroned in the collective subconscious as
stay-at-home versions of the Ladies of Llangollen, an identification that would
have astonished them, as we can instantly understand from what they wrote
about the Ladies themselves. Somerville's own nephews and nieces served
during the Second World War, and some of them discovered during it the
capacity for sexual relations between those of the same sex. This capacity
would seem to exist in far larger numbers of people than the statistical
proportions of homosexual to heterosexual would suggest.[17] In the course of
the Second World War, homosexuality was present in prisoner-of-war camps
and among WAAFs and WRAACs with a degree of openness and acceptance
that was lost after the war. Edith Somerville's niece and god-daughter Diana
Somerville found her partner Nancy Eastwood during the War and remained
with her for the rest of her life.

It is now recognised that sexual love may exist between pairs of men and pairs of women as profound and lasting as that of heterosexuals, but if we read the understanding of later years back into mid-to-late nineteenth-century Ireland we are in danger of wilfully misreading facts and giving them a meaning that did not exist earlier. Diana Somerville, for example, understood her aunt's experience in pairing up with another women to have been the same as her own, and was quite unable to accept that photographs of Edith Somerville showing her in ball gowns, in the nude, and in acting make-up, were of her godmother, though their provenance was unimpeachable. Some of them were signed on the reverse by their subject. Strenuous eagerness to see Somerville and Ross as 'in denial' of a sexual love for one another has blinded some researchers to the sexual presence of men in their lives; and to their evident understanding that their own relationship was familial, as of close sisters. Such a blinkered view of Somerville's papers was taken by Louise Collis (also a lesbian), who was the researcher for her father's biography of Somerville and Ross of 1968.[18] This biography was not well received by the family. 'I don't know who this book is about, but it's not about anybody *I* ever met,' was the reaction of Edith's niece Katharine. Many other dismayed nephews and nieces, of every sexual persuasion, denied the accuracy of the reductive portrait of Edith given by Collis when his book was published; and the 1968 Sotheby's sale catalogue of Somerville and Ross manuscripts in particular pointed out that a key letter between Ethel Smyth and Somerville had been mistranscribed by Collis to give a meaning that it did not have in fact.

As we shall see, the decade 1878–88 in Somerville's diaries contains, unnoticed by the Collises, frequent references to flirtations and to two more serious relationships. Rose Marie Salter Townshend and Sylvia Townshend Lovera both knew an Edith Somerville who delighted in men, and Canon Claude Chavasse gave the opinion, in writing, that 'when she was quite old she seemed to be in love with our huntsman'.[19] The surviving early papers suggest a vigorous sexual interest in men; but due to her grandfather's spoiling Edith seems to have come very late to a realisation of what was permitted and required of her sexually by her class, so that at first she formed unsuitable attachments to males who were 'out of bounds', a theme that pervades all of her fiction. Her loss of confidence may date from the collision with her parents, at the age of nineteen, which convinced her that she could not do as she pleased.

Women's suffrage campaigners of the late nineteenth and early twentieth centuries, like Somerville and Ross, were fighting for the rights of women to be educated, to take part in public life, to administer their own finances and to own property in their own names. They lived their lives in affirmation of the capabilities of women in professions, capabilities other than those of the traditional sexual role in childbearing, and did not want to live lives that were dominated by their sexuality. They turned their energies outward from the nursery and took 'another way'. Although they certainly had deep affections for their comrades, which they may have valued more than transient sexual passions, they were not fighting for the rights of women to have sex with one another, as most did not understand that this was possible. In their generation and in their society the problem of sex was embodied in the male, and sex was naturally penetrative and reproductive. Somerville and Ross were able to discuss together the men with whom they were involved, as soulmates can and do. Soulmates are not infrequently comic duos; it is only relatively recently that women have gone public and taken the stage as comedians and worked in pairs. Walters and Wood, French and Saunders show the same kind of high-speed mutual intuition that the writers must have had, and their case is a helpful parallel. Laughter can hold at bay the problematic – sex, defeat, decay.

Their laughter and the laughter that they bring to their readers was not meant to be cruel, as Katherine Tynan came to realise; she and they and Lady Gregory all acknowledged the power of innocent laughter, and that it may teach and heal.[20] It is the laughter of neighbourly banter over the Anglo-Irish fence on which they were sitting. When *Some Experiences of an Irish RM* was released in 1899, Charles Graves in his *Spectator* review placed them among the elect as great humorists, among whom, at that time, there were few women: 'if there were many women writers like Miss Somerville and Miss Martin the discussion whether their sex is deficient in the sense of humour would be not merely otiose but impertinent'.[21]

From quite different backgrounds, Ross from a literary family of the patrician Anglo-Irish type and Somerville from a more hearty one of the Army and Navy hunting and shooting type, they might stand as representatives from Shaw's Heartbreak House and Horseback Hall.[22] In Heartbreak House 'the pleasures of music, art, literature, and the theatre had supplanted hunting, shooting, fishing, flirting, eating and drinking', but on the other hand there was Horseback Hall, 'a prison for horses with an annexe for the ladies and gentleman who rode them, hunted them, talked about them, and gave nine tenths of their time to them, dividing the other tenth between charity, churchgoing (as a substitute for religion) and conservative electioneering (as a substitute for politics). It is true that the two establishments got mixed at the edges ...' By a happy chance Somerville and Ross came together on such an overlap of edges.

As a working relationship it functioned most successfully in the decade 1888–98. When Violet Martin became a semi-invalid after a hunting fall in 1898, the strain of regular writing was too much for her; in the following years we find Somerville set up as a landlady, renting out property, and as a farmer, in partnership with her remarkable sister, from 1908 to 1946. She still wrote in partnership with Ross, but on a much reduced basis. The Somerville sisters were members of an important group of reforming landlords who were practical farmers, under the leadership of Sir Horace Plunkett and his Irish Agricultural Organisation Society. Its motto, 'Ní neart go cur le chéile', meant 'No strength without combination' and applied equally to co-operation between women themselves, as in the United Irishwomen, and between classes and religions. Only those landlords who had practical working knowledge of farming and stockbreeding were to survive with house and lands, and Drishane with its lands was saved by Edith's dodge of becoming an agricultural tenant of her brother, the heir Cameron.

Her long, ninety-one-year life is seldom examined in its thirds. The first third, for which the records have been missing for some time, formed her, and it was a time of emotional and sexual turmoil. The central third came under the influence of her friendship with Violet Martin, with whom she shared her feelings about what had happened to her before their meeting. The last third, after Violet's death, was given to her home and family, as a result of which Drishane survived. To be dazzled by Violet Martin, and place Edith Somerville in her shadow, is understandable, but shortsighted.

She was a product, and not a unique one, of the peculiar circumstances of her class and sex in Ireland in the second half of the nineteenth century. In essence she was a lady farmer, who, like the Toler Aylwards, the Gore Booths and the Gubbins sisters, had learned to trade in livestock and manage farms in order that their houses and lands should survive. Her subsidiary activities, painting, illustrating and writing, were certainly remunerative 'irons in the fire' as she called them, but for the last third of her life might be described as recreational. Somerville and Ross as a literary firm existed most productively from 1888 to 1898. Violet Martin's invalidism and decline to her death in 1915 prevented the firm from developing the power that had been shown in *The Real Charlotte*, which shows a knowledge of intense sexual passions. In their twenty-eight-year association they wrote only five novels. For pecuniary reasons tied to the RM series, of which there were two further volumes in 1908 and 1915, they were forced to 'pot-boil' during the periods when Martin could not write. Their literary association was, by this accident, effectively aborted. Edith became a *rentier* and farmer to make a sufficient income. Despite all the outward signs of emancipation and professionalism, both women stayed in their family 'cage' by choice, for as long as possible. Ethel Smyth's sour reaction, when she realised that Edith could never be her lesbian lover, is in its way apt: Edith was, she expostulated, 'just a stone in a tribal necklace'. Perhaps we might reach an understanding of why that position might be a satisfying and even desirable state of being to a woman placed as Edith Somerville was.

CHAPTER I

# Family backgrounds

... Nonsense about being 'English'! I don't mind if you say 'British'
if you like, but the only pallid trickle of *English* blood comes from
one marriage, when Hester Coghill married Colonel Tobias Cramer
*a pure-blooded Hun* – if not Jew! You might just as well say you
were German! ... My family has eaten Irish food and shared Irish
life for nearly three hundred years, and if that doesn't make me Irish
I might as well say I was Scotch, or Norman, or Pre-Diluvian.

Edith Somerville arguing with her brother Jack in 1923[1]

E ACH ANGLO-IRISH FAMILY with gentry pretensions had its own origin
myth, though their origins were extremely diverse, and undesirable parts
fell away, or were pushed, to be lost to memory. We find elements of hopeful
fiction in *Burke's Landed Gentry of Ireland*. The Somervilles in Ireland were
self-made men who became landholders through marrying into the gentry.
Snobbery caused Edith Somerville to hide her lowly ancestors and to invent
replacements of higher status. Not only did she publish a fictitious family tree,
but she painted two fictitious family portraits: one of her legitimate ancestor
William Somerville and one of a Reverend Thomas, whom she affected to
believe came of a line of clergyman. She distressed the paint surfaces, framed
them in antique frames, and pretended that she had bought them at auction.
Tremendously pleased with the success of her work, she wrote to her friend the
painter Alice Kinkead describing the paintings, but warned: 'They are a secret
so don't mention them to my little brothers.'[2]

The letter to her brother above shows the order in which Edith Somerville
thought of herself – Irish, British, Scottish, Norman. She came of a class that
was Anglophile, but the section of the combined Somerville, Coghill and
Townshend families that is of interest and relevance in any study of Edith
Somerville is the section that defined itself as Irish, and acknowledged Ireland's
status as a nation among the other nations that made up the United Kingdom.
In these families there was a fashion for 'Twinning', which meant having a

13

soulmate, both of one's own sex and the opposite. The four men who represent
the 'nationalist' group (Boyle Somerville, his Twin Bertie Windle, Nevill Coghill
and his Twin Claude Chavasse) discarded their family religious beliefs. Boyle
was Edith's favourite brother, and Bertie was her male 'Twin', born in the same
week as her. They also studied the history of Ireland and were aware of the
wealth of Irish literary and legal sources before the English language came into
being; and they were proud of their connection by marriage with the Cameron
family, who had been Jacobites, and eventually became commanding officers of
the Cameron Highlanders. Bertie Windle converted to Catholicism, and Boyle,
Nevill and Claude became devout Anglo-Catholics.

Except on the subject of the suffrage for women, Miss 'Facing-both-ways'
Edith Somerville had a chameleon-like tendency to sympathise with a range of
political points of view, without divulging her own in public, but she and her
brother Boyle were privately at one in their discussions of the future of Ireland
as a country and as a nation. Claude Chavasse's memoir of Nevill written for
*To Nevill Coghill from Friends*[3] shows us that within the strictly Unionist
families of Castletownshend the grouping of Twins that leaned to revolutionary
ideas saw itself as 'Nationalist' with a capital N: Boyle, he says, 'spent many
years charting the reefs and islands of the Pacific and around Australia, a skill
which he was later to employ in exact records of the many pre-historic
monuments of West Cork. He was a devoted Anglo-Catholic and an ardent
Irish Nationalist ...'

Like the Irish, the Anglo-Irish gentry were passionate about good breeding,
of animals and humans. Whatever their origins, having arrived in its pages,
*Burke's Landed Gentry of Ireland* was their bloodstock book and a necessity to
them like the Bible or Bradshaw. It was what the more earthy of them called it,
a 'stud book'. Claude Chavasse demonstrates this point by reminding readers
of his memoir of Nevill of the strong strain of Irish blood in his descent:
'Students of heredity may be interested to know that both his parents, who were
first cousins, inherited the blood of the Doyles of County Carlow, which is said
to be what cattle dealers call a "good strain".'[4] As many of the families that had
come to Ireland from Britain instantly went up a social class on account of the
native Irish being assumed to be 'beneath' them, it is forgotten that they were
often from British yeoman stock themselves. It is one of the distinguishing
features of Somerville and Ross that they apprehend the class range from high
to low in both English and Irish society: they understood that the Irish reverence
for genealogy and for bloodline status was of a different order from the English
reverence for power and wealth. In Ireland, high status was given to learned
families, who preserved knowledge of the law, history and the creative arts:
social standing was not inevitably linked to material possessions. This

understanding of Ireland's love of family and relationship came to the writers from their great grandparents' generation, for their families were descended from an able class of legal administrators and Irish parliamentary orators who had fought against the Union with all their might – Grattan, Plunket, and Charles Kendal Bushe, ancestor of both Somerville and Ross. They fought for Catholic Emancipation and for the continuance of the independent parliament for Ireland. In the Union debate of 1800, Castlereagh, then chief secretary for Ireland, had so bribed wavering Irish members with titles and money that he had bought himself a majority of 42 in a House of 234. Bushe was nicknamed 'The Incorruptible' from having refused a massive bribe from Castlereagh. Only 96 Irish members faithfully supported Grattan. Descendants of this group of Grattan supporters who felt themselves to be Irish rather than English would be naturally disposed to a form of Irish home government. Lecky quotes Bushe speaking against the Union in his *Leaders of Public Opinion in Ireland*:

> For centuries the British Parliament and nation kept you down, shackled your commerce and paralysed your exertions, despised your character and ridiculed your pretensions to any privileges, commercial or constitutional. She has never conceded a point to you which she could not avoid, nor granted a favour that was not reluctantly distilled. They have all been wrung from her like drops of blood. and you are not in possession of a single blessing (except those which you derived from God) that has not been either purchased or extorted by the virtue of your own Parliament from the illiberality of England.[5]

Bushe's wife, Nancy Crampton, wrote to her son Charles, Rector of Castlehaven, in about 1843, after her husband's death, to complain of the state of the country, and the ruin caused by the recent Poor Law legislation: 'Useless however to complain. England has the *might* that supersedes the right, and we are punished now for our own folly in consenting to the *Union*. Just what your Father predicted – "when Ireland gives up the *rights* she has, what right has she then to complain?" How true this little squib of the poor dear Chief. Happy for him he did not live to see the ruin he predicted!'[6] Squib is a word that did not change in its political meaning, Edith Somerville used it in 1932 to describe her own writings in support of the Irish Free State President, William Cosgrave.[7]

In the confusing welter of family connections that surrounds Somerville and Ross, their distinguished ancestor Charles Kendal Bushe (1767–1843), who linked them, stands out like a beacon. Educated at Trinity College Dublin, he became a barrister with an extensive practice. He was MP for Callan in the Irish Parliament by 1797. His career was not blighted by the prominent part he played in opposing the Union: he was Solicitor General for Ireland 1805–22 and Chief Justice of Ireland 1822–41. He was a star to breed from. James Martin of Ross in County Galway married his granddaughter Anna Selina Fox; James Martin's sister Marian Martin married his fourth son Arthur; Admiral Sir Josiah Coghill, 3rd bart., married his eldest daughter Anna Maria; Admiral Josiah's daughter Emmeline Coghill married his second son, the Reverend Charles Bushe; and her brother Sir Joscelyn Coghill, 4th bart., married his granddaughter Katherine.[8]

The Bushes were Welsh, reputedly descended from a fabled prince, Cadwgan Fawr, who had battled against the Normans. They settled in Glamorgan, and from here they drifted via Somerset to Ireland. Originally named in Welsh Daullwyn (two bushes) the family translated and simplified its name into Bushe and, moving across the Bristol Channel to fresh fields, served for some generations with distinction as churchmen in Somerset. The Bushes came into Ireland with the Army of the Commonwealth,[9] Colonel John Bushe being rewarded by Cromwell with lands in County Kilkenny on which were built the houses of Kilmurry, Dangan and Kilfane. The Reverend Thomas Bushe, Charles Kendal's father, married Catherine Doyle of Carlow. Her native Irish family, of marked literary and artistic ability, turned Protestant and become distinguished in military service, and was renowned for its powers of speech and the speed of its wit.[10] Arthur Conan Doyle belonged to the branch that had remained Catholic.

Charles Kendal Bushe's political association with Grattan and Plunket was further bonded by marriage: his cousin Gervaise Bushe married Grattan's sister, his daughter married Plunket's son. Bushe's letters to his wife, used as a source by Edith Somerville when she wrote *An Incorruptible Irishman* (1932),[11] show a keen awareness of that remnant of a class of Irish Catholic gentry which had all but disappeared by the time that Trollope came to write his first novel *The Macdermotts of Ballycloran* (1847) and *The Kellys and the O'Kellys* (1848) out of his experiences working as an administrator in the postal service of western Ireland. Travelling on the legal circuit, Charles Kendal Bushe attended the great fair days and saints' patterns of Catholic society. He went to see the barefooted pilgrims making the penitential ascent of Croagh Patrick; out of tradition the pilgrims all wore ragged and common clothing, but, writing to his wife Nancy Crampton on 10 August 1810, Bushe noticed that 'those of the upper Class are discovered by the delicacy of their hands and feet'.[12]

Bushe and his descendants knew that they had displaced native families with a passion for genealogy far surpassing their own. In many cases the new arrivals had no idea of their own immediate ancestry, or did not care to make it public. In Castletownshend, the Anglo-Irish knew perfectly well that the local families of O'Driscoll, O'Mahony and O'Donovan (some of whom who now constituted their tenantry or were servants in their houses) had been displaced and dispossessed by force. Castlehaven Castle, into which the Reverend Thomas Somerville moved as Rector of Castlehaven, had been the seat of the O'Driscolls; Raheen Castle, on the opposite side of the estuary, had been an O'Donovan stronghold. At the time of the Troubles of the 1920s, the leading local O'Driscoll politely alluded to this when he desired to buy back ancestral lands from Hildegarde Lady Coghill.[13] The most knowledgeable genealogist of these local families was the lawyer Eoin O'Mahony (the 'Pope'), who was held in respect by Edith Somerville despite the age gap between them. In his review of Rosemary ffolliott's invaluable book on Cork families (*The Pooles of Mayfield*, 1958), we hear a disdainful tone of voice as he lays bare the distinction between the breeding of the native Irish aristocracy and those who displaced them.

> When Conchubhar O Mathghamhna, or O'Mahony, of Castle Mahon, Bandon, was killed in the Desmond Rising at the age of twenty three, twelve thousand acres of his lands were granted to Phane Becher, the son of a London haberdasher, at an annual rent of less than three half pence per acre. The townland of Knockanemeela now Mayfield, four miles west of the present town of Bandon, was given by Becher to the Adderleys who sold it in 1628 to Thomas Poole, late fuller of Charfield, Gloucestershire. Nine generations of Gaelic speaking Pooles farmed this land until the house was burned to the ground in June 1921.[14]

Generally, those who came to Ireland as Protestants after the Reformation were much less likely to be assimilated than those who came earlier, like the Martins – families that were called 'Old English' and who shared Catholicism with their tenantry. In Castletownshend Church the list of rectors from 1403 shows the critical break between Irish and Cromwellian, when 'O'Driscoll, O'Callaghane, O'Driscoll, Cormac' gives way to 'Basse, Pratt, Stukely'. In his review Eoin O'Mahony was keen to notice the existence of landlords that had been close to their tenantry, using Irish (as the Pooles and Edith's grandfather and his brother did) in their relations with them. He also observes an Anglo-Irish gentry tendency to marry into the upper layers of Irish families who had become Protestant, like the O'Donovan branch at Lissard, and he gives the specific example of John Townsend's marriage to Lady Catherine Barry, 'who in turn was descended from MacCarthy Reagh and O'Driscoll ... the native stock always outbreeds and prevails over foreign blood whether animal or human'.

To any of the refined and educated ladies of the women's movement, who were trying to shift the emphasis from a woman's body to her mind and soul, all this insistence on fleshly breeding would have been distressingly farmyard in tone, but to Somerville and Ross it was meat and drink, the motive force of their plots. Inheritance dominates them, just as in reality it utterly dominated their own domestic lives – particularly in *Some Experiences of an Irish RM*, where Flurry Knox does not know if he will inherit from his grandmother, and in some sections of *The Real Charlotte*, where Charlotte Mullen forges her way over the earlier legal dispositions of Julia Duffy; the reader needs a strong head and concentration to pick a sure route through blood relations and mere hangers-on. Charlotte Mullen and Julia Duffy both aggrandise their breeding. They are both daughters of agents to landed estates, both from native Irish families that had been Catholic and had converted to Protestantism and become anglicised through an urge to better themselves under new masters. In the 1890s, when *The Real Charlotte* was published, some landed families began to rediscover or re-invent their lost Irishness in the Celtic Revival. The Gaelic League had been founded in 1893, and spread rapidly. There were landlords who spoke only Irish and French, and wore saffron kilts. Each family made its own adjustments; unlike the Martins with their Norman Irish descents, the Somervilles were apparently quite obscure. It was only by attaching themselves by marriage first to the Townshends and later to the Coghills that they and their ancestry were drawn into the light of west Cork gentry genealogy and into the margins of *Burke's Peerage, Knightage and Baronage*.

Boyle Somerville and his elder sister shared a passion for Somerville genealogy. They also shared an awkward secret.[15] They were descended from a Reverend William Somerville who, during the time of the Covenanters, had been an Episcopalian minister at Leswalt in County Galloway in Scotland before moving at speed as a refugee from his battlefield of a parish in 1690 to Lough-in-Island in County Down. Accompanying him was his son-in-law William Cameron, Minister of Inch, and ancestor of a distinguished line of soldiers who did not enter themselves in *Burke's Landed Gentry of Ireland*. The Somervilles and Camerons had appeared in Ireland not as colonisers or rapacious Cromwellian soldiery, but had fled there as to a sanctuary. From 1894, when Boyle employed an Edinburgh genealogist, the Reverend Walter Macleod, to search the Edinburgh records, they must have known that they were descended through the Reverend William from Edinburgh Burgess skinners.[16] They preferred not to believe this, and Edith, aided and abetted by Boyle, constructed a more desirable tree, roping in Sir Patrick Agnew of Lochnaw and a Royalist clergyman in order to produce a family descent more comfortable to live with, and to offer up to a society that was hypersensitive to class.[17]

Walter Macleod was perfectly sound in his research, and his papers show that the Irish Somervilles' ancestor, the Reverend William Somerville, a one-off clerical sport in a line of Burgess skinners, had married exactly within his own class by marrying Agnes Agnew, the daughter of Andrew Agnew, Burgess of Stranraer. In Castletownshend, the parentage of Agnes Agnew was a heated subject of debate, but nothing could move Edith Somerville from the conviction that Agnes was of aristocratic breeding and the daughter of a baronet. Consequently, the sections of *Somerville Family Records* concerning the history of the family in the Scottish Lowlands are a fabrication by a very good fiction writer.

Walter Macleod sent Boyle Somerville facsimile copies of the Edinburgh Guild Register, which showed that their rightful but unwanted ancestor, the rich Burgess skinner John Somerville, Deacon of the Skinners of the Burgh of Edinburgh, had been the curator of the natural son of William the Master of Somervell (heir to Lord Somerville), who was dead *c*.1605. The Edinburgh Council Records note a dispute over the payment of maintenance (twelve bolls of oatmeal yearly out of the mill of Carnwath) for the deceased William's illegitimate children. William's bastard son James claimed unpaid maintenance from his mother Jean, who had married again, to the hatmaker David Lindsay. These facsimile records can only ever have been read for annotation by Edith or Boyle, or possibly, much later, by Moira Somerville, who succeeded Edith as mistress of Drishane; the references to the natural children James and Helen Somerville, 'bairns procreate betwixt the deceased William Master of Somerville … and Jean Somerville', have pencilled exclamation marks beside them. The services of heirs in chancery show that of the two male children that the Reverend William brought with him to Ireland, when he fled from the armed Covenanting mob who were coming to expel him from his Galloway manse, the younger one, Thomas, remained in Ireland eventually to become Rector of Castlehaven parish, and the other, William, returned to Edinburgh and his hereditary family occupation as a Burgess skinner. On 18 March 1725 it was recorded: 'William Somerville skinner in Edinburgh is served heir general to his father the late Mr William Somerville at Leswalt.'

Edith and Boyle could not bring themselves to believe all this; but, ironically, these Burgess skinners were of the Somerville tower house of Plean in Stirlingshire and had a perfectly clear and legitimate descent from the Lords Somerville of Couthalley Castle, Carnwath. Neither Boyle nor Edith read up enough Scottish domestic history to realise that great Scottish families quite often diversified into trade in their younger branches. These would blithely return to well-bred type should the topmost branches fall. What we learn from this concealed episode is that, despite the traditional family bonhomie with all classes, Edith in particular among the Somerville siblings was privately quite perverted by snobbery; this in part was the attraction of the Martin family, for whatever had befallen them in the way of bankruptcy, their bloodlines were a thing to revere.[18]

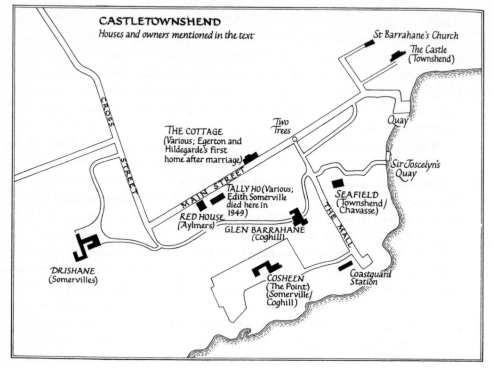

**CASTLETOWNSHEND**
*Houses and owners mentioned in the text*

St Barrahane's Church

The Castle
(Townshend)

CROSS STREET

Two
Trees

Quay

THE COTTAGE
(Various; Egerton and
Hildegarde's first
home after marriage)

Sir Joscelyn's
Quay

MAIN STREET

TALLY HO (Various;
Edith Somerville
died here in
1949)

SEAFIELD
(Townshend/
Chavasse)

RED HOUSE
(Aylmers)

THE MALL

GLEN BARRAHANE
(Coghill)

DRISHANE
(Somervilles)

COSHEEN
(The Point)
(Somerville/
Coghill)

Coastguard
Station

1  A map of Castletownshend, known as CT, with its principal houses.

When Tom, the Reverend Thomas Somerville's son, lost an eye in an accident at Trinity College Dublin, he gave up the option of following his father into the Church and became a merchant. In doing this, he was simply reverting to family type; he had links with his Uncle William in Edinburgh, the Burgess skinner, and certainly knew and could have made use of Scottish family connections in trade. Having written the Somerville connection with trade out of their history, Edith and Boyle affected to believe that 'Tom the Merchant', the only member of the Castletownshend branch of the Somervilles to become seriously wealthy, had acted out of character in going into trade. Records published in Rosemary ffolliott's *The Pooles of Mayfield* show how sensitive Cork high society was about families in trade; clearly, 'Tom the Merchant' was not accepted as being out of the right drawer, even if it was full of money.[19]

Castletownshend today still bears traces of Tom the Merchant's reign. He had built up a small fleet that traded with the West Indies and Newfoundland in sugar, salted provisions, rum and wine. The round tower on Horse Island was built by him as a harbour mark; his, too, is the huge range of the storehouse that fronts the quay at the bottom of the precipitous village hill; and he built Drishane, adding to a pre-existing Townshend farm building a weather-slated Georgian block facing straight down the village street that visibly linked his house with his place of work and storehouse.[20] From Drishane or the Mall House, with his telescope he could keep his eye on his shipping business. As the Somervilles married into the Anglo-Irish gentry and left trade connections behind them, the entrance to Drishane was moved a few hundred yards up Cross Street, and the old horribly public gate-opening that looked directly into the Drishane main door was blocked up.

In 1789 Tom the Merchant's daughter Judith Barbara married the heir to the Fleming estate, Becher Fleming. She is one of the earliest Irish Somerville women of whom we know more than their marriage date and the birthdates of their children, which *Burke's* records rather than their own date of birth. She was very characterful, and tales of her doings were told and retold – such as that she lived to be over ninety without ever lying on a sofa or sitting in an easy chair, and that in the week before she died she danced a jig. She bore twenty-three children to Becher Fleming, and showed Somerville female characteristics – toughness, fecundity, physical vigour into old age, and another not quite so desirable feature, said to have been passed through Judith to her eldest son Lionel: 'the ferocious temper of the old Somervilles'. An explosive temper was inherited by Edith Somerville and by her brothers Boyle and Aylmer. She had to curb hers while her brothers did not.[21] Rosemary ffolliott remarks on Judith and Becher's marriage: 'Her father's prosperity being derived from "trade" gave rise to certain unpleasantness in the county. Tom's friends and relations, jealous of his money making enterprises, looked down their aristocratic noses at this low fellow who dared to do better than they. Not that any of them felt any scruple in accepting the handsome portions he gave his daughters at marriage.' Judith's sisters married into the Reeves, Becher, Hungerford and Townsend families. Even after their father's death in 1793, 'the sneers went on'. Then they, too, felt compelled to do what Edith and Boyle were later to do, and concocted a family tree 'setting forth their gentle blood'.

The Somervilles spread downwards into that class called half-sirs. Edith's grandfather's brother had qualified as a doctor and practised as a GP in Union Hall. His family lived in Park Cottage there and was known to the Castle-townshend (hereafter CT) family as the 'Porks', as their refined pronunciation of English rendered 'Park' as 'Pork'. Doctor Jim's skill as a doctor and his use of Irish in his widespread practice made him popular high and low. Through him and his family, Edith met Somerville cousins that were less than half-sirs. She wrote to her brother Cameron of meeting one who was so confused by being introduced to Edith, the famed (though long retired) MFH, that he curtseyed as he shook hands with her.[22] She described him as 'good hearted' but nevertheless 'a scrog'. The provision of handsome dowries to Tom the Merchant's daughters seems to have emptied the family coffers, and in the succeeding generation the bankruptcy of a friend for whom he had stood surety meant that Thomas Somerville the third crashed down to rock bottom, so that Drishane was stripped of valuables by bailiffs. The family edged back to financial stability by judicious marriages to wealthy women.

In landholding terms, compared with the Martins the Somervilles were very small beer, and the intimate knowledge of the workings of a down-at-heel Anglo-Irish family that had merged at its edges into the host class of native Irish, that is shown in the creation of the Knox family of the RM series, must have its origin in Cork rather than in Galway. Outside the walls of Galway city, the county was more remote and suffered less from the forced Protestant settlements of Cork. Flurry Knox, whose male ancestor had married into the MacCarthys who persisted in using Florence as a male name, is introduced by the RM, Major Yeates, in 'Great Uncle McCarthy':

> He was a fair, spare young man who looked like a stable boy among gentlemen and a gentleman among stableboys. He belonged to a clan that cropped up in every grade of society in the county, from Sir Valentine Knox of Castle Knox down to the auctioneer Knox, who bore the attractive title of Larry the Liar. So far as I could judge, Florence MacCarthy of that ilk occupied a shifting position about midway in the tribe. I had met him at dinner at Sir Valentine's, I had heard of him at an illicit auction, held by Larry the Liar, of brandy stolen from a wreck. They were 'Black Protestants' all of them, in virtue of their descent from a godly soldier of Cromwell, and all were prepared at any moment of the day or night to sell a horse.[23]

Edith Somerville's bourgeois family background on her father's side gave rise to a self-conscious awareness of rank, bloodlines and breeding. She was very conscious of the distinction of her grandmother's Townshend family, the largest landholders in the area, with whom the Somerville men had intermarried twice, but it was through her mother's family the Coghills that she acquired the link to Lord Chief Justice Charles Kendal Bushe that made her a second cousin of Violet Martin. This family had a most exotic ancestry. Originally they were a Yorkshire family who had gone in for the law, but Sir John Coghill had moved to Ireland on becoming Master in Chancery in Ireland. He married into the Cramer family of Ballyfoile, County Kilkenny, but his son Marmaduke, a very plain-looking man who became Chancellor of the Exchequer and MP for the University of Dublin, died unmarried in 1738. He had lived first at Belvedere House in Drumcondra, but then had built the splendid Drumcondra House, where he lived with his sister Mary, also plain and unmarried.[24]

Reputedly, they did not marry on account of their ugliness. The Coghill estates eventually devolved upon John Cramer, the grandson of Marmaduke's sister Hester, who married Oliver Cramer of Ballyfoile in 1700. The Cramers were in origin happy-go-lucky middle-Europeans, and handsome. Tobias Cramer was a soldier of fortune from Lower Germany who had come to Ireland, and his grandson Tobias, who served in Ireland under Cromwell, had been granted the estate of Ballyfoile by the Protector. His great-great-grandson John Cramer assumed the name of Coghill and became the 1st baronet of the line in 1778. The Cramers brought with them good looks and a pleasant, sociable temperament. The 3rd baronet, Sir Josiah, Vice-Admiral RN, who had served under Nelson at the battle of the Nile, fathered the ten daughters who were to be the mother and aunts of Edith Somerville, and whose marriages linked her to a host of powerful families and provided her with a large support group of male cousins. As they dominated her childhood and youth, a list of these daughters and their marriages is helpful.

The Admiral married first Sophia Dodson, who bore him three daughters:

1. Caroline, who died unmarried in 1885, aged 81.

2. Emmeline, Aunt Emmie, who married in 1839, the Reverend Charles Bushe, son of 'The Chief', and Rector of Castlehaven. Godmother of Edith Somerville, her first child was Constance, who was herself only eighteen when she became Edith's minder and mentor. One of her sons was Seymour Bushe, the distinguished lawyer and 'Saymore Bosh' of Joyce's *Ulysses*.

3. Josephine, who married in 1844 George de Morgan, and became the mother of Joscelyn and Sydney de Morgan, who were frequent visitors to CT. Joscelyn had hoped to marry Ethel Coghill, Edith's female 'Twin' who married instead James Penrose.

Sophia Dodson died in 1817 and the Admiral married a second time in 1819. Confusingly, he married Anna Maria, the eldest daughter of 'The Chief' Charles Kendal Bushe. In other words he married the sister of his daughter's husband Charles Bushe, the Rector of Castehaven. Another road began to lead the Coghills to Castletownshend. By this marriage the Admiral had daughters:

4. Rosanna, who married the wealthy John Aylmer of Walworth Castle. She died with him and her eldest son in the railway accident at Abergele on 20 August 1868. Her two remaining sons Percy and Eddie became wards of her brother Sir Joscelyn, and were very close friends and financial supporters of their cousin Edith in her struggle to become independent.

5. Aunt Sydney married in 1854 the Reverend Samuel Windle. Their son Bertie, who was to be Edith's male 'Twin', converted to Catholicism and became a distinguished academic and President of University College Cork.

6. Aunt Alice married in 1850 the Reverend George Ray, and lived in Yorkshire.

7. Aunt Florence never married and lived with her brother Joscelyn until her death.

8. Aunt Georgina married in 1860 the Reverend William Chavasse. Their son Henry ('Hal') Chavasse was eventually to settle in CT in Seafield with his wife Isobel Fleming: they were the parents of Claude, Kendal and Paul.

9. Adelaide Coghill married in 1857 Thomas Henry Somerville of Drishane and became the mother of Edith in 1858. Cameron (1860), Joscelyn (who died young), Boyle (1863), Aylmer (1865), Hildegarde (1867), Jack (1872), and Hugh (1873) followed her.

10. Aunt Sylvia married Thomas Greene, Secretary of the General Synod of the Church of Ireland, and became the mother of Conyngham (Frank) and Herbert. The Greene house at 49 St Stephen's Green was the Dublin base for the Coghill sisters when they were in the city. Herbert, a classical scholar and Dean of Magdalen College, Oxford, was to remain Edith's faithful suitor for many years, and never fell out of love with her.

    To Admiral Coghill's great relief, two sons were achieved among this flock of daughters – Joscelyn (b.1826) and Kendal (b.1832). As brothers they were very close, Joscelyn having saved Kendal from drowning, when he fell through ice, in 1841.[25] Joscelyn was a painter and a pioneer in photography and in psychical research, a subject that interested the entire family. He was a Vice President of the Society for Psychical Research, a yachtsman, an actor and singer. Kendal was a colonel of the 19th Hussars, and a veteran of the Indian Mutiny. Edith's fixation on fair-haired horsemen with golden moustaches and bright blue eyes seems to begin with him; ever generous to his nephews and nieces, his army pay gave him a certain independence from Coghill financial problems. Generous dowries to eight of the Admiral's ten daughters had drained the family resources. The last of the Coghill family money was to disappear in a French shares scheme concocted by a swindler called Bourget. A later letter reveals the sum lost to have been £40,000.

    Ethel Coghill, Edith's soulmate and female Twin, described Sir Joscelyn her father in her memoir, explaining a great deal about the nature of the unusual family that came to Castletownshend and changed it:

He was a real Peter Pan – a boy who never grew up in many ways, full of enthusiasms of all kinds, whether it were yachting, music, painting, writing, acting, photography, spiritualism, speculation – all had their turn and he flung himself into each and all with a fervour that lasted at fever heat for a time. At one time after my mother's death [1881], he and his brother Kendal took a house in London for some months. To it they brought a considerable amount of the family plate and a presentation set of gold belonging to my Uncle, as well as my grandfather's medals and other valuable things. They left the house for some weeks in charge of two maids, who promptly brought in their young men, cleared the house of nearly all the valuables and had the cheek to order a sumptuous luncheon in my father's name and a landau in which they went either to Ascot or the Derby, I forget which. My father was in Ireland when the telegram came to inform him of what had happened. I did not see him for some time afterwards. By then, he had come to look on the thing as a huge joke. Nothing was ever recovered, but he felt as though he had been part of a Sherlock Holmes mystery, and this compensated him for everything he had lost.[26]

There was in the Coghills a strain of careless good nature and flippancy quite different from the social tone of the cluster of families into which Violet Martin was born. The more conservative Martins did not cast their net so wide for partners, marrying instead within a restricted range of 'Old English' and Irish families. The Martins claimed to have been in Galway city since the time of Richard de Clare, 'Strongbow', the Norman invader.[27] They were one of the fourteen families known as 'The Tribes of Galway'. During the reign of Queen Elizabeth, Robert Martin, High Sheriff and Mayor of Galway, deciding to move out to the west of the city, began an appropriation of land starting with Ross, near Oughterard, twelve miles away. He moved on to Dangan, Birch Hall and Ballinahinch. The Ballinahinch estate itself extended to almost 200,000 acres. The Martins lost this land at the time of the Famine. The last of the family to live there was Mary Martin, 'The Princess of Connemara'. Her grandfather had been the celebrated 'Humanity Dick' Martin, the founder of the League for the Prevention of Cruelty to Animals. After the Famine, the Ballinahinch family left Ireland, resettled and flourished in Canada. Archer Martin of this Canadian branch visited Violet Martin and her mother at Ross, by then the main seat of the family, in 1887/8 when he was writing his history of the family, and he met Violet again on another Irish tour in 1912.

Until the mid-eighteenth century, the Martin family was Royalist and Roman Catholic, but Violet Martin's great grandfather fell in love with

Elizabeth O'Hara, a Protestant, and in order to marry her, he became a Protestant himself. His six children were brought up as Protestants, but on his deathbed he reverted to Catholicism. His eldest son Robert married a Roman Catholic – Mary Ann Blakeney of Bally Ellen, County Carlow. So it came about that the rites of both churches were celebrated in Ross. The eldest boy was Violet Martin's father, James, who was born in 1804. He took a law degree at Trinity College Dublin, but before he was twenty-one had decided to marry. He returned to Ross with his wife, who bore him four daughters, dying at the birth of the fourth. It was not until he was forty that he married again, to a characterful twenty-two-year-old woman who, among other things, was well educated in Latin – Anna Selina Fox, the daughter of Charles Fox of New Park, County Longford, and his wife Katherine, daughter of Chief Justice Charles Kendal Bushe. Charles Fox had died young, and Katherine had returned to the home of her father, 'The Chief', at Kilmurry House in County Kilkenny. The broad-mindedness of the Chief Justice extended to the education of women. Anna Selina Fox, his granddaughter, was given a Latin tutor as well as a music tutor. She was a daring rider, and her daughter wrote of her: 'In her outdoor life she was what, in those decorous days, was called a "Tomboy", and the physical courage of her youth remained her distinguishing characteristic through life.'[28]

Anna Selina Fox married James Martin in 1844; after the birth of yet another daughter, the years of the Famine began. In 1846, to great rejoicing, despite the deteriorating conditions for the Ross people, Robert Martin was born – the first son in the family for forty-two years. During the famine Marian Martin (James's sister), James himself and Anna Selina ran a relief kitchen at the Ross gates. Aunt Marian also ran a school for the estate children, where she caught Famine fever, but survived. After Thomas Martin of Ballinahinch caught the fever and died, his family evaded the Famine and the wreckage it brought down by moving to Canada. Determined to hold on to Ross, James Martin was unable to survive financially without taking some form of paid employment. He became a leader writer for the London press. He was a stern and authoritarian man; in his daughter Violet's opinion, all of his eldest son Robert's fun and vivacity came to him from his mother.[29]

Robert Martin was sixteen when his youngest sister Violet was born in 1862. Their sister Geraldine wrote about her birth: 'She was the eleventh daughter that had been born to the house, and she received a cold welcome. "I am glad the Misthress is well," said old Thady Connor, the steward; "but I am sorry for the other news." I think my father's feelings were the same … [she was] a dear little child but quite unnoticed in the nursery. Charlie [the baby born before Violet] was the child brought forward. I think the unnoticed childhood had its effect. She lived her own life apart. Then came the reign of the governesses and their delight in her'.[30] Violet was, if unnoticed, a child of a controlling disposition, and a tomboy herself. On a visit to another Big House she found a rusty pair of spurs in an old stables. Riding astride and using the spurs, as well as wielding an ashplant, she enjoyed subduing an intractable mule. Guests' horses, safely stabled at Ross, were taken out and put through their paces while their owners were indoors with her mother. This was an extreme of tomboyism not reached by Edith. She was never allowed to ride out without a man of the family or a groom in attendance, and remained horrified by women riding astride to the end of her life.

The firm of Somerville and Ross was to be a compound of two distinct halves. Compared to Ross, nothing could have been more different than Somerville's start in the world at Drishane. Edith was the first and adored child, spoiled by her grandparents, with the special attention of her godmother's daughter Constance Bushe; Martin was the last of a long line of unwanted daughters growing up quite a solitary little prodigy. She did always have the consolation of a special closeness with the sister next to her in age, who married Cuthbert Dawson and who is the 'Edith' of her diaries where her writing partner features generally throughout as E.Œ.S. The personal connection between Somerville and Ross has a tone of reverence and formality that only flooded over into overt emotion when Somerville came to memorialise Ross after her death in 1915.

These very different families, Somervilles, Coghills and Martins, were bound together as a group in Irish society by descent from Charles Kendal Bushe. When Ethel Coghill invented the word 'Buddh' for his descendants in 1885, and compiled a Buddh Dictionary of their slang words with her Twin Edith, it seems as though Buddh and Bushe were interchangeable. His descendants had very strong, substantial legs. There was a family joke that 'no-one could doubt the solidity of their understandings' – 'understandings' being a euphemism for legs. In time, this contracted into 'Bushe leg' or 'Buddh leg' as a term of approval for the characteristic inheritance of athletic limbs. Through his good influence in this group of families, women had come to have an easy equality with their menfolk, riding and hunting with them, and, most importantly, they talked in mixed society. Delight in remarkable flights of speech is evident from the diaries of both authors at an early age. Before they met one another, they had thought deeply about the best way of recording such flights in writing. Edith referred to the peculiar words that the Buddhs invented as the 'froth on the surface of some hundred years of the conversation of a clan of inventive, violent, Anglo-Irish people, who, generation after generation, found themselves faced with situations in which the English language failed to provide sufficient intensity, and they either snatched at alternatives from other tongues or invented them.'[31]

All Buddhs loved telling stories using Irish accents. It seems schizophrenic, but Canon Claude Chavasse, who was brought up in Castletownshend at the beginning of the last century, insisted, 'we had two voices, one English and one Irish.'[32] When Edith herself was recorded by the BBC reading *The Dane's Breechin* in 1927, only Percy Aylmer in Wales, Ethel Coghill in England and her dogs in Castletownshend realised that it was her voice doing all the characters when the broadcast was transmitted.[33] Of all things, when a stage version of the RM was being scripted, Ethel and Edith fought over taking and playing the part that they both saw as the plum – Mrs Cadogan, the Shreelane cook. There was no dispute as to who was to play Flurry Knox: this was tailor-made for Joe Coghill, Ethel's brother, a brilliant mimic and quick-change artist. In their separate families, Somerville and Ross both grew up with a collector's ear for speech, and in the same way that folk music collectors of the time were taking down Irish tunes in musical notation, they began recording whole tracts of conversation winding a way to a punchline. Their admiration for native speech in English was clearly expressed in their essay 'The Anglo-Irish Language' of 1910:

> Ireland has two languages; one of them is her own by birthright; the second of them is believed to be English, which is a fallacy; it is a fabric built by Irish architects out of English bricks, quite unlike anything of English construction. The Anglo-Irish dialect is a passably good name for it, even though it implies an unseemly equality between artist and material, but it is something more than a dialect, more than an affair of pidgin English, bad spelling, provincialisms, and preposterous grammar; it is a tongue, pliant and subtle, expressing with every breath the mind of its makers.[34]

Edith looked upon the arrival of Anglo-Irish families in Castletownshend as successive waves of invasion. For a century or so, the Townshends adjusted to the Somervilles and had the place to themselves. Edith's description of a cartoon that was an imaginary portrayal of the Coghill invasion of CT by Constance Bushe, illustrates her innocent use of the word 'aboriginal' in complete ignorance of the later meaning with which it was to become laden by the politically correct. The description seems also to hint that she had some notion that her father's family had 'Red' blood running in its veins rather than the desired 'Blue'. It was a picture showing 'the supposed indignation of the Aboriginal Red men, i.e., my grandfather Somerville and his household, at the apostasy of my father, a Prince of the (Red) Blood Royal, in departing from the family habit of marrying a Townshend, and in allying himself with a Paleface. In that picture the Red men and women are armed with clubs, the Palefaces with croquet mallets. It was with these they entered in and possessed the land ... The Paleface females surge in vast crinolines; the young Red man is encircled by them ... my grandfather swings a tomahawk, and is faced by my Uncle, Sir Joscelyn Coghill, leader of the second wave of invasion, with a photographic camera (the first ever seen in West Carbery) and a tripod.'[35]

Edith grew up among companions who were mostly male; as a result she and Ethel and Violet Coghill did everything adventurous that the boys did out of pride in being their equals. Edith followed where her intrepid cousin Percy Aylmer led. To ride as well as their boy cousins and brothers did, if not better, was a matter of prime importance. They broke out of the traditionally restricted female domestic sphere, by showing themselves to be fearless riders; they were allowed to hunt, thus displaying their skill as riders to the outside world. We often find in their papers the old-fashioned distinction between 'him outside' and 'her inside'. The horse carried them into the 'outside' world, away from domesticity. From their grandfather's relaxed attitude in allowing them to ride, hunt and frequent the farmyard developed the Somerville sisters' career in stockbreeding, farming, dairying and horse-coping. The fact that the CT children, unknown to their elders, had such adventurous childhoods may have had something to do with the strict division between adult and child: children were kept out of adult doings, and not expected to intrude upon adult conversations or social events in any way. Some of the Buddh Dictionary family words for children and related matters are quite antagonistic to them. After describing some of the more horrifying secret scrapes that she passed through with Percy Aylmer in her 1923 memoir *Wheeltracks*, Edith concluded: 'What our fathers knew we neither knew nor cared. Nor did they. Anyhow, it had been early borne in upon us that fathers didn't matter.'[36]

Apart from the fact that Edith and Violet were the daughters of matriarchies, what is most important to remember about both writers is that neither the Somervilles nor the Martins were Cromwellian in origin, and that their families' connections with England had been brief; England was used only as a staging post for the Somervilles on their journey to Lowland Scotland, and for the Martins on their journey to the West of Ireland. They were unembarrassed by their families' presence in Ireland. Their long roots in Scotland and Ireland account for the independence of their vision as writers, so unusual as to surprise and delight their English readers. They came from an *ancien régime* accustomed to a Union of Kingdoms; their families possessed family trees whose roots curled round kings of Scotland, Ireland and Wales. It was common for the snobbish to flaunt the fact that their families had been 'Royalist'. In the mêlée of the United Kingdom this gave them quite a few kingly options; in this diversity of royal lines and in the inventiveness of genealogists, like Edith herself, in supplying much-desired family trees, there was much material for writers of comedy.

The Celtic Revival of the late nineteenth century began a social re-fragmentation in the British Isles. What began in the arts coalesced in due course with the movement for political independence. Some families who had dumped their Celtic origins and become anglicised began to be proud of them. Here was a heated subject of discussion. Had England absorbed the Celtic Fringe, or had the Fringe absorbed the English? Were not the English themselves a Fringe that had taken many wives and layers of administrators from those peoples whose lands they 'shared'? The Bushes' career showed how the Welsh passed smoothly and silently in translation into the English administration. Their great ancestor Cadwgan Fawr is also the ancestor of the Earls of Cadogan, whose descendant, George Henry, became Lord Lieutenant of Ireland (1895–1902). The English pronunciation of Cadogan preserves its original Welsh inflections. Somerville and Ross give his family name to the RM's Shreelane cook, with the note that 'her name was made locally pronounceable as Cay-de-gawn'.[37]

Hybridity was hardly a thing peculiar to the Anglo-Irish. The Tudors shifted from Wales to stand as kings of England, just as the Stewarts shifted later from Scotland, causing an influx of Welsh and Scots into the court and administration who became anglicised, speedily casting off their Celtic languages or provincial accents. The most powerful of all families in the Elizabethan administration was the Cecils, Earls of Salisbury. Their Welsh name, Seissyll, retains only in its English pronunciation, Sissil, the whispering hint of their Glamorganshire origin, shared with the Bushes. The family became completely anglicised. This also happened in Irish families anxious to get on under English rule. A family called Nihill, a name that means nothing to most of us, became distinguished in the British colonial legal system; shorn of its 'O' their anglicised name conceals its origin – O'Neill.[38] In the nineteenth century Ireland's native population that had become anglicised was attempting to throw off its Englishness along with its landlords. Those landlord families who were most anglicised stood the least chance of surviving. The present-day Townshends of the Castle at Castletownshend, under the direction of Rose Marie Townshend, who married William Salter, are a model of survival by adaptation. What we read about in Somerville and Ross is a society trying to make sense of its hybridity. Their favourite literary figure was a trope – 'a figure in which a word, either from need or for purpose of embellishment, is shifted from its proper meaning to one similar but not proper to it'. If it were possible to live a life as a trope, then Edith Somerville lived it. In her lifetime the two burning political questions of Irish independence and women's suffrage were resolved; she seems to have held conflicting views on them. But her experience of life fell out as it did as a result of two of her brothers' failure to get to grips with problems that they left to her. She lived life as a stand-in for the heir's wife and as home farm manager, a capable woman in a place left vacant by her brothers Cameron and Aylmer.

It was her eldest brother Cameron's duty to marry, produce an heir, and keep up Drishane. He did none of these things, and at the bankrupt end was in the position of having to sell his family lands. He and Edith's brothers Boyle, Hugh and Jack went into the pay of the armed services; and Aylmer married an English heiress. It was the stay-at-home Aylmer who had a talent for farming and for hunting a pack of hounds; but after a year as manager of the Drishane Home Farm he grew tired of the struggle and had left it to his sisters by 1910. A keen golfer, he moved to England, where eventually he became manager of a golf course. Except in private letters to her sister Hildegarde, Edith never criticised her brothers Cameron and Aylmer for the choices they made. But in a letter to Ethel Smyth in July 1922 during that time of architectural cleansing when Big Houses were being burned to the ground in 'The Troubles', she acknowledges the numbers of Irish landlords who have fled to England, casting off their troubles with no thought of return. Such a landlord, she wrote, desired nothing but to forget his loss – 'to forget also his own people and his father's house in the thrills of a daily potter round the Suburban golf-course'.[39] But for both Somerville sisters, who never threw off their love of home, leaving Ireland was unimaginable.

# CHAPTER 2

# *Family predicaments*

Ireland was at that time completely under crown rule and Anglo-Irishmen were proportionately far more heavily represented in the Army and Navy than were their English counterparts. The reason was largely financial since it was cheaper to live in the services if you enjoyed serving overseas. Anglo-Irish gentlemen had neither coal, railways nor industrial sites to exploit and their rentals had begun their catastrophic fall. There were a few Castle appointments and they sometimes took in each other's washing by becoming land agents – targets at times for their employers' dissatisfied tenants – but, if they were to keep up the smallest place for three generations, the only possible hope was to marry money ...

Nora Robertson, *Crowned Harp* (1960), chapter II

COASTAL WEST CORK DOES not have large areas of rich farming land, so that rents for its small tenant farms had never been high. Many acres were administered by the land agents of absentee landlords, a profession entered by some of those cousins of Edith Somerville's, like Claude Coghill, who were younger sons. Self-made men could make themselves a place here, settling on the fringes of the vast landholdings of grand families, like the Townshends of Castletownshend. Formerly a Townshend holding, Drishane House in Castletownshend, east of the market town of Skibbereen, was built and had lands put together around it by Thomas Somerville, son of the Rector of Castletownshend, and a successful West Indies merchant who flourished in the second half of the eighteenth century. His descendants were to live precariously off this creation of 'Tom the Merchant'; after a bankruptcy in the following generation, the family, for example, could not afford an expensive commission to a cavalry regiment for his grandson Thomas Henry, born in 1824. His military career began as an Ensign in the 6th Foot, Warwickshire Regiment, then he rose to the rank of major with the 68th Durham Light Infantry, and by his early thirties was a lieutenant colonel in the 3rd Buffs. On leave in

Castletownshend, he met Adelaide, the sister of the wealthy amateur artist and photographer Sir Joscelyn Coghill, who had moved to the village with his family, and whose brother Kendal served in the top-notch Hussars. Henry and Adelaide married on 27 June 1857. Adelaide was the tenth daughter of Admiral Sir Josiah Coghill and his second wife Anna Maria, who was the daughter of Charles Kendal Bushe, Lord Chief Justice of Ireland. After her wedding she travelled by troopship with her new husband to Corfu, where he was then stationed, and where on 2 May 1858 their first child was born and christened Edith Anna Œnone. The baby thrived, completely untroubled by the racket of living in a barracks; she loved the military band of the Buffs, and became infatuated with the sound of its bass drum, so that even as a baby she was conditioned to noise, hurly burly and soldiers.

At the age of ten months, baby, father and mother returned to Drishane. While Colonel Somerville went to India to serve with the Buffs, Adelaide and her baby settled in with her in-laws. Young Mrs Somerville was to hold the subsidiary position of mistress-in-waiting for almost quarter of a century. Grandfather Somerville, the 'Big Master', ruled Drishane and its lands until 1882, by which time his favourite and first grandchild Edith was twenty-four years old. The relationship between these two was intense: it had the effect of distancing Edith from her parents and of making her father, in particular, pale into insignificance beside her grandfather. From him and his Townshend wife Edith acquired an inflated estimation of her importance and powers which was to be rudely destroyed.

In Edith Somerville's late teenage years she was made aware of the fact that her parents were facing financial ruin and that any escape from it, and survival for Drishane, depended in the long run on her brothers doing well. The last available family money was spent on giving them enough education to get into Woolwich or the Royal Naval Academy. Family connections were traded on shamelessly in order to put them there, for they had a highly placed 'Good Fairy' both in the Army, General Cameron, and in the Navy, Admiral North. Edith's eldest brother was christened Cameron to keep alive the link with that family. Legacies from relatives were of the utmost importance, and handouts from wealthier connections like godparents among the Townshends or Coghills were gratefully received; foreign travel and art classes in London came to Edith as a bonus when she tagged along with the Coghill family party. Sheer chance favoured the brothers. Rich elderly relatives could make or break the fortunes of the young. The £500 that would have come to Edith and her father, had not their cousin Emily Herbert persuaded Aunt Fanny Somerville, Mrs Herbert, to change her will in Emily's favour, was lost to them at a time when it could have established Edith in Paris and made her as independent as her cousin Rose

Barton[1] or her friend Alice Kinkead.[2] Without her small inheritance, Edith was limited to short terms of study in Paris, and tied to her home; so it was by this mischance that she came to know her cousin Violet Martin, and took up with her a career in writing rather than her preferred option of painting and illustration. The realisation that her brothers would always come first with her parents, and that she must make her own way, was extremely painful to her after being spoiled as chief grandchild by grandfather Somerville and her Townshend grandmother. Her parents did not allow her the leeway that her grandparents did.

From 1858 to 1873, Adelaide Somerville was preoccupied by the sequence of births of her eight children. When Edith was four in 1862, Adelaide gave birth to her third child Joscelyn, a sickly boy who lived to be only two years old. Edith and Cameron, the heir born in 1860, were very much in the company of their Somerville grandparents, living with them in Drishane, and with their Coghill aunts and uncles. Uncle Kendal was to remain Edith's model of the ideal man, and, with one dark-haired exception, she was to fall for horsemen just like him – athletic, blue-eyed men with fair hair and moustaches. It is not surprising that with her two elder children Adelaide was later to have a more difficult relationship than she had with those born after Joscelyn, and the two elder children, unlike the rest of their siblings, did not marry. Edith's first memories were of the Rectory at Castlehaven, where she often stayed with her godmother, her mother's sister Aunt Emmie Coghill, who was married to Charles Bushe, the Rector. Their second daughter, Constance Theodora Antoinette Bushe, was Edith's first mentor as a painter, and Edith remembered Constance from the time she was about four years old, when Adelaide was absorbed in the care of the ailing baby Joscelyn: 'She took me into her care; I slept in her room, and I remember awakening one night with a light in my eyes, and finding that she was making a drawing of me; the only time, I expect, when she could trust to the model to keep still.' Emulating Constance, Edith began to draw at an early age. In the Coghill Archive is an album of drawings dated at Drishane, 12 November 1869.[3] It was given to her as a gift by her mother. For an eleven-year-old girl they show a remarkable talent for caricature, and a taste for punning wordplay. A drawing of two tinies scrapping in the sea is captioned 'Sea urchins'; a study of a very plain woman is captioned 'A sweet poetess'; 'A yacht scene' shows a woman throwing up over the gunwales. Acknowledging a formative influence on her when she was very young, Edith referred to Constance as 'my patron saint in art'.[4]

For Constance, Edith felt an adulation all her life. When she became an invalid and moved to London, her home was Edith's favourite port of call when in the city: 'Her sofa in the flat in Wynnstay Gardens became a central point, a place of counsel and refreshment, a haven of peace, for everyone who knew her.

She was ageless and timeless, as one believes angels are, a spirit so rare and enchanting that it seemed as if Death could never touch her, because she had already put off all that was not purely spiritual.' Constance belonged to the earliest generation of organised women suffragists whose cause was like a religion to them; they had the same high-minded independence of character as the women of the Non-Conformist churches. The Anglo-Irish poet Eva Gore Booth, born in 1870, who shared the same temper of mind as Constance, actually hitched together Non-Conformist Christianity and women's suffrage in her work as a suffrage organiser. She wanted to draw women away from a simply animal destiny, and to make them understand that there were dictates of their individual mind and spirit to be listened to, as well as dictates of the body.[5] A strong tendency to idealise certain adult women, free spirits all, was carried through this first part of Edith's young life where the biographer has to rely heavily on telegraphic diary entries and intermittent sidelights from her memoirs.

With her gift for friendship, Constance Bushe may well have influenced the development of Edith's own easy way with people, men and women of any class. When Violet Martin first came to CT in 1886, she found it very difficult to make any special kind of connection with Edith owing to the numbers of her admirers, and what Edith says of Constance might with some justice have been said of Edith twenty years later: 'One laughed at her for her troops of worshippers; one grumbled at their innumerableness, their eternal presence, their immutable resolve to sit at her feet, and stay there. But that, possibly, was because one was of the company, and two of a trade don't agree – let alone twenty ...'[6]

In those huge families with an embarrassment of daughters, like the Coghills, who made a joke of Admiral Coghill's exclamation on the birth of yet another daughter, 'More Rubbish!', we cannot be surprised that one or two of the girls grew up self-consciously aware that they only reduced the family fortunes, by having to be dowried, in contrast to their brothers, who added to it when they married.[7] Neither should we be surprised when some of these daughters worked out that financial independence through their own efforts would benefit both the family and their own self-esteem. As an illustrator Edith Somerville was earning money from card manufacturers like Raphael Tuck at the age of sixteen, and later turned down nothing that might earn money, from modelling to accepting a West Cork agency for the sale of bicycles.

A recently re-surfaced memoir by Ethel Coghill Penrose, Edith Somerville's first cousin, and elect female 'Twin', has at last provided intimate details of a period in her life that has remained almost a blank.[8] Because of the peculiar situation of the class into which she was born, Edith Somerville experienced an unusual degree of sexual liberation in her early years. Less sure of their social and financial position, young males in her class were becoming less confident and overbearing, and females were allowed both to express themselves force-fully, and to have a certain amount of power in the management of estates on behalf of their absent brothers. Within the group of cousins with whom she grew up Edith had a male 'Twin' as well as a female; he was not an outgoing man of action like Percy Aylmer, but a bookish and thoughtful boy. He had difficulties in his relationship with his father, who was a vicar, and gave up God for a while before becoming a Catholic, explaining that he wanted a God 'who was a friend and not a policeman'.[9] He was another first cousin: Bertie Windle, son of her Coghill Aunt Sydney. Bertie's male 'Twin' was Edith's favourite brother Boyle.

Supportive comrades were a necessity of life to the children of such large families. Mothers seemed to try to control their large broods as a flock, and showed favour to the male children. Edith's mother Adelaide Somerville was quite overpowering. Her firstborn son, Cameron Somerville, born after Edith, was unable as a child to find the strength of character and independence that marked his elder sister after she had come through her early twenties. He remained mentally overpowered by his mother, and later by his elder sister who, at his request, succeeded her as mistress of Drishane in 1895. Though a charm-ing and humorous man, his nature was indecisive, ineffectual and secretive. The accident of their births, Edith coming before Cameron and outshining him, of her taking the place of adored first grandchild with her grandparents who lived in Drishane, were for Cameron cramping disabilities from which he was never able to escape. Cameron had taken refuge in the world of music, as his sister took herself to the world of hunting. Outwardly, as a grown-up, Cameron was a big, jolly and sociable man: his behaviour as eldest son and heir, in dealing with money, was naturally not like that of his sisters. He went his own way without reference to what was best for his family. He disliked being cramped in an expensive lifestyle. His baby grand piano went all over the world with him on his army postings. His secret life of playing on the stock exchange and getting into such debt that by 1940 Drishane was on the brink of falling into the hands of creditors shows us a man formed very early as an evasive singleton. His four brothers were very different from him – forceful, bold men who could be irritated by their soft elder brother.

Adelaide took an interest in Edith when her young ones were safely through babyhood, and when she might have been ready to be broken in as a model daughter, to be put on the marriage market. But by this time it was too late, for Grandpapa Somerville had already had the time of his life training his eldest grandchild as a rider and treating her as an equal. Quite extraordinarily, when he took morning prayers in Drishane he stood holding hands with Edith at his side, as if she were the heir, facing her brothers.[10] Edith, much beset by her brothers, prayed at such times that she might miraculously become a boy, an ambition she later abandoned with no regret. In such households it seemed to be the luck of the draw if an adult formed a close relationship with a child. It was unusual between an adult male and a female child, but far stranger things happened than Edith being brought up as though she were an honorary boy by her grandfather; she merely became an 'Amazonian' rider and outdoor woman. Another Anglo-Irishwoman of Edith's type, but an only child, Nora Robertson, who became mistress of Huntingdon Castle, Clonegal in County Carlow, wrote: 'Although my father always professed not to have wanted a son, he brought up his only child as half an able-bodied seaman and half an early pioneer. We tied reef knots, spliced ropes and made fires and wigwams, despising the incompetent. I don't know how I ever got over it. Perhaps I didn't.'[11] Like Edith, but in the next generation, she steered the Robertson house and lands safely through all difficulties, capitalising on their Slaney fishing by letting it out. Apart from her memoir *Crowned Harp* she wrote two classics – *Thrifty Salmon Fishing* and *More Thrifty Salmon Fishing*.

Edith grew up knowing that several women in the family, who were wealthy heiresses, had been able to choose a husband who was beneath them socially, and much less rich. Encouraged to think of herself in the same gilded bracket, she formed relationships with such men, and only later came to the realisation that she had no such monetary power to break with convention. Her sister broke no rules by her marriage within the close circle of Coghill cousin-hood. Because she married and had four children, Edith's sister Hildegarde tends to escape notice as a feminist pioneer in community health, who was as well an able farmer and stockbreeder, a crack shot and bold rider. As young girls from Horseback Hall, encouraged by their grandfather, both the sisters got into that area where everything that was really important happened – the yard. This was a relatively classless place where skill with animals was the only measure of worth. The influence of a strong male mentor like their grandfather on girls in early life was ineradicable. Edith's grandfather was completely unlike her father, who was very much overshadowed by him. He was a dandy, a famed rider and hunter, a Magdalen man who had made the Grand Tour and brought back Canova etchings from Rome. He read Turgenev, whose *Hunting Sketches*, like the works of Maria Edgeworth, give a voice, and emotions, to the peasant classes. Edith read both these writers in her grandfather's library. He spoke Irish in dealing with his men, and in 1868 concealed in Drishane a Fenian in flight from the law. He had a quirky sense of humour, putting up a standing stone on his land 'to puzzle posterity'.[12] He, rather than her mother Adelaide, formed the foreground of Edith's early life. This did not inhibit her emotionally. As a girl she was emotional and physically demonstrative to those she loved.

Her mother's Coghill sisterhood was overtly and physically affectionate. They all called each other 'Darling' even when they were annoyed with one another – 'Darling, I don't think you're *quite* telling the truth' being a catch-phrase. So we cannot be surprised that the men of the family, who were in the minority, were remarkably good at comfortable physical contact with the young and the old.[13] As serious students of mesmerism and the psychic world, Uncle Kendal and his nephew Egerton were very effective with the elderly and ill as masseurs and sick-bed attendants. In those enormous families, invalids and the mentally disadvantaged were maintained within the family circle. Sir Joscelyn's invalid children Gerald and Beatrice Coghill both needed special care, and the greatest possible comfort was given to the old of the family at the ends of their lives. If the Somervilles' Drishane of the time may be categorised as a barracks, the Coghills' Glen Barrahane rated as an asylum. In her youth and middle age Edith shows this comfortable, reverential, Coghill physicality. She made icons of objects belonging to her 'Darlings', like her locket containing some of her grandfather's hair. To those who did not know her well she was, apparently, a physically remote woman as she became elderly, a crusty shell having overlaid the sparky young woman who was her younger self. But her diary, the Buddh Dictionary of family language and her letters to her brother Cameron show that this is indeed what she had once been.

Some letters between Edith and her mother survive; once Adelaide had discovered that her eldest daughter was not tractable, Edith became one of the fascinations of her life. Just as Adelaide's determination to make her children thoroughly competent musicians stood them all in good stead (particularly Cameron and Jack who became Commandants of the Army School of Music at Kneller Hall), so she had a lifelong effect on the child Edith by insisting that her handwriting be modelled on clear copperplate. Her main grudge against Edith was in not taking enough care of her appearance, in being too much of a clowner in her facial expressions and in her use of brogue. Of an early portrait photograph Adelaide wrote to Edith: 'I am glad to see that one can be got of you that is neither an idiotic grinner or a self-grave-digger which up to this all your photos have been', but she rejected another as being of 'the Amazonian type without any doubt and there is a saucy, horsey, slangy expression in the face that I cannot say I like'.[14] Though Edith controlled her temper and behaved in the presence of men, with her mother there were stormy rows and passionate outbursts, during which she might threaten to throw herself into the family vault in disgust at the world. These melodramatic outbursts relieved her feelings; they were variations on the well-known adolescent theme of 'I am so depressed I want to DIE' and were, like Uncle Kendal's roaring explosions, a safety valve. They were expressed with the aid of an awful, arch, gallows humour that also came into play when she was irritated by pushy social climbers or disruptions in her class hierarchy; thus we might find the irritant person labelled as a 'sweep', 'grocer', 'lout', 'flapper' or worse – words that might be used in calmer circumstances quite innocent of negative meaning. This was something that her mother and aunts did, and is classified in the Buddh Dictionary of family language as 'blorting': the language was intemperate but indicated a passing irritation and gave no guide to the inner workings of the mind. The callous and flippant slang of the Twins, Ethel and Edith, was caught from the English public schoolboy chaff of their male cousins and is easy to mistake for jeering. Its actual tone is suggested by the Buddh Dictionary definition of 'Scut', which was: 'one who is at once pert and contemptible. This epithet nevertheless does not denote ill-feeling.'

What emerges most clearly from Edith's early letters to her mother is her passionate love of horses. She was distraught when in 1877 Colonel Somerville had to start selling the family horses in order to pay debts. The horse so threatened was Edith's own Psyche, which was to be sold so that the family could attend a Vernon wedding. At this wedding she first cast her eye on Sydney Vernon, young brother of the bride. She marked him as a 'good egg' and mentioned him to her mother: 'I contrived by deep strategy to decoy the youngest Vernon boy Sydney to look after me.' From London, staying with Aunt Emmie, Aunt Zoe and the de Morgans when she was preparing to enter the South Kensington School of Art, Edith wrote to plead that Psyche be kept, and also suggesting an unusual route home via the railway to Bandon: 'all the weddings in Europe would not be worth that – I am simply wild to see her – don't you think she could meet me at the steamboat, and I might ride along by the side of the train? and you might go inside'. But Psyche was sold for £9.10s. By her next letter Edith had met up with Herbert Greene, her first cousin and admirer, who was 'eating his dinners' to become a barrister; from him she discovered what her cousins the Aylmer brothers had done recently at Oxford and Eton: 'Fancy, Percy is rowing in the 3rd Trinity boat. Eddy is also a great swell in one of the Eton eights. PS You never said that Sukey [her pronunciation of Psyche, tutored by her suitor Herbert, the classicist, with her own spelling] should come to meet me to Cork or Bristol. Kiss Peter for me.' Peter 'who must have broken hearts as well as horses' was her beloved horsebreaker Peter Donovan.[15]

Staying with cousins, the Camerons in Neville Street, she passed her entrance exam to study at the South Kensington Scool of Art where she experienced what she described as 'Three months of a most useful breaking-in for a rather headstrong and unbroken colt ... from a lawless life of caricaturing my brethren, my governesses, my clergy, my elders and betters generally, copying in pen and ink all the hunting pictures, from John Leech to Georgina Bowers, that old and new *Punches* had to offer ... I passed to a rule of iron discipline.' Her first female fellow students were a motley crew, and Edith was amazed at the eccentricities of some of these girls, who, naturally, had grown up without any notion of working or learning in a group. She herself remained untidy and careless of her workplace surroundings all her life, though fussy about her appearance and dress in public. Her mother reacted to some complaints sent in a letter: 'We were greatly amused at the Queen of Filth's strictures on her painting pals.'

The Twins had an ambition to earn money by writing a sensational best seller. Frequently we find in Edith's diary the entry that Ethel had come up to Drishane from Glen Barrahane and 'we conflagrote'; of these efforts only their *Fairy Play* survives complete. Though Ethel was to leave Castletownshend on her marriage in 1880, because she married out of the Coghill circle, she and Edith remained soulmates and shared the same sense of humour to the end of their lives. Without the stimulus and generosity of the next-door Coghills, Edith would never have become an independent woman, and this was as much to do with Edith's friendship with Egerton Coghill as with his sister Ethel. Ethel's autobiographical memoir, written at the age of eighty-one in 1938, works backwards and opens with a listing of changes and inventions during her life-time in order of importance that immediately gives us an insight into the Twins' different range of interests, apart from the paramount one of young men from 'egglings' to 'good eggs', which was a way of marking out the more attractive from the as yet unformed.[16] Ethel had been all her life a great traveller, so her list begins unsurprisingly with 'Train services as we now have them; I can remember seeing a train in which all the luggage was packed on top of the carriage'. She carries on listing with 'Bicycles ... Electricity in all its various forms and uses ... Women's Suffrage ... Telephones ... Broadcasting and television ... Motor Cars – movies and talkies ... Aeroplanes.' For the mature Edith the Suffrage came first, and as for transport, she never fell out of love with the horse, though even in her eighties she deeply enjoyed being driven fast in a motor car. At the opening of Ethel's memoir and at its very end we find a fundamental difference between the Twins. Ethel died in Hampshire. Like so many Anglo-Irish she had repudiated the country of her birth, and would not have her grave in Ireland. In Ireland: 'Times have changed, and as I see it all, for the worse. It is better to shut the book and to leave it and its memories for my great-grandchildren to read.' In contrast to her Twin, Edith's life was spent in coming to terms with New Ireland and fighting a rearguard action to preserve her family home with its lands. She lived and died an unashamed Irishwoman and was always a countrywoman, whereas her Twin was more of a sophisticate and Anglophile.

The Coghills were far richer than the Somervilles and Ethel was born into a life of cosmopolitan ease. Most of the Coghill lands were in County Carlow, but these were unattractive to her father, Sir Joscelyn, compared to other options. Ethel Coghill was born at the grand family seat in Dublin, in Belvedere House, on 18 May 1857; this building is now part of St Patrick's College, Drumcondra. As the house was leased to religious orders, it survives, as, nearby, does the bigger and grander house built by Marmaduke Coghill that he named Drumcondra House (now the Vincentian All Hallows College). Ethel was the fourth child and the first daughter of Sir Joscelyn Coghill and his wife Katherine Plunket. When she was three months old, Sir Joscelyn moved his family to Switzerland, as he had a passion for painting Alpine scenery. The Coghills were often to return in a large family group to the area around Lucerne, where German and French tutors would provide the children with perfectly accented languages. But their chief playground was not abroad: from about 1850, the family had taken sailing holidays in West Cork. As well as being a painter and photographer Sir Joscelyn was also a keen sailor, and when he discovered that a favourite sister, Emmeline (who had married Charles Bushe, Rector of Castlehaven), lived on the brink of fine sailing waters, he took a house in Castletownshend. His son Egerton, who eventually succeeded Sir Joscelyn, was born in Malmaison on the village hill in 1853. The influx of Sir Joscelyn's sisters, some of them unmarried, into CT during the summer enchanted the young men of the neighbourhood. It seems to have been after the marriage of his sister Adelaide to T.H. Somerville that Joscelyn decided to make his headquarters in CT; he bought and rebuilt the old house then called Laputa, and renamed it Glen Barrahane. It is a sign of his interest in Ireland that he discarded the original name, that of Gulliver's floating island (given in celebration of the visit of Dean Swift), and acknowledged instead the local Irish saint.

Edith, born on 2 May 1858, and Ethel, born on 18 May 1857, bonded instantly when they met in the Glen B schoolroom. They both had the same problem of being over-run with noisy brothers, and this simple accident of circumstance made them both fluent speakers, controversialists and embryo feminists. Ethel was first aware of Edith as a fellow toddler-sized bridesmaid at the wedding of their Aunt Georgina (Gig) Coghill to William Chavasse in Castletownshend church in September 1860, but they did not band together as 'Twins' against their brothers until they were sharing the same schoolroom. In her memoir, Ethel expresses a horror of the gross amount of childbearing put upon her mother's generation, in the quest for male heirs: 'I cannot say how things were in other families but, certainly in ours the patriarchal system was followed to what now, even to my eyes (and how much more so to those of my great grandchildren), appears an almost unbelievable extent. My father and mother were first cousins, their mothers being respectively Anna Maria Bushe and Charlotte Bushe, daughters of Chief Justice Bushe. Anna married Admiral

Sir Josiah Coghill, and Charlotte married John Plunket (afterwards Lord Plunket). Anna Maria was Admiral Coghill's second wife, and she and her predecessor between them produced sixteen children, only two of which were boys.'[17] At a time when women were supposed to be still, silent, opinionless creatures, these Coghill sisters gave each other confidence, which their own girl children inherited from them along with eloquence and executive power. Their type was abroad in France and was known there as the *maîtresse femme*. As the males of the Anglo-Irish gentry class into which they married were in a predicament, in the process of losing wealth, power and confidence, they nearly all dominated their husbands. Edith's mother Adelaide Coghill, in particular, was a dominatrix almost to the point of domestic tyranny.

Ethel was against large families: 'I have had, before death diminished their number, no less than seventy-eight first cousins, with the result that it was almost impossible to meet anyone who was not in some way either a member of the family or connected with it in some remote degree. Where nearly all the cousins were pleasant, agreeable and clever in one way or another, the temptation to cultivate their acquaintance to the exclusion of outsiders was very great and tended to keep us in a sort of fenced enclosure – a large enclosure certainly, but still an enclosure, with "the family" inside and everyone else looked upon with a sort of kindly arrogance as "outsiders" to whom we were civil and polite, but, with some rare exceptions, never intimate.'[18] Ethel chose to marry an exceptional 'outsider', rather than her first cousin Joscelyn de Morgan; by doing this she left the charmed circle, with its London / CT axis, to be a land agent's wife far away in County Meath, north of Dublin. It was because Ethel was thus leaving the circle by marrying 'out' that Edith was so bereft in 1880.

Sir Joscelyn and his brother Colonel Kendal were born towards the end of a sequence of ten girls. When Joscelyn married his first cousin Katherine Plunket, all his unmarried sisters lived with them until such time as they themselves might marry. In such extended families, Big Houses like Glen Barrahane were crammed with all sorts – spinsters like Aunt Florence, wards of court like the orphaned Eddie and Percy Aylmer, permanent invalids like Gerald Coghill, and girl children who were taught at home. At Glen Barrahane, the new additional building included a big dining room and schoolroom. The building work was haphazard and crude with ill-fitting doors; a local boat-builder robustly fended off any criticism: 'Ah! Sir Joscelyn don't care for a bit of straight work, he'd rather be looking at crooked mountains.' One of the results of the poor building was that the schoolroom, where Edith and Ethel were taught with their brothers before they left for their various public schools, was infested with wild life of various kinds. It is a sign of Edith's unusual character that two caterpillars who moved in to the schoolroom were befriended by her and christened Glumdalclitch, (because of the Swift connection they all read *Gulliver's Travels*), and Friskarina. At this time in her life Edith had a marked talent for doctoring sick and damaged animals, later extended to humans.

The variety in ages of the Coghill and Somerville cousins meant that they split into distinct quartettes. Edith and Ethel were partnered by Claude (Joe) Coghill and Cameron Somerville. Edith's happy connection with Joe, who was a year younger than her, as a dancing partner and a fellow actor, began in their early teens. These four used to act out pantomime-like dramas. The amateur theatricals at CT were quite remarkable in the obvious delight that all the young took in dressing up in drag: Cameron could carry off old ladies and mothers-in-law to perfection. Janey Butt and Sylvia Townshend liked particular uniforms, Sylvia having a genius for playing London bus conductors, and Janey looking magnificent in a Zouave costume. Edith liked to play hero parts, but had been known to relinquish the part of hero for that of a clergyman, as she liked the black robes that were choice items in Sir Joscelyn's extensive 'acting press'. As clergyman, she would preside over the marriage of the hero and heroine.

A letter to Ethel, her 'Ducky Pet', *c.*1880, gives the camp theatrical tone: 'In "Marriage" I was the man – an adorable *jeune premier*, in a cork moustache, a silver headed cane, wellington boots and a jerry hat – (o, yes, I had an ulster, too) In this capacity I made love to several Butts and ran away with one of them.'

The Twins had a memorable success with a cruel parody of *Romeo and Juliet*, described as 'an elaborate farce' by Muriel Currey, of an anti-romantic kind;[19] during this period, when they described themselves as 'flappers', they seem to have been heartless creatures. Although she could do Mark Anthony in a toga, Ethel was often the beautiful heroine in dire danger, and Claude could act anything, but was particularly good at bridesmaids. The most fetching photograph of all in those records of theatricals is of the burly Boyle Somerville in blackface and drag as a pantomime dame. The theatrical inventions of the elders seem to have been no less remarkable than those of their young. Ethel remembered a play written by Aunt Emmie Plunket in French. It opened with Egerton as a shepherd addressing his sheep, who were Cameron and Gerald with sheepskin rugs tied round them, and ended with an address to Hymen, Nevill Coghill dressed up in a sheet. When this group of children grew up, their skill with theatrical make-up, and dressing down, was such that they could disguise themselves so successfully that their own parents did not recognise them. This was done famously by Claude Coghill when he appeared at Glen Barrahane in the guise of an itinerant second-hand carpet seller and sold his parents a carpet, borrowed from Drishane; and by Louie Penrose, who went overland to a quay, where her father was about to come in with his then yacht

*Ierne*, dressed in the guise of an apple seller, and successfully sold him apples when he strolled ashore. These 'sells', as they were called, show that the CT young used two voices discriminately and could drop into brogues that were absolutely convincing.[20]

From the memoir by Ethel we know what was the staple reading of Ethel and Edith in their early teens. Aunt Florence read Shakespeare to them from Bowdler's edition, Lady Coghill read Scott, and Miss Mann, their most successful governess, read them Dickens. In the summer of 1873, Edith joined Ethel and the Coghills at Clarens in Switzerland, where both of them were thrilled to the core by their first opera. They went to Vevey to hear *Zampa*, a stormy romantic work by the French composer L.J.F. Herold. Ethel wrote: 'She and I lived in a fine frenzy of excitement and admiration for weeks after it, Edith filled pages in her sketch book of portraits of the hero from memory.' They bought a piano arrangement of the opera for four hands and played it endlessly together.

This was the year in which, at the age of fifteen, Edith started to keep her diary.[21] She arrived in Schwitz (now Schwyz) to find the 'usual crowd of relations'. In June all the young caught measles and passed the disease from one to the other over the whole summer. In July, on the 15th, Edith enters 'Heard from Papa and Mother has a baby. A boy, that is all I've heard.' This was Adelaide's last child, Hugh. Early in August the Coghill party travelled back to Britain. Edith was the last of the children to develop measles, and she was isolated in a London hotel with her Aunt Florence for company until she returned to CT. Aunt Florence and Aunt Emmie were the best of company for any child interested in the arts. Emmeline 'Emmie' Plunket, favourite sister and lifelong companion of Katherine (Lady Coghill), was the cleverest of all the women with whom Edith came into contact as a child. A keen astronomer interested in the calculation of time, her *Ancient Calendars and Constellations* was published by John Murray in 1903. Aunt Emmie did not marry and lived in the household of Sir Joscelyn Coghill, her brother-in-law. In 1874 Edith began to enter the names of paintings that she had made under the tuition of Aunt Emmie – portraits of 'a gorgeous old fisherwoman' and 'old Howrahan'. A French mademoiselle taught the Coghill and Somerville children with the aid of plays that they acted out in costume. In this same year they were all taken to the first ever pantomime presented in Cork, and Adelaide Coghill began to read Dickens to her children, starting with the 'not half bad' *David Copperfield*. On 4 September 1874 Edith enters in her diary: 'I am reading up for the TRIN. COLL. SCHOLARSHIPS.' It was not until two years later that she actually sat the scholarship examinations. At this stage in 1874, as a graphic artist, she is already earning money from two greetings card manufacturers, Page and Raphael Tuck, describing it as 'a regular business'.

With Joe Coghill, her favourite dancing partner, she learned ballroom dances, and practised them wearing the ballgowns in which she took such an interest. Edith's nickname, until Joe married in 1885, was 'Mrs Joe'.[22] The first grand ball she attended was at the Hungerfords' Cahirmore in January 1877. Some of Edith's ballgowns survived in the Coghill dressing-up box for years. The eighteen-inch waist of these gowns, and of her first red hunting waistcoat, horrified her nieces.[23] Her coming-out ball had been at her parents' friends' home, Dunkettle House, in the year before. It was held there as it was more convenient for Cork gentry to travel to Dunkettle, close to Cork City, than for them to go to Castletownshend, far in the remote west of County Cork. The owner of Dunkettle was Thomas Wise Gubbins, whose family had made their money in trade at Limerick. He and his wife were close friends of Henry and Adelaide Somerville; their daughters had been born deaf; it was through familiarity with this family that all the Somervilles were used to sign language and the emphatic use of facial expression that made them expert in the parlour game of charades called 'Dumb Crambo'.

Neither Edith nor Ethel was in any way excited by education until they were sent together to Alexandra College in Dublin for a term in 1875/76, after which they both decided to sit the examinations for women held by Trinity College, to see how clever they were, as they felt themselves to be 'advanced females'. They lived in a rented house in Harcourt Street with a 'chip' or chaperone, and here Conyngham (Frank) and Herbert Greene, their first cousins who lived on Stephen's Green, assisted them in their preparations. 'I am afraid a good many of our supposed hours of work were excessively rowdy!' Ethel wrote, but nevertheless she won a Junior Scholarship and Edith won a First Class. The women sitting the TCD examination had to remain anonymous and were given numbers, so that when the results were published in the newspapers only the numbers and not their names were made public. Although they were perfectly capable of doing so, neither of them made a fuss about following up any form of higher education at that time: both must have sensed the looming financial difficulties that already made providing for their brothers' educations and placements enough of a problem for their parents.

They returned to CT and to an 'entirely irresponsible life'. Though they had noticed there were bad patches, they had no inkling of the catastrophic seriousness of the financial troubles beginning to beset their parents. Ethel wrote: 'I think back with some shame that we had, apparently, no duties except to amuse ourselves, and that we did very thoroughly. Edith and I invented a system by which all our male cousins were supposed to be our nephews, described by my Uncle Tom Greene as "the most bare-faced system of flirtation I ever heard of", in which remark he was more than justified. It is rather strange that no serious complications arose from these summer flirtations. The system of chaperonage enforced by our elders was entirely illogical. No chaperone was considered necessary for the long mornings spent in the boats, but a picnic was quite another matter ... Herbert and Frank Greene, and Percy and Eddy Aylmer were the 'nephews' in chief.'[24] Ethel described the seasonal waves of entanglements with 'nephews' dying down as each winter set in and the boys returned to their colleges or barracks, leaving Edith and Ethel 'still only semi-grown up' to write and illustrate comic strips and ultimately to produce their greatest effort, the *Fairy Play*, a version of *Sleeping Beauty*, that was revived, revised and acted by three generations of CT children after them. Neither of the Twins lost the English public schoolboy slang, and the coarse gallows humour that they learned from their male cousins (the Greene boys were at Harrow, and the Aylmers at Eton): 'Hideous', 'Brutal' and 'Pukey' being everyday exclamatory adjectives.

Edith laughed at the unexpected, and frequently skimmed over serious questions by changing the subject. Regarding the future of Ireland, something must have been working itself out in her father's mind, without reference to anyone else in the family, except perhaps Boyle. Grandpapa had already proved himself sympathetic to the Irish cause. Writing to her mother at this time, Edith makes the flippant comment: 'I laughed at the idea of Papa's voting for a Home Ruler ...' before passing on to another joke. When the Coghills were away for Christmas in 1877, Ethel wrote frequently to her 'Beloved Twin', telling her of the music, discovering Wagner, and complaining of the lack of 'good eggs' or dancing partners. She had found an American who looked proficient, but danced with him only to discover that the 'American hold on partners is very different'. The family had taken their servants with them, Lady Coghill refusing to be separated from her maid, Hurly. The family acted in a performance of *She Stoops to Conquer* in which Sir Joscelyn took the part of Hastings – 'a most touchingly beautiful Hastings and I quite fell in love with him in his white wig and black moustache and eyebrows' as Ethel described him to Edith. Egerton was Tony Lumpkin. However, Hurly was not impressed with the play, exclaiming to Joe: 'Ah what foolery it is talking of *She Stoops to Conquer* – sure I stooped often enough and yet I never got a husband.'[25]

During the summer of 1878 spiritualism was rife in CT, with table turning, ouija board communication, and automatic writing all keenly practised by the Coghills. In her diary on 25 August Edith wrote, after deciding to sleep with Aunt Flo in Glen B: 'Aunt Flo's basket trunk has suddenly (11.30 pm) become possessed of an evil spirit and has waved its lid about of its own accord. I am going to sleep with her in my character as materialiser and strengthener.' Under the observation of Uncle Kendal, Edith received scripts from a long-dead Coghill ancestress.[26] This experience does not seem to have marked her in any

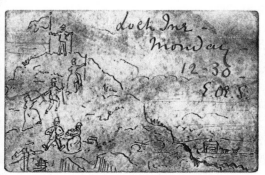

2 Edith Somerville's invitation to a picnic at Lough Ine. This is the only surviving item from the correspondence between Edith and Hewitt to have passed through the Postal System; a concealed exchange of letters was enabled by the 'Cobbian Post', as it was called in Edith's diaries, whereby the Coastguard Officer Francis Cobb carried letters back and fore along the coast in his Naval cutter.

serious way. Matters spiritual were relatively marginal. Sexual maturity came to the Twins in their late teens.

In between the seemingly superficial flirtations with cousins, both Ethel and Edith had cast their eyes further afield, over the fence; 1878 was a significant year for both of them. Edith had a serious relationship with Hewitt Poole in this year at Easter, running on into the autumn. Hewitt, related to Edith through his great grandmother, a Somerville, was staying with his mother's family, the Flemings, at New Court, to the west of Skibbereen.[27] He was a very handsome man, athletic, and with mesmerising sea-blue eyes, fair hair and moustache. But he was poor, and young, and only a Trinity College Dublin student, not yet having begun on his career as a railway engineer. He came to CT with his sister Lilla for a tennis party on 4 April; they were both first-class players, and immediately stood out in the crowd. Edith and Hewitt, with whom she 'walked circuitously' alone rather than with the usual crowd, were mutually attracted. After their meeting, her diary records that they exchanged poems and letters by return of post. Hewitt sent a poem first, on the 14th, Edith sent one back on the 15th, and he sent another on the 19th. These are now destroyed, but Edith kept her dance cards with his name on, and he kept two mementos of her all his life, hidden from his wife – a studio portrait photograph of Edith and an invitation to a picnic at Loch Ine for 8 April, done in sketch.[28] Unrecorded in her diary, the correspondence may have gone on through the summer, as another admirer of Edith's, Charles, the son of the Sealys, then tenants at Malmaison, became jealous. On 13 June, Edith had, her diary records, 'a terrible row with the Seal about letters of affections. A choice complication.' As we shall see, Charles Sealy 'the Seal' was still on the scene a year later, unlike his rival. The method of communication between Hewitt and Edith seems to have been 'the Cobbian post' via Lt. Francis Cobb, the Coastguard Inspector for the Skibbereen Division of which Castletownshend was the principal station.

Hewitt's circumstances were against him, he was not the heir to the family home, Mayfield near Bandon (the heir was his first cousin, who had the same name); he had a sketchy education from Bandon Grammar School before going up to TCD, eventually to study engineering, but taking an arts BA first. From a landed gentry point of view, as a prospective son-in-law his prospects were bleak. Nevertheless he was extremely popular as a country house guest, being so good looking, and an excellent dancer, rider to hounds and games player. In CT Glen Barrahane attracted great numbers of visitors like him through its tennis courts, and billiard room where highly competitive billiards and pool was played between young men and young women. Apparently, only one single letter survives from this period when Edith was writing and receiving those 'letters of affections' that so upset Charles Sealy. It is quite unique in its familiar tone and appears to be an apology from Hewitt for his failure to set off to the Lough Ine picnic on 8 April because of foul stormy weather, which caused its cancellation. It is addressed on the outside to Miss Somerville, but on the inside to 'O thou that playest upon the timbrel'. He was staying with the Jacksons near Kilcoe and had hired a horse, Leary, for the occasion, which he sent back to Skibbereen. 'It is now the time when *you were* to start; I presume you will await a brighter moment ... I suggest the return of Leary ... hoping thereby to save some portion of my wrecked fortune, lost to horse hire. Pray for the boy Brickly who takes back Leary – How about the game of Pool today? I think it suitable weather for it or *Blindmansbuff*. H.'[29]

Hewitt was much at Drishane in early September, staying there from the 10th. Edith's comments on games and dances with Hewitt are similar to her later high-spirited involvement with Barry Avonmore: 'Played "grab" after dinner, am still quivering from the effects' and 'played, after tea, quadrille. Madly exciting.' Blindman's Buff was an ever-popular game that facilitated close physical contact. From Edith's diary entries, which never mention him in detail again, it seems possible that Hewitt made some hopeful declaration to Colonel Somerville on the night of 16 September, 1878. In the morning Hewitt was gone, seemingly under some kind of cloud, as he never came to Drishane or CT again. In November 1880 he was to marry his cousin Mia Jellett, to whom he had been unofficially engaged while he was in West Cork in 1878. Hewitt was a flirt, and Mia was ashamed of the jealousy that consumed her when she knew that Hewitt was staying with the Townshends at Derry, or with the

Flemings at Newcourt. Letters survive between the married couple that show that Mia could not let rest her suspicions about Hewitt's involvement with someone else; but he never confessed.[30]

It must have been painful to Edith to see the happy course of Ethel's engagement to James Penrose, announced in June 1879, but she laughed at the 'toodle-noodling' of the pair and wrote to Cameron at the end of that month, 'I will go on to my other half and speak of my loathsome Twin. You have heard the bare outlines of her "goings-on" by this time, but you never, o never, can know what we, who live, so to speak, in the thick of the engagement have to suffer.' Fatalistic diary entries made a month before Ethel's wedding, at the end of November 1880: 'I will work. I will paint' might well relate to seeing a description of Hewitt's wedding in a newspaper, because as we shall see later Ethel's wedding itself was vastly enjoyed by Edith and her attendant brides-maid's man, Joe Coghill.

After some false starts, Ethel had fared much better than Edith in her choice of man, though he was an outsider. In the summer after the Twins had finished at Alexandra College, when Ethel was nineteen, Sir Joscelyn had taken a house in Fitzwilliam Place to present Ethel at Court, at one of the Lord Lieutenant, Lord Abercorn's, 'Drawing Rooms'. As well as going to a round of afternoon teas 'which were well described by Nannie Martin as Irish Stews', Ethel went to a big fancy dress ball given by Mrs Roe at the Dublin Exhibition Buildings. 'In the middle of one dance, I found myself lassoed by a chinaman's pigtail, and, on turning round, found the Chinaman was Jim Penrose; this may be looked upon as an omen!'[31]

There were financial difficulties, and possibly social ones. Ethel was twenty-two when she became engaged to Jim Penrose in June 1879; she did not marry him until 30 December 1880. Although Edith was deeply miffed that her 'Twin' Ethel was marrying and going to live out of reach in faraway Athboy in County Meath, letters from the summer of 1879 showed that, at least on the surface, she had rebounded from the misfortune of the year before and was merrily flirting with another. This time she had chosen a member of the aristocracy, and again there was a family connection, and again she made an ill-fated choice. Her great-grandfather Charles Kendal Bushe had a distinguished colleague called Barry Yelverton.[32] They both became comfortably wealthy as lawyers in Ireland, but in the 1790s they took different routes in their careers, when Bushe campaigned against the Union and Yelverton accepted and promoted it along with the bribe of a title. For this betrayal, he was detested in Ireland, and his family was tainted by his disgrace. Although he had been a mere schoolteacher when he attracted a Nugent heiress, who married him, Yelverton and his descendants took to the ways of the idle aristocratic rich. His great-grandson

was to bring down further, and worse, odium on the family by making their surname a byword for immorality. Born in 1824, Charles Yelverton, fourth Viscount
Avonmore, became a social outcast. He was the villain of the celebrated Yelverton
Trial, a widely reported and sensational court case that went on from 1859 to
1868 and was widely reported in the press. Yelverton had contracted an
irregular marriage with a Roman Catholic girl, Maria Teresa Longworth, at
Rostrevor in County Down in 1857. He had arranged it as a theatrical sham, to
keep her quiet. He lost any sympathy he had from the public when he revealed in
court that he had taken sexual advantage of Miss Longworth because she was not
'a lady'. In fighting the case in the courts, he bankrupted his estate. Repudiating
Miss Longworth as his wife, in 1858 he had married Emily Marianne, the widow
of Professor Edward Forbes and was to have three children by her. She was the
youngest daughter of Major General Sir Charles Ashworth. It was his undeserved good fortune that she, who took the title of Lady Avonmore, was a
strong and long-suffering woman. In supporting her husband, she endured
decades as a social pariah; but she herself was supported throughout by her
eldest sister, Caroline Laura, who had married Col. Alexander Cameron in
Cork, and thus become connected with the Somervilles.[33] The validity of Miss
Longworth's marriage was upheld in the Irish Courts in 1861, but annulled in
the Scottish Court in 1862, the Scottish judgment being confirmed in the House
of Lords in 1864. In the judgment of the Irish Court, Lord Avonmore's children
by his second union were illegitimate. The disgrace of his trial and the Irish
verdict were never to be lived down.[34]

Lord Avonmore was cashiered from the army in 1861 and banished from
his clubs. With his wife and children he fled abroad to live at Biarritz. (His
discarded sham wife did not keep quiet. Miss Longworth, or Teresa Yelverton,
who became a novelist, published *The Yelverton Correspondence* in 1863.) In
the slang terms of Edith and Ethel's flapper youth, Lord Avonmore was a very
bad egg indeed. Twenty years after his disgrace, he thought it was safe to be
seen in Ireland again. During the Crimean war, when he was serving with the
Royal Artillery, he had come to know Lt. Colonel T.H. Somerville through his
sister-in-law's marriage with Lt. Colonel Alexander Cameron. Like so many
others who were connected through the Bushe family and 'The Chief', Charles
Kendal Bushe, Lord Avonmore began to holiday in Castletownshend, which
was an excellent cheap and convivial place in which to retrench. The
Avonmores rented Glen Barrahane from the Coghills while they were away.
Long-ago kindness between their families, and the link with the Camerons,
encouraged the hope that Lord Avonmore's past might be overlooked here.

When the Avonmores first took Glen Barrahane during the winter of 1877,
socialising between Drishane and Glen Barrahane was intensive. Barry, the

Avonmores' eldest son and heir, was then a Sandhurst cadet, and a well-made young man, with his father's thick and curly dark hair. Outgoing and full of fun, he fitted in with the Castletownhend young like a long-lost relation and provided what Ethel and Edith referred to as 'fresh meat'. His army leaves were noted carefully and by late 1879 some of the CT young had taken to going up to the Avonmores' house, Belle Isle on Lough Derg in the extreme north of County Tipperary, during vacations to sail on the Shannon lakes with Barry as their skipper. He was commissioned 2nd Lieutenant on 30 January 1878. Because of the lack of money neither he nor his younger brother Algie was given English public school education, and Barry had to make a living for himself as a career soldier. He loved the Army, and may have hoped, by distinguishing himself, to rehabilitate the family name in Ireland and restore its reputation. The Avonmores took Glen Barrahane again at the following Christmas.

Barry stayed on in Castletownshend after Christmas 1878. We have a glimpse of him as one of that still-remembered group of tearaways who raced in a bathchair down the precipitous CT hill, on either side of which were the main street houses. As ever, Mrs Cameron was accompanying her sister Lady Avonmore, with her two sons Ewen and Maurice, Barry's first cousins. Edith described the scene to Boyle: 'Barry and Maurice Cameron got out the Glen B bathchair and were tobogganing down the hill in it all the morning. They started just below the Cobbs and swooping round the two trees used to fly right down the hill only pulling up a little before the Castle hall door.'[35] Less simple-minded amusements were dreamed up as well. Edith's brother Cameron, whose nickname was 'Chimp', was persuaded by Maurice and Barry to dress up as an old lady, a 'Miss Fleming', and visit Glen Barrahane for tea. Edith dressed him in an assortment of Adelaide's old clothes and he was taken in to be introduced to Lady Avonmore and Mrs Cameron by Barry. 'The Chimp talked in a little high falsetto and when Lady A politely asked him to sit down and take a little tea I really thought I should have died. However, down squatted the Chimp and began to make company talk.' Then Barry's sister Alice asked Miss Fleming to sing 'Home They Brought Her Hero Dead'. Strangling with laughter, Cameron could just get a few notes out intermittently as he accompanied himself on the piano, but these strange vocals were understood by the uninitiated to be delivered under the influence of the song's emotion. 'Everybody in the room except Lady A and Mrs Cameron subsided into orgies of suppressed laughter. Barry wept upon Papa's bosom while I cried down his back ... all around the room were heard low sobs blending with the shrieks of the Chimp at the piano'. Lady Avonmore was steeling herself to give thanks to the singer for her song when Cameron turned round from the piano: 'and seeing Lady A cowering beneath Punch to hide her laughter ... thought she had discovered him and suddenly wound up in a bass roar'.[36] Even so, Mrs Cameron only realised what the trick was when Barry went up and thumped Cameron on the back and congratulated him on his acting.

Suddenly all the fun was over. Ethel's eldest brother Nevill, the Coghill heir, was serving with the South Wales Borderers in Natal. At the end of January the news came through that on the 22nd he had been killed by the Zulus during the battle of Isandula. Nevill had been riding out of danger when he turned back to help the wounded Adjutant, Lieutenant Melville, and they were both unhorsed after crossing a river. Nevill, who had injured his leg previously and was unfit to ride, was carrying and dragging Melville up a ravine when the Zulus caught up with them. Ethel was distraught at the news, her agony made worse by her fears that Nevill's body had been mutilated, as was common practice. Castle-townshend went into mourning, and all festivities and entertainments ceased. A friend of Nevill's had been killed by the Zulus on the same day – John Hodson, Lieutenant in the 24th Foot. The Hodsons, in the elder generation, had served with Uncle Kendal in India, and after their shared loss at Isandula the family kept up its friendship with CT for decades.

In the joyless atmosphere Maurice and Barry (who had been promoted to full Lieutenant on the 20th) left at the end of February, leaving the place 'very empty without them'. Forming another brother and sister quartette, Barry and Cameron with Alice, Barry's sister, and Edith, they had made so much noise that they were known by the collective noun 'The Row', making a type of happy noise that must be carefully distinguished from the painful 'Row' of arguments between Edith and her mother. A letter from Edith to Cameron of April 1879 shows that Edith was writing regularly to Barry at his barracks and vice versa. Barry had lost a regimental shooting match. He had scored a bull's-eye, but on the wrong target. Edith sent a decorated envelope to her following letter to Barry with a cartoon depicting the ridiculous incident. It had been pinned up in Barry's mess and caused widespread mirth before he tore it down. 'However in a truly Christian spirit he sent me what he calls "coals of fire" in the shape of a little spoon brooch with a mouse crawling along it to eat a pearl in the bowl – A delicious little thing.'[37] As there was already a foreboding of Coghill financial ruin, there was great rejoicing when Uncle Kendal's racehorse Vienna won the Baldoyle Steeplechase and £600.[38]

An undated letter to her mother, which must come from this year, describes another gift from Barry to Edith while she was in London and he was with his regiment. This might be a birthday gift, which would place it in early May. For all his fun and games Barry was serious in some things. He was a keen craftworker and had made Edith a personalised present. 'Barry's gift has arrived. It is a delicious delightful little ivory prayer book with my initials awfully well cut out of half a crown'. Barry took his position in the local community around Roscrea very seriously: he served on the Select Vestry of Lorrha Church from 1879 to 1881, when he began to soldier out of Ireland. The lakeside setting of the Yelverton seat, Belle Isle, and the character of its young Master have not previously been recognised as elements used in the fiction originated by Edith before and after the death of Violet Martin, from their very first novel. We see them particularly in *French Leave* and in the yachting scenes of *The Real Charlotte*, but also in the setting of the *Big House of Inver*, which is hard by a tower house just like Belle Isle.

Some of the Avonmores were still in CT at the end of July. Edith wrote to Cameron, stationed in Barbados, on 28 July 1879 when Barry's sister Alice Yelverton was in her room. The letter shows how 'romances' sprang up among the crowds of cousins; it shows also that Joe Coghill and Cameron were another pair of elected 'Twins', and that Alice was attracted to Cameron, as Barry was to Edith:

> The faithless Alice is here, in my room, and my poor child I must tell you that she has deserted you for your Prophet [Joe] – she will doubtless endeavour to lie with her usual veracity, but believe me who speaks more in sorrow than in anger that she is not to be trusted. [Here Alice joins in, writing in her own hand.] Edith is a liar. Don't believe a word of this history. I *am* faithful and I am sure you will say I am quite right to take up with the other half of you as your dear self is so far away, instead of some stranger.

Edith went up to Belle Isle in the middle of August and did not return until the beginning of November. When Edith arrived there, Lady Avonmore was away with her husband, the token adult chaperone was Barry's Aunt Mrs Robson who sailed all day, and Edith took over the running of the household. The engaged-to-be-married Ethel wrote: 'I was somewhat amused at the idea of you having assumed the reins of household government when you know in your heart Ducky you can't tell the difference between a shoulder or a leg in its raw condition.'[39] Neither Barry nor Edith could have cared less about this defect, as both of them seem to have been by nature hardy pioneers who could endure any domestic discomfort for the sake of fun. During the whole of this late summer she raced the Shannon lakes in the Yelverton's eleven-ton yacht, *Virago*, and slept on board an eight-tonner, the Jacksons' *Haidee*, where she set up quarters with her supposed chaperone, Mrs Sydney Robson, a noted racing yachtswoman. Mrs Robson had with her at all times a pet white cockatoo which was troublesome. An incident was laid away in Edith's mind to re-emerge in the RM story 'The House of Fahy' twenty years later. Barry and his friend Maynard Hay had their quarters in the *Virago*. They left their yachts for social events in the house. The diary entry for 29 September is 'decorated the hall all the morning, danced all night'. Writing to Boyle at the end of October, she described her enjoyment of the sailing life: 'We had some fine racing. You would not believe what good sailing you get on the lake here ... I have experienced two bad runnings aground. One was just in the entrance of the Shannon into the lake. Barry was in command but we had a pilot on board who was supposed to know every pebble in the place.'[40] It is a commonplace of interviews with Edith's relatives that they emphasise her detestation of sailing, and could also remember her phrase 'I have been shipwrecked'. We can make a safe assumption that sailing was put behind her, shut away in a closed compartment, along with everything that life at Belle Isle offered her. Boyle Somerville certainly knew of Edith's involvement with Barry at Belle Isle, as the same letter reveals that at this time Boyle was serving on HMS *Shannon* with Ben Yelverton, a cousin of Barry's, who was exchanging letters from *Shannon* with Mrs Robson, Edith's sailing companion, at this time.

Edith wrote to Cameron in Barbados on 28 August 1879, a letter in which it is quite clear that Barry was more than a passing fancy: 'It is a bore Barry getting so little leave as he must be off next Saturday, and the male Seal [young Charles Sealy] has not, as you suggested, superseded him. A steady skirmish is kept up between him and me, but I grieve to say the old Uncle is not here to help in the row.' Barry's uncle, keen to marry him to a suitable girl in order to safeguard against the horrors of anything like Lord Avonmore's clandestine marriage to Teresa Longworth and social disgrace, had sent advice to Edith on how to handle his nephew, how 'to pierce even that outer covering that so comfortably encloses Barry'. Edith's letter to Cameron describes scenes of what Edith and Barry considered to be 'fun', such as a 'scrimmage that culminated in Barry and me putting Mrs Robson's sponges in her bed and filling her bath with turf. But since then our energies have principally directed to taking each other's chairs and saying the smartest things in the most painful voice we can rise.' Barry was a very physical man, and, like Joe Coghill, enjoyed carrying Edith around bodily and rough-housing with her, an activity that was called 'bear fighting'. A dance at Belle Isle was described to Cameron at a point when Edith was already exhausted by a bad dancer, and Barry claimed her back during what sounds like the Breakdown, the last, conga-like dance of the small hours of the morning that wound through the lower rooms of the house. She wondered how her body was going to recover from the fact that yet 'another Beast should lean on my back until it nearly broke, and then run rings round me as if I was on a flypole. These things and many worse were done to me,

Dear Chimp, and yet I live.' The entire company at Belle Isle must have been impressed by the enthusiastic horseplay of Barry and Edith. Maurice Cameron, then a naval cadet, had been at Belle Isle, but had returned to his ship from where he wrote to Edith on 20 August: 'it has struck me that you ... without the pacifying presence of the SOOTHER [himself] maybe having rather a rough time. I therefore enclose a few trifles in weapons [some pins] hoping they may be of some service. They are calculated to penetrate even that outer covering that so comfortably encloses Barry. They are purely for defensive, and on no account to be used for, offensive purposes ...'

With a party of other yachts, the *Haidee* and the *Virago* sailed up the Shannon into Lough Ree. All the sailors, Edith included, attended the Artillery Ball at Athlone on 10 October. Barry got leave again and re-appeared to join them in a different yacht, the *Flabdab*, on the 21st. In this one he had a mate, noticed in Edith's diary: 'Mr Hawkins, who is a small and amusing R[oyal] E[ngineer].' Hawkins was a painter, who did some work with Edith on 'several great pictures'. His appearance and name was borrowed for the male villain of *The Real Charlotte*. As Barry was never a publicly declared suitor, Edith seems to have been free to take a simple pleasure in responding to male admiration. Another cousin of Edith's called Sydney Vernon, whom she had met two years before at a family wedding, joined the yachting party. He evidently 'flopped' on Edith, commissioned five water colours of Lough Ree from her and began an enthusiastic correspondence, to which Edith responded. After Edith had returned home and Barry had gone back to his regiment, Sydney Vernon visited CT in late November and stayed, partnering Edith in tennis and games, until 8 December. He seemed to be a great success with her. There is some duplicity in the way she describes Sydney to her brothers later as uninteresting when one does not gather this from her diary entries of November.

The diary is over-populated with Sydneys at this point; she was writing also to Sydney Robson, her sailing companion, who sent to Edith a photograph of 'her brutal cockatoo'. On 6 December when the CT households were preparing for the Avonmores' arrival, Edith told Cameron that she was annoyed that Sydney de Morgan had to leave to spend Christmas in London with his own parents: 'I regret to say that Sydney de Morgan is off this week, just before the Avonmores come which is the most awful nuisance. Apart from the violin side of the question he would have been lovely fresh meat for Alice,' she complained to Cameron in Barbados. Edith's Christmas greetings had to be sent three weeks in advance, so they were sent in this same letter of 6 December. Her seasonal greetings explain why Cameron was called 'Chimp': 'Bien Xmas, and two happy new ears. I don't like the ones you have now, they stick out too much, and are fringed with red, which is not aesthetic.' The inquisitive Cameron showed an interest in Edith's affairs of the heart, but she attempted to preserve a degree of privacy behind a smokescreen of flippancy: 'You ask, Dear Child, where I have bestowed my young affections, I tell you franchement, Eddy [Aylmer] is the sole possessor of my heart, Sissy's, Lotty's, and Ethel's (only she is too much afraid of Jamesie to say so). He has just been gazetted to the 20th Huzzars [sic] and means to be transferred to the 19th to be with Uncle Kendal. He has a lovely yellow moustache and is nicer than ever. Barry is quartered at Haulbowline now ...' Hardly a letter concerning matters of the heart failed to mention possible brides for Cameron. In this summer the daughter of Lissard, Melian O'Donovan, entered upon the social scene, and was a runaway success at dances: 'You can't think how nice and pretty she looked, and she has £500 a year. See that for you. Mother says she will save her for you.'

Adelaide Somerville was given to making rather bald pronouncements. Speeding up to a crescendo during an argument over what was going to be found when the nearby reservoir was drained for cleaning, her voice rang out triumphantly with 'Dead Babies!' At Christmastime in 1879, there was another Drishane house guest called Miss Forbes, who had an understanding with a young man who was away in Africa. In his absence Miss Forbes enjoyed flirtation, and, like many others, her eye had been taken by the attractions of Joe Coghill, who was then only nineteen. Noticing this, Adelaide said: 'There is no doubt she thinks a boy in the hand is worth a man in the bush.' In public neither Edith nor her mother showed a sensitive attitude to young love. Writing a letter to Cameron in Barbados at the end of November, Edith had entertained him with an account of 'the great Martin elopement case' which had featured in the Irish newspapers. This is the first detailed mention in Somerville's papers of the person who was to become her writing partner 'Ross', Violet Martin:

> a great niece of old Aunt Bessie's called Nannie Somerville (vulgar looking) went up to the Alexandra boarding house, and at the dear Alhambra Lectures she met Violet Martin. And when they saw one another their hearts leapt out to one another, they knew that they loved with a love passing the love of women. Then Violet brought Nannie home to Morehampton Road very often, and at Morehampton Road she encountered the lovely and fascinating Charlie [Martin, Violet's brother, then sixteen] – can you be surprised that a wild and mutual attachment was the result? ... about three weeks ago Charlie eloped with her ... a clergyman refused to marry 'infants' ... they went from church to church ... [then, exhausted, Charlie] went to tell Nannie's Aunt Elizabeth what he had done ... [meanwhile] Robert Martin had got detectives to check all steamers ... at eight in the evening Charlie walked in with Nannie 'crestfallen' ...[41]

Clearly there was a great relative difference between the sexual experience of Somerville and Ross more than five years before they met. Edith at this stage was flippant, flirtatious, and contrary with her parents, but ready to admit to her brother that she was seriously interested in Barry Yelverton and not in Charles Sealy. She was quite prepared to have a high-speed flirtation with Sydney Vernon, for entertainment's sake, while more important matters were clarifying themselves. In 1880 Edith appears to have struck against a major difficulty with her parents; and it seems most likely that this difficulty was over Barry Yelverton.

# CHAPTER 3

# *Escaping the cage*

Those brief but intense visits to Paris come back to me as almost the best times that life has given me. To be young, and very ardent, and to have achieved what you most desired … all these privileges were mine. I may have taken my hand from the plough and to *cultiver mon jardin* in other of the fields of paradise, but if I did indeed loose my hand from its first grasp, it was to place it in another, in the hand of the best comrade, and the gayest playboy, and the faithfullest friend, that ever came to turn labour to pastime …

Edith Somerville, *Irish Memories* (1917), chapter IX

POOR LAW UNION GUARDIANS (appearing in the diary as 'Plugs'), of whom Edith's father was one, were organised into regional Distress Committees to disburse relief early in 1880. One of these met in Drishane, as the Toe Head area to the west of CT was among the first to fail in bad times. The Somerville girls assisted their parents with the distribution of relief. Edith left for London on 8 March to stay with the Camerons at 5 Neville Street. There she attended art classes, and shared music lessons with Maurice Cameron, with whom she went to concerts regularly, and there Sydney Vernon called on her. On 14 May she had a violent altercation by letter with her mother, the culmination of a series of heated letters flying back and forth between them from the 9th, which continued until the 22nd. On the 14th Edith wrote in her diary: 'to my horror another letter arrived which was one larger, angry question which I have left ignored for days'. These letters were all destroyed; we might guess that they concerned either money, and how Edith was to support herself if she did not marry, or the future of her relationship with Sydney Vernon or Barry. She could hardly have been unaware of the effect of her flirtations on Herbert Greene, her first cousin and declared suitor who was approved by her parents, and marriage is most likely to have been the subject that led to this altercation.

On her own, and apparently at her own decision, on 26 May she went to the Vernons at Kettering, where she stayed with Sydney and his mother.

Bafflingly, this was another relationship that flared up briefly; but a description of Sydney written from Kettering to Cameron suggests some kind of flippant dismissal of a man who had been extremely popular with her only two months before: 'Only Mrs Vernon (Cousin Gertrude I call her with surprising fluency) and the young, very young, man Sydney are here. Mrs V is delightful ... endowed with an extraordinary natural belief in me. I pine for someone to laugh with, Sydney is a worthy lad but deadly withal.'[1] Then, leaving the Vernons on 3 June, she went on to Cousin Gendie, Mrs Miller Mundy, who approved of Sydney Vernon and was impressed by his First Class degree, at Thornbury Park before returning home on the 8th.

Here at Drishane, four days later, she moved into Jack and Hugh's old bedroom and rechristened it 'The Studio'; she associated this workroom with a new beginning and healthy resolutions, leaving it unclear as to what exactly had come to an end. At home in May and June she was learning to use a special pen called a 'Multoscript', for making multiple copies, that Barry had sent her. In her diary she wrote: 'Have made a deadly resolve to get up before breakfast and worry the piano. What agony is my future position ...' We cannot tell if this is flippant or serious, but this is the year when Ethel married and Edith came to some kind of understanding with her mother, having had a major fight. Like many girls in a crisis who had yearnings for independence, at the beginning of July she cut off some of her long hair, to her mother's horror. Short hair for some women was a kind of tonsure, signalling that they were making no bids in the marriage market. Nothing survives to suggest the reason for the timing of this demonstration, surely made against her mother. It occurs one month after their altercation by letter. That Edith was profoundly depressed and irritable is suggested by a further row with her mother; but on the surface Edith maintained her pawky, chaffing manner, particularly towards Ethel, who was escaping by marriage from the family predicament in which Edith was trapped.

During the summer of 1880, while his family were at Castletownshend, Barry posted about to various army camps on manoeuvres.[2] The Army disliked leaving regiments in any one position for too long. The barracks at Skibbereen kept an outpost in the grounds of Lissard, seat of The O'Donovan, from where they were easily inveigled to attend dances and parties at CT. A letter to Cameron from Edith on 7 August mentions that the Rifles (Rifle Brigade) had left 'the O'Donovan's camp' to be replaced by the Worcestershire Regiment. It also remarks 'apropos of Barry I have not an idea where that excellent youth is –Alice is at Belle Isle.' Edith was conducting an intensive correspondence with Maurice Cameron at this time. And the faithful Herbert Greene arrived for his summer vacation on 11 August.

In August, Coghill finances unfroze sufficiently to allow the legalities of the marriage settlement for Ethel and Jim to be drawn up.[3] Edith, writing to Cameron to tell him this, incidentally reveals the identity of one of Ethel's previous lovers, another 'nephew', the son of Aunt Josephine Coghill: 'As [Uncle K's] rents are coming in, Jim and Ethel are to be married either in November or December. The prelims were gone through this morning, and I believe Joscelyn de M[organ] is arranging the settlements! rather what you call the Irony of Fate, and somewhat rough on Joscelyn to have to arrange her marriage with another man.' Aunt Josephine had married into the extraordinary family that produced not only the mathematician Augustus de Morgan but also the potter and novelist William de Morgan, who, like Edith, was to abandon art for the more remunerative novel-writing.[4]

Colonel Somerville was entangled with his tenants in complex bluffs and double bluffs over the payment of rents. Edith explained to Cameron that the tenants all claimed that they would like to pay their proper rent: '"Sure the poor Colonel wants his money, he have a severe and heavy family" (NB this is the first time we have proved a source of income to our parents),' but that she was sure that the tenants would ask the Colonel to give them receipts only to the amount of Griffith's Valuation 'to prevent their getting into a row with the [Land] League'. Ethel's wedding began to take up everyone's time, as the date was finally fixed for 30 December: 'Glen B will be crammed to the roof and it ought to be great fun. How I wish you were home ... If only you had got into Barry's Regiment instead of this idiotic 4th.' This shows her innermost thoughts about the wedding: she was expecting it to be fun. But on the surface she was melodramatically cross about Ethel marrying and mordantly flippant, writing in her diary on 19 September: 'More talks of Ethel being married. I mean to study the art of suicide practically, I rather incline to chloroform as being at once clean and picturesque if you only stiffened yourself into a good position.' Whatever was troubling Edith, she could not share it with Cameron, or with Ethel, with whom she no longer shared a bed or shared confidences, as she was completely taken up by the Penrose family and was to drop out of CT society.

On 11 October Uncle Kendal was badly hurt by a fall from his horse when commanding the cavalry during a violent demonstration by protesters on the 'Boycott relief expedition'. Captain Boycott was Lord Erne's agent. Troops had been sent in to Fermanagh to protect the Boycott family and their workers who had been drafted in. The Castletownshend families followed all the military and political manoeuvring with intense interest. The Somerville brothers, who were away on service, tried to follow it through their letters from home. Edith's letters to her brother Boyle show that he was of a similar outgoing and active character to her. Less cautious and subtle than Cameron, Boyle always understood and shared Edith's belief that Ireland could manage herself far better from Dublin than any London politicians could, while remaining an independent member of a four-part United Kingdom. (In this, they knew themselves to be upholding the anti-Union views of Charles Kendal Bushe – that the Irish themselves, through their own native administrative class, could best rule Ireland;[5] the Union of 1800 had disastrously removed the seat of government from Dublin to London.) Their letters, consequently, have a political slant sharper and more detailed than those between Edith and Cameron. Edith considered Cameron's political vagaries after he retired as merely silly, notably when he decided to join Boyle as a Sinn Feiner; but the letters of Boyle and Edith are of serious interest in showing how two pro-Irish Big House inhabitants first perceived and then adapted to revolutionary ideas. They agreed with Parnell that Irish landlords should have a place in a nationalist movement. On 27 November 1880 Edith described the nature of the Land League to Boyle; he had asked for a precise description of the agrarian reform movement that had sprung up. It was:

> a well organised society headed by Parnell and other Irish M.Ps ostensibly for the purpose of lowering the rents and giving fixity of tenure, ie leases for ever – but really to separate Ireland from England and make a Republic of it. This League has established branches all through Ireland (except in Ulster where the Orangemen are too strong for it) which branches serve as a kind of courts of appeal and redress for tenants against their landlords. Almost all the tenant farmers have joined the League, and although they are bound to pay pretty heavy subscriptions to it, they find it so useful to them in enabling them to cheat their landlords and so obliging when they require a little murder or rick-burning done, that they have joined it, gladly ... The head branch of the League published an edict that no rents were to be paid over Griffiths Valuation, made during the worst time of the famine, intentionally 25% below letting value *at the time*: the land's value having since 1846, risen 25%, you will see that this valuation is 50% under the real valuation of the land. Naturally the landlords refused to accept this, in which case the League directed the tenants to pay nothing and insinuated that the man who shot his landlord or agent under the circumstances was only '*executing* a rack-renting Tyrant'. Any tenant who violated these orders was to be anathema, his hay burnt, his cattle mutilated and his supplies of food stopped. This cheerful game is called 'Boycotting' as the show specimen of the type is a Captain Boycott ... Down here most of the men have, after a protest, paid up; but so intense is their terror of the League

that they have either refused to take a receipt, or else asked for one for 'Griffiths' only, as one of Papa's tenants said: 'it was as much as his life was worth if it was known that he had paid his full rent'. The others did not come until Papa sent them a hint that he was ready to *borrow* money from them, when 2 sneaked over and paid partly and will probably give the rest by degrees.

Harry Townshend, living at Seafield, had received death threats; he had been sent letters smeared with blood, illustrated with a coffin and the words 'lead' and 'black death'.[6] Under the strain, his wife Minnie broke down and she left for the safety of Dublin while Harry had to be guarded by two policemen wherever he travelled on open roads. This period in West Cork was described in the second novel written by Somerville and Ross, *Naboth's Vineyard*, the village being hardly disguised.[7] 'Captain Moonlight' appears in this novel; Parnell was not averse to using the threat of violence by the anonymous Captain and his followers. When he was asked who would take over if he were imprisoned, he answered 'Captain Moonlight'. Parnell was imprisoned in October 1881 and released on 3 May 1882.[8] On 30 November, St Andrew's Day, 1880, in Edith's diary we find the resolution: 'I will work. + I will also paint' inscribed around either side of a cross. It is difficult to understand what inspired this. It does not relate in timing to Ethel's doings, to which in any case Edith was adjusted. It might relate to Hewitt's wedding on 8 November; but it is difficult to link it with anything in her relationship with Barry, which, though unofficial, apparently continues long after this date and seems to have come to some kind of a crisis in a row with her mother in 1882. However if she had been forbidden to marry Barry in May of this year, or Barry had been fobbed off with the necessity of a waiting period until he had established himself in the Army, this might explain her *angst*.

Writing to Boyle of the Christmas Day before the wedding and the accompanying Coastguard ceremonial, she described it as 'a regular Naval Demonstration in favour of Ethel'; and she was able to joke, about a mix-up in the church music, that she was not responsible for Ethel's 'choice of hymns' [hims]. She kept Boyle informed, too, of the state of the country, which was 'pretty quiet here, but at Clonakilty they have boycotted Mr Bence Jones and there have been horrible outrages in the Schull area – cutting off ears, burning ricks ad lib ... They expect a rising in January when the Coercion Bills are enforced (ie taking away the general permission to carry arms and making it possible to put a man in prison on suspicion without any definite crime being committed ie the Habeas Corpus Act being suspended) ... and [they] have flooded Ireland with troops, 30,000 of them are in the country now. I wish they would send us a few to Skibbereen ...'[9]

Not all the Drishane land was productive or easy to farm; some of it was a rocky coastal strip, from which it was difficult to scratch a living. The same letter tells of a rare Somerville eviction: 'You remember that Papa evicted [for non-payment of rent] a woman, Peggy Roche, from Castle Haven ten years ago. He had to give her an awful lot for "compensation for distress" with which she set up a public house in Skib and was very happy. However, the Leaguers went at her and would have re-instated her, after ten years, but she implored them to let her alone. She "was making money in the town which was more than she ever did in that divil of a place". So that thanks to her bad farming we escaped a row. In other parts of the country people have not been so lucky, and the Leaguers have hunted up tenants who 20 years ago had gladly given up their holdings, being handsomely paid to do so, and shoved them in again.'

In *Irish Memories* (1917) Edith gives a clear-eyed account of the poverty of the West Cork farming land in their neighbourhood and of the failure of the Government to mend a system that had itself failed to recover from the Famine: 'The years of the eighties were years of leanness ... Congested Districts Boards and Departments of Agriculture had not then arisen. Successive alterations of the existing land tenure had bewildered rather than encouraged the primitive farmers of this southern seaboard; the benefits promised were slow in materialising and in the meantime the crops failed. The lowering or remission of rents did not mean any immediate benefit to people who were often many years in arrears. Even in normal years the yield of the land, in the district of which I speak, barely sufficed to feed the dwellers on it; the rent, when paid, was, in most cases, sent from America, by emigrated sons and daughters. There was but little margin at any time. In bad years there was hunger.'

The reference to America prepares us for the returning emigrants of the novel *Naboth's Vineyard*. A generation after the Famine, some Irish Americans returned, comparatively wealthy, to the old country. They brought an entirely new political and economic perspective to their surviving relatives, making them question the *status quo* and look with interest on the Land League. Some of the landlord class took in this new perspective. An awareness that the family income could hardly support the education of her brothers sunk into Edith. At the turning of the year she made another 'deadly resolve' to get up before anyone else, as this was the only time of the day that she could be unbothered by company; the house slept soundly until Donovan the steward made the rounds at seven. She had resolved to push herself out of bed and practise, to 'worry at' the piano alone. It was a long-lasting resolve. When Martin Ross was first in CT in the summer of 1886 we find that they start to work together, completing the Buddh Dictionary that Edith had begun with Ethel, at the crack of dawn, before the house awoke.

In 1880 Barry was supposed to have spent Christmas at Drishane and to have attended the wedding, but he had to cancel: 'heard from Barry saying the 37th is ordered to Kilkenny and so can't come. Disgusting.' Edith wrote in her diary. As they shared a light-hearted and high-spirited daftness, Edith was unaware at that point that Barry was serving with cavalry detachments used in controlling violent disturbances and was frequently in real danger. The day of Ethel's wedding, headed 'The Hideous Day' in Edith's diary (30 December), was an organisational triumph, the only flaw being something that was slightly off in the wedding breakfast food, but that did not manifest itself until the day was safely over. The Coastguard Captain Cobb was very gifted at scene painting and theatrical effects, and for Ethel's wedding he excelled himself. She had a pro-cessional walk up to the church over sails spread all up the steps, and on either side of it an avenue of coastguards in white dress uniform. Neither Jim nor Ethel was nervous, and they were smilingly surrounded by close relatives old and young. Edith was one of the seven bridesmaids, Jack and Hugh were the pageboys in sailor uniform carrying Ethel's train, which Edith described to Cam as being 'as long as one of Miss Young's domestic narratives'. As soon as the married pair started to move out of the church, Edith and Joe, who was Edith's 'bridesmaid's man', belted up to the organ loft and played four-handed both Mendelssohn and Wagner's wedding marches in a 'stormy rendering' that 'nearly killed the hapless [Sam] Chard who was pumping'. The part of the wedding that Edith 'enjoyed most was the return to the carriage. Joe and I were rather late, but we weren't going to hurry. We swaggered down that sail-path, I with my tail well-spread and the Prophet [Joe], a vision in clean linen and shining hat. I am sure they preferred us to the miserable Bride and Bridegroom who had none of that graceful ease and suavity etc. etc. ...' The wedding breakfast and the cutting of the cake were at Glen B, a ceremony that later deteriorated into a bread-throwing brawl, with Joe picking on the two haughty hired waiters from Cork, who, despite their 'clerical looking' appearance, drank five bottles of champagne between them.

No sooner had the village recovered from the wedding, than next day there was a ball at Lissard. Numbers of guests were ill after the Penrose wedding breakfast, including Edith who was, she wrote to Cam: ' – O my darlin' child – rachin and scraching and roaring for the basin ... well – I was very bad all that day, so was Mother, so was Bock [Bess Somerville of Park Cottage]. The Prophet [Joe Coghill, who was banned from going to the ball by his mother] came up and gave me negus and spiritual consolation. Suddenly his Mother changed her mind and said he might go and so we all said we will go too – Melian [O'Donovan of Lissard] expects every man to do his duty and if we die she must only bury us in the back garden. So we went and it was a capital dance.' Edith had 'some very good turns' with Joe Pike, Joe Coghill, Dr Greene and 'a few chosen others'.[10] As though it marked the end of some halcyon period, after the wedding a change came over CT society: the Coghills decided to travel again and left the country en masse – a sign that Sir Joscelyn was perturbed by the agrarian situation in Ireland, for he had decided to move his family abroad again for a whole year in Germany and Italy. Perturbed for the same reason, Edith's parents decreed that it was no longer safe for any of the young to go racketting up to the Yelvertons at Belle Isle.

During 1879 over 1,000 families, amounting to over 6,000 people, had been evicted in Ireland for non-payment of rent. The potato crop had again failed in 1877–9, causing widespread destitution; previous experience did not prepare the Government to deal with the return of famine. The Land War began in August when the Compensation Bill was thrown out by the House of Lords.[11] The bill had been designed to compensate evicted tenants with sums of money paid to them by their landlords. Ironically, it was a non-evicting landlord who became the first victim of the Land War. Lord Mountmorres of Ebor Hall, County Galway, was shot dead on 25 September 1880. Parnell refused to condemn this murder, blaming the House of Lords and the Government for precipitating it. At the beginning of January 1881, Lady Avonmore wrote to Edith to tell her that Barry had been badly hurt at Kilkenny, having been stoned about the head by Land Leaguers during a demonstration.[12] A prime target, Barry's identity must have been well known, and his decision to serve further afield and out of Ireland must have been affected by this attack. The situation was to become progressively more violent over the course of this year. Writing to Cameron in the summer, Edith described the alarm rising in isolated houses: where summer open-house parties used to be the rule, now there was alarm over death threats and the violence to animals and property becoming more prevalent. 'I hope we are all right down here, but really I am very glad we are not at either Belle Isle or the Jacksons. The people are so perfectly brutalized and reckless that except one had plenty of ammunition and men to use it one would have a very poor chance in a lonely house in Tipperary ... I heard from Barry in Kilkenny he says he has to do the Polis's dirty work and patrol the roads at night'.

Giving up on Ireland for a time, Barry had applied for a posting abroad, so that soon both he and Edith, with the help of Egerton, were to leave Ireland for a wider world. At the beginning of January Egerton and Edith painted still lives in the Studio together, before he went away to study in Germany. It was hardly surprising that Anglo-Irish with the means to do so should take themselves out of the country until such time as it became less disturbed. At the end of the month, Edith went to England to stay with Aunt Alice and the Rays at Finghall

Rectory. She moved to the Coghill house in London in March, where she discovered that her Aunt Katie Coghill had got permission for Edith to stay with them in Dusseldorf for three months. Ireland was best avoided: Adelaide wrote to Edith in London on 9 March describing the Land League riots in Skibbereen. By the spring of 1881, with his Twin, Herbert Baxter, Egerton had settled in a studio in Dusseldorf, and he prevailed on his Aunt Adelaide to allow Edith to work with him there when she arrived with the rest of the Coghills on 18 March. This was the first intensive art training that she undertook abroad. She shared a private studio with Eva Le Mesurier. Her tutor, in private classes, was Gabriel Nicolet, a very talented portrait painter who became a good friend of Egerton's and a visitor to Castletownshend.[13] He was a strong influence on Egerton and Edith in their use of pastel. Because the School of Art did not admit women students, the chief pleasure of Dusseldorf for Edith was musical. She attended the twice weekly orchestral concerts at the Ton Halle and joined one of the mixed-sex choirs, a *Gesangverein*, and sang alto at the three-day May *Rheinische Musikfest*: 'The Abbé Liszt was one of the glories of the occasion. I saw him roving through the gardens of the Ton Halle with an ignored train of admirers at his heels; an old lion, with a silver mane, and a dark, untamed eye.'[14] She took to drawing caricatures of her fellow concert-goers on her music programmes – a lifelong habit caught here from German art students.

The family party returned to CT on 1 July, minus Edith. Jim Penrose, on holiday with Ethel at the Penrose seat Woodhill, came down to fetch her from Passage in a two-horse jingle, to take her to stay with them en route to home. He had been forgiven for taking Ethel away: 'The excellent Jim', she called him in her diary. True to her vow of November 1880, Edith had brought her painting up to amateur exhibition standard and joined the Irish Fine Arts Society [IFAS], exhibiting first with them in March 1881 at the Molesworth Street Gallery in Dublin. Other painters exhibiting were her uncle Sir Joscelyn Coghill, and her friends-to-be Helen O'Hara and Fanny Currey. It is typical of her flippant perversity that the first oil painting that she exhibited publicly was entitled 'Mostly Rubbish'; this lost painting was presumably a 'dead nature' study featuring a fascinating ashpit, or possibly an interior of Edith's room. By the date of the IFAS Exhibition in Cork of November in that same year, she had progressed to less freakishly-titled studies: 'Study of a Head', twice, and one 'Sunflower' shown along with the not-for-sale 'Head of a Sick Camel at the Dusseldorf Zoo.'[15] The Cork IFAS shows included Rose Barton, Mildred Butler, Egerton Coghill and Ethel and James Penrose. In the early 1880s, Edith's paintings were priced at about two to three guineas. For comparison, a study by Mildred Butler 'One of the principal streets in Castletownshend' was priced at 5 guineas, a painting by Sarah Purser called 'A sketch in summer' was 12 guineas while Edith's canvas, 'The Little Goose Girl', was 3 guineas. The men and women of the painting fraternity continued to wander at will over the Irish landscape, regardless of any political agitation. Others were more worldly: by late 1880, for instance, when Hewitt Poole went on honeymoon to Killarney with his wife Mia Jellett, like any Anglo-Irishman at the time with any nous he carried a revolver.[16]

Ethel wrote to Edith from Woodhill later during the summer to describe a vast Land League meeting in the centre of Cork at which Parnell spoke. Ethel had a gift for writing that was developed later in her children's books; her description of the crowd and its sound reminds us of the Twins' shared passion for operatic drama. On that day James Penrose was staying in the Cork County Club with a few other gentlemen, and when the crowd in the Mall became so big they unwisely went out onto the balcony to watch. They had put on their hats and coats and stood impassively watching. Parnell and the political activist Father Eugene Sheehy, a 'Land League Priest' who had recently been released from jail, passed underneath the balcony in their carriage. The crowd was cheering wildly, and hats were being waved and thrown into the air. The crowd immediately perceived the Anglo-Irish insult to Parnell, and roared, when the gentlemen on the balcony stood watching without removing their hats. The carriage stopped. The roar of the crowd intensified. Then Father Sheehy made a brilliantly theatrical miming gesture – it was impossible for anything that was said to be heard – taunting the gentry with his release from captivity. Ethel wrote: 'Jim and about a dozen men on the Club balcony didn't take off their hats and the recently released Father Sheehy stood up in the carriage with his arms crossed [and glowered at them]. Then he flung his arms wide and the crowd hissed and groaned.'[17]

In the summer of 1881 we find a sore subject rising to the surface in family letters. Placing one's male children in a safe profession, preferably out of Ireland, became necessary for peace of mind. Adelaide Somerville's favourite, and spoiled, son Aylmer was not as receptive to education as Jack and Hugh, who as small boys were successfully 'crammed' for free by Edith in German and French, and were bright enough to make it by this route into the Army and Navy cadet schools. His future was a subject of fraught debate; because there was no money to buy him a start in anything, his parents began to consider the merchant navy as a possible career for Aylmer. Edith discussed this with Cameron in a letter of 7 September 1881:

> From what we both know of Aylmer's readiness to be led by anyone he happens to be with more especially if that one is a cad, we fear that in one cruise he would come back well versed in all the most ungentlemanly

habits he could possibly pick up, e.g. drinking, swearing and card playing (not to say swindling). The real place for him is the Army; where he would be under discipline and in the company of gentlemen, but unfortunately Papa cannot afford to send him to Sandhurst ... [if he could get into the Indian Army] he would get on capitally and be able to live on his pay quite easily. It is an *awful* pity he should be allowed to go to the bad as he is a very nice boy, his only fault being his absurd follow-boyism, which makes him copy anything he thinks grand or swagger and has not sense enough to keep clear of cads. He is hail fellow well met with every dirty boatman in the village, simply from soft-heartedness ... the only alternative is the merchant service, an utterly abominable profession, in which he loses caste, manners and morals, and from all I can hear does not get anything to make up in the way of pay.

Cameron was due home on leave and Edith reminded her 'Lovey' and her 'Darling Cam' to bring home what was most important: 'Now farewell my trimbuilt wherry, bring *every note* you possess with you – I thirst for duetts.' Boyle also came home on leave in September and he and Edith set to together to make do and mend the battered furbishings of the house: 'spent the entire morning doctoring old chairs with Boyle and glue' she wrote on the 3rd. Despite all the company to be entertained, Edith read in September and October Trollope's *Phineas Redux*, Henry James' *Roderick Hudson* and Miss Mitford's *Cousins*, but struggled with *Middlemarch*. All the time she practised at copying anatomical drawings, and acquired another skill more deadly: Jim Penrose taught her and Ethel how to use revolvers. The Avonmore family had stayed at Glen Barrahane long into the autumn of 1881; but with Barry about to go abroad they were changing their routine, and Lady Avonmore eventually leased a house in London. Fearing that he might be murdered by 'Leaguers', she was relieved that Barry was leaving the worsening military situation in Ireland, though he had to wait for his new posting. But the habit of making a joke of anything was still strong, for someone unknown sent a joke telegram to Drishane on 20 October: 'Parnell arrested. Gladstone still at large.' On the following day the Land League was proclaimed an illegal organisation.[18] On 7 November Ethel Penrose had her first child: 'Ethel is the haughty proprietor of a daughter. Poor old Twin was awfully ill – but all right now thank god,' Edith wrote in her diary. At the end of November, the ailing Lord Avonmore was moved to Bordeaux for treatment of asthmatic bronchitis. Writing to Cameron about the Avonmores on 20 November, Edith reported: 'Alice goes with them, Barry will stop with his regiment at Roscrea. It would be great fun if we could get him down for Christmas.' Jokingly, Edith referred to Barry as 'Beast', and we may have a reference to him in a letter of December 1881 from Ethel, now Mrs Penrose, to Edith. A new piano had been installed at Drishane in addition to which Edith had been suffering from extreme irritability from her mother. The monstrous Row which now broke out between them dates from early 1882. It is possible that this single reference by Ethel may give a clue as to the reason for the Row, which might have been exacerbated by Edith's moony playing of Schumann and Schubert lovesongs, which her mother detested. Ethel, writing from Switzerland, expresses her pleasure in the fineness of the new piano: 'I am sure, on it, Aunt Addy will even become reconciled to the Nameless Beast'. The previous worst Rows had been in 1878 when Edith was an over-emotional nineteen-year old, coincidentally the year of her relationship with Hewitt Poole, and in May 1880. It had been started by a melodramatic outburst from Edith, obviously depressed and thinking deathly thoughts of throwing herself into the tomb again, but for a change announcing that she wanted to be cremated and not buried in the family vault.[19] By 1882 she was a hardy twenty-four and must have clarified in her mind the reasons for her difficulties with her mother. She was happy for Edith to marry within the cousinage, ideally to Herbert Greene, and thus stay within her reach, but did not want Edith to be lost from the family by an unfortunate marriage, or by entering an artist's profession in London or abroad.

Money was in short supply. The 1881 Land Act coming on top of the foundation of the Land League by Parnell and Davitt in 1877 jammed the gentry into a progressively tightening corner. In her diary on 8 January 1882, Edith recorded some of the highly effective Land League tactics: 'Uncle Josc's tenants have paid up £300 and refuse to give more. The amount due is £1,600. Pleasing prospect for Uncle Joscelyn until eviction forces the brutes to pay'. Later in the month she noted cruder tactics closer to home: 'Micky Collins [of Farrandau] was punished for paying his rent by two of his sheep being killed last night by his friends and neighbours.' On 27 February she wrote to Cameron, and in passing explained that she had been having a light flirtation with Captain Ewen Cameron, brother of Maurice, whose portrait she later painted on 6 March; this *pas de deux* was so noticeable that young Harry Morgan, another admirer, had become openly jealous: 'Harry is perfectly frantic with jealousy ... Ewen is not much of a dancer – he dances a rather fast *large* step and wants plenty of room, and as he doesn't do polkas he only took the flure [*sic*] 3 or 4 times. I think in a big room he would be very nice, and he holds you well ...'. When Ewen and Edith had been sitting out, Harry Morgan had butted in and Edith was 'borne away by the loutiest of all the rising Morgans'. This was not as offensive as it sounds to the modern ear: Jack and Hugh were cheerily addressed as 'Louts', hence the term 'Lout Hole' for their room.

Early in March she helped Ethel and Jim Penrose with the design of the memorial window to Nevill Coghill, killed in the Zulu War three years before, for St Finbarr's Cathedral in Cork. She had to make a sketch for it of the 24th's Queen's colours, that Captains Melville and Coghill had carried out of battle. She had the good news that two of her paintings had been sold in the Irish Fine Art Society exhibition just before she went abroad again. Whatever subterranean wrangling was going on between the impulses of her mother and those of Barry, Edith kept her sights on work and repeated her Dusseldorf visit in the spring of 1882. She left London on 28 March. This year she stayed with the family of her fellow art student, May Goodhall.

Her tutor was Carl Sohn, who taught both landscape and portaiture.[20] While she was immersed in her art education with May, her mother sent her the news of her grandfather's death. It made her ill with grief, and Mrs Goodhall put her to bed, where she wept through her waking hours. She wrote to her mother: 'Darling darling grandpapa … I wish I was at home   … I have never half been grateful enough for his fondness and goodness to me … Please keep a little bit of his hair.' The lock of her grandfather's hair was set into an *in memoriam* locket which she kept around her neck, to kiss in remembrance of him.[21] The Goodhalls were the most sympathetic friends she could have had in this event, and in a week she returned to studio life. Her tutor, the 'delightful' and red-bearded Carl Sohn, encouraged her landscape studies, where her greatest gift lay. In a letter to her mother at this time, we have one of the earliest mentions of Edith's passion for red hair, a thing that stayed with her through life. She wrote of her tutor's criticism of her last studio work, a portrait: 'He liked the colour of the Italian boy very much and said many other things which, together with his red beard, have combined to make me hopelessly in love with him.' As Edith's attachments to the men in the Drishane yard were to older ones like Peter Donovan, who had white hair and bright blue eyes, or Tom Connell, who was fair, this was a curious taste for her to have acquired. Nothing appears to explain it. Despite her happiness with Sohn, she became restless. Noticing the lack of exhibition facilities for women painters, she began to feel frustrated by the segregation of women art students as mere amateurs from the professional young men of the Art School. It appears that women were chiefly tolerated as a sub-group as they provided an income for hard-up painters as tutors to them.

Edith returned from Dusseldorf to spend a month in London, where she went about with Herbert, going to a memorable performance of *Patience* with him on 3 July, the day before she went back to CT. There was intensive socialising with officers from the barracks in Skibbereen during the summer. The Avonmores were in CT for a holiday during this year. A letter from Jack, at school, to his eldest sister, shows that Edith had a special connection with them, and also that she was not a morning person: 'I wonder are you a lazy pig of a morning and what does Lord and Lady A say to you for that? how is Algey getting on and how many birds has he shot with his catapult, ever your loving Brat Jack.' Ethel had a son and heir for Jim on 21 October, Edith entered in her diary; this was Dennis, her godson on whom Edith doted: 'Ethel has a young son – he is beautiful and intelligent.' To complete their happiness, Jim Penrose got the agency for Lord Darnley at Athboy with 'a fixed salary of £600 a year'. Sixty guests came to a ball in Drishane on 28 November, when the dancing went on until 6 o'clock in the morning. A regimental piper had come with the Kings Own Borderers, who played reels and schottisches for the dancers. For the third time in her diary Edith marked St Andrew's Day with a cross, reminding herself of her vow. The officers from the barracks at this period were extremely musical, and, in combination with the family instrumentalists, a performance of Haydn's Toy Symphony was achieved. Though seemingly happy in her social life, by her twenty-fourth year something had made Edith consider spinsterdom. In December she recorded in her diary, apparently unconnected to anything else, the remark of a housemaid: 'I think I will never be married. I'd love to be an ould maid. A single life is airy.'

The ever-sympathetic and attentive Egerton understood her frustrations in Dusseldorf and began a campaign to move to Paris, where women painters were more easily accepted by the professional painting fraternity. She wrote in *Irish Memories*: 'I do not regret those two springs in Dusseldorf but still less do I regret the change of counsels that resulted in my going to Paris the following year. "When the true Gods come the half-Gods go" and, apart from other considerations, the Dusseldorf School of Art only admitted male students, and ignored, with true German chivalry, the other half of creation.'[22] The idea that she was created only as a half-being with the potential of joining up with her other half and thereby becoming whole somehow floated in her thoughts despite her airiness.

The later novels of Somerville and Ross were to dwell on an Anglo-Irishwoman's struggle between the desire for independence and adventure and the desire for a compatible partner with whom to replicate their mothers' exercise of power as the mistress of a Big House. Edith may have seen this as merely exchanging one cage for another. Through her brother Cameron's failure to marry, as a spinster sister Edith was to achieve both seemingly incompatible desires, with sex discarded, in 1895 at her mother's death. But, in the early eighties, for Edith the struggle of choosing between a career and a possible marriage was a live issue. Her novel *French Leave* (1928) was written twelve years after Martin's death, and five years after she had turned down an affair with the enthusiastically lesbian Ethel Smyth. It has a heroine who is quite closely modelled on Edith, and she chucks art for Lord Corran. As we know that Edith subsequently made a comfortable income for herself by writing and painting, marrying Barry in the mid-eighties against the wishes of her family might well have been a disastrous move for her personally. Undoubtedly she knew that children would have dominated at least the period 1885–1900, for she had the example of Ethel to observe. Colonel Somerville and his wife were keenly interested in the financial standing of any young man who presented himself as a suitor. The dismissed Hewitt Poole must have seemed a hopeless prospect, and Barry not much better, even had he been born legitimately of a socially acceptable father.

With the failure of rents, the Avonmores were now in worse financial difficulties; when they appeared in CT, Belle Isle was let to shooting or sailing parties. The combination of difficulties may have been too much for Adelaide, who may not have known of the true state of the Coghill finances, and may have retained until her death in 1895 an overestimation of the wealth and consequent grandeur of her family. In her eyes all the world knew that Barry Yelverton, the lawyer colleague of Charles Kendal Bushe [the 'Incorruptible' who turned down Castlereagh's bribes], had accepted his bribe and the title of Viscount Avonmore in order to carry the Act of Union; and, even worse, all the world knew of the moral disgrace of his great-grandson, whose children were of dubious legitimacy. Through no personal fault of his own, Captain Barry Yelverton of the Hampshires carried a taint of moral and financial corruption that would have rung alarm bells in any genealogically minded stockbreeder's calculations. As Edith was to write herself in 1910, 'the dirty drop is always a danger in a pedigree'.[23]

The letters between the Somerville sisters have a lot of detail on horses and their maintenance and hunting; Edith's favourite Peter Donovan, the horse-breaker, was still working around Castletownshend in January 1883, as Edith reminds Hildegarde in a letter: 'You never returned my precious Peter's list.' At the beginning of February 1883, all the Somervilles went to stay with the Gubbins at Dunkettle in order to attend a Masonic ball in Cork. A few days after the ball the Gubbins loaned Edith a mare, and Mrs Gubbin's habit, for her to hunt with the United in company with their daughter May (Marion), who was a six-footer like Hildegarde, and was to become a faithful friend. In March and April, Edith went to stay with Ethel and Jim at Athboy, where she painted and sketched and made music with her hosts. She was low in spirits: 'began a very original book "my trivial life and misfortune, by a plain woman"' she wrote in her diary on 16 April. She went back to CT to welcome Egerton on his return with their tutor M. Nicolet, who was painting a portrait of Colonel Kendal Coghill. The Colonel was about to retire from the Hussars. Earlier in

3 Charles Yelverton,
4th Lord Avonmore.

4 His son Barry Yelverton,
5th Lord Avonmore.

the year Edith had written to Cam: 'Uncle K leaves the service in June I grieve to say – and will devote himself to art and hunting.' A boon companion, much loved by all his nephews and nieces, Uncle K played a strange wind instrument called a saxhorn, which he sometimes played in church accompanying the organist, and sometimes played on board yachts when he was sailing. His sister Mrs Somerville in early May planted out an entire flower bed with chickweed seedlings, having mistaken them for asters. The whole of the episode was given to Lady Dysart of *The Real Charlotte*.[24] She remained boisterously domineering over her eldest daughter. On 6 May Edith entered in her diary, after a terrific political row over a recently defeated parliamentary bill that Gladstone lost by only three votes: 'Mother says I am nothing but Chamberlain and would have voted for the Affirmation Bill.' Charles Bradlaugh, the radical parliamentary colleague of Joseph Chamberlain, and an atheist, had requested the right to affirm rather than take the oath on the Bible. Thought was being given to earning income: as a money-raising speculation Edith began to assemble quotations for the Mark Twain Birthday Book, giving apt quotations for every day of the year.

Joe Coghill turned up for a holiday in early August, and he and Edith fell back into their old ways, cutting each other's hair, and playing the fool all day long. Her diary entries show that the desire to cut off one's hair was not in the least peculiar in a girl: 'Joe came up and we cut hair (all Sylvia Townshend's among other trifles)' and the next day: 'fine day, did more hair cutting, having a general mowing before Joe goes'. This is a most interesting entry. Sylvia Townshend was CT's most high-powered man chaser, so perhaps there was a vogue for the gamine look. There were changes at Belle Isle in this year: in April old Lord Avonmore died and Barry became the 5th Viscount Avonmore.[25] If Adelaide Somerville disapproved of Barry as a husband for Edith on account of his possible illegitimacy (he was considered to be so in the eyes of the Irish courts), his lack of money and his father's well-publicised immorality, she was overlooking the fact that they were very well suited in the hope that their obvious interest in one another would pass. Like Barry, Edith was an untidy, careless creature, impervious to dust and dirt, and was consequently known as Slummy and The Queen of Filth to her intimates. It is likely that, when we read her later criticism of Barry's unkemptness, we are hearing an echo of her mother. For example, we last hear any detailed description of Barry in a letter to Cameron dated 3 September 1883. Like her earlier dismissive description of Sydney Vernon after she had been through a flirtation with him, this is surely an attempt to put Barry at a distance. He had been at Drishane briefly, sailing in to CT on a yachting trip with friends: 'He is perfectly unchanged since the old Row time. In fact I am vaguely disappointed in him. He is as jolly and noisy and goodnatured as he always was but he has no manner (not manners). He is exactly like an easy going schoolboy; has filthy hands, eats live winkles with a clasp knife and doesn't seem a day more than 15 or 16. All the same he was great fun and is just as great a bear-fighter as ever. I only wish he had a little more of the "ormy accent" and swagger, and that he did not yacht and make friends with such cads as his two ship mates'. One of these shipmates was the playboy son of a wealthy Cork tanner named Dunn; nevertheless to Edith he was a 'cad' whose brogue, table manners and bearing she criticised. This supercilious attitude to the middle classes in trade, particularly in this specific case of a tanner, prepares us for the lengths to which Edith and Boyle were to go in order to avoid acknowledging their descent from Scottish Burgess skinners. Her diary entry on Barry's visit shows a new, crude consciousness of class and its gradations. She thinks Barry's companions are second-rate, if not third. The girl who never gave a thought about what people might think of her and her friends has changed; she has become sensitive to status and wealth.

Her letters to Cameron contain turns of phrase concocted to amuse him, and about this time in her life she began to realise that such humour was a marketable commodity. She was aware that in England there was an audience appreciative of 'Irishisms'. She had been stung by a drowsy wasp at the end of the summer: 'I cannot conceal from you that I was in severe pain and the next day half my head was as big as the whole of it (this thoroughbred Irish shorthand is worth millions in the English market.)' To Cameron she also confided her thoughts on men, whom she met at dances. Describing a dance late in October she wrote: 'I think I only knew three people there, (I mean dancing men) ...' She organised a dance for the local soldiery at Drishane at the beginning of November: 'I only asked the younger ones from each house "giddy flurtin" gurls.' She showed three pictures in the winter IFAS Show in Cork, one of which was singled out for praise in the notice of the exhibition in the *Cork Constitutional*.[26] When she went to see the exhibit, Edith was pleased with the way her paintings had been hung, and noted in her diary that she admired: 'Some lovely O'Haras and Curreys.'

Edith was staying in London when Barry turned up again at CT towards the end of the year. An undated letter to her mother describing another gift from him, evidently from late 1883 as he has become the new Lord Avonmore, shows that Barry was still thinking of her. He had found a barnacled block of exotic wood in flotsam while sailing and sent it to her in London for her to carve. It had been roughly labelled, with no letter to identify the sender, but it was an appropriate gift. In the Glen B Studio they had done craft work together; Barry had designed his own headed notepaper, with a drawing of the Avonmores' yacht, which Edith herself used when short of her own. The letter to her mother is important in that it identifies Barry as Edith's 'Skipper', which was how he signed his letters to her, only one of which survives: 'I had no idea Lord Avonmore sent that block of wood. Tell him with my most respectful compliments that it never arrived till the 2nd (being wrongly directed) and in that case the sell always reacts upon the seller. Tell him also that only for the respect that I own him as my Skipper, I should be inclined to suggest he wanted to send me something to remind me of himself. I believe a Barnacle generally pre-supposes a G – – se ever your loving Edith PS What *did* it mean?'

It may have meant that Barry was going to hold fast, like a barnacle. Adelaide showed her hand clearly in late December of 1883 when, in all the fraught discussion about funding Edith's art training, she herself volunteered to give to Edith the £100 left to her by her sister Florence, who had died unmarried on the 20 December after a long and agonising illness. Edith took the survival of Aunt Florence's spirit after death as a matter of course. Though they ceased to be practising spiritualists in their middle years, Edith and Cameron retained throughout their lives a fixed belief in the survival of personality after death.[27] Edith wrote to Cameron about Aunt Flo on the day of her death: 'It is a comfort to think she will have a happy Christmas – you can't imagine what sufferings she has gone through, and we can only be thankful they are over at last.' There was family conflict over the plans for spring, conflict as to the city in which Edith and Cameron were to take a vacation together. Cameron needed to go to Germany to brush up his German for an application to the army staff college, but Edith did not want to study in Dusseldorf again. On the next day she wrote again to delay the start date for the family leaving for abroad. 'I don't think I *could* start on the 6th [of February '84] as my gowns wouldn't be ready ... Papa won't say yes or no, it is impossible to get him to discuss the project or to suggest any plans of household economy to render it more feasible. In fact as Mother said this morning "He is intentionally just letting it drift, in hopes it may all come to nothing" – it is too bad of him, as if he would even say definitely "I won't go" we should know where we are and what to arrange ... I heard from Egerton, strongly urging Paris for me, he says the work there is what I want, and what would do me real good ... my real object is not pleasure but work and I know I should get the latter in Paris of a better quality and with less distractions ... Sweeny has not yet collected the November rents which makes the financial troubles all the worse – in fact I see plainly that it would be quite impossible either to ask or expect that we could go by ourselves to Dusseldorf ... nobody but Minnie [Townshend] realises how I *pant* to get away and work – but it can't be helped. I was born in a pecuniary rat cage, and I suppose I must "take the consequences" of such a situation and be thankful that I *have* escaped once or twice – and I can't vampire the whole family for the sake of my dirty self.'

This funding of Edith's art education is an important financial intervention by Adelaide. The Somervilles were exceedingly short of money. By funding Edith, they were ensuring that she did something that would absorb and distract her in a manner and in a place that they knew about, and after which their daughter might manage to make a living for herself. This is strangely special treatment for a woman who was, after all, twenty-five. It marks a quite critical point of acceptance by her parents that she was to aim at being a professional artist. There is no evidence to explain why Adelaide felt the need to give her daughter this life-changing gift. If her parents had, in effect, twice prevented Edith from making an unsuitable marriage, the explanation may be that they were offering her an alternative route to that normal for a girl in their class; perhaps more significantly, the effect of it would also be to tie Edith, in a spinster state, to Drishane. Adelaide may have calculated that Drishane would need a household manager while the boys were away; certainly she herself shows a strong dependence upon her eldest daughter, expecting from her the support and organisation that should properly have been carried out by the other-worldly Colonel Somerville.

Full of gratitude for her mother's generosity, Edith wrote to Cameron to cancel the proposed trip with him to Dusseldorf on 23 December 1883, as she had agreed with Egerton that Paris was where she would get the best teaching: 'I must take any opportunity I can,' she explained, telling him that Mother was funding her: 'I feel mean enough taking her little private store for *work* with the hope of repaying her, but I could not take it for Skittles, and Dusseldorf for three months would not be more than that. Remember, like Dives, that you in your youth had your educational good things and to me they are only coming in my old age – and I *can't* afford to keep my miserable talent in a bag any longer or I shall find by painful experience that tho' Art is long, Life is short. Dear Child, forgive me. It isn't my fault – our poverty and not my will consents.'

The early days of January 1884 were taken up by incessant arguments with Edith's mother about chaperones for her in Paris; these were referred to in Buddh shorthand as 'chips'.[28] When a young woman was travelling through or staying in an unknown place, some female had to be found to sleep with her for safety's sake; this was a serious duty of the nearest male relative. Egerton was writing to Edith from Paris arranging her *pension*, and making all smooth with her parents; he was established as a pupil of Adolphe Bouguereau at Académie Julian.[29] She crossed to stay with the Coghills in London on the 31st. A family party left for Paris, arriving on 5 February. Egerton's painting companion Herbert Baxter acted as chaperone to Edith, and he took her to Colarossi's where she was entered as a student on 6 February. The women students here were not amateurs playing at art. The studio day involved getting up at 7.30 and working from 8.30 right through until evening meals. There was a change of model between the morning and afternoon sessions.[30] Edith studied at Colarossi's again with May Goodhall as her painter companion and bedmate. The family attitude to the move to Paris, and Edith's own reaction to it, is described in a passage in *Irish Memories*:

> Of old, we are told, Freedom sat on the heights, well above the snow line no doubt, and, even in 1884, she was disposed to turn a freezing eye and a cold shoulder to any young woman who had the temerity to climb in her direction. My cousin who had been painting in Dusseldorf, had moved on to Paris, and his reports of the studios there, as compared to the possibilities of work in Dusseldorf, settled the question for me. But the point was not carried without friction. 'Paris!' They all said this at the tops of their voices. It does not specially matter now who they were; there are always people to say this kind of thing. They said that Paris was the Scarlet Woman embodied. They also said: 'The IDEA of letting a GIRL go to PARIS!' This they said incessantly in capital letters ... and my Mother was frightened'.[31]

Eventually Edith arrived in Paris with what she described as a 'bodyguard' of her mother, Cameron, another girl cousin and May Goodhall. After three weeks the bodyguard party was bored out of its wits, and they left. May Goodhall and Edith sighed with relief and moved into a cheap *pension* near Colarossi's. Her tutor in this first spring in Paris was Dagnan Bouveret.[32] She loved the characterful models and thrived under the ferocity of her tutor's criticisms; as someone who came to strict art education so late in her life she did far better than might have been expected with a moderate talent. Her French seems to have been quite serviceable and colloquial. From this first year in Paris there is a diary entry about *poste restante* mail: 'Went to ask about the letters Cam says he sent me. If he is playing the common April Fish he will be sorry.' April Fish: Poisson d'Avril, is the French equivalent of April Fool, later used as a title for an RM story.

Her fellow students were women for whom their training in Paris was intended to give lifelong distinction as teachers and professional artists, to fit them for an independent life and income. Most of them seem to have been very poor, managing on very small funds, so that, like Edith, they had to cram as much as they could into the time that they could afford to stay in Paris. They were Bohemian, some of them short-haired, and their manners seemed unusually free after the relative formality of Dusseldorf. Edith wrote of them later: 'Colarossi's never took a "day off". Weekdays, Sundays and holy days, the studios were open and there were *élèves* at work. Impossible to imagine what has become of them, all those strange, half sophisticated savages, diligently polishing their single weapon, to which all else had been sacrificed.'[33] In Paris, Edith learned to make do. She discovered that she could use her tin hat box as a foot bath, and, in extremis, could even bath out of it in sections. Her necessarily cheap rooms rarely had easy access to a *salle de bain*. All through her life she was to amuse some and alarm others with her mixture of the Bohemian with the *grande dame*.

More of her childhood friends were marrying, and some for love rather than money. Her cousin Sissy Payne Townshend, sister of Charlotte 'Plain' Townshend, who was later to become Mrs George Bernard Shaw, had succumbed to the charms of a delightful but penniless Captain Cholmondeley of the Rifle Brigade. Hugh Cholmondeley, with a love of horses equal to hers, was to become a dear friend of Edith's. She wrote to Cameron: 'They will worry along comfortably on £4,000 a year – which is what Sissy will have if not more – why oh why did Egerton let her go out of the family? I believe he might have had her if he had tried hard enough …'

Edith wrote to Cameron from Paris on 28 March 1884, describing her daily routine and her tutor: 'Dagnan Bouveret is becoming very attached to me, he has been very amiable.' The women students all roomed together in the same warren of a *pension*: 'we play in and out of each other's rooms like rabbits.' Ethel and Jim came over to see what her life was like as an art student for a week in May. In return for all the care Mrs Goodhall had given Edith, the Goodhall girls, Janie and May, were invited as guests this summer to Drishane for their vacation. Edith left Paris for London on 12 May, stayed for almost a month with Uncle Kendal and Uncle Joscelyn at their house in Penywern Road, and returned to CT on 4 June. On the 21st the whole of CT was invited to inspect the Fleet, then at Bantry. Boyle was serving in HMS *Agincourt*, on board which they were given luncheon. With all the sailors and soldiers about, there were many dances 'Navy and Army assisting nobly.'

In this summer Edith had seen a lot of a Captain Pennyman, nicknamed 'The Coin', and at a party in Drishane with him and some fellow officers early in September, one of the captains, who was a Blavatsky enthusiast, organised a table-turning session and spirit writings that 'got onto dangerous ground'. 'Captain K' then tried mesmerising Edith and made her 'towed and guided' go across a room to pick up a newspaper to bring it to him. She was disturbed by this, and told Cam: 'we had better play tennis and let the spirits alone'.[34] From her diary entries at this time it is clear that her mother inspired a crass streak of contrariness and independence in Edith. On 26 October she wrote: 'Very fine. Of course because it was Sunday I could not paint. This thing will make a Jew of me: I can't stand it much longer. Music indifferent chiefly owing to Mother singing the Jubilate when I was worrying away at the Benedictus.'

That Edith was still in very low spirits for some reason and needed cheering up is suggested by another development in 1884. Other well-wishers came forward: Percy and Eddy Aylmer had written to Mark Twain in the previous summer to request his permission for Edith to edit and illustrate a 'Birthday Book' giving quotations from his works for each day of the year. Evidently Edith knew Mark Twain's work intimately.[35] A quotation from the RM that became so famous that in England its original source was forgotten: 'being economical with the truth', as Flurry Knox was described by Edith and Violet Martin, is in fact a re-working of a Twain *bon mot*: 'The truth is so valuable that we must learn to economise with it.' Both of the wealthy Aylmer brothers adored Edith, and both shelled out large sums on her behalf during their lifetimes. Eddy Aylmer at this point paid ninety-five pounds to have *The Mark Twain Birthday Book* printed. Through Remingtons it was to sell very well and earned Edith a regular sum from royalties. On 2 November Edith wrote jubilantly to Cameron, 'The dear Mark [Mark Twain, which was the pen-name of Samuel Clemens] gives full leave to publish and treats it as a compliment ... he is a brick.'

She went up to Dublin before Christmas to see the Greenes, then crossed to
Aunt Alice to attend Ripon Ball with the Rays, staying at Finghall Rectory. While
there she finished the proofs of the *Mark Twain Birthday Book*.[36] When she got
back to Drishane she began a portrait of Hildegarde at the same time as Egerton.
To his delight, Barry had been promoted Captain on 16 November; he and all of
the serving soldiers of the CT circle were on the alert. In early 1885 the Egyptian
war began to build up to the crescendo of the race between the Generals Garnet
Wolsely and Butler to reach the besieged General Gordon in Khartoum before the
Mahdi did. Keen to take part in the relief expedition, and to distinguish himself,
Barry had applied for secondment to the Nile from his Regiment and was posted
to Egypt, which had been a British protectorate since 1882. Serving under General
Garnet Wolsely, he took part in the cross-country attempt to reach General
Gordon. He wrote a letter to Edith expressing his happiness with the bold
adventure of the expedition. This last letter from him was destroyed, along with
the rest of his letters, bar one accidental escaper, by Edith herself when she had to
reduce her papers by burning on leaving Drishane in 1946. Barry was struck down
by a virulent fever before the victory at Kirbekan in February 1885, and died after
three days' illness on the 13th. Edith wrote to her mother from London en route
to Paris on the 19th: 'Isn't this news about poor Barry terrible? We had seen it in
the Morning Post but hoped, as it was not in the other papers, that it was not true
– Poor Lady Avonmore – I think of all her troubles this is the greatest. It really
seems too sad to be true I will write to poor Lady A from Paris but I *dread* doing
so with all my heart'. Lady Avonmore responded instantly to Edith's letter. Edith
wrote to her Mother again: 'Poor Lady Avonmore is inconsolable about Barry I
got such a heartbroken letter from her this morning. The poor thing has heard
nothing from Egypt about his illness, all she got was a telegram from the Horse
Guards announcing his death. I wish I knew where Eddie was [also serving in
Egypt at this time] he might be able to find out for us particulars of his three days
illness ...' Edith saw Lady Avonmore on the way back from Paris. She told
Cameron by letter on 26 April: 'Lady A seemed utterly broken-hearted – you
would hardly know her – she sent her love to you and thanks for your messages
about poor Barry ...' The regimental chronicle of the Hampshire Regiment
recorded the death of Captain Lord Avonmore and the deep regret of his brother
officers of the Second Battalion, then stationed in Hyderabad: 'with his regiment
he was a general favourite as those of us who knew him personally can testify'.
There is a memorial plaque to his memory in Winchester Cathedral. Barry was
succeeded by his younger brother Algie, the 6th Viscount Avonmore, but when he
died in 1910 the title became dormant, his wife having borne one daughter. The
collateral Yelverton heirs of the viscountcy, descended from the brother of the
third Lord Avonmore, settled in Australia and New Zealand.

There can be little doubt that Barry Yelverton largely inspired young Lord Corran in Edith's 1928 novel *French Leave* – an Irish landlord who must decide on how and whom and where to marry, on how his heirs will face the New Ireland, and on how to survive in a country that does not want him. The male lead of her first novel *An Irish Cousin* is given Barry's middle name, Nugent, and like Barry, he frequents the south of France. Edith had acted as the mistress of Belle Isle in the absence of Barry's parents in the summer of 1879. Like a long locked-up dream written into being, the novel's protagonists marry and stay on in Ireland rather than fleeing from it with the majority of their class. The romantic themes of her novels show a repetitive pattern, which has been little examined in relation to her life before 1886. They combine elements of her experiences with Hewitt Poole as well as with Barry Yelverton, and it is in *The Real Charlotte* that we find a clear example of such a fictional combination. Here there is a secret correspondence between Hawkins and Francie, in which Hawkins conceals his previous engagement to another woman. Hewitt had concealed his unofficial engagement to Mia Jellett during the period in 1878 that he was involved with Edith in a privately delivered exchange of letters. Also given to Hawkins and Francie are a series of sailing mishaps the like of which Edith only experienced with Barry on Lough Derg in 1879. Hardly any of Edith's nephews, nieces or cousins realised or even suspected that her youth, before she met Violet Martin, was completely sealed-off, unknown territory, and had not been sexually uneventful.[37]

A handwritten commonplace book of quotations, now marked distractingly with a capital 'M', shows that Edith kept a collection of emotionally significant love lyrics and poems dating from her late teens to late twenties, just as she kept sheet music and love songs from the same period. Violet Martin came to know well the favourite German love songs that Edith sang often at musical parties; she had been given them by Cameron in two music albums from Dusseldorf: Brahms' *In deinen blauen Augen* (Opus 59. Song No.8; see below), *Die Lotusblume* from Robert Franz's *Album of Lieder*, and a song called *Liebesgluck* by E. Geibel.[38]

> Your blue eyes are so still
> I can see into their depths.
> You ask what do I hope to see?
> I see my own well being.
> I was burned by another pair,
> and the scar still hurts,
> Yet your eyes are clear
> and cool like the sea.

A later letter from Violet Martin to Edith in 1887 shows that Edith herself wrote about lost love even after Martin was wandering about at the edges of CT life; after criticism from Martin, she published two love sonnets in *The World* in 1889, printed at the end of the next chapter. She went to enormous lengths to conceal her authorship of these sonnets. In Edith's commonplace book a quotation from Morris ('When I was young and green hope was in sight') lies beside a superficially lighthearted verse of W.E. Henley's:

> You babbled in the well known voice,
> Not new, not new, the words you said.
> You touched me off that famous poise,
> That old effect of neck and head.
> Dear, was it really you and I?
> In truth the riddle's ill to read:
> So many are the deaths we die
> Before we can be dead indeed.

Another entry, a quatrain from Burns set to the still familiar haunting music, 'Ye Banks and Braes o' Bonny Doon', surely shows that Edith had won love and then lost it, or put it away from her. Edith's version is unusual, perhaps from a song book with its own variation on the words:

> Thou'll break my heart, thou bonny bird
> That sings upon the bough
> Thou minds't me o' the happy days
> When my fause Luve was true.

However we interpret their relationships, it cannot be said that either Barry Yelverton or Violet Martin were in any way false to Edith, neither did they have the remarkable blue eyes that inspired the Brahms song *In deinen blauen Augen*. This would suggest that for Edith the damaging relationship was with Hewitt Poole, who already had a secret unofficial engagement to Mia Jellett before he took up with Edith, and who married the determined and suspicious Mia just before Ethel married Jim Penrose. Whatever had marked Edith emotionally before she met Martin, she was very determined to hide it. In 1925 Edith instructed Hildegarde, in a will made before travelling on the notorious French railways with Ethel Smyth, to destroy all her papers from before 1886.[39] This was not done; Hildegarde assembled Edith's personal papers in a trunk, which remained substantially as an outlier to the post-1886 papers. Though all of Edith's papers were moved down to Tally Ho, this trunk was later to have a different fate from the other papers that went out of Drishane in 1946. It did not travel to Gloucestershire with the rest. As we shall see, Edith was later ashamed of her behaviour as a racketty young woman, and wished to edit out what had happened to her before meeting Martin; what little survives suggests that the celibate spinster feminist, who when old was a crabby martinet with the young, was a very different animal in her youth.

Apart from the disaster of Barry's death, in many ways 1885 was to be a good year during which Edith made progress as a professional graphic artist and as a writer. She continued to show interest in young men, and socialised. In early February she went to stay with Captain Pennyman's family at Ormesby Hall, Middlesborough. From 21 February to April 12th she was again at Colarossi's Studio in Paris, studying under Gustave Courtois.[40] She roomed with a convivial pair from the year before, Miss Marion Adams, an American, and Miss von Poncet, a German. 'To me was allotted the humble role of scullion. We had rooms in a tall and filthy old house in the Rue Madame, one of those sinister and dark and narrow streets that one finds in the Rive Gauche, that seem as if they must harbour all variety of horrors, known and unknown, and are composed of houses whose incredible discomforts would break the spirit of any creature less inveterate in optimism than an Art student.'[41] To save money she learned to cook on a spirit stove, and practised strange domestic economies to make every *sou* count. She ate a lot of fried bacon and eggs, and *frites* from street sellers. In her letters from this year in Paris we first see comments critical of her English fellow students. Another German fellow student, a Fraulein Wirth, 'knew I was not English by my voice … in fact the English are, without exception, such a horrid crew that I am proud and thankful to be able to say that I am Irish.'[42] Although proud to be identified as Irish, which was not at all a common stance in her Anglophile society, she was still finding it difficult to come out as an independent woman, and taking cover behind male relatives was to remain a failing.

Crossing back to London, she explained to her mother her arrangements to ensure that she did not sleep alone *en route*, returning to the Rays: 'I have written to Uncle Kendal to let me have May Goodhall to sleep with me on Sunday night and I will go to Finghall on Tuesday by the first train.'[43] She wrote to Cameron when she was re-established at Finghall Rectory; she had not written to him while she was in Paris, time there being too precious. This year she had some tuition from Egerton's old tutor Gabriel Nicolet: 'I left Paris on the 12th – in tears and fury and the night train – they had ordered me off a whole week before I expected to have to go, and you may imagine how real mad I was … Nicolet seemed really delighted with what I had done in my seven weeks.'[44] At Finghall Rectory she took part in an amateur theatrical production of *The Sorcerer* with Egerton and Joe Coghill. The Coghill brothers were very expert with stage make-up and for her acting part had transformed Edith into an elderly woman. A description was sent to Cam: 'Once I half lost my head and actually spoke one of my sentences in a fine Cork brogue but I recovered and the rest went capitally ... Joe invented any amount of business that fetched the house splendidly ... Egerton got an encore for "My name is J.W." but that was the only one ... heaps of people utterly refused to believe that I was not an old woman of at least sixty ...' The crowded house party was utterly chaotic in its sleeping arrangements. It was obviously a very necessary part of a male relative's duty to make sure that in such circumstances one's womenfolk were not placed in improper situations. Edith wrote to Cam explaining that Joe 'got kind little Auntie May to come up and dine and sleep with me on Sunday night'.

Ethel and Jim were at the *Sorcerer* performance: 'I meant to come straight home but Ethel and Jim laid violent hands upon me and carried me off home where I stay until next Monday.'[45] She did not tell Cameron what she had done in his name: May 1885 saw the publication of a piece of comic prose by Edith in *Home Chimes* (she had submitted it to the magazine under her brother's name). It was an account of a production of *Macbeth* by a travelling company of actors given in the Skibbereen town hall. An income from the popular press seemed a growing possibility. The *Mark Twain Birthday Book*, published by Remingtons, sold out its first edition in two months, so a second thousand was being printed. Her royalties earned £12. 10s. per thousand. In this year, after Barry's death, two interests materialised that were to develop into lifelong habits of mind. She began writing down notable speech and words with precise intonations, and met her first hardline woman suffragist, Fanny Currey. It is clear that her interest in vernacular speech, the compilation of the Buddh Dictionary of family language, and suffragism were all established before she met Violet Martin, an event that she did not particularly mark at the time. And during this summer of 1885, during which two of Edith's 'playboys', Joe Coghill and Charles Sealy, married and became family men, and Ewen Cameron died at Quetta in Beluchistan, Ethel Penrose found a novel way to raise Edith's spirits.

Cameron had brought to Drishane a copy of E.P. Sinnett's distillation of Madame Blavatsky's theosophist doctrines, *Esoteric Buddhism*, and it caused a sensation in the family.[46] Edith loaned the copy to Ethel Penrose, who, with her fertile mind and adaptive skills, very quickly put Blavatsky and the Buddha to her own uses. Edith wrote to Cameron, who was stationed near Canton, on 27 May 1885 to explain Ethel's new theory. The descendants of Charles Kendal Bushe, Ethel declared, represented an incarnation 'of the Divine Essence that comes down now and then in the ages ... She herself is the Meath Buddh. Egerton and I manifested in Paris and Yorkshire. Aunt Georgina is the Buddh

**O**

**One of Them**. n. a man, not necessarily young, good looking or well-born, but is endowed with a subtle attractiveness, imperceptible to grosser intelligences, tho' for the keenly sensitive & possessing an overmastering charm. (deriv. from the number & variety of those gifted with this strange fascination, the uncomprehending scoffer would, at the sight of any low mean person, mockingly enquire if he also was "one of them"? i.e. those in whom the Twins have discerned the quality mentioned above. Mod Buddh)

**P**

**Paughmedear!** interjection. The last possible expression of a contempt too sublime for argument. (deriv. The only reply vouchsafed by a lady, of great moral determination, to the extortionate demands of a hackney-coachman. Mod.B.)

**Pajuda!** Interj. of disgust. (see Skewurge! Mod.B.)

**Pardiggle** .v.t. To expound to the ignorant or worldly those things which tend to edification. (O.C.

**Peggory's Crowders**. n. Term in Buddh medicine (deriv. Rev. 2.)

**Perch** . pro. Why. (deriv. Perché. Italian . gr.)

5 Buddh Dictionary definition of 'one of them'.

of Northern Italy – you and Boyle [then in Japan] enlighten the East ... At first
we thought all the family were Buddhs, but on reflection I think that it requires
the touch of Coghill blood to bring out all the true qualities. The Bushe drop is
content with Nirvana but the Coghill is the power that makes us get up and
spread ourselves' – poor Jim Penrose was made very cross by all this fey Buddh
fantasy, and roared about 'self-conceit', but Edith and Ethel told him, maddeningly, 'that if he is patient and good and does what the Meath Buddh tells him
he may rise to high rank as a Chela ...' Ethel and Edith started to list Buddh
words. This same letter gives us a hint that Cameron was privately shaping up
to be the life-long bachelor of the family. Edith had passed on to Mrs Kerr, the
Drishane housekeeper, Cameron's remark that there weren't many heiresses in
Canton. She replied: 'Thank God – Thank God – They won't ketch him.' In
June Madame Blavatsky was exposed as a charlatan under strict investigation
by the Society for Psychical Research, of which Sir Joscelyn was Vice President,
but this does not seemed to have unduly affected any of the CT spiritualists.

On 30 July Mr Rivington, who had offered to act as agent with any articles
she might write, succeeded in placing her 'paper' on art studios with Cassell's
*Magazine of Art*. By 26 August 1885, at CT for her summer vacation with Jim,
Ethel with Edith started to write a first version of the Buddh Dictionary. This
manuscript is now lost; we do have a second clean copy, dated 1888, containing
the hands of Edith, Herbert Greene and Martin, but this first version must have
had only the hands of Edith and Ethel.[47] In a commentary on the coded
expressions used by the young ladies of CT to grade the skills of young men at
dancing – 'Egg, Fresh Egg, Eggling' – Edith writes to Cameron on this same
day: 'It is a most invaluable expression and has been incorporated into the
Buddh Dictionary.' The same letter gives an account of a ball at the barracks in
Cork, where Edith and Hildegarde wore much admired gowns made from
Chinese silk that Cameron had sent them; before the music started Edith had
instantly identified and bagged the best dancer, a 'good egg' called Captain
Cautley, but Bess Somerville had poached him from her. There were some 'most
wild people' there and they had gone to their beds in the Imperial Hotel at 5
o'clock in the morning. Tacked on to this letter is a comment of Aunt Gig's on
Edith's coarse and insensitive humour, which was shared by her mother. At
some remark of Edith's her Aunt Gig had exclaimed: 'Edith would laugh at her
own mother's grave'; then, Edith carried on, 'the mother in question went off
into shrieks of unfeeling mirth.'

At the beginning of September Edith read Trollope's *Autobiography*, 'and
am spitting over its unaffected egotism.'[48] On the 4th she noted in her diary that
she had sent the text of an article called 'West Carbery' to Mr Rivington, so she
was motivated enough to keep trying at articles for the popular press. At the

end of the month Fanny Currey came to stay in CT, invited by Egerton who had met her through an exhibition of paintings. She was the daughter of the Duke of Devonshire's land agent at Lismore Castle, County Waterford, an agency that was later to be held by Jim Penrose. Edith describes Fanny to Cameron in a letter of 30 September 1885. A woman suffragist, a respected journalist and painter, in manner Fanny Currey was very like Ethel Smyth. Edith had not met the type before and her comments make it quite clear that the type, though fascinating, is not her style at all. 'Miss Currey is a great bone of contention, Harry, Papa, and Aunt Gig loathe her. Egerton, Uncle Jos., I and I think Minnie love her wildly – Mother loves her when she is talking to her but at other times reneagues. I admit her manners are rather brusque and manly and she is cruel plain – but she has such intelligence in her face, and is such fun, and is such a good fellow into the bargain that I love her with a reckless ardour.'

An evening party took place in Drishane at which there were twenty-five people, only seven of whom were men; 'It is one of those occasions which make one think seriously of the future state, moreover all the eighteen women sing.' Miss Currey took no notice of gender whatever and talked away through thick and thin. Edith sent a further instalment of a description of Fanny to Cameron in mid-October: 'She is excessively plain, but is not at all self-conscious (a thing as distressing in a plain, as it is offensive in a good looking person). She has good manners and is very pleasant and has lots to say, but unfortunately she has a trick of saying it like a man. Also she smokes cigarettes in the most unaffected way in the world – she is I suppose about 40 ... the rest only see what is bad in her and she is probably the best abused woman in CT (and that taking Emily Herbert, The Seal [Miss Sealy, aunt of Charles Sealy, the male Seal at Malmaison], her friend Mrs Pemberton and Madame von Nertz into consideration, is a big word)'. 'West Carbery' had gone to Cassell's Magazine for approval. A local hunt was re-organised, and in October we hear of a meet of the West Carbery Hounds, at Hollybrook.

How far Edith in her manner and approach to men differed from Miss Currey is brought out later: 'I like her as she is awfully amusing and clever to talk to and I forgive her her manly manner – a thing I detest – as it is to a great extent eccentricity. She has the great merit of telling an Irish story to perfection.' Edith gave an account of one of Fanny's stories, concerning a woman who, while under the influence of drink, had jumped out of an upper window to fly. It shows a careful attempt, with suspension marks and stress marks, to give the manner of delivery. The doctor said to her: 'Well, you won't be flying out of windows again.' She replied: 'Well, Dããctor, the fly'n was agree'ble enough, twas the pairchin [perching] was unpleasant.' Egerton's painting friends Adrian and Marianne Stokes were staying: 'We go out in gangs every morning to paint,' Edith wrote to Cam, very impressed with the Stokes who were 'awfully clever and they are better than any master to me in fact'.

The Drishane rents remained a problem; by the end of October Colonel Somerville had offered new low terms to his tenants: 'If they don't take them and he evicts them, no-one will take the land as the boycotting system is so perfect that not a man dares to take an "evicted" farm,' Edith explained to Cameron. At the same time, Cassell's sent the proofs of Edith's studio article, having entitled it 'An Atelier des Dames' and named her as author.[49] At this point her mother intervened like a Fury, and forbade Edith to sign her name to the article in full; she wanted her to sign it with her initials only, if not a pseudonym, but it was too late to change. This ruling would grow into an enormous bone of contention when Edith started to write novels. She was confined to bed with bronchitis during November and read *Adam Bede*, *Barry Lyndon*, and Turgenev's *Fathers and Sons* in an 'infamous translation.'

By December 1885 the withholding of rents had so far affected Colonel Somerville's income that he was on the brink of removing Jack and Hugh from their prep school, and had put his two best horses, Lucifer and Sorcerer, on the market. Badly depressed by this, as Jack and Hugh were her special protégés, Edith went to stay with Fanny Currey at Lismore at the beginning of December. There she found herself pitched into heated discussion of the predicament of Anglo-Irish landlords. 'They say Gladstone will gladly chuck the Irish landlords to Parnell. Mr Stuart of Dromanagh said they would be glad to get 15 years purchase for their land – but the tenants know that by waiting they will get it for nothing.' While she was staying with Fanny, her mother sent on a letter from the *Graphic* accepting a comic strip that Edith had drawn, based on a ridiculous story about an ostrich that Boyle had sent to her from the China station.

In the all-pervading financial gloom her income from illustrating became of the utmost importance. She was paid 3 guineas for her 'Ostrich' cartoon strip for the *Graphic*. On 30 December she wrote to Cameron: 'between ourselves – most of the tenants have paid up – with 15% reduction ... the small boys can remain at school ...' For all Ethel's declared horror at yearly childbearing, it came upon her, too.[50] Five years to the day that Ethel and Jim were married, Edith wrote to Cameron: 'Ethel has another son (No. 5) he is to be called Evelyn Cooper – Mary Ingham suggests Omega – But I fear that would be bitter irony ...' The same letter shows how pleased Edith was with the success of her cramming of her youngest brothers. For them to get assisted places with the Army and Navy was a great boon to their parents. Hugh had been given a nomination for the Navy. Edith went on to describe him to Cameron as 'clever and very sharp – Jack looks very delicate – He is much the same weedy leggy shrimp that you were – only me dear he works three times as well as you ever did [and should get] into Woolwich flying.'

Egerton's painting friends Adrian and Marianne Stokes were staying in the village again in December; she in particular gave good advice to Edith on selling her work to journals. Her mother's Christmas present to Edith this Christmas was a massively constructed easel, a significant sign of growing confidence in her daughter's future art work.[51] Cassell's paid 12 guineas and £3 for the letterpress of 'West Carbery': her prospects seemed good. Minnie Townshend and Edith were reading a manuscript story of Ethel's called *Peacock Feathers* to give critical comment: Ethel was to have a moonlighting part-time career as a childrens' author, often using Edith as her illustrator. On the 29th a party of Flemings came over from Newcourt to Drishane to organise and practise for a charity concert in Skibbereen which the Pooles were to take part in; Edith helped to choose the programme and conducted the choir practices over the next week. Her diaries have a summing up at the end of each year, sometimes in the Memoranda, sometimes on the last day of the year. The 1885 diary ends with a record of a happy and sociable day with the Stokes and the Townshends, and some tennis with Hildegarde and the boys; but the page for 31 December closes with the musical annotation of the song *Love Farewell*.

The concert in Skibbereen on 7 January was attended by numbers of Flemings and Pooles. Hildegarde and Jack sang well and were much applauded; Edith played the violin and sang two songs, one with Hewitt, now a father of three: 'Sang "Friendship" with Hewitt Poole and "Bid me Goodbye" by myself', she wrote in her diary. To open 1886 her literary career progressed well with Mr Remington contracting to produce the third edition of the *Mark Twain Birthday Book*. Edith received threepence from every half-crown copy sold. Cassell's *Magazine of Art* paid 5 guineas for the first article on Paris studios. She was reading Turgenev again, who was an author brought to her attention by her grandfather, this time *Nouvelles Muscovites*. Funds appeared from somewhere to pay for a stove 'The Dumpy', to warm her studio, which was installed on the 11th.[52] Four days later she ends her diary entry with: 'am trying to write a small invention story' so that she must have been encouraged by the publication of her first story in *Home Chimes* to try another. This new story was eventually published as 'A Night in the Suburbs' in the magazine *Argosy*.[53]

On Saturday 16 January, in the middle of notes on who was where, we find 'Violet and Selina Martin arrived at Tally Ho'. Their mother was Anna Selina Fox, the widowed Mrs Martin of Ross House, County Galway, who had wandered from relation to relation in an aimless, but economical, kind of way since her youngest daughter Violet had finished her schooling at Alexandra College in Dublin. The Martins' house in Dublin, in Northumberland Road, was let as often as possible. They were in such financial difficulty that their country house was leased out as well while they scraped along elsewhere, living off friends and relations as much as they could. When they met, Somerville and Ross were not at all alike, and their experience of life had been quite different. Somerville herself brushed away the importance of the first third of her life in her memoirs. As sources have been difficult to locate, the existence of her own beguilingly written accounts has been dazzling and distracting, being chronologically jumbled in the extreme. Her diaries are densely packed with facts, but facts that have been hard to interpret in the fog of slang, nicknames and secrecy over her affections. Misled by *Irish Memories*, biographers have persistently read Violet Martin's meeting with Edith in January 1886 as being for them both an awakening into emotional life and happiness through their working partnership. In fact, at the time nothing remarkable happened, apart from the low-key opening of a close friendship, and more than a year passed before any thought was given to writing a joint work of literature. Their own accounts are frank statements that they made the choice of a professional alternative to marriage in a practical way. The position of unmarried daughter of a Big House was an old and perfectly adapted institution which they converted to their own uses.

The unknown territory of the first third of Edith's life had, in fact, been full of incident and fraught relationships, and conflict with her parents. Marriage had indeed been a possibility from which she had turned away. Both Edith and her 'Twin' Ethel Coghill had shown a tendency to notice the sexual attractiveness of men who were of a lower, or poorer, or outcast class: instead of such men remaining invisible to them because they contravened the dress and manners codes of their class, they sized them up as sexual partners. They both found, as the 'Buddh Dictionary' of family language tells us, 'overmastering charm' where they should not have been looking.[54] This unblinkered view of men had caused difficulties that were insuperable for Edith. Girls married in their late teens then, and the loss of looks that put a woman 'on the shelf' could set in by the mid-twenties, by which time Edith's looks had been spoiled by barbaric dentistry. To avoid the forced choice of either having to get married, or of being a financial burden on one's poverty-stricken parents, the 'other way' of earning a living was a sensible solution. Ethel and Edith had a creative urge to write together from an early date, they slept in each other's rooms, stayed up all night and 'conflagrote' works that they dreamed might bring them success; Ethel let go of this dream, but not Edith. After ten increasingly uncomfortable years in the marriage market, for Edith a paid co-operative working partnership with another woman would have represented a peaceful relief, a coming into calm waters on an even keel; or it would have done, if they had not considered their families first.

In 1886, by the age of twenty-eight, Edith was a martyr to her bad teeth, suffering frequent 'swole face' through abscesses; the dentists who worked on her teeth removed the nerves of many of them with a ghastly little instrument like a steel bottle-brush, which no doubt simultaneously introduced infections even as it took the nerve away. She had four false teeth by the age of twenty and was used to leeches being placed along her jawline to reduce the swelling caused by the repeated infections of her jaw. One of her front top teeth was completely black, and was not given a primitive crown until her second stay in Dusseldorf. There are some unfortunate photographs surviving that show her hollow-eyed and puggy appearance at such times. By 1886 her looks were faded, her remaining teeth blackened wrecks, and all her contemporaries, bar the professional independents, were married and mothers. She spent 1882–5 in a dithering state, unable to decide if she had enough talent and character to support herself as a professional independent woman. She knew that she did not have enough character to break away from her family and marry against the wishes of her parents. She was quite incapable of being a solitary, absorbed in solitary work; she always wanted a close companion, male or female, present while she was working. A great deal had happened to form the character of Edith Somerville before she met Violet Martin, and her diary shows painfully clearly that Violet and her mother were not too welcome during their first stay in Castletownshend, as they were taken – cruelly but accurately – for spongers battening on the Coghills and Somervilles at a time when money was getting tight. In her 1917 memoir *Irish Memories*, Edith was to give a glowing fictionalised account of her meeting and her working with Martin, as though nothing of particular note had happened to her before 1886. Close reading of the diaries, Ethel's memoir, and Edith's letters to her brothers give us a corrective view.

In the first novel written by Somerville and Ross (*An Irish Cousin*, published in 1889) the heroine, Theo, dithers in love between two men. One, Willy, has fair hair, grey eyes and a moustache and speaks in a low, fast Cork voice, the other, Nugent, has dark hair, blue eyes and speaks in a more cultivated manner. The romantic passages of this novel were written by Edith alone, and the dramatic plot rests on the sort of complications that beset the Yelvertons when Barry died and Algie his brother married out of his class. What the heroine feels when she thinks she has lost both men may be compared to Edith's description of what her meeting with Martin meant to her, which was 'another way' alternative to marriage. *An Irish Cousin* has a happy ending, in the arms of Nugent, but at the moment when all was seemingly lost and Theo was making written arrangements to leave Ireland, she sat: 'feeling that I had done something akin to making my will. The best part of my life was over; into these past three months had been crushed its keenest happiness and unhappiness, and this was what they had amounted to. They had none the less now to fall into the background, and soon would have no more connection with my future life than if they had never been.'

Among the quotations from love poetry that were edited out from *An Irish Cousin* for the 1903 edition was Michael Drayton's 'Come let us kiss and part'. They were chosen to express the emotional state of a woman who has given up a lover, but a lover whom she is bound to meet again. We find this theme repeatedly in the fiction of Somerville and Ross; only in 'High Tea at McKeown's' does a dismissed suitor (a 'penniless pup' of an engineer) re-appear, now rich and thus acceptable to the previously disapproving parents of his lover. It uses the familiar image of a passionate love fading away to almost nothing, yet still retaining a spark of life, a metaphor that repeats throughout Somerville's work, and seems to describe a love defeated by adverse circumstance:

> Since there's no help, come let us kiss and part,
> Nay, I have done: you get no more of me,
> And I am glad, yea glad with all my heart,
> That thus so cleanly I myself can free.
> Shake hands for ever, cancel all our vows,
> And when we meet at any time again
> Be it not seen in either of our brows
> That we one jot of former love retain.
> Now at the last gasp of love's latest breath,
> When his pulse failing, Passion speechless lies,
> When Faith is kneeling by his bed of death,
> And innocence is closing up his eyes,
> Now, if thou would'st, when all have given him over,
> From death to life thou might'st him yet recover.

We shall see that Somerville was to describe her meeting with Ross as 'a hinge, the place where my life and hers, turned over': this is a metaphor chosen by a woman who did not mince words in dealing with what the less forthright Ross called 'the central physical point of life'. Somerville knew the difference between a hinge and a hasp and staple.

# CHAPTER 4

# Violet Martin comes to Castletownshend

The outstanding fact, as it seems to me, among women who live by their brains, is friendship. A profound friendship that extends through every phase and aspect of life, intellectual, social, pecuniary. Anyone who has experience of the life of independent and artistic women knows this; and it is noteworthy that these friendships of women will stand even the strain of matrimony for one or both of the friends ...

Edith Somerville, *Irish Memories*, chapter XXVIII

IN CONTRAST TO EDITH, Violet Martin's early life, particularly after she had left Ross for Dublin, was lonely. She formed an important relationship with a stray sheepdog, which she was eventually allowed to keep. The rescue of this animal was utilised in one of her earliest stories 'The Dog from Doone'; it parallels the story of Edith's published by *Argosy* in 1887, called 'A Night in the Suburbs'.[1] In both stories they write in the persona of one of their brothers, as a military cadet, and undergo a psychological trial. Violet's cadet rescues a grey and black sheepdog that had escaped from the sack in which its owner had tried to drown it and lived wild, avoiding mankind. Starving, it had come close to a Big House, where the cadet befriended it: 'I made a bed for him with my rug, and he accepted it, and looked me in the face as man to man. A bed, recognised and ordained, means to a dog the Franchise and the Old Age Pension all in one.' The dog then saves his new master from drowning in a bog hole when he is going cross country in mist after spectral hounds. The story is suggestive of the importance that Violet's stray held for her, and her understanding of the simple animal necessity for a safe place of rest, and privacy: 'A bed, recognised and ordained'.

At Ross she did have friends among neighbouring families, but saw them infrequently, the remoter Big House estates being sufficient unto themselves. One neighbour was Daisy Burke of Danesfort, later Countess of Fingall, who remembered Violet Martin for her infectious sense of humour even as a girl:

'She was so alive. You could see the wit and fun bubbling up in her',[2] but she was also self-contained, reflective, and withdrawn during bouts of illness. When she left Ross in 1872 at the age of ten to live with her mother in Dublin, she attended Alexandra College where she continued to be self-contained and reserved except to those who knew her well. She was a quiet thirteen-year-old lower-form girl when Edith Somerville, aged seventeen, and her cousin Ethel Coghill, aged eighteen, attended the same school for a term in 1875.

After Christmas 1885 Mrs Martin had decided to descend, with her daughters Selina, Violet and Katie, on her Bushe cousins in Cork; she sent two daughters in advance. On 16 January Violet entered the journey in her diary: 'Left [Kingsbridge] 9 am Cork at 2, Skib at 6, Somervilles carriage Skib – CT.'[3] That anyone should take a short let in CT in the dead of winter was a clear sign of retrenching and the strictest economy. After a brief diary entry of Edith's noting that Violet sang in the church choir: 'Thank goodness as we are fairly badly off', it was immediately impressed on CT that she had poor health, as she then took to her bed, 'seedy'. Violet revived when her friend Rose Helps arrived with her mother. The first detailed remark about the Martins in CT comes in a letter to Cameron from Edith on 27 January. It had been noticed, especially by Harry Townshend at Seafield, that Mrs Martin, who had only arrived on the 24th, had a tendency to 'borrow' things and then forget to return them: 'Harry [Townshend] drew up a delicious code of rules as how far and in what degree Nannie was to sponge upon the family … she carried off Mother's Cork Con[stitutional] before Papa had read it.'

By 13th February, the professionally charming 'Nannie' Martin had persuaded Edith to make a portrait of her, a small water-colour head, completed on the 15th. Neither Violet's diary entries, nor Edith's, show any sign in January or February that they particularly noticed each other in the throng. Violet was very taken with Harry Townshend, Aylmer Somerville and 'Aunt Adelaide', and the Coghill sisters Violet and Beatrice were much taken with her. The two Violets together became known as 'The Onions'. When Edith began a portrait of her brother Aylmer in the regimental uniform of Methuen's Horse on 7 February, 'Violet M. came up to keep him quiet.'[4] Edith was also working hard at her story 'A Night in the Suburbs' and made a fair copy to go to an editor on the 23rd. We do not have a detailed mention of Edith in Martin's diary until 27 February when she notes that she 'sat to Edith', for the portrait, 'hinted' out of her – that is to say scrounged – by Mrs Martin, that was completed by the end of the first week of March after five sittings. 'The Martins' moved about en masse as a party, attending teas and dinners. According to Edith's diary she 'began to paint Violet' on 1 March. Before this she had noted Violet Martin with 'Miss Helps and many others' littering the Studio, and then again at a

6 Uncle Kendal asleep. Pencil drawing from an 1880s sketchbook.

crowded musical party on 29 January: 'Violet plays very well'. Edith first saw Violet riding, hunting on a borrowed horse on 2 March, commenting 'she rides right well'; and to general amazement, as Violet was practically blind without her pince-nez, which could not be worn when riding. She just rode after a lead rider, and quite soon Edith was the rider she followed.

By 10 March the fact that the Martins were very good company is overcoming Edith's dislike of Nannie Martin. She wrote to Cameron on that day: 'I hope the Martins will be able to get a house [for the summer] I like both Violet and Katie Currey [Martin's married sister] very much – but Nannie certainly is an awful old soldier – nevertheless she is so amusing, and such good company, that by hardening your heart to her hints and bunches [the Buddh term for scrounging] you can get on very well with her'. Despite her dislike, Edith's diary shows that she had been so far charmed by Martin's mother that she had taken her hint to paint Violet for her, describing the hint as: 'Nannie has attacked me about doing a portrait.' Edith told Cameron in the same letter: 'I have just painted a panel of Violet (Martin) wh. is fairly like her.[5] I am hard at work at your Mule riding performance for the Graphic ... there has been a rush of babies all over the family ... Ethel's letters are most depressing, she has now

5 children and says she spends her life blowing their noses – Music – Art – Riding – everything has to be sacrificed to these children – Kitty and Dennis were all very well but the others are the most uninteresting little beings ...'[6] In fact Edith lost her heart to Dennis, 'the only one I really love'.

Knowing Ethel's situation as a married woman and mother, and difficult as it was for Edith to make her own private space within the Somerville family, she was grateful that she was free to pursue her own interests. There were further surprising developments in getting to know the Martin family. Violet was so clearly hampered by her short sight that it was amazing that she should even think of riding to hounds, often on unknown borrowed horses, but she did. On 17 March Edith wrote to Cameron: 'Violet Martin was out and rode awfully well. She is very blind and rode to my lead, and we were not the last (this, with modest pride)...' Years later, when Edith looked back at her first comments in her diary on the Martin family, she found some phrases very unflattering to them, and wrote over these phrases with bigger bolder writing. For example, after the entry 'Had tea at the Martins', on 20 January, we find overwritten on a following remark: 'The east wind is appalling'. It is possible that the first intimate thing that Edith noticed about Martin was bad breath, which was a Martin family failing with their snaggle teeth and digestive maladies. In the years to come Martin was to suffer from a long-running toothbrush joke. 'Sisterly candour' was a Coghill speciality. We do not know how many times Martin said to Edith, 'I thought you would have your jest about toothbrushes.'[7] The cousinage that was related through Charles Kendal Bushe shared various resemblances, so that it is unsurprising that the Martins merged in so comfortably at CT; Edith saw Mrs Martin's strong resemblance to Aunt Alice, and Violet had a singing voice uncannily like Ethel Coghill's.[8] Before Edith left for France, Violet had achieved the position of her protégée, but was one among many, male and female.

Violet Martin was at first out of her depth in her new company. Emulating their brothers, the girls of the Somerville and Coghill families ran wild, loved horses that they rode very fast, and contrived to have adventures without the knowledge of their parents, even leaving their homes after dark by shinning out of windows. A witness to the wildness of all the girls was the general servant, Mary Anne Whoolley. In their notebooks Edith and Violet were to record some of her speech under the title 'Bally-Whoolleyana'. At the back of Notebook 10 we find Violet's record of an outburst of speech made by Whoolley early in 1886 when Edith had come, via the Glen B back avenue and the Main Street back gardens, to the kitchen door of Tally Ho in the dark and in disguise as a 'Fairy Woman' said to be haunting the village at the time.[9] Violet and one of her sisters were in the kitchen with Whoolley, who had opened the door when something made a noise against it from the outside:

*magazine of art. Feb. 1886*

7 A Ladies Studio in Paris, from the first article written and illustrated
by Edith Somerville, published in 1886.

Faith the tears ran from me eyes with the fright. Whin I wint to the doore
I seen this thing like a big mountain fallin' in on top o' me, and the big
white head bobbin' up an' down. Twasn't her tail frightened me at all but
the head. I don't know what curse I said but indeed it must be somethin'
bad, I thought I'd never bolt the doore agin' her, me hands was helpless
like, and she rushin' in on me. But indeed it wasn't till I see *your* face and
yer ears as red as blood that I was frightened all together. Faith if I was
in the house be meself I'd never tell me name after it. And that other lady,
the crayture, shure she threw the egg from her with the fright. Amn't I
after wiping it up this morning. Ah! thim's ever and always arch, the
same as they was and they children – and t'is worse they're getting'
accordin' as they're getting' oldher. And the marrid' gintleman [Claude
(Joe) Coghill, married to Maude McVeagh, 25 June 1885] the worst o'
thim. As for thim others, oh my! Gallopers! They'd be out til mornin'!
Them'd gallop the woods all night like the deer.

Edith had called at all the houses on the village street where she knew she could
give a good fright. She must have known every inch of the village to walk

around its back quarters in the dark. Violet Martin calmly notes after the record of Whoolley's words: 'Miss Somerville had come to the door of the Cottage [a sign of failed recollection, they were in Tally Ho] with a white gauze petticoat over her head.' Edith's diary also tells us that she had made up her face, aiming at the appearance of 'an old fairy woman' reputed to be in the neighbourhood. The 'Gallopers' among the Coghill girls most alarmed Whoolley; Ethel's younger sister Violet came in for special opprobrium: 'Miss Coghill's like a young gintle-man, hoppin', hoppin' up and down and into every place.' Though headstrong, Violet Martin was at this stage prim and proper; she had not been in company with such wild girls before. Hildegarde Somerville and Violet Coghill nicknamed her 'The Doll' because of her stiff, controlled manner; but not many months passed before she had been converted, chiefly under Hildegarde's tuition, to the easier ways of CT.[10]

Following her usual pattern for spring, Edith prepared herself for study in Paris. Soon after she left on 20 March, Violet began to compose an affectionate letter to her, dated 28 March. This was a twenty-page missive containing a description of a hunt ridden on Sorcerer. It had poured with rain and this time she had no lead from Edith to follow: 'how much I missed your company and protection – one does miss a comrade very much on such occasions …' It is clear that they already shared the same zany sense of humour, as Violet described a ridiculous incident during the hunt with the concluding comment: 'My dear, if you had been there we should have forever disgraced ourselves.' She shows from the beginning in her letters to Edith a minute interest and disposition to control. She did not like the unknown – the world of Edith's larger life in Paris – or know how to come to terms with events like Seymour Bushe's elopement with a married woman, at that time a sensation in the Irish newspapers. He was the son of Charles Bushe, the Rector, and the brother of Edith's revered Constance. Much regretted by his legal colleagues, he had left the Irish Bar to live with his Lady Kathleen in Paris, but later practised in London. 'Paris I resent so will say nothing about it – I have a feeling you will meet Seymour – how interesting if you do …' It is signed 'Yours afftly. V. Martin.'[11] When Edith wrote to her mother on 30 March to describe her doings in London en route to Paris, she asked for thanks for this letter to be passed on: 'Tell Violet that I was enchanted to get her letter which was a most admirable one and over which I laughed considerably.' Edith did not have time to write to anyone but her mother, and these letters were read aloud at Drishane at meal times. Violet would not have heard all, as she was based in Tally Ho with her mother. The same letter to her mother that passes on thanks via Mrs Somerville to Martin describes an interview with Mr Williamson, sub-editor at the *Graphic*, and it shows that Edith had taken an important step forward in self-esteem after two sessions of Paris training. Mr Williamson was on the brink of taking a cartoon strip ('Mule Ride in Trinidad') and was discussing terms with Edith, when he said:

> 'thirty shillings a page is the usual amateur price' – 'But I am a Professional,' I said with dignity. 'Ah yes – I thought the drawing was very good. I am sure we shall be able to arrange – we vary our price very much according to the work – these we can photograph direct – others we have to re-engrave in order to correct errors in drawing – We shall be very glad to see anything you can send us – Your subjects are very fresh' (here a very imperfectly concealed grin) 'and well-drawn – We were all very much amused by the ostrich pictures.' They pay ten days after publication and will send the ostrich money to Paris.

From a note in her diary, apparently Edith did think at once of writing to Violet and started a letter, but this was never completed and posted, and Violet took offence at the long silence; she spent her time with Hildegarde and the Coghill sisters, Violet and Beatrice. On 1 April her diary records that she went with her mother to visit Emily Herbert at the Point House, so that though she later disclaimed any part in the creation of Charlotte Mullen of *The Real Charlotte* from the model of Emily Herbert, laying her at Edith's door, she had in fact met the woman. In May, while she was in Paris, the *Graphic* was preparing for press their second cartoon strip of Edith's, 'A Mule Ride in Trinidad'; the figure model for this had been the strapping Boyle Somerville home on leave before posting to HMS *Audacious* in the China Seas. Boyle was always obedient to his eldest sister's wishes. Heroically, he had posed in his underpants in the winter draughts of the Studio. He caught 'flu as a result. Quite often, Boyle and Cameron were to be within range of one another in their Army and Navy postings around the world; wherever they were they sent exotic gifts in very good taste to their sisters. At Drishane while Edith was still working in Paris in 1886 a parcel of Chinese silk garments, one yellow, one blue, had arrived from Cameron in Canton for his sisters. Edith sent a message to Violet via her mother that shows she already had a respect for Violet's taste in clothing. 'I will leave it to you and Violet Martin to decide for me. I must have a tea-gowny garment of a better sort – I suppose I *must* let Hildegarde have the yellow – but tell Violet to purge her soul of all prejudice, and then, having taken a solemn oath on the Mark Twain Birthday Book, let her dispassionately choose for me – I will abide by the decision.' The reason that Edith did not want to wear the blue was that it would tone with her bad front tooth, which was blue-black.

The most important work done by Edith in Paris this spring was a set of drawings made in the clinic of Louis Pasteur on the Rue d'Ulm on 1 May. She

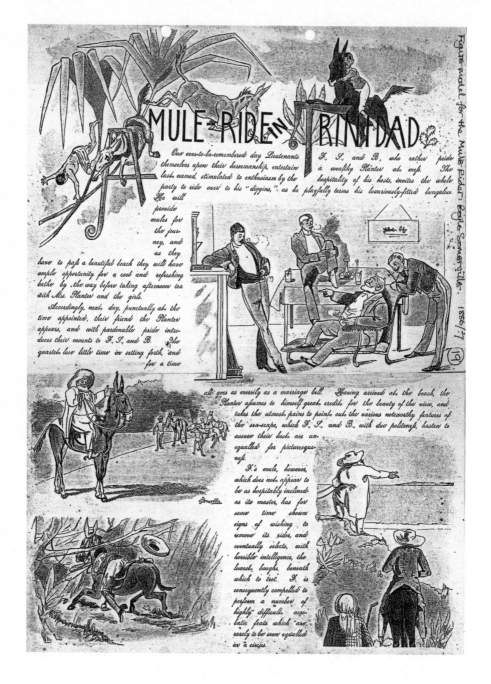

8 Comic strip *A Mule Ride in Trinidad*, published in the *Graphic*, it was drawn in
Paris in April 1886. It was based on a story collected by Cameron Somerville,
and the model for the mule rider was Boyle Somerville.

drew both Pasteur and his patients. She wrote to Cameron five days later: 'Did you hear that an American girl and I went off to see Pasteur the other day? There was a crowd of the most varied sort of patients in the little garden outside his door. Russians, peasants in every possible costume and a perfectly adorable Arab in a grey burnous and with one of the most beautiful faces I have ever seen …' Pasteur had been terribly busy and had not time to speak to them after they had asked for permission to draw, but he gave them 'a bow and a smile only but it meant we might stay in the room and see an operation.'[12] Egerton, whose paintings were in a different class from Edith's, had a painting hung in the Salon this year. 'The Old Cobbler', later shown as No. 2 in a posthumous exhibition of his works in 1964 at the Ashmolean in Oxford entitled *An Irish Impressionist*.

An undated letter from Edith in Paris to Hildegarde survives from this spring; Aunt Louisa Greene, who was a published authoress, had sent Edith a criticism of her story 'A Night in the Suburbs': 'I must wait now for that very visionary 5 shillings until I get home and can make the alterations she suggests.' Egerton's painting friends the Stokes were in Paris at another studio: 'Marianne doesn't want to come [to Tally Ho!] because she thinks CT too frivolous a place for solid work, in which respect she is quite right … will you tell Violet Florence that my next letter to them parts shall be to her – Tell her it is not ingratitude but simply incapacitude that has hitherto prevented me from answering her perfectly delightful letter – sections of which I have read out to understanding persons.' But there was still no time for writing to Violet. On 18 May, nine weeks after her first unanswered letter, Violet wrote again to Edith who was almost at the point of returning home, only eight pages this time:

> My dear Edith, you know and you should blush to know that there is no reason in the world why I should write to you but there are people to whom it interests one to write irrespective of their bad qualities and behaviour – as I have heard each of your letters declaimed I have felt that I should like to make merry with you over many things therein but have been daunted by the thought of your many correspondents – you have one fatal fault you are a 'popular girl' a sort I have always abhorred, so bear in mind that theoretically you are in the highest degree offensive to me … if you were not such a popular girl I could say very nice things to you about coming home …

By this date, 19 May, the Martins had moved down to the Mall House on the Mall leading off from the Main Street at the Two Trees down to the Coastguard Station. Martin was collecting funny stories in written form to amuse Edith, and this letter contains one later used in the RM story 'Lisheen

Races Second Hand'. Martin was not working at her own writing, she was swept up in the frivolities of CT summer society – 'somehow CT inertness has me in its grasp' – and though she was aware of the morally reprehensible 'business-like waste of time', she succumbed to it and began to blossom socially. She blossomed particularly in the company of Hildegarde, who persuaded Martin to dress in a sheet – 'heaven in the way of comfort' – as a Grecian lady for a Fancy Ball: 'Hilda and Violet [Coghill] play with me very nicely and I begin to think they are the nicest and best people I have ever seen. Yours ever, Violet Martin.'[13]

Violet entered in her diary for 16 June: 'Went up to Drishane and up to meet the returning Edith – a pale and dwindled but fashionable lady.' Full of ambitions, Edith returned to work in her Studio, but as summer came on, so did 'The Wave' build up. 'The Wave' is defined in the Buddh Dictionary as: 'A phenomenon known only in Castletownshend, where, during the summer season, idle multitudes throng from house to house overwhelming or absorbing all with whom they come into contact.' The wave all too often washed up in Edith's Studio, where it lifted her off course and set her to teaching new dance steps or popular songs. By the beginning of June 1886, Edith and Violet had realised that no serious work at all could be done in the waking hours of the throng of pleasure-seekers, and Violet decided to join Edith in her pre-breakfast sessions in the Studio, participating in the working sessions that Edith had instituted in 1880. Martin had an ambition to write serious political journalism, and earn by it.

She had already made an attempt to act as an amanuensis to an established writer, and had earned by this. Willy Wills was an elderly-seeming cousin in his late fifties when he struck up a romantic friendship with Violet Martin.[14] He was chiefly famous for writing the play *Charles I* for Irving, and adapting *The Vicar of Wakefield* for Ellen Terry as the play *Olivia*. He wrote novels and poetry, but by the early 1880s was running out of steam and eager to have an energetic collaborator. He sent money to Violet with undated letters like this, from *c.*1885:

> My dearest Violet
> I am sure you will credit me with a true affection and an earnest wish that I could serve you and help you which would make me *very happy* do be good to me and don't be angry for I want a little pleasure all alone as I am – accept the enclosure – I am a fairly plucky man – but I confess I am all in a twitter venturing so far – you know I am doing well, *Yours* WGW

Violet evidently discussed the plots of plays and novels with him in great detail, for another letter from him insists: 'I don't think I ever met any lady half so intellectual as you – I really think so – we'll conspire and we'll make plenty of money', and another: 'I am swarming with plots and would like to talk one or two over with you.' Violet did manage to get onto a solid footing as paid co-operator and amanuensis to this vague and unaccountable man, it seems at her own suggestion. She worked as editor and proof-reader on his verse drama, *Melchior*, published in 1885, for which she was paid by cheque. But when she found such happiness in the society of Castletownshend, and began to write to him of its delights, Wills became offended: 'Pal of mine. I detest hunting. I hate lawn tennis and I have a morbid loathing for a fly pole – I on the other hand love chatting nonsensical strolls with my young paragon of everything – Jolly and good VM and pretty VM'.

It is then clear on this evidence that it was not Edith but Violet who had more recently done joint work as a professional writer when they met in 1886, and it would be to Violet – with her intimate personal connection with Wills – that his joint work with Edith's Aunt Louisa Greene in Dublin had more immediate significance.[15] Wills and Greene had written and published *Drawing Room Dramas in Verse* in 1873, but in 1886 they published a thriller *Whose Hand? Or the Mystery of No Man's Heath*. The question of which of the two writers, Somerville or Ross, first impelled them to practise writing together is extremely difficult to answer. As we shall see, Somerville's account in *Irish Memories* was only a convenient fiction.[16] Martin was not without that subtle, managing suggestiveness that marked her mother's character; we find it in many of her letters dealing with the improvement of Edith's written work. It was also Violet who master-minded the reviews and publicity for their books, using the connections gained through her brother Robert in London. They wrote their first novel as a light-hearted speculation, and had no inkling that writing novels together, any more than journalism and illustration done solo, would bring them an income. It was fun, and might just be remunerative.

Though they shared a zany sense of humour, and Edith wrote, 'Martin and I were not accustomed to take ourselves seriously', they did quite quickly come to recognise each other's serious intention to be independent in a society that was superficially only intent on pleasure-seeking and flirtation. Edith had moved on from what she called in 1917 'the varying, yet invariable, flirtations and emotional episodes of youth', which for most of her fellows had been 'resolved and composed' by marriage. She described herself and Martin in 1886 as being 'well stricken in years ... not absolutely the earliest morning of life; say, about half past ten, with breakfast (and all traces of bread and butter) cleared away'.[17] They were twenty-eight and twenty-four. Female maturity, associated with gynaecological fitness, came early then; many girls were married, mothers and mistresses of households, before they were twenty. Edith still places a

misleading emphasis on their ages at the time they met, trying to anchor Violet
Martin at the twenty mark, whereas in fact she, four years older, was twenty-
eight. What she is contriving to do is paint out the decade 1878–88 and her
own 'emotional episodes'.

The familiar name for the Studio was 'The Purlieu', as Adelaide had
compared it to 'the revolting purlieu of some disgusting foreign town'.[18] Here
Edith painted and Violet wrote. And it was here, according to her later account,
that the idea for writing a novel crystallised in Edith's mind, when they were
idly, and separately, doing something else. Apart from Wills and Greene, Mrs
Hungerford, the sensational novelist famous for *Molly Bawn*, was also a
relative by marriage. She was rumoured to earn £1,000 for a 'Shocker' novel;
this fact, too, may have contributed towards their ambition to write together.
The novelty and fun of sharing such a private workplace was enough at first.
While Edith was away in Paris Violet seems to have written a curious account
called 'A Day in the Purlieu' on 2 June in response to Edith's draft short story
'A Night in the Suburbs'. As Edith's workplace was also shared by her brother
Boyle, it is also possible that the piece is by him. To reach the Studio from the
second floor of the house, they used a door in the apex of the loft which had
passed through so many successive uses – servant's bedroom, nursery, boys'
bedroom and now workroom-cum-Studio. At ground level under the mid-
section of the loft was the open throughway into the yard. Up the right-hand
wall, once through the archway, was a short open stair. This gave access to the
Studio quite unobserved by anyone in the main block of Drishane. Servants with
a knowledge of the inner workings of the house came by this route to Edith; Violet
and Edith left by it when they heard unwanted company approaching from the
house back staircase. Or they could decamp into the house if they heard
unwanted company approaching by the yard. This was Edith's own domain.

From Edith's memoirs it is not easy to get a clear-eyed picture of the room
that was of such importance in her working life. It was, after all, only a cold
and draughty added-on outbuilding, and it needed a pioneering spirit to live
and work in it. But we have a delightful child's-eye view of the room from
Edith's godson Paddy Coghill, who wrote an account of his 'Aunts' in 1952.
The Studio was, he wrote, 'Lit by a low window and two skylights, both of
which leaked, it was like the cavern of the winds … It was, to my mind a place
of singular and hideous discomfort, and there the two of them would sit,
huddled in rugs and surrounded by fox terriers. It was crowded with easels,
canvasses and all sorts of painting and hunting impedimenta. For me as a child
it was a sort of Aladdin's Cave, which filled me with envy and wonder at the
exciting lives led by grown ups. But looking back, it is a mystery how they endured
the discomfort and a still greater mystery how they triumphed over it …'[19]

Drishane had many rooms of indeterminate use; up on the bedroom level only the master and mistress seemed to be ensured a permanent resting place. Hildegarde and Edith seemed to be ready to decamp from any bedroom at a moment's notice; guests might be luckily placed, or not. In the year that Violet Martin arrived in CT, the 'Brats' or 'Louts', young Jack and Hugh, had only just graduated to beds in the main block after Aylmer's departure, thereby vacating the 'Lout Hole', leaving it free to metamorphose into the Studio-cum-'Purlieu'. It is touching that the family used the term 'the bed' as if it were a generic term, and nothing personal: nobody said, 'My bed'. One of the common expressions in Drishane for an overdose of guests was 'Throng as three in a bed we'll be'. Girls and young women, boys and young men were used to doubling up with each other or guests if need be. This only caused difficulties if the attached dogs did not get on. Boyle, Jack and Edith at various times had dogs who slept not on, but in, their owners' beds. The bed was where the body happened to be stowed at any particular time. This is startlingly clear in what might be Violet's first known piece of Studio work, 'A Day in the Purlieu', which survives among the papers left in Drishane:

> Day was slowly and chilly breaking over the Galley head, and a few of the bits were beginning to drop promiscuously about the House. All the family were in the Bed; and as a sharper fragment than usual of the broken light fell on it, they pulled up their blankets, and turned away from the windows with an air of resolve – which not even the terror-laden foot or the tobacco-laden breath of Donovan [the steward] should shake – not to budge until the prayer bell should ring. All of the family, I say, were in the Bed, all, that is, except Two.

This piece might equally well have been written by Boyle Somerville, who shared the same keenness for work with his sister Edith when he was home on leave. The timing of the house was ruled by bells and gongs. By 1886 it was Adelaide who conducted morning prayers, which waited for the entry of Edith and Violet as they scurried in from the back quarters. The gong called to meals, and in the evening it was sounded before the dinner gong, as the signal for dressing. Those in riding clothes or any kind of outdoor wear discarded their muddy outer layers, took off their riding or yard boots, cleaned up and dressed for dinner; the gong for it was struck later. It was perfectly possible to respond to these calls to duty, or to eating, from the Studio. The difficulty with the existence of the Studio was that it became a source of entertainment for every visitor in the place. Violet bemoaned the difficulty of working there, and the fact that the stated aim of the institution was not taken seriously. But she is perfectly aware that for Edith merely to have established the room as a work-place is an achievement. The motto that they fixed on the Studio door was 'Ah! It'll do!' The account of 'A Day in the Purlieu' closes: 'The sun goes down on the wrath, the hungry wrath, of the Two ... The Philistines descend into Ascalon and Gath, and the uttermost parts of Skibbereen ... finally the sun, just missing Toe Head by an inch drops into America, and the shadows and smells of evening settle down on the Purlieu.'

From a letter by Edith to Cameron later that summer, of 22 July, we learn that Adelaide had noticed that Edith and Martin 'worked' together, for their own amusement, and was puzzled. Adelaide's comments on the pair, that also come incidentally in a diary account by Edith of the new tenants of the Castle, are intriguing: 'Lady Maidstone and her entourage have taken the Castle ... Violet Martin says we shall feel like Huck Finn with all these Dukes and Kings around – How do you talk to a Duke?' ... [visitors were in the offing] 'and in about ten minutes I shall have to spread a feverish layer of superficial tidiness over all my most cherished camacs – "What have I done" says Mother in a burst of pathetic indignation "that I should have two dirty old maids squatted down upon me?" – What indeed? And the worst of it is that they [the visitors] aren't dirty and we shall have to be clean ...' This is an interesting implication that her mother had something to do with having an old maid daughter on her hands. The letter to Cameron is also one of the last to refer to 'Violet Martin'. Towards the end of the summer a decree had gone out that, to prevent confusion with those Violets of the non-shrinking variety, Miss V. Townshend and Miss V. Coghill, who was the chief instigator of Martin's remaining in CT as a guest, Violet Martin would be known simply as 'Martin'.

The weather had been foul, but Edith and Martin had managed some riding: 'she is right good on a horse and as plucky as they come, and knows well what she is about,' Edith wrote to Cameron. Martin had quickly understood that when in Drishane it was possible by cunning to avoid visitors with whom one did not want to socialise. A visitor turned up on the doorstep one day catching them all short. 'Martin slowly and sadly lay down under the sofa – at least I saw her no more – Hugh had no false pride about bolting, and did so. I got half way up the stairs with mother following [saying] "I *can't* go in as I am – I must fly and change me dress", she fled – then I said with a high heart and a flashing eye. Shall it be said that a Buddh shrank from a suburban? Never!'[20]

Edith was still concerned that Cameron find an heiress to marry, for a following letter reminded him: 'My dear, whenever you do marry – and may that day still be distant – marry the nice girl with money and not the one that hasn't.' In September Hugh left for *HMS Britannia*, the naval training 'ship' where Boyle had been schooled before him.[21] On the 9th Edith went over to Lismore to stay with Fanny Currey for a painting holiday. Here she found and read *Daniel Deronda* and Rossetti's *Poems*. She did not return until the 18th. Martin was bed-hopping about, sometimes sleeping with Hildegarde at Drishane, or with Violet at Glen B or with her sisters who were staying at the Mall House. Martin's diary entry for the day of Edith's return shows that she was forming an attachment to Edith: 'Did nothing in particular, too excited by the prospect of the return of E Œ S. Went to Constance's in the afternoon to fill up the time till 6.30 when Aylmer and I walked up the Skib road in torrents of rain and met the Bart and Edith. Dined at Drishane and spent the night in the bed.' Martin had been a shining success in CT society. On 25 September Martin changed her status in CT from tenant to Guest, when, at the suggestion of Violet and Beatrice Coghill, she was invited by Sir Joscelyn to extend her stay after the departure of Mrs Martin and her daughter Katie. Beatrice was given to 'flopping' on people with a consuming passion. She had a 'flop' on Martin at this time.

Martin moved from the Mall House to Glen B on the 28th: 'Had lunch at Glen B and gradually moved into residence there.' She was depressed by her nomadic existence: 'How I loathe giving up houses and packing,' she entered in her diary on the next day. Her brother Robert Martin's engagement to Connie Roche was announced at the end of September. For him this was a marriage of convenience: she was rich, he was poor. Typically Robert made a quip that did the rounds, saying that he preferred 'the Union to the workhouse'. This was the kind of heartless joke that Martin disliked from her brother, though she did not approve of Connie Roche. She did not plan to attend their grand London wedding. In October, Edith and Martin worked together on preparing for the press the illustrations and text of Edith's cartoon strip on palm-reading. Martin enters that she had worked on 'the letterpress for chiromancy pictures'. *Chiromancy and Its Consequences* was to be published in the *Graphic* on 8 January 1887. Edith does not flatter Martin, or Hal Chavasse, the male model. When Hildegarde went off to the Flemings at Newcourt on 7 October, Martin moved into Hildegarde's room next to Edith's for a couple of days, but her main base was at Glen B, and her diary frequently mentions doings with 'B&V' – Beatrice and Violet. Disinclined, but also too short of money, she was not present at Robert's marriage to Connie on 20th. Then the village was rocked to its foundations. Martin wrote in her diary on the 26th: 'Hildegarde's engagement to Egerton announced. Sensation.' Like many another Anglo-Irish pair, they were first cousins, and their financial prospects were as black as could be. After a few years, Martin was to christen them 'The Dowager Lovers' as the pair were to spend seven long years in waiting for family finances to be propitious enough to allow them to marry; but knowing they had to earn the most they could on their own account, they started working together as photographers and selling their prints of seascapes and landscapes to visitors.

Early in November, Martin's keen interest in politics infected Edith to the extent that 'Martin and I rode to Lissard to convert Madame (The O'Donovan's wife) to Primrose Leaguery.'[22] [Had] forgotten that Gendie [Mrs Miller Mundy, nee Townshend] wants me to set up a habitation here [i.e. a Primrose League branch] and has designed *me* to recruit for the loathely concern. The more I have to do the more redly Radical do my feelings become.' This diary entry of Edith's is a good indicator of her surface flippancy, and refusal to be serious. Never did she share the wholehearted Unionism and intense interest in politics that so marked the character of Martin, her sisters and her brother Robert; and some Cork neighbours did take her for a political Radical as a result. One of her family nicknames in the key at the end of the Buddh Dictionary is 'Mrs Chamberlain', but it is not clear if this was given solely on account of her political radicalism.

The *Graphic* brought out the cartoon strip 'Miss Neruda Jones' on 4 November; Martin had modelled for the girl violin student, and was even less flattered by this than by the chiromancy strip. A week later, Edith and Martin began to write up the old Buddh Dictionary, with Herbert's encouragement and co-operation. Martin's diary records the writing out of the dictionary from 11 November to 12 December, where it is described as 'Buddhing'. Full of vigour and optimism, Edith began a major redecoration and cleansing of the Studio. It was being perfected as a place of work. With no visitors to bother her, she attacked the room, stripped it and whitewashed it. The room had been the old Nursery. There were five layers of wallpaper, she told Boyle on 26 November: 'I have no doubt that all kinds of loathsome diseases were sandwiched between those papers, measles, scarlatina, whooping cough and sudden death (my old Nurse Pardoe died of heart disease in that room) ...'; she follows on with a prized remark in dialect, one that we find later used in the story 'Matchbox' in *All on the Irish Shore* (1903): 'I heard a story of a horse. A man was asked "Could he lep?" He said, "Is it lep? If there was forty men and their wives, and they after him with sticks – an' he wouldn't lep a sod of turf." This tale is Martin's. I like the notion of the married crowd all appealing in vain ...' Though at this time they had no inkling of the purpose to which they would put their collection of speech in dialect, Edith and Martin were consciously writing them down as perfectly rendered as they could. They appreciated their entertainment value at first as elements in letter writing and as spoken anecdotes.

On 1 December the household auction at the Rectory marked the end of the Bushe era, and the installation of a new Rector. It was to take some time for the incoming Reverend Harry Becher to find his feet in CT, for there was no chance of him ever replacing Charles Bushe, and to learn how to co-exist with its opinionated womenfolk was to prove beyond his powers. As the church

9 The comic strip *Miss Neruda Jones*, published in the *Graphic*, November 1886.
The model for the violin student was Martin Ross.

organist, Edith did not co-operate with Mr Becher as she found him unsympathetic. The Rector must have been pained by the lack of proper reverence for
the male shown by Edith and her cousins. The unrestrained nature of the
conversations between the young women, known as 'squaws',[23] who frequented
the Drishane Studio gives us an idea of the scorn with which these young
women regarded the conventional man-hunting flirt; for example, an aside in
Martin's diary recorded that 'Hilda Fleming [of the Newcourt family] would
dote on a tongs'. On 8 December a letter arrived from Herbert on the subject of
the Buddh Dictionary from Magdalen College 'with glossary, and full of noble
enthusiasm'. Then a large part of December passed Edith by in a daze as she
had another bout of her 'swole face', associated with rotten teeth and infected
gums. She was dosed with laudanum and was looked after by Hildegarde and
Martin. In sickness, the 'Squaws' were a very present help in time of trouble to
each other, and they changed rooms and beds with bewildering frequency in
order to be of service. Laudanum was an effective painkiller but had unwanted
side-effects in causing a kind of drunken loss of muscular control. Martin
entered in her diary for 12 December: 'Poor H did not get one chance of
sleeping with the Doll [a nickname for Martin] as E's face was bad and we
wouldn't let her sleep alone ... they were very sorry to say goodbye to me.'

On that day Martin left to spend Christmas with her mother in Dublin, the
season to be followed by a tour of cousins. She wrote to Edith from Ballsbridge
on the 14th: 'I don't know when I have been more depressed than at leaving CT
– and more especially Drishane – and more especially you – "but no matter" ... I
don't know how to say what I should like and what I feel about the way you all
united to spoil the Doll – It would take a Doll of superior mechanism to mine to
say it all ...' Mrs Martin was pleased with her daughter's new free berth in CT,
and told her of her 'deep sense of the moral and physical improvement' in her
after her stay there. But Hildegarde's loosening-up influence had evidently only
gone so far, for she writes across the head of the letter, 'PS I have not sent love to
anyone – I hate doing it – I think it absurd'. To close her letter she had simply
ended her last paragraph and written 'Martin'. Even so, in her letters to Edith we
find a much more open expression of affection. Edith's to her are full of humour,
crazy descriptions of dances and entertainments and racy accounts of hunts; what
was personal was an awful, joking tone of intimacy that could cheerfully castigate
Martin as anything from 'The Queen of Pig's Feet' to a 'a white rat' when she was
ill. Evidently Edith did not spare Martin from comments on personal hygiene.
Such frankness was a product of sibling familiarity in Castletownshend, and it
meant that Martin was 'in', adopted as one of their kind.

The surviving series of letters between the two writers begins on Edith's side
with a description of a dance at the Maxwells' and a hunt with the Conners of

Manch. We can compare the version of these events written to Martin with the version written to Cameron, and we find whole phrases repeated. Edith wrote letters to her brothers away in the Services and to 'the boys' Jack and Hugh, with a machine-like constancy, so this is hardly surprising. While Martin and her mother, known as Nannie Martin, were in Dublin, a visitor admired the oil panel portrait of Martin by Edith. Nannie was a woman of stupendous vagueness, and Martin heard her mother respond: 'Yes, Miss Myers, I think it *is* very good, it was done by Miss Coghill, a cousin of mine.' Martin's Christmas gifts from CT came up to her in parcels. Edith sent a fur cap – '(same as her own) a delightful gift.' The most expensive gift was from Beatrice and Violet, an opulently bound volume of Tennyson.

On 3 January 1887 Edith's first fox terrier arrived: Patsey 'two months old, small, wizened and well bred, and bursting with intelligence'. In February Edith and Hildegarde went off to stay with Fanny Currey, taking Patsey, who had rapidly become a sort of accessory, in a carpet bag. Patsey took to travelling so well that he was soon to be taken to Paris with Edith, in the same conveyance. From Lismore Edith went up to Ethel and Jim at Athboy where she rode with Jim to some meets of the grand Meath Hunt, and where the field was often as many as 200 riders strong. She wrote to Hildegarde that it was impossible to work at Ethel's: 'beyond taking some of the "terrible sensationalism" out of the "Night in the Suburbs" I have been able to do no work here'. She complained of her 'gashly [sic] existence' with the noise of all the babies. But she had fallen for Dennis: 'The only one I really love ... a dear little chap and the best-looking.'

From Athboy she went on to Paris. Edith told Cameron that the Martins planned to return to CT at the end of July, but that she might see Martin in Paris if she could get permission for her to come over. The Greenes in Dublin had been scandalised at the 'Bohemian idea' of the two of them racketting about Paris without a chaperone, and an illegal dog, Patsey. Edith also had to deal with Cameron's irritation over the fact that their brother Aylmer was still 'unplaced' in a profession: 'It is no use storming in your letters – I quite sympathize with you but Papa and Aylmer are alike in a certain form of delay – Papa from kind heartedness and Aylmer from longing that something may turn up to save him from the ranks, if I were only in his place I would be a sergeant this minute.' Aylmer was quite soon saved from the ranks by marriage to a rich girl.

After staying with her mother and Aunt Marion at Jubilee Hall in Bray, Martin crossed to England.[24] On 24 February she went to stay in London with her brother Robert, who had made a name for himself as a writer of popular songs and revues, and his wife Connie at 48 Leinster Square in Bayswater. She met up with Edith en route to Paris via Dublin and they crossed to London together. Edith was still aiming at an independent income from illustrative art.

Egerton had been of great importance to Edith in helping her gain independence as an artist, and she revered him as a painter and a close friend: 'no words can tell how nice he has been, and how improved he is, in every way since this engagement – so different to his uncertainty of last summer, that got on his nerves, I think, H. is lucky to have him,' she wrote to Cameron. Having fought for it, Egerton had invented a word 'inder-bloody-pendence' that Edith gladly borrowed from him. Egerton's life had been changed utterly by the death in 1879 of his elder brother Nevill, for the spotlight had suddenly fallen upon him as the heir to the Coghill baronetcy. As a younger son, he had been apprenticed as an engineer at Erith Engineering Works, to prepare him for a profession. When his elder brother died, it was thought, too optimistically, that it would no longer be necessary for Egerton to earn his living, and he took to the study of painting. As a carefree art student Egerton had long hair, earrings and Bohemian clothes. In photographs from this time he looks like an inauthentically clean extra in a stage version of *Trilby*. But with his new responsibility as heir had come eventually a revolution in his appearance – a military 'short back and sides' haircut and a moustache.

Apart from their journey to London from Dublin, Edith did not see Martin in 1887 until she joined her in Paris. On 2 March Edith wrote to Martin from there, and that her letters to Martin were less personal than Martin's to her is shown by her closing instruction: 'I have just written home so feel weak but I think it is due to you to send you a letter, and if you have found Minnie's whereabouts in town [London] you might make an occasion to go and declaim its contents to her.' Sadly this letter gave no address to which Martin could respond. She replied the following day, having found out the address from a 'Castle T-ite' in London: 'What makes you so awfully clever? Who but a person with a really great mind would have thought of writing from Paris and giving no address ... You are I should think "In your glory" surrounded by American art students with their excellent comic paper jokes ...' Here we find early notice of a difference in subtlety of humour, which persisted throughout their career together. Edith wrote back on the 11th full of praise for the work of her cousin Rose Barton. It opens 'My dear child ... I know I shall talk in a twang soon. I hear nothing but Amurrican but they are a nice people ... I live in groove and you must get there, too, before I can write anything that will amuse you ...' Martin was not convinced by this excuse for short letters: 'I wonder you can talk such offensive rot about your letters and your uninteresting groove – Go to, my dear, and invent a better class of falsehood next time. When I find your letters uninteresting I shall cease to correspond with you – you bet.'[25] She was very keen to discover where Edith went to church, but never found out.

Edith seemed to miss the stimulation of her mother's rows and criticism. On the 12th, she wrote a letter to Adelaide trying to persuade her to come and live with her in Paris: 'I don't see why you shouldn't – to live here is amazingly cheap … it would make all the difference to me your being here as I should hate being away from home a whole winter. Yet that is what I ought to do if I am to become really successful.' She was terrified of one of her tutors: 'He is rather down on me as he thinks I am a mere flaneur who comes here for sport and gets sick of it in a couple of months – and yet wants to paint pictures – I don't dare show *him* Paley Dabble [a comic strip]. He would scarify me for such un-serious work.' Obviously Edith and Martin had no thoughts of operating professionally as a working pair at this point, more than a year after they met, because they do not know each other's plans: 'If you have room it would be nice to have Martin down for a time in the summer – But perhaps they may take the Mall? I know nothing on the subject and she has not mentioned it.'

On 27 March Martin wrote again to Edith, sending her for her amusement a story of a mishap with a large harrier at Ross that had a fit of hysterics on seeing Martin in her hip bath, followed by distressing digestive complications. It closes with the comment: 'The whole thing makes quite a nice little story.' It also reveals that Martin did not approve of what she saw as the crude humour of Edith and her American fellow students, with their 'vulgar practical jokes – it cannot be right to excite the earnest feelings of others unnecessarily. This you will remember I have often had occasion to repeat to you …' But Edith revelled in the Americans' sardonic, deadpan ripostes. Marion Adams had borrowed Edith's continental Bradshaw's Railway timetable. When she handed it back Edith said, deadpan: 'Did you enjoy it?', to which Marion replied, equally deadpan: 'O yes! I stayed up all night to see how it ended.' Edith had a super-correct and obtrusively Christian chaperone at this period called Miss Newstead, who bored her considerably. She wrote back to Martin to thank her for sugges-tions of subjects for comic strips: 'My dearest child … [I am] most grateful …' and then passed on to Miss Newstead: 'I do not like them as good as she is – If I had to choose between the poor but saintly curate and the wicked Duke I would take the Duke immediately, and advise you to do the same …'[26]

Martin had experienced difficulty in getting permission to join Edith in Paris; just as much as the Somervilles, Mrs Martin seemed to associate Paris with vice. Edith had to put her mind at rest: 'Wrote to Nanny Martin after dinner to try and let Martin come over as there is some rooted idea in the family that it isn't proper', she wrote in her diary on 23 April. More than once she complained: 'It seems I cannot go to Paris without a married grandmother.' She wrote to Cameron telling him of the plan: 'I hope Martin will be able to come over for a week or so, just to see the Salon before I go – it would be great sport going round with her – She is the best company possible and an awfully good sort and I hope you will meet her whenever you come home.' If Martin could get to Paris, both of them wanted separate rooms, describing them as 'more airy' than a shared one, but in the event Edith could not get a room anywhere near hers and they eventually shared. Martin's unconcealed neurotic fears, of ghosts and sudden disasters sent by a Parisian *mal occhio*,[27] had persuaded Edith that to put her in a separate pension away from the rest of her gang would be a cruelty.

On the 29th she entered in her diary: 'Heard from Martin. Her mother has given in.' Martin crossed to Paris on the next day. She did not really enjoy her rather airless experience of cheek by jowl Bohemian life with art students. She did not speak French and had observed all the hurly-burly silently. Back at Drishane in mid-May, Edith wrote to Cameron: 'Martin joined me on May 1st, we stayed til the 10th ... we tore round generally and saw all the pictures and most of the churches and lived for about 2*d.* a day, by the dint of economy and *cremeries.*' Martin showed how very quick-witted she was on the boat home when she concealed Patsey from an approaching Customs Officer by stuffing the amiable little animal up her wide sleeved coat, leaving the slower-witted Edith dogless and innocent: 'with the utmost candour I showed the man the contents of my carpet bag – they must have surprised him – a large green carpet bag exclusively dedicated to one dirty handkerchief, a gnawed crust of bread and a filthy painting blouse; all red-hot from the puppy's person.'

Back in England Martin left Edith to go down to Portsmouth to visit her sister Edith Dawson[28] and wrote from there at the end of May: 'I must say an artist's trade seems the pleasantest all round especially when it gives an opening to your cousin to come and improve her mind in Paris. I think I was a sort of dumb dog over there and assumed a sort of aristocratic languor all the time – so it seems on reflection – but I was inwardly full of enthusiasm and pleasure – so don't make any mistakes about that ...'. With her sister Edith, Martin watched Queen Victoria's Jubilee Procession from Lady Waterford's balcony. Martin was from a rigidly Unionist family, much more patrician than the easy-going Somervilles, and she was one of the voluntary contributors to a book of sonnets published by the *Irish Times* in celebration of the Queen's Jubilee. Martin's sonnet is a production showing strong Unionism and an equally strong sexism: it describes the new year, Jubilee personified in her poem as 'him' and 'He', inaugurated by the Royal Visit to Dublin:

> ... In far other guise
> We welcoming stood to watch him drawing near,
> Bearing on his young brow a word that here
> And henceforth 'mid the throng of centuries
> Crowns him. He consummating comes, and cries
> From far a Royal name – a name most dear ...

Edith did not restrain herself from criticism of this volume, 'puke' being part of her reaction.[29] Social life in London with her brother and with the Dawsons between London and Portsmouth was quite hectic, but on 27 June Martin went to her old friends the Helps at Kew, where she socialised with their neighbour Warham St Leger again. From CT, in June Edith went off painting with Fanny Currey in the Youghal area. Afterwards Hildegarde joined them for a sailing trip on the yacht *Miriam*, and on it Edith nearly drowned. When they were sleeping in their berths on board in Youghal harbour, Edith went up on deck, sleepwalking. Hildegarde was woken by some unsleeping sense of danger and shot up on deck to lay hands on her sister just as Edith was about to saunter overboard, followed by the faithful and unsuspecting small dog Patsey. Hearing of her near disaster, Percy Aylmer, her childhood companion in scrapes, wrote to her from Walworth Castle: 'My child, I always knew that you were not born into this world to go out of it by such an effeminate way as drowning, you seem to have had a narrow escape ... may you always be as lucky ...' The letters give some other examples of Edith sleepwalking at this time, and these episodes would suggest some form of suppressed emotion. She was working secretly at a pair of sonnets on lost love, not revealed to Martin for criticism at this point.

When they came back, at Drishane there were dances, musical evenings and tennis parties. When in funds Cameron was always financially generous and helpful to his elder sister; he commisssioned a portrait of Drishane. Martin wrote approvingly: 'It shows great nobility on the Chimp's part to come down with the ready as he does.' The painting was a much-admired one.[30] During July at CT, Edith also painted a successful portrait of Violet Coghill, and spent a lot of time racketting about with her. They went together to a festive meal in Ross Carbery to celebrate the installation of the new Bishop, where they both ate huge quantities, Edith told Cam, she being encouraged by 'the village Violet, than whom I know no solider or more dependable, or whose aid I value more in the matter of a simple gorge'.

The most intensive work that Martin and Edith did in this summer was a revision of the Buddh Dictionary, first started by Edith and Ethel in 1885, and worried at in the summer in between. The words listed in the Dictionary cast light into a tight corner of the Anglo-Irish mind of the time, revealing a mentality under threat, in retreat, withdrawing into a private world, and concealing many things under flippancy.[31] Ridiculous as many of the words seem, they were in use throughout the lives of Edith and her sister, and were to be very useful as a code in their letters of the 1920s which were being opened and read by Irish Free State censors. We cannot read their letters without its key. For instance, it is only because of the Buddh dictionary definition of 'hints and bunches' that we know that Mrs Martin was disliked in CT for being an unscrupulous scrounger. The entire code was invented to preserve private communications when in the company of outsiders, or before domestics. Manuscript the second is annotated with details of its production: Edith was Editor 1 and Martin Editor 2.

## Some frequently used Buddh words

**A-pers,** preposition. Apres. Expression used as a reminder that the conversation is not fitted for the ears of the domestic (derivation French).

**Absquatulate,** v.i. Generally used in the imperative tense as a command to children to remove their superfluous presences. 2. To retire (derivation Ab-from .Squat- to sit, to crouch. Derivation Old Coghill)

**Blaut,** v.i. and n. Violently to express immoderate fury. (more probably Blort from snort and Blast. Ed. 2.)

**Bosom-salad,** n. A vegetable structure, used for purposes of concealment and decoration (derivation Greene)

**Bunch,** v.i. and n. An imperfectly veiled attempt to extort a favour. Takes the prefix 'Ever Thine' (derivation from the nickname 'Bunch' of an old lady, famous alike for her rapacity and her powers of obtaining what she wanted by ingenious hints. Old Coghill)

**Camac,** n. An equivalent for any known substantive (derivation unknown, Greene? Any unnecessarily complicated and costly contrivance for effecting a simple purpose.)

**Chip,** n. feminine. The elder Buddh woman.2. One who is erroneously supposed to be the sole prop of morality and order (derivation Chaperone, Greene)

**Coghelian,** adjective. Applied to any sluttish device for evading a proper system of repair or arrangement (derivation the perverse ingenuity of the Coghills, Rev. J.Bushe.)

**Cretacious,** adjective. Expensive (derivation Chalky, Old Coghill)

**Dwam,** n. A heavy and half unconscious state resembling coma (derivation Old Coghill)

**Fresh Egg,** Good Egg, Eggling. Terms applied to male partners in the dance, denoting their varying degrees of merit (derivation American, Modern Buddh)

**Falconising.** Paying visits. Preying upon unwilling friends (derivation Old Coghill)

**Flop,** noun. A lavish and unreserved depositing of the affections upon one whose reciprocity is wholly superfluous (For the most part a feminine practice) (derivation Modern Buddh)

**Glaum,** noun. The horrible laying on of an uncanny hand. A witch-like clutch (derivation Old Buddh)

**Gub,** noun. A vague pursuing horror, the embodiment of the terror of darkness. By the superstitious it is conceived capable of inflicting unimaginable injuries. The person enduring this pursuit or possession is said to be gubbed (derivation Modern Buddh)

**Howling-wolves,** noun. Young men of a dangerous attractiveness. The Chaperone's natural foe (derivation obvious Fox)

**Hussy,** v.i. and t. To pander to masculine vanity (derivation Modern Buddh)

**Hugger-Muggering,** v.i. pres.p. The illicit clustering together of young persons to the neglect of their social duties (Chiefly a feminine practice) (derivation Old Coghill thro' the Anglo-Saxon 'Hegian' to hedge in)

**Jobation,** noun. A premeditated reproof of unusual length and severity to which the prudent will not attempt a reply (derivation Old Buddh)

**Kanat,** noun. An artful and dangerous person; capable of treacherous and flagitious acts (derivation Old Buddh)

**Leebarkation,** noun. A flirtation of a resolute character (derivation Martin)

**Mawse,** v.t. To abuse, to scold. The prerogative of elders and betters (derivation from Mause Heddrigg, Old Mortality [novel by Walter Scott]. Old Coghill)

**Sink,** noun. Either Drishane or Glen Barrahane. Varies with the person employing the term. (derivation the well-known capabilities possessed by these establishments, for absorbing and assimilating property other than their own. Modern Buddh.)

## Terms and Phrases from the Buddh Dictionary

**One of them,** n, a man not necessarily young, goodlooking or well born, who is endowed with a subtle attractiveness imperceptible to grosser intelligences, tho' for the keenly sensistive possessing an overmastering charm (derivation, from the number and variety of those gifted with this strange fascination, the uncomprehending scoffer [Herbert Greene, identified as 'the skoffer' at the end of the dictionary] would, at the sight of any low mean person, mockingly enquire if he also was 'one of them' ie those in whom the Twins had discerned the quality mentioned above. Modern Buddh)

**Pig's Foot,** n, term in the Buddh pharmacopeia. The ultimate and more complicated form of any slight accident or ailment which has been wilfully neglected – as an abscess caused by an insignificant burn etc. (derivation Fox)

**The Pigs are out**. By this is conveyed the fact that some person is in a dangerous state of irritation, or that there has been a general blowing up by those in authority (derivation 'The pigs are out and running through the pratie garden' – author unknown – from which comes the idea of aggressiveness and destructive onslaught. Old Buddh)

**Purlieu**, noun. A receptacle for rubbish, literary, artistic, bestial and human.

**Scrip**, noun. A reason or excuse for coming unexpectedly to a meal in the house of a friend. See Bunch.

**Sassoferrara**, noun. A burst of violent abuse, a blowing up (derivation Old Coghill)

**Scoops**, noun. The mother of. Term in hymnology, applied to melodies which are dear to vocalists of the portamento school.

**Sheba**, noun. Any new and prized possession which is calculated to excite hopeless envy in those to whom it is displayed (Deriv. Queen Sheba's despairing resentment at the sight of King Solomon's high class furniture. Rev.J.Bushe.)

**Squaws**, noun, pl. Young unmarried Buddh women of the highest and most confidential type (derivation Modern Buddh)

**Sylphing**, pres.p. Posing with conscious grace in the hope of attracting attention (derivation Modern Buddh)

**Themmish**, adjective. An attractive and loveable youth – not necessarily of the upper classes. (Derivation see 'One of them')

**Unbung**, verb. To release the pent up flow of Chip conversation which from absence or some other unavoidable cause has been temporarily checked (derivation see Bung)

Early in August Edith wrote to Cameron to tell him how much she was enjoying Cousin Gendie (Mrs Miller Mundy) and her guests at the Castle, one of whom was to change Aylmer's life: 'I have a great belief in Cousin Gendie and petticoat pressure. She is really a most delightful woman – *too* amusing and extraordinary – you can never guess what she is going to say ... There are two Miss Sykes (I think Boyle knows them) coming to the Castle next week – Ten thou apiece – we are counselling Aylmer to go in for one of them. Gendie declares she will give him all her help as he is just the sort of young man she would have gone in for herself. She says 'First I was pretty, then I was intellectual, now dear child I am *Good*.' 'Tis she is the doty woman.'[32]

Edith sent five paintings to the Dudley Gallery exhibition in October. One of them, 'Cutting for a new line', is a painting of earthworks for part of the Bandon-Skibbereen extension railway, on which Hewitt Poole was the engineer.

As Edith later remembered it, when she was painting a landscape of the Lissard Lake for Herbert Greene in the Studio, and talking, Martin was immediately taken by Edith's suggestion that they might try to write a story together. What was called 'The Shocker' started to come together, to be published finally at the end of 1889 as *An Irish Cousin*. Edith's diary entry for 4 October had: 'began to invent a plot for a penny thriller'. It was definitely on the stocks in October 1887. We can track quite closely from Edith's diaries how its invention came about. In the course of their pre-breakfast early morning work in the Studio, they had cobbled together an article on Youghal and had sent it off to Oscar Wilde, a friend of Sir Joscelyn's, who was editor of the *Woman's World*. On 26 September Edith heard from him: 'He will take the Youghal article ... wrote to him. Martin and I began to potter at the Wild Corner in Carbery encouraged by Youghal's success.' From 29 September for three days Edith simply enters: 'Toiled at Carbery.' Then on 4 October she enters: 'Began to invent a plot for a penny thriller.' It seemed to lie in compost for a while before its next mention: 'Vaguely discussed the "shockeraun"' is noted next on the 15th. Martin's niece Muriel Currey, in her invaluable notes on her Somerville diary transcripts, remarks here that the Shocker 'really began as a joke', seeing it as a kind of running gag that was taken up by the family, and the authors had to keep writing further and further episodes to satisfy the family's demands. But when we look carefully at the date sequence, it looks very much more as if the encouragement given to them by Oscar Wilde had had an immediate effect upon their confidence in making them think of attempting something bigger than an article.

In a frivolous letter to Cameron on 26 October, Edith gives an account of a visit that she and Martin made to the old Townshend house, White Hall. On the envelope, Edith's handwriting when she was an old woman declares boldly: 'White Hall "Irish Cousin"'. The account inside of the visit to the house of kind Townshend relations at which they arrived ravenous from their ride and 'ate a huge tea' bears no resemblance to the Gothicised account of the inspiration for *An Irish Cousin* of 1889 later written by Edith in *Irish Memories* of 1917, when she conflated it with an experience she had on her own. Also running counter to *Irish Memories*, Martin's later letter of 21 August 1889 does not identify their own visit to White Hall as the trigger for the novel: 'I seem to remember very much the beginnings of the Shocker just now when ... you told me of the old maniac's face at the window over the White Hall door ...' Continuing its opening vein of frivolity, Edith's letter to Cameron has a paragraph showing that he kept up his theatrical appearances in drag: 'I do hope you will be photographed as a girl – *and still more* that you will bring back that nice pink gingham frock home as when you outgrow it I know it will make a lovely summer frock for me. You might buy the other one second hand from Major

Davis, as if he is 6' 7" it ought to be just about Hildegarde's length.' The discrepancy between the tone of this letter and the doom-laden later account of the genesis of their first novel in *Irish Memories* is so large that we might suspect that as an old woman Edith remembered not what was actually in the envelope addressed to Cameron in 1887 but her later fictionalised version.

Now that writers no longer manually write their scripts with pen and ink, the sheer laboriousness of clean-copying 100,000-word novels is easy to overlook. But Edith clean- copied almost all their novels up until her discovery of efficient copy-typists after Martin's death. Her copying took an immense chore off the shoulders of Martin, and it is an absorbing question whether she was consciously aware of using Edith as an amanuensis. Edith herself, with her gallows humour echoing a comment of her partner's, used to refer to herself as the 'hack and amanuensis' to the genius of Martin.[33] Miss Hingston, the palmist who read both their palms just before they set to work together, gave this reading, which was carefully recorded by Martin in her diary, just as Edith recorded her own:

> Line of affection shows great warmth of affection – extreme fidelity but not much passion. Will have many friends and will be trusted by both men and women [Martin comments in the margin here 'interesting – scarcely human'] … is proud – naturally low spirited rather than high. Delights in theatres. Tragedy more especially. Has large reverence. A good deal of superstition – a little credulity. An immense amount of conscientiousness, A tendency to bother about trifles. Likes her own way. Delight in planning and organising – but often fails to carry out her plans. A little apt to take her colouring from her surroundings, is sensitive and sympathetic – is a most delightful companion on account of a certain amount of adaptibility … Great deal of tact. Is more of an idealist than a realist, not enough brain power to carry out her aspirations – ought to make money by her own exertions. Is given to castle building. Is irritable, not excitable. Has great dislike to hurting other people's feelings.

Whatever its inspiration, their first novel had a most extraordinary genesis. At first the family had laughed at them and their novel – 'that nonsense of the girls' – and Edith thought that the fact that they were cruelly persecuted made them want all the more to succeed. Written in bits and pieces that were exchanged by post and read by those interested members of the family as separate episodes, the 'novel' was assuming some size by December 1887, when we begin to read about its construction in their letters. Martin stayed at Glen B for Christmas, when discussions raged as to the plot of 'The Shocker', but left for her family in

Dublin at the beginning of January. They tried to tie up all the novel's loose ends before Martin went: 'Martin came up [from Glen B]. Shocker all day. Very Exhausting.' Working alone in the Studio, Edith finished the clean-copying for a publisher on the night of 21 January, 1888. Meanwhile Mrs Somerville had read it: 'Mother has begun to read the shocker and loathes it for many reasons.' Fortunately Minnie Townshend was of a quite different opinion, and by post Ethel gave approval also.

Her mother had been complaining of the want of romantic passion, and Edith decided to supply this want. She wrote to Martin on the same day to tell her of the changes she had made to MS pages 71 and 72:

> ... I know you must loathe me sticking in these putrid things and then fighting for them – I couldn't help it – as I got the feeling of it one night in bed and wrote it there and then. Please goodness we will have many a tooth and naily fight over it next month – but don't let us combat by post: it is too wearing. I pity you – I was just saying how odious it must be for you having these things jumped on you. She [Hildegarde] says you are ever so much too refined and too anxious not to have anything in your book that was ever in anyone else's book; I think that is true – Mother has complained bitterly of the want of love interest ...

Edith's additions met with her mother's approval: she thought the last chapter '*very* good'. But 'The Shocker' was turned down in its first version by Sampson Low, and the manuscript passed on to other readers. The novel involved all their close friends and relations. Hildegarde, who had very good clear handwriting, made a complete MS copy to enable more relations to read it and comment. The plot takes for granted the readers' understanding that gentry men had illegitimate children by their tenants and servants, but the rigid outward rules of gentry society still enforced social outlawry on Willie Sarsfield, who marries his lodgekeeper's daughter: he has to emigrate to Australia with her to start a new life. Later novels were to dwell on gentry women who fell for men of the tenant and servant class; in this event there was no way out by escape to a new world.

In the novel, the heroine Theodora, at a dinner party, is impressed with the way in which Henrietta O'Neill, at the opposite end of the table, has managed to keep up an unceasing flow of discussion with her gloomy Uncle Dominick. Suddenly he breaks out into loud-voiced anger:

> 'You amaze me,' he was saying. 'I cannot believe that any sane person can honestly hold such absurd theories. What! Do you mean to tell me

that one of my tenants, a creature whose forefathers have lived for centuries in ignorance and degradation, is my equal?'

'His degradation is merely the result of injustice,' said Miss O'Neill, coolly adjusting her *pince-nez*.

'I deny it,' said my uncle, loudly. His usually pale face was flushed, and his eyes burned. 'But that is not the point. What I maintain is, that any fusion of classes such as you advocate would have the effect of debasing the upper while it entirely failed to raise the lower orders. If you were to marry your coachman, as according to your theories of equality, I suppose you would not hesitate to do, do you think these latent instincts of refinement that you talk about would make him a fit companion for you and your family? You know as well as I do that such an idea is preposterous. It is absurd to think that the natural arrangement of things can be tampered with. This is a subject on which I feel very strongly, and it shocks me to hear a young lady in your position advance such opinions!'

Uncle Dominick is the villain who comes to an appalling end. With his mistress, one of the servants of the house, he had, cleverly and undetected, contrived the murder of his elder brother in order to inherit his house and estate for himself. The plot of the novel was at this time a subject of heated group discussions within the family. It owes much to Le Fanu's *Uncle Silas*, and to Edith's knowledge of the Yelverton scandals, although the social scene and dialect throughout is that of Cork. The legal emphasis is changed from that of the Yelverton scandal, from fake marriage certificates to fake death certificates, though there is the same play with a crucial time lapse. The geography of the house of the fictional Durrus and its lands, described as overlooking Roaringwater Bay in County Cork, suggests Belle Isle. The deep pool within easy reach of the house, in which Uncle Dominick eventually drowns himself, is paralleled by the deep inlet of Lough Derg that the Yelvertons had adapted as a mooring basin for their yachts. In particular the violent ending and final scene were hotly debated, and were to be drastically changed for the second edition of 1903. But hatred between brother and brother, on account of inheritance, remains the mainspring of the plot. Because the 3rd Viscount Avonmore had run into financial difficulty, his brother, who had not, gave an allowance to his nephew, the heir Charles Yelverton, Barry's father, on condition that he did not marry, so that his own son might inherit Belle Isle and the title.[34] This may explain why Charles thought the fake marriage with Teresa Longworth a good idea. But he immediately regretted it and repudiated it, as the wealth of Emily Marianne Forbes, Barry's mother, might have enabled him as 4th Viscount to bypass his uncle's schemes; but it was all brought to nought by his seduction of Teresa, and the expense of his trial.

A letter of 1 February 1888 from Edith to Boyle shows that she was still trying to cram two occupations into a timetable only fit for one, as she worked in the time that was left over after the primary claims of her household. She was painting the very large canvas 'The Goosegirl' for exhibition, at the same time as hacking irregularly at the manuscript of *An Irish Cousin*. The novel did not achieve its final title until far too late. It actually went to press under the title of *An Experiment*, having started off as *Durrus: An Experiment*. This first effort was memorable for disagreements and last-minute changes; they can hardly have thought they could make a living out of such a painfully argumentative and time-consuming method of producing a text. It was Edith who wrote the romantic passages, Mrs Somerville and Hildegarde flatly giving as their opinion that Martin was too fastidious for the writing of these.

Martin had been with her family in Dublin and Kilkenny, but at the end of the month Edith wrote to Boyle: 'after this week I hope to plunge into the Martin-and-my novel. It has had a most tremendous success with the private critics to whom it has been submitted – but the 2nd part is still to be written. Martin comes here on the 3rd to bear me companie, as soon as the Hejira begins. Seafield [the Townshends] to London on the 7th, Mother and H to Glandovan on the 15th, Papa's High Sheriffing begins on March 17th and then I hope to take my picture under one arm and our novel under the other and away with me to London ... the tenants have paid up more or less, and by shutting up this house we shall economise a bit – which is exceedingly necessary these bad times.' By mid-February there was hardly time for diary entries. Martin wrote on the 17th in her diary: 'Shocker in possession of today and of every day – with the exception of hurried constitutionals.'

When Edith wrote to Cameron on 22 February, the engagement had been announced of Aylmer and Miss Emmie Sykes, and she told him: 'You and I and the Busto [Boyle] dear child, may now retreat on the highest dusted shelf available as in the opinion of all the world we have utterly and entirely sunk, in that we have been bested by our younger brother and sister ... Martin and I are working like blacks at our story as I want to take it to town with me next month ... This ought to fetch your birthday. Blessings, blessings dear Child be upon you, and *never* reveal that you have the misfortune to be the junior of your venerable but still vivacious sister.' Despite the Shocker, Edith still managed some reading for light relief. On the 29th she noted in her diary that she had read Darwin, not the obvious title, but his *Expression of the Emotions in Humans and Animals* that had been published in 1872. This must have been to aid her in her illustrative work.[35]

They both left for London on 26 March, Edith en route to a theatrical house party in Yorkshire and Martin to visit her sister Edith. The experience of writing a novel together had passed from being fun to being hard work, and also a source of conflict. Martin was exhausted by it, and not too keen to repeat the experience. Languishing with her sister in Portsmouth, she wrote to Edith in Yorkshire on 17 April: 'I have had a notion of a feeble kind for a story in my mind for a little time and will try conscientiously to work it. But indeed I don't feel it my line – I feel more like writing pompous papers on emigration and such things and even occasionally vex my soul with wonderings as to what germ of truth may be in Fenianism.'

While in London Edith did a round of editors, including Oscar Wilde at *Woman's World*. She did not find him attractive in person, no matter what the effect of his good opinion had been on her career, and described him to Martin in an undated letter: 'He is a great fat oily beast. He pretended the most enormous interest ... but it was all of no avail ... He languidly took the sonnets [Edith's, later published by *The World*] and is to return them by post. He talked great rot that "French subjects should be drawn by French artists" ... He assumed deep interest in the "Miss Martins", asked if they were all married: I said "Mostly all". He was kind enough to say that Edith was so pretty and nice – and bulged his long fat red cheeks into an affectionate grin at the thought of her. He then showed me a book of very indifferent French sketches – was foully civil and so goodbye. I then took Carbery [the article on the stocks after "Youghal"] to *Cassell's Family Mag.* office. A dear little intelligent vulgarian in charge – such a relief ...'. Still looking for contacts, she met up with Mr Rivington in person; he was helpful and attractive as well: 'I hope you will see Mr R – a very nice man – I could love him if I got time – but go inside me if you get a chance ...' She had met Connie Martin: 'She said she had heard *nothing* of any of you since you left town – and asked if I had – I told her I had heard on professional business – but I believe she wants a letter.' At the end of this month a letter from Edith to Martin gives the only hint of a cause of disagreement over the ending of *An Irish Cousin* : 'I think to end with a kiss would be rather cheap – and I like the little human commonplaceness of the finish better.'[36]

In Yorkshire, Edith sang the major part of 'Little Buttercup' in an amateur production of *Pinafore* and attended dinners and dances with others of the cast. During rehearsals, Edith demonstrated that she was completely unembarrassed by physical contact with young men. She had to train the female chorus to be 'forward' with the sailors of the male chorus: 'We wanted them to be very loving, and at last in despair I plunged into the chorus, and my dear, wogged a young auctioneer in the most abandoned way.'[37] Edith was successful in promoting physical familiarity: 'now they hug each other nearly as much as Captain Corcoran and I ...' She got through her part by acting the fool: 'you are quite right in feeling that Dumb Crambo [mime] is my strong suit – I don't know how to begin to act ...'. The reviewer of the production in the local newspaper still singled her out for her drollery and 'powers of facial expression'.[38]

In a letter to Martin from London on 15 May, she described having to sight read an accompaniment to a cellist called Grove: 'I was in a blue funk all the time, as he was a faultless professional who doesn't try to do more than he knows how. Then, my dear, I sang "In Deinen Blauen Augen" – modified approval except from 2 or 3, and then I warbled a little thing that I believe you know, very suitable for open air effect – called "the Wearing of the Green". It is wearing a little white at the seams now, but is still a good grand article ...'[39] Mrs Martin seemed to be planning a holiday at her old home in Galway, and sent an invitation via Martin to Edith to visit her and her daughters there, but she answered: 'I am awfully afraid I don't see my way to it', money being too tight. Edith had no inkling of what was in Mrs Martin's mind.

Meanwhile Martin's mother made a decision that diverted Martin's life for the next eighteen years. Moving in a counter direction to the Anglo-Irish tide, Mrs Martin decided to move back to Ross after a lapse of fifteen years. No sooner had she made this decision than she had asked Hildegarde and Edith to join her and Martin during the summer, without a notion as to the condition of the house, which had been ill-treated by its tenant and was in a bad way. Edith wrote to Martin: 'Mother is disgusted at your Mother reneging off to Ross and no wonder – my sentiments will not bear being put on paper ...' Martin, being something of a hypochondriac, told Edith every last thing about her numerous malaises, most frequently dysmenorrhea, not always getting sympathy. There were many patent medicines and painkillers for the menstrual problems besetting her, and Edith was astonished at their frequency: 'It is my firm belief you have the divil three times a week. It is perfectly ridiculous affectation. You never wrote to me yet that you weren't bedivilled ...' [40]

Martin was staying with the Helps in Kew on her birthday, the eleventh of June. All of her CT cousins were lumped together as 'the squaws'. She had 'Congratulatory letters from the squaws – with notice of gifts. Excellent but misguided women.' Martin's letters to Edith from Ross start in June 1888. The move to Ross can be dated precisely from a letter to Hildegarde from Kew, written on 16 June, when Martin wrote: 'I go over to Dublin on Tuesday morning ... until I land the furniture and muck generally at Ross on the following Saturday.' While in London, Martin had visited the Irish Exhibition at Olympia with Warham St Leger, assistant editor on *Black and White*, contributor to *Punch* and neighbour of the Helps.[41] He and she had almost missed the last train back in to the city, but while Martin ran flat out, 'behind me were smothered crowings and yelps from my wholly futile companion – who when furiously asked why he was laughing could give no reason except that we were running to catch a train of importance – and that emotion always took him that way – Idiot.' This visit was to bear fruit in Martin's first article, 'Olympia to Connemara'; written about the exhibition, it was accepted by Edmund Yates as editor of *The World*, and published at the end of August.

To Hildegarde, Martin described a boat trip up the Thames to Teddington, where she had pulled an oar for about six miles 'and had something of an appetite for a monstrous high tea provided at the house of two bachelors of the party on our return'. The bachelors were St Leger and his fellow writer Henry Pottinger Stephens, who were joint authors of a thriller called *The Basilisk*, published in 1886. When we search for their inspiration to write a novel together, there is no need to assume that Edith and Martin were solely inspired by knowledge of Willy Wills and Aunt Louisa Greene writing thrillers together, as Martin knew of this other instance on her own account. Willy Wills and Aunt Louisa had published *Whose Hand? Or the Mystery of No Man's Heath* in 1886 as well. Pottinger Stephens was the joint author of a series of thrillers with another colleague; *The Basilisk* was his only work with St Leger. What Somerville and Ross did in writing novels together was not in the least unusual at the time they set forth on their career, and there has been a revival of the practice recently.

Warham St Leger had been privileged to see and discuss the Buddh Dictionary with Martin, and had delightedly suggested elaborations of some of the definitions. He was a Cambridge man, and Martin enjoyed comparing him with Herbert Greene. Sending Edith one of St Leger's helpful comments, on a word that had baffled Herbert, Martin wrote on an undated fragment: 'Ha Ha Miss, and Ha Ha Herbert and the whole lot of you. Is not the Cambridge man valuable better than the Oxford scholar who makes language his study?' At a tea party in Kew that St Leger was hosting, Martin had become involved in a spontaneous round of instantaneously composed sonnets, and had not been found wanting. Edith was amused by Martin's account of this, and was inspired herself to join in with a pun on the pronunciation of Warham's name: 'Very kind you were at that St Leger tea party. Do you like Warham cakes or cold ones? – I hope they disagreed with you. *Be sure* you send me Rose's criticism of the Shocker. I am most curious to hear it.'

Edith described Martin's labours at Ross in the phrase 'setting a razor to cut down trees', but her brother and mother were pleased at her important part in extending the Martins' nominal hold on Ross for just a few more years. In a complicated settlement, Martin and her mother were tenants of the Land Commission, a tenancy that seemed to be kindly, as it passed on Robert's death to his widow. Muriel Currey remembered Martin at Ross in her old gardening clothes, with a leather belt that held a small hand-axe, for chopping away the

stems of ivy on the old trees. Martin's love of Ross was as deep and fixed as
Edith's of Drishane; for both, their family houses were the dominating passion
of their lives. When Martin returned to Ross, she confided in her friend Maud
Morris at Spiddal that she was 'to make enough money by her writings to buy
back from the mortgagees her old home, Ross, that was all she wanted ...'[42]

The house and estate had been maltreated by the tenant of the last fifteen
years. Martin had loved this place and had had to leave it when she was ten
years old. She returned, aged twenty-six, hardly prepared for almost two
decades of intensive house maintenance and stewardship. Her diary is laconic:
'Place looking well bar the loss of trees and shrubs – house much dilapidated –
Mama and Nurse Barrett its only occupants. Sleep in the pink room.' A letter
to Edith of June 27th gives a fuller reaction: 'I miss some of the best trees –
blown down, cut down, and what not. Everything looks ragged and unkempt –
but it is a fine free feeling to sit up in this window and look abroad ... to be
lonely or anything like it – it does not enter my mind – The amount of work to
be done would put an end to that pretty fast. There is literally everything to do
except the tremendous pioneer sort of work that Mama got done in the garden
which was as the people told me "the height of yerself in weeds" ... We inhabit
five rooms in the house – the drawing room made for the present a kitchen! I
could laugh and I could cry when I think of it. I am not gubbed [troubled by
ghosts], as an empty house is not nearly as appalling in that way as a full one.
Everything wants repairing, papering, painting – and there is no money to do it
...' To her surprise Martin found that she needed particular clothes for local
society: 'Will you ask Violet to send all the things of mine that are at Glen B?
One wants clothes here for tennis parties I see. People are more advanced in
their ideas than one would expect ...'

Their letters had become more complex as Edith and Martin had fallen into
the degree of intimacy that shared the most private feelings. Edith had told
Martin about Herbert Greene's feelings, expressed in a sonnet sent to her at the
beginning of the year. Herbert seems to have had a rather unstable and gloomy
temperament, and had taken Edith's repeated rejection of his marriage proposal
with a plunge into depression. He wrote a sonnet on the painting that Edith had
completed for him, influenced by Shelley's 'Ode to the West Wind':

'On a Picture': O'Donovan's Lake by E.Œ.S.

So late! So late! How fast the hours are flying!
How soon the world, and we therewith, grown older,
Sink into shadow! Night winds breathing colder
Their sad lament across the lake are sighing;

O'erhead the melancholy sea bird crying
Sweeps westward, night rolls down the mountain's shoulder.
Scarce, should she come now, could mine eyes behold her.
Day dieth fast – and hope with day is dying.
Oh horror of great blackness grimly falling!
No moon shall cleave thy blinding folds asunder.
No star illuminate thy murky cope.
Oh thou that tarriest, hear my passionate calling!
But a brief space, no cry shall sound thereunder.
Still the light lingers, – is there yet a hope?

In addressing her as 'thou that tarriest', Herbert obviously cannot see that Edith's intention to earn her own living is a very serious aim, or that her feelings towards him were not romantic. His love sonnet may be compared to two of Edith's, published in October 1889, that may have already been composed by this time, and which show her love to have been fixed elsewhere, and unhappily. She took them with her to London in April 1888. At this stage Herbert was thirty-one years old and Edith thirty. He had fixed his idealistic love upon her in his late teens; she must have felt something for him as she kept even his baby letters to her. In 1877 he had written exultantly to her from his desk in his examination hall, having completed his Oxford Entrance Papers. He was a man of very fixed and strong convictions, and his strongest conviction that Edith was to be his wife remained a rock solid reality to him. Edith was awed by him, especially after he took a First that she had not expected, and quite unable to upset him by trying to send him packing, so he remained a fixture as her suitor.[43] Her unwillingness to give direct offence to men is a clear indication of her innate conservatism and was an ineradicable element of her femininity, whereas Martin was quite capable of talking sharply to men and contradicting them. Despite the seemingly last-ditch effort of his 1888 sonnet, even in 1898, ten years later, by wilfully misreading her evasions, Herbert thought he had won her. Unfeelingly Edith sent on Herbert's heartfelt plea to Martin with the simple remark 'Herbert sent me a sonnet', for independence was far preferable to life with Herbert.

The emotion that Herbert inspired was irritation, but clearly another man had inspired much deeper feelings. Martin had by now seen Edith's private commonplace book and its collection of love poems and songs. In their letters of July and August there is much discussion of a rondeau and the two sonnets by Edith on the subject of lost love, rejected by Oscar Wilde, but accepted by Edmund Yates and eventually published by The World in October 1889. Martin made careful suggestions for the improvement of the poems, which show that she was familiar with the contents of Edith's commonplace book. She warned

# TWO SONNETS.

## FULFILMENT.

I SAT that night, and watched the fire dying;
   The embers still were glowing red and bright,
   "One touch," I thought, "and they will break in light.
But let them die." Close at my heart were crying
Old longings, all unheeded. Then defying
   Memory stooped down, and kissed me through the night,
   And took my tired soul with treacherous might,
And lit the love that in my life was lying.

There came a step upon my lonely stair,
   My heart beat in my breast like a wild bird,
"He has come back!" I said, "my heart, come back."
I raised my head. Ah! he was standing there
   With kind forgetting eyes. He spoke a word,
When—crash! the embers fell all dead and black.

---

## AFTERWARDS.

I LOOKED into the happy past through tears,
   And saw the lost days shining back to me,
   As one who sees a jewel deep in the sea
Gleaming—a wavering splendour that appears
And vanishes in darkness. Memory clears
   Life's depths, and shows the days that used to be :
   Wraiths of dead hopes—a shadowy company,
And Love low lying 'neath the rushing years.

Dead alike hope and heart-break. I have wept
   Long since my tears away; my eyes are dry.
No more with whitening cheek and quivering lip
   I watch for Sorrow; now she passes by
My empty heart, where long her home she kept,
Dwelling in fateful Love's high fellowship.

       D. R.

10 Edith's love sonnets published in *The World*, 1889.

Edith against unconscious imitation of the last verse of Burns' *Banks and Braes o'*
*Bonny Doon* and specifically to avoid the metaphor of the plucked rose and the
abandoned female lover left with only the thorn.[44] None of the earlier drafts of
Edith's poems have survived, for there was considerable re-shaping, and nowhere
in the surviving letters between Edith and Martin is the male lover identified.

They also discussed the prospects for future writing and it seems that
Martin wanted to avoid any obvious division of labour in their texts, although
there was one: 'You know I don't mean that you are to write exclusively love-
making and improprieties.'[45] At Ross Martin fretted about the spirit inhabitants
on the top landing of the upper storey, where only she slept: 'the ghosts will
undoubtedly eat me, but the room is delightful ...' In contrast to Martin, Edith's
life passed in a round of dances, balls and concerts. She sent a critique of the
Powells' dance, where the male dancers were all too young for her: 'To begin
with there was not one man who could dance. In the second place there was not
one man. I may be vitiated but I like men at a dance.' She watched the course of
a touching flirtation between Violet Coghill and Phil Somerville of Park Cottage
to relieve her boredom. The same letter shows her sympathy towards men who
had transgressed; Maurice Healy, similarly inclined, in his *Old Munster Circuit*
had referred obliquely to Seymour's 'domestic tragedy': 'Seymour [Bushe] and the
Lady Kathleen are now in Devonshire – I think his two years of wandering have
been penance enough, without his own people making it difficult for him.'[46]

Martin began to enjoy the visiting circle at Ross. The Morrisses at Spiddal,
from another of the 'Tribes of Galway', were old friends of the Martins. Lord
Morris was a distinguished lawyer, Lord Chief Justice of Ireland, and an Irish-
speaking Catholic. He had a fine library of Irish books and manuscripts; the
area around Spiddal was famous for its connection with the learned family of
Mac Firbhisigh, historians to the O'Dowds. Spiddal House was a Moorish-
influenced re-creation, and getting bigger; Lady Morris loved building extensions
and used concrete enthusiastically. Martin went there on 6 August: 'Nothing
could explain the length of those 11 Irish miles, or the loneliness of the road. It
was like mid-ocean and a slight mist tended to increase the unboundedness of
the stretches of moor and bog ... The wind blew tremendously up in those
altitudes and it and the grey hilly country and the mist were at last a sort of
intolerable nightmare. We descended at last to the coast and beheld a sluttish
large village spread along the shore, a fine black looking salmon river, young
trees, and finally the Morrises' house or fishing lodge. Civilisation in Siberia
could not be more surprising. They are a pleasant people – you know what he
is as to agreeability and to brogue and she shrewd and kind ...' The Morrises'
daughter Maud was to be Martin's closest friend outside the family in Galway.
She had passed through a deeply unhappy affair, but had recovered and was to

marry later. Martin described her in a letter to Edith on the following day: 'Of Miss Morris I am much enamoured – not very pretty, but a taking short sighted way with her head (which *indeed* I haven't got) not very anything except nice ... she has a delicious accent only enough to be emphatic – and is as clever as you want ... I never met better company. I bore you about her, but I know something about her which makes me take a great interest in her – as a study – I can't tell it but it is a melancholy thing.'

Martin's sister Geraldine Hewson was at Ross, and had told her that she had met Edith ten years before.[47] On 19 August Edith wrote to Martin with a plea: 'I am glad you have Geraldine. Give her my love, although I know I am not in the least the same woman that she thinks she met ... Do not try and collate your edition with hers, it would not help you and I would rather you did not know how many parts of a fool I was. I daresay I am just as many now, but they are different parts. I should like to meet Geraldine again, but I would have a kind of envy and dread of that shadowy idiot of nineteen that was getting between her and me all the time. It would be a fine thing to be back there again, and to know better, but I suppose anyway, one would get there – i.e. into the wrong place – just the same? There are only a few people who know how to get just the best they can out of their time.' It was when she was nineteen that Edith had fallen for Hewitt Poole. By the same post Martin sent a draft article to Edith for her opinion, which was fulsome: 'The whole paper is a triumphant proof of what I have always held, that if you have got the hang you can go it lively. You have style, originality and sentiment and I am blowed if I know what more you want ... You are just bound to succeed if you put your back into it ...' Edith felt that Martin's writing was 'immeasurably superior to anything I could do ...', but there was with Martin always the problem of impetus, and her pace of working at her own articles was snail-like compared to the production of joint texts. The prospect of joint work seemed to recede the more firmly that Mrs Martin settled at Ross. Edith complained: 'I wish you were here or I was there. It would save much time and trouble.'

Edith was very upset when the family coachman, Tom Connell, left the Somervilles at the end of August. There was some personal difficulty here that was never explained, but Edith disliked his new young wife. Sprucing himself up, and preparing to move on to his next post, he had shaved off his moustache, further upsetting her. He was a superb horseman and groom, a great loss to a house where the stables were so important. Edith wrote a letter to Martin, now lost, expressing her feelings. Martin's reply survives: 'What am I to say of the loss of Tom? I am truly sorry, but see the force of what you say. Sing him the Coolin touchingly – it was the lament for the love-lock – why not for the moustache? ... no-one will ever love Sorcerer as Tom did ...'[48]

One source of trouble in the family was now gone forever, as Aylmer was well settled with his Emmie. Seething at her mother's boasting to Emmie of Aylmer's ungovernable temper as a boy, Edith had written to Cameron at the end of June to exclaim at the wealth of Mrs Sykes, Emmie's mother: 'Mrs Sykes gives Aylmer anything he wants. I think you had better come home and marry her – she is only 43 – and has, from the brewery, £10,000 a year. It is so much simpler and better to go to the Fountain Head at once instead of fooling around with the 2nd generation ... Martin is now at Ross, I grieve to say and I miss her here very much indeed – there is every chance of that brute Ethel going abroad with Jim during his summer holidays – so I am rather in want of a playfellow – as Egerton naturally absorbs most of Hildegarde. I hope Martin will get her Mother to come down here as soon as she has had enough of Ross. I wish Boyle was going to meet her – altho' I know that young women usen't to be his line still she is such an awfully good sort that I know he would like her – she is the very best company I know.'

Martin was forgetting the pleasures of good company and becoming depressed at Ross, on discovering how much had changed in their fifteen years away: 'How much better if we had never left Ross – we are weighed down with giving a little work and a little wages to people who are far too old for field work. There is a terrible bitter spirit. The young are prosperous, the old get left, and no-one cares a button for anything but their own gain ...' Martin was still alarmed by the spirits dwelling outside her bedroom door on 'the awful ghost-walked landing'. She had intended to go down to put her letter on the letter-tray in the hall ready for the early post, but finishes 'blow the early post – I am too frightened to go out of the room.'[49]

At Drishane this autumn there was much to do in preparation for the marriage of Aylmer Somerville to his Sykes heiress; it was not a love-match: like Robert Martin he made a sensible decision. Emmie had £500 a year, and it was her money that funded the re-establishment of the West Carbery Hounds of which Aylmer was to be Master from 1891 to1903. Boyle Somerville arrived back on 8 September in plenty of time for the wedding. All the Somervilles went to England for it on 3 October. Afterwards Hildegarde, Boyle and Edith went off to visit a friend of Boyle's to keep him company until his leave was over. They returned to CT on the 10th. Martin was extremely sympathetic to Hildegarde and Egerton when Aylmer married, sadly comparing their unknown and clouded future with Aylmer's 'run of luck'. Sir Joscelyn and Kendal Coghill, who were inveterate optimists, had been taken in by a fraudster; there was no sign of the French shares scheme called 'Bourget' bearing any fruit for them, and never would be. In some way, the Catholic Church had become involved in Bourget's swindling schemes. Martin, like Edith, was extremely hard-headed about the making of money: 'it will take more than the sight of the ready to make me believe in a combination of Bourget and Jesuits', she wrote,[50] and she lacked Edith's crazed generosity to her loved ones when she was in funds.

Engrossed in what the Martins called the 'Restoration', Mrs Martin was to release Martin from Ross only infrequently. After three and a half months Martin had a break of three weeks in CT at Glen B and Drishane; she was already there when the sisters returned from Aylmer's wedding. On 26 October she finished her article 'A Delegate of the National League' and began to write with Edith the short story 'Slide 42'. Quite unexpectedly while she was in CT their novel was accepted by a publisher. On 2 November 1888, Richard Bentley and Son offered £25 on publication and £25 on sale of 500 copies of the Shocker. Martin wrote in her diary: 'Got a letter from Bentley announcing that the birthday of our lives had come ... All comment is inadequate – went dizzily to church, twice.' Edith's diary entry is almost the same, recording their repeated church going: 'went to church twice in a glorified trance.' Encouraged, they thought that the short story on the stocks might have possibilities for expansion. But on 5 December Martin had to go back to her mother, via the family in Dublin: 'Got up with deep loathing in candlelight, and hauled myself out of Drishane, being accompanied to Skib. by the good Edith and Hildegarde.' She was back at Ross for Christmas with her mother on the 14th. A letter of Edith's to her there reveals that the Coghill money that later sank without trace in Bourget's scheme was £40,000.[51] Doing the Christmas round of old tenants at Ross, Martin called on the Widow Leonard and her family. She sent a description of the visit to Edith; in its candour it gives us an idea of Martin's looks. After giving her strong drink, the Leonards plied her with compliments: 'It's not that you're lovely but so commanding. Indeed you have an *imprettive* (imperative) look about you. Sure we're all enamoured by you.'

At the close of Martin's 1888 diary we find a newspaper clipping with a whimsical poem by Warham St Leger – *An Autumn Lay*. It has a pencilled note on it by the author, identifying it as a poem written after an expedition with Martin rowing at Wirgleswater. Alongside the clipping Martin has written a quotation from Dowden:

> Oh wild sea voices, victory and defeat,
> But ever deathless passion and unrest;
> White wings upon the wind and flying feet,
> Disdain and wrath, a reared and hissing crest.
> The imperious urge, and last a whole life spent
> In bliss of one supreme abandonment.

Here too, as in Edith's diary, we find a part of the palmist Miss Hingston's character reading, with underlined the sentence: 'will have simply an unclouded married life.' Though in *Irish Memories* Edith claimed that marriage was a condition to which neither of them had aspired, she may have been whitewashing the background of their early lives.[52] The surviving letters from St Leger to Martin, 1888–95, do suggest that there was some kind of romance between them. She prized his letters, his poems and his good opinion. She sent him shamrock on St Patrick's Day, which every year he planted out and succeeded in growing on. They liked mucking about in boats together; he wrote to her after she had returned to Ireland at the end of June in 1890: 'there has been a sad relapse into the realm of slate colour and it is most difficult to believe the afternoon on the river really took place in the present dispensation. I wish you were coming back in a few days when the rain is over and gone and the mellower summer sets in.' His letters, quoted later, on Martin's literary work show a clever sympathetic man who was extremely quick-witted and perceptive. With an unromantic return to earth and normality at the end of Martin's 1888 diary, along with the poetry we also find Mrs Anderson's recipe for dropsy and anaemia. At the end of Edith's diary we find a more painful record on 30 December: 'Heard from Bentley saying we have bothered the printers with our corrections and additions.'

On the traditional New Year's Day hunt at the Conner's Manch in 1889 Edith rode one of her most exciting hunts with the West Carbery; she sent an obstacle-by-obstacle account of the run to Martin at Ross.[53] The accounts of hunts are the most vividly written of all her letters to Martin. When she re-read what survived of them as an old woman, she bundled them all together as being 'mostly about hunting'. The public nature of these letters, which might be read to a meal table or tea party, gives them the air of a radio script. This letter of 1 January has the concluding suggestion that Martin should send it on to Ethel Penrose 'like a good child' to save her writing the same account twice. Sending her confirmation that her painting was now of a good standard, on 1 February the Royal Hibernian Academy accepted 'Retrospect' for exhibition.[54] (This study of Mrs Norris was the largest canvas she ever painted.) Enjoying the adventure of the zig-zag railway journey, Edith set off for Ross on the 4th. Because of lack of money she had not been able to go to Ross in the first phase of the 'Restoration'. She finally arrived there and stayed from mid-February to early March of 1889. A letter to Boyle on 11 April describes the household: 'very pleasant quarters, having Martin, Katie [Martin's sister Mrs Currey], Murray [Moolah's Nurse], Moolah [Katie's daughter Muriel], Mush [dog], Selina [Martin's sister unmarried] and Patsey [dog] as co-inmates. I do *not* sorrow that Nannie is in Dublin. We are remarkably airy under the present regime and I ask for nothing more ...' Once again Edith reverts to the home she will share with Boyle when they have struck it rich, Poulavawn Lodge: 'I wonder should we have a house all on one storey – like a bungalow – ? Of course we shouldn't get as good a view but it would be cheaper.'

At the back of Notebook 10 [55] in Martin's hand we find an account of what might have been Edith's first night at Ross before Mrs Martin had left for Dublin. Featuring in the event were other visitors to be entertained, a new batch of domestic fowl that Mrs Martin kept indoors to acclimatise before releasing into the vast backyard, and the same kind of vague apportioning of beds and bedding (that can only have been campaign beds of the most mobile sort) that we find at Glen B and Drishane. The three storeys of Ross rose up around a central stairwell and sounds on all levels reverberated far and wide within it:

> The daughters of the house are snubbed in favour of strangers, and have to take each other in to dinner – after the meal they lie in wait in the hall, while incessant music is made by the hostess and the strangers to each other. At 12.30 while the former peals forth Eurydice, a massive tea equipage is brought in and ink-black tea poured out by one of the aliens ... [later] ... in the bedrooms the strangers huddle together and are interrupted in the midst of loud criticism by one of the ladies of the house ... [at this point Mrs Martin seems to have recalled her duty to the just-arrived guest and showed her all over the house] including the nursery where 'poor little Annie' is pointed out, a monumental sleeping nurse, at 2.30 am. At 6 the quackings of ducks rise from a neighbouring apartment. In the next room low and incessant whisperings attest the fact that Mrs Martin and three others have passed the night there *en masse*.

Edith travelled on from Ross to stay with Ethel at Athboy from 9 March to 3 April when she returned to Ross. While at Athboy, on 15 March she went up to Dublin with Ethel to see her painting 'Retrospect' hung in the RHA Exhibition. An interesting letter reached her at Ethel's, sent on, from Boyle who was then in Auckland, New Zealand with HMS *Dart*. It told her that he was singing the song 'Parnell Aboo!' at Navy concerts. He and Edith took their nationalist sympathies too far for many of their friends' and relatives' liking. Writing from Athboy, Edith described to Martin a hunt with Jim Penrose and the Meath Hunt. 'Just a few tinting words – the rest will keep until next week – remember I have to write to home, Hildegarde and Boyle ...' Among the 'tinting words' she revealed that she had a disaster while hunting when her hairpins all came loose and her hair fell down all round. Her hair had been described by a fellow hunter as a 'Chestnut Wealth', which was a description she blithely transferred to Martin in *Irish Memories*.

Back at Ross, to her mother's joy, Martin's talent had been confirmed and commended by a distinguished literary man. Her second article 'A Delegate of the National League' had found a publisher, the same who had published her first. Edmund Yates, editor of *The World*, wrote a 'deeply flattering' letter to Martin accepting it and asking for more of her writing. Yates 'possessed the main merit of a first class editor: he chose his contributors with discrimination and gave them a free hand ...'[56] He promoted the career of George Bernard Shaw, who was music critic of *The World* from 1890 until Yates' death in May 1894. But on 7 May there was an end to rejoicing when Edith's little dog Patsey ate strychnine poison laid for rats at the side of the Ross avenue. He died despite everything that Edith could do for him. Muriel Currey comments in her transcript of the diaries at this point: 'This is my first clear impression of D [Edith's nickname in the family]. I remember the misery of that night and the despair of D. and Martin.' Edith went back to CT, arriving on 11 May. Muriel Currey never understood the connection between herself and Edith. She thought the mutual liking was explained by her resemblance to Martin, but in fact she was like Edith herself as a girl, both in appearance and in her character – noisy, lively and physically intrepid. After Edith had gone Martin mentioned that: 'The Roberts thought Moolah wonderfully like you.'[57] When we find a contrast between a young hunting woman and an older, as we do in *Sarah's Youth*, it is a study of an interaction between Edith's young and old self, as John Cronin has already remarked, but we can now identify the young woman whom she saw as a *Doppelgänger*.[58]

At Ross, Martin worked away at her article for *The World* (then called 'Education', later 'Cheops'); she wrote to Edith on 18 May to tell her how much she appreciated her as a colleague: 'you take the highfalutin' out of me I think – I feel you saying "Well, but I don't see" and then I don't see either, but it is very good for me. Let us take Carbery and grind its bones to make our bread – Cut my dear! – it would be new life to me to cut it – and we will – and we will serve it up to the spectator so that its mother wouldn't know it.' This was over-optimistic of Martin. They ground the bones of an area much wider than Carbery, and its mothers did know it. The extensive 1903 re-write of *An Irish Cousin* was necessary to cover the tracks of Edith's too-close modelling of her complex plot on the Yelvertons, ancient and modern, and to cover up the appalling coincidence of the fate of Algie Yelverton, who married out of his class in 1890, with the fate of Willy Sarsfield. Though Martin had such high hopes, it was proving difficult for Edith and Martin to work together. Mrs Martin was determined to use her youngest daughter as a helpmeet at Ross, and thus made it difficult for her to draw up a timetable for literary work: 'That old beast N[annie] has never written to say when she comes. Martin is still uncertain, we have now written and begged her to wire ... so perhaps she will do so – she is just trying to dodge so as to stop Martin', Edith wrote to Hildegarde.[59] During this period, the long-suffering typesetters of their novel, which was being set for Bentleys, had been wrestling with frequent changes made to the text still called *An Experiment*, the subtitle of the first section of the first edition of *An Irish Cousin*. The proof-reader dealing with them stoically wrote at the end of his letters: 'we remain, dear mesdames, your etc etc.' when his patience must have been near exhausted.[60] Mrs Somerville had insisted that the family name could not be used 'in trade' and Edith showed particularly idiotic vagueness over her nom-de-plume (or non-de-plume, as she called it). Not only did she try Giles Logan, a name chosen by Bentley, before the soon-discarded Geilles Herring, but there is one, deleted, even earlier, and easily the most awful – the pen name of Somerville Grubb. She had suggested the composite Somerville Ross as a convenient compound, but Martin decided to stick to two separate names. We shall see Edith use the initials DR on her *World* sonnets at the end of this year. D, or Dee, was her family nickname, and she may have borrowed Martin's toponymic 'Ross', perhaps because she was there when she had to think of a pseudonym. It was Bentleys who, losing patience, invented their own nom-de-plume for her – 'Viva Graham' – causing an explosion of rage from Miss Somerville, who wrote to complain, presumably not in the words of her diary, at 'the putrescent puke of a name they have fixed on me'.

Martin came down to CT at the end of May and returned to Ross on 12 August to help with the summer visitors, although Robert Martin and his wife were at the Castle as tenants from mid-August to mid-September. After Martin had gone, on 19 August Edith entered in her diary: 'Heard from Fanny Currey sending Suffrage papers to be signed. We most did.' Hildegarde and Edith both joined the Women's Franchise League at Fanny's instigation, as did Martin separately from Ross. Writing was something they were merely speculating about: 'You should paint and illustrate, and take a share in a story of some kind – as little share as seemed good to you, or as much', she wrote to Edith on 29 August. An amicable sliding scale of payment seems to have been in operation until Martin's hunting accident in November 1898. Income from *The Silver Fox* (1897) was split three-fifths to Martin and two to Edith. Among her letters to Edith in August is one that shows Martin's pleasure in her friends who are happy in love: 'Rose [Helps] has got Dr Cupid – for the first time – so I feel happy about her.' On the 31st, Martin wrote to commiserate with Edith for having to open a ball, in the first dancing couple. 'I pity you ... or I should pity you if I did not know you were well able to do it.'

Robert Martin and his wife Connie had taken the Castle at CT for late August. After she left he stayed on alone, and he performed at a concert on 5

September in the Town Hall at Skibbereen, singing his popular songs 'Killaloe' and 'Ballyhooley' inimitably. The *Skibbereen Eagle* reviewer loved him: 'This genial, this fascinating son of the Dear Old Sod.' 'Mama is very pleased at this graceful allusion to herself', Martin commented to Edith. At the last moment the Chimp was run in as an accompanist: 'he was a tower of strength and imparted a moral courage such as – for me – only he and Hildegarde inspire'. The concert, and socialising, took up most of Edith's time: 'Don't expect to hear from me for some time, too harrassed', she wrote to Martin, on the night of the performance. Edith was to realise the enormous influence that Robert had with journalists and theatrical and literary people in London through the coverage given to *An Irish Cousin*. Martin wondered when she would be revealed to the public as 'Miss Ballyhooley', but in fact this did not happen until the 1901 reviews of the first volume of RM stories. When, in one of his letters, Boyle revealed to Edith that he was writing a play, she responded by suggesting that she showed it when finished to Robert, and then went on to imagine it as a London hit: 'we will realise enough for you to come right home and build Poulavawn Lodge – I also keep that little dream up my sleeve.' Money matters were deeply depressing, she explained to Boyle: 'I think Bougie [the Coghill French shares scheme] is through ... If I sell him [her comic song The Kerry Recruit] I shall instantly begin another similar work: hateful though such games are we must work out our own salvation, as Bougie can't be relied on.'

In Castletownshend this summer, Robert Martin had a thoroughgoing flirtation with Violet Coghill, to the anguish of his wife.[61] Martin was disapproving, for apart from anything else her brother had only just become a father. Robert had married Connie Roche, it appears with ulterior financial motives, on 20 October 1886. His only child Barbara Zavara had been born on 14 July 1888. Male sexual mores seem to have been quite lax among some family connections, Lord Avonmore to the fore. Seymour Bushe's scandalous elopement with Lady Kathleen, the daughter of the 4th Viscount Hawarden, when she was the wife of Gerald Brooks, was to reach the newspapers and cause rifts within the family that never healed. We find missing sections of letters quite frequently in the Somerville/Ross correspondence, and, remembering those 'left-handed families' of illegitimate children, these are quite likely to have contained discussions of matters too scandalous to keep. Violet Coghill, who had a strong physical resemblance to her first cousin Edith Somerville, after a most adventurous youth as a flirt, settled down as a medical doctor after 1900 and lived with another lady doctor, Lina O'Connor, in North London.

Buried in household doings at Ross, Martin had been very much ground down by the problems of running the house, and by the struggle to finish an article. Of working together again she wrote on 15 August: 'I do not feel in the least like writing anything more just yet – I suppose it will come, but at present I think of nothing but the atrocities of bad servants and the knavishness of hangers-on – and feel a profound and paralysing depression on these subjects. I feel tired of the whole show, and find the machinery of life more trouble than it is worth – But no matter – one goes careering on somehow, as Mr St Leger said when finding fault with his own career.' By her next letter, on the 20th, Martin sent corrections to proof copies of Edith's two love sonnets sent by Edmund Yates' printer, Robson. 'They look very well in print …The dashes and full stops break up the thing a bit – but the two that I altered seem to make it all right – I of course put "head" for "eyes" – Now it will be a matter of great interest to see what Edmund pays for them – and when they will appear…' Edith had repeated the word 'eyes' in two consecutive lines at the close of her first sonnet.

Although Martin's solo writing is lapidary and stylistically smooth, producing a joint text with Edith seems to have been at first unhinging. At the end of a letter from Martin to Edith of 21 August from Ross, we find a remark that relates to the beginning of the year, when they were making a very bad impression on Richard Bentley by making continual changes to the setting of their novel text. It seems clear from Martin's remark that their arguments raged to and fro, each argument resulting in a change of setting. It is really not surprising that Richard Bentley was to put in a fairly low offer for the manuscript of *The Real Charlotte*; Martin wrote: 'I seem to remember very much the first beginnings of the Shocker just now – when I was humping over the Dumpy [the Studio stove] and you were mucking with paints at the window you told me of the old maniac's face at the window over the White Hall door – and remember you were the person who suggested that we should try together to write a shocker or story of sorts on that foundation – and you also were the person who lifted us through the first chapters. But no matter. We little thought that I, at Ross, should take *The World* to see my own writing in it, and should see the shocker in large type heading Bentley's list therein. Goodnight whatever. Here's luck to the Shocker and even if it doesn't do much to making our fortunes I do not think it was time wasted. It taught us a lot – in a literary way – and I don't think we shall ever forget it. And the long time that we fought over it, it was my fault – Isn't that true? Yours ever. Goodnight again – you were a nice woman to write with.'

The discrepancy between Edith's later account in *Irish Memories* of the inspiration for writing *An Irish Cousin* and Martin's account in her letter above, reminds us that we should treat Edith's two published memoirs with caution. She concocted an episode in which they both rode to White Hall and saw their incarcerated relative. She wanted to make Martin's part in the invention of their first novel to be larger, just as she wanted the Somervilles' family tree to be grander than it was, so she adjusted reality accordingly. She was a fiction writer and a strong-minded, self-interested optimist. When she called herself 'Miss Facing-Both-Ways' it was a description that chimes perfectly with her brother Boyle's description of the armed but cautious CT village nationalists as the 'Sitting-on-the-Fencibles'; it was a sign of her sympathetic nature to see all points of view and keep her own private. This was an advantage in a writer who was to specialise in the recording and rendering of conversation with all classes. It is obvious that in fiction she was unafraid of tackling romance and physical passion, whereas Martin was afraid or too fastidious, but it is very difficult to track her political beliefs, in an area where Martin was a Unionist luminary. Their partnership was very oddly assorted, the whole bonded together by the one shared talent for humour, and need of money.

An Irish Cousin, by Geilles Herring and Martin Ross, came out in Bentley's autumn list and was a considerable success on account of excellent publicity. On 16 September Martin wrote to Edith from Ross to give congratulations on the reviews the novel was receiving. The Observer review of 1 September began: 'If, as we suppose, the two gentlemen whose names figure on the title page of this novel are novices in fiction, they deserve the warmest congratulation on the unqualified success which has attended their efforts. An Irish Cousin is quite one of the best Irish novels of the generation. The texture of the story is slighter than Hurrish, but the truth to detail is more striking, and the dialect more faithfully reproduced than by Miss Lawless. Above all, the book is brimful of humour, which emerges even in some of the most tragic situations. As a picture of ramshackle Irish provincial society An Irish Cousin is inimitable ...' The Sunday Times featured the novel, 'a jewel of a book', as its Book of the Week on 22 September. Their first review, opening with 'Messrs Herring and Ross have accomplished a rare feat ...', was in The Athenaeum on 31 August; described by Martin as a 'flourishing critique', it gave them more pleasure than all those that followed, as it first made public their success, a thing of which they had only dreamed. Their delight in the joke of being taken for men never tired, and the tiny, ladylike Martin took deep amusement and pleasure in being called 'Mr Ross'.[62] Lady Gregory wrote to congratulate Martin on the novel; and Mrs Martin sent on some compliments and advice sent to her from Lady Gregory's husband, Sir William: 'The Irish dialogue, too often revolting in Irish novels from the writer's ignorance, is excellent and racy of the soil ... I am sure she will gain fame and popularity but tell her from me not to hurry – the greatest care and finish are necessary for a well-assured and permanent success.'[63]

It is Martin who makes an overt statement that shows that their writing together brought to them a new kind of pleasure in remunerative work: 'I think the two Shockers have a very strange belief in each other, joined to a critical faculty – added to which writing together is – to me at least – one of the greatest pleasures I have. To write with you doubles the triumph and enjoyment having first halved the trouble and anxiety.'[64] Together they were to embark upon a literary career of novel writing that neither of them would have attempted alone. Had they not joined forces, Edith could have developed as a writer and illustrator of comic pieces, and Martin could well have become a leader writer. The fact that together they were to produce on the one hand *The Real Charlotte* and on the other *Some Experiences of an Irish RM* in two quite different registers suggests that their combined powers, from the point of financial remuneration, were in sum far greater than their parts.

Martin was very good at pulling strings, and finding them in the most unlikely places. She used her charm naturally and instinctively. Through her brother Robert, she was known to a number of prominent Anglo-Irish journalists like Charlie Graves,[65] and she networked further to men like Edmund Yates, who was her first powerful champion, publishing her first article in August 1888. He was a strong supporter of education for women, and as editor of *The World: A Journal for Men and Women* he employed the novelists Miss Braddon and Mrs Lynn Linton on his staff. In 1889, before *An Irish Cousin* was published, Yates had accepted Martin's second article, 'A Delegate of the National League', which appeared in *The World* in July, and took a third, 'Cheops in Connemara', that was published in October. While Martin was having a success with these solo articles, which were serious in tone, Edith was trying to make an income from publishing the illustrated sheet music for a comic song, 'The Kerry Recruit'. One of the drawings used for its illustration was of Herbert Greene, transfigured. At this point they had no idea that writing together would be financially worthwhile; they were still trying to find their most profitable natural *métier* separately. They helped one another out with their separate efforts. After Oscar Wilde had rejected Edith's love sonnets, which he had received in April 1888, it was Martin who sent them on to Edmund Yates at *The World*.

The reaction of Cork booksellers to 'The Kerry Recruit' and the reaction of the sub-editor of *The World* to Martin's July 1889 article show that major adjustments were needed, in those politically troubled times, to find the correct tone for writing about Ireland. The sub-editor wrote to Martin: 'If you can choose a subject with which a little more sunshine can find its way, or, say, a little of the proverbial Irish humour, for your next contribution, it will, I think, be desirable. This sketch is excellent, but from its subject is necessarily a little heavy. Pardon this suggestion please.'[66] Although selling in England, Edith's offering to the public did not sell as well in Ireland and particularly not in Cork. Again she had been supported financially by a male relative in publishing: the

Aylmers had paid for the printing of the *Mark Twain Birthday Book* and this time Cameron had paid the London printers Day and Son £46.17s. 6d. for an edition of 5,000 copies of the 'Kerry Recruit'. Cork was not impressed. Day's travelling salesman Mr Perry reported back: 'he says the feeling amongst the booksellers there is that it is making game of the Irishman, and consequently do not buy so largely as they might.'[67]

Both writers were mortified by any suggestion that they 'made game of the Irishman': the give and take of drolleries intended to entertain, to which they were accustomed in their dealings with their Irish neighbours, servants and tenants, is easy to parody, difficult to capture. A paragraph from Edith's *Mrs Maloney's Amateur Theatricals* gives a forewarning of the coming political correctness that was to despise Robert Martin's comic songs, once much loved and performed high and low: 'Ireland nowadays does not seem to be a favourable spot in which to pitch one's dramatic tent. The traditional pleasure loving Irishman appears to linger only in the plays of Mr Boucicault, and the stern, high-souled being who represents "New Ireland" has no sympathy with such frivolities as music or theatre.'[68]

On 29 September Edith recorded in a notebook a character reading of her hand by Miss Hingston. Edith obviously had a complicated set of lines for they seem to suggest that she would have many relationships or 'engagements'. But the start of the reading was uncanny: 'Is not given to flirtation – in the ordinary sense of the word – but manages to make herself agreeable to the opposite sex – Has passed through two flirtations successfully – One was rather troublesome (to both parties) – there will be rather a long period without any serious affair of the heart ...' A précis of this reading was put into her diary: it leaves out the line 'One was rather troublesome (to both parties)'. This is a very interesting document that she has taken the trouble to record, giving us a fragment that tallies with her concealed dealings with Hewitt and Barry.

When Edmund Yates caught up with his sub-editor's comments to Martin in November he was not pleased, and wrote to tell her: 'for heaven's sake don't take any notice of requests for "Irish Humour", but let me have some more in your own delightful style'.[69] When Martin asked him to help with publicity for *An Irish Cousin*, he was droll: 'Depend upon my doing everything in my power to further the interests of your Irish Cousin. You are "Martin Ross" and not "Grilled Herring"?' At the end of December, Martin sent a 'charming' portrait photograph of herself to him, and he sent one of himself in return 'from the gentleman who has the honour, occasionally, to act as your editor.'[70] At this stage the fifty-eight-year-old Yates was a grand specimen of a mature man, weighing sixteen stone. They finally met in June of 1890 and were very pleased with each other. When Yates was desperately ill in 1892, and writing to her as he recovered, he reminded her in a letter 'your photo adorns my literary over-mantel'.

It is quite remarkable that, although Martin's first article came out in July, within the month she had been contacted by the newly formed, but short-lived, Women's Franchise League. She may have had her name put forward by Fanny Currey. She was sent a paper to sign: 'It was rather interesting to see the women who had signed, put down in different classes, doctors, heads of Education things (all the Girton professors signed) – Art and Music – among which did I see Fanny Currey, Agnes Zimmerman and other familiar names – Authors and Journalists – under which head I propose to put my name, in very good company. I certainly think it is absurd that the people that Mama employs should have a vote, and that she herself should not have one. After all, most women who have to stand alone and manage their houses or places themselves are competent to give as intelligent a vote as Paddy Griffy or Sam Chard ...'[71] But it was not until almost twenty years later that Edith and Martin were to give strong, overt public support to the suffrage campaign, after they had seen and heard Mrs Pethick Lawrence and Christabel Pankhurst in action at the Hyde Park 'monster meeting' in 1908. Neither of them relished public meetings, and it was to be the more public-spirited Hildegarde who organised the first Women's Suffrage meeting in Skibbereen in 1897.

With the September reviews of An Irish Cousin came hope that by serious novel writing Edith and Martin might earn their keep. Boyle wrote in the highest delight to Edith: 'wild and frabjous joy at the reception of Geilles and Martin ... Mother's radiant letter of 18th came today ... another extension has been put on the Buddh umbrella by the appearance of this work.'[72] The mothers had been converted to active support of their daughters' career, impressed by their earning power. Edith wrote to Martin: 'Mother's last suggestion is that you and I should live three months about at each other's houses.' But this was never to be. Already, on the strength of their reviews, a publisher called Langbridge was sounding them out about a second novel. Martin had written to Edith on 4th September: 'I send you back Mr Langbridge's letter. I think a little more money might be skirmished out of him ... If he would say £20 down, it would be well worth it. I should not seem too keen about it, as it is certainly not a brilliant offer. Those two extra fivers seem remote. At the same time we might be very glad even of the £15 by the time we got it – I know I should – and I should much enjoy writing with you if it could be managed. A few more high class reviews might make him raise his price.' Two days later, she assessed the chances: 'You shall write another story with me or without me it would be too bad to let go such an opening as we now have, and I am not man enough for a story by myself.' Martin was so short of money that Edith offered to send her some on a long loan, as she was prone to do when any of her nearest and dearest were in a fix. She was aware that she earned much more than Martin, and felt quite happy when she had any spare to prop her up until she made a success: 'Talking of money – shall I say what I have said so often before. That I really do not want that which you wish me to take – and that you are so kind to me that it makes me half sick to think of it – I can't believe it. I feel it all the time "Oh Edith, this is not health." But no more on this topic.'[73]

A fragment probably from early September this year survives in the letters between them: it is a postscript to a letter from Martin: 'I quite forgot to say a most interesting thing – Mr St Leger went to see Rose [Helps] on Sunday – and praised the Shocker in the most ardent ways. Couldn't put it down till he had finished it – thought the crime well nursed to the end – Moll gave him the creeps – Irish delineations most telling – prophesies great things – for *me* not for you – the poor hack and amanuensis – thought it so like the way I talked (principally in words of four syllables) in fact said all he could. But no letter of any kind has he written to me about it – "and am I then forgot, forgot – it broke the heart of Ellen". If he doesn't send me a review of it in the Sunday Times, reeking with lies and flatteries I shall have no more to say to him – Rose has asked him to a boating party, and will further draw him out. He is ill, poor creature – and seems in a poor way …'[74]

Martin came down to Dublin to be treated by her dentist on 26 September, where Edith joined her for the same reason, bad teeth and infected gums. They returned to Ross together on 4 October. At last *The World* for that week printed Edith's two sonnets together, paying her £1 for them.

*Fulfilment*
I sat that night, and watched the fire dying;
The embers were glowing red and bright,
'One touch,' I thought, 'and they will break in light
But let them die.' Close at my heart were crying
Old longings, all unheeded. Then defying
Memory stooped down, and kissed me through the night,
And took my soul with treacherous might,
And lit the love that in my life was lying.
There came a step upon my lonely stair,
My heart beat in my breast like a wild bird,
'He has come back!' I said, 'my heart, come back.'
I raised my head. Ah! He was standing there
With kind forgetting eyes. He spoke a word,
When – crash! the embers fell all dead and black.

. . . . .

*Afterwards.*
I looked into the happy past through tears,
And saw the lost days shining back to me,
As one who sees a jewel deep in the sea
Gleaming – a wavering splendour that appears
And vanishes in darkness. Memory clears
Life's depths, and shows the days that used to be:
Wraiths of dead hopes – a shadowy company,
And Love low lying 'neath the rushing years.
Dead alike hope and heart-break. I have wept
Long since my tears away; my eyes are dry.
No more with whitening cheek and quivering lip
I watch for Sorrow; now she passes by
My empty heart, where long home she kept,
Dwelling in Love's high fellowship.                    DR

Because of Edith's secretive nature, it is not easy to identify the source of inspiration for these sonnets on which she worked, fitfully, for over three years. The 'kind, forgetting eyes' imply a relationship long enough and intimate enough for the partners to have argued and disagreed violently. Only Barry was seriously involved with her over a long period, and we might suppose that his death caused her terrible regret that she had parted from him without a clear understanding between them. All references to these poems are concealed and indirect both in the diaries and letters: on 9 October Edith noted in her diary 'the World of last week held two sonnets of an unexpected sort in it ...' and on 13th November 'Martin got £4 from the World – one more than normal which is strange ...' Martin's diary entry for the same day has 'Got cheque from the World – £3, and one more which I passed on to its owner.' They show a respect for each other's privacy: there was no privacy in Big Houses, servants and relatives trailed in and out of rooms regardless. Perhaps both writers were aware that their diaries, lying around, could be read by anyone curious enough to look, and deliberately left out, or disguised, any revelations. The sonnets belong to a painful emotional life that Edith had put behind her when she made a success as a writer. She certainly used the sexual emotions that she had experienced, again and again, in her fiction, but did not apparently repeat those depths of experience. This would accord with the usual phasing of intense sexuality in the late teens and twenties.

Literary success with an independent income was to be consolation and balm. On the 15th Robert Martin wrote to Edith and Martin at Ross. He had obviously been talking to his friends about the future work of Edith and Martin. Edith entered in her diary: 'Letter from Robert saying that Ward and Downey would treat for a new shocker.' They heard from Ward and Downey themselves on 23 October. There followed a series of communications, as quite obviously they had been marked out as worthwhile prospects by publishers: 29 October: 'Heard from Bentley offering £100 and £125 on 2nd 500 copies for 3 vol. Book'; 30 October: 'Heard from Ward and Downey offering £125 for 3 vols. but making no mention of a royalty'; 2 November: 'Wrote temporizingly to Bentley and W&D.' On 30 November, shelving decisions, they went down to Athboy to Ethel and Jim for a fortnight. Then they both went on to CT, where Martin stayed over Christmas.

In 1889 they spent the greatest amount of time physically together, writing their first novel; after this year, there are more demands on their time through family ties, and they habituate themselves to collecting material and writing it up when they are apart, so that the business of producing texts when they are together becomes less time-consuming and more streamlined. On 31 December Edith wrote in her diary: 'Good accounts of the Irish cousin. Eason says he never was so much asked for any book, which fact forms a good ending for 1889.' Boyle was also pleased with progress during the year. Writing to Edith again after the New Year, Boyle shows that he is in on the joke of calling Martin 'Mr Ross', as intimate friends did for the rest of Martin's life. 'My dear Geilles (pron. French) the wife of Martin, well a year has been put behind us, and for me at least it has *flown* and flown pleasantly too. We have both found work that suits us in it and altogether 89 is a candidate for red lettering ... our design [the cover, Plate 14], I must say, does look swagger. The first artistic work of mine that has ever been multiplied for the benefit of a hungry public ...'

# CHAPTER 5

# *Commencing authors*

Slaney put away her best hat, and felt that there were yet many hours till bed-time. Those who lay out with a confident hand the order of a day's events would do well to prepare also an alternative.
Yet Fate, had, after all, reserved a blessing.
*The Silver Fox*, 1897, chapter IV

BOTH EDITH AND MARTIN were in Drishane, working in the Studio, until the spring of 1890 when 'gaddings about' started up again. On 4 February Edith heard from her printer Mr Day that 'The Kerry Recruit is selling well in Dublin, but failing in Cork because the Nationalists think it is an antidote to their valour.'[1] When, in their diaries, they recorded their work on their next novel, they continued to describe writing as 'shockering' and to the new novel as a 'shocker'. The short story 'Slide 42', for which they were paid five guineas, was expanded during the year into their second novel *Naboth's Vineyard*. Unusual in being set in an Ireland without reference to any major characters in its gentry class, it has a love affair in which a woman foolishly pursues a lover whom she has previously spurned, and has a tragic ending. 'Slide 42' was first published by the *Lady's Pictorial* in the 1890 Christmas number. Edith notes the completion of the clean copy of the novel on 12 March, when she posted it off. It was to be published by Spencer Blackett in October of the following year, 1891.

There was much socialising with the Castle in March, where cousin Gendie, Mrs Miller Mundy, was in residence, and there was an expedition to Bantry on the 6th to see Boyle on board his splendid ship HMS *Shannon*. On 3 April Martin was delighted to note in her diary that '*The Observer* has mentioned the *Irish Cousin* as one of the books that prove Irish literature is not on the wane.' After dealing with a difficult part of *Naboth's Vineyard* Martin had settled down to a long solo article on the subject of marriage, 'In Sickness and in Health', at a less hectic pace than when writing commissioned to a deadline. It was not until the end of her writing career that Edith was to write her own essay on the same subject, 'For Richer for Poorer'; the two essays show that both authors had given a good deal of thought to this thorny topic. During April Martin read Willy Wills' *Eugene Aram*, simply remarking in her diary that she had 'finished' it. Drishane started to over-fill in mid April, so Martin moved back to Glen B on the 18th, and switched back to her article. On 1 May Edith entered: 'Martin finishes "In Sickness and in Health"'. The next day was Edith's birthday. Their lack of money at this period shows in the quality of their birthday presents to their friends and to each other. Martin: 'Presented E with a handsome ball of twine, it being her birthday.'

On this day they added an item to their collection of newspaper clippings of court reports.[2] Sir Patrick Coghill was meticulous in his arrangement and notation on the various bundles of material in the vast archive that he inherited. One miscellaneous deposit he has classified as printed sources; this is a gathering together of newspaper cuttings containing verbatim reports of speeches in court. Edith and Martin had started to collect these around 1888, as soon as they had recognised them as a prime source of raw material. They had noted the type of humour that produced 'Laughter in court' but were not to work it up into extended comic stories until the writing of the RM series ten years later, most notably in *The Boat's Share*, which features a fish dealer named Honora Brickley. This gives us a good chronological guide as to the length of time they nurtured material before using it. On 2 May 1890 the *Southern Star* carried a report from the Skibbereen petty sessions regarding a summons for abusive language and being drunk in a public place brought against Hanora Hurley, fish dealer, of Skibbereen. She had been celebrating the birth of her last child, a son. When the chairman of the petty sessions, Captain Walsh, delivered his verdict: 'Fined ten shillings and costs', Hanora Hurley burst out: 'Oh Good God (laughter) Well that I may have another son now, and, begor, I'll pay ten shillings more for him, thank God (great laughter). But I wouldn't care about daughters at all. I'd rather have one son than a creel full of them (renewed laughter). Whenever I has a son I'm sure to take a drop.' The frank lack of appreciation of daughters was found from the top to the bottom of the range of social classes. Somerville and Ross's indebtedness to the *Skibbereen Eagle* was acknowledged in *Wheeltracks*: 'I have preserved some of these records ... so diverse is the point of view, the sense of humour, the standard of honour or propriety, the laws of social etiquette – [it is] like intercepting fragments of intimate wireless messages that are passing between two far-off planets.'[3]

Also finding time to read in this spring, Edith was converted to enthusiasm for Kipling's writing by reading *Soldiers Three*. Little more than a month after its completion, Martin's essay had been to a reader and been vetted. On 7 June *Blackwood's Magazine* wrote to her and 'fulsomely' accepted 'In Sickness and in Health'. On the next day, and less fulsomely, the friends accepted Spencer

Blackett's low offer for *Naboth's Vineyard*; both went to London on 17 June, Martin to stay with Robert at Leinster Square. They relied when they could upon the services of a hairdresser in London rather than Dublin. Their diaries record the establishments that they patronised for hats, shoes, dressmaking, hairdressing, dentistry and later health cures. On the 21st Martin entered: 'We had our hair day.' Sure of their smart appearance, this prepared them for an onslaught on publishers and editors. Martin saw Edmund Yates, 'who was very civil and took the Goleen article to read. Fatherly in manner.' Then they both went to Bentley's: 'Saw Mr Beard, the manager, a very civil young gentleman with beautiful manners. They yearn for more of our work.' While in London, Martin was examined by Bram Stoker's doctor brother William: 'He says I have anaemia and ordered many pills and stuff.' This diagnosis was later swamped out by the advice of many other doctors in London, Ireland, and abroad, who did not identify anaemia as the cause of Martin's ill health, but it was to be confirmed and reinforced fifteen years later after an examination by Dr Eleanor Hodson in 1906. They struck luck in the *Lady's Pictorial* office with a commission: a series of travel articles on a tour of Connemara, the writing of which earned them £21 each.

At the outset of their career joint earnings were meagre: Martin listed them at the back of each diary. On average in 1890 she was paid £2 or £3 for a solo article, about £5 for a joint story, and her half of the royalties of *An Irish Cousin*, from the year before, brought in the largest amount: £37.11s. Edith, distinctly better off, always picked up extra cash by the additional payments for her illustrations and cartoon strips.[4] But writing popular articles for newspapers was a more immediately remunerative way of earning money than writing novels. On leaving London, Edith went back to CT, while Martin went down to her sister Edith Dawson at Portsmouth for a week. She visited the Helps at Kew en route to Ross, where she was installed with her Mother by 9 July. Edith then joined her at Ross where, because they needed the money urgently, they at once piled into the first of their Connemara articles, before they had actually done the tour. Martin notes in her diary on the 12th: 'Began at the first Connemara article, find it hateful, but Edith gets along all right.' A symptom of Martin's ill health was sudden fatigue: she was liable to fall asleep at any moment during the day, though she found sleeping right through the night difficult. They took constitutional walks with the dogs to break from writing in the afternoons: 'Went down to Annagh Point in the afternoon and fell asleep and E made a sketch of me.'[5] This sketch survives; again, it is not in the least flattering, and shows the imperious look that so impressed the Leonard family. On the 17th, Warham St Leger sent her a copy of his *Ballads from Punch*, with which Martin was very pleased: 'they are excellent.' Like the novels of their relation by marriage, William de Morgan, copies of this popular volume were spread among the family; the connection of the author with Martin was not a secret.

From Ross, Edith wrote to try and persuade Cameron to join them on the Connemara jaunt; she was prone to get as many 'playfellows' as possible on 'sprees' throughout her life. It is difficult to believe that Edith had any sexual designs upon Martin when we read:

> Pig dog, why don't you answer my letter? How is your choleriac tum? Are you coming to Connemara with us? We hope to start next Tuesday or Wednesday ... My Paris Copyists comes out in the Art Journal next month, I think, as I have just got proofs of it ... I hope you are stirring up the Ridleys about the Kerry Recruit – make them all write to the different Regiments about it. You know they said they would, and now is the accepted time ... If Connemara is a possibility for you, write and let me know. It would be a tight squeeze, but I think we could pack you in, and we should have a *lovely time*. So do try.[6]

Without Cameron, who had other ideas about how to spend his leave, Edith and Martin left Ross to tour Connemara from 22 July to 2 August. After serialisation, the articles, which were rather crudely heightened in a Somervillian comic style, were later published in book form by W.H. Allen as *Through Connemara in a Governess Cart* in 1892. That over, Edith left Ross on the 5th to visit the Franks at Merlin Park, and was back at Drishane on 9 August, to plunge into her neglected horsey life and to prepare for showing. On 6 September she went to Brittany in a farewell party with Cameron, whose leave was ending, and a group of his friends to St. Jacut sur la Mer. Both writers were prone to take off on such sudden jaunts, leaving the other to fret over loss of writing time on their new novel, which had acquired a nickname, as kin to their first. As yet it was but vaguely plotted.

The 'Welsh Aunt' was inspired by the doings and person of a relative. The character of Emily Herbert, nicknamed 'The Cadger', provided Edith and Martin with the raw material for the prime mover of their most substantial novel. She was the niece of Edith's great-aunt Fanny, of the Point House, who had married a Herbert. It had been expected that Aunt Fanny would leave a substantial legacy to Colonel Somerville, who badly needed it. It was discovered later, in 1908, that Aunt Fanny's original will had left £4,000 to Edith and her brother Jack, her favourites.[7] But in her last illness Emily Herbert had prevailed upon Aunt Fanny to change her will in her favour. Having been Aunt Fanny's companion, Emily became her nurse and keeper. Her brusqueness and short temper did not make her fitted for this position. Aunt Fanny had died in that

1 Drishane, home of the Somervilles, Castletownshend,
near Skibbereen, County Cork.

2 The Castle, home of the Townshends, Castletownshend; when Jane de Burgh Townshend
was widowed she was considered not competent to run her son Maurice's estate in his
minority, during which a cousin, Charles Loftus Townshend, became estate manager.

3 Glen Barrahane, home of the Coghills, Castletownshend,
near Skibbereen, County Cork.

4 Ross House, home of the Martins, near Oughterard, County Galway.

5 Colonel Kendal Coghill, 1832–1919, in the uniform of the 19th Hussars. Violet Martin came to love this man as well as did his nephews and nieces: 'Nothing would ever surprise me about him, his reading the Lesson in Church, or dancing in front of the Salvation Army, or opening a faith healing establishment at the Point. He has such strength of character he would carry out anything he thought to be right.' He served under Sir Bartle Frere, a fellow Haileyburian, during the Indian Mutiny; he promoted his eldest nephew's army career. After attending Haileybury school, by 1879 Nevill Coghill had risen quickly to the post of *aide-de-camp* to Bartle Frere when he was killed during the battle of Isandula in the Zulu War. The events of the Mutiny marked him for life; in 1909 his nephew Egerton took him back to India to those scenes where horrifying acts had taken place, to help him erase old memories.

6  Egerton Coghill with his painting companion Herbert Baxter. Violet Martin came to
know Egerton at the end of his career as an art student. In May 1894 she was in Paris
with him and Hildegarde after they were married when he criticised some passing,
seedy, art students: 'They might get their hair cut, *at least!*'. Writing to Cameron,
Martin commented, 'Then one reflects that he once went about Paris with a jellybag
Tam O'Shanter and earrings. He really looked this time like a very smart major'.

7 Edith Œnone Somerville at Alexandra College. This photograph taken in
Dublin in 1876 clearly shows the regular oval of the bone structure of her face.
This was to be destroyed by brutal dentistry, by which her jawline was deformed;
recurring abscesses in the roots of her teeth were to reduce her to plain
ugliness in many photographs of the eighties.

8 Hewitt Poole as a student at Trinity College Dublin.
He entered TCD in 1874, and took his BA in 1879. After an arts degree
he settled on a career as an engineer and took his B.Eng. in 1882. He married
Mia Jellett in 1880. The timing of his periods of study might indicate that the
necessity of taking a professional qualification was tied to his decision to marry
Mia. The period from Easter to Autumn of 1879, one in which he was a
familiar at New Court, his mother's family home, and Drishane,
was one in which nothing was settled.

9 Edith Somerville and Egerton Coghill acting in *The Sorcerer*, 1885. From Gilbert and Sullivan Edith acquired a store of melodramatic exclamations that peppered her conversation and letters.

10  Martin Ross in 1886, still stiff and formal, her appearance in contrast to
Edith Somerville, in artist's disarray and huge straw hat.

11 Martin Ross dressed for a fancy dress ball in 1887, as a Grecian lady in a table cloth, with Jim Penrose in attendance.

12 *Retrospect*, Edith Somerville's largest painting, circa three and a half feet
by five. The subject was Mary Norris, a 'thundering good' model, who had been
a very good-looking woman; in this pose she was uncomfortably wary of
the mirror facing her. A frequent prop of Edith's appears here, her crucifix.

13  Herbert Greene, Dean of Magdalen College Oxford and distinguished classical
scholar; long-time suitor of Edith Somerville's.

14 The cover of Somerville and Ross's first novel *An Irish Cousin*, by Edith and her brother Boyle, 1889. It shows Boyle's strong archaeological bent, using a penannular brooch for the capital I and a drinking horn for the capital C.

15 Group photograph of 1890 showing Edith and Martin together, dressed
in high fashion for a family social event. Correct hats were something of
an obsession for both of them.

16 Group photograph from 1891 'The Waxworks'.
From the left, back row, Herbert Greene, — ?, Ethel Coghill, EŒS,
Violet Martin, — ?; front row, Egerton Coghill, Violet Coghill.

17  Joe Coghill acting, *c.*1890, with his sister Ethel and his daughter
Hebe, both to be doctors.

18 The wedding of Hildegarde and Egerton 11 July 1893.

February 1886 when the Martins had just moved into Tally Ho, so that it is only in Edith's diaries that we find the painful details about Emily. On 27 January she wrote: 'my blood boils over when I think of her devilish cruelty to that unhappy weak minded old woman'. Aunt Fanny died on 20 February and was buried two days later, her will being read on the day of her burial. Edith's diary entry for the 22nd was: 'then they read the will and with the breaking of the seals, hatred, malice, and all uncharitableness got out. In effect Emily got everything. Except about £500 to the Somervilles, of which Papa and I get £50 each. It is a curious instance of the power of will – Emily's will in particular.' On 8 March Emily settled at the Mall House, to Edith's fury: 'Agony, rage, despair' she scrawled in her diary. But Emily's crude money-grabbing had so horrified CT that she was boycotted socially and only a month later she left.

Emily died less than a year later. Edith wrote that: 'She who inspired Charlotte had left this world before we began to write books, and had left, unhappy woman, so few friends, if any, that in trying to embody some of her aspects in Charlotte Mullen we felt we were breaking no law of courtesy or honour.'[8] A drawing of 'Charlotte' from the back survives in Edith's sketches, in which she depicts her as stocky, with a powerful frame barrelling forward. Her manly, overbearing manner was of a type that Edith found fascinating, if ultimately repulsive; it was a manner we find her responding to in Fanny Currey and later Ethel Smyth, as if she were charmed by it. There are a few short descriptions in Edith's letters of Emily and her doings. In her readiness for a physical brawl Emily was a virago like Fanny Currey; a reference to her in a letter from Edith to Cameron of 7 August 1881 shows not only her interest in politics but that she was physically powerful to the point of being a thug: 'Emily Herbert has just returned from London and is in great form – she got an admittance to the House [of Commons] for one night and ever since talks of the members as if they were her intimate friends, or enemies, as the case may be. She got into a row on the G.S.&W. [Great Southern and Western] line'. On her rail journey back to Skibbereen, as the train had a pause for thought before it came into the station, an old lady in the carriage with Emily thought she could get out. As there was no platform, Emily tried to prevent her from getting out, but very roughly. The old lady started to fight her, strongly. Edith carried on: 'I am convinced the old woman believed that she had got into the clutches of a female Lefroy, as she fought so wildly to escape from Emily's clutches that they actually broke the carriage door.' While the fight was going on, the train had drawn in to the station platform. The wiry old lady nipped off, leaving Emily to face an enraged station master who presented her with a bill for £2. 8s. for a new carriage door.

By thwarting Edith over a substantial sum of money that would have given her the wherewithal to be a financially independent woman, Emily had made herself fair game for copy once she was safely dead. A revenge was taken, from which Edith benefitted financially – a setback was turned to the good – but it took a painfully long time. Of all their books, *The Real Charlotte* had the most prolonged gestation. It was worked on in snatches over a period of three years.

From Ross Martin wrote to Edith, who was painting at St Jacut: 'If only this dreadful Welsh Aunt were written – I feel horribly anxious about it – everyone says that the second book is the test – and here we are having doldromised over it for a year.' A fragment, undated, belongs to this time. Quickly Martin had consigned their last effort 'Naboth' to the dustbin and was depressed about the future in joint writing. She described to Edith a tea party when she was cornered by a local lady who knew she was a writer and asked: 'But how do you manage about the spelling – does your editor correct that?' I managed to say that dictionaries were now cheap. It was apropos of Naboth. We are a distinct failure in Oughterard in a literary sense. Bear up – Miss O'Flaherty and Mrs Sparrow said something polite about Naboth. The rest is silence, and even Mama no longer expects anything else …'[9]

Martin was obviously beginning to feel that her youth and energy were slipping away as she fought to restore Ross, for two days later on 18 September she wrote to describe her feelings about coming across an old press photograph taken of her serving at a stall in the Dublin annual Masonic Charity Bazaar *c.*1885, only five years before: 'Then I was counted "one of the fairest flowers within the mossy barrier" by the *Lady's Pictorial*, now you wouldn't pick me out of an ashpit, or know me from one, with my filthy old clothes covered with the tracks of gorchings many and fierce.' The atmosphere in Ross was most uncomfortable, with Mrs Robert Martin and her mother-in-law incompatible – as the old and new mistresses – who, as a compromise, had set up two separate establishments within the house, over which each of them ruled. Up until late September it was planned that Edith should go to Ross. Martin was so short of money that she had to sell shares, a thing that Edith was dead set against doing in her own finances.[10] Martin was at Ross, apart from a visit to the Morrises at Spiddal on 29/30 September, until 23 October, when she joined up with Edith at Fanny Currey's at Lismore and made for Drishane.

She had tried to get Warham St Leger to visit her at Ross during September. He answered her invitation on 23 September: 'The idea of the lake, and the punt and real remote country, is very tempting. I should like to be able to set out, like a man in a German song, and wander across England to some suitable sea point and take shipping and then trudge pilgrim-wise till in some sunset I should see you and there would be much to say.' St Leger's sense of humour was just as subtle and bizarre as Martin's. He described an acquaintance, Oswald Crawford, to her as 'a large, patronising, diplomatic, feminine sort of a man with a brooding manner towards girls and women, like a hen who has been accustomed to teaching at Sunday School'. His was a different humour from that of Martin's brother Robert, who came with Martin on the visit to the Morrises. It was at the dinner table here that the inebriated and unsubtle Robert 'shouted down' everyone else in re-telling stories that Martin had told him in the first place and made her feel sick with embarrassment. Writing to Edith from Spiddal, it is apparent that they both rated particular letters to one another as a prime source for their fiction, and marked them for such later use: 'we went for another walk along the shore, in a pure cold daffodil sunset – with the Clare hills melting from their own exquisiteness – and the sea as delicate and innocent as you please, with a thumping breaker along the beach ... [the walkers came to a graveyard in a sandhill half washed away by the sea with bones lying about] ... ideal to the last extent and certainly to be elsewhere made famous.'

Martin dithered about travelling when she had a period, as she found the process harrowing enough without the added physical pain and tension.[11] The friends' menstrual problems were personified as the workings of a malignant, male, devil who was referred to as 'the divil' or 'the Prince of Darkness'. She made Edith delay travelling in order to avoid this coincidence: 'I know your beastly divil comes on Sunday week, thread for thread with mine.' A fragment, possibly a part of the same letter, shows Martin's erratic attack on work schedules: 'Now my dear friend you talk very gloriously about the advantage of having finished Connemara before you come here. It is indeed a beautiful scheme, all the more lovely and fairy like from its total impossibility ... We should polish off these articles a thousand times faster and more satisfactorily together than apart – at least as far as I am concerned. If you didn't insist on my co-operation I should not be surprised at you writing the whole set in the fortnight – but if you are dependant on me the chances are not good. At the same time I shall do what I can – at any rate we can clean up and weed together ... The St Leger is pretty happy over his book ... he has had capital notices ... The Daily News jumped on [it] in a leader, but that was the only crusher – and who cares what Radicals think ... He mentioned a paper called the Gentlewoman as one that wished for novelties ... but I do not feel drawn to Ladies' papers – I even abhor them – and antagonistic yearnings towards the incomprehensible and Wordly [sic, a pun] stir within ...'[12]

But at last Edith and Martin were back at work at Drishane on 28 October. On the following day Martin made a momentous entry in her diary: 'Made a start at the Welsh Aunt' and so did Edith in hers. This working title and pet name for the novel was later to become The Real Charlotte. The difficulties over finding a suitable workplace with the fewest possible sources of interruption caused complicated plotting and planning by post. Trying to organise a major attack on the novel, Martin had wanted Edith to come to Ross, but in the event it was she who went to Drishane. Edith's painting certainly got in the way of writing. In September, she had been painting keenly on her holiday in Brittany with Cameron; a picture from this holiday, 'La Plage, Saint Jacut sur Mer', was exhibited at the Royal Hibernian Academy in the following year. Although her paintings, and Egerton's, have since been shown in the loose category of 'Impressionist', they were both middle-of-the-road *plein air* painters, belonging to a more traditional school like their Parisian tutors. They admired Corot and recognisably belong to that school of Irish painters who were influenced by Bastien-Lepage and worked in Brittany.

Short of cash, Martin had been kept penniless and immured at Ross by the slowness of the *Lady's Pictorial* to publish their articles and pay up. When Edith got back to Cork from Brittany, there was a letter waiting for her from Martin, who was trying to get Edith to come up to Ross: 'the sooner you can come, without seeming unkind to your family, the better. I *must* make money – so must you – and the Welsh Aunt is an awful business ... Hang the old *Lady's Pictorial* why won't they start these articles – or even answer my letter.' As by this stage Martin had gone to stay with the Morrises at Spiddal, Edith responded to her there: 'The Welsh Aunt is our best chance and will you honestly tell me if you are able to work as we ought to work. Not if you are willing, I know you are that, but genuinely *able*? ... I would rather die in the workhouse than kill you by making you work when you are not fit for it. The only thing is if you don't work with me you will be toiling about the vile house and I don't know which is worse for you ...' This letter has a reference to the excellent sales figures of the just-published book *Ballads from Punch and other poems* edited by Warham St Leger. Edith chaffed Martin about her 'Cambridge man' just as Martin chaffed her about her 'Oxford man'. St Leger does seem to have been a delightfully humorous man in contrast to Herbert Greene, and Martin's chaff about him has a sharp edge in it that we do not find in Edith's about St Leger: 'I am awfully glad the *Poems from Punch* are going well – you might have told him so, with my love, only I know you answered his letter by return of post. Ye slut. Alice Riddell has just had a daughter ...'

The parts of *The Real Charlotte* written at Drishane in 1890 were Chapter II, draft dated October 29; Chapter III, draft dated November 4–8; Chapter IV, draft dated November 10–15.[13] Edith was still working as an illustrator on a wide variety of fronts. Her own relatives were a fertile field to till in themselves. The *Kerry Recruit* had been an attractive proposition, as it was a song popularised by the singing of her cousin Harry Plunket Greene; she was also being employed by Ethel Penrose as the illustrator for her children's story *Clear as the Noonday*. Martin stayed at Drishane until 22 December when she returned to Ross to be with her family for Christmas and the New Year. For the train journey back to Ross Edith had loaned Martin Cameron's copy of *Dorian Gray*: 'The only reason I can imagine for the Chimp lending it to you is that he thought you wouldn't understand it. If it is what I darkly surmise it to be, it is the most daring beastliness I ever struck – but keep this to yourself – Certainly I should be afraid to own to having read it, to a man.'[14] Established back in the Ross household, Martin was writing articles for Edmund Yates' journal *The World* despite many visitors, as the restoration of the house had been such a success that numbers were calling, and some were staying on. Another sign that Ross was having something of an Indian summer was that Robert organised a tenants' dance in the coach house on New Year's Eve 1890. It is a surprising fact that the Martins continue to refer to the people on their old lands as 'tenants', and even more surprising that as 'tenants' such numbers of them appear at this traditional egalitarian entertainment at the turn of the year. Martin commented on the human difficulty of brutally discarding under the dictates of politics those ties of friendship that had grown over generations between landlords and their servants and tenants. She described the Ross New Year tenants' dance in her diary:

> Robert, Connie, Mama, Selina and myself went out to the coach house and we were given a great welcome – about three hundred people there – Robert gave a speech – a very successful one and Jimmy Lee sang his song. Peter Bawn the albino fiddler played a jig and Robert danced with Anne Connor and I with Andy Welsh ... [Martin became tired with all the dancing and crept away before the end while her brother] sang songs and danced hornpipes – I went to bed and was thankful.'

This dance was written up in the RM story 'Oh Love! Oh Fire!' and used as the background to a scene where Flurry Knox, inebriated, dances a jig with his grandmother in what appears to Major Yeates RM as an 'extremely scientific' way. When the gentry danced with their tenants, the young men of the gentry felt it a challenge to dance as well if not better than all comers. The super-flexible Brian Somerville, second son of Boyle, was the best male step dancer in the generation of Edith's nephews and nieces, as in her own were Jack and Aylmer. Robert Martin was skilled enough to dance exhibition hornpipes for his ex-tenants. Transposed to the RM story, Major Yeates comments: 'They say that jig was worth twenty pounds in Mrs Knox's pocket at the next rent day; but though this statement is open to doubt, I believe that if she and Flurry had taken the hat round there and then she would have got in the best part of her arrears.' Borrowings from the life of Robert Martin are as prominent in the RM as those from the life of Aylmer Somerville. It was Robert and his brothers who became involved in a trail of deceptions after unhitching a Ross carriage horse and racing her in the interval between bringing the family and taking them away from a race course – the theme of the RM story 'Occasional Licenses'.

Martin was to stay at Ross from late December until the end of April when she finally got away and settled in with the Coghills at Glen B. It had been impossible to organise any concentrated writing together during that time for many reasons. In a letter of 15 January 1891, Edith at Drishane was trying to see her way to a clear space for writing in, while completing and sending off a series of illustrations: 'I hope that our plans will soon begin to crystallize a bit. You may depend upon me going up to Ross. If only for a month, it would be better than wasting that month; and if Ross is to be shut up at the end of next month, you must either come here or we must meet at Ethel's – all the same I don't care about that, as I think it is rough on Ethel, as you and I, when immersed in literature are more trouble than we are worth.' In the Skibbereen district, the Toe Head people were in difficulties again, and relief work went on through this early part of the year. Edith ran a campaign to collect money to help the poor and needy. In her diary she notes that she went with Cameron around Toe Head on 30 January: 'Sickened and stunned by the misery. Hordes of women and children in rags. Gave as many bread and tea tickets as we could but felt perfectly helpless in the face of such hopeless poverty.' Egerton Coghill ran the Relief Committee for the area, as did Robert Martin at Ross, in an area equally in distress.[15]

On 7 February Edith went up to Ross, and was astonished at the changes that Martin had wrought in the house with painting and decorating. Martin was working at the story 'The Bagman's Pony' that was taken verbatim from Uncle Kendal, whose experience it was, and here, too, Edith went out with Martin on relief work at a place called Porridgetown, its name a memory of earlier Famine days. They spent their breaktimes walking with guns, and trying to perfect their shooting, without much success. Edith went on then to Ethel and Jim at Athboy on 8 April. At the end of the month, possibly the reason for her being unable to go to Athboy with Edith, Martin was in charge of the reception at Ross of the Lord Lieutenant's party at the request of her brother Robert, who was travelling with the Zetlands.[16]

Martin was based in Glen B from the end of April to 5 September, before there was any forward movement in joint commissions. Writing to Edith at Ethel's on 13 April, she asked: 'Could you stay with Ethel until this Monday fortnight? It would, I think, be better all round … but if you are in a hurry I will come – of course I want to be off – but many things weigh on me. Let me know about this as soon as you can. My ideas will want shaping – Violet [Coghill] says I can come any time.' Finding writing time was a sore trial. During this summer a large group photograph was taken of the tableau-cum-charade called 'The Waxworks'. Edith wrote to Boyle on 25 August to give him the good news of Cameron's new billet as ADC to General Cameron at the Cape, where he was to spend almost three years before posting to India. Some work had been done: 'We are into the second Volume of the Welsh Aunt but have been much delayed by the concert and waxworks [a tableau], it is very hard to work down here in the summer.' The concert, at which Robert Martin 'brought the house down with "Mullingar" and sang "Killaloe" as an encore', raised funds for the purchase of a new draft of foxhounds. Edith was depressed that she saw so little of her brothers, and told Boyle: 'I do hope and trust that you will try and get a home billet for the next few years; it is too dreary your spending all the best years of all our lives out at the other side of the world.'

A major event amidst all the boating and tennis of the summer was Aylmer organising the revived West Carbery Hounds with a great deal of local support, and with the financial backing of his wife. The foxhounds arrived on the last day of the month. They were whipped into shape quickly: the first meet of the hunt with Aylmer as MFH was at Lissard on 8 September. But hunting had to be abandoned, for at last Edith and Martin were sent by the *Lady's Pictorial* to Bordeaux to cover the wine harvest in a set of articles. These were to be gathered into a volume later – *In the Vine Country* was published, again by W.H. Allen, in 1893. They set off on 25 September and made a circuit, Martin starting from the Helps at Kew – Paris, Bordeaux, Paulliac, Oxford and back to Kew again. Martin's original suggestion for the series title, 'From Cork to Claret', was rejected as being 'too subtle' for the reading public.[17] Eventually given the more sober title by Allen's editor, *In the Vine Country* taught them both a great deal on the illustrative front. They were given a Kodak to snap studies en route, from which Edith could later make sketches. This proved a good working system that she used from then on when she was strapped for time. Hildegarde had come to London to see them off, and it was she who first fathomed the workings of the box camera. To her fury, all of Edith's drawings were later re-drawn by the slick illustrator and *Punch* staff artist F.H. Townsend. When she got back to Drishane she wrote to Boyle: 'Martin and I have been away on a business tour in France ... It is disgusting to think that we only got £20 for it. However, as Mother says, every good critique claps £20 on the price of the Welsh Aunt, so we shall take it out of them somehow.' On its release their novel *Naboth's Vineyard* was taken very seriously by reviewers and well received. There was a particularly good review in the *Daily Graphic*, which had published Edith's illustrative work, and it shows that some reviewers had tumbled to their real identity and sex:

The issue of a new story by the two clever ladies who gave us *An Irish Cousin* serves to remind us of the instructive fact that Irish fiction is practically in the hands of Irish women, and, let us hasten to add, in very safe hands too. Gerald Griffin and Samuel Lover, Charles Lever and Sheridan Lefanu have left no literary descendants in the male line. Mr Rudyard Kipling, who, though he has Irish blood in his veins, has never set foot on Irish soil, has proved by his creation of Mulvaney that he has a real insight into Irish character. But for faithful pictures of Irish home life and Irish scenery we must go to the author of *Hurrish* and to the authors of *Naboth's Vineyard*. What strikes me about these writers is their impartiality, and, in the case of the joint authors of the last-named work, their keen sense of humour – qualities which many male critics deny to their literary sisters. There can be no question that the Home Rule agitation has exerted a sterilising influence – in men. It is, perhaps, then owing to the eternal law of compensation that we meet with a double portion of it in the writings of Irishwomen.[18]

After the French tour, and a weekend lavishly entertained by Herbert in Oxford, Martin disappeared on an intensive round of visits.[19] She was at Kew with the Helps on 22 October when Warham St Leger called to present her with Marie Bashkirtseff's *Journal*, a thoroughly Bohemian choice of gift. By 21 November she was at Chatham with the Curreys, then moved to Canterbury on the 26th to be with Edith and Cuthbert Dawson. She crossed back to Dublin to see scattered Martins and Bushes in the city and on 7 December travelled down to Skibbereen, where she was met by Aylmer and Edith Somerville. There was a new time-consuming element on the scene: Edith gave a great deal of her attention to the care and maintenance of Aylmer's hounds, the pack of the re-established West Carbery Hunt. With Martin she worked at writing up the series of twelve articles for Mr Gibbons of the *Lady's Pictorial*.

Unusually, Martin spent Christmas at Drishane and did not leave that house until she had to move to Glen B because of Easter visitor congestion at Drishane that lasted from 14 February until 27 April, when she moved back in. The 'Vineyard' series of articles had been finished on 6 February. Then they were able to return to serious writing; it cannot be described as a full-time profession. Hunting regularly, they went out twice a week to meets and dined out frequently. There must have been an improvement in Somerville family finances, as on 20 May Edith entered in her diary that she and Hildegarde were to get 'an allowance to dress on, £26 each'. Edith and Martin had gleaned a few hours a day for writing over a stretch of four months; in consequence *The Real Charlotte* shows as much careful work in its finish as does the much shorter

novel of 1897 *The Silver Fox*. On the first day of June they took a break, and
visited the Curreys and Penroses at Lismore.

The Welsh Aunt had been progressing, and was coming to its dramatic
crux. On 8 June 1892 Edith wrote in her diary 'Wrote feverishly. The most
agitating scenes of Charlotte. Finished Francie.' They wrote the final chapters
in a favourite out-of-the-way corner of the orchard field at Drishane. The
decision to send their heroine Francie Fitzpatrick to her death in a fall from her
horse had been a difficult one, for which the family reviled them. Although she
is deaf and blind to her surroundings through her self-absorption, Francie's
urban *insouciance* is shown in her ignorance, shared by her lover, of the finer
points of riding and country manners, an ignorance that was fatal to her. On
horseback she crowds the funeral procession behind the coffin of Julia Duffy,
her horse rears wildly when the keen is raised and throws her to her death. The
abrupt coming together of the speeding lovers on horseback and the slow march
of the funeral procession for Julia, whose lands have been misappropriated by
Charlotte, the villainess of the piece, is worked with delicacy and sure control
of all the strands woven through the novel.

Their work station out of doors at Drishane was perhaps even more of a
sanctuary than the Studio. It was where the writers went to escape unwanted
summer visitors, and, in 1915, it was where Hildegarde came with Edith to be
out of the way while Martin was being buried. The tragic overtones of *The Real
Charlotte* may have put off publishers' readers. Bentley's were to offer only an
unacceptable £100 for it, and it was then turned down by Smith and Elder. The
manuscript eventually passed on to Ward and Downey. Martin was at Ross for
the summer with her mother until 11 August when they went together down to
visit Aunt Marion, Mrs Arthur Bushe, in Bray. She returned to CT at the height
of the summer visitor season on 17 August. In this summer Aylmer and Dr
Jennings founded the Skibbereen Agricultural Show, from which any profits were
to go to the West Carbery Hounds that had been re-established the previous
winter, and the Show had increased visitor numbers. There was no room for
Martin at Drishane or Glen B. Making a demonstration of independence, she
moved in to The Cottage with the holidaying Rose Helps, renting the house from
Maurice Townshend of the Castle. Her Mother came to stay too. Herbert was
reigning as the chief occupier of Edith's time. In this year he had presented her
with a skiff called the Miri Chi (meaning 'My Girl' in Romany) and lorded it in
the stern of the boat giving instructions to women rowers.[20] Martin was to
remain a tenant at The Cottage until early April of the following year, when she
moved back to Drishane and her Mother nipped into The Cottage in her stead.

When Mrs Martin moved in, her tenancy was rather informal and she
should have made way gracefully, as Egerton, who was, born of necessity, a do-

it-yourself enthusiast, was getting the house ready for himself and Hildegarde. Later Martin mentioned this awkwardness: 'she has a kind of dislike of leaving any place as you can remember when she hung on in the cottage while Egerton was breaking holes in her bedroom wall.'[21] In November 1892 *Through Connemara in a Governess Cart* was published to moderate or subdued notices, reviewers recognising it as the light journalism that it was. Warham St Leger had a review copy, and he told Martin: 'I have been studying the pictures with great desire to see you in them.' In her own abode Martin was laid low over the Christmas period with a bad cold. Even so she and Edith wrote an article together for *The World* on 'St Stephen's Day'.

Edith and Martin did some novel writing work as well at The Cottage, as it was less congested than anywhere else in CT. On 8 January 1893 Edith completed the clean copy of the first 45 chapters of the 'Welsh Aunt' for it to be taken by Boyle over to Mr Bentley in London. On 4 February they 'actually and entirely' finished the Welsh Aunt. Although as an old woman Edith claimed that nearly all their books had been written in Drishane, careful examination of their diaries shows frequent exceptions. A part of *The Real Charlotte* was actually written in The Cottage, shortly to be Egerton and Hildegarde's first home on their marriage. The future for Egerton as a landlord looked grim, and though he made attempts to set up as a professional artist, like Edith he never truly escaped the cage he was born in. Despite its artists and rebels CT was a Unionist enclave under threat, and it behaved like one. On 17 March, St Patrick's Day, Martin had entered: 'Left off [writing] to go to Anti-Home Rule Service at the Church, where everyone was, and we bellowed the National Anthem.' Edith had gone over to London for some lessons at the Westminster School of Art, so that the offers being made by Bentley were discussed between them by post, and turned down. Martin did take in some overflow guests at The Cottage; that same night, she noted: 'V. Coghill slept here.' At this stage only an amateur medic, like Edith, Violet Coghill was treating Martin's mother for lumbago with massage. Martin had less than two weeks in Drishane, able to work peacefully in the Studio, before she had to move back to Glen B. She set off north on a round of visits from Dublin on 20 April.

Five days later Martin joined Edith in London. Ward and Downey had been reading the MS of *The Real Charlotte* since 14 April, and were pondering on what to offer. Low offers had already been made by Bentley and Allen. At the end of the month, Edith and Martin joined up with Hildegarde and Adelaide on a visit to Herbert Greene at his college in Oxford. They were in Oxford for the May Day celebrations; Herbert was then the Dean of Magdalen College. Edith wrote: 'a party more bent on triviality and foolishness has not often disgraced the hospitality of a Scholar'. Although Herbert remained to Edith all her life a man 'with whom it seemed unwise to trifle', Martin found him so irritating that she cheerfully misbehaved in Oxford. Martin had ways of wounding with a quick lash of the tongue – 'What is Herbert writing these days apart from errata?' being a good example from a letter to Edith from Ross to Drishane, where Herbert was looming in the Studio. When Herbert took the party of women on to the roof of the Bodleian to admire the view, Martin, determinedly not doing what was expected, was entranced, and then inspired, by the sight of the ventilation shafts going down into the Upper Reading Room. She was overcome, Edith wrote in *Irish Memories*, by 'an uncontrollable longing to shriek down it in imitation of a dog whose tail has been jammed in a door. (An incomparable gift of hers that has been the making of many a dull dinner party.) I have often wondered what the grave students in that home of learning thought of the unearthly cry from the heavens. Sirius, as it were, in mortal agony.'[22] Of course, their appalled host didn't think that this was in the least funny. Herbert turned white, and rushed them down the stairs.

After Oxford, Edith went to London intent on clothes, before returning home. She patronised a dressmaker called Gare, and her passion for particular materials and colours in her dresses, as in her hats, was pronounced. She only spent a small proportion of her life in hunting rig, but the majority of photographs of her to be reproduced are taken with the West Carbery Hounds, or country day-kit, giving the quite misleading impression that she lived in a riding habit like a Lady of Llangollen. This has rather delayed any general appreciation of her sartorial or jewellery-collecting passions. On 9 May she wrote to Hildegarde : 'I went to Holmes this afternoon and after an agitated half hour have decided on a reppy poplin biscuit colour – Deep revers and rolling collar of mirror velvet that faints from purple to palest heliotrope, ditto bars on sleeves – A full white silk undershirt-thing – (the body a short one, like my black, with sleeves to the elbow) The whole trimmed with rich gold gimp – to cost from 5 to 5 and a half guineas. The skirt to have three rolls for itself with gold gimp – Holmes thinks it adorable – it was my idea – Do look in the third drawer of my chest of 'draws' for the black and chenille trimmed belt of my black dress and send it to me. I want it badly.'

Martin carried on after Oxford and London to Kew where she stayed with the Helps. On 16 May, via letters, at last they made their decision on *The Real Charlotte* and sold their novel to Ward and Downey for £250.[23] At the end of the month Edith's favourite editor Mr Williamson gave them a commission to tour in North Wales. Martin travelled to Welshpool in North Wales on 14 June to meet up with Edith for their tour, which was to be written up and serialised for the magazine *Black and White*. The tour took them a mere eleven days, for they were back in Ireland on 26 June, Martin returning to Ross and Edith to Drishane by the 28th. The tour writing contains a description of Llangollen and its Ladies whose lives as they describe them contrast so strangely with the two flippant young women who travel to see their home. There is a great contrast, too, between the tone of their tightly controlled novel writing and the tone of their early journalism, that almost amounts to the contrast between mature and immature.[24] Riding together before getting to Llangollen, we get a picture of the pair as little more than giggling sixth formers about to visit a curiosity. Edith features in the account as Miss O'Flannigan. Their horses, on a road, were agitated by the approach of a steam roller, and they nipped through a convenient gate:

> we burst through into the shadow of tall evergreens, tearing out a hold-all buckle in an encounter with a gate post. We were startlingly confronted inside by an old lady in a mushroom hat, carrying a spud and a garden basket, and wearing an expression of complete and unaffected amazement, which, considering all things, and especially the fact that Miss O'Flannigan and I had fallen into maniac laughter, was a pardonable lapse of good breeding. Pointing to the traction engine, we endeavoured to explain ourselves ... The old lady stirred neither hand nor foot throughout the occurrence and for all we know may have been a rustic detail added, in wax, by a proprietor of a realistic turn ...
>
> [they arrived at Llangollen] ... if it is seen on the way into Wales instead of on the way out of it, it will occupy with fitting distinction its place in the crescendo of Welsh scenery, undiscounted by the coming fortissimo: to be one of the last notes in a diminuendo is quite a different thing.
>
> Probably it was the two unparalleled persons known as the Ladies of Llangollen who did most for its fame. They ran away from their Irish homes to go and live there, which, in itself, from our point of view, suggests eccentricity. Perhaps it was in lifelong penance for this act that ever after they wore riding habits, summer and winter, indoors and out. After a fortnight spent in riding habits we could appreciate such an expiation, even though the equipment we had dedicated to the Tommies [their horses] did not include powdered hair and cartwheel felt hats. Pardonable curiosity might well have caused any traveller by the Holyhead coach who could scrape up an introduction to climb the hill to Plas Newydd; but it was not upon curiosity alone that the ladies relied for society. They had the agreeability that could at will turn the sightseer into an acquaintance, the means to weld with good dinners such acquaintanceships into friendships; and aesthetic taste, the best part of a century ahead of its time, that taught them to frame the grotesque romance of their lives and appearance in antique and splendid sur- roundings ...[25]

Nothing much was done in the writing line this summer during the preparations for the wedding of Hildegarde and Egerton on 11 July 1893. This pair did so well on behalf of their children that it is difficult to catch up with their own personal economies as a married couple. For their honeymoon they chose to live like gypsies for a fortnight and hired a punt, with a tented tarpaulin cover for sleeping at night, to punt all the way down the Thames. The two were popular on their own accounts, and their wedding was celebrated in the village street with displays of flags, bunting and a great banner reading 'Cor Unum Via Una'.[26] Their particular and personal closeness to Edith and Martin is shown by the fact that the worries over their financial affairs were a shared burden, and if either Edith or Martin was short of money they borrowed from Hildegarde and Egerton. Toby Coghill, Egerton's grandson, was often to exclaim on the gypsy-like existence of the Coghills in CT during that twilight when the landlords weren't quite dead and gone and New Ireland was not yet: 'They were hanging on by their fingernails!' However, some money had been found to marry Egerton and Hildegarde in style, the bachelor Uncle Kendal being always generous.

Edith wrote to Hildegarde after the wedding day was over in a state of emotional exhaustion. During the morning the sisters had begun to drink champagne while Edith was dressing Hildegarde 'to keep ourselves stiff'. By the end of the day they had quietly drunk at various moments, apart from the celebratory meals, a bottle each. After the carriage with the bride and groom had gone Edith wrote: 'I went up to your room and found the dogs lying in moody coils with their backs to the world, and I thereon put my face down on their backs and wept and the Tothams [her personal dog Dot] licked up my tears with avidity. This is a fact.' Egerton's dog, the Irish water spaniel Pastel, was also bereft, and fixated on Jack as a substitute: 'Pastel haunts Drishane and often sleeps with Jack.' The married couple in their punt on the Thames had good weather, but in Ireland it was foul, Edith wrote to Hildegarde: 'I don't like speaking about the weather as my language becomes coarse and uncontrollable.' Between downpours, Ethel Penrose and Jack, Herbert and Edith spent days carrying things to the Cottage to prepare it for the return of the newly-weds.

On 3 July at Ross with her mother and sister Edith, Martin had been horrified by the arrival of a War Office telegram. Her brother Charlie, in an Indian regiment, had been killed at Taipeng, where he served as Adjutant of the Perak Sikhs.[27] His wife Lucy sent a following telegram to explain that it had been a 'horse accident'; Major Seymour Clarke, the author of *The Genealogy of the Martins of Ross*, described Charlie's death as happening while he was 'tent pegging'. Mrs Martin adored her sons, and her grief was extreme. In her diary Martin wrote: 'A dreadful afternoon. No-one knowing what to do or say.

Thank heaven Edith [Dawson] and I were here.' Later Martin found that the accident, very like her own to come, had happened when Charlie was attempting a big jump with a partly trained horse; of her siblings, he had been the child next to Martin in age and suffered like her from crippling short sight. Both were bad at judging the size of obstacles. When his horse swerved and refused at the last moment, it lost its footing, Charlie was thrown and his horse fell on him. Martin remained with her mother, rallying her, and dealing with letters of sympathy.

A letter from Edith to Hildegarde of 22 July of this year dates two photographic nude studies that the sisters made of each other for a French publisher who was assembling a volume of such amateur studies for the use of art students. A letter from the publisher has survived which reveals that Hildegarde herself used the male pseudonym of Henry Collins for some of her photographic work (see p. 206). There does not seem to have been much prudishness about nudity among the free spirits of CT, for, like the sisters, others including Egerton and Boyle swam unclothed down at the private Dutchman's Cove. The photographs, which do not show the sisters' faces, were referred to as 'the backs' and were mounted in one of the Drishane albums since lost, but they survive as prints in the Coghill Archive. There was eight years' difference in age between the sisters, during which time teenage girls had been liberated from the deforming bands of tight stays that rendered the lower ribs vestigial and pushed forward the upper, thus increasing *embonpoint*. In consequence Edith has an hour-glass waist in comparison to her younger sister. Despite the many visitors, there was no convivial companion for Edith, and in the same letter to Hildegarde, she writes: 'I fear there is no chance of Martin coming here for some time; it is very unfortunate and I am very lonesome with no-one in your room.'

On their return Hildegarde and Egerton began their married life in The Cottage. Prototype do-it-yourself fanatics both of them, out of financial necessity, they spent months scraping, cleaning, painting and papering their new home. Egerton made a wonderful glass house cum conservatory on a concrete base, glazed with old stained-glass windows and photographic plates. Edith and Martin tried to get back to work by post. *The Real Charlotte* was in proof stage, but it was summertime, and Herbert turned up for his usual vacation. We have some evidence in letters that gives an impression of the manners of the man who failed to charm Martin. A letter from Edith to Hildegarde describing the difficulties of dealing with him is dated 6 August 1893:

> Herbert is really too provoking with his stirk [animus] against the grass
> court – his sisters are all mad with him for his rudeness, but of course he
> does not consider that he can be rude to any of the family, his theory is

that such civilities are merely conventional usages of other places. They do not obtain in CT. This is in itself exasperating. I must say he is a most wearing person in his madness for expeditions or exercise, and in his resolve to boss everything, and his conviction that he knows this place better than we do becomes very maddening ... Then I must say he riles me awfully in his persistently ignoring that I have any work to do, and yet every morning I have to undergo the same botheration about playing tennis (on the gravel) or going out in the boat – I hate seeming ungrateful and he is a very good fellow but a more tactless creature I have seldom met – Martin and I are worrying on with the Welsh Aunt through great disadvantages ...

Edith liked looking at handsome animals and humans, as objects of admiration, and it is ironic that she particularly liked the looks of Herbert's sister Constance [Consie], who was also down for the summer. She had written to her sister earlier in the month: 'Consie is quite charming – in a sort of way as I can flop on a poem or a picture so do I upon her – She has lovely turns of the head, especially at the piano.' The same letter has the surprising note: 'I enclose a bit of a letter from Martin that will amuse you I don't want it back', and also the gruesome information that the new draft of hounds had killed and eaten an old hound called Solomon from the original pack in the kennels. The details later turned up in the RM story 'The Whiteboys'. It is hardly surprising that the surviving letters between the writers are fragmentary, as so many bits of them travelled around the family like this. Boyle sent £5 this summer to the Reverend Walter Macleod to research the Somerville family tree in the Edinburgh records. Writing work was very much in the background, with a tour abroad commissioned for the autumn. Edith complained to her sister: 'I don't know when, if ever, Martin can come here. I think we shall start for Denmark about Sept. 6th or so.'

Martin remained at Ross with her mother until then, when she set off to London to stay with the Dawsons. Edith Somerville joined her here for their tour of Denmark, commissioned by the *Lady's Pictorial*. They went abroad on 9 September and crossed back three weeks later. This tour, unlike the others, was never published in volume form, but was included as an item in the miscellaneous volume *Stray-Aways* of 1920 as 'In the State of Denmark'. It is light journalism again, written to earn money while they reserved their concentration for their novel. Back in Ireland Edith met up with Jack in Dublin and carried on to CT while Martin had an appointment with her dentist Corbett. From the amount of dental detail in their diaries, both women could have written quite substantial specialised biographies of their teeth, which were the bane of their lives.

The last discussions over the final form of *The Real Charlotte* took place in October/November 1893, when the novel left their hands. On 7 December Martin left for Ross and a subdued Christmas with her mother, for they were joined by the widow of Charlie Martin and her two children. Martin was further disturbed by the suicide by drowning on St Stephen's Day of a local boy in an incident that she later wrote into a short story and a novel.[28] Her diary of January 1894 names the boy as Shauneen Holloran of Pribawn. With relief, Martin left Ross on 13 February to join Hildegarde and Egerton at The Cottage in CT. The manuscript of *Beggars on Horseback*, the Welsh tour, was perfected and sent off on the 21st. On 15 March Edith wrote to James Pinker as the new editor of *Black and White*, about future work for that magazine; he was the replacement for Mr Williamson, who had moved on to *The Hour*. By some process they later could not account for, Pinker was to become literary agent for Somerville and Ross. Martin moved back to Drishane on 28 March, but soon left it again for a spree abroad. Edith, Hildegarde and Martin went to Paris on 5 April and were at first in the Hotel de la Haute Loire, but then economised. Edith slipped back into her old ways as an art student.

When *The Real Charlotte* was published in May 1894, in the three-volume 'three-decker' form that was popular then, Hildegarde was keeping Martin company while Edith worked at the Académie Délécluse. They had rooms in a run-down art students' quarter on the Boulevard Mont Parnasse, at the corner of Boulevard Raspail. Hildegarde, who was on a quiet shopping spree stocking up for the annual Saint Barrahane's Church Bazaar in mid-August, was cook. Martin was writing the series of articles *Quartier Latinities*, illustrated by Edith, to be published by the magazine *Black and White*, which had been commissioned by their old favourite and staunch admirer Mr Williamson before he left it for *The Hour*; sub-editors of his on *Black and White* were Warham St Leger and Williamson's successor at *Black and White*, Somerville and Ross's literary agent-to-be, James Pinker. The well-known double portrait of the authors at this time was taken, on 8 May, at the request of Mr Gibbons at the the *Lady's Pictorial* for a *Real Charlotte* publicity shot.

Returning to Ireland on 8 June, Edith and Martin were not to see each other until the end of October, and even then, although Martin was in CT, Edith went off to France. On the 26 June, the day after her return to Drishane, Martin noted an: 'Excellent review of Charlotte in the *Graphic*.' This gave much-needed encouragement. The first reviews of *Charlotte* from family and critics were painfully unfavourable, but gradually in time some enlightened reviewers, in the *Athenaeum*, *The World* and the *Daily Chronicle* for example, began to swing public opinion. Some reviewers abused the book; on 16 June Edith wrote: 'Got a *Westminster Gazette* with furious abuse of Charlotte's disagreeability.'[29] But the dire response of the family hurt them, Jack's being the most critical, as did a Sunday *Weekly Sun* review by T.P. O'Connor in which he labelled them 'shoneens' – Irish apers of the English who were perverted by snobbery. Martin realised that despite this it was an excellent review, 'one of the best and best-written notices we have had'. Such negative reaction may lie behind an eventual swing in their joint novel-writing towards a lighter tone, away from what was described as the 'dirty Irish realism' of *The Real Charlotte*. O'Connor's review also blighted their reputation in Ireland for some time. But the book was disliked by English reviewers for other reasons. The review in the *Lady's Pictorial* is an example of the kind of misunderstanding that was common: 'English people who read this book will be confirmed in their mistaken idea that Ireland is a nation of barbarians, for the authors have forgotten unfortunately, that without light and shade there is no real art, and as their story grew under their hands the light that glimmered in Volume I went out completely ... was it worth while to expend such an amount of cleverness upon such a sorry crew?'[30]

Writing to Martin at Ross at the end of the summer, Edith sent the great news that Violet Coghill had been accepted as a student of medicine: 'Violet has just heard from Frau Doctorinde Jex Blake saying she must to *Edinburgh* to pass an easyish preliminary exam and then work there all the Winter! She means to try!! It is well for her that Katie will be at Glen B to tend the Bart.' Edith may have been so badly affected by the negative response to Charlotte that she took to other occupations in disgust. She had more than one way of earning money, and supplemented her earning from writing with horse-coping and painting; it was touch-and-go whether co-operative writing with Martin was worthwhile. In November Edith went over to Shropshire to stay with Sissy Cholmondely at Edstaston, taking with her her new mare Novelty, on whom she hunted with the Quorn and the Cottesmore Hunts.[31] She left her mare, displayed to perfection to prospective buyers out hunting, with a dealer, and carried on to Paris, where she arrived on 1 December. She worked with her old friends at the Académie Délécluse again. She heard from Sissy that Novelty had been sold for £100. Martin had a collapse in health before Christmas and went to ground in Drishane for two weeks. She made no diary entries over this period save: 'kept over Xmas by a cold.' She went home to Ross on New Year's Day. In mid-January of 1895, a sign that perhaps too much Bohemian Studio life was not for Martin, she went to visit Andrew Lang and his wife in St Andrews[32] while Edith was off again to Paris for another term at the Académie Délécluse, to her old haunts and old friends. While at St Andrews Martin had sent a set of reviews of *The Real Charlotte* to Warham St Leger. He wrote to her on 22 February:

Very many thanks for sending me the reviews and notably T.P. O'Connor. It is amusing and interesting to observe the limitations of the reviewers. So many put themselves in the position of a teacher correcting an exercise – The 'Sunday Sun' is marred only by a rather pathetic sort of loyal petulance. He knows that these people are so and can't quite forgive you for saying so. Hence he falls back on primness and repartee and says you are a 'Shoneen' to wit, which is a very fascinating expression. He might as well argue that George Moore is a domestic servant and prove it by 'Esther Waters'. The Pall Mall Gazette notice is certainly a very good one but the writer seems to be afraid of letting himself go. I don't know what he means by the book being 'too photographically minute'. That's just what it isn't. It is the fine observation of what is significant that makes your writings so true and vivid. 'The Real Charlotte' is perhaps a bit above the minds of the professional appraisers.[33]

An undated letter from Edith to her mother from Paris survives from this January. It might suggest that Edith considered her writing career to be done with, making way for art: 'I spent in book writing '87–'94 – and six most valuable ones at that – I am getting on with my work ...'. Too low to plan ahead, Martin wrote to Edith in Paris from St Andrews on 16 January 1895. In her letter she always shows an awareness of where Edith is and what she is doing, a kind of constant awareness that did not exist in Edith, who was in general too preoccupied, regarding Martin. After a complete account of the appearance and manner of Andrew Lang there is a desolate review of Martin's present situation:

*How* can I meet you in London on the first of March when I am hifling [rushing] straight back to Ross in a fortnight[34] – There to stay indefinitely? But it is no use to talk of plans. It requires special firmness and hardihood to carry out any – and also money. As to that two pounds that is between us, I will if you like say no more – take it as a series of Christmas presents, to extend over thirty or forty years – but you know it is nonsense that you should pay my way to CT. Why shouldn't I pay your way to Ross the next time you go there? It is a very strange thing that I should be so much more successful at Drishane when you are not there – but it is a fact. A child might have played with your mother throughout – therefore I did so with a success that terrified myself. Everyone liked me much better, and I was much nicer to them. I cannot explain how or why, but it is so. I suppose that people used to think that I only cared for your society, and I have always told you that I am at my worst when you are by. It is quite true. You make me shy and cross in some mysterious way – and I think your mother is like that too. She prefers your company to anyone's, but it seems over-stimulating. So don't tell me again I can't get on well with your mother. I can get on with her forever when you aren't there. It is you who fight and then my heart takes part with you and I turn horrible. It is a very intricate position and one that has often made you justly angry with me, but believe me there is a basis of good feeling and always was, and it has often lately touched me to see how your mother has suppressed in talking to me the home truth that in earlier days would have flown from her lips, and would have roused the spirit of combat in me. This is a strange dissertation, and confused, but I thought of it all a good deal while you were away in Paris – and I think I had better stay at Drishane only when you are away in Paris – and I am sure Hildegarde would agree with me. She used daily to cross herself regarding the Millennium harmony. But for all that your mother and I would rather fight and have you there – strange as it may appear. [The letter gives a minute account of her own health, and closes with:] I do hope you are not dying of cold in Paris. I hate reading accounts of the bitter cold – I am afraid of your coming out of the hot Studio into the biting air. Walk plenty and keep up your stove. I hope the club fires are good – you are very precious, and you haven't anyone to bully you or take care of you ... Don't be killing yourself to write. It isn't fair when you are so busy – Yours ever, Martin.

Discussion of *The Real Charlotte* raged in St Andrews, and Martin was pleased to be able to lay the invention of Charlotte at Edith's door.[35] Though Edith was let off letter-writing duty, others wrote to Martin from Cork. The CT coastguard officer's wife, Mrs Warren, had taken to writing poetry, and some of her verse had reached Martin in St Andrews. Mrs Warren had asked both Edith and Martin to give criticism: 'When shall I be able to give it to you in person. It seems a long way off – more than is good. If it means May we shall hardly know each other. *How* could I go to Paris – I should have no reason for such extravagance ... I am all right about money for the present ... You are – very much what you always have been, in offering to stand by. If it were not so awfully foolish I could put xxxs in that place, like the children – You will understand that I have *not* done so because I don't want you to laugh at me.' On 1 February Martin went down to London to stay with Edith Dawson with whom she went to see Oscar Wilde's *The Ideal Husband* – 'extremely amusing and quite proper' – and searched for and found a dress pattern that Edith wanted. Always careful with money, Martin tended to buy cheap tickets with

Go To 171

decaying Big Houses. The roof beams were originally laid well away from the chimney linings, and plastered over, but with the passage of years the plaster of the flue eroded to expose the beam-ends. Trapped sparks then ignited the end of the beam and with a slow burn crept along to a space where they could erupt into something bigger. Martin entered in her diary for 17 May: 'providentially William and Wat [the Lee brothers] were in the garden. They, I, and Hildegarde who leaped from bed, fought the flames then half a dozen men came from round the country and all was put out by 6 o'clock. It was an awfully near shave of destruction.'

When Edith and Nannie returned they found the contents of the gently steaming Ross House out on the lawns, including all the dining table silver, which Hildegarde had thrown out onto a nesting duck under the dining room window. She and Martin had organised a human chain using every container available, and had been part of it, to bring water up from the lake. Edith told her mother that they had done: '– "what'd kill six men" – as one of the servants said to me in awestruck tones'. Edith then left the two heroines at Ross to take Nannie off to Aran, where Martin was to join them later after Hildegarde returned to Cork. The fire at Ross was to provide the last dramatic scene of the last story in the first twelve of the RM series, 'Oh Love! Oh Fire!' The title was significant in its implication that the marriage of Sally the aristocrat and Flurry the half-breed could literally bring the house down.

Edith and Nannie descended on a rented house in Kilronan on Inis Mor of the Isles of Aran. Edith found the air 'tremendously bracing' and the island full of picturesque models: 'I have never seen such fine, easy, graceful movers as all the people old and young.'[39] But never a drawing was Edith able to make of them; to all those graceful movers hers was an evil eye: 'if they are drawn they die the following day.' Martin wrote: 'At the first sight of the sketch book the village becomes a desert; the mothers, spitting to avert the Bad Eye, snatch their children into their houses and bang their doors. The old women vanish from the door-steps, the boys take to the rocks.'[40] The holiday, described by Martin to Hildegarde in a letter of the 22nd, had started disastrously for Edith and Martin as both of them were prostrated by 'the divil' in the form of menstrual pains, and they at first crawled about in slow motion. They struggled with domesticity. The house, Killrany Lodge, was strangely equipped, with two saucepans to its name and one monstrous teapot, and no spoon bigger than a teaspoon. As the Martins were frequent travellers to Aran, Martin knew the captain of the Aran boat, Neal de Largy, and what he had been doing the night before she travelled over: 'I found Captain de Largy perfectly sober, and apparently without a head [hangover], but reeking of a morning peg ... I sat and read on deck all the time and talked to Mr Johnny Joyce ...' Edith had arrived some days before and was already sunburned.

No continuity

restricted dates: 'I can't stay on until you come – my ticket is up – but you must come to Ross – I have any amount to say but must stop. How about your rocky interior?'

But, after all, Mrs Warren's poetry did get passed on in person. Ships that passed in the night, fleetingly Martin met up with Edith in London on her return from Paris on 27 February where she was staying with Constance Bushe. The next day Edith returned to CT, and Martin to Ross. Martin had been loaned by Edith a copy of the first number of the *The Yellow Book*[36] — Edith, to Martin's astonishment, had enjoyed it. A fortnight later Martin commented: '[I] am very glad you did not read aloud the Ballad of the Nun. It is disgraceful, to the point of spoiling a very beautiful thing – and the idea of the Virgin Mary coming down and being a porteress while the young lady was off on the ramp like any dog or cat is almost noble in its novelty. But beautifully written it is, and I wish it were a little less degraded – I do wish people would give up making the central physical point of life its central point of happiness, of intellect, of interest …'[37] In the poem a hitherto devout young nun, the apple of her Abbess's eye, is overcome by lust. She breaks out of her convent, discarding her clothes as she runs to a nearby town. She throws herself at a young man, experiences sexual fulfilment and learns the true meaning of life. Showing a considerably coarser humour than Martin, Edith enjoyed the Ballad, and adapted it, with alterations to suit her humour, in *Irish Memories*. Casting herself as the Abbess and her dog Dot as the nun, her adaptation runs: 'She loved her more and more, and made her Keeper of the ashpit.' Gallows humour again, but the jest is about emotions that have turned to ashes, even as burned letters in a rubbish pit. The letters in the ashpit of the story 'Lost, Stolen or Strayed', in *Some Irish Yesterdays*, prepare us for what was to happen to Edith's most personal letters, when after a long passage of years they had lost their hold on her.

Back at work in the Studio on 18 March, while Edith was making the drawings for the story 'Bocock's Mare' she noted in her diary: '"Slipper" alias "Pack" posed for me for 2 hours, sketching. I let him go, he said "Good Day Miss, we'll know each other agin".'[38] Her model was a celebrated Skibbereen character, renowned for his skills with horses and hounds, and a heavy drinker. He had attached himself voluntarily to Aylmer's service with the Hunt. Three years before they thought of the cast of characters of the RM stories, Edith had met and captured graphically one of its chief players-to-be.

In early May Hildegarde and Edith went up to join Martin at Ross. While Edith drove Nannie Martin over to lunch with neighbours, Hildegarde (who had been ill and in bed when the alarm was raised) and Martin together dealt with a major household disaster. A chimney caught fire, and the conflagration spread along the beams into the roofspace. This was a common happening in

GO TO 170

Martin was uncomfortable with the people of Aran: 'I don't like the natives, they are savages pure and simple – their manners are a dreadful come down from our nice Wat [Lee] and Matt [Kenealy]. They have also the air of not caring to have good manners and of wishing to rook you.' Edith and Martin were keen to find out, from people like the Island's parson, what impression Miss Lawless had made when she was staying to research for her novel *Grania*. The answer was hardly any. A woman failed to recognise the title of the novel 'in any pronunciation that Edith could impart to it', and they concluded that Miss Lawless had drawn upon her imagination 'almost altogether'. Annoyed and thwarted, Edith had to give up any attempt to draw the natives in their picturesque dress: 'Not a creature will allow Edith to draw it. They think they would die if a picture was made of them.' Hildegarde was a champion camping cook, and Martin lamented that she was not with them, as the concocting of meals was a trial: 'We regret your absence daily – wholly on selfish grounds. You and Egerton and half a dozen more could easily share our room. It would hold four beds and still look unfurnished.'[41]

Martin's Mama still had all her old charming, and scrounging, ways: 'Mama went alone to church, and returned with mint and vinegar for mint sauce from the Rectory – where she had never before been.' The whole party returned to Ross the following week. One of Martin's most powerful essays was written up from this stay in Aran. It is the first essay in the volume *Some Irish Yesterdays*, published by Longmans almost ten years later in 1906. At Ross from 30 May to 10 June, when she went to stay with Ethel and Jim at Lismore, Edith with Martin struggled at the writing-up of the Danish tour. The visits to Athboy and the hunting with the Meath pack were over, for the Penroses had moved from Athboy to Waterford. Jim Penrose had become agent to the Duke of Devonshire, and taken up his palatial quarters with Ethel in Lismore, where Edith and Martin were to be frequent guests.

In June 1895 Edith began to receive a series of travelogues from Herbert Greene, who took summer boat cruises on which he seemed to do nothing but think about Edith and sit on deck writing to her.[42] In 1892 he had sent a fifty-nine-page account of his travels, in 1895 he sent some sections of sixteen pages. On 6 August he wrote to her of being in one of his well known depressions – 'one of my savage fits, but of unusual strength'; he was writing to her sitting alone in the bows of the boat, having been reading a complete Tennyson and making notes of the number of times the poet used the name 'Edith' in his poems. The emotionally inarticulate Ulick Adare of the novel *Dan Russel the Fox* of 1911 seems a close relation of Herbert's. He is cast in the novel as the ineffectual man of thought in opposition to the madly attractive horseman and man of action, John Michael Fitzsymons. Herbert took his 1895 cruise alone, the friend, Ulick Burke, who was to have accompanied him having died suddenly. His letters show a tortured mind, unable to stop hoping that one day Edith would give up her independent life and marry him. So fixated on Edith was he, and so immovably self-assured intellectually, that he could read, as he was to do in 1898, her distracted failure to say 'No' as 'Yes'.[43]

For another man the path of love did run smoothly. At about this time Edith received from Boyle what she described as a 'mad rhapsadody' [sic] on his feelings at having fallen in love with Mabel Allen in Sydney and on having his proposal of marriage accepted. Both Martin and Edith, delighted, had written to congratulate him. He replied to his sister: 'Please give my love to Martin ... and thanks for her words of congratulation. If she or you only knew (I am not sure, however that you don't, my ladies?!) what the glorious happiness of being *unrestrainedly* in love is ... My darling Edith, it is so supreme and thrilling that no one, not even a poet, has or ever can put down on paper the majesty of it ...' Boyle, like everybody else in the family, knew that Martin had a *grádh* for the famous Warham St Leger of *Punch*, and that his letters were important to her. Towards his sister the reference to her possibly knowing unrestrained romantic love is more puzzling. He would never have realised that she wrote the pair of *World* sonnets in 1885/6 that reveal that she did know, and surely Boyle must have guessed that Herbert was unattractive to her. No letters have survived from Boyle to Edith from 1885 that tell us what he thought of Barry's death, though he would have known there was a connection from 1879. When he married, Edith had to put away her dream of bungalow bliss with Boyle on his early retirement; she never thought of an independent home for herself again.

At the end of June a reporter came to CT to interview the writing duo for *The Minute*.[44] They had laughed at one of the first questions, which was: how did they feel about the general assumption that they were men? 'Oh, yes,' replied Miss Martin, 'they used in the old days to take it for granted we were *men* and then after a long correspondence about MSS., we would perhaps walk in to an editorial sanctum and – the effect was amusing.' The interview is valuable as it shows that Martin was also, by now, fictionally explaining the impulse to write together in the same way as Edith, with a slight geographical variation. 'How came you, then, to think of writing together?' It is Miss Martin who answers: 'Oh, we had both written a little separately before, my things being often semi-political. And we had seen a curious old house near Cape Clear, belonging to a kinswoman of Miss Somerville's, which suggested a background for a story.' They admitted that they did not publish some of their best stories: 'Our sense of humour and gratitude for hospitality are frequently in conflict.' The interviewer was determined to get some idea of how they wrote together, and recorded Edith's response, ending: 'It's rather amusing that we have *three* separate styles, which have developed themselves unconsciously. There is our joint style, Miss Martin's own style, and mine. It's like blue and yellow which together make green!' The interview, with accompanying photograph, appeared on 1 July, 1895.

A week later the Conservative Women's Unionist Alliance asked them to act as canvassers in the Norwich area during the run-up to the General Election. Edith and Martin crossed to East Anglia for their work in the Braintree and Witham area, returning to Ireland on the 19th – Martin to check in with her mother at Ross and Edith to CT. While they were in East Anglia, Edith wrote to Hildegarde in a fury to complain that Martin's plans were yet again to be interrupted: 'Her filthy sisters want to hunt poor Martin back to Ross and all they want her to do is *arrange a bedroom for Jim's two boys*! As if Nannie, or even Selina couldn't do that – I am in a fury – She would only stay there a few days, but I had hoped she would travel home with me, and you must write and expostulate at being thrown over, for such nonsense! She is so absurdly good and obedient to them that I can hardly rouse her to revolt.'

The news came to CT that Violet Coghill was to train with Dr Jex Blake at the London School of Medicine for Women, a source of great pride to the suffragists of the family. Martin re-appeared in CT on the 27th, on the day that Gibbons of the *Lady's Pictorial* sent the much-needed cheque for 75 guineas for their Danish tour articles. Edith won first in the hunter class with her mare Dodo at the Skibbereen Show, a fine advertisement for the horse-coper. Suddenly there was an abrupt shift to literary work, and the creation of a novel, *The Silver Fox*, that was to be Martin's special effort. On 8 August, recorded in her diary, there was a 'Letter from Mr Williamson asking for a story of 26,000 words,' for initial serialisation in *The Hour*. Though CT was teeming with summer visitors, only four days later the book had been hatched and christened. On 12 August Edith recorded: 'Wrote to Williamson re. "Silver Fox"', and they worked on it when they could. Martin stayed in Drishane until there was a re-arrangement of sleeping berths on 15 August. Cameron had been staying with Hildegarde and Egerton at the Cottage; Martin changed places with him, but moved to Glen B at the end of the month, when Aylmer and Edith were away at the Dublin Horse Show, until 12 September. She then spent a fortnight in Drishane before going back to Ross on the 26th. Great, but unappreciated, care was taken over their novel, of which Martin wrote the major part. Noted in Edith's diary was the fact that Mr Williamson wrote to say that he 'fears the Silver Fox is too good for his public'.

Edith wrote on 10 October to congratulate Hildegarde on being pregnant; she was nervous at the physical trial to come, but Edith assured her: 'You are so big that you are safe to have a good time, it is the little creatures who suffer.'

But her sister did suffer, despite her large physique. The contrast between Edith's sensitivity in private and her coarse gallows humour in familiar company shows a marked determination to put aside her sensitivity in public in favour of the comic: perhaps she had spent too much time with racketty young men in her youth. The same letter to her sister shares her delight at Boyle's engagement. At the end of the month Edith was involved in a brawl in print with Rhoda Broughton who had attacked Edith over her 'ferocious jocosity' on the subject of vivisection in her article on Pasteur in the *Lady's Pictorial*; they came to an understanding in the letters column. One at Ross and one at Drishane, neither Martin nor Edith felt at this time particularly enthused about writing together, and there was in neither of them a great creative urge.

Any work, however desultory, on the *Silver Fox* was halted when suddenly at the beginning of December, at the age of sixty-three, the vigorous Adelaide Somerville was stricken with pleurisy and additional complications that baffled her doctors. This was to be a death that marked Edith much more than that of her father. She had been confrontational with her mother, and had rebelliously refused to be everything that she had wished. For her part her mother had treated Edith very carelessly, not noticing her in her crucial early years, and openly preferring her sons and flirting with them. As the eldest child Edith had been farmed out to Constance Bushe during her mother's subsequent late pregnancies and childbirths. As Edith matured, her mother had become fascinated by her, and in her last agonising hours it was Edith that she wished to have by her. After a dreadful night sleeping in her room with her, Edith sent a man riding hard to fetch Dr Hadden with morphia. Hadden's assistant was a young doctor O'Meara, who came when Hadden could not, and he is mentioned for the first time in a letter to Martin on the next day. While they were waiting for Hadden, Edith sent for Egerton and Uncle Kendal, who both used mesmerism and massage to calm Adelaide. As soon as Hadden came and injected morphia, her breathing became laboured, but by the evening she was breathing shallowly. She was peaceful when she stopped breathing about midnight on 3 December. Edith wrote to Martin: 'Poor Papa is wonderful – so gentle and good and so utterly and entirely heartbroken. It would wring your heart to see him. It was all so sudden – we had about eight hours in which to face it and till the last we hoped. Everyone is more than kind. Keep well, be careful of yourself – Love from Hildegarde – Ever Yours Edith.'

Another letter followed on during the night when Edith could not sleep: 'I can't go to sleep. I have tried but it is no use, so I have lighted my candle and will try to think that I am talking to you … I know you will tell me it is morbid and foolish but most of the things that come back to me are of words and actions that I was sorry for even at the time – and now – … And then I feel as if I have never been a bit demonstrative to her or ever let her know how I felt – except indeed when I was angry or provoked. I know she took pleasure out of us all, but I feel now as if I might so easily have done so much more. That there were so many times when I was snubbing or beastly – I don't say all of this for you to contradict me – but because I must get it out of my heart … How could you ask me to run away down to the Cottage and let Aylmer bear the brunt alone? It wasn't like you and I can't think you wished me to do it. For one thing I should have gone mad there. It has been, up here, incessant arrangements and giving of orders and seeing that things were done and that H didn't do them. Her pluck was quite splendid but yesterday afternoon she broke down (in health I mean) and Egerton and I drove her to bed in my room.' Edith had to be careful to keep her father and sister far enough away from Adelaide's room that they did not hear the sounds of the men taking the coffin up and carrying it down. Hildegarde was five months pregnant with her first child, Paddy. 'As for Egerton I need not tell you of him. He has been everything – so helpful and tender and absolutely unselfish … I can remember that when at about half past eleven, we were taken in to see her for the last time, the two nurses were standing with tears running down their faces, one on each side of the bed, and I can see that young Doctor O'Meara's pitiful face as he held her pulse. I can't believe it now. I can see her stumping up from Glen B to lunch, with her eyes on the ground, planning "I'm an awful planner" she always used to say, …'

Martin had written to Hildegarde on the 5th, sympathetic and prayerful. She was devoutly religious, as well as determined to keep the sisters out of the funeral arrangements: 'make Edith sleep at the Cottage if you can – Don't let her sleep at Drishane for these few days and do my dear – please keep away from the ceremonials of all kinds – stay with Edith out of sight and endure it – there are others to do these things. You have still Egerton – you have Edith and there is that coming life that gave your mother such pleasure to think of …' Adelaide's funeral occasioned an extraordinary demonstration of sympathy from local people, and not only among the Somervilles' own tenants; relays of six men carried her coffin from Drishane to the Castlehaven graveyard. Edith's diary entry records the interesting fact that her mother was keened. 'They keened her. The whole country was there.'[45] The keen was a loud Irish lamentation for the dead, it was unstructured, and at the inspiration of the mourner. The road had been swept clean before the bearers. The Somerville vault in Castlehaven was opened by the coastguard officers and lined with moss and white chrysanthemums. Edith ended her letter 'O, dear Martin, it is a comfort to write to you, but how Hildegarde and I wish you were here. After the two of us, no-one knew her in and out as you do … it is very nearly one o'clock and my candle also is burned out, but I feel better and as if I should go to sleep now – I can hear Miss Dody [Dodo, the mare in hand] kicking like a little fury. I cannot praise Sylvia and Zoe and Grace enough – I could never forget their kindness through it all especially Sylvia – Ever Yours Edith. H is sleeping with me which is why I went to bed without writing to you. She is asleep now.'

Martin had longed to come to Drishane to help. Writing three days later, Edith suggests that Martin might come in about a fortnight 'Till the Chimp is gone and the servants settle down I am afraid I ought not to ask you to come ... Don't think of me as moping, or the like o' that. I have more to do than I ever had in my life, but I am glad to go to sleep when I get into bed. Father Lyons preached a long sermon about mother on the chapel yesterday and "spoke most beautifully" they all say. He ended by saying the prayer for the repose of the Souls of the Dead from their Office. They say all the chapel was crying. It shows their powers of emotional sympathy. Half of them could hardly ever have seen her. I must stop. You think too well of me – Don't say the things you do. They only make me ashamed. Yours ever, Edith.'

Martin had become close to Adelaide. Mrs Martin wrote a letter of condolence to Edith, and remarked: 'To Violet nothing can ever fill the gap to her. No new friendship [can] supply the place of your mother to her.'[46] At Ross, Martin received a sad Christmas gift from Edith: 'the silver buckles that she and I gave to Aunt Adelaide last year.' She finished her diary with a résumé of the family whereabouts, made up her accounts of her income from writing, and on the 31st 'wrote to Edith and EŒS'. Muriel Currey makes an intervention at this point in her transcript: 'D. [Edith] of course had to take over the running of Drishane, but she never makes any reference to household affairs. There must have been an enormous staff of servants in all the houses at Castle T. No cook could ever have known how many people there would be for luncheon or dinner. Everyone just ate or slept where they happened to find themselves.'

Martin returned to Drishane on 4 January to find 'Uncle Henry a good deal changed, the house quite different'. She had been 'met by Edith and Hildegarde, the former looking rather bad, the latter fairly well.' Edith was at hand when her sister went through a difficult childbirth on the 18 March. Her first son Marmaduke Patrick was delivered by young Doctor O'Meara, who took much care over the recovery of the mother, and by late April 1896 Hildegarde was herself again. When Edith tried to arrange with her father for Emmie, Aylmer's wife, to housekeep in her stead while she was away in Paris, she was irritated by his flat refusal. She wrote to Cameron to complain of his soft character and that he 'insists on doing it himself (while Emmie is champion at it!) It is his madness for doing women's work and doddering about the house instead of seeing after the sorely needed things out of doors. Moreover, as Martin says, *anything* that amuses or interests him is to be encouraged, though I fear this amusement will be pursued at Aylmer and Emmie's expense. It is a thousand pities he isn't an old lady: he would give his eyes to be one I know. H and E go to the Cottage in 10 days time.'[47] Later in the year a drunken butler had to be sacked because of his 'insolence to Papa', which was another sign that the Master was losing his grip.

Martin was valuable to Hildegarde in carrying around her baby while she caught up on sleep. Writing to Cameron on 28 March Edith had described him: 'Marmaduke [a name soon discarded in favour of Paddy] improves daily, but is awfully like Egerton, and that is *not* a pretty type for a baby; however he may grow out of it ... my longings turn Paris-wards. It is always the place that sets me firmer on my feet than any other, and would be the most thorough and cheap change that I could get. Kinkie is there and a lot of people that I know and this is the time when the weather is perfect. One grand point about Paris is that any clothes do, and I should have no expense in that matter, which would be inevitable if I went anywhere else.' This is one of the earliest familiar mentions of Alice Kinkead, nicknamed Kinkie, a Galway doctor's daughter, and a painter who later turned silversmith. Because Edith had, as Kinkie believed, saved her life by tending her through a fever in Paris in 1894, Kinkie addressed Edith in her letters as 'Dear Doctor'.

Aunt Georgina (Gig Chavasse) was returning to CT, and it would be the first time that Edith had seen her since her mother's death and burial. In the same letter Edith wrote to Cameron: 'I dread seeing her, she is a sort of caricature of Mother in voice and manner, and even in looks there is a family likeness that makes seeing her horribly painful. It is *too* hard that Mother who of all others would have gloried in this baby [Paddy] and would quite have enjoyed all the fuss, should not be here – there is hardly a day that she is out of one's mind. Hildegarde is very plucky and we don't let her talk, but I can see how it tells on her. Martin must, I grieve to say, go back to her mother very soon – She *says* next week but we might get her to stay a little bit more. I really can't think what we would have done without her had she not been here when the trouble [Paddy's fever] began last week.'

On the 11 April Martin joined her mother in Dublin. Very briefly, she saw Edith on the 20th when she was staying overnight at the Greenes', en route for a stint in Paris with Alice Kinkead for a month at Académie Délécluse. She and her Mother were back at Ross on 16 May. While Martin was at Ross for the summer, Edith tried to arrange for a compatible painting companion to join her in CT after Paris. Her first choice was Constance Bushe, but she was not free: 'I am deeply sorry to say; I have asked Kinkie instead,' she wrote to Cameron on 25 June. Though she had pushed *The Silver Fox* onwards, Martin had spent most of

June inactive, feeling ill with toothache. Edith was not very sympathetic: 'I am so sorry for you that I must write and tell you so. I do hope you will have sense and get that *beastly* tooth out. You will never have comfort until you do.' After two solid pages on horses, and Aylmer going to sell at Bandon Fair, she suggested, 'Do be here then and we will go a-coping again. It is about the third of August'. Edith closes her letter by getting back onto the subject of teeth again: 'Dot is squawking and I must stop to go out. My first and last word is get rid of that tooth. I hate to think of what it has made you suffer. My love to Geraldine [Hewson] Yours Ever -You are the Queen of Pig's Feet – Edith.'[48] 'Pig's Foot', a Buddh word, was 'a term in the Buddh pharmacopeia – the ultimate and more complicated form of any slight accident or ailment – which has been wilfully neglected.'

Edith sold Dodo for £50 to a brother officer of Cameron's. The proofs of *The Silver Fox* were dealt with by post; Edith had left much of the novel to Martin and had not seen a finished ending. On 8 July she wrote in her diary: 'Martin sent the end of "The Silver Fox" which I think is *very* good.' She went to London on the 23rd for a week among the editors, and to get a new habit and a hard hat. While in London she entered a competition to draw a man on a bicycle in forty straight lines sponsored by the Advance Cycle Company. On 1 August, meeting up with Edith en route in Cork, Martin came down to CT to stay in Glen B, moving up to Drishane on the 12th, when at last a fairly peaceful three months ensued. Boyle married and brought his Australian wife to meet her vast tribe of in-laws; Mab was a highly trained and gifted pianist with very striking looks. Boyle had fought off a previous attachment of hers and thrown the previous attachment's engagement ring into Sydney harbour. Under inspection by the tribe, Mab swept all before her. Edith wrote to describe her to Cameron: 'She is a most charming creature, and the more one sees of her the more one likes her – I would give anything for her to be living here, but I suppose it is quite out of the question.' Boyle and Mab were to spend many years in naval quarters, and their children were to know CT only through summer holidays and Boyle's leaves until his retirement from the Navy in 1924.

To her delight, Edith won the competition for the 'Advance' bike, which arrived on 3 October, and gave huge entertainment to the entire village; she accepted the West Cork agency for the firm.[49] During October, the Drishane household was prostrated by colds; Martin, who was back there again, made herself very useful as a nurse and helpmeet to Hildegarde and baby Paddy down in The Cottage. On the 17th Edith wrote to Cameron: 'I am thankful to say Martin is here too, tho' "ye can't tell a day from an hour", as Eliza says, and she may be hauled off at any moment. How deeply do I wish that she were really, as Hildegarde and I call her, the third sister! It makes all the difference in the world having her here – Hildegarde is over her cold ...' In November, Edith took herself off to Paris and shared rooms in the Boulevard Mont Parnasse again with Kinkie: 'a *very* nice girl and it is such a comfort her being Irish, so much more seguashable' (the Buddh word for one 'who gives peaceful and good company'). In a disaster that would affect their literary income, during this month their favourite Mr Williamson's new magazine *The Hour* went bankrupt, and his cheques were dishonoured.

Martin left for Ross on 11 December, travelling as far as Dublin with Edith who was going up to visit the Greenes. Edith attended a musical evening at which her cousin Harry Plunket Greene sang, and among the audience were many CT familiars, described in a letter to Martin. Madame de Bunsen came up to Edith, very taken with her black and white velveteen blouse: '"May I ask Paris or London?" I said "Skibbereen". "Ah, alors, c'est le façon de le mettre!" It was highly gratifying.' To the intense relief of his family, Cameron passed his exams, and gained promotion to senior Captain. He was posted to Malta for September, and arranged home leave for Christmas. Boyle planned to come over from London to CT for a week on 2 January. On behalf of his wife, Edith objected: 'I think it is a pity and I don't like his robbing poor Mab of a week when he only has six left ...' Boyle had completed seven years' hydrographic surveying in Australia and the Western Pacific, and was about to begin nine years service in HMS *Egeria* in the Eastern Pacific.

Martin was with her family for Christmas, and was not to leave Ross until 13 March. In Galway at the New Year Martin spent time with the Morrises at Spiddal again and came across Yeats through her connection with Lady Gregory. Though she was apparently living in the wilds, Martin was able to send Edith hot news about London and the *Savoy* magazine, and a description of Yeats in poverty and aesthetic dress: 'He is thinner than a lath – wears paltry little clothes wisped around his bones, and the prodigious and affected greenish tie. He is a *little* affected and knows it – He has a sense of humour and is a gentleman – hardly by birth I fancy – but by genius. Arthur Symons, who was here with him, was not much liked I think – just a smart little practical man of letters, who knows how, and has no genius at all. Bad luck to him, he has written an account of Aran in this last number of the *Savoy* not badly at all – very culturedly – it is not illustrated, fortunately, and this is the very last number of the *Savoy*. It is a failure, and has ceased. There are one or two awfully good pictures by Aubrey B. in it – Yeats is writing a strange and mystic novel about the southernmost Island of Aran ...'[50] Edith was to have dealings with Symons many years later, when he was no more likeable.

Some idea of the demands on Edith's time made by being Mistress of Drishane is given by a letter of 13 January 1897. It begins: 'It seems ages since I wrote to you, but I don't know if such is the case.' Edith was sending some drafts to Martin and also trying to organise another trip to Aran, possibly in May or June, with Kinkie and her sister. She was also suffering from gout, which immobilised her. In CT, whenever a female relative might need painkillers or help during the night, as a matter of course beds were moved, as in: 'Hildegarde slept with me thinking the gout would play on me' or when the pregnant Hildegarde moved into Edith's room for the comfort of her company during the days between their mother's death and burial.[51] To distract themselves from the foul weather the sisters and Aylmer took to learning Irish at classes with a Mrs Ward, and later with Carrie Townshend. Edith's letters to Cameron of this period have sections written in careful Irish hand.[52] They used the three volumes of the series of Irish Books issued by the Society for the Preservation of the Irish Language, and O'Growney's primers. A survivor from the period of enthusiasm for Irish was the volume *The Youthful Exploits of Fion*, published in 1896. The difficulty of the language, particularly in its pronunciation, defeated this enthusiasm in time. The early part of this year has many diary entries mentioning that Edith was packing violets for Hildegarde; she had some for sale, and found the climate was mild enough for them to flower all winter through. They were such a success with florists that she decided to expand the area under cultivation.

There was an important entry on 31 January in Edith's diary: 'Heard from Pinker. The Badminton [*Magazine*] is giving us £18 for the "Grand Filly" and wants us to do a serial for them. Wrote to Martin at great length.' This lost letter would have been of great interest, as it must have laid out the groundwork for what was to become the RM series. *The Silver Fox* had begun publication in serial form on 3 February. It was being set as a single volume by Lawrence and Bullen when Edith went to London in April 1897, carrying the article then simply called 'Aran' with her. Pinker took the article to place it for them, Edith suggesting *Black and White*. In this hunting season, Edith became an acting MFH when Aylmer was away. Her letter book as MFH shows how alert all local people were to the red fox as a pest to the farming community, a danger to domestic fowl and young animals. It was also at that time the main carrier of rabies in Europe, transmitting it to the dog population. A rabid dog had run through the village, biting a child; but although Hildegarde immediately ran up and sucked the wound clean, the child eventually died. Later in the year dumb rabies was to strike the West Carbery pack. Martin came down from Ross on 13 March 1897 to work: 'Martin comes tomorrow and then Work begins and the deer knows (as Jack says) when it will end – so don't expect many letters from me', she wrote to Cameron. For light relief from work, Martin joined the Irish classes: 'Aylmer has finally abandoned the Irish classes and Martin works in his stead, she makes an awfully good fist of it.'

In the offices of Lawrence and Bullen Edith had an eventful meeting with Mr Bullen, Hedley Peek his partner, and Pinker. It was to give a new direction to their career. Parts of *The Silver Fox* had struck Mr Bullen and his partners as ripe for development by the authors. Here was formulated the idea of a series of comic stories around a cast of characters. 'Then they all – including little Pinker – swore we had got hold of a very good thing in this serio-comic hunting business – "To use literary slang" – said Pinker – "this is *your own stuff* and no-one else does anything like it".' How long and hard Pinker was going to have to harry them before he saw any such stories was mercifully hidden from the optimistic Lawrence and Bullen. Closing her letter from London of 25 April, Edith wrote to Martin: 'The end of it all is – my Lady Anne, that you must come back to Drishane or else meet me in a desert place as soon as possible, get your insides tidied up by Willy S. [Stoker], and buckle to. Some other Irish devil who can hunt and write will rise up and knock the wind out of our sails, and we can't afford to be jockeyed like that. *The Silver Fox* money will make us fairly independent – of course you take the usual proportion 3/5ths wasn't it? and that ought to give you a good lift and you need be in no hurry to pay me that loan until Christmas ... The Bad Mag [Badminton Magazine] ... has wafted us to glory – It has a great and searching circulation, touching people that read nothing else ... I have no time to do more now than say your letter interested me, I hope you will get the physic safely – Yrs ever Edith.'[53]

Pinker had hammered home the going rate of a pound a page and his thoughts about book rights for the series in a letter on 7 March, but family concerns soon put all Pinker's plans out of their minds. Writing with Martin was not top priority for Edith: with all its complications Drishane was, for the same letter has the mournful complaint: 'I don't look forward to going home. I suppose it would be too selfish for you and me to hike off somewhere to work and peace. It *would* be too selfish – say no more and let us shut our eyes to the "vision splendid".' This is good evidence: a flat statement that shows that their writing work was done in the time that was left over to them after their duty to their families was done first. Some of the difficulties at Drishane were caused by the construction of a new septic tank, as the disgusting old one had been partly under the house: 'It seems we have been living on a typhoid breeding morass', she wrote to Cameron, sending with her letter a diagram showing the new route of the drain away from the house and its termination.[54] On Cameron's last leave, he and Edith had constructed a magnificent star-shaped flower-bed: 'Aylmer only just found out in time that Papa and the plumber had agreeably arranged to have the cesspool *under our star bed*! a thing that had cost us tears of blood in the laying out and that was already full of growing lilies, etc.! etc.!' From mid-March as well all hands available had been working with Hildegarde in the planting up of her violet farm; a whole field was planted and all the violets were rooted and healthy in the spring. In May Edith wrote to Cameron in a state of exhaustion: '*Res angusta domi* has been heavy on me of late and it is almost impossible to isolate one's mind, even though one's body may be safe in the Lout Hole [Studio].' The quotation from Juvenal was one she had picked up from Herbert; meaning 'the trials of family life', and she was to use it quite often.

There is a diary reference on 30 May to a Women's Suffrage meeting in Skibbereen, convened by Hildegarde. The women gathered there agreed on a campaign of letter-writing to MPs sympathetic to the suffrage cause. Any long stretch of serious novel writing for the authors seemed to be out of the question. The summer did not improve in that respect. In July, Edith and Aylmer disappeared to Cahirmee Horse Fair, prospecting. While Edith was away Martin had collected together a series of old stories for Pinker, who was going to try and sell a volume of them to a publisher. This was the origin of *Some Irish Yesterdays*, not to appear until 1906. On the 27th July Edith went to London and then, a great indulgence, on to art classes at Midhurst with P.H. Calderon, RA, the distinguished animal-painter. She came back to CT on 10 August, had to move out of Drishane, as it had been let, and moved in with the Warrens of the Coastguard Station for a fortnight. Martin went to Ross. It is unlikely that Pinker ever fully realised the extremely haphazard and fractured nature of the working partnership in temporal terms, but his optimism at selling a series on the back of 'A Grand Filly' was to be sorely tested.

Later in August another wandering hydrophobic dog infected the old foxhound Countess with dumb rabies. She carried it into the kennels and the whole West Carbery pack had to be shot, on 22 August. This was an act that was carried out with great bravery by the kennel huntsman and whip Tim Crowley.[55] The infected hounds had become restless and a marksman could not take sure aim, so Crowley trusted that they would not attack him and went in with a revolver, taking them each by the scruff of the neck and killing them cleanly. Edith wrote to Martin while he was doing this: 'You are right not to want to keep dogs. Countess has had to be shot, with dumb rabies, and every hound must go too. Poor Aylmer met me on my way back from Church with a white face – I couldn't think what was wrong, and then he told me ...' Dr O'Meara had rushed over from Skibbereen to confirm the diagnosis by examining the first hound to be infected, Countess, and then he condemned the pack: 'they are all in the top of condition – hard muscle, and fit for anything , and they must all be shot – One can't think of it even ... If it had been at any other time of year, before the young entry were in, or while the mothers were out – but it isn't – The benches even must be burned – They never were so fit or such a good lot as they are now – It is just heart-breaking,' Edith wrote to

Martin. 'I have no heart to write to you – It is so sudden and so smashing a calamity.' Since 1891, Aylmer Somerville had bred and worked the West Carbery pack to a state of perfection. The quick sympathy and help that came to him instantly from his fellow Masters of Foxhounds meant that very soon replacement drafts came from English and Irish Hunts. By the end of September, new kennels had been built, on a site given by Edith's father, and thirty couple were housed in them. Martin came back to CT, and the new pack, from Ross on 8 October.

In November reviews of *The Silver Fox* started to appear. This novel, ranked very highly by Arnold Bennett, has for long been completely forgotten, but, like Mr Williamson its begetter, the reviewers of 1897 acknowledged its quality. Bennett wrote:

> *The Silver Fox*, by Somerville and Ross, is within its limits, a perfect novel. The style exhibits a meticulous care not surpassed by that of Henry James. It actually repays a technical analysis. It is as carefully worded as good verse. There is a reason for every comma, and the place of every preposition and conjunction. All prose which pretends to be artistic should be as meticulous as this. Yet in fact the quality is almost unknown. Except in Henry James and Pater, I know of no modern prose of which it can be said that the choice and position of every word and stop has been the subject of separate consideration.

In the *Spectator* of 13 November the reviewer wrote that it was: 'brilliantly written ... the story is remarkable for the impartiality of the authors, for their true instinct in the selection and contrivance of incident, and for the self-restraint which has enabled them to condense within the compass of less than a couple of hundred pages materials for a story twice that length.' The *Daily Chronicle* of 10 December gives some choice quotes, then continues: 'but we cannot do justice to this book by quotation. Its method and its writing are so good that they tempt us to say its authors have nothing to learn from the French novelists ...'

Though it is short, *The Silver Fox* contains some of the duo's most controlled and powerful writing. In it they play their usual game of placing sections on English high life up against Irish country life, English sophisticates against Irish countryfolk, and intellectuals against bluff hunting people. Their creation of Lady Susan French, unsympathetic though she be, captures the reader's attention from start to finish. The Irish heroine, Slaney Morris, dislikes the English set in which she finds herself at Hurlingham on visiting her cousin Hugh, who has married Lady Susan. She watches some of them skating from a distance through a window:

they seemed to Slaney over-dressed and artificial. No doubt they were screaming inanities to each other, as were these other English idiots in the room behind her. How ineffably stupid they were, and how shy and provincial they made her feel! How could Hugh have married into such a pack?

[Hugh brings his wife and friends to his home in Ireland; they all go to visit Slaney]

As she [Slaney] came into the lamplit hall to greet her visitors, Lady Susan and Major Bunbury realised in their different ways that she was better looking than they had believed. Her dark hair rose full and soft from her white forehead, in the simplicity that is often extolled, but is seldom becoming; her complexion was pale and tender with western air and country living, the refinement that was so ineffective at Hurlingham was here pervading and subtle. Lady Susan looked hard at her, and promoted her at once and ungrudgingly from the ranks of non-combatants ...

Edith and Martin used each other as models; the description of a woman like Slaney gives us their idea of what attractiveness is in a gentlewoman. We can see from photographs that in the 1890s neither of them, yet, were in appearance what Lady Susan so helpfully classifies as 'non-combatants' in the sex war.[56] In Edith and Martin's world, non-combatants understood their place in the world and behaved accordingly. Pie Fox, a cousin of Mrs Martin, was a very plain woman, like Fanny Currey and Emily Herbert. Pie led her own life, and had an enchanting sense of humour. Once, when she was walking home after dark in Dublin, an amorous drunk attached himself to her hopefully. Pie said firmly, 'My good man. Take me to a lamp post.' In The Silver Fox, and later in Dan Russel the Fox, we find the non-combatant contingent of womanhood carefully included under sympathetic observation, particularly those unmarried sisters who merged into their married brother's or sister's households, effectively in the position of an upper servant. There is a brilliant scene in Dan Russel the Fox where Mrs Delanty enters her kitchen wet and tired after hunting. Here she is relieved of wet garments and given hot tea by a sympathetic and servant-like being who is only identified as her elder, plain and unmarried sister, Janetta Scanlan, in a muffled aside at the end of the paragraph. Such was the authors' love of their families, and readiness to be of service to them, that they do not seem to have apprehended that by the time of their arrival at middle age they themselves had slipped from one classification to the other.

The novel The Silver Fox features a railway engineer, Wilfred Glasgow, with an omnivorous appetite for women of a breadth demonstrated by his falling for

Slaney and for Lady Susan. He is a convincing portrayal of a womaniser, playing the field while in secret having a wife. He brings about the fateful workings of the plot by driving his railway line through an old rath and felling a hawthorn tree held sacred in the neighbourhood. Somerville and Ross's men are not all hopeless cases; the type of whom they approve is not flashy, has easy manners and a subtle sense of humour. The man who will marry Slaney is singled out early on by his reaction to Lady Susan after she has ranted about the eccentricities of Irish hunting, the last straw for her being provided by an energetic cow who had grown emulous and joined the tail of the hunt. Putting a stop to her criticisms which he realised were annoying Slaney, Major Bunbury chips in sharply with 'She was a clinkin'good jumper.'

In December, dental matters dominate the diary again. Edith, who had had many of her teeth removed as they rotted at the root after turning black when the nerves were removed, was brought low by an infection in her lower jaw that completely incapacitated her. She must have been extremely ill as she lost stones in weight and became bony. She stopped writing her diary. Martin tended the invalid; she was at Drishane for Christmas, a rare event. In closing her diary for 1897 she made her accounts, placed the scattered members of the Martin family, and ended: 'EŒS and I working at hunting story.' This was the prototype of the RM. In January 1898 all of Edith's lower teeth were removed, and as we see from photographs after this date her lower jaw came forward with an unfortunate effect on her appearance if she did not consciously arrange her facial muscles. For two months before Christmas, she had become increasingly ill with what was in effect poisoning. She was in no condition to repel boarders when Herbert Greene made a point of renewing his proposal of marriage at Christmastime. In a deep depression caused by her illness, Edith did not respond to his proposal with the usual negative. Believing that at last his object had been achieved, Herbert told his mother, Edith's Aunt Sylvia, that they were to marry. Sylvia told her sister Georgina the good news and she wrote to Edith to congratulate her:

> Dearest Edith
> although you have not written to announce the fact – yet having been told it 'on the best authority' I must send you a line of hearty congratulations on your engagement to be married. You were very clever to keep your secret so well, but now as it is out of the bag I suppose there is no use in trying to capture the feline again. I hope you will have a very happy future in store for you. I hope that the changed state will not bring art and literature to an end. Hildegarde will find it hard which to rejoice or bemoan, as she will wish to share in your happiness and yet CT will be a very different place to her without you ... ever your loving Aunt Gig.[57]

This period in Edith's diary was left blank and filled later from Martin's diary. Somehow Edith extricated herself from this awkward situation with Herbert and her Aunts. The episode was overlaid by more pressing events. Boyle's wife Mab, with her first son, came to CT at this unfortunate time. Martin described to Cameron her 'arrival last night with her enormous, glowing, determined, muscular baby … he [Raymond] arrived here rampant and Mab like a boiled rag. She is a very pleasant fact in a house – always nice to look at – always exuding amiability and nice music – Boyle is to be envied, I think …'[58] Their baby son Raymond was now the Drishane heir.

Edith had to manage Drishane inside and out. Her father had quietly lost his grip on life after Adelaide's death. When Henry Somerville died on 17 March 1898, Martin's reaction shows how very reserved she still was about intruding on the close Somerville family. Martin had been telegraphed the news. She had herself been called away from Drishane on 18 February to help her sister Edith Dawson, who had fallen ill at Ross. She wrote to the Somerville sisters instantly; to Hildegarde she wrote: 'I should give anything to be with Edith and you and feel miserable at having gone away before all this terrible stress fell upon you both. It is a comfort to think of Egerton, and all that he is in trouble. But who can fend off the pressure and the dreadfulness of these days – so much to do and all of it miserable. Thank goodness you are better able to bear it than when your mother died … I wish Edith had thought it better for me to come today – but she knows best. Perhaps Ethel has come – at all events you and Edith have each other to look to and that is a great deal – but it is wretched to sit here and think …' Edith's communications with Martin were at this point telegraphic. She had to write to her brothers, and her grief was fully expressed to Boyle and Cameron. Martin's diary entry simply reads: 'Hear from EŒS and Hildegarde. The latter wants me to go to her – accepted – sent notice of Uncle Henry to *Irish Times*.'

So, though Edith did not ask her to come down from Ross, Hildegarde did, asking for Martin to join her at Glen B. This is one of those clear instances showing that at certain stages of black depression Edith was best left alone, and both Hildegarde and Martin respected the fact that there was no talking her out of it. On the 19th Martin wrote to Hildegarde: 'You are very good – I feel it very much that you should have me at such a time. It gives me a feeling of being truly bound up in your affairs – for good or evil – and I don't want a more comforting thought than that just now – Of course I will come. It is what I have been longing to do, but I do not like the thought of giving you trouble – Thank you awfully for what you said about lending me money – but I am allright about that …' Some time was allowed to lapse before she joined Hildegarde; Martin arrived at Glen B on 1 April.

Now that both her parents were dead, Edith constructed an icon that hung at the head of her bed for the rest of her life. She hung studio portraits of Henry and Adelaide together with the ebony and silver crucifix she had brought back from France; a portrait of Martin eventually joined them.[59] In her memorialising instincts Edith was not the average Church of Ireland Christian. Where she acquired the reverential religious habit of kissing the relics of the dead, as she kissed her grandfather's locket of hair and later Martin's Claddagh ring, it is not possible to say with any certainty. If it was acquired in her childhood, then she was emulating, and keeping company with, Catholic servants far more than her parents or grandparents realised. They had been concerned that the small Edith was spending so much time with the servants and stable boys that she would talk in a brogue, and vetoed it, but the child was very observant, attentive to differences and retentive in memory.[60]

On 18 April Edith had a letter from Cameron, now Master of Drishane: 'he wishes the status quo ante to be preserved,' she told Hildegarde. There was a difficulty for Cameron in dealing with his younger brothers; a later letter between the sisters shows that he tried to dominate them in an annoying way.[61] In the place of acting 'woman of the house' he seemed to prefer to rely on his elder sister, rather than Emmie, the wife of Aylmer. This was quite contrary to the usual order of precedence: married women ranked over the single, regardless of their age and experience. The problem of who was to housekeep at Drishane was quite crucial, but it was at this point shelved while those most closely affected attended to their failing health. On 12 May Edith and Martin got away, via Cork and the dentist where: 'E got new flashers in'.[62] With a new smile Edith went on to join the Coghills in Aix-les-Bains, nicknamed 'Aches and Pains', for a cure in the waters, while Martin went to her sister-in-law Amy Martin's new house Paveys, in Langton Green. Edith wrote to her here on 12 June: 'heard from EŒS who has settled to start from Paris tomorrow night and meet me at Étaples Wednesday afternoon.'

Both writers had been in poor physical condition at the beginning of 1898, Edith much the worse of the two. But it was not until 16 June that they took anything that could be described as a rest cure. Martin apparently had complications from thyroid and anaemia hanging over her. Apart from her recent jaw abscesses, Edith suffered a common complaint among women who had ridden sidesaddle for decades: failure of circulation in the right leg that was crooked up on the crutches of the sidesaddle, leading to varicose veins and gout. By the late 1890s she was suffering periods of crippling pain. Martin wrote a series of secret letters from Étaples giving a health progress report to Hildegarde back in Glen B. A letter to Hildegarde shows that Edith quickly caught on to this: 'Keep Martin's note for me to read. She wont show it to me. I believe it is compact of lies.' She thanked Hildegarde for giving her the chance to take the break: 'The extraordinary freedom from all earthly care, what I shall eat, and what raiment I shall put on, and *no* visits, and *no* afternoon tea parties has done more for me than even the good food – I wake wondering what *must* I do today, and then a wondrous tranquillizing consciousness of entire irresponsibility flows like balm over me. I am getting strong hand over fist and several people have said how much better I look – I think I am also putting on flesh. Martin is also thriving here. Her wretched neuralgic ears have, so she says, healed in the most marvellous way, instead of booming and aching and singing all the time she now never feels them and has only had one bilious attack in three weeks instead of 2 in every 3 days. We have not tried any joint writing as Dr Rendell has strictly forbade it, but she is writing (at her usual snail's gallop) at an article... Is Eddy [Aylmer] in the place? Give him my love if he is.'[63]

There were lots of Edith's fellow pupils from Académie Délécluse in Étaples. Edith was out walking and painting as soon as they arrived. Her passion for red hair was unabated. Martin wrote: 'she is out at it all day, [painting] with hideous little red haired children ... she *would* walk and overtire herself and I did not know enough to stop her ...' In the previous November, Martin had been alarmed by the physical strain involved when Edith was breaking the young horse Cara Dil: 'I am sure that the absence of housekeeping and brothers is excellent for E. now ... I hope Crowley [kennel-huntsman] is reducing Cara Dil to order, as if E got a fall and hurt herself it might be very serious. The rheumatic gout would fasten on the joint nearest and she might lose the use of it for ever ... Ethel [Penrose] also has written saying that Dr Rendell spoke very seriously to her about E saying that her constitution was broken down and she must avoid *all* fatigue of mind and body – I think this life is just the thing for her at present ...' They were to be joined by friends from the Paris studios: 'Kinkie and Miss Deane ["The Dean" of Edith's letters] are to be here very soon. Then indeed the cycle of Irish brogues will be complete'. Her last remark is a clear acknowledgement of the different regional intonations of Anglo-Irish speech – the four of them representing Ulster, Munster, Connacht and Leinster in their voices. The group at Étaples was described as 'a pleasingly Irish-American gang' by Edith as they were joined by the Americans Helen Simpson and Anna Richardson.[64]

But there was to be no real lasting peace. At Étaples on 16 June Edith got a cross letter from Pinker. It had been a long year and more that he had been waiting. She entered in her diary 'Heard from Pinker again. He said that Watson of the Bad. Mag. is shrieking for hunting stories.' Then a wet day arrived, so wet that they all stayed indoors, and in free conversation – enlarging upon the ideas they had talked over in December – Martin and Edith talked into being the cast of the RM stories. Then the weather changed again: 'we sat out on the sand hills, roasting in the great sunshine of Northern France, and talked, until we had talked Major Sinclair Yeates, RM, and Flurry Knox into existence. 'Great Uncle McCarthy's' ghost and the adventure of the stolen foxes followed, as it were, of necessity. It has always seemed to us that character presupposes incident. The first thing needful is to know your man...'[65] They began to write up the stories before returning to Drishane. They sent the first story to Pinker on 29 July. Muriel Currey exclaims at this point in her diary transcript: 'It must be remembered that except for "a scrap of work in the morning", the whole day was spent picnicking and sketching in the country with the "Irish party."' They crossed back on 11 September.

An important letter of 1 July survives from Martin in France sent to Cameron in Japan. Cameron had evidently written to Martin about the future of Drishane. It is oil for troubled waters:

> I well understand what you feel about Drishane and Edith – I should feel it, in your place – and of course her one wish is to do what you want – Throughout she has been ready to either efface herself or take up the reins – and Emmie and Aylmer are also only anxious to do what you and she prefer ... It is a wonderful thing to see so many people so anxious to do what is best for everyone – and one does not see it too often. It is very good of you to say what you did about my staying at Drishane – and to put it that way – I feel it very much – more than I can say – it makes me think of so much that Drishane has been to me – and how more than kind you have all been. I often wonder how it was that you all conspired to make my life happier than it ever was, but so it has been and I hope we shall all be together there yet ...

With the continual travelling about it was an achievement for Edith and Martin to be together in one workplace for as much as a month; this was a dreadful drawback telling against the production of manuscripts in one smooth flow from beginning to end. As soon as they got back to Drishane, Hildegarde was able to take her family off to Weymouth, she herself having become ill in the meantime. She could not eat and slept very little. Martin wrote to her in Weymouth, urging her to search for appetising food for herself: 'An empty sack will not stand, as Nurse Davin said.'[66] In her childhood, Martin had spent so much time in the care of her 'Nurses' that she retained a large store of their admonitions and often used them. She had not stayed long at Drishane before flying off again; she described her gaddings about to Hildegarde in an undated letter: 'I went up to Dublin for two days to see Jim [her brother] before he went back to Ceylon, and saw at the same time masses of my family. Mama and I stayed at Emily Barton's and out at Alma Brook's were billetted Jim, Edith, Cuthbert, Connie and Barbara. My journey down here was marked by an incident which will not do for reading aloud to Egerton.' [An old woman had peacefully urinated in her corner seat of the carriage, a pool spreading on the floor, then got out at Mallow. A gentleman then rushed in and sat in her place. He kept his face straight all the way to Cork, and so did the other two occupants of the carriage.] 'Emmie housekeeps away and does it very well, and Edith has all she can do in looking after the violets and the outside things, and doing the writing for the B[adminton] M[agazine]. We did a record day's work to get off the last instalment – working for eight hours with only pauses for meals. It was bad for Edith, and we must not let it happen again ...' The Bushe telegraph was a very speedy conductor of news. As the RM, in the episode called 'Great Uncle McCarthy', made his first appearance in public, Robert Martin reported back to his sister the reaction from his Clubs, before Robert had realised that Edith and Martin were actually the authors. Martin explained to Hildegarde: 'Sir William Russell [war correspondent of *The Times*] at the Garrick said to Robert, "The best thing I have read in years about Ireland is an article in the *Badminton* about an Irish R.M. You ought to read it." The provoking thing was that Robert did not know for some days afterwards that E & I were the authors so he could not blow our trumpet ... Paddy has just gone past in his pram. I am afraid his Aunt Dee and his cousin Martin have not much time to play with him. Perhaps he will value their attention all the more – Love to Egerton and all – I hope you will be soon back ...'

Hildegarde became pregnant again on her rest cure, and very depressed in consequence. Edith tried to cheer her up: 'think of Paddy's excitement ... it will just make his life twice as happy, and make him a child, instead of growing up into an old-fashioned imp ... I really can't help congratulating you ... a second edition of Paddy will be very eagerly welcomed ... I am sure Mother knows and is as delighted as she was before ...' [67] The Somerville brothers and sisters were trying to come to an agreement over the best way to keep Drishane running as a household after their parents' deaths, and she added: 'I have just written a jobation to the Chimp on the accursed subject, and hope he will accede to Emmie's wishes – *Nothing* should I loathe so much as going in harness again.' 'Jobation' was a Buddh word meaning 'A premeditated reproof of unusual length and severity, to which the prudent will not attempt a reply.' Contrary to Sir Patrick's later opinion that Edith could think of nothing more splendid than to be 'Miss Somerville of Drishane', it should be noticed here that what she did for Cameron in keeping up Drishane was the taking on of a loathsome 'harness'. This is a very good example of the way in which she over-ruled her own feelings to please her male relatives throughout her entire life, wishing to show them generosity.

In the stables Edith was training up her hunter Cara Dil. Some of her horses became so attached to her that they seemed to behave as affectionately towards her as dogs; describing Cara Dil to Hildegarde, Edith explained: 'she has the most winning ways in the stable and would lick me all over if I let her'. This was akin to being elected an honorary horse, and is one of the pieces of evidence that best shows Edith's empathy with animals, like that of the best vets. She was called 'the Mother of the animals' at Drishane, though she did, less frequently, nurse humans successfully. Her horse-coping was at this stage more remunerative than writing. 'Great Uncle McCarthy' was the first item of the October 1898 issue of the *Badminton Magazine*. On 13 October Pinker paid £18 4s. 6d. for this first RM story. The authors earned less than ten pounds apiece; Edith could sell a trained horse for £100, and could have brought-on three a year. For her, writing was not so remunerative, but it was Martin's only means of earning a living. At last they seemed to have struck the right note with the reading public, and Pinker was delighted.

But fate struck too. Between the publication of No. I and Nos. II and III, Martin had a disastrous fall when out hunting on 1 November. Edith, who had been riding just behind Martin, entered in her diary: 'Martin rode Dervish at a fixed pole into the seven acre field; he took it with his knees and fell right over it, pitching Martin in the mud and apparently falling on her. Mr Purdon [RM] and I picked her up. Thought her dead. When recovered found her shoulder bruised but no bones broken, and only a few small cuts on her face.' Muriel Currey comments here: 'My mother [Martin's sister Katie] always said that she ought never to have hunted because she was so short sighted that she could not see what she was riding at ... It became obvious that she had damaged her back very severely. My own impression is that she never recovered from this fall.'

At first, Edith was unconcerned over the accident. Her letter to Hildegarde written on the same day, at 4.45 when they were back in Drishane, was quite laconic, describing the fall as a 'wonderful escape ... she was just at Morgans [Bunalun House] so everything was handy. Luckily there was six inches of mud where she fell which saved her ...' But Edith was wrong, it was not a 'wonderful escape'. In the weeks that followed Martin could not walk without excruciating pain, and spent weeks prostrate with low spirits. She had to be drugged to sleep, and at the worst times Edith slept on a couch in Martin's room, to refuel her with painkillers during the night. It was her first calamity on horseback and it broke her nerve. Though she made herself quite soon get on a horse and ride sedately, she did not hunt again until 1909. Most catastrophic of all, she was even less fit for concentrated writing work.

This put Edith into a terrible predicament, for they were bound to the production of the series of stories, twelve of them in monthly instalments; but by exhaustive efforts they kept them coming: 'Trinket's Colt', RM story No. II, appeared in November, and III, 'In the Curranahilty Country', in December. After Martin's fall, they had most difficulty with writing 'The Waters of Strife' in the second half of November. The worst was over for Martin then, but the series was completed only by a wholesale cannibalising of the letters between Edith and Martin from 1886. From the first long funny story that Martin had sent to her in 1887 when she was in Paris, about a large harrier at Ross, Edith had marked them with notes like 'save this story' to try to ensure that it came back to her if it went on circuit around the family. Martin herself had written at the end of that tale 'the whole thing makes quite a nice little story.' Soon it became a sport in the family to identify models, and the origins of plots. They were alarmingly careless about modelling characters on recognisable personalities.[68] In his letter criticising *The Real Charlotte*, Jack refers to the fictitious 'Charlotte' as Emily (Herbert), and mentions not the fictitious Julia Duffy, but instead their Aunt Fanny: 'The death of Aunt Fanny was about as vivid a thing as I have ever read.'[69] The character model who caused most controversy was to be Flurry Knox. Maurice Healy was to give a detailed account of what he thought was his original, Hugh Irvine of Roscarbery, in *The Old Munster Circuit*.[70]

Martin was at Drishane for the Christmas of 1898. She made a long entry to close her diary: 'Started the year '99 at Drishane with a bad back, the consequence of Dervish falling on me out hunting on November 1st. H and E also there. Emmie and kids at York – Mama, Edith, Selina and Cuthbert at Ross and well. Geraldine and Co at Gowran. Katie and Co at Newcastle. Robert in London. EŒS and I working at a series of sporting stories in the Bad Mag of wh 3 have already appeared.' She had to be carried up and down stairs; her headaches prevented her from working for any length of time. On 10 February she wrote in her diary: 'We decided to break up *A Man of the People* [an unpublished novel] and use the pieces for the Bad Mag.' Some of it ended up in *An Enthusiast* (1921). Parts of the manuscript of the unpublished novel are now at QUB and TCD; it has an unusually graphic record of a disagreement between the authors. Over the sentence 'His smile had a quality that made it hard for any woman to look at him unsympathetically' is scrawled in capitals 'PUKE'.[71] It is most likely that the critic is Martin. Towards the end of the month she began to walk about more comfortably. Nothing of any particular note except packing violets and writing the RM happened until 18 March, when Egerton's Twin and painting companion, Herbert Baxter, suddenly collapsed and died of heart failure. Martin wrote in her diary that he 'died in about an hour and a half. The nurse, the doctor and Egerton were there and did everything that could be done, but he could not be saved. Edith and I went down to the Cottage in the afternoon. Egerton very much cut up.' Although Baxter's family turned up for the funeral and arranged his affairs, he, too, like Martin when her time came, had become so much a part of CT as an adopted relative that he was buried in it, and not taken back to his family burial ground.

In June both Edith and Martin went to cousin Gendie at Thornbury Park, and from there to London where a specialist examined Edith's crippled leg and recommended a cure at Aix. They both went to Ross on 24 June and wrote there at RM story No. XI, 'Occasional Licenses', which gave them immense trouble. The long haul 'desperately at work' on the story was over in essence at the beginning of August 1899, when Edith went to Ethel and Jim at Lismore, then on to Dublin and the Horse Show. At Ross, Martin still worried away at polishing the story; she wrote to Edith, who was immersed in organising a dance, about a problem with her mother, who had annexed a piece of material that Martin had given as a Christmas gift to the Ross servant Bridget: 'it was yielded, with I may say, bitter disgruntlement on Mama's part. This transpired this morning. It is very typical of all things here. We are but poor namby-pamby people after all. I am so glad I was not at that dance as you were short of men. This sounds like the most degraded shyness that is really only the deep conscious-ness of superfluity. I am working at XI – badly – I am very stupid and not the least clever, except at mending blinds and dusting the front hall and writing cold boiled ...'[incomplete].[72]

At the end of August Martin made a throwaway flippant remark in a letter to Edith about the laborious writing of 'Occasional Licences', No. XI of the RM series, making a joke about the Ladies of Llangollen, whose house they had visited on their Welsh tour in 1891. In *Beggars on Horseback* they had boggled at what they considered to be the 'grotesque romance' of the two Irish ladies who had left their family homes for rural bliss *à deux* in the depths of North Wales. This had seemed to them quite inexplicable behaviour, and seriously anti-social. They had stuck in Martin's mind with negative connotations. She was never seriously concerned about the quality of their light-hearted joint work, knowing that if one made a slip the other would mend it: 'I hae ma doots when you say that you find No. XI very good – however I daresay you will pull it together – I never could tell the wearisome grind of those blessed hags of Llangollen.' Staying with the Morrises at Spiddal, Martin rode a pony at Cloghreva; riding up from the lake back to the house was for her the 'first time in a saddle since my fall'. It had been ten months since her accident. She went with Maud Morris to stay at Lissadell as a guest of Lady Gore-Booth. Both authors were in a poor way; Edith had become lame and had to go abroad for treatment. On 1 September Martin wrote in her diary: 'Heard from ECES who is on her way to Aix.' On the 28th Martin went to Paris to join up with Edith for a long break away from Martin family cares.

The twelve stories for the RM series were collected together and published in one volume by Longmans as *Some Experiences of an Irish RM* in November 1899. Not every reader fell under their spell. An Irish reviewer took them in a very serious spirit:

> The picture they give of Irish life is ... so depressingly squalid and hopeless ...The food is appallingly bad, and the cooking and service, if possible, worse. No one in the book, high or low, does a stroke of work, unless shady horse-selling and keeping dirty public houses can be said to be doing work ... On the whole the horses and hounds are far more important than the human beings, and the stable and kennels are only a degree less dilapidated and disgusting than the houses. Not a trace of romance, seriousness or tenderness, disturbs the uniform tone of the book.
>
> Such is the picture of our country given, I believe, by two Irish ladies ... A more unfeminine book I have never perused, or one more devoid of any sentiment of refinement, for even men who write horsey novels preserve some tinge of romance in their feelings towards women which these ladies are devoid of. A complete hardness pervades their treatment of the female as of the male characters.[73]

Muriel Currey in her commentary on her transcript of Edith's diary makes an important point on the completion of the first twelve RM stories. She sees in the fraught session of writing the series from 1898 'a remarkable study of their attitude towards writing. It was a bore, a nuisance, an interruption when at CT. References to it are embedded in accounts of going round everyone's houses and long lists of the same people coming to tea every day. All this of course resulted in much-resented "hurry up" letters from the "wretched Watson" [editor of the *Badminton Magazine*] ... Dee [Edith's name in the family] was prepared to work all day long in the Studio, obviously so much preferring drawing to writing. Well, as Dr Johnson remarked, nobody writes except for money.' Muriel was not alone in this opinion. A detached observer of Violet Martin, whom she saw regularly at Spiddal, was Lord Morris' daughter Maud, later Mrs Wynn. She, like Muriel Currey, made a comment that suggests the overwhelmingly practical and financial aspect of Martin's career as a writer: 'It was a curious thing about Violet Martin that her one great ambition was to write serious prose on serious and important matters. Her perfect stories gave her no pride nor pleasure, beyond their lucrativeness, she often told me.'[74]

From 1900 to 1903 Edith undertook no new dual contract with Pinker, leaving Martin free to recover full health as best she could. As a reward for

completing the RM, they established themselves in Paris at the end of
September 1899 and lived for five months in an apartment on the Boulevard
Edgar Quinet, in a flat belonging to their friend May Barnard. Hildegarde kept
an eye on Drishane, which was unoccupied by family or tenants. A far cry from
Edith's impecunious student days, they had a *bonne à tout faire*. Alice Kinkead
had a studio in Paris at this time, which was a magnet for the Irish women
studying there. The number of old friends in the city provided them with a
comfortable social life; Martin idled and wrote. And Edith, out in the mornings
at Délécluse, kept making finds of remarkable new friends. Her appreciative eye
for handsome men never ceased to rove. She found a simpatico young American
with whom she set up a morning illustration class. This was the brilliant black-
and-white draughtsman Cyrus Cuneo, then in his mid-twenties: 'He was small,
dark, and exceedingly good looking, with a peculiarly beautiful litheness, balance,
and swiftness of movement, that was to some extent explained by the fact that
before he took up Art he had occupied the exalted position of "Champion
Bantam of the South Pacific Slope".' The morning studio used by Edith's classes
was occupied in the afternoons by the lady pupils of Whistler, who was then
teaching in Paris. A few of these students, being American and used to a free
country, objected to the rigid teaching of Whistler, left him, and joined the
independents of the morning class. Edith wrote: 'The models, whether fair,
dark, red, white or brown, had to be seen through Mr Whistler's spectacles, and
these, judging by the studies that were occasionally left on view, were of very
heavily smoked glass.'[75]

Because of their independent income, which was to be stabilised and
fortified by the RM, roughly averaging £300 a year, Edith and Martin were able
to take breaks from their families and conduct their lives on the model of the
free-and-easy young American women, daughters of wealthy fathers, who lived
in Paris, studying whatever subject attracted them. These clever, light-hearted
women amused Edith and Martin a great deal, and their company was itself a
tonic for Martin. Her letters mostly survive only in isolated fragmentary
clumps, but fortunately a letter from this winter in Paris to her mother at Ross
was preserved in Edith's papers. It is dated 25 November 1899. Although
Martin's bodily state was feeble, the letter is full of her gaiety and her droll
observance of independent women doing their own thing:

> Nothing very interesting has happened here since the night of the 'Leonids',
> the Shower of Stars that was to have happened last week. There was much
> excitement in Paris, at least the newspapers were excited. On my way to the
> dentist a woman at the corner of the Boulevard was selling enormous sheets
> of paper with *La Fin du Monde, a trois heures*! on them and a gorgeous

picture of Falbe's comet striking the earth. It was then 1.30, but I thought I had better go to the dentist just the same ... The Rain of Meteors was prophesied by the Observatory here for that night, and Kinkie and the Lady whom we call Madame La La arranged to spend the night in our sitting room (which has a good view of the sky in two aspects). We laid in provender and filled the stove to bursting, and our visitors arrived at 9.30. It really was very like a wake at the outset. The stipulation was that they were to call us if anything happened. I went to bed at 10.30, E. at midnight, and those unhappy creatures sat there all night and *nothing* happened. They saw three falling stars and they made tea three times (once in honour of each star) ... in the awful dawn they crept home, and I hear, turned up at the Studio looking just the sort of wrecks one might have expected. I believe they did see a light go sailing up from the dome of the Observatoire (which we can see from here) and that was a balloon, containing a lady astronomer, Mademoiselle Klumpke (who is, I believe, an American) and others. She sailed away in the piercing cold to somewhere in the South of Switzerland, and I believe she saw a few dozen meteors. Anyhow, two days afterwards, she walked into Kinkie's studio, bringing a piece of mistletoe, and some flowers that she had gathered when she got out of the balloon down there.[76]

Many of the women in the circle of Edith's fellow painters in Paris were much more independent than she was; they were not tied to their families, or their family houses. The place that Edith took as managing mistress of Drishane could very well have been taken by Aylmer's wife, Emmie Sykes. On her marriage, when she came to live in Drishane as a young bride in 1888, Adelaide Somerville was still reigning as its mistress. On Adelaide's death in 1895, the entire Somerville family had propelled Edith into being a substitute Adelaide as the only way of making life bearable for their father Colonel Somerville, who would never accept Emmie as Mistress. When he died in 1898, the dominance of Edith continued, at the command of his son Cameron, and against Edith's own wishes. Emmie had been most adaptable, accepting that Edith had taken the position of Mistress of Drishane preparing for one of two things: the day when, even yet, Cameron might take a bride, or the day when his heir was chosen from among his brothers' children. Boyle had the seniority of rank in this case. After 1898 Emmie stood in as Mistress when Edith was away, and was a most reliable maker of all things smooth, since like Hildegarde she had charm. But she also was away this winter of 1899, and Hildegarde made a decision that was to be far-reaching. She sent into the empty Drishane her right-hand woman, Joanna Minnehane, to strip and clean it. Edith had been warned by Martin that Ross had rotted and fallen to pieces through being shut up for long periods of time with no human presence. Dry rot, wet rot and woodworm could eat a house near to death in one inattentive generation. The sisters were determined that Drishane would survive in good heart, in Somerville hands; but they kept it up as a hearth and home for their brothers in an extension of their own childhood. No heir grew up in the house as they had, there was a generation missing in it through Cameron's failure to marry. So Edith continued as Mistress of Drishane, fossilizing as a mother-substitute. Not one of her brothers considered that she might do anything else, as it was to their advantage to have the house and lands maintained by such a manager.

By a complete fluke, one other letter of Martin's survives from Paris in November 1899. It is written to her favourite sister Edith and in its tone and content makes starkly clear the focussed intelligence and political nous that the Martin sisters shared, on a level not reached by the Somerville sisters. Conversely, Martin was simply not interested in the minutiae of dairy farming or painting and drawing. The letter to Edith Dawson gives a withering account of the political ignorance of the art students in Paris. At the time the French press was having a field day attacking England over the Boer War:

> The French papers are realising that a mistake has been made in the attacks on the Queen, and the better ones are saying so. But the *Patrie*, the *Libre Parole*, and all that fleet of halfpenny papers that the poor read, have nailed their colours to the mast, and it seems their idea is to overthrow their present government by fair means or foul. As long as this government is in there will be no quarrel with England, but it might, of course, go out like a candle, any day. I daresay you have heard the *Rire* spoken of as one of the papers that ought to be suppressed. We bought the number that was to be all about the English, and all about them it was, a sort of comic history of England since the Creation, with Hyde Park as the Garden of Eden. The cover was a hauntingly horrible picture of Joan of Arc being burned. The rest of the pictures were dull, disgusting, and too furiously angry to be clever. We had pleasure in consigning the whole thing to the stove …
>
> The students here, with exceptions, of course, – appear deaf and blind to all that goes on, and Revolutions in Paris, and the War in the Transvaal, are as nothing to them as compared with the pose of the model. In every street are crowds of them, scraping away at their charcoal 'academies' by the roomful, all perfectly engrossed and self-centred, and, I think, quite happy. Last Sunday we went to a mild little tea party in a studio, where were several of these artist-women, in their best clothes … No-one talked

anything but Art, except when occasionally one of the hostesses (there were four) hurriedly asked me what I thought of the Rubaiyat of Omar Khayyam, or *how* two people managed to write together, just to show what good hostesses they were, while all the while they tried to listen to the harangues ... Poor things, it was very nice of them, and I was touched. There are about half a dozen, that I know here, who take an English paper; it is a remarkable thing that they are nearly all Irish and Scotch, and have baths.[77]

In the middle of December Edith and Martin had an acceptance from the Northern Newspaper Syndicate through Pinker to pay £30 each for six articles of 2,500 words each. It was a legal contract that bound them to a set of fixed dates and deadlines. This they were to regret, as Martin was never again to be fit for a full-time working life. But the turn of the century brought a much more disastrous change that would alter the course of Edith's life, and, in consequence, Martin's.

# CHAPTER 6

# A popular success with the Irish RM

*Some Experiences of an Irish RM*
A prolonged prose version of the Ballyhooley Ballads would be an
accurate description of the book. The authors go to the cockney
state for their Irishness and their Irish brogue. The sketches are by
a man of the superior race, who looks on astonished, bewildered
and occasionally amused by the duties of the inferior race. The
incidents are made up in almost equal parts of drinking, fighting,
horse racing and fox hunting. It is fair to say, however, that there
is not a spice of malice in the book. The travesty is too grotesque
to be offensive. It is like the caricature of the absent master which
the naughty schoolboy draws on the blackboard. For all that,
there is a rollicking, irresponsible good humour about the book,
which is at times irresistible. It is Lever gone mad.
Review from the *Freeman's Journal*, 10 November 1899

THE NATIONALIST REVIEWER in the *Freeman's Journal* seems to have
identified Martin as Miss Ballyhooley, sister of Robert 'Ballyhooley'
Martin, the celebrated songwriter and creator of the Ballyhooley Ballads. His
dismissive reaction to the RM series, that it was a grotesque travesty, a caricature, was a common one from the Nationalist camp, which took the myopic
and ineffectual Major Yeates, the Resident Magistrate (RM), as of a 'superior
race' and for the central character, rather than the unobtrusively masterly Flurry
Knox, who stage-manages so many of the RM's 'experiences'. It is a reaction
that lives on: *Chambers Biographical Dictionary of Women* (1996) describes
Somerville and Ross as being 'known chiefly for a series of novels making fun
of the Irish'. To Edith at the turn of the century reviews were of marginal
interest compared to Martin's health, which remained variable, with alarming
slumps, or to the news of the Boer War. Jack was serving under General Redvers
('Reverse') Buller, who was defeated at Spion Kop in January. Percy and Eddy
were in action under siege at Ladysmith, serving with General George White.

Some of Edith's fellow art students joined up: Mr Holloway from Cyrus Cuneo's class was 'off to enlist with the Cape Mounted Rifles'. Edith and Martin in Paris had celebrated the start of the new century comfortably in May Barnard's flat, hoping to avoid the 'flu epidemic that was at its worst in London. Martin polished up her formal high-class French by doing half an hour a day with Mademoiselle Barot, in exchange for her teaching a half hour of English.[1] Edith was conscious of the class difference in their spoken French, but thought it was too late to change her own fluent but 'horrible femme de ménage dialect'.[2] The future in joint writing seemed rather doubtful with Martin unfit for it. Edith was always revitalised by Paris, and she had happily flung herself back into her old Studio routine, but little good seems to have been done for Martin's health. She was still 'looking like a ghost'.[3]

Edith wrote to Hildegarde to persuade her to join them in London after they left Paris on 1 March: 'I think that if Uncle Josc's rooms [Bolton Studios] are still unlet you ought to come over and clump there with Martin and me. You would see Boyle and Mab and would be on hand with Emmie and would help me to buy the needed things for Drishane wh. would be a most serious responsibility for me alone … I am sure Egerton wouldn't mind bossing the babies.' The future of Drishane was in doubt; Edith thought that Emmie and Aylmer should move in and take care of the house on Cameron's behalf. During this winter, while Edith and Martin were in Paris, Hildegarde did this duty and Edith reiterated her pleasure that she had sent in Joanna Minnehane to clean it. 'Martin says that was the way Ross rotted to pieces only having men in to light the fires and open windows and letting filth accumulate. I think the Chimp ought to hire Joanna permanently (until something else is settled) – it is only false economy to stinge four or five shillings a week to let valuable things go to decay.' Edith had no time to go into 'the vexed question of plans, but I will anyhow most gladly accept your offer of staying with you until my way is clear'.

Had these plans come to anything, the literary firm of Somerville and Ross would have been happily attached to Hildegarde and Egerton at Glen Barrahane, while Aylmer and Emmie would have run Drishane and the farm. In the long run this would have meant the survival of Glen Barrahane as well as Drishane, but at this point their bugbear, 'the irony of fate', came into play again. Emmie had caught the 'flu; as she was pregnant and run down, the infection rapidly turned into pneumonia and she died at her mother's home in York on 13 February, which was, strangely, Barry's death date fifteen years before. Edith did not immediately cross to England, as the 'flu epidemic was worse in London, and she was 'terrified' of Martin catching it in her weak condition. 'She is not fit to be left by herself for a night, much less a fortnight.' Economy played a part in this decision also. There was nowhere for Martin to stay free with relatives before joining up at the appointed time with Edith Dawson at Buxton, so they stayed put in Paris. Edith wrote many letters, to Aylmer and the Sykes, and one on each of three consecutive days to her sister.[4] More than any other letters of Edith's, they show her very strong mothering instinct and understanding of parent/child relationships. On 14 February, the day on which she received Aylmer's telegram, she wrote, instantly understanding Cameron's situation: 'If he [Cameron] would like to let Aylmer live in Drishane with me I would take care of him.' On the next day Edith wrote again: 'It is very hard to see why a little gentle useful Mother-thing like that should be taken and useless cumberers, like plenty I could name, are left ...' Having failed to get black mourning wear because she was too tall and thin for French ready-made clothes, Edith shelved buying them until her return to London and meeting up with Hildegarde.

On the 16th, after Emmie's mother had written to her, she wrote to her sister: 'Poor poor Mrs Sykes – Her letter just tore my heart' and confided to her sister her awareness of difficulties ahead for Emmie's children: '*Don't* let Aylmer make any arrangements that shall cut him off from Gilla, she *ought* to live the greater part of her life with him – If she doesn't he will never feel that she is his child or she that he is her father: and some day, when it is too late, he will regret it – she might grow into being the greatest comfort and companion to him, which Sonny [Desmond], being at school can't be, and if she is handed over bodily to Mrs Sykes there can *never* be the same feeling. I do feel very strongly that it is for his and their moral advantage that he should stick to his children and not renounce what may now be responsibility but will some day become a help and a pleasure ... How you and I will miss Emmie at every turn no words can say! She was the most sympathetic, ardent, delightful little standby at every possible juncture.' But Aylmer was already thinking of going to the Cape to join his friends in the Cape Mounted Rifles, and Drishane was to be let.

On 28 February, the day of the relief of Ladysmith by Redvers Buller, Edith and Martin returned to London, staying briefly at Sir Joscelyn's Bolton Studios rooms in Earl's Court. A London specialist, Dr Armstrong, diagnosed after an examination of Martin 'malnutrition and starvation of the nerves' and had prescribed spa treatment and the 'cutting off of all sugars'. Another doctor had prescribed the same for Martin's sister Edith Dawson. Edith wrote to Hildegarde from the Admiralty, where she was waiting for Boyle to come out of an interview on 15 March, describing Martin as looking as though she had been 'skinned', with her nerves all on the top like Cara Dil. 'She is in dungeons of despair about herself and thinks it is such a nuisance for me.' Both Martin sisters went to the Derbyshire spa town of Buxton and shared rooms at 10 Broad Walk. Edith met up with Hildegarde in London on 24 March and they returned together to CT. Martin was at Buxton from the end of March to the 10 May, when she returned to Dublin, en route for Ross. She did not see Edith again until 20 June when she joined the Coghill household at Glen B, there being no room at Drishane. She was very weak through the summer; her diary entries are sparse, sometimes consisting of little more than 'bed', 'slack' or 'lay in garden'. Nineteen-hundred was the most unproductive year for joint literary work. Edith was already thinking of improving her alternative means of earning a living, should Martin not recover.

This summer, among the visitors, Edith's painting friend Mabel Royds was over in CT; she sailed with Uncle Kendal, who loved flirting with lively women: 'Uncle K is much in love with Daisy [Morrough] but I shan't be surprised if my girl cuts her out, as tho' not half as pretty she has twice the brains.'⁵ In August, Violet Coghill, finished with her studies at the London School of Medicine for Women, was at Glen B on vacation; now a qualified doctor, she was over with her friend, fellow doctor and colleague Lina O'Connor. The Somerville sisters were very aware that they were among a new breed of professional women: 'The doctors are very well and are addressed as such.' The home farm made Drishane self-sufficient, even with the summer influx: 'We hope to begin on the oats this week,' Edith wrote to Hildegarde in the same letter, and carried on with a description that shows how efficient the Drishane kitchen garden must have been: 'Phil Large's yacht has been in. I was d- - - civil – asked them to tea and in ecstatic gratitude for their not being able to come sent them masses of vegetables and flowers.'

The Martins' doctors decided to try spa treatment again and on 15 October Edith Dawson met up with Martin, who was so weak she was being bath-chaired about Dublin, at Buswells Hotel. They returned together to Buxton. Very concerned over Martin's health, Dr Violet Coghill followed them there to check up on the treatment they were taking. Edith wrote to Martin describing the visitors and guests at CT, including an account of a dinner party where Boyle's wife Mab met Joe Coghill for the first time: 'Joe was delightful and sang and jack-acted for, or rather to, Mab, with highest success … Joe is really nicer than Eddy in many ways – Far more useful. He drove me to Rineen [to paint] and can and will do any mortal thing he is asked – except tell a story in less than twenty minutes. He says a friend of his told him he had at first read the R.M. "economically", a scrap every night – then he had galloped through it, and then, (and not till then he was *thankful* to say,) he had been told it was written by two ladies! Mr Purdon today told me that whenever he was tired, and cross, and bored, he read it, to cheer him up! Are we really going to be bracketted with Sponge's Sporting Tours? [Surtees] It almost looks like it … '

Literary work was shelved. The Martin sisters left Buxton after two weeks of treatment to stay at Edith Dawson's club in London. Martin dined at

Robert's in high society and met up with Edith Somerville for an 'unsatisfactory' conference with Pinker on the 31st. She then left London for Lowestoft to stay with the Dawsons at their country home, moving on 15 November to stay at Gravesend with her sister Katie's family, the Curreys. On 5 December she returned to the Dawsons in London, then went on with them to Portsmouth and Southsea where she spent Christmas. Edith sent a Christmas gift to her there: 'got present of tin tea basket from EŒS a delightful gift'. Though she was invalid, this itinerary of Martin's for late 1900 is indicative of how little time the writers actually spent together in writing, and makes us realise the prime importance of their separate note-taking and the postal exchange of drafts in their literary work. During these blank years lost to invalidism after Martin's fall, they were accumulating separately enough material to put together a set of eleven stories in 1904/5. It was very unusual for them to spend more than half of the year patchily together in the same place, and even then time for writing in was hard to come by. They existed as a pair most concentratedly in print, and in the dialogue of their letters. Sometimes, so many months passed between sightings of one another that they could be shocked by the changed appearance of their 'Co-Operator'. Photographs were taken of them separately if a magazine featured Edith on her own, for she was to be frequently in the sporting press after becoming the first woman Master of Fox Hounds in Ireland in 1903.[6] On 22 December, 1900, Martin's diary records: 'went out onto the Strand and bought a copy of *Madame* with picture and notice of EŒS in it'.

Edith began 1901 by organising a large-scale raffle for one of her landscape paintings, of Rineen, in aid of the West Carbery Hunt. The raffle was drawn in the town hall at Skibbereen, the gathering being overseen by two of her favourite hunting henchmen. Edith wrote in her diary: 'Dr Jennings made a harangue about me and was seconded by Mr Purdon [RM]. So home with nearly £17 for the good of the Hunt.' Martin returned to a berth at Drishane on 14 January where she immediately went to bed with a cold. It was imperative to produce some finished articles and short stories as in December 1899: as they seemed to have forgotten, Pinker had contracted for them to write regular pieces for a newspaper syndicate, and they had not been as productive as he could have wished. On the 26th Edith wrote in her diary: 'Began to try and write a story with Martin', but two weeks later she conceded: 'Tried to do a little at the Syndicate thing. Martin not able for writing.' On 2 April the hunting season finished, and on the following day Edith took a major decision that was probably influenced by her despair at the minuscule amount of literary work produced this spring, and the consequent lack of income. She wrote in her diary: 'Settled definitely that I would buy the Mall [House] and the Atkins' house from Percy.' She bought the ends of leases from her cousin Percy Aylmer.

'The irony of fate' had cast its muddling shadow on the Mall House. From the schedule of effects attached to Edith's will after her death it appears that the Mall House lease was made over to Edith, when she was three, for ninety-nine years from 26 March 1861 by her Townshend grandmother whose favourite she was. As the lease had been administered by her menfolk and sold on to Percy, Edith appeared to be unaware of its history, and certainly none of her menfolk thought it necessary to unravel the complication. Putting aside concentrated literary work on account of Martin's incapacity, she intended to make an income from letting houses and became a *rentier*. By 9 April Edith was supervising the workmen who were demolishing unwanted walls and building stables at the back of the Mall House.[7] Whether this was a wise move or not is debatable, in years to come it absorbed a great deal of her attention, and because she had the farm as well from 1908, it was to prevent her full-time return to literary work. Ironically, their fortunes were at last about to change with the growing reputation of the RM, published just before the turn of the century.

On 18 April there was a leading article in the *Irish Times* on the RM; this had been inspired by another article by Stephen Gwynn in *Macmillan's Magazine* in which Edith and Martin had one of their own. Stephen Gwynn described *The Real Charlotte* as 'probably the most powerful novel of Irish life ever written'. Pinker was delighted by the publicity. Martin was managing to do 'a little writing' every day by late April. On 13 May Edith went to London to shop for furniture and fittings for the Mall House. When she got back, she had to entertain Mr Meredith, the son of the novelist George Meredith, who was a representative of the publishing firm Constables. He was head-hunting, but was taken riding on hunters to distract him: 'Aylmer, like all the other men, flopped for Mr Meredith ... [and] took him off our hands.' Martin left at the end of May to join her mother at Ross. In Drishane a party of invalids was assembling to go abroad.

Ill health had struck Hildegarde, and consequently in this year a regular route to the French spa town of Aix les Bains was laid down for parties of CT residents taking spa cures abroad. Summer breaks were quite often used up in taking cures for whatever physical accident or ailment had befallen them in the winter; 'pig's feet' continued to trample hardest on Martin, who was never deposed from her throne as the 'Queen of pig's feet'. Apart from the complications caused by her hunting accident, she suffered from congenital ailments throughout her life, whereas the Somerville sisters until their old age mostly suffered reverses in health from the physical demands they placed on their tough constitutions. Accidents were frequent in their outdoor lives, and increasingly so when they took up farming for their livelihood. In July 1901 Edith and Egerton took Hildegarde to Champex, near Aix, to get help for

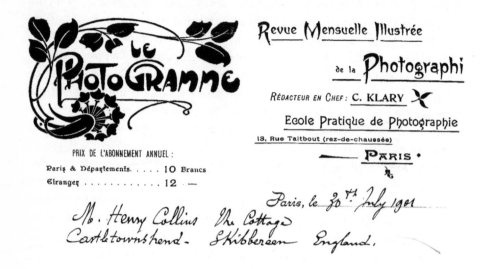

**11** Letter to Hildegarde Somerville from *Le Photogramme*, where she is disguised
as M. Henry Collins. Her work was known to Snowden Ward, it has not been
possible to discover if the nude studies of Edith and Hildegarde appeared
in the volume planned by M. Klary.

Hildegarde's damaged back: this had been caused when Egerton, lifting her up
into her side-saddle, had heaved her upwards with such strength that she had
been thrown over her hunter, and had landed on the base of her spine.[8] Edith
was treated for gout, and Jack, who joined the party in London, came with
them for treatment for his hand that had not healed since he was wounded in
the arm and hand while serving in the Boer War.

Meanwhile, from Ross, Martin went off on a slow-motion tour of connections; in August 1901 she joined an extended house party at Coole, to which
writers and artists seemed to come and go in an informal and unaccountable
manner that must have annoyed the household staff. Alice Kinkead had been of
the party but had left before Martin called in for an afternoon and stayed the
night after dinner. She dined with Lady Gregory, W.B. Yeats and her godson
Robert Gregory, who was then a student at Oxford. Martin had not been at
Coole for twenty years, since the christening of Robert. She described Yeats,
who was still at this stage an impecunious poet, to Edith as: 'A cross between a
Dominie Sampson and a starved R.C. curate – in seedy black clothes – with a
large black bow at the root of his long naked throat. He is egregiously the poet
– mutters ends of verse to himself with a wild eye, bows over your hand in dark
silence – but poet he *is* – and very interesting indeed – and somehow sympathetic

to talk to – I liked him – in spite of various things – and I got on well with him, so far. He gave an opinion of me to Augusta of which I feel inclined to repeat only the remarkable adjective, 'simple' – I didn't know that I was that nor perhaps did you. It is strange to talk of "deep subjects of life and death" without any self consciousness, and I must say he induces that, and does it himself. He is not at all without a sense of humour, which surprised me. He thinks *The Real Charlotte* very big in the only parts he has read, which are merely quotations in reviews ... But he doesn't approve of humour for humour's sake – (here Miss Martin said beautiful things about humour being a high art) ... Today Augusta made me add my initials to a tree already decorated by Douglas Hyde, AE and more of the literary crowd ...'9 This description of Yeats remained fixed in Edith's mind, so that when she herself actually met him, by then successful, well-dressed and well-fed, at the Greenes' in Dublin in 1933, she was astonished at the entrance of what appeared to be 'a country-gent'.

At Ross, Martin helped her sister Geraldine, who had been ill, to recuperate in the fine weather. Edith tried to put some order on the writing timetable in a letter to Ross towards the end of July, for it was urgently necessary for them to write up stories for the new book on the stocks: *All on the Irish Shore*, published in 1903: 'I want to be back as soon as may be after that, [September 2nd] as the garden and the hounds claim attention, and I don't see why we couldn't work here very comfortably. September always suits you here and is generally bright and dry, and if November proved too bad you might go up to Saint Andrews. Mrs Coghill [Hildegarde] and I wish to say that if you find your health can't stand it, we will pay the cost of your ticket here, as it is by *our* wish that you are coming – I have abandoned the thought of Cushendall – No time, and too late in the year, but I hope I may get to Ross about Monday or Tuesday week – But listen, *I won't go if I am made to play the organ* and you may just tell them so.'10 We should notice the formality of this letter, practical and sisterly, written more than fifteen years after Martin had become a CT familiar, and the fact that Martin was a boon companion to both sisters. Edith went back to London from Champex on 19 July and spent a week there shopping for household necessities for her letting property before returning to CT on the 26th. She had to stay in Glen B as Drishane was let, and carried on with her work on the Mall House. From Glen B she wrote to Martin on 2 August, at about seven in the morning:

The reason that I don't write is that I have too much to say and no time to say it in ... I have the divil [period] and I have just prowled downstairs, got these materials, met little Miss Oliver, and hinted an excellent cup of tea out of her, so now I can at last write to you as Bridget won't call me until 7.30 – The Mall as you have doubtless realised is the cause, it *is* the cause – my soul ... [after descriptions of the Mall work, details on dog breeding purdah follow: the female dogs all went on heat together] ... Maria [Egerton's water spaniel Pastel, Maria in the RM stories] just been immured. Egerton was, I hear, furious, because H and I kept wondering "*where* poor old Maria could be", and being seriously anxious as to whether she had died in secret of her own surpassing stench. At last he very crossly told H that Maria was shut up, and was made still more angry by H's uncontrollable amazement that it should still be thus with her – Personally, I should as soon suspect Madame de Bunsen [an aged and very distinguished relative of the Townshends at the Castle] ...

Martin must have laid down some kind of successful musical moratorium at Ross, as no organ-playing in church was required of Miss Somerville. From Drishane Edith joined Martin there on the 13 August, and from it they made a trip to Achill. En route they stayed again with Mr McKeown at his hotel in Leenane where, Edith told Hildegarde: 'Martin is already looking better for getting out of the fuss and worry at Ross.' Mr McKeown had been so pleased with their notice of his establishment in *Through Connemara in a Governess Cart* of 1892 that he cut their bill. He was therefore 'A man to be encouraged'.[11] His name reverberates again in 'High Tea at McKeowns' (1903). On this trip Edith and Martin recorded material for the remarkable story 'An Irish Problem', eventually placed as No. 8 of the collection *All on the Irish Shore*, at a sitting of the petty sessions court in Clifden. A closely observed and recorded interchange between two magistrates (a doctor and a store owner, both of whom speak Irish), an interpreter for the Irish-speaking plaintiff, Darcy, and the defendant Sweeny, opens in a comic vein but becomes colder. Darcy was 'a peasant from the farthest shores of Western Ireland, cut off from what we call civilisation by his ignorance of any language save his own ancient speech, wherein the ideas of today stand out in English words like telegraph-posts in a Connemara moorland.' Sweeny, with a cunning command of English, perjures himself in a multitude of ways, then is brought to judgement. The piece ends with regret that the English tourist who may attend such petty sessions will never be able to understand a man like Sweeny: 'How can they be expected to realise that a man who is decorous in family and village life, indisputably god-fearing, kind to the poor, and reasonably honest, will enmesh himself in a tissue of sworn lies before his fellows for the sake of half a sovereign and a family feud, and that his fellows will think none the worse of him for it.'

Back at Ross, Edith and Martin were pleased to read 'a good notice' of the RM in *Punch*. Mr Meredith continued to pursue them by letter, trying to acquire them as authors for Constables, as did Edward Arnold, who wrote: 'how anxious I am to have the chance of securing some of your work. Have you not got something – anything, that you would allow me to see? Amusing books are so rare, that it is a positive duty for the few who have the power to write them to continue doing so in the interests of the community.'[12] The petty sessions story went very well; at Ross they finished the manuscript, and christened it 'An Irish Problem', on 27 September. As a result, despite her plans Edith did not get back to Drishane until the 28th. By this time Martin was back at Buxton again with her sister Edith on yet another cure.

The manuscript of No. 9 of *All on the Irish Shore* was passing between them by post, and an article for the editor, Mr Maxse. Edith decided to finish it herself, as Martin was not up to literary work: 'Don't knock your head up; I think you may trust me not to do anything very awful; it wants so little, and I know that you aren't fit for hair-splitting and adjective weighing, which I shouldn't do, and wouldn't mind if I did ...' Martin's health was not Edith Somerville's only cause for concern. In October, when Jack Somerville was given a hero's return from the Boer War by the villagers and tenants, Edith had become distracted by the livid wound in his hand, already treated at Aix but failing to heal, which might, among other things, have affected his piano playing. The family had tried to keep Jack's return a secret, she wrote to Martin, but 'ordering his bedroom was enough, and more than a notice in the Times, and all the Village turned out'. There was a bonfire and tar barrels, and every single person there wanted to shake hands with Jack and welcome him home safe. 'His hand is ever so much better and has a normal colour and consistency, tho' still much shrunken, and last night he actually got a spoonful of soup to his mouth, without disaster but that was a tour de force ... the masseur fears another operation may be necessary ...' Eventually Jack regained full use of his hand and instrumental skill, but for a while Edith, the organiser of concerts and entertainments, had the use of his fine bass voice only.

While Martin was away, Edith wrote an article on her own for the *Country Gentleman*, 'A One Horse Country'. Jointly they were offered £20 by the *National Review* for 'An Irish Problem', the fruit of their note-taking at Clifden petty sessions. From Buxton Martin had gone to Dublin where she attended an Abbey Theatre performance of 'Diarmid and Grania', by George Moore and W.B. Yeats, on 28 October with her niece, Eileen Hewson, Geraldine's daughter. She described this to Edith, and though her description is lighthearted, it shows her powers of memory and observation very well:

I thought Diarmid and Grania a strange mix of saga and modern French situations – George Moore and Yeats were palpable throughout – the former in the situations the latter in the beautiful writing here and there, and in the peculiar simplicities that arose. It was hardly a play for Eileen I am afraid – the biblical terms not being shrunk from to describe the progress of the emotions of Grania who was excessively French in her loves. In the first act she is on the verge of an enforced marriage to Finn; she states without any contemptible subterfuge her reasons for objecting to this, and finally deludes Finn's friend Diarmid into falling in love with her and taking her away from the marriage feast a la young Lochinvar. He only yields after much lovering on her part – then curtain. The next act is sometime afterwards, and the really novel position is that she has become tired of Diarmid. I give George Moore some credit for that. Never was anything like her ecstacies of love for him in the first act. She then falls in love with Finn, which she might have done in the beginning and saved the writing of the play – and the curtain is Diarmid's discovery of them in howlts [locked together with sexual intent] and his resolve to go and hunt an enchanted boar … The last act is Grania's noble endeavours to dissuade him from the hunt, amid much thunder and lightning out in the woods. He makes one or two as backhairy [intimate] remarks to her on her conduct as George Moore would wish and retires to hunt the boar. After interludes there is a banging and roaring at the back and Diarmid is carried in to make dying speeches to Finn and Grania and to be carried off to a funeral march, with Grania striking attitudes all round the place. Finally the court humorist, alone on the stage, says "grand will be the burning of Diarmid, but grander will be Grania's welcome to Finn". If this is the lofty purity of the Irish drama I am indeed mystified … still there are great points in the play – and unusual moments …

At this time in Dublin, Martin made a second call at the Abbey, described in an undated fragment, after she had been seeing what there was to be seen in Dublin; she was clearly quite determined not to get mixed up with the Abbey set, despite knowing Augusta Gregory so well. She did not attend an exhibition of paintings by Nathaniel Hone and J.B. Yeats because she had heard that Yeats was there 'incessantly' with Maud Gonne, and feared that she would be forced to be rude to her. She did catch sight of Maud Gonne at the Abbey: 'I saw her at the Irish play on Friday night, and thought her looks terrific. The features still handsome, the nose salient and short but the badness of the expression was startling … Yeats was with her in a box all the time, except when he was with I think Augusta Gregory in a box opposite. I never looked his way, I daresay the Irish Literary Revival was quite disastrously unaware of my presence in the shades at the back.'

By November, when the Northern Newspaper Syndicate were harrying them with terse communications like 'hurry up', Martin had gone to join her sister Edith Dawson in Portsmouth. On the first of the month the *National Review* featured an article on Somerville and Ross. Readers of this article might have imagined them writing in an ivory tower. The reality was that Ross had become a heavily populated glorified boarding house for the tribe of Martin, and CT in that year cannot have been described as restful. To Martin, staying with her sisters was a good and preferable option. Glen B had a rebuild involving the demolition of interior walls, and the building of the Aylmer brothers' Red House next to Tally Ho, which was itself being extended, loomed over the village street at its top end. 'I think both houses will look five times too big for their little patches of garden,' Edith wrote to Martin. She was hunting concentratedly; what writing they did, like the piece 'A Record of Holiday', was done by post. They did not see each other from the end of September until mid-February. Martin stayed with the Helps at Coleshill in mid-November, and went from them to the Dawsons in Portsmouth for a month. Edith lost track of her, writing on 23 November: 'You *said* you were going to the Gun Wharf "the end of this week" so I address there, but in much uncertainty ...', sending on a missive of Pinker's. Martin went back to Ross for Christmas with her mother, and eventually met up with Edith again at Ethel Penrose's in Lismore.

They were working at a set of eleven stories eventually titled *All on the Irish Shore*; this was a miscellany, with a disparate cast of characters unrelated to the inhabitants of the RM's Skebawn and its environs, their setting for the fictional version of the Skibbereen district. Edith started the New Year with a lot of children, nephews and nieces, out hunting; she was pleased with the progress of her godson Paddy Coghill as a rider. And in January she began excavating a famous pond and rock garden.[13] A letter to Martin from 29 January 1902 shows that their agent Pinker, who was not without self-interest, had entangled them with the Northern Newspaper Syndicate without fully explaining the terms, which proved very complicated financially; and they were paid later than ever as a result. Incidentally, in this letter a source of stories is revealed – the servant Matt [Kenealy] at Ross. 'Just a line to say that the MS arrived at about the same time that I got back from Connonagh [WCH Meet] and directly I had tea I started in to copy. Was that good or was it not? I think it is awfully good and I grudge those precious Matt stories going to that rotten Syndicate – I will try and get Pinker to extract some coin from them; I can't see why they shouldn't pay us, especially now that they have 4 up [i.e. stories I- IV out in magazine form].' Matt Kenealy is disguised in *Irish Memories* as 'Rickeen', and has a chapter to himself.

On 15 February the *National Review* wrote to Edith, 'asking me and my distinguished Co-Operator for another delightful Irish sketch'. Went and met

13 A Somerville and Ross manuscript with an intrusion. Edith Somerville was the
godmother of Hildegarde's eldest son Paddy, who was to succeed to the Coghill
baronetcy. She indulged him greatly, and in her eyes he could do no wrong. Whereas
all other nephews and nieces knew that they were on no account to interrupt Edith
and Martin when they were working, Paddy was able to intrude upon the scene
with impunity. Here he walks into the room, climbs up on Edith's lap and joins
in on the script of *All on the Irish Shore* on 15 March 1902. Over-indulgence
by his mother and aunt no doubt contributed later to Sir Patrick's
solitariness, and iron rule over his family.

'Distinguished Co-Operator at the station'.[14] They went to Ethel at Lismore for
two days, and passed through Cork on the 17 February on the way back to
Drishane. The enervated Martin was in slow-motion. Her diary enters: 'I
shopped languidly and lunched at Baker and Simpsons, Edith shopped wildly,
and did not lunch.' Her diary entries were still brief and fragmentary. By the
27th Martin was too seedy to work again, and Edith 'began to try a Syndicate
muck' on her own. She distracted herself from problems by working on the
pond. Boyle was home on leave and helping her. Laid back as ever, Hildegarde
and Egerton went off for a day, leaving their two young sons in the mud with
their aunt and uncle. On 15 March Edith entered in her diary: 'Perfect day.
Spent most of it at the pond with Boyle, making steps and a disposition of
boulders and stepping stones. Paddy and Bubby [Nevill Coghill] wove through

all. Realise that to tend them successfully needs the imagination of a Shakespeare, the strategy of a von Moltke and the long suffering of all the Apostles. But they are good little things.'

The base of the pond was concreted and then it was filled. The excitement of the pond overlaid the mention of writing work in diaries: nevertheless somehow in this spring six Syndicate items were written. On 30 May even the pond took second place with the arrival of Pinker. He had come to discuss the volume that Mr Meredith had eventually persuaded them to write for Constables, and to bribe them into more of the RM. On 3 June Edith notes that: 'Pinker made large offers for a further series of RM stories.' The Constable volume was *A Patrick's Day Hunt* with text by Martin and illustrations by Edith. They were muddling along with the series of stories and by 7 July would have finished 'The Dane's Breechin', ninth in the eventual series of eleven.

Martin's ill-health was still a medical mystery; she had stayed with her sister Katie at Gowran in June, from the 7th to the 11th, but then had another medical check-up with a Dr Philip, who suggested a private nursing hospital for a period of rest. She spent a part of early July in Miss Scott's Nursing Home in Dublin's Lower Leeson Street before getting to Ross on the 13th. To alleviate her tinnitus Dr Philip had tried syringing Martin's ears frequently, with some success. From Ross, Martin joined Edith on the 28th in Dublin for six weeks to tag on to a holiday in Jersey with Boyle and Mab and the children. Here, in a house near St Helier, they perfected the combination of Edith's seventeen pictures with the 4,000-word text of *A Patrick's Day Hunt*. They left Jersey on the 19 September, spent a week in London, then parted again, Martin going to the Dawsons, and Edith back to Cork. In London on the 23rd, Elliott and Fry had taken a publicity photograph of them, Edith in a borrowed habit, Martin in a tea gown.

Edith managed to get back to CT in time to fortify Hildegarde for the delivery of her third child Ambrose on 30 September, performed by Dr Lina O'Connor; knowing his sister's desire for a girl child, Boyle exclaimed 'Oh Ambrose! That thou were Ambrosia!'[15] Martin immediately wrote to Egerton to congratulate him, and give him her thoughts on preserving the well-being of Hildegarde. She did not mention that her own health was veering wildly: after a sudden severe reverse she had to go back into a nursing home in London, Miss Parry's, from 28th October to 11 January for complete inactivity, quiet and isolation from worry. But none of her smallest doings could be kept secret from the Bushe telegraph. Her diary entry for 8 November reads: 'Post card from EŒS reviling me for writing letters because I had written a post card to Mama. Was much upheld by consciousness of rectitude.' She was being treated by a Dr Tooth and undergoing a course of massage for her back.[16] Her efficient and effective masseuse, who became a dear friend, was a North of Ireland woman, Nora Tracey. Boyle Somerville called on Christmas Eve to deliver the CT-ites' presents, including a silver photograph frame from Edith. While she was in the nursing home manuscripts came and went and 'The Connemara Mare', eventually placed at third in the published series, was finished and sent to Pinker. Martin made an unusually intimate diary entry at the end of the year: 'Close the year in bed, much fatter than I began, head moderate, digestion ever so much better, back pretty fair – Poorer in pocket but richer in friends than ever.'

*A Patrick's Day Hunt* was published in an edition of 5,000 in mid-November; a month later 3,000 had been sold in Britain and 1,000 in America. This was a good beginning for 1903, their popular reputation having been firmly established by the success of the RM stories; now they became celebrities in the British sporting literature world. Jack wrote to Edith from London to say that 'the PDH was the book of the season'. The first edition in 1899 of *Some Experiences of an Irish RM* of 1,500 copies had sold out in a few months. The repeated editions (Longmans had printed ten impressions by 1901) made them financially comfortable at last, or would have done if they could have stopped themselves from generosity to their relatives and pet causes. Editors and publishers fell over themselves to propitiate Somerville and Ross; they were waiting for the next set of stories, a sure-fire gold mine, and manoeuvring to publish them. On 22 January Edith 'Heard from Pinker that Longmans want a PDH for next Christmas.' This inspired her to plan the illustrated volume *Slipper's ABC of Hunting*, published in 1903, which she concocted on her own, and of which her writing partner disapproved. Martin left her rest home in mid-January to stay with the Dawsons where she entered in her diary: 'Regretted in some ways the peace and shelter of the Rest Cure.' At this time Edith was with the Cholmondeleys at Edstaston in Shropshire, deep in their agricultural doings. As they were so wealthy, Hugh and Cissie had horses and livestock of the best, but they were also introducing reformed agricultural practices and were to advise the Somerville sisters when they began to farm, before they came under the wing of the Irish Agricultural Organisation Society.

When Martin was in London in March staying at her club, the New Century, in 1903, she took her brother-in-law, Cuthbert Dawson, her sister Edith's husband, with her to a meeting in the *Spectator* office for moral support, since Edith Somerville was bogged down in domesticity and unavailable. Busy as Edith was, she remembered to send Martin shamrock for St Patrick's Day, just as she did to all her siblings who were out of Ireland. St Loe Strachey[17] was the *Spectator* editor at the time: 'We had tea in Mr Strachey's rooms. There were there Mr S – large, capable, Jewish looking, 43 years old – shaved except for a *tiny* black moustache, kind and all there – and modern – and stirring [their word for a physically attractive man].[18] There was Charlie Graves, and Eric

Parker – a nice quiet young man now editor of *Country Gentleman* ... Mr Strachey sat down before me and said that he owned the *Country Gentleman* as well as the *Spectator* and would we allow them (him and Eric Parker) to make a bid for the new serial rights of the new RM for the *Country Gentleman*. I was not to commit myself, or to think of taking a penny less than we were getting elsewhere – you can imagine that I temporised and said Pinker – on which Eric Parker brightened up and said he had the highest opinion of Pinker – and was delighted that we had an agent – Mr Strachey said resounding things of the RM ... Mr Graves said he had had a very nice letter from you (bother you – coming in behind me) and that you and I wrote much alike ...' For all the urging to produce a sequel to the RM stories of 1899, for seven years the reading public and Pinker was kept at bay with this year's *All on the Irish Shore*, 1903, the two illustrated volumes by Edith, *A Patrick's Day Hunt*, 1902, *Slipper's ABC of Foxhunting*, 1903, and a volume of old essays, *Some Irish Yesterdays* of 1906. Martin was in permanently poor health, failing to recover from the hunting fall of 1 November 1898, and Edith was overworked as the manager of Drishane, and her own houses. Neither of them felt inspired, but played-out. They were in their mid-forties, a period of life that revealed others of the Martin sisters to have poor constitutions.

The proofs of *All on the Irish Shore* arrived on 6 February; it was published at the beginning of April, and well reviewed, particularly in the *Spectator* of the 18th. The linked pair of stories 'Fanny Fitz's Gamble' and 'The Connemara Mare' enshrine some of the Ross tenant Matt Kenealy's speech.[19] A lover of horses as passionate as Edith, he had described a mare that he had sold on but that had not forgotten him despite a long passage of years; she heard his voice on a village street 'and she turned in to me with the cart! "Ho, ho, ho!" says she, and she stuck her nose into me like she'd be kissing me. Be dam, but I had to cry. An' the world wouldn't stir her out o' that till I'd lead her on meself. As for cow nor dog nor any other thing, there's nothing would rise your heart like a horse!' The notebooks recording spoken words are now in Queen's University Belfast. Often they recorded the speaker, or sender in written form, of the pieces. Sometimes there is a pencilled note of the eventual relocation in the published work. Not all of it was used in published stories. The most densely packed Notebook 10 is an Admiralty Ledger once belonging to Boyle Somerville. Edith has written on it 'HMS Ship "Irish Memories" January 1886–19?' but the actual date of the ledger in Navy time seems to be 1897. When, in 1946, Edith destroyed papers in order to reduce the amount that went with her to Tally Ho, she made notes on the material that did move with her. This volume has a note in the handwriting of her old age: 'NB The contents of this book are copyright and are strictly reserved by E Œ Somerville.'

Working on her own, Edith during this spring made the illustrations for *Slipper's ABC of Hunting*. This was a purely money-making venture and Martin feared that the accompanying verse, described as 'doggerel' in a letter to Pinker on 24 February, would harm their reputation. This did not occur to Edith, and the publication gives another instance of their different natures and Martin's care not to offend her. After London, she had gone up to her mother at Ross on 19 March, and settled in for six weeks with the prospect of eventual relief from a rest cure abroad. Then Edith met her in London and they set out for Paris en route to Aix for the curative waters, which they took from 8 to 27 May and were back in London on the next day. While based there, Edith went off for the weekend to Cousin Gendie at Thornbury Park, and Martin socialised with the Barton girls. They crossed back to Dublin on 6 June, Martin travelling from there to her sister Katie at Gowran for a week, to turn up at CT a week later. Here, at last, at CT together some work was done: they worked hard on a manuscript revision for almost a month with the usual interruptions before returning to London on 18 July. A sure sign of their rising reputation was that Longmans was re-issuing their earliest work. From mid-June to mid-July they had been working at a new edition of their first novel *An Irish Cousin*; they made major changes, and the rare first edition reveals that what was cut related to the love affairs, Edith's original contribution. They must have felt very strongly about this as, according to Edith's diary, they: 'Wrote to Longmans and offered to forego royalties on the Irish Cousin so that he could with them bribe libraries to give up their old editions.' Consequently copies are difficult to find.

They removed all the chapter heading quotations which include lines from Edith's commonplace book of love poetry, and one of her favourite love songs, from Schumann's *Dichterliebe*; they changed the prophesied fate of Willy Sarsfield, as it horribly predicted the fate of Barry's brother Algie who married disastrously out of his class, and then fled to the Klondike.[20] They completely removed the character of Aunt Jane, the acting mother to the orphaned heroine Theodora, perhaps because Aunt Jane had too open an antagonism to Irishmen as husbands: 'Men were regarded by her as the natural foes of cleanliness, economy and piety. And of all men she considered Irishmen to be the epitome of their sex's atrocities.' Aunt Jane had tried to prevent the marriage of her sister to Theodora's Irish father: 'That ne'er do weel Irishman! A creature that tis well known had to leave his home for heaven knows what wickedness! Did you never hear that a bad son makes a bad husband?' In the course of the novel Theodora comes to know two Irishmen very well, and marries one of them, thus proving her Aunt Jane wrong.

When it seems that she must abandon her love, the heroine shows an extensive knowledge of tragic love poetry concerning a discarded and a suppressed love. With Rossetti and Heine, the quotations, all edited out, include lines from Tennyson's *The Two Voices* ('"What is it thou knowest, sweet voice?" I cried / "A hidden hope," the voice replied'); lines from Scott's *The Antiquary* ('Remorse she ne'er forsakes us;/A bloodhound staunch, she tracks our rapid step'); lines from Drayton's 'Come let us kiss, and part', and from *Love's Labour's Lost* ('"Uncover ye his face," she said; /"Oh, changed in little space"'). As the writers had become well known in Ireland, their fictitious characters were widely believed to be portraits in thin disguise, and were identified by readers, rightly or wrongly. For example, Lady Gregory was convinced that Martin had modelled old Mrs Knox of the RM series on her mother, but there are other elements in the composite character: old Mrs de Burgh of Kilfinnan and Mrs Annie Townshend of Whitehall.[21] Too many details in *An Irish Cousin* pointed to the Yelvertons, in the elder and the younger generation; the changes must have been made to prevent reader recognition as well as to improve a novel which did show signs that it was a first attempt.

From London Edith then went, on the spur of the moment, to stay in the country for some art classes at Stanford near Liphook in Surrey, at the edge of the Hampshire Downs. It was Boyle who kept the closest tabs on his eldest sister's movements. These were never easy to follow. On 22 May 1903 Boyle had written: 'I can't make out whether you have been to Aix, or even, if you have, this will find you at home again – I suspect you hardly know yourself in the fearful whirligig of plans and chops and changes in which you live.' In August Longmans published the new revised edition of *An Irish Cousin* of 1889. After visiting relations, Martin joined Edith at Stanford, where Longman sent them six copies of the revision. On the 18th, Edith made a triumphant entry in her diary: 'Went to the class. Back at 12 and did some writing. Have begun another RM!' Then Edith left Stanford for CT family duty. At the end of the month Edith moved into Glen B to look after that household while Hildegarde and Egerton went off to Aix. Martin stayed with the Helps at Coleshill and then went back to Ross on 19 September. Her only adventure from Ross was to stay with the Morrises for a weekend at Spiddal on 8/9 October. By this time, through the RM, Martin's reputation was such that numerous guests would come to specially arranged dinners at Spiddal to have the pleasure of meeting her. In her memoir published in 1937, Maud [Morris] Wynne gave an account of Martin preparing for such a dinner party. It shows Martin's pernickety standards in dress and finery unabated. She was late in coming down dressed, and Maud dashed up to her room to see if all was well. She found Martin almost in tears because she had forgotten to pack evening shoes, and her feet were peeping out from under her long yellow silk evening dress in the 'strong common sense laced boots of the period'. Maud tried to find a pair of court

Flurry Knox

Slipper

Sally Knox on Cockatoo

Maria

12 Some of the cast of the *Irish RM*, drawn by Edith; characters like
Flurry Knox and Slipper, and Old Mrs Knox of Aussolas became literary
immortals in the first decade of the century.

shoes in the house that would do, but Martin went down eventually in her own footwear and great embarrassment. Maud wrote: 'No debutante could have been more fussed and put out.'[22]

*Slipper's ABC* came out at the beginning of October, 1903. On the 14th, Martin joined the household at Glen B: 'Where E is watchdog over the Bart [Sir Joscelyn], Beatrice, Paddy, and Miss McLeod [Beatrice's minder].' Even so, Edith was hunting twice a week. She had succeeded her brother Aylmer as MFH of the West Carbery Hounds, a position she was to hold from 1903 to1908. Nothing is noted in Martin's diary for the next week, showing that her time was fully occupied, even to exhaustion. The reason was that they were re-reading *The Real Charlotte* to check for errors to be corrected in the new edition. On the 26th, Hildegarde and Egerton arrived back, refreshed, while Martin and Edith went back to Drishane, worn out. Though we can gather no sign from her diary entries that Martin's physical strength was returning, it evidently was, as she hunted with the West Carbery on the next day, from Innisbeg. She did not accompany Edith on a trip to London in November, but worked at editing and polishing the new edition and helped Hildegarde with the violet farm packing. It seemed that, through the RM, even in Ireland their reputation was spreading by word of mouth, and being re-interpreted en route. On 17 November, Edith wrote in her diary: 'I had a letter from one Bodkin, editor of a paper called "The Irish Packet" offering to "consider" a story if we would write one about better society than the people in "The Experiences of an Irish Policeman".' Tugged by invisible apron strings, Martin took a lift from Percy Aylmer in his motor to Cork on 23 December and went to join her mother at Ross for Christmas. On Christmas Eve she 'sent off lots of Kodaks of myself as Christmas cards'.[23]

She celebrated Christmas at Ross with Mama, Selina and her old friend Nellie Somerville; Edith Dawson arrived to join them on 7 January 1904. At this time Edith Somerville was staying with Boyle and Mab at their house Mill Hill in Newcastle, where Boyle was temporarily stationed. Martin had just recovered from 'flu, and when Edith Dawson arrived she in her turn went down with the disease. Edith wrote to Hildegarde from Boyle's: 'The enclosed has just come [a letter from Martin] I absolutely smile with fury at the thought of Martin, only just over influenza, sitting up all night. Why can't E get a nurse for herself – and where is Cuthbert? Next thing we shall hear she is ill again – I wish she had no relations in the world nearer than second cousin.' It is easy to see why Martin was a different and happier person at CT where she was fussed over; her family used her quite thoughtlessly at times. Edith was right in supposing that Martin would become ill again. On 3 February Edith and Martin met up at the New Century Club in London for a serious meeting with Pinker on the 5th. Afterwards, to recover her equilibrium, Martin, who was keen on carpentry, bought a beautifully-made wooden plan-chest for their literary papers.

Drishane was now being let out regularly in the hunting season. From London Edith was sending advice to Hildegarde on how to deal with some arrogant English tenants whom she was managing in Edith's absence: 'I think it is quite unconscious, but sooner or later all English people betray their underlying conviction that they have taken Ireland and "all that in them is" – now that I have blorted a little I feel better'. Later she wrote about the same tenants again: 'It is the old story of the Conquered race having to pay tribute to the Saxon Caesar, and *don't do it.*'[24] While Edith went back to CT and Glen B, Martin went up to stay with Boyle and Mab in Newcastle. Here, on 7 March, she suffered some kind of severe relapse, which so alarmed Boyle that he wired to Edith for her to come immediately. She arrived on the 9th. Martin wrote in her diary: 'EŒS arrived about 8 am having come over by Kingstown. She could only remark that I was like a white rat – and immediately began to catch cold.' To Hildegarde, two days later, Edith wrote that she was 'horrified' at Martin's appearance, 'white and thin … Private. She is now worrying over the accursed affairs of Ross …' They both went to ground with Lady Allen, Boyle's mother-in-law, at Maxwelton House, Edgeware, on the outskirts of London, while Edith tried to organise a getaway to the sun.

Edith's instant response to any severe illness was to go abroad, preferably passing through Paris. True to form, she started to move the inert and fevered Martin, first to Paris on 17 March. They took the night train south on the next day, travelling in a first class ladies' carriage, no economy necessary this time. Changing at Narbonne, they arrived at the haven they sought on the 20th and stayed there until 2 May. It was only Edith's second season with the hounds as Master, but she had quickly handed them over to Aylmer:

> and started for London at a moment's notice, with an empty mind and a Continental Bradshaw. In the train I endeavoured to fill the former with the latter, and, beginning with France, its towns and watering places, the third name on the list was Amélie-les-Bains. 'Warm sulphur springs, which are successfully used in affections of the lungs. Known to the Romans …' [she then met on the train a woman who knew and loved the place and recommended it unreservedly] … I went next day to Cook's; they had never heard of Amélie. No-one had ever heard of it, but I clung to Bradshaw and my nice woman, and in three days we started, in faith, for Amélie, Martin with bronchitis and a temperature … we stayed at 'Les Thermes Romains Hotel'. We went there because we liked the name; we stayed there for six delightful weeks, from the middle of March to the beginning of May, and irrational impulse was justified of her children…[25]

It was known that Martin had bronchitis and asthma, but at Amélie a doctor diagnosed her as having emphysema. However, she gradually recovered, and was able to walk long distances in the clear dry air; the family heard of the pleasures of the place and Percy Aylmer joined them for a while. It was so delightfully cheap that Edith wrote long letters trying to persuade Hildegarde to join them as well, and to take the third bedroom in their suite: 'Martin and I would love you to be here.' Edith took hot sulphur baths for 'my back, the Seat of Scriggles'. In Amélie they 'discussed the new RM', and may have sketched some stories. A rejuvenated Martin turned up at Glen B with Edith on Monday 9 May, to Hildegarde's delight walking in easily, just in time for tea. She settled in for a working summer at CT; but it was not to be. Martin left for Ross on 18 July where she stayed until 23 August, strongly advised to keep away by Edith for as long as possible. Drishane was in chaos with a major rebuilding programme. The house was 'full of masons and carpenters, all in raging passions, and sending for me every five minutes to demand the head of Danny Boy on a charger. I have thought of ... fleeing to Tally Ho, but find that I *must* stay here so as to keep the peace and save Danny from dismemberment. You are well out of it.' Only the hardiest souls were in it: May Goodhall had come over for a fortnight to paint with Edith and moved into Martin's room for the end of July until Edith left for the Inner Hebrides.

Having a companion in work was still a necessity. While Martin was still at Ross, she went up to visit her friend Madge Robertson and her family at Pennyghael on the island of Mull and painted there from 9 to 23 August, in company with Hector Burn-Murdoch and his wife Jean. At Ross Martin worried over her sister's health; Edith Dawson was ill again in this summer. There was some unusual feature in the malfunctioning metabolism of the Martin women that remained undiagnosed, save vaguely as 'malnutrition'. It may have been thyroid, but in its late stages had the symptoms of dropsy. Edith was pleased that Martin was not in CT. The worst of the turmoil at Drishane came with the installation of a new kitchen range: 'You are well out of it,' Edith wrote again to Martin, and continued: 'I *must* dine out otherwise I couldn't dine at all – the dining room carpet is up and this room [the Hall] is part kitchen part servants' hall – Ellen bears it like a saint – Katie has even laughed – so things might be worse – Hildegarde arrived from Castle Freke [from a dance] this morning at 6.30 and then went to bed ...'

Summer was a time of intense preparation for showing horses, at local shows and in Dublin at the Royal Dublin Society. The showing of quality horses kept up Edith's reputation as a horse-coper, sales from which constituted an important part of her disposable income. At the Skibbereen Show, Bridget took 2nd in the Hunter class and Joker 2nd in the Jumping.[26] As usual, Ethel and Jim

Penrose had been in Glen B for their annual holiday before going on to Switzerland. Ethel often stood in as a reader and critic when Somerville and Ross manuscripts were in a stage of development, passing between Edith and Martin by post. In this summer a letter mentions Ethel giving criticism on an early version of 'The Boat's Share' (at first numbered 3, later displaced by 'Poisson d'Avril'), which eventually emerged as No. 6 of the *Further Experiences*. The disruption, dust and dirt caused by the builders and the new kitchen range went on: 'I am *thankful* you are out of the house – I have read through attentively 'The Boat's Share' and I think Ethel and I wronged it. In fact I think it really is rather good, and so is the island one ['The Last Day of Shraft', No. 7].'

Jack, who had very good Japanese, had been passed over for service in Japan on account of favouritism shown to a man with connections but 'only three words of Japanese'. Edith was furious: 'next year for certain (the W[ar] O[ffice] says) Jack shall go to Japan. But will Japan be there for him to go to? Or will it be an extension of Manchuria? It is most sickening.' Other men of the tribe of CT cousins were doing better. Edith's 'Twin', Bertie Windle, reappeared on the Irish scene in this year. He had taken a degree first as a medic and taught in Birmingham University as a pathologist for twenty years. He was head-hunted for the post of President of Queen's College, Cork.[27] While in this post he served also as Professor of Archaeology, a passionate interest to him that he shared with his cousin and male 'Twin', Boyle Somerville. He was to be a source of advice and comfort to Edith during his time at Cork.

Martin was back in Drishane at the end of August. On 27 September they finished 'The Boat's Share', and sent it off to Pinker. They planned out story No. 4 before both Edith and Martin went to London on 15 October; they separated on their return to Dublin a week later. Martin went back to Ross, Edith to CT. While Martin was at Ross, Edith made the illustrations for the stories in the new RM set done so far. By the time that Martin returned to Drishane on 4 November, the weather had turned foul, so that they worked at No. 4 concentratedly for a solid month before there was a catastrophe. On 5 December Edith sprained her ankle in a fall, and took to tea partying and socialising, being unable to hunt. On the 21st she entered in her diary: 'Martin's head struck work, so did we.' On the next day Martin went up to join her mother at Ross. There was a large gathering of Martins in the New Year: 'lots of boys at Ross for Christmas,' Martin wrote in her diary, but the Indian summer of Ross was nearly over, for at the age of eighty-two Mrs Martin's health was failing.

Pinker must have been driven to distraction by the on/off progress of their work. Martin went back to Glen B on 5 January, but was called away from CT to care for her mother on 4 March. During February they had done some work on story No. 5, 'A Conspiracy of Silence'. Martin was able to return to

Drishane at the end of March when her mother had recovered a little. All this spring Edith was involved off and on with preparing the Mall House for tenants. In April, when Mrs Martin went into a nursing home in Dublin, Martin went up from CT to settle her in. Physical overwork began to tell on Edith, and Hildegarde became concerned about her sister's symptoms. She was examined by Dr O'Meara, who found that she had developed an irregular heartbeat, palpitations and breathlessness. He recommended an examination by a specialist, but this was put aside until the late summer, plans for which holiday, at Aix, were laid this month. On 30 April Martin wrote to Edith from Dublin:

> It will be delightful if we can get Hildegarde to Aix. It ought to be a very entertaining party, and remote from interruptions ... I must tell you that Augusta [Lady Gregory] was here yesterday, and was rampant that I should write a play for the Abbey Street Theatre, protestations of total inadequacy were put by as the idle wind – want of time ditto – apparently they want what they are good enough to call a Shoneen play. I suppose that means middle class vulgarity ... It seems to me that they want now to rope in the upper classes and drop politics ... Augusta was enraptured when I divulged the fact that you had faint aspirations towards a play ... 'a week at Coole would do it – We could give you all the hints necessary for stage effects etc. ... the characters and plots picked from your books ... I will look through them at once.' I gave no further encouragement of any sort and said we were full up ... I couldn't face Edward Martyn – he is too idiotic a rebel – so I didn't come in for the tea party on the stage, for which Augusta told me she had cut 98 sandwiches (I don't think '98 was intended) I also saw Yeats in the distance looking very like Kinkie! He had implored me to come and hear his play – and acknowledge that blank verse perfectly spoken, is the proper vehicle for poetry – and I was sorry not to be able to tell him that I thought it perfect for *acting* but that for reading to oneself the charm of metre and rhymes was as the power of different sorts of music – I had the pleasure of telling him that I thought it a sin to throw such beautiful weapons out of his armoury. He assured me his plays were full of lyrics. He does write well I must say – I am going to Saint Patrick's today with Mama and Flynn – It is the Easter music again ...

Martin went up to Dublin again on 17 May to see her mother safely off back to Ross with her minder Flynn. On the next day there was great excitement at Drishane on the return of Cameron from India on six months' leave. Edith immediately started a round of visits to relations with him. They were with Gendie, Mrs Miller Mundy, at Thornbury while Martin went ahead and

waited for them at her Club in London. The family party was assembling to go
to Aix, where Edith, under doctor's orders, was 'to do nothing more or less'.
Hildegarde, Cameron, Edith and Martin were joined by Percy Aylmer. They
were at Aix for 3–26 June, Edith doing absolutely nothing while her system
slowed down. On the way back they dallied in Paris for 1–4 July, then engaged
briefly with their editors in London before crossing back to Ireland on the 8th.
Edith spent the rest of July organising a successful concert and bazaar to raise
funds for a village hall, which was the brain-child of Egerton. Their profits were
£92.10 shillings.[28] Martin was back at Ross on 10 July. Her sister Edith
Dawson, probably disliking the open-house lack of privacy of Ross, had set
herself up in her own dwelling: 'had tea with Edith in her nice little house
Waterfield,' Martin entered in her diary on the 12th.

On that same day she first noted that: 'Robert not well'. Like his sisters,
Robert suffered from a respiratory disease; coming home to live with Mama
had its drawbacks as Ross was, like most unmaintained Big Houses of the time,
freezing cold, damp and draughty for a large part of the year. Martin returned
to Drishane for August on the 3rd, in time to join an important social event.
Cissie and Charlotte Townshend turned up for lunch on the 7th, Charlotte with
her husband, George Bernard Shaw, who was 'agreeable and quite affable'.[29] As
a brilliant writer for the theatre, GBS was to be a helpful advisor and critic to
Edith in years to come, when she tried to adapt some of the RM for the stage.
In the hope of getting some peace in which to write, Martin went with Edith to
stay with the Penroses at Lismore from the 17th to the end of the month. But
they still had not finished story No.5 when they got back; it had been begun on
23 February, more than five months before. The rate of progress of their joint
work on these RM stories was excruciatingly slow compared to Edith's solo
work or joint short articles. We know that they had argued and wrangled to
excess over An Irish Cousin, and even returned to the argument after a ten-year
gap, but it is quite possible that the same fraught discussions and repeated version-
ing were carried on as a necessary part of their creative process throughout their
career together. It does not help to clarify this difficult point that Martin, who
was brutally neat and tidy at her desk, threw away drafts if Edith hadn't already
stored them out of the way, so that the surviving field of reference is thick with
the topmost layer of finished manuscripts in Edith's 'clear commercial hand.'

Back at Drishane on 1 September, Martin had a letter from her sister Edith
with 'a poor account of Robert' and she made arrangements to travel back to
Ross the following day. She found her brother 'not suffering but the nights
terribly restless', living with his sister Edith in Waterfield. He refused to die in
Ross, and was to show his disgust with his tenants in the same way that many
Anglo-Irish landlords were to do. They repudiated Ireland, and their ancient

family burying places. His mother was at Ross, and his estranged wife was staying at the Railway Hotel in Oughterard. On the 10th, Martin wrote in her diary: 'I went over to Ross in the morning and came back with Mama, who saw Robert for the last time.' On the night of the 12th/13th Robert 'passed into a deep sleep about 9 o'clock. He slept more and more quietly til 3.30 on this Wednesday morning when he passed out of life in perfect peacefulness.' He was fifty-eight years old, he had no male heir and no house and lands to bequeath; it was the end of the line that connected the family of Martin with the house and lands of Ross.

Martin moved from Waterfield to Ross to support her mother. The funeral was at mid-day on Saturday, 16 September. Martin wrote in her diary: 'He is buried at Oughterard by his own wish – to the great anger of the tenants.' Few of his London socialite and theatrical acquaintances made the journey to the funeral, but Robert's Irish friends were there – Hugh McCalmont, Charlie Callwell and Bob Martin.[30] Edith wrote to Hildegarde, who was on holiday, on the 23rd, explaining the difficulties of the youngest daughter of Ross: 'Till Edith [Dawson] gets another house – or *builds another room* – Martin has to mind her mother.' There was another worry in that Hildegarde was pregnant again for the fourth time with the baby both sisters determinedly called Katharine, and her deliveries had been increasingly difficult. Edith's letter carried on: 'I suppose if it be Katharine far from requiring pity you will rejoice – I *trust* you may be right and the signs and tokens point to a female "For they are by far the more amiable sex" as Miss Currey's grandfather said. Still the prospect of a winter of discontent and no hunting is not very cheerful, and I cannot pretend to say I like it. It must be of a very determined and hardy nature if all your *appalling* sightseeings did not daunt it.'

Edith was suffering her own difficulties. Nominally in charge of Drishane, she had to co-ordinate the financial contributions of her brothers to the upkeep and maintenance of the place. With none of her brothers permanently on site, irritating problems arose that placed her at a public disadvantage. They were trying to keep up a house and lands which, even in combination, they had insufficient finances to maintain. Edith wrote to Hildegarde on 29 September:

> Cameron, having ordered the green-house, promising to pay £40 down, and the rest at Christmas, departed, telling Strawson that Miss Somerville would give further orders. Accordingly I made all sorts of plans and arrangements, got the old house down and ordered the new one. Then came a letter from Strawson asking for the £40 promised, before starting work. I sent his letter to Aylmer. After a week another letter from John Strawson, again demanding money. I wired to Aylmer (who is still

recuperating his overworked constitution at Lahinch) and heard this morning that "he hasn't a penny at the bank", and Cameron had taken the £40 to India! You may faintly imagine my lawful rage – I had, of the two, dissuaded the job. I had said, and I was right, that fifteen shillings worth of timber would have held the old house up for a long time, but Aylmer himself suggested using Collins' fine and Cameron eagerly agreed. Now the old house is swept, everything will die, and "what to say to Strawson I cannot tell" – the longer I live the less opinion I have of men's business capacity. With but few exceptions they are impulsive and untrustworthy and *dishonest* – in our family anyhow.

At Ross, Martin wrote endlessly at replies to the flood of letters of sympathy on Robert's death; for almost a month with her sister Selina she helped her mother. On 11 October she threw off the demands of the house and went to the lawyer Robinson: 'and concluded the raising of my charge on Ross at a cost of £18'.[31] On the next day she was back in Drishane, leaving Selina in charge of her mother. She settled down to writing. On 26 October Edith entered in her diary 'Brooded over story 6' but two days later remarked that 'it patched slowly'. This is a valuable remark, suggesting the joining together of small sections of finished pieces, like a pointilliste painter structuring his painting, or an embroiderer stitching sections. Perhaps the story 'patched' so slowly because at this time Edith was absorbed by nursing a hound puppy called Rainbow, whose death from combined distemper, dysentery and eczema she staved off. During this hunting season, Edith was overcome with pride at her hound puppies, Graceful, Clarion and Carbery, which she had bred and reared herself, becoming notable and reliable in the hunting field.[32] She told Hildegarde that the success of her young hounds gave her solace during the fiasco of the Drishane greenhouse demolition.

On 29 November, 1905, at the age of seventy-nine, Sir Joscelyn Coghill died, and life changed dramatically for Hildegarde and Egerton, who inherited the baronetcy and a load of troubles. Early in December Edith published another one of her solo productions, a pamphlet for the hunting fraternity on hound puppy walking, reviewed favourably in *The Field* and in *Horse and Hound*. Martin spent Christmas in CT, an unusual event for her, but returned to her mother at Ross for New Year's Eve. Before she left on 27 December, Edith noted that they had finished No. 6. There had been a slight improvement: a writing time of four months compared to the five months of No. 5. Martin moved from Ross to her sister's house, Waterfield, early in January 1906 but isolated herself in Naughton's Hotel on the 24th on account of a streaming cold. Edith went up to Dublin from CT on the 26th to the Greenes, travelling with the two little dogs, Candy and Sheila. With a cousin she went to the Abbey Theatre to see *Riders to the Sea* and *The Eloquent Dempsey*, and was enchanted by the acting of Fay but 'indifferent' otherwise. From Dublin on Wednesday the 31st Edith wrote to Martin giving the name and address of a nurse, highly recommended by the Windles, who could come at once to care for her mother, who was declining fast. Two days later Edith joined Martin at Waterfield to give support to her during Nannie's last hours. The doctors could do nothing for her, saying that her heart was in a state of gradual collapse. She recognised no-one for the last ten days of her life. Edith stayed with Martin for a week from the 2nd, and tried to distract Martin with work by talking over the next RM story, No. 7. And yet another stop-gap volume was in the offing: on 3 February she 'Wrote to Pinker about the summer volume that Longmans wants us to bring out.' This was *Some Irish Yesterdays*, quickly nicknamed by Martin as 'the rubbish book'.

Martin entered in her diary on the 8th: 'at 6 am laboured breathing until 9.45 when she ceased to breathe. Amy [Charlie Martin's widow], Edith S and I, the Nurse and Annie were there', and on the following day: 'Spent the day in a maze of telegrams, arrangements and distress. Alfred Jackson came at once and undertook everything – ECES invaluable.' Edith wrote to Cameron: 'I needn't say that Martin, with her peculiar fidelity, feels it, and will continue to feel it, harder than anyone and at this moment she looks the most miserable ghost I ever laid eyes on. I am going away tomorrow.' Edith left because Waterfield was too small to hold all the family that were gathering for Nannie's funeral. Vast numbers of local people gathered also; Mrs Martin was known and loved far and wide; she had been a familiar figure driving in her trap drawn by her pony Killola. Unlike her son Robert, she, who had struggled through the Famine at Ross with her husband half a century before, made no break with her tenants and tradition. She was, Martin wrote in her diary 'buried in Killanin. Killola following the hearse with the pony carriage filled with all the flowers. Tenants met it at Rosscahill, and carried the coffin from the turn to Killanin to the vault, which was lined with moss and ferns by Alfred Jackson. All that friendship and good feeling could do was done – all the men of the neighbourhood there.' Nurse Dodwell, the friend of the Windles who had come so quickly to assist Mrs Martin, stayed on 'to help, and to see the poor people and others who came'. Before leaving Galway, Edith had persuaded Martin to keep Sheila with her for sympathetic company. This had been an inspired thought. For one thing, it forced Martin out of the house twice a day for walks. Martin went to stay with old friends, the More O'Ferralls at 'Balyna' [*sic*], Moy Valley,[33] before returning to Drishane on 21 February: Sheila 'travelled 3rd with me with complete success.'

Various difficulties about the future were being worked out in Martin's mind. Having come through the death of her brother and mother in the space of five months, and being in poor health, we might suppose that she had decided where she herself wished to be buried. She had a horror of the graveyard at Oughterard; after her mother's death she broke her connection with Galway. She had never liked her brother Robert's wife Connie, who now moved in to Ross with her daughter Barbara, but they were not to use the house as their main dwelling. Martin shifted her base from Ross to CT, moving about between the households of Hildegarde and Edith depending on the bed situation. Martin was back in Drishane by late February, when Edith told Cameron that Martin was 'more like herself and we are at work again on Number VII of the new R.Ms.' Cameron was chastised in this letter for allowing his mortgage debt to the bank, which was apparently his system of running an overdraft, to stand at £1,000. As the heir to Drishane, he could raise such a sum on the security of his inheritance. This was a discovery that Edith found extremely alarming, as she herself panicked when her overdraft approached £100. Thirty-four years later, shortly before Cameron died, it was revealed that his financial state had only worsened and he was trapped in the pocket of a Skibbereen Bank manager.

Early in March they started assembling their 'new' volume: 'Hunted for MS for summer book, found "literary remains" in all sorts of forgotten purlieus.' Edith wrote in her diary. Later in the month, she was shocked when a cousin of Martin's, Zoe Callwell, published an article in *Blackwood's Magazine* in the style of Somerville and Ross, posing as a 'Miss Martin of Ross'. Edith flew into a passion, telling Cam that it was 'the most offensive stealing of another's thunder that I have ever known for a long time ... Martin is so maddeningly full of goodness and family feeling, and rot, that she wouldn't get into a comfortable rage. She only laughs idiotically ...' This was, as Edith realised, a reaction that failed to impress Zoe, and indeed she went on to write a volume in the same style.

At first 'the rubbish book' was entitled *Solos and Duets* as it contained pieces by both working together and alone, but Longman did not like this title and changed it.[34] They were more intriguing and marketable as a pair of women writing together; the manuscript went off, with twenty-two drawings by Edith, on 22 April. In May Edith started rebuilding 'The Beach House' with one of her favourite workmen, Jerry Leary (known as Jerry the Slow), but took a break with Martin in London for the first fortnight of June. On Martin's birthday, the 11th, Edith gave her a Kodak camera. She was then drawn away from writing with Edith by a commission to write a memorial portrait of Robert from Sir John Henniker Heaton, an MP, who failed to impress her when she went to London to meet him:

He is common and unclean, self important, tactless and vulgar. Good-hearted I am sure, and really devoted to Robert – but I don't wonder at Robert's feeling toward him. He has obviously force of character and an excellent opinion of himself. He has a stomach, and a large capable face, like a pale Falstaff – looks about fifty. I should say his literary sense was naught. Probably I was tired and captious but he was abhorrent to me in connection with Robert. The gist of it all is the book is to be crown octavo – and as well as I can make out, my part is to be about 15,000 words! He said 'about twelve columns of *The Times* – but you write all you like, and we can select what is wanted. – I at once said that I was too busy to write stuff that might not be wanted, and he seemed quite surprised – I don't think that he at all realises the position, or that I am a professional writer. I shall not put you in a passion by telling you any more of his recommendations and advice ... I fear Old Henniker disliked me; it was so very hard to be in the least nice to him ...[35]

This letter from 10 July written at the New Century Club shows Martin in decided contrast to Edith, who could never have brought herself to retort in person quite so sharply to a man, but used humour and diversions in similar situations. Her dislike would not have been so overt, but instead shared with her intimates later. Edith came back on her own from London: 'That odious and idiotic Martin won't cross with me as she wants to go and see Rose Helps ... going 3rd from London to Cork [alone] is *not* enjoyable', she complained to Hildegarde. It was not only the Somerville sisters who were in a financially perilous state. Boyle could not be sure that he would gain promotion in the Navy and was thinking of early retirement. Edith wrote to Hildegarde on the 30th: 'I think I shall advise him seriously to study architecture as if he has to leave the Navy at 45, he ought to have some trade, and with his taste, inventiveness and capacity for figures and mathematics he ought to be a very good architect. I don't know what his pension will be – Hamilton Currey got £300 as a Lieut. – with promotion on leaving – B ought to get more having served as a Commander.' Martin did not begin to write Robert's memoir until the end of August when she was staying with Edith Dawson at Waterfield. She visited Ross, where Robert's widow Connie was staying, and was numbed by her feelings, inexpressible to Connie.

While Martin was at Ross, Edith had a revolution in her writing life and dealings with publishers. She employed a typist, Miss V. Plunket, to type the manuscript of the second series of RM stories No. 8 and No. 9, 'A Horse! A Horse!' Up until this time Edith had laboriously clean-copied every page of their work. She went to the Dublin Horse Show at the end of the month, and when she returned started cubbing twice a week. Dr Violet Coghill was looking after young Paddy and old Kendal in Glen B. Joint writing was fitted in around other events. Madge Robertson was staying on a painting holiday with Edith, and Martin had stayed on in Dublin. Edith wrote to Hildegarde to explain why there had been no writing lately: 'Martin has been coming every day this week and putting off as often. Finally yesterday a wire "May I stay for the Phoenix Park Races?" so I don't suppose she will come for another week. I am, in a way, glad, as she would only be killing herself tearing after Geraldine [Martin's sister, staying in CT] and 'til Madge has gone work would be impossible.'[36] In any case the memoir of her brother Robert absorbed Martin when she returned to Drishane in mid-September. A break from this fixation came at the end of October when she went with Edith to stay with the Penroses at Lismore. While they were there two excellent reviews of *Some Irish Yesterdays* appeared, one in *Punch* and one in the *Spectator*; the book had been published on 5 October.

The last essay of the book, 'Children of the Captivity', written by Martin, is her tribute to Connemara talk:

> One might safely say that this bare and still country carries an amount of good talk, nimble, trenchant, and humorous, to the square mile that the fat and comfortable plains of England could never rival. It has been so for centuries, and all the while the sons and daughters of Connemara have remained aloof and self-centred, hardly even aware of the marching life of England, least of all aware that Ireland holds the post of England's Court Jester. Others of their countrymen, more sophisticated, more astute, probably less agreeable, have not been slow to realise it. Perhaps they would have refused the Cap and Bells had they known what the privilege entailed.

'Children of the Captivity' also has a criticism of Kipling's use of brogue:

> It is strange that the error of making Irish ladies and gentlemen talk like their servants should to this hour have a fascination for novelists. It is not so very long since that, in a magazine, I read of a high born Irish Captain of Hussars, who, in a moment of emotion, exclaimed: 'Howly Mither av Hiven!' ... it is with diffidence that one arraigns one of the most enthralling of living story tellers. Few of his works have been more popular than 'Soldiers Three' yet to me and others of my country, it is the narratives of Private Mulvaney that give least pleasure. 'Gurl' for girl, 'Thimber' for timber and 'Quane' for 'Queen' are conventions that have unfortunately proved irresistible ... But, after all, right or wrong, pronunciation and spelling are small things in the presentment of any dialect. The vitalising power is in the rhythm of the sentence, the turn of phrase, the knowledge

of idiom, and of, beyond all, the attitude of mind ... to stud the page with 'ut' and 'av' instead of 'it' and 'of' is of no avail. Irish people do not say these things; there is a sound that is a half-tone between the two, not to be captured by English voices, still less by English vowels. ...

In some practical matters Martin was more happy-go-lucky than Edith, as we can gather from Edith's comments to Cameron in a letter of 13 September, 1906: 'Martin has always wished for a Kodak of her own but now, having got one, she never uses it, or when she does, she exposes the same lot of films twice, and does every stupid thing in the world, *especially* never having it when she chiefly needs it. She is in Dublin now and says she will be back by the end of the week. I hope she will as we ought to get on with our work ...'[37] Edith was aware of Pinker and bank managers breathing down their necks.

The year 1906 was a bad one on many fronts, due to the ill health of Ethel Penrose, who was almost blinded by an eye infection, and of Geraldine Hewson, Martin's sister, who, like Martin, suffered severe headaches and had also become totally deaf. Geraldine was at this time living in a cottage in CT. A colleague and friend of Dr Violet Coghill's, Dr Eleanor Hodson, had moved into the Mall House as Edith's tenant, and found herself called upon for medical advice so often that she might easily have started an early form of well-woman clinic. Apart from the painting, Madge Robertson was staying in CT to recuperate from an accident. Edith described for Cameron an afternoon outing that summer: 'We had the most deplorable Cripples Home Picnic the other day, personally conducted by Martin and me – Ethel the Blind, Geraldine the Deaf, Madge Roberston the Lame. We made merry over the Hospital Ship in which they were ferried over to Reene but it was most melancholy. Thank goodness Ethel is really much better, and will, I hope, get absolutely allright in time, but she is very helpless in black goggles and a heavy cardboard shade ... I am *mighty* hard up just now as no subs [West Carbery Hunt subscriptions] have come in and many outgoings have gone out – but I hope times will mend. Martin is still busy with the memoir of Robert, so our other work is standing still.' Ignoring financial restrictions, Cameron had been trying hard to get Edith to join him in Japan, but she wrote to explain that she had read and heard so much about it that she felt she knew Japan 'as well as you or Lafcadio Hearn. Anyhow it could wait until we are both out of debt.'[38] Being 'in the black again' was never to come to Cameron, and to Edith only at the end of her life. Extraordinarily it transpired that Cameron had not read Lafcadio Hearn's book on Japan, and Edith, generous as ever, sent him Hearn's double volume with the heartfelt note: 'It is melancholy to think that such a clever man, and an artist, should never have been clear of money troubles.'

On 21 November Edith wrote a letter to Cameron that shows that the hunting fall in 1898 had affected Martin's head, though the connection between her damaged back and spine and her frequent headaches may not have been recognised. Martin was in Dublin: 'Martin's tickets don't expire until Saturday and I don't expect to see her till they do – Her head is still far from being the thing and I am feeling very anxious as to how we are to get ahead with our work. It is *absolutely* important to us both, financially, to get these things written [the Further Experiences]. It is no use my tackling them alone – Good or bad they wouldn't be the same thing, and neither public nor publishers would be content. I am thankful she has not been here lately, as the weather has been horrid, and today is thick fog and howling wind, a combination known only to West Carbery.' The transference of landholding from landlord to tenant had gone on wholesale since the Wyndham Act of 1903, and by 1906 the workings of this transference had become labyrinthine. Edith tried to explain to Cameron in this same letter of 21 November how their own lands were affected. She puts forward here the idea of safeguarding Drishane lands by becoming Cameron's agricultural tenant, and working them herself. Though nothing could have been better for the succeeding male heirs, for Edith it was to mean more than thirty years of constant financial worry, and a huge investment of her own time and money:

> [there is] a wave of buying going on and on all sides one hears of sales. Egerton's men are mostly buying and he hopes they may all come in. The danger now is for landlords who hold untenanted farms (like yourself) – Jim [Penrose] says there is a commission for purchasing these and cutting them up into 'economical holdings' – so far, of course, this is not compulsory, but the fear with this brutal government is that it may be made so. It makes me feel very nervous. I even talked to Aylmer about *my* taking one of your farms and buying it under the Act. The worst of it is that they won't accept for purchase any tenancies subsequent to 1902 of more than £30 per annum – I would of course leave it to you in my will, and as I would be an agricultural tenant they couldn't compulse it out of me. I think it is worth considering. If Aylmer or Boyle took it, you might not like them to leave it away from their children (unless one of them succeeds you) which is why I suggest my taking it, as that would come to the same thing as your keeping it. I might even put horses on it, as Harry Becher does, and make a little money besides paying rent. The fine could be deducted from the £400 of mine which is already in the property. It would be maddening to have to give up Farrandhau or Farrandeligeen on compulsion to any ruffian whom the estates commission might want to give it to.

Edith was right to be alarmed about Cameron's personal finances, as he enjoyed playing the stock exchange. On 11 October she wrote to Cameron and Boyle together, as they had coincided at a place called Shwebo on the coast of Ceylon, and had also met up with Martin's brother Jim. The Somerville brothers were sharing a bungalow: 'I am glad you met Jim Martin [ – ] I have only met him once, but I thought him very nice, and Mother fell desperately in love with him. I hope he has not "deluded you" to chance all your income in rubber! It seems a fascinating gamble, but I should live in terror of a German chemist inventing a substitute ... as they did with indigo whereby they ruined all the indigo planters...' Martin's brother Jim was at this time a rubber planter in Ceylon. Boyle was commanding HMS *Sealark* on the Ceylon Coast Survey. There were more deaths in the family. At the end of November, Martin's half-sister Emily, daughter of James Martin's first wife, who had married Augustine Barton of Rochestown, died at the family home in Merrion Square. She was the mother of the painter Rose Barton. Though only forty-four, Martin must have felt ominous forebodings. At last in the middle of December Dr Hodson, who had seen her briefly once before, examined Martin thoroughly. She wrote in her diary: 'Eleanor Hodson examined me again and said anaemia was mixed up with my disorder.' Her medication was changed.

Pinker does not seem to have kept his authors well informed about their sales. To her surprise and amazement on 9 December Martin saw an advertisement for their new book, making much of the fact that it was in its ninth thousand after three months. They began to cast a cold eye upon him. As she always did, Martin made a résumé at the end of her 1906 diary on New Year's Eve. 'At Drishane with E Œ S. Influenza at Glen B and Tally Ho – and everywhere in the British Isles. Sylvia Greene [Herbert's mother, Edith's aunt] hanging between life and death as the result of an attack – Kendal Coghill pretty bad from it in London. Edith D at Waterfield – Geraldine and Eileen at Blackrock. Katie and Co spending final days at Newcastle. Hamilton [Katie's husband] has been Sec. of the Scottish Primrose League. Our *Irish Yesterdays* published in October has got to 9,000, including American and Colonial copies.' Edith's diary entry on the last day of the year included 'Martin's crockey head still keeps her from work.'

It was not until 1907 that the return to Skebawn, Flurry and Major Yeates worked its way out satisfactorily on to the written page. It was only on 2 February that they sent off the typescript of 'A Horse! A Horse!' to Pinker. At the same time they responded to a request from the *Grand Magazine* to supply 100 words on the subject of 'our best story' and had chosen 'The House of Fahy'. The prestigious Lyceum Book Exhibition showed two of Edith's black and white illustrations; Arthur Rackham had been one of the judges. But money was still tight: however much Edith earned, she never seemed to have any in

hand, and the hounds were a great expense. She was in financial difficulties with
the running of the West Carbery Hunt, one of her chief supporters at this time
being Morgan O'Donovan. He came to Drishane on 4 April to do the hunt
accounts with her; they were depressing, but he was supportive: 'Decided to go
on – idiotically from most points of view.' In this spring, Edith and Martin were
with the Penroses at Lismore from 12 April to 3 May; here they did some light
reading as their hosts kept up with all the latest books, and had a good library.
The Western islands were beginning to draw students of Irish literature and
folklore, and to be written about. Edith and Martin were interested to read
other writers' reactions to 'the Aras of the Sea'; Edith read Synge's book on
Aran and though it 'first rate stuff'.[39] A reviving Martin went off on a tour of
friends in June, but before she left Lismore they had finished 'A Royal
Command', later RM story No. 2 in the *Further Experiences*. She stayed with
her new friend Nora Tracey, her masseuse, at Radway in Bishop's Teignton in
Devon, and seemed ready for anything. It was a sign that Martin's health was
improving that she attended the 1907 Derby with the Pinkers, and stayed with
them as their guest. Edith wrote in astonishment to Cameron: 'Little Pinker
now drives a four-in-hand in the summer! It is far more profitable to keep
people to write for you than to write yourself.'[40]

Early in July, six years after Emmie's death, Aylmer married again; his
second wife was Nathalie Turner, daughter of W.B. Turner of Ponsonby Hall,
Cumberland. There were to be two children of this marriage – Gilbert, and
Elizabeth, who later married Captain Paul Chavasse. After the wedding a CT
family party had taken off for Champex – Jack, Hildegarde and Egerton, Edith,
Madge Robertson and a Mr and Mrs Wilson. Egerton and Edith found it
difficult to find anything paintable, and the party's chief amusement was music-
making. Edith had long stretches of time where she did not know where or how
Martin was, and the uncertainty of her health and the constant possibility of
over-riding doctors' orders made plans terribly difficult to pin down. From
Champex she wrote: 'I am wondering when I shall hear from you as to our
plans and what you can do, and where you will go ...' Mrs Wilson was a trial:
'She was a Miss Knyvett – a good family – and has all the English anxiety to let
you know it.'[41] Soon Champex was abandoned, and on 7 August Martin joined
Edith in Devon at a holiday house taken by Egerton and Hildegarde.

Drishane was let for August so Edith had to hitch on to her sister's household. When they travelled back through Dublin at the end of the month, Edith
and Martin were immobilised at the Greenes' in Dublin when Martin got
lumbago in her back, Candy got broncho-pneumonia and Edith caught something like it with a terrible cough. They were in Dublin for the Horse Show.
Getting their distress signal, Hildegarde came on 31 August to nurse them all.

On top of all this, Jim and Dick Martin came to the invalids to say goodbye before going out to Ceylon, where Dick was going to be a tea planter. After they left, Martin was sunk into 'a deep and deathly depression'. As happened so often at low times, Ethel Penrose 'swooped down' in her motor and took them off to Lismore on 4 September where there were 'large fires everywhere and much comfort'. They were back at Drishane on the 29th, but there were still no diary entries from Martin; and Edith had made no headway in making Cameron face the Land Commission and Drishane's future. 'I most deeply agree with you in *loathing* the Act, but I feel it is a case of needs must, it is better to arrange your manner of going yourself, than to be driven out by those devils in the Land Commission. I knew you would keep the Castle and orchard, and the fort [Knockdrum] and Horse Island. What a hard unjust thing it is that a man is forced to sell his birthright!'[42]

Martin's diary entries began to pick up again on 16 October, when she was taken by Dr Hodson in her car to hear a celebrated court case going on at that time in Skibbereen: 'A delightful counsel for the defendants A M Sullivan made the best of a bad case.' As we know from his memoirs, the delightful A.M. Sullivan had noticed Edith and Martin taking notes in court some years before – 'two girls studying the scene before them' – and had wondered who they were. By the time he published his memoirs in 1952 they starred in his opening remarks.[43] Still in the Far East, Cameron had settled into a new billet and wrote to Edith describing his new companions, apropos of whom she wrote back: 'I hope your new menage (not womenage) is going on smoothly – I quite agree with you – either all men or all women (I prefer the latter) a mixed crowd inevitably creates rows.' This is an interesting reflection on CT society, which had a good share of womanisers and manisers and a rolling boil of sexual intrigue.

At a meet at the Clock Tower in Skibbereen on 4 November Edith was delighted by solid support from the town dwellers and followers: 'Dr Jennings took the Cap. In all £5.15 shillings. A record.' All through the month they worried away at the writing of story No. 12, 'The Whiteboys', the last in the second RM series. The opening of this story can be analysed, as the sources are available, to show the density of references packed into the pages of these stories. Because of their experience with the introduction to the Buddh Dictionary, in which they were fortified by Dr Johnson's recommendation of 'frigid tranquillity' in the face of defeat and dismissal, they used him as a touchstone, and in this story twice. It opens: 'It has been said by an excellent authority that children and dogs spoil conversation. I can confidently say that had Madame de Sevigne and Dr Johnson joined me and my family on our wonted Sunday afternoon walk to the kennels, they would have known what it was to be ignored.' Mr Knox's pack was about to be augmented by the purchase of three couple of old white Irish hunting hounds from the pack of an ancient Irish head of a family, old O'Reilly of Fahoura. Two incidents with the existing hounds in kennel are taken straight from letters to Hildegarde on pages one and two, including the killing of the old hound Solomon by the new draft in 1893. At Fahoura the huge and stately old man rises from his chair to greet Flurry and Major Yeates with the greeting made to Boswell and Johnson by a highland chieftain who knew of Boswell's family but disdained to know the name of Johnson: 'Your father's son is welcome, Mr Florence Knox, and your friend ...' He gives them drink, a choice of old port or old potheen, and starts to talk of his hounds, 'in my family, seed and breed, this hundred years and more', giving an anecdote that is a précis of one recorded in Notebook 10. It was told to Dr O'Meara by a Mallow hotel-owner: 'At the funeral of the Huntsman of the Duhallows there was a great concourse of farmers, all anxious to help in carrying his coffin. There was some delay about getting the key of the graveyard and the farmers took the coffin in straight over the wall. They said he shouldn't be looking for a gate now, he never did it in his lifetime.' Showing the writers' tremendous compression of rich material, this anecdote is reduced to one and a half sentences in the published story. Martin never forgot Sir William Gregory's good advice of 1889 on 'care and finish'.

In Notebook 10 there are loose letters containing material that might be of use. Many friends and relatives fed this source of supply. On 9 December Edith Dawson wrote to Martin to tell her of 'the nine foxes that came round Gormanston when Lord Gormanston died'. Spectral foxes flit through the novels and stories, like *The Silver Fox* (who turned out to be real) and 'The Dog from Doone' (made of mist, but pursued by a pack of hounds). On the 15th, the *Sporting and Dramatic* printed a full-page picture of the West Carbery Hunt. Only its woman Master and the fame of Somerville and Ross had brought this distinction to this small and impoverished hunt. Martin was still not returning to her former vigour as a diarist. For the first time at the turn of the year, there is no Martin family record of who was where.

The first entry to leap out in Martin's 1908 diary is in red. On 14 January: 'sent off the typewritten MS of last RM story to Pinker.' It had gone to England with Edith. Two days before, Martin had written, 'E went to London via Lismore by the early train and I entered into residence at Glen B.' In London Edith was making a deal with the *Graphic*, 'who are to begin our stories in the summer number.' Jack accompanied her for moral support. In February Edith Dawson became dangerously ill with double pneumonia and Martin was with her at Waterfield from the 14th to the end; her son Lionel had come in time to be with her when she died four days later. This death was one from which Martin never recovered. Edith had been the sister closest to her in age and in temperament; Martin stayed on in Galway with Edith's husband Cuthbert. She went with him on 30 April to attend a Land Commission court to hear the widow of their old steward, Thady Connor, plead her case against her daughter-in-law, who was making a joint claim on Thady's land. 'After the production of Thady's will, the daughter-in-law's name was crossed out. Home in satisfaction.'[44] There are no diary entries by Martin from the day of Edith Dawson's death until mid-April. During March, while Martin was away, Edith Somerville had decided to pass the hounds on to another Master. She had discovered that in five years she had spent £850 of her own money in keeping them. Morgan O'Donovan agreed with her to advertise for a new Master. She kept at work and by the end of March she had finished the illustrations for the new RM. A possible new Master, Major Burns Lindow, wrote at the end of April and was to appear on 8 May; a difficulty for him was that he would need stabling for hunt horses as well as a house. But he refused to buy the hounds and have to build stables as well.

As though they could not get rid of one problem without getting another to replace it, in April 1908 Edith and Hildegarde made a far-reaching decision. They agreed that they would run the Drishane farm together in order to save it for Cameron's heir. Their brother Aylmer, who had run it and was an experienced farmer, was going to leave Ireland. Edith wrote to explain the situation to Cameron, at a time when Boyle was home on leave: 'I quite expect that he and Nathalie [Aylmer's second wife] are going to chuck this place. They are able to give up their lease at the end of seven years and that unluckily is next year – I think it is a bad thing all round. Aylmer will turn into a foreign watering place loafer, and the children will have no real home. Also Tally Ho having been made hideous and unwieldy at great expense, to please them, will now be flying back on Egerton and Hildegarde's hands ... I suppose that Egerton and I will be able to manage your affairs; we shall have to try, but Aylmer is a clever farmer, and we know next to nothing ... Here is Boyle and as the Queen of Sheba demands instant attention I can say no more'. She finished the letter later: 'Boyle looks very well and is a most satisfactory Sheba ... how I wish you were with us!' Martin was still at Oughterard with Cuthbert when she had 'two shattering pieces of news' from CT on 5 May: 'Longmans payment of £337.10. being one and Hildegarde has measles.' A week later at CT, Edith, the retiring MFH, received a tribute from her fellow hunters: 'Morgan O'D came over and said that he had collected nearly £50 with which to erect a tombstone to me. Begged to be allowed to build stables for the Hunt with it.' Martin did not pack up her things at Waterfield and return to Dublin until 25 May; she met up with Edith there two days later. On the following day they heard that Major Burns Lindow had decided to take Shana Court, by the two trees on CT main street, and the

Hunt. They were back in CT at the end of the month, but bedless: 'Drishane being uninhabitable because of the painters', their standby Glen B was crammed and no work could be done anywhere in the place. Beguiling Hildegarde to come with them, they went to London on 19 June.

Edith, Hildegarde and Martin went off to London on a deliberate spree. They saw the Horse Show and the Exhibition, but most importantly they attended the 'monster' Women's Suffrage meeting in Hyde Park. It was calculated that there were 240,000 people in the Park. It was very orderly; the suffragettes had put up twenty platforms in a large circle of about a quarter of a mile in diameter. First off the CT party, which included a 'loudly complaining' Jack, fought their way to hear Mrs Pethick Lawrence speaking, and were impressed by her pleasant manner and way with hecklers. She managed to keep a melodious tone in her voice despite having to project it very firmly. Edith described the scene to Cameron: 'The leaders are many of them ladies and highly educated ones, but it is the middle classes (chiefly) and the professional classes who are backing them and therein lies their strength.' Edith and Martin realised that the platform surrounded by booing and howling youths, who were ringing handbells to try to distract the speaker, was the station occupied by Christabel Pankhurst. They fought their way close to her to see her in action: 'She is a *very* extraordinary girl. She is only about 20 and has just taken an Ll.D degree in Edinburgh. She is not tall but has a good figure and a most interesting face. A sort of typical revolutionary, she stood with head flung back, fronting the crowd dauntlessly, and emphasising her very able speech with the most picturesque and effective gestures. She has beautiful hands and uses them with amazing effect. Her voice carried better than any of the others. The last act in the performance was a bugle call, after which the multitude lifted up its voice and its hats and roared "Votes for Women!". I had climbed a railing so I could see away over the heads of the packed masses and I never saw anything more extraordinary than the sudden outburst of men's straw hats on sticks and fluttering pocket handkerchiefs when the shout was raised ...'[45]

On the following day they attended a Suffrage meeting at the Queen's Hall at which Christabel spoke again, introducing to the packed assembly one of the movement's founders Mrs Wolstenholme Elmy. Mrs Pethick Lawrence made a brief appeal for monetary support and £300 was collected in hats in ten minutes. For light relief they went to a music hall and saw the celebrated Maud Allen, only to be shocked by her 'indecent' performance. 'I suppose we (VM and H) are not up to date but it seemed to us a singularly indecent show.' Hildegarde and Edith returned to Drishane leaving Martin in London making intensive calls on relatives 'with a vague promise of following us the week after next'; this was a wise move. At the beginning of July masons began to demolish the side wall of Drishane to insert the new front door, and the RM stories began to appear in the *Graphic*. By this time Martin had gone to visit first the Dawsons at Lowestoft, and then Nora Tracey in Devon. On 16 July she went to Cheltenham to see Frannie Taylor. She reappeared at Drishane on the 21st: 'where was Edith Candy and Sheila and the new and beautiful front door.' Though much disliked, regular tenants at Drishane funded summer travel, as well as its renovation.

On 4 August Edith and Martin went to stay with the Cholmondeleys at Edstaston Hall and plunged into local horsy life at the Wem Horse Show. On the 11th, while the Chomondeleys, as paying tenants, then travelled over to holiday in Drishane, Edith and Martin went to Montreuil. There they joined a group of friends who had gone ahead of them, and were met at the station by the American painter Helen Simpson. Advance copies of *Further Experiences of an Irish R.M.* were sent to them at Montreuil by Longmans on the 29th; Martin had an uplift of spirits after its publication and excellent reviews. They returned to London on 13 September, where Edith shopped at high speed for necessities, and then went to Ethel in Lismore on the 16th. They were back at Drishane two days later.

Edith tended to capitalise any diary entry that was momentous. On the 25th September Morgan O'Donovan had convened a special meeting of the hunt members: 'the great and terrible day of the presentation of the Hunt Testimonial. MORGAN MADE A SPEECH AND GAVE ME A SILVER HORN, a list of subscribers' names, framed, and a cheque for £47.13 shillings.' After this fulsomeness the contrast with her current finances was all the more painful. After telling Hildegarde: 'At the function I wore that Exeter blue dress and a new and rather nice Woodrow hat', she revealed that Burns Lindow, the replacement Master, was screwing as much as he could out of Edith for his purchase money: 'All this is thoroughly English and no more than one ought to expect, yet it is hard to remember how different are their ways from ours.' And still they had guests. Martin's friend and masseuse Nora Tracey was staying at Drishane: 'No trouble at all and a nice creature.'[46] On 8 October Edith entered in her diary: 'Made up my bank book. Have £2 2s. 6d. to face a frowning world.'

Edith was riding to hounds under the new management. Burns Lindow was not very good as a Master, and seems to have been too pig-headed to acknowledge a woman as having anything worthwhile to tell him about what was a very difficult and quirky hunting country. There was a surprise on 8 November when Edith's fox terrier Sheila, who had somehow evaded a complete and strict incarceration during her last heat, gave birth to five puppies on Edith's bed in the early morning: 'All alive and Sheila herself wonderful considering her bad illness beforehand,' wrote Martin in her diary. The unlooked-for puppies took up a lot of time, but Edith was dead set against the drowning of complete litters of pups or kittens, telling Cameron that it was bad for the mother's future health to do so. Cameron had no qualms about destroying complete litters; Edith was to be very angry when he drowned the litter of kittens born to his cat Buchanan.[47]

At Drishane for Christmas and the New Year 1909, Martin again did not enter her habitual account of the whereabouts of all the close members of her remaining family. On 7 January a telegram came from Geraldine in Kilkenny to say that Selina was very ill with acute bronchitis. In her diary Martin wrote: 'Up at six and left by the 8.25 with Egerton who was starting on his trip to India'. But by this time Selina had already died 'quite peacefully'; she was not taken back to Galway to be buried. Ross House was beginning to fall back into the dilapidation that it was in when Martin and her mother returned to it in 1888. Barbara Martin, Robert's daughter and its nominal heiress, was there infrequently. There were nephews of Robert Martin's who might have made an arrangement with the Land Commission such as Robert had, but none came forward. The Ross servant Julia Lee wrote a letter of condolence to Martin that describes the half-alive house, falling again into decay:

> Dear Miss Violet
> it was only today I heard from my Granny of Miss Selina's death indeed I am awfully sorry for her but I hope God had seen her prepared to go after all her years of preparation and that her soul may rest in Heaven.
> My heartfelt sympathy in all your troubles, indeed you have had your share for the last few years and I trust God will give you strength to overcome them and live long to forget.
> ... It is sad seeing all the family out of Ross now – and it doesn't seem like the old place at all – all its beauty is destroyed since the woods has been cut down. All the timber is cleared out now and the fellers are cutting Captain Martin's wood up in Doone. It was a North of Ireland man who had the shooting this season ... Wat [Lee] and his wife are living in the house during the winter... – believe me it is a serious loss to all the boys of the place that there is none of the Martin family in Ross and its everyone's wish and prayer that Master James will yet reign in our midst ...[48]

The West Carbery Hunt was in an unhappy state, with conflict between the new Master and many of the regular riders. Muriel Currey had started hunting during the winter of 1908/9 and makes an important intervention in her transcript of the diaries to explain what became of the ill-fated Major Burns Lindow: 'I have very clear recollections of that unfortunate winter. The position got worse and worse; Major Burns Lindow was inexperienced and ignorant of the country. A clever man, which he was not, would have played up to D. asking for her help, but he ignored her. All the time she was criticising his every mistake with the result that he made more. The whole village combined against him and his wife and treated them as pariahs. Every afternoon there was an indignation meeting in one house or another.' The situation became so tense on the hunting field that Edith had abandoned regular hunting by 9 January 1909.

She was otherwise occupied with agriculture. At the end of the month the arrangements for the joint farm at Drishane fell into place. Aylmer had reconsidered leaving: 'Hildegarde and I of the one part, Cameron of the other, Aylmer manager. To start with about 25–30 cows. My £400 that was in the property being absorbed in a half share of stock etc.' On 3 February 'The Drishane House Dairy' formally began operation. At opportune moments Edith and Martin talked about a new novel. Then the WCH Master resigned, but he was asked by the more polite members of the Hunt to reconsider his resignation, and returned to the field. On 9 March both Edith and Martin hunted from a meet at Lissard, Martin 'going great guns and none the worse'. Edith simply notes after the Patrick's Day Hunt: 'Finish of the worst season ever known in West Carbery.' Martin's diary was blank through February and March; but on 9 March she had entered that she went out hunting again at the Lissard meet. She was especially amused to be accompanied by her young niece Muriel Currey, her sister Katie's daughter, ecstatically riding Edith's beautiful Tarbrush. And she notes that she hunted again on St Patrick's Day in a field of twenty-two riders. Evidently Martin must have been benefitting from Dr Hodson's advice, and she took heart. With the hunting over, she went with Edith to see Pinker in London and they were so optimistic as to sign an agreement: to have written 40,000 words by 30 June for Methuens. This was to be *Dan Russel the Fox* of 1911.

By March, after just a month as farmers, Hildegarde and Edith had become so perplexed by keeping farm accounts, which kept getting mislaid in miscellanea, that they decided to sacrifice a bedroom in Drishane as a farm office. Writing to Cameron, she said: 'We are nothing now if not commercial. I have been doing accounts all morning, and feel that the courtly language of trade is most natural and appropriate.' She had just applied to the Board of Trade for a loan to subsidise the building of a Cow House. With the help of their dairymaid Delia Fahy, they were experimenting with the production of cream cheeses. She told him that Martin had started to hunt again, with no ill effects. 'Her nerve is as good as ever it was. Since it doesn't kill her, it will do her good.'[49] Leaving the farm in Aylmer's hands, after seeing Pinker in London they went abroad via Paris and Genoa to an Italian coastal resort for a holiday.

Edith's diaries, though telegraphic, sometimes have jottings recording peculiarly intense experiences. In 1909, on 10 April, when a quartette made up of Edith and Hildegarde, Martin and her friend Nora Tracey were staying in an hotel at Portofino, after much persuasion a Russian played the piano for his fellow-guests after dinner. The episode appears in *Irish Memories* as a worked up piece, but the diary entry shows the raw instantaneous record of feeling. 'A very old Russian was asked to play. A grey heap of ashes from which flames suddenly burst. Die Walkürenritt, slashed out of the heart of the terrified hotel piano. Never heard the like. Electrifying.'

The published piece covers a page, and reminds us of the thoroughness with which Adelaide had trained all her children as musicians, and how she had inculcated a lifelong sensitivity to music:

> An old Russian Prince had come to the hotel, a small, grey old man, feeble and fragile, in charge of a daughter. Gradually a rumour grew that he had been a great musician ... there was a long resistance, but at last the old Russian walked feebly to the piano, and seated himself on so low a stool that his wrists were below the level of the keyboard. I saw his fingers, grey and puffy, and rheumatic, settle with an effort on the keys. He looked like an ash-heap ready to crumble into dust. I said to myself that it was a brutality. And, as I said it, the ash-heap burst into flames, and Liszt's arrangement of 'Die Walkürenritt' suddenly crashed, and stormed, and swept. There was some element of excitement communicated by his playing that I have never felt before or since ... then, when it was all over, the old ash-heap, waiting for no plaudits, resigned himself to his daughter and was hustled off to bed ... As for the hotel piano, till that moment poor but upright, after that wild ride it could only remain prostrate, and could in future only whisper an accompaniment ... It transpired that the Russian had been the personal friend of Wagner, of Schumann, and of Liszt, in the brave old days at Leipsic, and was one of the few remaining repositories of the grand tradition.[50]

We should notice the simile of stirred ashes bursting into flame, an echo of the simile used in her *World* sonnets of 1889, twenty years before, and one that re-appears in *Notions in Garrison* of 1941. It is clear that emotional expression, transmuted and refined, was for Edith possible and acceptable in music. The emotional anguish that she sang about in German in her favourite *Lieder* surfaces in the love scenes of her novels but never in any personal papers. Her response to the expressionist paintings of Jack Yeats was horrified and uncomprehending. She never grew out of her childhood training in concealment and control, and learned well the lesson that as a woman she should be subservient, attentive and helpful to her menfolk.

Back at Drishane 6 June, Edith wrecked all the summer plans by twisting her ankle in a rut and breaking two bones in her leg. Drs Hodson and O'Meara gave Edith chloroform and set the leg in plaster. Martin was watching Edith anxiously: 'Towards dinner time she got a sort of nervous collapse which defied Eleanor [Hodson] and Katie Plunket, and O'Meara was sent for at 10 p.m. She was better when he arrived and he thought it nervous – the result of a shock and chloroform and morphia.'[51] Pinker and Methuen were put on hold. Showing great recuperative powers, by 21 July Edith was walking again. Eleanor Hodson was caring for the limb and gave instructions to Hildegarde and Martin on bathing and massage for the foot. Two days later a family party set off for Dublin to join up with the Cholmondeleys at the Dublin Horse Show. They all went to see *The Playboy of the Western World* (and 'did not care for it' – Martin; 'disliked it very much' – Edith) and Shaw's *Blanco Posnet* ('very strong and quite harmless' – Edith). Edith had a fine horse up for sale at the Horse Show, Kingcup, but did not sell, because he got stage fright and bolted out of the ring. On the 28th Edith went back to CT but Martin went to the Persses at Roxborough, then on to call on Ross people like Matt Kenealy and the Lees. She was at Coole for a weekend with Augusta Gregory, where she went riding with Robert Gregory on 18 August. She was back at Drishane a month later. A Mr Beamish was hunting around Skibbereen with an informal pack, and both Edith and Martin rode out with him.[52] It was clear that Martin was hunting with pleasure again, and at a meet at Drishane on 29 October rode Edith's big horse in hand, Condy. She was much improved in health and rode out on idle jaunts: on 10 November Dr Hodson rode Solomon, Edith rode Tarbrush, and Martin rode Condy on a pleasant ride over to Park Cottage to see the Porks. On the 22nd it was Hildegarde's turn to disappear for a rest cure with Dr Hodson: 'The excellent news that Paddy has got a second scholarship into Haileybury arrived just before H started for Bath with Eleanor for a cure.'[53] Very little was done in the way of writing.

At Christmas day dinner, everybody descended on Glen B for a gigantic game pie that Hildegarde had composed. She had three lady doctors staying as guests, her sister-in-law Violet Coghill, Eleanor Hodson and their colleague Lina O'Connor. They made a return meal at Drishane on the 27th when: 'Hildegarde and the three doctors dined here'.[54] Hildegarde was at the centre of a feminist cell concerned with medical care in the community. Eventually she set up a District Nurse, and through the United Irishwomen and their first-aid classes brought about changes in primitive conditions of home care for pregnant and nursing mothers, the elderly and the infirm – primitive in Big House and cottage alike. Finding a cure for Martin remained an intractable problem; though she was so close to these medical women, and not shy of consulting male doctors, her persistent malady remained a mystery. Their contract to write 40,000 words by 30 June had been a hopelessly optimistic ambition, and six months later at Christmas their diaries reveal little about progress on their current novel. To the fore in Edith's is livestock and stockmen and holiday tenants, which are seemingly of more importance. Their agent Pinker would have been aghast had he known the number of claims on the time of Edith Somerville, which were remote from the profession of author.

# CHAPTER 7

# The late novels: Ross's death and Somerville's reaction

Buckley has a little farm of 9 acres in Tracarta that he bought from you, under the act, for £70. He has advertised it for sale, with a rent of £6 15 shillings, and he has already *refused* £206 for it. O! I hope and pray that I may live to see English and Scotch landlords served in the same way!

Edith Somerville to her brother Cameron, 19 January 1910

THE COMPULSORY PURCHASE and re-distribution of land was not the only worrying topic in family letters. Edith and Martin watched with alarm as the Suffragettes became more and more daring, and imprisonment with forcible feeding was introduced. 'The danger of forcible feeding has been proved up to the hilt and every one of these poor martyrs for a principle has had to go straight to nursing homes, with ulcerated nose and throat passages, and in the most pitiable state in all ways,' she wrote to Cameron.[1] At the election in January 1910 she and Martin had bought every available newspaper and followed the political news avidly: 'I believe the Suffragists have detached a lot of voters from the Liberals and though I know *hundreds* of people are entirely of your opinion as to the Suffragist militants' methods, I believe that they have gained, among the working-man class of voters, more than they have alienated among gentlemen. My own feeling is that though I hate these tactics, still they show the enormous conviction of the suffragettes and the W[omen's] S[ocial and] P[olitical] Union at least shows that women's powers of organisation, and their fidelity to one another and to their principles, are all factors that may be relied upon (contrary to all the conventional theories on such points) ...'

In Drishane they were delighted that William O'Brien had been returned, but Maurice Healy was beaten by five votes ... 'O'Brien is really an honest man and in one of his speeches he said that until this idiotic boycotting of a quarter of the people of Ireland (i.e. Protestants) ceased they could not expect to get any measure of Home Rule worth having "You might as well ask England to let you massacre them at once".[2] The MP for Mallow, William O'Brien, was a nationalist who had become convinced that the only way forward in Ireland was by co-operation between unionists and nationalists.[3] He had just founded the 'All for Ireland League' with six other Cork MPs, the organisation having as its watchwords: 'Conference, Conciliation, Consent'. It is noticeable, more and more, at this time that public positions, once the special preserve of the Protestant landed class and its hangers-on, were being taken by Catholic Irishmen. In January two new medical officers were appointed to the Skibbereen district, Doctors Burke and O'Meara. Edith was pleased that Dr O'Meara had 'got the Infirmary'. As well as being their medical man, he was a great friend and ally of the Coghill and Somerville families; as a women's suffragist he was most involved with Hildegarde and her projects.

Their social circle widened as they became more involved in the suffrage cause. On 12 February Edith and Martin went to the suffragist Blakes at Myrtle Grove, Youghal, for the weekend. Edith slept in 'Raleigh's Room' and Martin in 'Spenser's'. Edith's diary comments, 'Very comfortable, no ghosts apparent.' Then, back at CT, one of their brothers made a decision that affected the Somerville sisters' lives drastically and permanently. On 14 February, Aylmer shocked his sisters by deciding, after all, to go and live in England, leaving the farm without a manager. While Edith and Hildegarde were adjusting to becoming managers themselves, Edith and Martin had another nasty shock: 'Heard from Methuen asking about advertising for the new book which is not half written.' At this time Methuen's were adding to their list a group of women authors who were involved in the suffrage movement.[4] The 'new book' was the slowly maturing *Dan Russel the Fox*. But cows, not books, were in the foreground.

Hildegarde wrote an account of the Drishane herd for the *British Friesian Cattle Society Journal* : 'In the Spring of the year 1910 two ladies, with little or no practical knowledge of farming, found themselves in the unanticipated position of joint managers of a farm of about 300 acres in the extreme SW of Ireland. The farm's principal attention was given to milk production, butter was made in small quantities only, and the bulk of the milk was sold as such, in a neighbouring village.'[5] Hildegarde and Edith supervised the weighing of the milk yield morning and evening with a spring balance weigher, keeping daily lactation lists. For their first two years they used a Stud book Ayrshire bull to breed from, achieving an average yield per heifer of 517 gallons. They were to improve on this later when, in the spring of 1912, Hildegarde, being an avid reader of farming newspapers, read an article praising the newly developed breed of British Holstein Friesians.

Converted by the logic of this article, the sisters changed their breed of bull and between 1915 and 1920 the herd of six pedigree and fourteen half-bred Friesians was to give an average yield of 728 gallons. Though reduced over the years, their herd was finally sold off only in 1946. The hard daily work and care taken over their dairy herd must not be overlooked as a key element in their lives for thirty-five years. The milk record books ruled the disposition of their time both for other work and recreation. There always had to be at least one sister in charge, of the milk records and the herdsmen. Very rarely from now on do we find the sisters going away together; if they do, when they return they write up the records from data kept in their absence by Richard Helen or Mike Hurley, who came into service with the Somervilles in this year. Born in 1880 in CT's Cross Street at the top of the village, Mike Hurley trained as a groom at Adare Manor with the Catholic Dunravens. His brother Patrick trained at Lismore Castle, on the staff of the Devonshires. Both brothers were superb horsemen, eventually becoming Huntsman and Whipper-in of the West Carbery Hounds.

The sisters were involved in every aspect of their cows' existence, from supervising impregnations to the more academic recording of yields and calf markings. Edith's art training came in useful for the individual record that had to be kept of the markings of each calf born into the herd. After a few years of cattle breeding they suffered from an over-production of bulls. Edith put this down to the mother-of-three-sons Hildegarde and her '*Male*-volent influence on the herd'. The young bulls were fattened for beef to 18–10 hundredweights. Both sisters worked in the yard with adult breeding bulls, animals of a ton weight; heavy yard boots protected their feet from accidental trampling.

The farm and its stock placed another heavyweight baffle between Somerville and Ross as a literary partnership. But it is doubtful if they could have written more than they did, even without it, on account of Martin's lack of stamina. With the death of her mother, Martin ceased to record in her diary her family 'who's where' register at the turning of the year. The annual summing-up ritual was reduced to her cumulative accounts of writing income. On 26 January she noted the invitation to Somerville and Ross to attend, as guests of honour, the Corinthian Club Dinner in Dublin in May for Irish women writers. They accepted without much enthusiasm, for to them their work was a 'business' and they did not feel themselves to be part of the 'high-souled' literary movement of the Celtic Revival. In February 1910, Boyle was home on leave. He wrote up papers for the Cork Archaeological Society from the data he gathered in surveying the stone circles of County Cork. Like his sister he enjoyed having fellow 'playboys'; as a playboy his wife Mab was by now *hors de combat* regulating the four children in her nursery. Regardless of the weather, he often persuaded Edith, and sometimes Martin, to accompany him. Martin wrote in her diary on 26 February: 'Bright morning which lured forth Boyle on Hurley's car to drive to see a Druid Circle beyond Connonagh accompanied by Edith and me.' One of Martin's Kodaks of Edith leaning on one of the stones and watching Boyle working survives from this expedition. Notable is the fact that Edith is wearing a hat of high fashion. She had also brought her spirit kettle and the makings of tea. The weather turned: 'Boyle took his bearings while Edith and I cowered behind a fence and made tea – in horrid rough wind.'[6] Boyle believed the stone circles to be early astronomers' observatories, used in calculating the calendar. How far he was influenced by his astronomer Aunt Emmie Plunket in this passion we do not know, but it is possible that, just as Constance Bushe instilled in Edith her passion for drawing, so did some powerful cross-generation transference take place between Emmie and Boyle.

Martin's diary is patchily filled in the spring of this year. There was good news from Longmans: 'Longmans is going to bring out all our books [seven volumes] in a uniform cheap edition at 3/6 crown octavo.' On 5 April the farming and riding element of CT society brushed itself up for the Cork Agricultural Show. While attending it, Hildegarde and Edith stayed with the Windles in the president's lodgings at the University. Planning an improvement to their stud, they bought a yearling bull at the Show. No sooner was the agricultural show over than the sisters were back in Cork for the Industries Exhibition at the end of the month. With fewer claims on her time, Martin supervised the timetable for literary work, and in this month an excellent article was somehow produced, sandwiched between cows and horses. *The Times* now had Somerville and Ross filed as reliable providers of quick copy. On 4 April Bruce Richmond, the then editor, had telegrammed them for a critique of 'the Joyce Book': *English as We Speak It in Ireland* by P.W. Joyce, which, despite all the counter-claims on Edith, they produced in double-quick time.[7]

They went up to Dublin for the Corinthian Club dinner on 2 May, Edith's birthday. On the next day they first went to their hairdressers; then began to dress after tea, 'Edith in black sequins over white, I in pink with gold.' The dinner was in the Aberdeen Hall. They were introduced to the Aberdeens 'in an enormous room with 200 guests'. The lady writers were at a top table, and Martin found herself with Land Commissioner Bailey on one side and Judge Ross on the other, and had good conversation. 'Lord Aberdeen, Lord O'Brien, Mrs Stopford Green spoke, the latter best of all.'[8] On the following day they were photographed at Chancellors with the rest of the women writers; and afterwards the photographers Lafayette took them, free of charge, for a publicity shot. Mr Bailey had captured them for dinner that night. Dining at Earlsfort Terrace, they met Mrs Stopford Green, Douglas Hyde, George Moore, Miss Purser 'and others of interest'. Martin, minus pince-nez, excelled at making social conversation with whoever was placed on her right and left, relying entirely on her hearing for understanding of nuance. She entered in her diary: 'I strove with a soulful gunner and George Moore – the latter very entertaining and discomposing and alarming.'[9] She was very short-sighted, and had been known to shake hands with butlers, and enter into high-class conversation with them.

On Sunday 8 May the church service nationwide was taken up by a memorial celebration for King Edward VII, who had been ailing for some time before he died. The church at CT was draped in black, a specific set of funeral hymns was sung and the service closed with the National Anthem. Martin was convinced that the political situation had been a factor in the King's death, particularly 'the ruction about the House of Lords into which the Radicals, Asquith, Lloyd George and Co have dragged his authority'.[10] Her diary was blank for the rest of May. She begins entries again with the return of Cameron on 5 June, 'very fit and well' on leave. Martin by now seemed to have the symptoms of tinnitus permanently added to all the others, and Dr Hodson began syringing her ears night and morning. On her birthday on 11 June we find in her diary what may be the first reference to her having a permanent room of her own at Drishane, one that she could decorate to her taste: 'yet another birthday. E gave me "The Book of Dublin Verse" – Cameron a black and silver stole brought from Suez – Hildegarde the cretonne with which my bedroom has been decked'; in spite of this, Martin often decamped from this room to Hildegarde's home so that Kinkie or Mabel Royds might be Edith's guest at Drishane when they came. It was Hildegarde's old room, next to her sister's, to which she was to return often after Egerton's death.

On 22 June Cameron 'went to England to enter on his duties as Commandant of Kneller Hall'. This institution was the Army School of Music where all its military bandsmen were trained. Martin left on 8 July to stay with Nora Tracey and her sister Beryl on holiday at Teignmouth for a weekend, and then joined up with Edith in London to inspect Cam's new quarters out at Twickenham: 'Very imposing building, and place of 60 acres with lake, nice garden etc. Edith just starting for London when I arrived, to call on Jack's future "laws" [Edith's brother Jack was engaged to marry Vera Aston Key]. Went round with Cameron and looked at things.' Kneller Hall, and its guest rooms, was to prove a boon to all the family as a base and free berth. It was especially useful in summer when Drishane was let. Edith returned from London and they did not leave Cameron until 6 August. They visited relations separately, then had a meeting with Pinker in London on 16 August, but they did not leave the city until 2 September, when they returned to Cameron for another week. Edith was still not recovered in health, and was taking a preparation of bismuth and chloroform for her heart palpitations. Drishane was let, so that finding a space to live in at CT was a problem. Edith wrote to her sister asking if they could 'go to you as p.g.s [paying guests] for a week … it would be agreeable socially.'[11] They were back at Drishane on 10 September, having been away for two months. If they were taking holidays from the farm, this was not an unusual length of time for one sister to be left in charge; indeed, it might have been an agreed maximum of time away, as Hildegarde and Egerton once or twice took breaks away of that duration.

With houses to maintain as a landlady, horses to run on Cameron's land, a farm to manage, and no time to write concentratedly, Edith was in a deep financial depression, and could not afford to entertain guests like her old painting companion Madge Robertson: 'I am too hard up to keep her for more than a fortnight or three weeks – unless Kingcup is sold I really don't know what to do,' she told Hildegarde. Her overdraft was by now standing at £135, with a limit of £200. 'I suppose my share of the farm and the Mall House is more than good [as security] for that, even if this wretched book failed, and, with luck, I don't see why it should, but that depends on health and *not* catching trains in a hurry.' Edith was continually exasperated by Martin having relapses because she had run for a train, or put her back out again by dragging a trunk along a platform. She was exasperated, too, by the limitations put on her by lack of money. She could not afford to go to Jack's wedding, but covered her shame with an excuse: 'I can say publicly that you and I could not be away together.'[12]

The Cork woman suffragist and playwright Miss S.R. Day, daughter of the MP Robert Day, head-hunted Somerville and Ross and persuaded them to act as president and vice-president of the newly founded Cork branch of the Irish Women's Franchise League (an all-Ireland movement). Miss Day wrote plays collaboratively with the suffragist and medium Geraldine Cummins, who was to become a friend of Edith's in her later years. On 24 September 1910 we hear of the first Irish Women's Franchise League meeting attended by Edith and Martin in Cork: 'I *spoke*! A very small affair. Martin and I concocted a very brief address which did allright. It was more a sort of Committee Meeting, the "Press" were there,' she wrote to Cameron. The text of her speech survives.[13] The society did extremely well over its first year of existence. They gained two hundred members, organised two rural branches in Skibbereen and Waterford, and convened sixteen meetings. Her first short speech came after a vote of thanks to preceding speakers:

> It is a great satisfaction that County Cork is awakening to the importance, shall I say the inevitableness, of the Suffrage movement, and I hope we shall not come second in the warmth of our welcome to Mrs Pankhurst on October 3rd. I think that the strength of the present Suffrage movement

lies in the fact that women have been educated, and have become workers. The great majority of self supporting women are suffragists, because they are aware of a capacity to vote, and of an interest in the matter to be voted about. I do not see how this tide of feeling is to be arrested. It is too late now to check it. The ruling powers should never have educated us, nor given us the right to hold property if they did not want us to vote. Those were fatal mistakes! And, unfortunately for the Anti-Suffragists, they are now past praying for.

Education and money are at the root of the question. It is *not* Physical force that governs, it is the money that employs the force. If women were richer they would have more power and influence, and, thanks to education, they will, as a class, become richer by their own efforts, with a corresponding increase of influence.

I think that two of the most valuable features of the Suffrage movement are that, First, It teaches women to believe in and to stand by each other; and Second, that it compels them to think for themselves ... It is, I think, most important that women should, more generally acquaint themselves with the questions of the day, both political and social, and should be able to give a reasoned opinion about them, temperately, and without exaggeration or bitterness. Every man, consciously or unconsciously, judges women by the women he knows best, and it rests with each of us to form that opinion. We are asking men to give us the share of power that should, in abstract justice, be ours. Let us show them that we are competent to use it, not only for our own advantage, but for that of the Commonwealth.

Edith carefully laced her speeches with humour, in direct quotation, just as she did in her profession as a writer. She closed this speech with an anecdote: 'It is time for us, in Ireland, to bestir ourselves, and to relinquish the more agreeable pose of Looking On. A friend of mine saw a man digging by the roadside, and four others were watching him. My friend said, "Well boys! This is the usual thing one sees in Ireland. One man working and four idle fellows looking on!" The man with the spade looked at him and said "There's five of them now, Sir!" I hope no-one will tell this story to Mrs Pankhurst.'

With some amazement Uncle Kendal discovered he had two women suffragists on his own doorstep. Edith was careful to keep calm with him, when he announced that the reason there was no point in giving women votes was that they were too unconscientious. 'I held up his own sisters and, of course, they were "exceptions"! I am so *sick* of being told "I would give *you* the vote, of course!"' She did manage to leave Uncle Kendal conceding that 'Mrs Pankhurst's character was above reproach.'[14]

Edith and Hildegarde made heavy weather of their start in farming, and even before Aylmer had abandoned the Drishane Farm, Edith had written to Cameron on 20 December of 1909: 'farming is the nearest way to bankruptcy in this country at any rate ... I hope that Hildegarde and I will keep in the narrow and grimy path that means money making ...Until Aylmer hands over the books I can't give you any idea of the financial status ... so far the expenses have swallowed up all the takings but what *either* were I don't know, and neither does Hildegarde.' As well as Aylmer, other long staying familiars of CT were leaving. Edith's fellow rower Loo Loo Plunket and her family were the next to pull out: 'Loo Loo is selling her boats (which is the same as burning them) and they act as though they had no abiding city here ...' Concerned over the sisters' clearly unprofitable first year of 1910 as farm managers, Martin went to Galway in September to stay with her sister Geraldine and her sister-in-law Amy at a rented house called St Brides. She was back in CT on the 20th, being collected from the station at Skibbereen by Dr Hodson in her motor. On 3 October Edith and Martin were stewards at the historic meeting of the Irish Women's Franchise League in the Cork City Hall at which Mrs Pankhurst delivered an address.[15] Lady Blake presided. Martin watched the celebrated guest speaker closely: 'she is small and quiet, [with] an excellent voice and manner and spoke very well indeed – there was a small disorderly section in the Gallery kept well in hand by Mrs P and also Lady B. Edith and I were stewards of the uppermost seats and sold literature ... we were afterwards introduced to Mrs Pankhurst – who was tired and quiet and impressive on that account as well as others.'[16]

Martin's damaged back must have improved as on 21 October she hunted with the West Carbery. She was still suffering from painful earaches that Dr Hodson was treating. On the 28th she hunted with her doctor: '[I] on Condy, Eleanor on Buttercup and Edith on Tarbrush.' Martin could now walk around easily with no ill effects. In December she rode another hunt on Condy, and her riding was described by Edith in a letter to her sister: 'a big field out ... including Miss Martin on Condy, who gave me an awful moment when she charged a high, thick, *fixed* pole across the lane on top of Killnavoodhea! Rita Morrough said to me "O, *did* you see Miss Martin? I got quite white when I saw her ..." Her face all the time being as red as a rose.'[17] On Christmas Eve Martin recorded in her diary that she went walking on the rounds of hands and servants with their Christmas 'boxes': 'went out to Mary Minnahane's with Edith for usual benefactions'. Her cumulative account at 1910 was £2,705 13s. 10d. Overall Martin had earned roughly £200 a year from writing. Just before Christmas Edith was delighted to hear the news that, after long faithfulness and waiting, Hewitt Poole of Mayfield was to marry her first cousin Grace Somerville of Park

Cottage, 'an excellent arrangement', she wrote in her diary. He was the first cousin and shared the name of the man in whom she had shown an interest thirty years before. On 29 December there was a big engagement party: 'Hewitt and Grace both here, very beaming.'

Although Edith's first cousins Percy and Eddie Aylmer were not permanent residents in CT, their wealth and influence was a constant comfort there. In January 1911 the wife of Percy's lawyer Mr Luxmoore took up a holiday residence in the Aylmer brothers' Red House. How little Mr Luxmoore himself knew of the complexities of the insider dealing between the nest of cousins was never revealed to him. He remained baffled, only aware that he did not know everything. The Aylmer brothers both supported Edith and Hildegarde by gifts, and Percy was about to make a large contribution to their farm. At the beginning of February, the Cork branch of the Irish Women's Franchise League dissolved and re-formed independently, changing its title to the Munster Women's Franchise League, retaining Edith as president. Apart from presidential addresses Edith was relieved from other work, all paperwork being dealt with by Robert Day's super-efficient daughter. 'Miss Day, Hon. Sec. does all the work and is A1.' In mid-February both Edith and Martin went to Galway to hunt with the Blazers: 'the fields are large, smooth and sound and are all boxed in by straight, regular walls made of awful, angular nuggets of limestone. Every angle fit to sharpen a pencil ... they well deserve to be called the Blazers, as I never saw such going.'[18]

On the 21st they left Galway to go to the Penroses at Lismore for a weekend. They were still writing *Dan Russel the Fox*, in a haphazard kind of way, but plans were liable to change at a moment's notice. Edith had caught a cold in Galway: 'If it is bad at Mallow I shall go on to Cork, and let M go to Lismore.' A far cry from the standards of the Blazers, the West Carbery was having poor hunting. On 24 February, having made her cold worse, Edith wrote in her diary: 'Drew the whole country blank in spite of assurances of foxes wherever they can be. Home in heavy rain and homicidal fury against the trappers and poisoners of this unhappy country.' In *Dan Russel the Fox* they included scenes of violent antagonism between farmers and huntsmen. Now owning their own land, and objecting to hunts passing over it, some farmers staked and wired their fences, or laid poison to kill the hounds. These topical details were drawn into their work. The MFH Gus Fitzsymons of the novel that they were writing had his troubles. Mrs Delanty explained to Katherine Rowan: 'He has the Dunnigans up against him now, and that's half the country, you might say! It's a very different story with the farmers now since they've bought the land; it's hat in hand me friend Gus should be to them.'[19]

At the end of March Edith supervised the men when eighteen young cattle were swum out to graze on Horse Island. Muriel Currey notes in her diary

transcript: 'a laconic "wrote" fills in a rare spare minute'. Edith had yet another
tooth out on 8 May. On the 19th, Martin, the enthusiastic Unionist, went off to
London with others to see the coronation of George V, staying with her sister
Katie and the Curreys. She was there along with Hildegarde, Nora Tracey,
Kinkie and Beatrice's minder Miss McLeod, but had a special ticket through her
old friend Alice Campbell, Lady Stratheden, on whose balcony she had a seat
to watch the procession:

> all the time a ceaseless cataract of carriages passed down St James Street
> for the Abbey – with scarlet and ermine laps and fronts showing very
> gloriously – and the coronets in their laps – one could see the glint of
> them (NB I had opera glasses) and perishing bare necks and long white
> gloves ... and the King's Watermen, and the Beef-eaters – and the Band of
> the Lifeguards – were completely delightful as one could have wished –
> They were so genuine and easy – [ Martin then left the Stratheden's balcony
> to walk in the streets and go up to high vantage points] McLeod and I made
> an expedition into the Mall as the procession was leaving Buckingham
> Palace and of course could not get near, but a boy was holding up a mirror
> on a stick and with a group of other scalliwags I saw the golden coach in
> the mirror exactly as I looked up into it ... From the roof of the chapel we
> saw the towers of Westminster Abbey – and heard its joy bells crashing as
> if you dashed your hand across a harp – that was when the King went into
> it – about 12 came the cannon, announcing that he was crowned ... [On
> the following day, based at the Lyceum Club, Martin saw the King and
> Queen again] ... She was in cream colour with the blue garter ribbons
> across – and a small hat with shaded blue ostrich feathers – and one noticed
> again the admirable poise of her head. There undoubtedly is something
> about her. A cleverness and grace – and pluck – one would imagine – I
> had a good look at Lord Roberts, and his lithe young figure and the way
> he was *sewn* into the saddle. Now this must go ...[20]

Back in CT on 27 April, Martin, Edith and Hildegarde attended the wedding
of Grace and Hewitt Poole in Union Hall church; the bridal couple were, Edith
wrote in her diary, 'both radiant, as was fitting'. The whole church-full then went
over to Park Cottage where there was a chaotic and lively party 'eating mixed and
unexpected delicacies til 4.30 when the Happy Pair departed'. The handsome
couple, who had not been at liberty to think of themselves for many years, were in
their fifties, and were yet to have seventeen years of married life.[21]

In May the accounts of the dairy farm had to be put straight. This was only
done with the aid of Ethel Penrose, who had a head for mathematics, and was

in Glen B and able to help. July was taken up by finishing the first part of *Dan Russel the Fox*; 61,000 words went off to Methuen on 22 July. Because of the dairy, only mornings were set aside for writing; a few hours a day was the most they could do for their novel. Nevertheless in August Edith sent off the second part of *Dan Russel* on the 7th, and then the last of manuscript went off: 'A great and incredible peace then fell.' During the peace Edith wrote to Cameron: 'Martin only got through by dint of every known tonic and restorative ... and once the harvest (oats) is through next week, we can, *if Pinker can get us some money*, talk about descending on you.' The typesetters at Methuen's were super-efficient, so the peace didn't last long, and just a few days later on 12 August the first batch of proofs arrived. They finished proof-reading by 1 September, and to celebrate the end of proofs, shows and harvest they went abroad, but first to Kneller Hall, leaving the three dogs in the charge of Mrs Kisby at Drishane. They stayed with Cameron until his greatest hour of military glory came. He was chosen to conduct the massed bands, with a total of 1,660 bandsmen drawn from 21 British and 25 Indian Army bands, at the Delhi Coronation Durbar: 'Cameron departed for India at 8am to command the Bands at the Durbar, Major Stretton with him as Musical Director – E and I went up to London by the 9.47 and dug out Eleanor [Hodson] at the Morley Hotel Trafalgar Square.'[22] The three of them then headed for Annecy and the Haute Savoie, Eleanor driving hired cars to explore from this base. This was officially a painting holiday: Edith and Eleanor painted while Martin saw sights.

They were back in Paris on 2 October, where Hildegarde sent to them the first review of their new novel on the day of its publication on the 5th: 'Dan Russel out today and has already been noticed very favourably by *The Times*', Martin wrote in her diary. This novel of 1911 reminds us, like the wedding of Hewitt and Grace, that – given the right conditions – sexual vitality springs eternal, or at any rate past the age of fifty. When she wrote *Dan Russel the Fox*, Edith was fifty-three years old. The sexual fixation of the heroine, Katherine Rowan, upon the beautiful young John Michael Fitzsymons is one of the most closely observed of a number of such *mésalliances* in the novels. As far back as the 'Buddh Dictionary' of 1887 and its frank admission of the 'overmastering charm' of a certain type of man socially beyond the pale, the character of John Michael, a centaur-like being who loves horses but is indifferent to humans, shows that the awareness of sexual attraction in his type of man never faded. Certain features remain constants of his type: he is in the position of a younger brother, penniless, very good-looking, and partly-trained as a vet, medic or engineer:

> John Michael was a younger brother of the old-fashioned tribal type, who existed happily, and pennilessly, under the suzerainty of his elder

brother. There had, indeed, been a vague period when he was 'going to be a doctor', during which he had acquired by some process of natural selection such facts as were of value to him when he relapsed into the state to which he was born, kennel boy, stable helper, and his mother's right-hand man. His dark good looks suggested some vagrant strain of the Spanish blood that has touched the western coast-people of Ireland, and warmed them like the Gulf-stream; his greatly-admiring mother had many times asserted that if 'Gustus [John Michael's elder brother] would only give Johnny the money to go to England, some rich lady would treat herself to him.[23]

Though a superb rider and huntsman, John Michael is withdrawn in female society through shyness and having been all his life overshadowed and bossed by his brother. He is chased through the novel by Katherine Rowan and Mrs Delanty, and eventually flees from them to America. Katherine Rowan is mesmerised by him. In the Fitzsymons drawing room: 'John Michael, on his music stool, was but two yards away from Miss Rowan, weighed down by a shyness palpable enough to touch a heart of stone. His red hands suggested icy ablutions at the pump in the yard; his dark hair was plastered down as if with the stable water-brush; he eyed Katherine from under his curling black lashes like a thing at bay. She felt that if so much as a twig cracked he would melt into the upright piano, even as Daphne was merged in the laurel.' What Edith describes in Katherine is a straightforward sexual fascination; she puts it aside in the end, to settle for a bystander, her faithful suitor, the man of intellect, Ulick Adare, who has to spend the novel in its margins, gnashing his teeth in rage, while his beloved is under the spell of the inarticulate but fascinating horseman.

The ebb and flow of their finances, directly linked to the publication of new novels, meant that publication days were associated soon after with visits to doctors and dentists for necessary repairs and consultations. Back in London, en route from Paris, Edith and Martin were staying at the New Century Club while they tried a new dentist: 'interviewed McAlpine apropos of new teeth – ditto Edith. My teeth must have gold plates and will cost £25!' wrote a shocked Martin in her diary. *Dan Russel the Fox* had rave reviews in *Punch* and *The Spectator*. On 12 October Edith went back to Drishane while Martin, staying in London, went to the Curreys for a week at Prince of Wales Mansions, then transferred to the Dawsons in Lowestoft. She returned to London on 2 November to meet up with her cousin the painter Rose Barton at her Club, the Lyceum. Rose had been very ill and was trying to recover from a terrible asthma attack that had precipitated a 'heart and general collapse'. Despite Martin's sympathetic concern over Rose's health and seemingly poor prospects of life,

Rose was to survive Martin by fourteen years, living until 1929. Martin stayed at the Lyceum until Edith arrived from Cork with her 'tiger and elephant book' for Pinker. This was the delightful children's book that was published by Longmans in 1912 as *The Story of the Discontented Little Elephant*. It was dedicated to Katharine (K) Coghill, Hildegarde's only daughter. Pinker was too ill to see them at this time and they were dealt with by his son, Eric, who 'did his best'. By now they both had serious doubts about the honesty of Pinker the elder.

In London, Martin saw yet another doctor, a Dr Parker, to check on a new and mysterious malady; of it she simply remarks in her diary: 'Dr Parker – nose and mouth better.' She was evidently showing preliminary signs of the tumour that was to kill her. Her teeth, ears, eyes, nose and throat were all under attack through the same unrecognised malignancy at the base of her brain. None the wiser, they returned to Ireland and Drishane by the Night Mail on 17 November. 'The dogs go very blissful at our return' wrote Martin. There was a new and interesting visitor in CT: Jem Barlow, a cousin of the writer Jane Barlow, was house-hunting in the village, having decided she wished to put down roots there. Edith and Martin took to her instantly. All too soon, there was little money left over from Pinker. With no hunt or hounds, Edith was consoled by friends inviting her to hunt with them. Edith wrote to Cameron to tell him that 'Jim M[artin] and Jim P[enrose] have begged me to go and hunt for a bit with them ... but I can't get away just now ...' and in a later letter explains, 'until you come home permanently and I can turn your sword into a ploughshare, I must be a farmer and must abandon the idea of going away for hunting, even if I could afford it.'[24]

In November, ignoring woman's suffrage, Asquith had put forward proposals to extend manhood suffrage that caused an outcry from militant and non-militant supporters of female suffrage alike. Edith wrote to Cameron: 'Asquith's last move "Manhood Suffrage" has maddened everyone, as Charlotte GBS says, in an excellent letter to the *Times* today "I feel as if Mr Asquith has spat in my face, and that of my sex!" Even the Anti-Suff papers are beginning to change their tune at the idea that any street wastrel, if he is 21 years old, can have his say in the disposition of taxes, while the like of myself is considered incapable and imbecile.'[25] As early as the first week of December, family members started drifting back for the Christmas holidays. Though Martin had 'her' bedroom, she was still required to move out of it to Glen B and Hildegarde's household in mid-December when Drishane filled to bursting.

On 15 December, Edith gave an address at a suffrage meeting in Cork entitled 'The Educational Aspects of Women's Suffrage'. She had become more confident as a public speaker, and though she never became accustomed to it, suffering horribly from nerves, her texts show that her arguments and style would have compensated for any flaws in delivery: 'Can we wonder that the field of intellect of many naturally able women is a very limited one? Women have been, and are being, brought up without any sense of duty to their country, without the least feeling of citizenship. That they possess either – and the work of the Churches and the Hospitals and the Public Health Associations is sufficient answer that they do – is due, not to Education, or to the encouragement of Comradeship, but to some innate and lofty emotion that impels them to self-sacrifice.'[26] Hildegarde also suffered from nerves when she was required to deliver votes of thanks and make introductory speeches in her work with Dr O'Meara to improve public health through the Skibbereen Rural District Council. She had also been elected president of the Skibbereen branch of the Women's National Health Association, founded by Lady Aberdeen in 1907 to combat tuberculosis. Edith wrote to Cameron on 24 April complaining of the sheer nervous terror that afflicted both of them before they stood up and spoke, and the 'goading force of conscience that makes us undertake these horrible things'. Horrible, but necessary, as another speech points out: 'Ladies, it is our business to see that we are not left outside the door when the conditions of our lives are decided upon. We have not joined this League for fun – It is not a Girls Friendly Society – our business is to let people know that we exist, and the reason why we exist, because we mean to have votes for women.'[27]

The women's suffragist Dr O'Meara and Hildegarde had a most harmonious relationship, serving together on boards of health and fund-raising committees, and they enjoyed each other's sense of humour. Notebook 10 records the two of them in conversation: 'Dr O'Meara has been attending the venerable Miss Duggan and her sister Mrs Allen. The one has never moved from the village of Glandore since before the wooden bridge was built. The other has seen it, but has remained in Glandore since then and has never seen the iron bridge. Dr O'M, paying a visit to HAC says "Well, Mrs Allen and Miss Duggan went to Cork today!" H, amazed says "What did they go in?" Dr O'M replies (almost indignantly) "In a hearse, sure!" Whereon H falls into paroxysms of laughter, and the Doctor is much offended.'[28] From Cork Edith went on to Ethel in Lismore, where their mutual friend Madge Robertson was very ill, until the 21st. Over the Christmas period, with all the young staying, Edith felt depressed over the loss of the hounds and the lack of seasonal activity in preparing her guests and their mounts for the traditional meets. In her diary Edith noted on 26 December: 'The first St Stephen's Day for 20 years without a meet in Skib.'

Martin's masseuse and friend Nora Tracey came to stay at Drishane with Martin again, and when a telegram came from Ethel on 1 January 1912, to say that Madge had died, Nora kept Martin company while Edith returned to Lismore for the funeral, taking with her from Hildegarde and Martin a shamrock-shaped wreath of violets and Christmas roses. Their minds were taken off the depression caused by Madge's death when they presided at a suffrage meeting, at which there were 'a good many men of all classes' in the Skibbereen Town Hall on 24 January. The speaker was Helga Gill, who was to become a popular figure on the Munster suffrage circuit. Dr O'Meara was in the chair: 'Miss Gill spoke for about 45 minutes on "How we won the vote in Norway" and was listened to with great attention and respect.[29] The chairman of the urban council proposed the vote of thanks and Edith briefly and success-fully seconded it. She and I sat on the platform and afterwards had coffee with the O'Mearas.' Martin had some mental stimulation when, on 29 January, a politico arrived to quiz her. He was a 'Mr Harold Begbie who is making a political tour of Ireland and is at present visiting the Bishop of Ross, who came with him.'[30] She took them to see the Village Hall, the funding and building of which had been master-minded by Egerton, all the while 'talking Unionism versus Home Rule.' Harold Begbie was to prove an eager letter-writer, though the correspondence between him and Martin is now lost.

Awkwardly, the editor of the *Spectator* asked Somerville and Ross to review *Old Irish Life*, by Martin's 'step-niece' Zoe Callwell, on 23 February. This was a controversial volume verging on the plagiarism of *By the Brown Bog*, and Edith was to remain unforgiving and angry with Zoe for the rest of her life. Delaying her decision until well through March, Martin simply refused to review it and left it to Edith: 'you have had my letter abandoning Zoe Callwell – Let you do it if you like – and speedily – I will not touch it – as I don't want to cavil and I don't want to praise.'[31] This letter was written en route to Coole for the weekend and closes with a description of Martin's second meeting with her Canadian cousin Archer Martin, who had become a faithful admirer of their work. He gave Martin the gift of a dressing-box with letters from him inside, 'expressing the opinion of the favour I confer on my family by belonging to it. He does not think they realise the magnitude of our work – they are very kind about it but they do not understand – is what he says. He is a most faithful creature and a valuable friend to us all. Now I must catch my train ...' Dated 20 March 1912, this is now the last surviving letter from Martin to Edith.

An undated letter survives in the TCD collection, from Martin to her cousin, the painter Rose Barton, that suggests that Martin was not quite an open book to Edith, for here we see a different reaction from Martin to her young and poaching cousin Zoe. The letter also makes clear that Nannie Martin, with her entertaining talk, had given Edith and Martin a priceless store of material. To Rose, Martin wrote: 'I see Mama's good stories of her own experiences pilloried and massacred – Zoe went down to Ross a few years ago and sat in Mama's pocket for two days extracting all she could from her. She did the same to Geraldine and to Katie, who did not realise altogether what she was at. She has every right to use her mother's stories, of course, and Mr Griffiths and all that lot – but, knowing that Mama had a daughter who used her stories freely in fiction, I think it was not cricket to go to that preserve. She then, as you know, published them anonymously and these were all credited to me, to the fury of my friends, who preferred my method of telling them. Katie has done all concerned the excellent service of fighting Zoe to a finish on this subject, and getting her to sign her own name to them ...' Changing the subject away from the talenapper Zoe, Martin goes on to say that she is exasperated, too, at the calls on Edith's time made by her household: 'Edith S and I struggle with our writing and she has much to do in the way of looking after the farm and creamery – I think she has forgotten how to be idle which is sometimes rather a disaster...'[32]

A letter from Edith to Cameron of 29 February mentions that Aylmer, like Boyle, had leanings away from Unionism. Edith described Uncle Kendal getting 'black as thunder' when Aylmer's wife Nat had said: 'Aylmer has turned Home Ruler! What shall we do with him!' Edith carried on: 'I didn't attempt to affirm or deny – I knew if I did I should have a squabble with him, and I hate that. One knows all the real arguments are against Home Rule being a success, but my sanguinity makes me rather take the O'Shaughnessy/O'Meara view ... I believe if the Yankee Rebel element could be eliminated, Home Rule might work all right, but it is always pouring poison into the country and keeping old wounds festering that would otherwise heal.'

Martin's brother Jim had returned to Ireland from Ceylon with his wife and children and set up in a house near Athenry called Rockmore. She went to see them there on 1 March, and was delighted with their choice – 'a snug little house with large rooms'. Edith came down to hunt among the Blazers with Jim. She rode her own horse Quinine, and Jim a brown mare who was, in comparison, something of an unknown quantity. They attended a meet at Athenry on the 2nd and another at Kilcornan on the 4th. Edith went back to CT while Martin carried on to visit the Redingtons. While staying there her friend Tilly Redington had taken her to see 'a wonderful wreck' – the remains of Tyrone House: 'In the afternoon Tilly Redington and I drove over to Tyrone House. A bigger and much grander edition of Ross – a great square cut stone house of three storeys, with an area – perfectly empty – and such ceilings, architraves, teak doors and chimney pieces as one sees in old houses in Dublin. It is on a long promontory by the sea – and there *rioted* three or four generations of St Georges – living with country women, occasionally marrying them, all illegitimate four times over. Not so long ago *eight* of these awful half peasant families roosted together in that lovely house and fought, and barricaded and drank till the police had to intervene – about 150 years ago a very grand Lady Harriet St

Lawrence married a St George and lived there, and was so corroded with pride that she would not allow her daughters to associate with the Galway people. She lived to see them marry two of the men in the yard ...'[33] Martin's lurid account of the St Georges reminds us that we should treat her hearsay facts with caution, since there was antagonism between the families of St George, French and Martin that coloured such gossip. Whatever the factual basis, through Martin's letter to Edith the family inspired the fictional account of the Prendeville family of the novel *The Big House of Inver* (1925).

Martin was with the Persses at Roxborough for two days before going on to Coole, where Augusta Gregory was 'just returned from her tour with the Irish Players in America.'[34] Her godson Robert Gregory was there with his two daughters, the eagle-eyed and dangerous 'Me and Nu', whose memoir of their childhood is required reading for the period.[35] Martin made a meandering round of calls on the Whites at Oughterard Rectory, followed by more Persses, back to Jim at Rockmore, then finally returning to Drishane on 11 April. She had been gadding about to friends and relations for six weeks. From Drishane on the 20th Martin went to Cork: 'for the big Unionist meeting to protest against the Home Rule bill.'[36] The Duke of Devonshire was there as the chief speaker, supported by Lord Midleton. At the meeting Martin met Kendal Coghill, who was at the time a house guest of the Bandons.

It was becoming clear that Irish Members of Parliament were so fixated on their rising Home Rule ambitions, and so bedazzled by the hopes held out to them by British ministers, that the cause of women's suffrage was quite out of the limelight. Edith had a talk with Miss Day, her honorary secretary in the MWFL, about this, in which Miss Day said: 'The sooner we Irishwomen are in a position to deal with *Irish*men in political affairs the better. To be governed by English Mackennas, Churchills, Buxtons etc etc seems to me a fate which deserves a special litany with a refrain of "Good Lord Deliver us!"' Edith commented to Cameron: 'I think she is quite right. I could not believe that any Home Rule Government could be as corrupt, incapable and unjust as this crowd. But when a typical member of an old Cork Protestant family says that sort of thing, one begins to realise what English Radicals have done to Irish loyalists.'[37]

Contrarily, and with immediate negative financial impact, Edith decided in May that she couldn't do without hounds after all and went to Skibbereen to discuss the revival of the West Carbery Hunt. She sent an advertisement to *Horse and Hound* for a hunt servant on the 9th. She repaired the kennels, and on the 18th she interviewed and hired the man who was to be one of her best huntsmen, Metherell, who had been with the Ledbury. The new hounds came a week later, and Edith's diary becomes packed with hunt work. On the 30th Pinker wrote 'demanding a story in ten days' and the diary went blank for two weeks. The awful collision course of Irish Home Rule and Women's Suffrage was approaching their point of impact. Regardless of the Pinker emergency, Edith wrote to Cameron to give him a résumé:

> Helga Gill says 'politics were never so muddled and *depraved* by Parties.' You may have seen that Lord R. Cecil and Philip Snowden are bringing in a Woman's Franchise Amendment to the Home Rule Bill. Redmond is terrified of the 50,000 solid and organised Ulster women, and personally is an Anti [Suffragist] – therefore he commands his Party, who are mainly Suffies, to vote against it. The Unionist MPs for Ulster are mainly Antis, but they and most of the Unionist Party are to vote for it, as it may split the Government and the Labour Party (it is believed) will vote for it also, in spite of the danger to the Government, or perhaps because of it, because they disapprove of the Government Strike Policy – and heaven knows what the result will be. 'Oh! The English Politics!'says Helga 'They are Party run mad!' And so indeed they are – Joe Devlin, T.P. O'Connor, Stephen Gwynn and many others are *pledged suffragists* and they will all vote against the Amendment and they say that of all the bitter hatreds between Redmondites and O'Brienites, no matter what may be the result their single resolve is to oppose one another.[38]

Helga Gill had told Edith that she had been in the House of Commons when the Conciliation Bill was beaten by 14 votes, because Irish members abandoned the suffrage cause in the hope of getting Home Rule, and had seen the horrible effect on F.E. Smith; she described him as a 'loathsome being' whose 'baboon antics' and yells of triumph were 'absolutely humiliating to human nature'. Edith commented to Cameron: 'I wish he would go over to the Liberals and let Churchill come to us. He is less of a cad, and quite as clever, so the exchange would be a good one.'[39]

In July 1912 the Farm work increased with its familiar intensity, again there was a glut of bull calves, and again 'our story writing has rather taken a back seat', Edith wrote to Cameron. The interesting new resident Miss 'Jem' Barlow, settled in; everyone liked her, as she was 'very psychic, gubby and literary-artistic'. She moved into a house on the main street opposite The Cottage. When Farm business obtruded too much it was a prelude to Martin taking off on a circuit of visiting until times might be more favourable to writing. On 20 July Edith wrote to her sister to comment on the engagement of Martin's niece Barbara Martin to John Mascie Taylor: 'if she goes to India for some years, it will be a wonder if Ross is not cut up into labourers' cottages by the time she gets back.' There had been no improvement in Edith's finances; sending birthday greetings to her sister for 1 August, she revealed that she had sold her much-loved Sunbeam bicycle in order to buy a new habit skirt, her old one having fallen apart.[40] In the middle of the month she had to write to apologise for being unable to pay a debt to Egerton for a coal bill: 'I was hoping Longmans would have paid up for the tail half of the Elephant before now, and I am in such very low water until he does. I *knew* I was letting myself in for perpetual money-mental strain when I took on the hounds again but I think they are worth it (at times anyhow).' Martin had wrecked her back yet again rushing to the station, and clearly she felt that Nora Tracey was a skilled masseuse who could help her put it right. 'She talks of Nora Tracey and Galway, but she is – in my opinion – quite unfit for battering. She is looking horribly thin and caduced ... I think she ought to have a Rest Cure at Drishane, with Judith to massage her, I wonder what Judy would charge per week?' Having sold her bike Edith had spent that money and now had none left: 'I have no money to buy stockings but I keep hounds – thoroughly Irish.'[41]

In September, Martin, who had a mind of her own, set off and went to the far North. In Drishane on the 28th Edith wrote to Cameron again: 'Martin is ramping round Ulster, and heard the Protestant Tom-Tom going at night! Very frightening. I hope she will write something about it for the Spectator ... but I don't know if she can get it written as quickly as may be necessary, as her gaddings seem to be continuous.' In Ulster on that day, Edward Carson organised a convention with the public signing of a Solemn League and Covenant by Unionist Anti-Home Rule Ulstermen in Belfast. There were 218,000 signatories of the Covenant, some signing in their own blood. Martin attended this huge public meeting as a reporter for the *Spectator*. She went up North to stay as a guest of Nora Tracey. Edith's worries about Martin failing to meet her deadline were groundless. The article, in the form of a letter to the Editor on 5 October, was headed 'The Reaping of Ulster', and had a tremendous effect upon its readers. Martin took her reader with her up north by train. At Lisburn she began to notice a difference in the people getting on board:

> To me, born and bred among the grave and dreamy faces of the West, apprenticed to Dublin life, seasoned in the South, these eyes and voices told a new story. Not an imaginative story, or a very sympathetic one; certainly not a long one; it would seem as if time were of more value here than conversation. They are quick movers, going about their business at a pace that is on equal terms with their brains; we can console ourselves down in the South with the entirely true reflection that if we moved as fast as our ideas we should be invisible to the naked eye ...

From the convention itself she gives an analysis of the speeches of Sir Edward
Carson and F.E. Smith; on the following day she attended church services, and
saw the banners on the Orange Halls 'that bore the unqualified statement that
these people would not have Home Rule':

> ... in the churches the hard and virile voices rumbled the confession of
> sin, and sang the National Anthem like a challenge ... When all was over
> the congregation filed into the Orange Hall and proceeded to the signing
> of the Covenant. There was no excitement whatever, and no hesitation;
> four at a time the men stooped and affixed their signatures ... In the
> Ulster Hall people were signing at about the rate of a hundred and fifty a
> minute; here there was no hypnotic force of dense masses, no whirlwinds
> of emotion, only the unadorned and individual action of those who had
> left their fields, and taken their lives and liberties in their hands; laying
> them forth in the open sunshine as a measure of their resolve ...

In a few days her "letter" was an influential success and many readers were
impelled to congratulate her. Charlie Graves wrote to Martin on 10 October
from his club the Athenaeum in London:

> Dear Miss Martin I thought you would like to know that Rudyard
> Kipling when I asked him today whether he had seen your paper on
> Ulster said 'Seen it? Why I've read it out aloud' and went on to say other
> honorific things as to the matter and manner of the article, in particular
> that there wasn't a single epithet that was out of place.[42]

Another writer who responded immediately was St Loe Strachey, the editor
of the *Spectator* himself:

> Dear Miss Martin, I must just write a line of sincere congratulation on your
> admirable article on the Ulster Covenant. Nothing could have been better.
> You avoid all the conventional horrors of the Special Correspondent and
> yet at the same time have not made your letter 'precious' but have fully
> brought out the high seriousness of the movement. Your comparison with
> the people of the South interested and amused me very much. I am such
> a Philistine that when I was in Ireland my heart went out to the Ulster
> people. I was captivated by their vigour and by the sense of 'will like a
> dividing spear'.[43]

On 12 October Edith wrote in her diary: 'Martin has much kudos for her
Ulster article. Copied into Belfast papers. Swept [meaning captivated] Rudyard
Kipling, and is read aloud at Unionist Committee meetings.' Martin went over

to Galway to Jim and Amy at Rockmore, from where she made a depressing visit to Ross. Robert's widow, Connie, was in bed, but her daughter Barbara, just back from honeymoon, was able to receive them. On 9 October Barbara had married John Mascie Taylor. She was to spend years with him in India, and sold out of Ross in 1924. Both Edith and Martin were becoming well known as public figures. With practice Edith's suffrage speeches had become more effective by careful pacing; she marked her scripts with instructions to herself on delivery. She gave a speech at a Cork suffrage meeting on 18 October:

> It is almost incredible that the valuable opinion of competent women should be denied to the State. Lord Robert Cecil was speaking in favour of Women's Franchise the other day, and he said that it absolutely frightened him to find how incapable he was of understanding the point of view of the Anti-Suffragists. When our Legislature accepts the votes of senile illiterates, and refuses those of Doctors, Teachers, Business Women, Graduates of Universities, writers and artists, one does indeed begin to feel frightened, and to realise that it is time to make a change.
>
> Ladies, I support the extension of the Franchise to qualified Women for four reasons:
>
> 1st – *For the Good of the State* – because the State has to make laws for women as well as for men, and wants all the help it can get from both sexes.
>
> 2nd – *For the Good of Women*. To educate them. To give them equal pay for equal work, and to raise their general status.
>
> 3rd – *For the Good of Men*. To enlarge their mental horizons and sympathies and lastly because Taxation without Representation is Injustice.[44]

Back at literary work Martin and Edith wrote a sketch, on 'A Western Hotel', in a leisurely way, then were interrupted by an urgent demand. On 5 November Edith made a diary entry that shows the speed at which commissioned work was produced under pressure: 'Wrote frantically at sketch for "Lady of the House" and at 5.30 sent Mike galloping to the post with it. Quite in the good old way.' Already under the influence of Sir Horace Plunkett and his Irish Agricultural Organisation Society through their agricultural work, the Somerville sisters, with Martin, had decided to set up a branch of the United Irishwomen. Edith wrote to her sister on 11 November: 'We are to unite as Irishwomen on Wednesday and the Ban Uasals [Ladies] come to the Castle next week.' Cameron joined them for Christmas and New Year. We can gather a lot of information about the relative brio of Edith and Martin at this time from the facts that were recorded in their diaries on New Year's Eve. Edith and

Hildegarde went off to the Ball at Hollybrook to dance into the small hours, while Cameron and Martin 'sat over the fire in the drawing room til midnight' when they turned in. The sisters came back at 2.30 in the morning.

On 14 January 1913 a lot of the children in CT for the Christmas holidays took horse with the West Carbery Hunt. They had too exciting a time, falling off horses with unexpected abandon. On the following day Edith entered in her diary: 'Horses and children none the worse for their tumblings about yesterday. I caught four loose horses and four loose riders, and there were five tosses in all.' We are reminded of Edith's grandfather and his delight in encouraging her to ride and hunt when she was a very small girl. Edith's niece Katharine remembered being in Drishane when the wealthy American horsewoman Mrs Hitchcock was talking to Edith. Edith asked: 'At what age do you think children should learn to ride?' There was a pause, then Mrs Hitchcock said, 'Oh … mmm … not before eighteen months.'[45]On the 16th, Edith wrote to Cameron, back at Kneller Hall: 'This can only be a scribble for early post as I am having a bye-day in the hills for the schoolboys who all go tomorrow … farewell, we are very lonesome after you and the Brown dog.' The West Carbery Hunt went out in a high gale on 8 February: 'It felt like a giant trying to wrench you out of the saddle. Eleanor [Dr Hodson], when we picked her up on the way home, had got past saying "Damn", and would only utter raven screeches of rage, like a Valkyrie.'

At the end of the month, Pinker made the legal arrangements for the German translation and publication of the RM. Somerville and Ross seem to have had a following in Germany, as their review scrapbook contains a notice from the *Frankfurter Zeitung*. In the same month Longman 'settled to take vol. of RM stories'. With the most diverse claims on their time it was to be two years before this third and final set of stories was completed. Edith was contacted on 14 April by the militant wing of the suffrage movement, to support the increasingly violent agitation: 'Heard from Mrs Cousins, head of the Irish Militant Suffrage movement asking me to support her in Skib. Wrote and said I could not back up militancy as I thought it was a tactical error.'[46] Much writing time was lost over a copyright case. It was in the second week of June that they first saw a copy of *By the Brown Bog* 'by Owen Roe and Honor Urse, whose flattery has taken the form of imitation'. This astonishing volume of barefaced plagiarism was published by Somerville and Ross's own publisher. The following day they wrote a 'vitriolic yet curbed letter to Longman' and wrote out a long list of parallel passages. By 10 June they 'had long letters from Longman and Pinker re "Brown Bog". Mr L climbing down head first.' When the book was reviewed in *Country Life* the reviewer naturally assumed the work was by Somerville and Ross and discussed the reason for their publishing under a new name. This assumption spread far and wide as the book was reviewed in other papers. Eventually on 5 July they had to send out letters to a wide range of papers and journals officially disclaiming authorship. Aided by the Society of Authors, they cleared their names and prevented further "Brown Bog" cloning from their work.

July was particularly fraught; in the middle of it, Martin wrote to Hildegarde: 'Edith would write to you too, only that she is packing a big box of your own – and has had her usual day of kennels, farm, then Dairy books, letters, and now the Ban Oosal [sic] and Miss O'Donovan and the organisers [United Irishwomen] to tea.' Edith herself wrote at the end of the month just before they went up to Dublin: 'What with farm and getting this house ready for the Aylmers, and hounds, and Choir, and Sassiety (tea parties innumerable) – and Constance Bushe's protegees coming to be cared for, I begin to feel that the stationmastership at Clapham Junction would be a pleasant lounge.'[47] Nineteen-thirteen was an important year in which they both fell under the spell of Sir Horace Plunkett. Martin first met him on 28 June, when he called to collect her with a friend from the Shelbourne Hotel to take her out to see his new house. First, she wrote in her diary, he took them to see his workplace – 'to Plunket House where we saw AE enormous and genial and then on to Sir Horace's delightful new house at Foxrock [Kilteragh] all sun and teak wood and verandahs'. The following day Martin was taken by Edward Martyn to hear his Palestrina Choir at the Marlboro' Street Chapel. Here she 'came in for second High Mass' and felt out of place in her grand dress, 'very gorgeous among the filthy slum people'. Plunkett had already come into contact with some Cork gentry when he spent a few years in the warm and dry American west, cattle ranching for the sake of his health, as he suffered from suspected consumption. His companions there included Richard Baxter Townshend and Alexis Roche, who was his ranching partner. Richard Baxter Townshend wrote the celebrated classic of the American West, *Lone Pine*, and was much loved by the CT young as 'Uncle Dick'. Claude Chavasse remembered being taught by him to lasso running cattle. Uncle Dick had tied the huge horns of a steer to the garden wheelbarrow at the Castle, and charged about on the gravel in front of the Castle shouting instructions at the boy with the rope.[48]

Until he retired from Kneller Hall in 1919, Cameron had little conception of the amount of work that Edith undertook on the farm during the early summer months in particular. Harvesting was the worst time for literary work, and to Martin this became an ideal opportunity for catching up with her sisters, nephews and nieces. Ethel Penrose realised the fraughtness of this period in the agricultural year and made a point of sweeping Edith away from Drishane as soon as the hay was in. The strain came off in late June in 1913. Hildegarde was away when Edith wrote to Cameron on the 16th: 'I know I haven't answered any of your long and most interesting letters but I am half dead with work, having four men's jobs on hand at present. And the Hay now, on top of all!' Edith wrote a letter on the next day to her 'Dear Partners' to tell them of recent cattle dealing:

> Dick [Richard Helen], who had been rather struck by the Jones' Ayrshire bull sale, laid down his cards when he heard of today's bargain, and said, "By gash, you bet us all". Before I leave the subject of the farm may I say that I cut one field of hay yesterday in blazing sun, east wind, and a high steady glass [barometer] ... Do you realise that I have in one week sold five bulls of our own breeding? All due to Hildegarde's *male*volent influence on the herd. Your exhausted sister Edith.

But by 21 June she was resting blissfully after her labours, with Ethel in Kerry for a few days at the Great Southern Hotel at Parknasilla. Her letter to Cameron from the Hotel gives us some idea of the gulf between their worlds, Cameron in the opulent upper ranks of Army society and Edith a farming countrywoman with country pleasures: 'Ethel has swept Martin and me off to this very lovely place in the motor. We go on to Killarney today and home tomorrow. I saw in the *Times* you were dining with the Regiment and I hope you got home fairly sober.' Back at the farm, a letter to Hildegarde, though meant to entertain, shows Edith's growing reliance on Mike Hurley, her groom and huntsman. She told her sister on 1 July that – when she had become involved in a tricky situation in the middle of a field with a difficult horse – she felt like the man who, in a similar fix, 'appealed to Mike "What'll I do now Mike?" and then when Mike told him, doing it.' In the middle of July an appreciation of Somerville and Ross by Charlie Graves was published in the *Quarterly Review*. It restored their confidence after their bruising experience with Longman and *The Brown Bog*. Edith wrote to Cameron on 26 July telling him to get a copy: 'See what Charlie Graves has to say about us! It is almost awful – and we wrote to tell him we felt as if we had died. It really is a valuable tribute and I hope Longman will take it to heart.'

After the Dublin Horse Show, they were to join a perfectly sober Cameron for a week at Kneller Hall, 12–25 August. Both Edith and Martin had begun to consult medically unqualified healers, described as 'quacks' by the more sceptical of their relations. After her homeopathic diagnosis in London Edith wrote to Hildegarde: 'I can imagine Eleanor's [Dr Hodson's] hellish smile of contempt.' At Kneller Hall there was always some musical event in hand. Bishop Taylor Smith was about to arrive for an open-air service: 'If I hear "Onward Christian Soldiers" again, I shall shoot the nearest thing, and rush, shrieking, into the family vault.'[49] With Plunkett's encouragement, Edith, Martin and Hildegarde had started up a branch of the United Irishwomen in CT. They began with Technical Instruction Classes under the auspices of the UI organisers. The first class mentioned in the family papers is on 26 July 1913, and Edith wrote to describe it to Cameron: '[the UI classes] have been an enormous success. As Martin truly says, it is a great thing to think that at least thirty girls in the parish now know how to make poultices, beef tea, and rice puddings. We are giving prizes and having a competition on Monday for the students, with an Exhibition of results. I am dying to turn our creamery into a Co-Operative one on Sir Horace Plunkett's lines. Martin is going to pay him a visit, for the Horse Show (Heavily Chaperoned, I hasten to add) and I will make her talk to him. Once the property is "vested" we ought to shut down the creamery, but if the farmers would run it on Co-Op lines it might be a noble and missionary work to help them in starting it.'[50]

When they were based in Dublin for the Horse Show on 27 August, Martin showed that while Edith was absorbed in the horse world, she could operate independently in another sphere. On the next day she entered in her diary: 'attended Suffrage Press Conference and gave my opinion to it against militancy', and on the following day she lunched at Horace Plunkett's house Kilteragh with the Maharajah of Mysore and his secretary. Plunkett had taken to Martin's company with enthusiasm. She was asked to lunch again on the next day, where she was 'the only female among eight men'. Then she took off on a visiting jaunt. But before setting off, on 1 September she wrote to Sir Horace about the United Irishwomen: 'I have thought about the United Irishwomen appeal ... If some kind of show or entertainment could be got up in Cork, for example, it would popularise the movement ... Dublin seems a long way off, when we speak of it at our meetings ... it would be a great matter to place the movement in a light that would commend it to the poor women, and bring its public aspects within their scope ...'[51]

Martin went first to Ballynahinch and from there on to the Morrises at Spiddal, where on 20 September she was at a noisy dinner party whose guests included Miss Gertrude Sweetman, Shane Leslie, Bourke Cochrane, and Miss Tilly Redington. She described the Catholic convert and Irish Nationalist Shane Leslie in her diary as 'pervert and Nationalist'. Meanwhile in Cork Edith managed to engage some excellent speakers for the Munster Women's Suffrage League; the industrial organiser Louie Bennett came to address a meeting in Skibbereen at which the visiting Miss Alice Kinkead and Miss Frances Perkins also spoke in support. Edith was in the chair and wrote to describe the meeting to Cameron on 19th September, incidentally describing her young guests:

[There were] 250 very respectable citizens, and no rowdy element though the entrance was only 3d. A Miss Bennett from Dublin, Kinkie and Miss Perkins spoke. Miss B was the speaker and did very well, thoroughly practical and interesting. Perkie surprised me; her manner was admirable, her voice very pleasant and what she said was very much to the point. Kinkie was fair, and I respected her the most, as she was by far the most nervous, yet stuck to it. I was as stiff and rotten as I always am and came home *dead beat* I don't know when I have been so done ... the poor schoolboys departed today and a peace so complete as to be melancholy now reigns. I am entirely pleased with Boyle's boys. I think them both [Raymond and Brian] quite exceptionally nice. Not as advanced in anyway as Paddy and Nevill, but clever enough, and Raymond has a clever face, and is full of notions. He is a most honest, unselfish fellow, a little hot, perhaps, but dead straight – a *very* nice body.

Martin had taken the opportunity to go up and visit Nora Tracey, at Ballybogey, in the North again. She went at a moment's notice, tacking it on to her itinerary from Dublin. 'That brute Martin has gone to Ulster – she never told me till just before she started (ie she goes tomorrow) I don't know when she will be home. She will probably be vivandiering about after Sir Edward Carson and won't come back till after the war' she complained to Cameron. Edith's reference to 'the war' here must be due to her dread that the political situation within Ireland would descend to armed violence between the North and South. Martin was back at Drishane on 10 October, nicely in time for a terrible panic over an article, 'November Day', that appeared in *The Times* on Saturday 1 November. Its writing and printing were done in one breakneck rush. On 29 October Edith wrote in her diary: 'Heard from Times asking for an article on opening meet of typical Irish pack. Began to do it'. On the next day: 'Oblivious of everything until 12.50 when Mike fled into Skib with the thing for *The Times* "To Open the Season" And we fell into a stupor of exhaustion.' It was in the paper in thirty-six hours. Edith was hunting twice a week; they were writing both RM stories and newspaper pieces.

For Edith at the end of November there was the upsetting news, which she sent on to Cameron, that Bertie Windle had got 'in trouble with the Gaelic League over his "stolen Oghams"'. Professor of Archaeology in Cork, as well as President of the College, Bertie had collaborated with Professor R.A.S. Macalister of University College, Dublin and together they had brought in to the safety of the University museum collection an important setting of large Ogham stones.[52] This caused heated controversy in the press. Gradually Nationalist opinion within the university had built up against President Windle, who was naturally seen by many as an odd combination of 'Castle Catholic' and 'West Brit'. As well as this, in personal dealings his Olympian manner and icy blue stare did not endear him to people. He was to be deposed in 1919 and leave Ireland to take up a post in Canada.

Charles Townshend and his wife Carrie at the Castle were fervent supporters of the Gaelic League; she played the Irish harp and also taught Irish. She taught Edith and Martin at various times. The Townshends were very keen to introduce Edith to the then President of the Gaelic League, Lady Desart. The same letter of 29 November goes on to tell Cameron that: 'Carrie T's adored Lady Desart head of the Gaelic League and of all sorts of Kilkenny Industries' was coming to CT. However, Edith turned down a call from Lady Desart because she was also President of the 'Anti-Suffs' [the Anti-Suffragists] and did not meet her. Martin's diary entries at this time were very patchy, and scrawled in fitfully. In Christmas week she only remarked on Hildegarde's Christmas Day pie at Glen B, of the 'usual vast dimensions'. Edith began the New Year of 1914 unable to hunt, having fractured her left wrist when her horse fell at a tricky place. This made finding time for writing less difficult, and the RM story 'Harringtons' was finished on 26 January. This story, like the earlier 'Waters of Strife', has a large element of the supernatural; Frank O'Connor in his review of the volume of stories said that it seemed to him to be the outcome of a collision between a funny story on a train and a ghost story on a bicycle. But O'Connor was to write an important appreciative article on Somerville and Ross some years later.[53]

The point had been reached in the lives of the Somerville brothers where they had to consider the conditions of their retirement. Cameron had planned to retire at fifty-five and live the life of an Anglo-Irish country gentleman with his sister as housekeeper and hostess. But in a letter from February 1914 the suggestion was aired that Cameron's appointment as Commandant of Kneller Hall might be renewed. Cameron, but not Edith, had doubts about the tenability of his position in Ireland, and only he knew his dire financial position, which he dared discuss with no-one. But Edith carried on preparing for his retirement and permanent return to Drishane, and renovated his room. On 25 March her diary notes: 'No one able to talk or think of anything but the Army Ulster crisis'. Prime Minister Asquith was considering sending troops from the Curragh Camp, near Dublin, to the North in the event of armed violence from the Ulster Volunteers. Fifty-eight British officers proffered their resignations in protest at the prospect of the military coercion of Ulster. Asquith drew back, learning from this that he could not rely on the Army in this quandary. The Volunteers in the North and the South continued to arm themselves.

For Cameron's fifty-fourth birthday, 30 March 1914, Edith and Martin both wrote to congratulate him. Edith's letter is bound up with the redecoration and refurbishment of his room. Martin's birthday greetings are on a closely written postcard: 'Dear Chimp – only a word of greeting to say Many Happy Returns – One thinks of next year, and it is a comfort to think that whatever may be the state of affairs here, we shall have the man of the house with us – if we all live – strange times indeed we are looking at, and may it all remain as a spectacle to us and far away ...' Martin was not to see how Cameron shaped up as Master of Drishane, as he accepted another five-year term of office in charge of Kneller Hall in order to be kept afloat by his Army pay. He eventually retired in 1919, four years after Martin's death. Cameron's room, the old Blue Room, was being repapered in blue and lined with panelling to take his collection of pictures. Edith was expecting it to be 'padded four feet deep with Japanese prints'. On 1 April she wrote to tell him that the carpenter Willy Driscoll had gutted the room, and all the old rotten wood and fitments were out on the lawn: 'it looks as though the house has been given a violent emetic'. The chaos caused by the builders, who were working at the kitchen range again as well, eventually became too much and Edith moved into Glen B. At the end of May Edith and Martin again went over to Ethel's in Lismore for a 'time of much enjoyed rest and laziness ... We are not – I need hardly say – having a holiday as far as writing is concerned, but the "Res angusta domi" is relaxed, which is something.' Their relaxation with Ethel did not last long, as Edith wrote to explain to Cameron that he could not expect a letter for a while: 'Pinker is sticking in the spurs and we shall have to foreswear everything superfluous in the way of writing so as to save our brains for the Work ...'

The story following 'Harringtons' was 'The Maroan Pony' which carried forward the cast into a new situation. A lady doctor, Dr Fraser, and her friend Meg Longmuir, are chicken farmers. They go to horse races with the RM, Major Yeates, and his family. A star rider called Lyney Garrett is riding against a local boy named Jimmy Kenny, who seems to have but one supporter shouting encouragement at him. Though we are supposedly seeing the scene through the eyes of the Major, now and again we are presented with an appreciative response to men's looks that is rather out of character in him. Standing amid tiers of people on a bank all yelling their heads off, the Major's party had wondered out loud who the local boy was: '"That's Jimmy Kenny," responded the man below, turning a black muzzled face up towards us, his light eyes gleaming between their black lashes in the sunshine like aquamarines. I recognized Peter Lynch, whom we had met before in the day.' The RM's way of dealing with those who were intoxicated and brawling by the end of the day, violent dispute having broken out between the Kennys and the Lynches and the supporters of Lyney Garrett, shows how well his judgement had matured after his years of service in Cork: '"Look here, Sergeant," I said oracularly, "take them to the water jump.

Build up the furze in front of it. Make them jump it. Anyone that gets over it may be considered sober. Anyone that falls in will be sober enough when he gets out." I have not, in my judicial career, delivered a judgement that gave more satisfaction to the public.'54

Through her suffrage meetings Edith met and talked to a wide variety of women in the movement. She consequently heard details of movements in military society from levels other than those her brothers frequented as officers in the Army and Navy. She watched the growth of the Irish Volunteer Movement, founded in a counter response to the Ulster Volunteers, with great interest. Writing to Cameron from Lismore, where she had been talking with Jimmy Penrose of the divided loyalties of the Curragh Mutiny in March, she told him: 'Most of the wise men here are full of apprehension about this Irish Volunteer Movement. It has, however one great merit viz that the warfare – if it comes – will be civilized by discipline. I met a girl yesterday who runs a soldiers' café, she told me that *numbers* of the gunners had plain clothes, and had they been sent to Ulster were going to have gone straight over to the other side!' The question of which side the Anglo-Irish gentry would take was a crucial one. As Edith went down with a heavy cold, Ethel and Martin left her to write letters while they went motoring; as a result Cameron heard more from Edith about the Irish Volunteers: 'I am sat upon for saying the gentry should join in, but though there are many practical difficulties, I can't help thinking it would be a sound thing, and a valuable safeguard.' Edith was envisaging gentry with nationalist sympathies joining the Irish Volunteer officer corps, to fortify a command structure and discipline. There could be no doubt that she never questioned the involvement of the Master of Drishane in whatever developments were to come in Ireland. The Volunteers drilled daily and celebrated the passing of the third Home Rule Bill Amendment with great processions; however, they had not yet reached a military standard of drill; on 27 May Edith wrote to her sister: 'The Volunteers that I have seen have been a negligible quantity.' But four days later she mentioned them again: 'The drilling goes on here every night, most diligently. I wonder of they will keep it up. They swear they are non-political and non-religious. I wish the Prod. men would join. It would be a great safeguard, and they couldn't refuse to enlist them.'55

Edith and Martin worked in Drishane through June and the beginning of July, while Hildegarde was away. Bed space was at a premium. A letter from Edith to her sister shows that Sir Joscelyn's yacht the *Ierne*, now converted to a houseboat, was used *in extremis* by the family when they had let, or given over to guests, all the space in their houses including their own bedrooms. 'If the Houseboat was unoccupied perhaps you would let me stay in her until the Show [Bazaar] is over?' A fund-raising Bazaar was in the offing when suddenly there was news from Ross. 'Martin has just had a wire from Ross to say that Connie [the widow of Martin's brother Robert] died there last night. Heart, Martin thinks. Poor creature – it is a desolate end – only servants with her.' She had died very bravely without complaining or sending for her daughter, who was stationed with her husband in India. Martin wrote of her to Hildegarde: 'it was never a very happy life' and carried on, 'if there is a row about Home Rule I suppose the Bazaar will be knocked on the head. It certainly is very row-ish now – a spirit is up in the country that will not easily sit down ... here comes a letter from you to E. – more about the bazaar – she must herself write to you – I turn to other themes – My name is aisy.' She kept Hildegarde up to date on Edith's health: 'she is out to the hay perpetually and that is good for her.'[56] Edith had been delighted, two days before, by the birth of an unauthorised and unexpected, but beautiful, foal to her mare Buttercup. She described it to Hildegarde with a stockbreeder's eye: 'The little filly is grand – I firmly believe she is the child of Marquis. She is the image of him. Buttercup must have formed her eye on him.'

The problem of Ireland and its risen spirit North and South was to be shelved by the Liberals at the outbreak of war. Percy and Eddy Aylmer were very wealthy, and had not stinted in the kitting out of their CT home, the Red House. Up in their sail loft, later converted into a flat used by Sylvia Townshend Gorges, Contessa Lovera, Percy had installed a radio mast, being a keen radio ham. On Sunday 26 July 1914 Martin entered into her diary: 'Percy heard on his Marconi mast that Austria is going to declare war with Serbia', and on the next day: 'a European War seems certain'. Britain declared war on 4 August. All of the Somerville brothers were to serve in it. Meanwhile, thanks to the English tenants' rents, Drishane had a major programme of refurbishment, painting, decorating and replumbing: 'I don't think there will be a farthing saved out of the Saxon's bloody gold,' Edith complained to her sister. Due to congestion with guests and workmen Martin was in Glen B from 28 July until 2 October. The next day she and Edith went to a suffrage meeting in Cork that turned bad. It had been planned to use the funds of the Cork suffrage society to buy and stock a motorised field ambulance for the Front. This proposition detonated a cloudburst of schisms.

Nationalist women did not want to support the 'English' war, pacifist women did not want to contribute any aid and comfort to acts of war, and Unionist women thought the right thing to do was to support their menfolk. This was a splitting in the ranks of the Cork women's movement that mirrored the rifts opening up in the National Union of Women's Suffrage Societies. From the moment war was declared, Irishmen had volunteered for the Front; there were very quickly casualties among local men: 'I am awfully sorry for poor

Maggie Hurley. I see from the *Eagle* that her man died of his wounds,' Edith wrote to Hildegarde on 14 October. Eleanor Hodson volunteered to the French Red Cross for one of their Hospitals in Paris and left CT. Edith and Martin saw the effect of the war on London when they were with Cameron at Kneller Hall from 8 to 24 October. Back in CT at Christmas time, the 'invaluable Aylmers' made themselves useful and joined the Glen B pie fest. It was a subdued Christmas. Two of the Somerville brothers were on active service: Boyle was in command of HMS *Victorian* on Atlantic convoy duty, and Hugh was serving in action on the North Sea. Jack was at the War Office. Aylmer was a recruiting officer and Cameron was at Kneller Hall. Quite soon the younger generation would be called up.

January and February of 1915 were taken up by the last RM story, 'The Shooting of Shinroe'. The war affected everything. Edith had difficulty in getting meat for the hounds, as even the scraggiest and most ancient horses that normally would have gone to the knacker's yard were being bought up by the Army. Knowing about the conditions at the Front for pack and draft animals from men of the gunners and veterinary corps, Hildegarde began fund-raising for the Blue Cross, the Red Cross of the animal world. On 27 February Candy, the 'Head Dog', became so ill that Egerton 'gave her the final peace' and took her away and chloroformed her. She was a great age, more than sixteen years old. She had been a puppy when the first set of RM stories had been published in 1899. In her diary Edith wrote on the 28th: 'Yesterday in the depths of our grief had to finish and send Longmans the story … it took the last ounce that was left in us.' Longmans was threatening to postpone publication of the new RM series until after the war, so they were relieved to get an offer from Nelsons via Pinker on 11 March to bring out a sevenpenny edition of their books, with £750 advance royalties. This they accepted.

By 19 March they were at work on a suffrage pamphlet, commissioned by Lady Robert Cecil for the Conservative and Unionist Women's Association, about the war work being done by various branches of the movement. It was entitled 'With Thanks For the Kind Enquiries' and was to be the last work they ever wrote together, talking, wrangling and laughing out loud.[57] Charles Longman had revised his plans and given *In Mr Knox's Country* the go-ahead for publication in June, and the proofs arrived on 1 April. Once free of the proofs, they went up to Dublin, where they visited Horace Plunkett at Kilteragh at the end of May and Edith made extensive notes on a tour of his experimental farm with his manager Wibberley, coming back via Lismore 'congested with information' to impart to Hildegarde.

On the journey to Lismore, 'an appalling trajet', their train had been full of drunks and troops. At first their carriage had not been invaded, as Martin who was in better form than Edith 'with a most menacing countenance held the door against the mob', but the mob had eventually broken through. Edith had been delighted with their meeting with Sir Horace's agricultural advisor 'Professor' Wibberley, with whom they had spent a morning at Kilteragh and who was 'a pet – Rather like Neville Cameron – not a gent, but just as nice, if not nicer than one, no swagger and humming with ideas ... I am so delighted ... that Paddy has taken up with a boy of his own class and age. What a pity there isn't a Camp at Skibbereen! It would have stimulated recruiting beside other advantages not necessary to mention.' Edith refers to the bygone years of sociable pleasure provided by the 'fresh meat' of the officers of the Skibbereen Barracks.

At Lismore Ethel took them motoring to visit the Abbot of Mount Melleray Abbey. 'He is a great farmer and says he found the Wibberley system *splendid* ... Wibberley has also been instructing on Sir John Keane's estate (next door to the Abbot) and has made a great success there also.' Impressed and convinced by the evidence, the sisters adopted the system of continuous cropping at CT also. The flagging Edith was taking a protein supplement in tablet form, and told her sister that 'Wib' was suffering from overwork in 'precisely the same way' as herself: suffering from loss of memory and 'lack of continuity of thought (unlike his cropping) – who says farming is not an intellectual occupation?'[58] She sent some of her protein tablets to Wibberley.

The War had a disastrous effect on the printing and publishing trade. Edith and Martin's incomes from writing dropped, so that the income from letting CT houses became all-important. Drishane was let from 14 July, so Edith and Martin moved to a house loaned to them in Lismore by Ethel and Jim. While here the reviews of *In Mr Knox's Country* started to come in. It was a relief that the Bence-Joneses had applied for a summer let of Drishane from 26 July to 15 September. All sources of income were drying up. Martin mentioned to Pinker in July 1915 that 'even a tenner is rather a rare object these days'. The worry and stress of the farm, the hunt and family finances finally broke Edith's spirit. She got writer's block. In her diary on 21 July Edith noted that she had done the Hunt Accounts with the help of Ethel and Martin: 'Made the pleasing discovery that expenditure was £200 more than the receipts.' On the same day Martin wrote to Pinker: 'Miss Somerville is very much worried over the fate of her beloved hounds and that and her manifold works at home have caused brainfag – the first breakdown of her wonderful capacity for work at a dozen different things – I daresay you are an expert in brain-fag – It is very distressing to an eager mind ... she must have most of the hounds destroyed if she cannot hold on [financially] ...' Pinker had written with the half-joking suggestion that, at the age of seventy-five, he came to live in CT and joined Edith as Joint-Master. Martin had responded that they looked forward to this imaginary event, 'when we shall all be five and twenty'. At this time the fifty-seven-year-old Edith was training a horse and Martin had passed on to Pinker a remark of Edith's huntsman Metherell: 'Her rides as if she was twenty five – the boldest rider ever I did see'[59]; so, although Edith was broken down mentally, and useless for writing, she had not lost her power over horses.

By the beginning of August, Edith and Martin had escaped to Kerry, on a holiday that was for the benefit of Edith's poor health. Martin was concerned over Edith, who was still very out of sorts and pulled down. En route to Cahirciveen they bought a *Spectator* at Mallow Station and read a 'refulgent' notice of their new book. Through Edith's friendship with some of the O'Connell family, descendants of Daniel O'Connell 'the Liberator', they had been sent to cousins of theirs who had opened their house as a country hotel. Martin wrote to Pinker to describe the country around Kinneigh House by Cahirciveen, on 7 August 1915: 'We are in delightful country here – with big scenery; bog and mountains, turf-ricks and little thatched cabins, groves of loosestrife, and forests of ragweed – little black cattle, three miles of salmon river and the War nowhere.' Attentive to agricultural conditions, Edith took in the significance of those 'forests of ragweed', deadly to grazing animals: they were a sign of land neglected. They found their host and hostess very agreeable. Mr and Mrs Fitzgerald – 'she a great-granddaughter of Daniel O'Connell the Liberator' – were the keenest of anglers, fishing for salmon on the River Inny.

On 11 August Charlie Graves wrote late at night in London to Martin in Kerry: 'I wonder did your ears burn tonight at about 7.30 when E.V. Lucas was holding forth at our weekly Punch dinner on the merits of *In Mr Knox's Country*. But I have a special message for you both from Rudyard Kipling whom I was lunching with at the Club yesterday. When I told him that I was going to write to you he said: "Please give them my respectful love, my compliments, obeisances and salaams." Those are his exact words. But he said a lot of other nice things which I will tell you some day, and he made me jealous by quoting passages from the book better than I could.'[60] They were so delighted with their holiday place that they stayed on into September. Edith painted, enchanted by the landscape and its colours. There are several survivors on canvas from this period, blazing with the purple of the loosestrife and the yellow of the ragwort. She wrote to Cameron on the 6th to complain of his letters' unreadable handwriting. She described herself and Martin getting headaches trying to decipher it, both of them using strong eyeglasses for close work by this stage. Their lifted spirits are reflected in the humour of their letters from Kerry. Edith asked Cameron: 'are you in training to write the thirty nine articles on a threepenny bit?' She was guilt-free in thinking of Hildegarde, left in charge of the farm, where she was having an inspection of stock by her

Professor Wibberley. 'Happy Hildegarde, now in the arms of Wib! (or partially so, he is about 5'5").'[61]

Recorded in Notebook 14 and dated Kerry, September 1915, is material later used by Edith in her articles 'Kerry I' and 'Kerry II' (later Chapter XXIV of *Wheeltracks*). Mag Barry, the cook at Kinneigh, had been a source of good talk and stories. The primitive arrangements in remote rural areas between surviving landlords and tenants seemed to be unchanged from medieval times: 'Rent is owed by Mrs Flib [a local contraction of Philip] of Bolus Head. In lieu thereof she tenders the services of her daughter in the house of her landlord, an accepted custom.' But an intense dislike sprang up between the daughter and another servant Joany Crohan. The landlord then discovered that there was an hereditary feud between the houses of Flib and Crohan, and Miss Flib retired home to her mother, leaving the landlord to go to law. The master gloomily said that 'now he would have to process the mother for the rent'.

On 7 September Martin wrote to Pinker about the proofs of their extracted RM stories being included with those 'Great English Writers' whose works were distributed free to the troops at the Front. He was not to hear from her again. Her last diary entry was made on the day before she wrote to Pinker: 'Got our copy of "Mr Knox" from H and struggled to make suitable extracts from it for the "Times".' They reluctantly left Kerry on September 17th, and Edith wrote to Cameron on the train between Killarney and Mallow to say that Martin 'had and has a bad go of neuralgia, caused by a tooth'. In Martin's diary there is the entry 'Left Kinneigh' written in on that day, but it is in Edith's handwriting. There is a photograph taken at the main door at Kinneigh at the end of August. A group sitting and standing round the door is saying farewell to a group leaving in a car. It is sunny, Martin is standing straight backed and sprightly, and Edith, who is looking her age, is sitting with a dog in her lap; both are looking at the departing guests and both wearing huge summer hats, Edith's the more elaborate. This is the last photograph taken of Martin, sent on to Edith by Maurice Fitzgerald.

They returned to Drishane where Martin became weak, didn't want to eat, and could only lie flat with what seemed like migraine symptoms. Dr O'Meara decided that abscessed back teeth were the problem, and on the last day of September a dentist removed them. 'But,' Edith wrote to Cameron, 'she has hardly been free from pain since, and O'Meara fears it is the nerves of the eyes that are causing the trouble. He says it is well the teeth are out, but though they may have been the original offenders, it is now other nerves that are giving the trouble. She is a perfect shadow, and is sickened by pain-killing drugs, so that she can hardly eat.'[62]

Martin was showing some symptoms that were alarming: her left eye had closed and she could not open it. Edith was to take her, on O'Meara's recommendation, to an eye specialist called McMahon in Cork. Aware of the efficiency and exaggerating tendencies of the Bushe telegraph, she asked Cameron not to say anything in London that might reach and alarm the Martin sisters. McMahon gave a course of treatment that caused a recovery, and by the end of October Martin was 'crawling' around the garden at Drishane. Dr O'Meara was pleased that she was picking up from what he described as 'a bad go of neuritis'. But on the last day of November, as Martin quite clearly started to drift in consciousness, Hildegarde and Edith decided to move her to hospital care in Cork. Two days later they drove with her to Cork after dark had fallen, not knowing that Martin was having a massive haemorrhage in her brain. Martin was received as a patient in the Glen Vera nursing home at 10 Sydney Place on the evening of 2 December. Edith obviously thought at this stage that Martin needed hospital treatment and rest, but had no idea how serious was Martin's condition. She wrote to Cameron: 'I do trust she will be out, and well, before you are over.'[63]

But by 4 December, Martin had slipped into a coma-like state, and only two days after her last letter Edith wrote to Cameron again:

> There is today just this to be said – She is no worse – and that is remark-able. The doctors were surprised. One of them said: 'Well there is just a shred of hope' – hardly that, I think, but still, not hopeless – but if her mind should be clouded it would be worse than losing her now. The tumour they suspect is at the base of the brain – near a very vital part, connected with the heart and respiratory system, but not so much affecting the mind. She is very heavily drugged – Jim Martin came last night … It is impossible to say what I can do, Martin's state makes plans impossible. She knows us, but cloudily, and with an effort. We have settled with her nurse not to see her unless she asks for us. The Dr almost insisted on our seeing her and I could see that it tired her. Her gentleness and docility and consideration for the Nurses fills them with admiration, drugged and labouring though her mind is. I should think that by Monday something more definite can be said. These things are sometimes lingering, running on for weeks – sometimes, as with Cecil Bushe's girl at the Red House – almost instantaneous. After her starting the week so well this sudden collapse was shattering. It is all a nightmare.

Nurse Tracy advised Edith that Martin must be kept quiet, but that Edith must be nearby, so that if Martin asked for her she could come immediately. By the 7th Edith told Cameron that Martin was sinking into unconsciousness more deeply with each day. She slept mostly but had said Edith's name. When

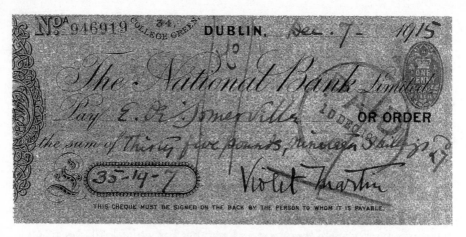

14 The last cheque written by Martin Ross, made out to her writing partner,
7 December 1915. Edith knew that she was Martin's executor,
but perhaps not that she was the only beneficiary.

Hildegarde spoke to her on 6 December she had answered to her familiar voice:
'You and Edith are always faithful.' On the 7th Canon Madden gave her the
Sacrament. More than two weeks before Martin died Edith was prepared for
her death and burial. After Canon Madden had gone, Martin said Edith's name
quite clearly and asked what time it was, she told Cameron: 'but she spoke
from this far-off place that she has been in throughout. Jim Martin is going to
have her brought to Castletownshend and I am glad of that – the desolate old
Ross place – like our own – is full and the alternative is Oughterard which she
and I hate. You must not think of coming over ... she would be the very last to
wish that you should have so great an expense just for a token, that is not
needed, of your feelings, and that reminds me that I have had *no* expenses
worth considering and your cheque shall be kept for you.'[64]

It is perhaps some form of flight from what was happening that caused
Edith to dwell on monetary matters and to plot economies at such a time, or
else an instant apprehension that her literary income might be at an end. She
had found staying at the Ladies' Club too expensive, and had been persuaded
by the Windles to move to the President's Lodgings at the university. However,
she was an extremely hard-headed and hard-up woman, and she was grateful
to Bertie Windle and his wife for their hospitality while Martin was in the Glen
Vera. 'These kind Windles have taken me in, and saved me much loneliness and
expense. I cannot tell you how truly sympathetic and considerate Bertie has
been ...' Certainly no-one could claim that Edith acted in any way as a
distraught or even emotionally upset woman at this time. She spent her days in
the vigil beside Martin's deathbed in arranging her affairs, including Martin's

burial, and in writing to her friends and relations. She was grateful that Martin had not understood that she was dying. Edith explained to Cameron that 'She has never, I think, known that she was really ill – it is no use trying to say anything: No-one but she and I can know what we were to each other – Dearest Chimp I know you sympathise and grieve.'[65]

In the Coghill Archive three letters, from 12, 16 and 20 December, survive from Edith to Hildegarde written from the Glen Vera. They show a complete matter-of-factness: 'I find her this morning very little changed. Her face has got *very* thin, but as she has not had half a pint of milk for a week that is not surprising. I met Dr Cremen and tried to get him to admit that her wonderful vitality gave hope – He said that if she *did* live she would be semi-paralysed in mind and body. He said he thought it would be the greatest misfortune for her to linger on ... Mrs O'Sullivan has no hope at all ...' Three of the night nurses said that they had heard a cry at twelve and at two in the morning during the night before, 'a child or a woman crying, *not* an animal'; searching and finding nothing, they thought it might be the Banshee. 'It is very strange, but it makes no difference to me now. What nice letters the boys wrote, and Nevill's was delightful and very entertaining as well ... I wouldn't let Ethel come up here this morning. I *am* thankful to have her, and also for your sake as I know it eases your mind about me.' A relation of Martin's, Mrs O'Hara, who was a Christian Scientist, was trying to help: 'She is hopelessly irrational about her faith healing, poor thing, but it has given her some pleasure, and I know Martin would not have liked me to snub her, or disappoint her ... Please don't write to me every day, as I know well how you are being killed with work of every sort and letters. You will only break down – Ethel's being here is just saving my soul alive. It is all a nightmare, yet I cannot wish it to end, and to look forward to a time when I can do nothing for her.'

Edith had still not recovered from the fatigue that had necessitated the holiday in Kerry, when Martin had been supervising Edith's medicaments. Assuming that Martin would be dead shortly, she decided not to be in CT at Christmas time 'wet-blanketting' the children, and to go to Ethel at Lismore. For, she explained to Cameron:

> she and Jim are alone, and they understand, and they loved Martin. It is no use to cry and weep as Norry the boat said, 'You might as well be dancing and singing'. Whether, as you say, I sit on the safety valve or whether I cried my grief to the four winds it would make no difference ... Half, and the best half – of my life and soul is torn away and there are no words and no tears that can cure my trouble – If it weren't for you all I would be thankful and joyful to follow her, that we might go together

as usual. But it is no use talking. I will try and do what she would like and look after things, just the same, and not break down or shirk – I suppose it won't hurt so much as time goes on. Life will go with a broken wing but there will still be a reason for standing to one's guns and 'carrying on'.[66]

This is the clearest statement that maintaining life at CT in keeping up Drishane was an actual physical battle and a sore trial. On the 18th Ethel Penrose had joined her in the watching and waiting, and it helped her to write letters about the herd and consult with her sister about the farm. It helped to think of Cameron: 'I do hope and trust that it won't be too long before you come home for good, and we must do the best we can for each other.' Edith sat beside Martin, whose breathing she could hear, writing to sympathisers. The Queen had sent enquiries among many of their readers. Reverting to Cameron's homecoming she asked him not to mind 'a heartbroken companion. It isn't that I don't love you all only that she was a part of myself, only unspeakably higher in every way, and nobler than any but I can know – You needn't fear I shan't pull myself together – for I will – only you must forgive me if I seem dull, or unfriendly, it will only be that I am trying and the task will often be too hard for me. I had to write all this because I am, like Boyle, unable to speak – and I am terrified lest I give any of you a wrong impression, or that you should not realise that a miserable heart sometimes seem like a surly one.' Mrs O'Hara kept trying to help, but on the 20th Edith refused her aid. 'If I *could* bring her back to a maimed and broken life, as it now must be, I would not do it,' she wrote to Hildegarde. Bishop Hearn came and sat with Edith, and he was a welcome comfort: 'I never spoke to a man with a more sympathetic, kind face and manner. No more now, I trust all are well and if you get a cold that you will mind it, ever your loving Edith.'[67] Three days before Martin died, with Hildegarde in the room, to distract herself with practicality Edith made a competent drawing of Martin's head. Martin's breathing ceased gently at 7.45 in the morning of the 21st when only Nurse Tracy was with her.

Through the last hospitalised weeks of Martin's life Edith kept a clinical diary of her condition, but she did not make diary entries until the morning of Martin's funeral. Her body had been brought down from Cork on Wednesday the day after she died, and it lay in the open coffin overnight in St Barrahane's before the altar. At that time there was a familiarity with, and reverence for the dead that seems strange to modern feelings. When Edith got up on the morning of the funeral she sent for the Glen B children including her niece K and Sylvia Townshend Gorges,[68] to show them how to make a letter-shaped wreath. This was a production-line item from the violet farm: customers could order a wreath of violets in the required initial. Edith seems to have found the familiar company of the young calming. Both K and Sylvia remembered two things from the day of Martin's funeral: Edith's deftness and composure in making the 'E' shaped wreath and then laying it on Martin's hands above her heart, and the sight of Jim Martin, a man they had not seen before, grim and black. Neither Hildegarde nor Edith could bring herself to be at the service in the church. They went together to the field where Edith and Martin used to sit and write, and wept.

The Galway Martins went back on the day of the funeral. Edith left for Lismore by the 12 o'clock train on Christmas Eve. At Lismore Edith found, sent on by Hildegarde, 'many letters. Notices of Martin in the papers, all alike saying a light had gone out.' Edith began to write her thanks in response to the 'wonderful flood of grief and sympathy and kindness'. In Lismore on New Year's Eve, writing letters in her room at the turn of the year, Edith stopped to write in her diary: 'The Cathedral bells are now ringing in 1916 – very cheerfully and tunelessly. This black, black year goes out in despair and tears.'

Two of Edith's oldest and dearest friends with great intuition gave her gifts that they thought would help her in grief. Percy Aylmer sent her a poem on the death of a comrade by Florence Nightingale, and Ethel Penrose gave her a volume of Rev. Basil Wilberforce's sermons: *New (?) Theology* [*sic*]. Wilberforce was a Christian spiritualist concerned to draw together spiritualism and Christianity. He was careful to stress what the two had in common, and to avoid any of the sensationalism that led many to believe that spiritualism was a form of black art, and could not be Christian. The particular passage that helped Edith was a form of prayer written to assist in bereavement in the family, adaptable for male or female:

> Suffer her to know, O gracious Lord, if it may be, how much I love her and miss her, and long to see her again; and if there are ways in which her influence may be felt by me, vouchsafe her to me as a guide and guard and grant me a sense of her nearness in such degree as thy laws permit. If in anything I can minister to her peace, be pleased of Thy love to let this be; and mercifully keep me from every act which may hinder me from union with her as soon as this earth-life is over, or mar the fulness of our joy when the end of the days has come.[69]

Edith made an album of the letters of condolence. Widely dispersed by the War, many of the letters came from men on active service, among them: Martin's nephew Lionel Dawson, RN (The North Sea); Boyle Somerville on HMS *King Alfred* (North Atlantic); Jack Somerville from the British Legation in Tokyo; Hugh Somerville, HMS *Earl of Peterboro'* (The North Sea); Eddy Aylmer temporarily at the Cavalry Reserve at Aldershot. Edith's tenant at the

Mall House, Dr Eleanor Hodson, wrote from the Hôpital de La Mothe, Paris; all the women's suffrage organisers wrote, including Mrs Corbett Fisher from the NUWSS and Miss Geraldine Lennox from the WSPU. People who had not known Martin personally wrote to Edith with the sincerest sympathy, such as Katherine Tynan and Rudyard Kipling.

A very informed description of Edith's state at this time was sent by Hildegarde to Kinkie. Kinkie had written frequently during Martin's last weeks, she had known Martin for years as a fellow Galway woman. Hildegarde had been unable to reply to any of Kinkie's letters until 28 December as she had a house full of children, had to do the Christmas gifts and presentations to the farm men alone, and was expecting Professor Wibberley again. She wrote to Kinkie:

> Edith is splendid. She just tries to go on and not make it hard for others but the mainspring of everything has gone and I don't suppose she will ever be quite the same again, it isn't possible. Thirty years of closest intimacy with someone of Martin's nature and then to lose her – it is a tragedy. For myself it means losing one of my best and dearest, but it is nothing to what it is to Edith. However, as she had to go, she went as she would have liked best, just slept away. No struggle or any horror, no knowledge of parting – with the most wonderful noble calm and happy look on her face – who could ask for better. Much love Dear Kinkie to you and Frances, May 1916 be a Happier Year to you and us all.[70]

The speed of the outpouring of memorial articles and appreciations was impressive. Katherine Tynan's tribute on 30 December was headed: 'Exit, the Spirit of Laughter'.[71] E.V. Lucas and Charles Graves made the mistake of assuming that Edith would be too distraught to deal with letters, whereas in fact she was churning them out, and they applied to Cameron for some details. They published articles on Martin using Cameron's information. E.V. Lucas's article, entitled 'The Two Ladies', appeared in the *Spectator* on 1 January. The endless Somerville and Ross controversy over who wrote what and how had started. Cameron was chastised severely:

> I am afraid you didn't quite get it right. It is *impossible* to apportion general responsibility in our writings but even to have said 'hardly a paragraph, a phrase etc etc' was written singlehanded by either of us would have been an exaggeration – even in the quotations Mr Lucas gave, some were hers, some mine, – If I ever said those words – which I hardly think possible – I was making far too sweeping a statement, and I

should be most awfully grateful if you would not continue to quote them – already various journalists have been tearing at me to write, to give them data for articles and make money out of what is to me a sacred thing – It distracts me this prying greediness and raking up every scrap of personal detail – Already someone has announced that I mean 'to go on writing as usual'... As if – even if I could bear to think of the future – I should be likely to make declarations about it !... *I don't know what I mean to do* – go on trying to live, I suppose, and that is sometimes more than I feel able for ...The books are the thing, not the wretched survivor of the 'once brilliant literary collaboration' (a phrase that has the power to cut like a knife). It remains that the hunt *must* be minded, and Hildegarde *must* be backed up over the Farm, and it is good for me, and right, to do my share.[72]

In her low state Edith was now attacked for the first time by sciatica, which was eventually to cripple her. She wrote responses to letters of sympathy, some of which she placed later in a memorial album. Among the letters of commiseration was one from Kipling, who wrote from Burwash on 6 January 1916:

Dear Miss Somerville, forgive me for intruding on your grief. This is only to say how deeply I feel for you in the loss that has come upon you. I owe a great deal of pleasure and more than pleasure to your stories of Irish life and all that they mean and seeing how closely you must have worked together and thought together I can guess a little what this separation brings with it to the survivor. Please do not trouble to answer, most sincerely, Rudyard Kipling.

The facility for producing spontaneous light verse of which Martin had been critical, like those speedily created to accompany *Slipper's ABC of Hunting*, had not left her. On the same day Edith sent a quatrain to Charlie Graves at *Punch*:

With Flurry's hounds and you our guide,
We've learned to laugh until we've cried.
Dear Martin Ross, the coming years
Find all our laughter lost in tears.

She went back to Drishane; with Hildegarde she sorted Martin's possessions and posted them to her sisters. Edith gave Cameron Martin's walking stick, 'Ryan Puck', a blackthorn that had belonged, Martin had maintained, to the last man hanged for sheep stealing in Galway. In the form of money it seemed at first that Martin left just enough to cover her liabilities, for she did not have many investments to be realised after her death, as Edith had. The sum – £78.15s. - which in the event did not cover her debts, shows just how close to the edge Edith and Martin were in their finances at this time, barely hanging on in the black. Martin's will was a very simple feminist one, unlike Edith's which was to be heavily populated by male legatees. Martin had revised her 1898 will soon after removing from Galway to Cork, on 29 March 1906, at Glen Barrahane. It could not have been more simply woman-identified:

> This is the last will and testament of Violet Florence Martin on this 29th day of March 1906. I, Violet Florence Martin, give and bequeath to Edith Œnone Somerville all my worldly possessions, of which I am possessed at the time of my death, or may be entitled to afterwards, to be disposed of by her as absolute owner and according to instructions which I shall give her.

The will was witnessed by Egerton Coghill and Hugh Somerville. By this will the copyright of Somerville and Ross works became Edith's alone, and Martin's literary papers and remains merged with Edith's. Before Christmas Edith had written to Pinker on business on 26 and 28 October, and on 4 November when she added, 'alas I have no better news, my dearest cousin is still ill ... she never was better than when we were in Kerry; we were planning much work when *I* should be fit for it ...' That Edith, who was still unwell, was lacking the will to go on at all after Martin was gone, something she did not admit to her siblings, was admitted openly to Pinker in a letter of the 28 December, when she explained that Martin was buried on the 23rd in CT: 'there I trust some day (and I do not care how soon it may come) I shall be laid beside her.' After Martin's death, it was not long before Pinker thought of encouraging Edith to write a memorial volume, but she hung fire.

Her mood of depression varied in intensity. A month after Martin's death she wrote in her diary: 'It was four weeks today. Sometimes it seems like a black hour, sometimes it might have been a hundred years of misery.' She was not completely inert; the writer's block of the previous August was gone. She sent a letter to *The Times* about the War Office circular to MFHs urging them to keep hunting going during the war. Her crippled leg was giving her such problems that Cameron insisted she go to Kneller Hall as his guest and get thorough treatment in London. She joined him at Kneller Hall on 22 February. From there she wrote to Pinker on the 26th, explaining the emerging difficulties of acting as executor for Martin: 'Her generosities and her charities had, unknown to me, outrun her bank account.' She went on to describe the strain of waiting for news of their menfolk: 'Paddy is now at Ypres with the R[oyal] F[ield] A[rtillery]. It is a horrible time to be alive – one has to fight on somehow, but it isn't easy. My brother Hugh has been hit, and had a narrow escape, but is right again.' The country was under deep snow. During Edith's treatment, all the members of the family who were in London came to her, so that her room 'was always full of visitors', Muriel Currey remembered. On 25 April Edith had a note from Muriel's mother Katie: 'a bad rising of Sinn Feiners in Dublin.'[73]

As the rebels in the Post Office had cut communications, *The Times* leader of 26 April had to make some speculations. It described the 'insane rising' as German-backed: 'it is evidently the result of a carefully arranged plot between the Irish traitors and their German confederates.' An Irishman called Thomas Polson wrote a letter to *The Times* on 2 May headed 'An Irish man's Remedy', suggesting that the 'invertebrate' government hang all the leaders and conscript the rank and file: 'The majority are simple misguided fellows, who, once removed from the influence of their leaders, would make as fine soldiers as any we have got, and they are already partly trained.' The Rising, and the fatal reaction of executing the rebel leaders, reports of which began on 7 May, triggered the writing impulse in Edith. Appalled by the executions of Pearse, Clarke and MacDonagh on the 4th, and guessing that more had followed, she sat up into the small hours of the night of 7/8 May writing. All of her brothers were serving in the British Army, and none of them ever knew that Edith was the 'Irishwoman' who wrote the first appeal for clemency for the Irish rebels in the letter columns of *The Times*.

### The Rebel Rank and File

Sir, it has been pointed out in your columns, and elsewhere, that the Sinn Fein organisation, which had started its career as a somewhat academic league of conventional patriots, began, by a singular coincidence, to give practical life to its ideals at the moment when the Liberal Government entered upon its reign of peace and love. A new spirit was breathed into Sinn Fein.

Love, as we all know, is blind: in the case of the large souled administrators of Irish affairs it was also deaf. Sinn Fein, unpropitiated by the indulgence of its rulers, proceeded to sharpen its claws.

Its officials were at no special pains to conceal either their methods or their opinions, and, as they found 'freedom slowly broadening down' they took every advantage of their favoured position. Financed by Germany, tutored by America, sheltered by England, the Sinn Fein propaganda ran through Ireland like an epidemic on a South Pacific island. The Gaelic

League was turned from its ingenuous programme of jig dancing and warbling passé treason in modern Irish, and was set to more effective issues ...

... I have heard of more than one state supported school in a remote part of Munster in which the greatness and generosity of Germany, and the reptile villainy of England, were given as themes for the essays of the 'little scholars'. The boys of nine or ten years of age, quick as ever to learn the romance of revolt, ready as ever to absorb sedition, as white blotting paper soaks up ink, have grown into these senseless, reckless, slaughtering idealists of today, out not for plunder or outrage, but out of the mad dream of Ireland a Nation. It seems improbable that any English Government past or present would propose that a couple of thousand or so of young men should either be hanged or imprisoned for life because they risked everything for a vision – 'Their country, right or wrong!'

But what is the alternative? To send them back to Ireland to be jeered at, admired, abused, to brood over their failure, and to plan, perhaps, a more excellent way; or to slam them into 'English dungeons' for as long as may serve to sour their wild blood and slacken their eager limbs, but not long enough to provide a time for repentance; and is eternity long enough for an Irishman to lay down his vision and take up with expediency and submission? Can prison discipline turn a thwarted rebel into a loyal subject, or sightless staring at the walls of a cell make a dreamer forget his dreams? England sat quiet while these lads were being taught disloyalty to her as assiduously as a Japanese child learns patriotism; the fault is not wholly on their side. Let her send out these captives to join their brothers in the trenches, there to find out what manner of man the German is. The mother of Shamus O'Brien, rebel of '98, had but one plea, but today it seems sufficient – 'The craythure is young. Ah! Spare him, my Lord!'

In his *Ireland a Nation*, Robert Lynd expressed the bewilderment of many at this time with his remark: 'There were not enough Irishmen in the Insurrection of 1916 to make up even one battalion of the Irish Guards.'[74] Edith followed the fate of the rebel prisoners, and the arguments of the Government with increasing despair. At the end of her treatment she saw Pinker in London on 18 May and formally discussed with him a memorial volume for Martin, and a collection of her pieces in one volume. He gave her a cheque for the sevenpenny Nelson edition of *Irish Yesterdays* made out in the usual way to both writers, so that Edith was forced to discuss this problem openly with him and think of its improbable solution. On 6 June her diary entry suggests that she could not push herself out of a slough of despond: 'Forget the deadly details that go to the making of each future-less and feature-less day.' But on 16 June she entered: 'Dined with Jem and did some writing with her and received communications of which I hardly know what to think. It was written for me (and with me) on Friday night – "You and I have not finished our work here. Dear, we shall. Be comforted."' Jem Barlow had turned out to be an amateur medium who used the conduit of automatic writing; she had been a great admirer of Martin's. She would have observed how the literary partnership worked, and she was so placed as to be able to comfort Edith, who found Jem sympathetic and entertaining. Though it is tempting to assume that Jem helpfully invented a spirit Martin to heal Edith's grief and enable her to write again, Canon Claude Chavasse did not so assume. He saw the automatic scripts as they were written and though he disliked Jem, nevertheless believed that she was an unconscious and genuine conduit for the dead Martin's thoughts. Since Edith's grandparents' generation, CT had been steeped in the psychical; apparitions and manifestations of the living and the dead, animal and human, were welcomed here. Automatic writing, where the medium rests a writing instrument on the hand, not grasping it, and high-speed scripts flow from it without word-breaks, had been practised in CT by Edith herself in her teenage years.

Thinking over her strange communication, Edith then threw herself into the toil of the harvest, and dairy farm work, not sure what to make of the lifeline that had come her way. By this intervention of Jem Barlow's Edith was rescued from despair. She had been unmoved by a suggestive passage in Martin's communication through Jem: 'Have you never felt me touch you?' Edith answered, 'No,' and Martin wrote, 'How strange that is.' In her Autobiographical section of Notebook 10 Edith gave an account of her early experience of spiritualism, and Martin's dislike of it, which had led her to put aside any thoughts of contact after Martin's death. Innocent and unprejudiced as a child, she had been used as a medium by her aunts and uncles, like her brother Cameron; 'thus it was that the idea of an indisputable force, unaccountable yet actual, grew up with me and my brothers'. Martin had no sympathies with this force whatsoever:

We had written many books together … We had hunted together, and had together shared nearly all interests. But she had not cared to inquire into things psychic. In fact she mocked at me, and told me I was an Athenian, who wanted '*Nothing else but either to tell or hear some new thing*'. And so I, with her, became immersed in strenuous and enjoyable this-worldly matters, and I forgot my friends the Ghosts, and abandoned the rather futile efforts that I had been making to develop the spark of psychic power that I believed I might possess.

Therefore it was that when she died the thought of attempting to summon her would have seemed like ignoring her wishes, and I never tried to do so ... But after a long half year of silence she was able to seize what – as she has since told me – was a long awaited chance ...

... my name was written in Martin Ross's authentic handwriting. It was as startling as a flash of light in a dark room. A few faltering sentences followed, faltering but of their essence they were their own assurance 'I feel that your mind is my workshop. I can only use what I find there. You must trust me.'[75]

At the end of the 1916 diary, in the notes pages, is a transcript of a sitting with Jem. Again it shows quite starkly that Edith was simply not suggestible, and can have carried no memory of Martin in the form of a physical connection. Jem wrote 'automatically' in the voice of Martin and Edith recorded her own response:

Martin: 'Do you feel me near you?' Edith: 'No.'
Martin: 'Can you feel me touch you?' Edith: 'No.'

Nevertheless the idea of Martin's company not being entirely lost to her gained ground and gave her hope. She became absorbed in farming activities again. There was no time to mope. She was as sympathetic as ever to her friends' predicaments. Old Mr McCarthy Morrough at Innisbeg had died, leaving his daughter Daisy unprovided for. Edith wrote to Cameron: 'Old cross men over 80 years old ought not to be allowed to make wills. Daisy says it was yards long and took two hours to read. The net result to poor Daisy who devoted the best 20 years of her life to the old savage, is that she now has to work for her living ... Certainly the French state-made will is a far more equitable thing. I must stop – I have lost my beloved pen and have no satisfaction with strangers ...' The Farm laid its claims upon her and she laid plans for its future: during 1916 care was taken to lay down legal agreements over the shares held in it by the various Somerville siblings. On 4 July she wrote to Cameron in a fury at a large percentage claim made by the long-absent Aylmer:

Aylmer has no right to expect more than two and a half per cent ... he has not been here for two and a half years and has done nothing in the matter of settling things (I am not blaming, merely stating facts) Hildegarde and I have been working the show, and Aylmer's awful wasted extravagances about machinery and the creamery do not improve his position. I should ask Aylmer, pacifically, what he is going on, and why he should have more than the two and a half per cent – I think you might quietly say that the very heavy expense to which he put you in the creamery (which he did without consulting you, or anyone) has crippled you a good deal and you think the usual agent's fees will meet the case.

The hay was in later this year, in mid-July. Hildegarde and Edith were out in the fields with the men: 'O that we two weren't haying. I am sick of the sight of dead grass and hot men. I have done nothing but "tend them" for what seems like a century and the end is not yet.' It was a relief to her that the Penroses were at Glen B for their annual holiday. Edith showed all over again her lack of confidence in practising as a creative writer on her own, and went right back to her earliest co-operative-work with her Twin. She distracted herself by reviving with Ethel the children's play, 'A Fairy Extravaganza: In Three Acts, By Two Flappers' with its punning title 'Chloral, or The Sleeping Beauty', which was then acted by her nephews and nieces. It was performed to raise funds in aid of the Prisoners of War Knitting Fund, and the Fowl Fund of the West Carbery Hunt. Writing to Pinker she described it as 'an old play written ever so many years ago by Mrs Penrose and me when we were flappers'. For the adults light relief was needed: the worsening war news brought tidings of the Somme. Dr Hodson had moved from her Paris Hospital to the abbey of Royaumont, west of Soissons, just behind the front line. It was one of the Scottish Women's Hospitals, and the remarkable Chief Medical Officer was Frances Ivens. In the makeshift operating theatres of places like Royaumont women surgeons gained extensive experience of surgery other than obstetric.[76]

Edith relied very much on the company of the medium Jem Barlow during the winter of 1916/17, but by February she had become so low in spirits that she wrote to Cameron to suggest closing up Drishane: 'Apart from money the slaughter of the poor hounds may be insisted upon (how much better to begin with the idiot asylums and "feebles" instead of these beautiful wise and faithful creatures) I don't see why you should have to run this place as well as Kneller Hall ... Hildegarde could take me and the dogs in ...'[77] In mid-January 1917, with Pinker's repeated encouragement, she had begun to write her engaging memoir, which is not a structured biographical study of Martin, but rather a rambling joint 'life and times' with a few personal purple patches. Edith did not think that she was writing alone, but with the help and guidance of her subject. She may have been impelled into the writing by a discovery in the papers that had been left to her by Martin. This was a box of fascinating old letters, including letters by Nancy Crampton, the wife of Charles Kendal Bushe, to her beloved friend Maria Edgeworth. Some of these letters have since been lost again, but were used for background details in Edith's later life of Charles

Kendal Bushe; the research papers for which she deposited in Trinity College Dublin include some of them.

Getting into the old habit of writing, she wrote an article about Irish hunting for *The Times*, 'The Peace Makers', on 16 March. She was obviously coming back to life, and was very interested in the outcome of the Irish Convention that was about to meet. She was, as well, inspired to intense interest in the work of the stained glass artist Harry Clarke. Cameron had been to see the Honan Chapel, a showplace of the arts and crafts of the Celtic Revival, in the university at Cork when he visited Bertie Windle in January, and had been so impressed that Edith went to see it herself on the 27th. Stunned by Clarke's use of colour, she wrote to Cameron to describe 'the quality of burning and furious brilliance, that I have never seen anywhere else. The blue robe, for instance, hits your eyes like a living flame or a blast of wind. Perfectly amazing, but not quite pleasant ... His windows have a kind of hellish splendour.' She had been discussing with Cameron the possibility of memorial windows in St Barrahane's for their grandparents for some time. On Bertie's advice she had contacted Harry Clarke, who came to Drishane on 4 April to discuss designs.

In March 1917 she first refers to writing with Martin as a regular event in her day: 'At seven I write with Martin as you know', but it is not until June that she confides further to Cameron that Pinker's suggestions of a memoir has taken hold: 'In confidence I am trying to put together a sort of memoir ... Pinker has seen a few chapters and been enraptured. You must know that Martin has never ceased to urge me to do it and she declared she would help me, and she is helping me, I am quite sure of it. By suggestion.'[78]In fact Pinker had much to do with guiding her through this period. Even by May her spirits had lifted greatly. The book was never intended to be a personal account of Martin Ross, or of the personal relationship of Somerville and Ross. She had been writing for two months and had produced six chapters totalling 25,000 words. She wrote to Pinker defining them: 'They are amounting to something that might almost be considered an account of Irish social life.'[79] Avidly reading newspaper reports on the Irish political situation, she involved herself in current affairs. She began an unsuccessful campaign by letter to try to ensure that women were represented as delegates at the coming Irish Convention. All the while she was worrying at a possible way of going forward as a writer without Martin. Then in one swift move on 22 May, writing from her bed in Glen B where she was holed up with a 'sharp gastric chill', she wrote to Pinker with her way clear ahead: 'I am including a great deal of Miss Martin's separate writing, and propose to keep our old joint signature.' She had found a solution to suit her predicament. Except in one instance no arguments or complications arose, and the stream of books was to continue under the names of two authors, one living, one dead. They published sixteen books together before Martin's death; after her death Edith was to publish seventeen titles, only three of them under her own name alone: *The States through Irish Eyes, Notes of the Horn* and the privately printed *Records of the Somerville Family* compiled with her brother Boyle.

On 13 June she went over to Ethel at Lismore for peace in which to write. Ethel gave her a room, the old smoking room in the Castle, and perfect writing conditions. She wrote in her diary three days later: 'Worked in the wide and wonderful smoking room in a peace that passed understanding.' Hildegarde took the whole weight of the farm work during harvest on herself this year. It was a thoughtful and effective service for her sister. Edith found time at Lismore to read: 'I am frightfully in love with Padraig Pearse's writings (a shot Sinn Feiner). It was sheer murder to shoot him. A mere poet and dreamer and a man of rare gifts and spirituality – wait til you read his book. Borrow Padraig Pearse from Boyle if you can – He is *enchanting*. It was a sin to have shot a poetic idealist, such as he, and very stupid,' she wrote to Cameron.[80] The renewed importance of Pinker to Edith at this time is made clear in a letter of hers to him on 30 June: 'I have no-one upon whose judgement I can rely, as, naturally, all my people view such matters with an even greater enthusiasm than I. So if you *can* give me any criticisms I shall be very grateful.'

The writing of *Irish Memories* that absorbed Edith until 20 September gave her great satisfaction and healing of grief. Then she went over to London with the last of the manuscript and to discuss illustrations with Mr Longman; the book went out of her hands. She stayed with Boyle and Mab and was with them for an air raid on 24 September: 'most interesting, saw star shells and searchlights and heard but could not see Gothas,' she wrote in her diary. She also was able to say farewell to her nephew Desmond just before he left for France. On another night she experienced one of the big bomb blasts that were so familiar to Boyle and Mab: '"Take cover warnings" given in time to be acted on.' Raids became so numerous in early October that she and Mab were sent out to Kneller Hall for safety. She returned to CT on 20 October. *Irish Memories* was so successful, its reviews so uniformly favourable, that a second edition was printed before the end of November. With no competent overseer, paperwork in Drishane had become disorganised: between them Edith and Cameron had managed to lose Harry Clarke's design for the memorial window in the post, and had to ask him to do it again.[81] She wrote to Cameron on 21 November: 'I had a magnanimous letter from Harry Clarke, who is indeed a gentleman, and a pet, I have written informing him of these facts ...' At the request of the Editor, she wrote an article for *The Times* on 30 December, 'Ourselves Alone'. Writing a novel alone was something she had serious misgivings about. The memoir and the planned collection of Martin's pieces were only bits of insulation to protect her from thinking of her own future as a writer, and her income. Her loss of physical mobility would have forced her to realise that she would need a sedentary means of earning money.

The success of *Irish Memories* continued. A third edition was 'selling well' by 6 January, there was a fourth before the month was out. The idea of continuing at novel writing without Martin appalled her, but she knew her own powers as a writer of short pieces perfectly well, and was writing articles under her own name with no loss of fluency and eloquence. Edith was very keen to explain the independent militant Irish position to English readers, seeing it as a phenomenon associated with an out-of-control younger generation revolting against their priests and parents. Her article on Sinn Fein, 'Ourselves Alone', written at the end of December 1917, was published in *The Times* on 8 January 1918. On 25 February she finished her eloquent suffrage appeal, '*Not* the Woman's Place', and this was published in April's *The Englishwoman*. Putting aside her misgivings, and relying on aid from an invisible Martin, she had brought herself to the brink of writing a novel. On 19 March we find the diary entry 'Began more definitely on the book. Very much frightened and cowardly.' This was to be the novel *Mount Music*.

She was more frightened of writing a novel on her own than she was of her isolated position in a house with sporting guns in it that were the object of raids. With practically all able-bodied Anglo-Irish men away serving in the war, raids for arms were made on Big Houses in the sure knowledge that they would only be inhabited by sisters, wives and ancient non-combatants. Elizabeth Bowen's novels from this period, like *The Last September*, dramatise this predicament, repeated with a different cast in Big Houses all over Ireland. Bowen depicts the tension in these households arising from the unspoken fear that trusted servants, from families who had been generations in the service of the place, were about to betray their employers. On 20 April Bunalun was raided and on the next day, Castlehaven Rectory. On the 25th Desmond Somerville's wife Moira wrote to tell Drishane that her husband was missing in action. When Edith was at a sitting with Martin her communication 'implies that he is wounded, and I fear severely,' Edith wrote in her diary. There was further news of Desmond via automatic writing, and the conduit of dead relatives. On 6 May: 'Martin says that she is sure that Desmond is alive and a prisoner'. This was confirmed a day later when Moira sent a wire: 'Desmond a prisoner and well.' The conviction would grow that the family dead were gathered about the living in a protective band.

Three letters to Alice Kinkead at this time express her growing confidence in her capacity to write novels again. On 22 February she triumphed, 'My writing with Mr Ross is *daily* and is more than I can possibly say to me. There are difficulties, limitations, but they are always decreasing, and don't make any real difference ...' The next account of joint-writing with the dead, a fortnight later, seems to imply that Edith herself did not use automatic writing in communicating with Martin but instead felt she was in some way intercepting her thoughts: '... you know Mr Ross helps me with these things – not by direct writing, but by "inspiration". It is not quite what it was in old times, I mean in point of jointness, but is very nearly, I believe.' At the end of April Edith acknowledges to Kinkie the effectiveness of her proceedings as first directed by Jem Barlow: 'It is a wonderful refreshment and renewal of life for me.' The same letter of 22 April complains, 'I continue to get demented letters about I[rish] M[emories]'. Numbers of people, many of whom were women who had lost their lifelong friends or partners, began to write to Edith about the memoir, but they were not all female or all demented. On 6 June: 'I had a most kind and friendly letter from Rudyard Kipling about "Irish Memories" and our other books.'

Returning to life and her various occupations, she picked up her palette and brushes again, and the haying was interspersed with painting. If they were particularly sympathetic, she enjoyed responding to her readers' letters. On 20 July: 'Had a line from Lady Kenmare enclosing an awfully nice one from Dame Ethel Smyth re "Irish Memories".' This was a letter that led to a new and different friendship. Edith heard from Harry Clarke telling her that the completed St Barrahane's window would be exhibited in Dublin at the end of the month. In September she went to Kerry to paint and called to stay for a few days with Lady Kenmare on the way back. She wrote to her sister after a week staying with the Kenmares: 'Contrary to expectation I like being there very much, and am much taken with them all. Lady K is most human and unaffected and pleasant with an excellent sense of humour and a power of zanying equal to your own.' Lord Lansdowne was a fellow guest; 'he always turned the conversation to rhododendrons if he found politics being dragged in ... he told me how he had caught old Lord Salisbury reading the RM in Downing Street, instead of doing his business, and how ashamed he was! ... They are all *quite* unlike RCs except on Sunday ... the only difficulty is in remembering that there *is* a difficulty'. Some very good tenants of Edith's had left, who had been much liked in the village: 'Such a loss socially; (even more so financially – A clean £5 on the first of each month has been quite nice)'.[82] Her book was about to earn her relief from money worries for a time. It was financial necessity that primarily drove her actions, and we can see the workings of it over this period of eighteen months after Martin's death where she moved from the successful completion of the memoir to contemplating another novel.

Clarke's window was installed and consecrated by 13 September. Compounding her worry about the firstborn Paddy, Hildegarde's second son joined up. At the age of eighteen Nevill Coghill was posted to Salonika, and, like his brother, serving in the Royal Field Artillery. Nevill always had an intense empathy with Edith and used to make the most surprising Somerville and Ross related finds. One of his strangest was on this 11 October: 'Heard from Nevill from front line trenches Salonika. He had found *An Irish Cousin* in a dug-out ...' The reader had obviously been inspired by the free copies of classic books issued to the troops, including the RM, to ask for other books by the same authors to be sent from home. At the end of the war, Irishmen who had served in the British Army found themselves in an anomalous position. The Irish had elected to honour the memory of the Easter Week rebels of 1916, and to delete from their memories the *c*.150,000 Irishmen who had volunteered for the Front, of whom a third were killed. With the British Legion it was the Somerville brothers who kept alive the Remembrance Day ceremonies in Skibbereen: they were held beside the memorial to an earlier Irish Rebellion. Though many Big Houses survived, in poor order, into the post-war period, of their owners there were very few, like Edith Somerville and her sister, who were to try to maintain working estates against the wishes of Ireland's new political rulers. True to its description by de Valera as a 'little Britain', CT celebrated the Armistice on 11 November 1918 with flags flying, bells, bonfires and fireworks, and Uncle Kendal fired his cannon. Not only did the Somerville sisters maintain what they had, Edith was about to expand Somerville landholding.

From her lifelong diary and letter comments about her periods of 'poverty' and lack of money in her bank account it is all too easy to misunderstand Edith's financial situation. She spent freely on what she considered necessary: keeping up the West Carbery Hunt through the war years had cost her dear, and she was crazily generous to her relatives when 'in funds'. She lived on her earnings from writing and illustrating but also on the interest from investments, a secretive aspect of her finances that has escaped notice but which ultimately was to save Drishane from falling into the hands of a Bank. Whenever she was temporarily 'in funds' she had invested some, and had also religiously 'put away' inherited money. She had shares in a number of corporations like United Steel, Lever and Canadian Pacific. Her stockbroker was Bethel Solomons in Dublin, who was also Hildegarde's. It was an inherited trait to look upon capital as untouchable, so that while moaning about her reduced circumstances and the difficulty of living on the income from the Drishane House Dairy, which she had run with Hildegarde since February 1909, she in fact had about £3,000 in shares. It was this capital in the background that enabled her to enter into extraordinary financial ventures like buying extra land for Drishane, or buying her brother Cameron out of Drishane lands in order to pay his debts, while at the same time complaining of personal poverty. It was as though her capital,

which included her own lifelong savings from earnings, was indelibly ear-
marked as 'family' rather than personal. Her yearly professional earnings can
be compared with the salaries of the first women surgeons who served through
the war, and very favourably, as the Scottish Women's Hospital surgeons earned
£200 per annum.

On 19 December 1918 Edith bought another 300 acres of agricultural land,
the Castletownshend Demesne Farm and Round O (the Rondeau field), for
£2,500 at auction. She described this in a letter to her godson Paddy: 'I expect
your mother has told you of hers and my latest gamble, buying the Demesne
Farm ... *everyone* is delighted that we have got it, and all the poor people seem
really rejoiced that we have it and that "it hasn't gone out of the family"... your
Mother's and my great grandfather was Richard Townshend of Castletownshend,
known as "The Munster Peacock" [he was a dandy] and we are therefore legitimately stepping into his shoes in holding the Demesne Farm ...Your Mother
now assures me that she lies awake every night, for hours, thinking how she
will evade the Court of Bankruptcy, but I think it is going to be quite allright
and that we ought to make a good business out of it.'[83] It later transpired that
this was done partly with the aid of a 'loan' from their ever-generous rich cousin
Percy Aylmer, who, just before he died in 1936, arranged his affairs so that the
sisters did not have to repay this sum to his estate. They were operating in a sphere
of high finance compared to their brothers who started to retire and return to CT
to live on their meagre Army and Navy pensions. Edith was to write in *The Smile
and the Tear* of this Townshend land, 'rescued and taken in hand in a flaming
moment of enthusiasm by two female tyros. They had no more valid reason for
this reckless act than that all their lives they had known its fields and fences, its
hills and bogs; that their dogs had hunted hares over its heather, and that, for
as far back as they could remember, they had lit Baal fires on the highest ridge
of its highest hill on St John's Eve. It had, as it seemed to them, implored to be
kept in the family, and they had been unable to resist its appeal.'[84]

At Christmastime the men home from the war still rode in their khaki to the
St Stephen's day meet at the Clock Tower in Skibbereen. Desmond Somerville,
Billy Morgan and Captain Telford were in uniform. They rode with Edith's
nephew and niece Ambrose and Katharine and six or eight young farmers. 'I
invited Captain Telford's men to come and run and a good many of them did
so, and tore about with the country boys in entire amity.'[85] In January, Sheila,
the dog 'twin' of Candy, who was fourteen, had to be put down after a fall.
Egerton did this service for Edith again. She was working at her novel with
some trepidation. On 4 February Edith had a letter, she wrote in her diary,
'from "The Thomas MacDonagh Sinn Fein Club" of Skibbereen forbidding the
hounds to hunt on "their lands" until political prisoners are released. Sent Pat

to Cullinagh to see the farmers, who sent a message that we were welcome as "flowers in May".' There were no violent developments out of this threat. On 17 March at the St Patrick's Day meet, Edith wrote in her diary: 'the hounds were cheered in Skib by (presumably) Sinn Feiners'. A month later she finished the novel, now called *Mount Music*, on 16 May, and gravitated to her agent and publisher. She was in London from 22 May until 9 June when she went to Dublin for an Agricultural Show. She was back in CT on the 20th. No matter how dire were her financial straits, she could not bring herself to cash in her shares. The consciousness that they were there in the background, however, must explain her lack of worry at living only just in the black at her bank's current account. She spent what was to hand as soon as it came there, and much was spent on travelling.

In May 1919 Cameron Somerville retired from his post as Commandant of the Army School of Music at Kneller Hall. He returned to Drishane as its Master, to take up his position at the head of the table opposite Edith. No wife had materialised. His heir would be chosen from among his brothers' sons. He kept silence about his disastrous financial affairs. In his first summer home in retirement the whole family was affected by the death of Uncle Kendal on 18 July, at the age of eighty-seven. Nearing death, he re-lived the moment when, nine years old and drowning, he was pulled up to the surface through the ice by his brother. His house, Cosheen or The Point, reverted to Egerton. Edith was helped out of her sadness over his death when she fared splendidly in later July, with an offer on the 28th of £900 from Longmans for *Mount Music* and a day at the Skibbereen Show on the 30th where the family won five first prizes and Paddy Coghill took 2nd in the hunter class on his horse Midshipman. When Paddy dismounted at the side of the course, he proceeded to sell his horse to an interested wealthy onlooker for £120, in the style of Flurry Knox. Even so, on that day Edith advertised the hounds for sale in *Horse and Hounds*. The pack went to Sir Dennis Bayley at Staniton Dale in Montgomery for £200. The loss of the hounds fell at a time when Edith knew she was losing her bodily strength and suppleness as a rider; coming so soon after Martin's death, the war and its aftermath mark a great period of change and physical decline in her life. But it never occurred to either of the sisters that the physical work of their farm was too much for them.

Until he came home for good, Cameron would have had no notion of the seasonal round, and more particularly the daily grind, of his sisters' farm. The harvest was the most active period of all. Vacations fell into place naturally after it in the late summer or in early autumn. On 21 August Edith got her copy of the *Skibbereen Eagle* 'with my farewell to the poor hounds', then went up to Dublin to stay with Sir Horace Plunkett for the Dublin Horse Show on the

23rd. En route to Killarney on 16 September 1919, in the Killarney train from Mallow, Edith finally met Dr Ethel Smyth, who had contacted her by letter so keenly. She wrote to Hildegarde: 'I like her very much ... she is very clever and has a touch of Fanny Currey, and is quite without swagger of any kind'. They were both members of a house party at Lord Kenmare's country seat near Killarney at which Edith met Ruth Draper (an 'impressionist' who was an American forerunner of Joyce Grenfell), young Lady Lovat and the writer Maurice Baring, brother of Elizabeth, Lady Kenmare. Edith wrote in her diary that Ethel Smyth 'sang and played enchantingly' and was 'a very interesting and affable companion'. In the same letter to her sister she shares her delight at the news of Frances Perkins's forthcoming marriage to Maurice Cameron (Major Sir Maurice Cameron's first wife had died in 1903): 'I quite agree with you that it is a good thing for *both* Frances and Kinkie, and I hope K will be mentioned in the marriage settlements! ... I don't see much chance of painting for this Society Butterfly. I *could* wish Lady K and Ethel S alone were here, it would be ideal.'[86]

Ethel Smyth wrote of her meeting with Edith: 'I have had the unhoped for, undreamed of good fortune to strike in my Autumn a new and perfect friend.'[87] What Ethel wanted in fact was a new and perfect lover, but this did not become clear for some time. The preliminaries took place by letters, hundreds of them. The social connections made at this house party widened Edith's circle of acquaintance quite remarkably. Through the promotion given to her by Ethel in Britain to her contacts in the women's movement, Edith became known to the circle of much younger independent women associated with Lady Rhondda's *Time and Tide*, founded in 1920. She came to know and respect Cicely Hamilton, who came as a guest to Drishane, and 'Christopher St John' (Christabel Marshall), later the biographer of Ethel Smyth. After leaving Killarney, Ethel came to see Drishane and its mistress on 25 September, and stayed until 11 October, but came back a week later for a further seven days. After three years of loneliness Edith had found someone with whom she could talk as freely as she had to Martin. Ethel understood that Edith was very lonely, and made a description of her that is surprising to a great niece who avoided Edith in the 1940s as a grumpy old battleaxe: 'Aloof, shy and reserved as she is, she has heaps of dash. Her almost insane diffidence irritated me at first, but after we had made friends I learned to respect it as much as her courage, and her unutterable soft heartedness.'[88] By 1 November Ethel had organised a London show for Edith's paintings.

Edith's friendship with Ethel Smyth, who was an enthusiastic lover of women, has for many years had repercussions on attempts to write her biography. Ethel Smyth had two biographers and admirers, both lesbian writers. The second, Louise Collis, had tunnel vision, failed to distance herself impersonally from her subject, and remained blind to manuscript evidence that did not fit her case when she came to treat of Edith Somerville – her case being that Edith Somerville, unknown to herself, was a suppressed lesbian who could not admit her sexual love for Ethel Smyth. Collis, who pronounces upon Edith Somerville like the wrong kind of teacher considering a not very bright pupil, writes magisterially of what she sees as Edith's fear and loathing of sex: 'It [sex] was also entirely connected with men in her mind, of whom she had a horror in the physical sense, being no bisexual.'[89] What we now know from the evidence surviving from the period before Edith met Martin, confirming the sense of some suggestive diary entries, shows that this is not a case that can any longer stand: Edith evidently had no sexual horror of men. When young she showed no horror or avoidance of physical contact with them – but quite plainly the opposite. The letters between the two women show perfectly clearly that Ethel falsely represented herself as composite comrade, guardian and friend as camouflage for her real aim, which was to seduce Edith Somerville. When she failed in this, she moved on to another woman and criticised Edith cruelly to her out of wounded vanity. Ethel's fixation on Edith lasted for seven years, and took three years to reach an overtly sexual crux. But apart from her sexuality, Ethel was a boon companion who revolutionised Edith's life.

Ethel Smyth was a prominent woman suffragist, who had been imprisoned for her beliefs, during a two-year period when she was enthralled by Emmeline Pankhurst. She had composed the music for the 'March of the Women' to words written by Cicely Hamilton. From an army family, she was loud and opinionated, full of an aggressive self-confidence, and a passionate musician. She bowled people over, and they either hated or loved her. William Plomer described her in his memoir *At Home* when remembering Rodmell and Virginia Woolf, with whom Ethel fell in love after falling out with Edith:

> Once at tea time indoors in the summer the click of the gate was heard and a second or two later there appeared in profile in one of the windows a stylish panama hat, sporting in cut and tilted slightly forward on a determined, military looking head with a granite chin, the head itself set rigidly on a square, parade ground chest and shoulders, which, lacking epaulettes, looked undressed. At a glance one might have thought this the top part of a Prussian field-marshal just back from shooting chamois in the Carpathians. The purposeful progress of this animated bust, in vivid relief against the old yew hedge, and without a glance to right or left, was as resolute as some old man-of-war called perhaps *Immitigable*, *Indomitable*, or *Impregnable*, carrying a great many guns and under urgent orders to ram and board a cornered enemy. But there was no

enemy, this visitor was not on any hostile intent, and, just as a man-of-war used to be called *she* was in fact of the feminine gender; she was a composer ... This high spirited woman addressed herself to life with a gusto more often seen in her generation than in ours. If her sensibility had been as conspicuous as her energy, her music might have been as attractive as her enjoyment of life ...[90]

Ethel in love behaved very like a man who, at the same time as wishing to possess the loved one, wishes to instruct and improve: in fact she behaved like Herbert Greene. The conviction that Edith needed Ethel as a sexual and academic tutor goes hand in hand with the notion that Edith was too dim to understand that she was a lesbian. Ethel was to educate her sexually as well as intellectually. Louise Collis comments on Edith Somerville: 'Many of the classics were unknown to her. Her history was deficient, her poetry scant. Ethel tried to improve her education, but with temporary success. It did not affect their relationship, the essence of which was mutual attraction and the finding of each other very good company.'[91] The American poetess Amy Lowell, fascinated by the relationship between Somerville and Ross, and dazzled by the latter, was to take the same patronising line in exclaiming at Edith's patient stupidity and lack of talent.[92]

It was a relationship that might have foundered at the start. When Edith first spent some time in Ethel's company she made the mistake of thinking that she might make tactful suggestions to improve Ethel Smyth's disastrous dress sense. It is not generally realised that Edith had a highly developed dress sense, as the common reader hardly ever sees photographs of her in anything but day dress, and country wear day dress at that, or hunting rig. Edith suffered tortures at the sight of Ethel sailing off to grand orchestral performances looking like a bag lady. She remembered the first time she dared to speak to Ethel about her clothes in a letter to Maurice Baring in 1945: '[I remember] a bitter fight with Ethel in a cab ... I hadn't known Ethel very long, but I rashly thought that I knew her well enough to suggest that a rather grand, old hat of Mary Hunter's looked rather uncomfortable with a distinctly shabby tweed coat and skirt. Ethel was immediately up in flames, and declared at the fullest stretch of her lungs that she wouldn't be dictated to. It was alarming but it didn't last.'[93] Edith's strictures had no effect whatsoever. In fact as she got older Ethel became more careless than ever of her appearance. At the Sadler's Wells performance of her opera *The Wreckers* in 1938, Edith described her appearance to Hildegarde: 'I've *never* seen her so badly dressed, more like one of George Belcher's "lydies" than you can imagine. The tricorne hat has been replaced by a perfectly awful old squashed black straw, trimmed with white daisies round it. A rusty black cloak, and strings of pearls over a very untidy grey blouse and a brown skirt. I've never seen her so like a caravan tramp woman ...'[94] Although she was notoriously careless in her working garb, Edith's good ladylike clothes, discreet make-up, and dislike of carelessness in formal society was one of the clear surface signs that she might not be what Ethel assumed her to be, but some years were to pass before their mutual fascination palled and painful sexual differences were laid bare.

CHAPTER 8

# Ethel Smyth, sexuality and high life

... the death of Violet Martin closed the long and brilliant partnership of the two Irish cousins who had delighted a whole
generation of readers by their vivid and impartial delineation of
the Ireland of yesterday ... The authors of *Some Experiences of an
Irish RM* have enjoyed a wide but singularly uncritical appreciation,
the great majority of their readers regarding them as the writers of
one successful book ... their other books were thus familiarly
described as not so good, or not nearly so good, or nearly as good as
the *RM* ... It is hardly necessary to add that, with few exceptions,
editors, publishers and reviewers aided and abetted this view.
  Charles Graves, 'Martin Ross' in the *National Review*, vol. LXXI

CHARLES GRAVES WAS one of the many who thought that Violet Martin
was the mastermind behind Somerville and Ross, and was expecting
nothing further in the way of original writing from the surviving partner. He
had praised *Irish Memories* and knew that Edith was putting together a volume
of pieces, including unknown work by Martin, published in 1920 as *Stray-
Aways*. Edith was keen to publish in book form stray pieces by Martin that had
been published in ephemeral journals. In all, the miscellany contains fourteen
pieces by Martin, seven by Edith, and two by the pair writing together; they are
described in Edith's introduction as 'the joyful moments of revolt by two
working women.' Her capacity for work returned. Edith's progress after Martin's
death was to a great extent influenced by her friendship with Ethel Smyth. As a
companion, the boisterous Ethel was in a different realm to the trim and subtle
Martin. To those who were not appalled by her she was captivating company,
and, regardless of her dress sense, bombast and egotism, she had friends among
the most distinguished writers, artists and politicians of the day. Through Ethel
Smyth, most importantly, Edith was introduced not only to practising homo-
sexuals but also to an intellectual circle that treated spiritualism with profound
seriousness, the circle of the Balfours and the Sidgwicks. She responded blankly

to the former, but with pleasure and interest to the latter. All these new acquaintances attended the London exhibitions of Edith's work organised by Ethel, beginning with a show at the Goupil Gallery in January 1920; the increased vogue for Edith's painting in this wealthy circle gave an instant and welcome increase in her income. At the Goupil she met the harpsichordist Violet, Mrs Gordon Woodhouse, and was taken in thrall by her musicianship and fey personality. The Goupil Gallery show had been organised by Ethel Smyth in November 1919; Ethel entirely deserved the title given to her by Edith: 'the very queen of advertising agents'. Ethel realised that Edith's paintings would attract people because of the link with her books; in her Goupil catalogue note, Ethel wrote: 'They will recognize landscapes they have known long since in another medium; the wild outline, the glowing colour, the haunting melancholy of this corner of Ireland.'

While the Goupil show was in preparation, the Somerville sisters were approached by local farmers to join them in an organisation to protect established Irish farming interests which were evidently not a close concern of the Government in Dublin, committed as it was to the redistribution of estates to the peasant proprietor, and absorbed in a larger struggle:

> Johnny Driscoll came to me yesterday and said that 'a few farms west' including Pat Connolly and Goggin and himself, want to start a branch of the Farmers' Union, and would we join? I said I was quite sure we would join anything non-political that is for the good of the farmers. He said they were dissatisfied with the Rural District Council, and the infamous roads and the high rates and nothing to show for them, and they thought this show (which is spreading through Ireland) might get influence and run better candidates for the elections next Spring. As it is strictly non-political and no more sectarian than the waterworks, I don't see why it shouldn't, do you? I would gladly join in anything of the kind only to show that there is 'no animosity' – I believe that we are now the only Ginthry left!¹

The letters between the sisters now begin to show the determined efforts of Ethel Smyth to capture Edith as a long-staying guest. 'Ethel Smyth is shrieking for me to go over and *stay over till Feb*.! Not Much!'² In Hildegarde's absence, Edith had to deal with a group of villagers, her sister's 'pet village-ocracy', who were taking large amounts of firewood from the woods, having been told they could do so by 'Her Ladyship'. Edith wrote that the next time she was asked for kindling she was to say that her 'brutal and ferocious sister won't let you – I don't care a pin what they say of me now that I haven't got the hounds.'³ This was not the only occasion on which Edith criticised her sister for her unthinking kind-heartedness and charm, which Edith saw as causing unnecessary complications, often coming home to roost in the shape of unwanted guests. From the strictly practical point of view, as guests, payers were more welcome than non-payers. Ethel Smyth and her sister Mrs Mary Hunter, a wealthy widow whose passion for celebrities had earned her the nickname 'Mrs Lion Hunter', had both succumbed to Hildegarde's overpowering charm. The Somerville sisters were amused by the 'flop' that the Smyth sisters had on them, which they saw as connected to the fact that the Smyth sisters' uncle was once a suitor for their mother Adelaide Coghill. In the same letter Edith wrote to her sister: 'We seem to hold a fatal attraction for the Smyths … Her Uncle, or Grandfather, wanted to marry Mother, so it is in the family.'[4] Hildegarde's easy, natural charm held sway over tenants, servants and neighbours high and low; and however inconvenient Edith may have found it at times we may be fairly sure that in large part because of it the Coghill and Somerville houses in CT were preserved from utter destruction.

Ethel herself scorned to use womanly charms, and her abrasive powers of attack often had the opposite effect to that intended. On the night of the Goupil Gallery opening she decided to act on behalf of Edith with her publisher, a move that was to enrage Edith's literary agent, Pinker: 'Ethel S[myth] tore Mr Longman to shreds at the PV [Private View] about the shameful printing of *Mount Music*. He was furious, and at length said "I've had enough of this!" and stumped away. He deserved it.' Apart from this altercation, Edith was glad to survive the crush of the opening, to which numbers of society people came more to inspect the person of Ethel's new lioness rather than her work. The obtuse object of their interest thought that the event was 'Quite like a wedding, with no bother of cake, rice or bridegroom.'[5]

It was to be two years before Edith understood that Ethel wanted to have an affair with her. As Louise Collis put it, Ethel 'wanted something more than a friendly handclasp and a peck on the cheek'.[6] The letters between the Somerville sisters before this understanding crystallised show clearly that the task of intervening between Edith and her family, and specifically her sister, was an impossible one for Ethel. Eventually Ethel dismissed Edith as a case of arrested sexual development. In January 1920 there are letters that show the pervadingness of the CT tribe quite clearly. When Ethel arranged for a holiday with Edith in Sicily to follow on from her London stay after the Goupil Gallery show, Edith assumed that Egerton and Hildegarde could come too, for Egerton was always Edith's most choice painting companion. On the 10th, penning a very big white lie, she wrote to them insisting that '[Ethel Smyth] is *genuinely* and extremely glad you are coming'. She felt she needed a painting break after the strain of London society: 'I am lashed to Ethel Smyth's war chariot wheels this week (dining and tea-ing) I tremble.' But by the 24th Egerton and Hildegarde had found they were too low in funds to travel: 'I bitterly grieve at not having Egerton to paint with and sympathise with him at having to chuck ... bother you and your finances, I am horribly disappointed.'[7] In fact when Ethel discovered that Edith had blithely assumed that Hildegarde and Egerton would be a welcome addition to their company, Ethel had written that, on the contrary, the proposed quartette would be 'a monstrous comedy ... you must be raving mad ... I want you and me to settle our affairs in peace and quiet.'[8] Edith wrote to Hildegarde on 5 February, her thoughts absorbed in their farm, though she was far from it: 'It is *sickening* you're not coming. When you are in Cork at the Show do try and poke out husbands for Lady Meath and Kitty. Bandon or Cork for choice.' She only bred from her best mares.

Ethel tried to explain her view of the situation a few months later when they had come back. Writing from Coign on 23 April 1920, Ethel tried to make Edith understand that her omnipresent family was exasperating: 'It is just that cheerful assumption that there is no difference (to one) between yourself and all your relations and friends that amuses me as a rule – Why – you are always lavishing your pearls about the path of the swine. Sometimes it angers me (for you I mean) ...'[9] Unaware of her obtuseness in Ethel's eyes, Edith had found time in London in January to visit Mrs Salisbury, a medium, who repeated what Martin had been communicating through Jem Barlow 'that we were to do some *new* work that would create much interest and comment'. Writing to Jem Barlow, she also described how she had a sitting with a medium who received automatic writing. In a trance state Mrs Penrose-Thackwell held a pen loosely, and while Edith looked on, the pen in the medium's hand wrote: 'I am Violet Martin speaking' – '*absolutely* in her own handwriting.'[10]

Before she left for Sicily, Edith told Hildegarde that she had discovered that their route was 'appallingly studded with Duchesses – Paris, Rome, Palermo – thank heaven for your Restaurant Gown!' She sent an emergency list of high-class clothing for Hildegarde to post to her, including her black hat with gold net over the crown: 'It might be a support to me with these awful women. I am a poor worldling, and wish I were eating flat fish at home, like Johnny Leary.' She had 'cleared' £260 from the Goupil show, but refused to tell cousins in London who asked how much she had made: 'I said tranquilly "I don't know"... I hate having my sordid private affairs discussed.'[11]

Because *Mount Music* boldly tackled a mixed marriage in the gentry class, Edith had been worried about the reception of the novel by her Catholic friends. Her first cousin and 'Twin', Bertie Windle, had converted to Catholicism and had experienced many of the problems that had beset the novel's leading man, Larry

Coppinger. She was intensely relieved when the Catholic Kenmares wrote to tell her of 'very good opinions, especially R C ones', and Bertie Windle and Martin's old friend Gertrude Sweetman both wrote with their enthusiastic congratulations. Ethel Smyth wrote a fulsome review later reprinted in her *Streaks of Life* of 1921.[12] In it she writes that 'this almost piercingly human book is the most beautiful the authors have given us' but makes no remark that of the two authors one is no longer living.

On 7 February Edith wrote to Hildegarde: 'Much as I enjoy the thought of Sicily, I should *love* to come home.' The trip to Sicily was written up and published by both writers in their memoirs. Ethel described the time in Sicily as 'magical', but it was not really that. From it henceforward Edith's lameness increased with the years. Having arrived in Taormina, Edith found that the Poste Restante sytem was defective and she failed to get family letters, apart from one from Cameron. She suffered terribly from mosquito bites, so badly that if she could not soon find a remedy (she had been pouring Sal Volatile on the scratched bites), 'I shall tell ES I will go home.' But Ethel would not hear of this. Then Edith got lumbago. On 20 March she wrote to her sister: 'Whenever I talk of going home E furiously says "Hish!" (just as Mother used to) and the thing gets no further.' Bolder than ever, Ethel had dropped a suggestion into Edith's mind that shows an attempt to detach her from Drishane and the sisters' joint farm altogether: 'there certainly is something in Ethel's revolutionary suggestion that we should sell out lock, stock and barrel! All the same I should hate doing it – we might as well pack up and go to New Zealand at once if we did.'[13] It is painfully clear that Edith had none of the relaxed recuperation on this 'holiday' that she used to have in her holidays with Martin and their friends. She wrote to Jem from Sicily, making arrangements for Jem to move into Martin's old room while Jem's house was let and told her: 'I shall be most awfully glad to get home again.'[14] Not wanting to face failure, Ethel did not play her hand in Sicily. She was overwhelmed with emotion when Edith absent-mindedly put her hand in hers sitting in a railway carriage; then she just as absently withdrew it with no comment needed. Edith was pleased with a find that she made in a jewellers, that she wrote to describe to her sister on 2 April: 'there is a dead bargain of a beautiful old Sicilian pearl and diamond pendant and chain going for 2,000 lire (£80). It really is a lovely thing – sell a cow and we will take turns in wearing it, and the Chimp's share shall be admiring us in it. It is something like this [drawing] It is set in gold and silver and there are 8 small diamonds in each link ...'

On her return to Drishane from Sicily, Edith, limping already on one leg, became crippled by sciatica or rheumatism in her good leg. When she arrived back at the house, a servant burst into tears at the sight of 'her that was always flourishing about as if she hadn't a bone in her body'. Ethel returned to the attack by letter, to try and convert Edith to a lover. The intimacy into which Edith had fallen with Ethel was interpreted by her quite differently, and she tried to laugh off Ethel's insistent harping on sex: 'It is so typical of you. You always pose as Diogenes, and as soon as anyone slips inside your guard into your tub, it instantly becomes a *lit conjugal*.'[15] On 7 June Ethel had been delighted by a letter of Edith's in which she had used a phrase that she used of Martin, that in effect she had joined hands with Ethel. This obviously had some huge personal and political rather than sexual significance for Edith that passed Ethel by, for she wrote in return: 'I have had your letter ... the one you wrote after blessed VM had told you not to stint ... and give all you could. And as I read, and for once felt, owing to your not stinting, what you meant me to feel ... that I have indeed "got a claw in" and hold a bit of you fast ... and again when you said your hand was in mine then time and space disappeared and there remained only the dizziness you must have known often in your life and the inexplicable frightening happiness that goes with it ... If one person amuses and enchants another, quite apart from other feelings they inspire, to such an extent, the result is an atmosphere in which ghosts are not at home.'[16] That she, vigorous and substantial, was being baffled by the ghost of little Miss Martin was irksome.

Ethel was aware of the solid existence of Martin as an unwanted attendant on her relationship with Edith. She tried to isolate Martin out of sight far above on a heavenly altar. On 11 June she wrote to Edith: 'You do not, how often have I said it, love a person because you deify them. It is because something in them combines chemically, if you like, with something in you and results in love.' Commenting on Ethel's strictures, Louise Collis explains: 'But Edith still had not grasped the lesson properly.' For she took advice from the otherworld Martin, who decreed: 'The soul must drive, not the body. Tell her that.'[17] Ethel was not pleased with this intervention from 'the impertinent ghost' but furious. Her letters to Edith became intemperate attacks on what she saw as prudishness and gentility. The physical intrusiveness of Ethel's attempt to possess Edith is evident in the phrase 'I have indeed "got a claw in" and hold a bit of you fast'; this prepares us for Virginia Woolf's reaction to Ethel's later fixation on her as 'like being caught by a giant crab.'[18]

The crisis of Ethel's pro-sex argument was in her letters of late June and early July, and in Edith's responses, now destroyed. When Edith insisted that her love for Martin had not been sexual and suggested that Ethel had a physical affair elsewhere with someone who might want one, Ethel was stung. Her sexual vanity made her obtuse: she saw nothing strange about recommending the superiority of manual stimulation to penetrative sex to a countrywoman who made her living as a farmer from stockbreeding. Writing on 25 June she explained:

Your instincts and education make you fastidious … and rather virginal. Your charm is to be thus. But don't you see that I am not all this – your law is not my law. That I can do and risk things that you *could not* – because in your case the inner sanction is lacking. I don't mind you feeling as you do – you and VM. It goes with your type. It is yourselves.

I should *not* say certain things before you that I would like a shot before Betty B[alfour] or Violet W[oodhouse] or Maurice [Baring] … I have others I can talk this foreign language with … The idea that I, who, I think, have more experience of life stored in my little finger than you have in your whole body (I mean of *a certain kind of experience*) should not be capable of judging whom to do what to, seems so odd to me …You innocent (I say it again) … You know I can put my shoulder to other wheels. Why, why shouldn't you imagine that I have *not* done so (and far more cleverly and energetically and patiently than any man would be capable of doing) for myself? I do feel – miserably sometimes "she *is* fond of me – but she does not really *see* me." What can I do to make you? Well – just have patience, I suppose. Life will do the trick.[19]

But it didn't. Edith seems to have responded to this letter with a severe and censorious reply that infuriated Ethel into insults: 'Certainly the being incapable of a certain kind of entrainment in matters physical is not a human being … I go with my father in preferring a "rip" to a spiritual pedant – a righteous pedant.'[20] It does not seem to have occurred to Ethel that Edith might have preferred sexual 'entrainment' from a man rather than a woman. From the evidence of her free-going relationships with young men in the 1870s and 1880s this is entirely within the realms of possibility. Geraldine Cummins, Muriel Currey and Rose Marie Salter Townshend have given abundant confirmation that Edith even as an old woman showed marked attention to handsome men of any age, and Muriel Currey makes a habit of remarking humorously on her interest in particular young workmen, and her desire for their company, in her diary transcripts.

As a relief from her rather painful correspondence with Ethel Smyth, Edith was cheered by the good company of Ethel Penrose and Jim, renting Glen Barrahane as usual, who came with their children for August. On the 21st, she wrote to Hildegarde: 'Ethel and Jim went this morning. Alas I shall miss Ethel *horribly*. I suppose I am better but not very much…my good leg is reduced to a pulp from disuse … the bad leg is only a medium for torture.' Ethel Smyth then appeared in person, and in good humour, and her 'excellent company' revived Edith's spirits: 'she has had the great good sense to realise that I didn't want constant companionship.' Edith was surprised to see that Ethel and Cameron, with the bond of music, got on very well together: 'she and the Chimp seem most successful, and call each other by their Christian names. But I don't expect it to go further on *either* side!'[21]

Although she was living in the familiar setting of a civilised and musical country house, Ethel Smyth found herself in a country under brutal military rule. She was a Unionist and British supremacist whose loudly declaimed anti-Irish views drove Edith into violent dispute with her. In March 1920 Thomas MacCurtain, lord mayor of Cork and commandant of the Cork No. 1 Brigade of the IRA, had been shot in his own home, apparently by the RIC. The hunger strike of his successor as lord mayor, Terence McSwiney, was the sole topic of political conversation. Edith wrote to her sister: 'I think all this hunger striking is the most remarkable proof of sincerity and fidelity to an ideal that could be given. I didn't think these under-bred venal men had such grit in them.' When McSwiney eventually died after a seventy-four-day fast, Edith ranked him with honourable men: 'I suppose most people will call him a fool – but so – therefore – are all Martyrs. It depends on the personal point of view of what is worth dying for.'[22] Despite understanding the seriousness of the issues faced by men like McSwiney, she thought that far too many Irishmen simply took advantage of the disturbed situation of the country to settle old scores with petty malicious damage, or to commit theft from the many abandoned Big Houses. Apart from her revolver in her bedside cabinet, Egerton had given Edith a shotgun that she kept on a rack in the kennels, and now this was stolen. On one of their walks together Ethel Smyth and Cameron discovered that Nelson's Arch, in the Castle woods, had been thrown down. Patrick Sheehy, editor, wrote a diatribe against the perpetrators in the *Skibbereen Eagle*, for the local fishermen and sailors were furious: 'The Arch' was one of their important seamarks on entering the harbour.

In September, Boyle and Cameron took Edith, with Isabel Chavasse for female company, to Dax, where they hoped that a course of treatment at the thermal baths would enable her to walk again. The doctor in Dax interrogated her. He understood himself to be dealing with a lady farmer. What did she do? 'I have a farm'. Here Isabel Chavasse did not help by volunteering the information that Edith was a 'Maitre de chiens'. By post, Ethel Smyth had given her opinion that 'foreign doctors *can't* understand "sportive" English or Irish women', and Edith explained to her sister that '[they] think we are all lumps of butter and jelly like these monstrous females here. *Never* have I seen such monuments of over-eating, and want of exercise!'[23] Edith's doctor suspected that the trouble had started with her lumbago in Sicily in the spring, and that it had been perhaps exacerbated by the rough Sicilian red wine. Edith underwent heat treatment and quite violent osteopathic manipulation and massage. Slowly she regained the use of her legs. Deep in Drishane Farm doings, Hildegarde

19 A wash drawing from *In the State of Denmark*, worked up in CT after their
return, to illustrate the tour of 1893. This shows the head of Violet 'Martin'
Ross from the back, and the profile of Violet Coghill; the Violets were staunch
namesakes and friends known, witheringly, as 'The Onions'. Edith used any models
to hand, even representing her mother as a Danish woman when necessary.

20  8 May 1894 *Lady's Pictorial* publicity shot on the publication
of *The Real Charlotte*.

21 Photograph of Edith by her sister entitled 'Clairvoyante'; in 1894 she
might still photograph well if she was free of teeth trouble.

22 Emmie Sykes, Aylmer Somerville's wife, and her brother-in-law Cameron
playing cards in the summer of 1895. This was a wash drawing carried
out by Edith at high speed and cropped violently by tearing.

23 Henry and Adelaide Somerville. After her parents' death Edith constructed
an icon from photographs of them placed on either side of her crucifix.

24 Hildegarde, Lady Coghill, dressed for the part of Cleopatra. She is
attended by her firstborn 'Paddy', later Sir Patrick Coghill!

25 Edith Somerville in hunting habit, taken in 1905, when she was master of the
West Carbery Hounds. At her breast on a watch chain is a whistle. She considered
it unladylike to blow a hunting horn. Consequently she used the whistle to send
signals to her huntsman, who translated them to the field on the horn which
he carried rather than the 'master'.

26 Egerton Coghill in a tweed cap, sailing jacket, sweater and wing collar. Possibly dressed for dinner on *Ierne*. Photographed by his brother-in-law Boyle Somerville.

27  A Kodak of Lady Coghill, Martin Ross and the medium J.E.M. Barlow.
This is one of the few photographs in which it is possible to appreciate the slightness
of Martin Ross in comparison with the statuesque Hildegarde Coghill.

28  Edith Somerville in her Studio in the 1920s. Her ancient straw hats were treasured, like many others, and used to dress models for illustrations. The room accumulated layers of papers and smothered objects; by the 1940s it gave offence to tidy-minded people. At the time of the Somerville and Ross festival of 1984, layers of late manuscripts, impacted in the damp, were peeled away from windowsills.

## IRELAND'S CHOICEST.

DOES Miss E. Œ. Somerville ever fail to win lovers for her Ireland? Not, certainly, among those to whom the high heart and the laughing eyes are treasures to be cherished wherever they may be found. In her new book, "An Enthusiast" (Longmans, Green, and Co., 8s. 6d.), she adds some notable portraits to her gallery, drawn, as always, with kindly humour and subtle perception; it is not, however, her happy hunting people that supply the models, but all the warring classes in the troubled land.

**Miss E. Somerville.**

The enthusiast is a man of the old landlord stock who, eschewing politics, devotes himself to constructive work among his farmer neighbours. But, grateful though they will be of the new understanding they gain of conditions in Ireland, most readers will follow with a more absorbed interest the story of the hero's heart; for, with him,

. . . A spirit in my feet
Hath led me—who knows how?
To thy chamber window sweet.

A moving story, told with dignity and restraint.

Among modern Irish novels and short stories none have a higher literary value than those written by Miss E. Œ. Somerville and "Martin Ross." Death has unfortunately broken that happy and fruitful partnership; but the surviving member of it has not laid aside her pen. Her new story, "The Enthusiast" (Longmans, Green, & Co., 37, Paternoster Row, London, E.C.4), is not in the least degree inferior to the best of those written in collaboration. Like "Tales of the R.I.C.," it depicts Ireland during the Sinn Fein "rebellion," but is written from a somewhat different point of view. The two books are complementary, not mutually contradictory, and no one who reads one of them should fail to make himself master of the other.

29  'Ireland's Choicest'. Reviews of *An Enthusiast*,
published in 1921, from Edith's scrapbook.

30 Ethel Penrose in her old age. The 'Twins' Ethel Coghill and Edith Somerville never lost contact with one another, but Ethel, like many of her family, abandoned Ireland after 'The Troubles' and 'The Treaty'.

31 Edith Somerville was still making money from horse-coping in her mid-seventies.
Here she is with Rathmore, wearing a fashionable striped cloche hat, a tweed jacket and
skirt, and a Cameron tartan tie. Both Somerville sisters wore Cameron ties throughout
their lives; the tartan pattern was Erracht, and symbolised their ancient Scottish link
with the distinguished military family who founded the Cameron Highlanders. Rose
Cameron Bingham supplied them with shawls in the same pattern.

32 The last photograph taken of the Somerville brothers and sisters before the murder of Boyle Somerville in March 1936. From the left: Aylmer, Boyle, Edith, Cameron, Hildegarde, Jack and Hugh.

33 When she was no longer able to ride, Edith took great pleasure in the riding triumphs of her nephews and nieces. At CT the young were encouraged to commune with horses at the earliest possible moment. Icelandic ponies were used to mount the youngest children. Here Faith Coghill, daughter of Ambrose, communes with Kelpie, who is held by Johnny Leary.

34 Edith Somerville, photographed for *Vogue* in 1948, the year before her death.

35 The graves of Somerville and Ross, in a choice situation, among family and friends.
The land drops away on the seaward side to a wide view of Castlehaven harbour.
Their heads are a few feet from the altar of St Barrahanes, their feet near a family
vault; nearby on the landward side are Edith's brothers Boyle and Aylmer.

wrote to her of the impossibilities of getting a Friesian bull imported, and Edith sympathised by letter: 'It is very maddening not being able to import a bull, let us hope Wib [Professor Wibberley] becomes the first President of the Irish Republic.' Back in London, walking with the aid of a stick, she was able to go a Wigmore Hall concert of Ethel Smyth's music.

After this it was safer to take a break at Ethel's home, Coign, rather than to go home, because by mid-October a typhoid epidemic had struck CT. On account of the disease the village was virtually a no-go area through the month of November. The feud between Michael Collins' men and English undercover agents in Dublin came to a head on 21 November on the day called 'Bloody Sunday'. On the morning of this day Collins' men shot eleven English agents in surprise raids. In the afternoon, for revenge, Black and Tans drove armoured Crossley tenders onto the pitch at Croke Park during a Gaelic Football match and fired indiscriminately into the crowd, killing twelve and wounding sixty. It became dangerous for the 'West British' in Ireland to identify themselves as loyalists, and it is clear that Edith Somerville, who detested 'West Britishness', came close to doing what her brother Boyle did in 'coming out' as a Sinn Feiner.

Edith wrote to her sister at the end of November: 'As for Dail Eireann I would as soon have it as doldromising Westminster. I think it is far more likely to help us out in this fix, and I haven't one spark of loyalty to England left. My sole reasons for not being a Sinn Feiner are geographical and financial! England has reduced Irish "loyalists" to destitution in order to conciliate the rebels, and failed, at that!'[24] The sisters were still using the Buddh words that had been filed in the Buddh Dictionary in 1887. 'Doldromising' means dawdling 'in a foolish and stupified manner'. The typhoid epidemic still raged in CT. Hildegarde wrote on 4 November that they had all been inoculated, and many of those over forty-five had been badly affected by the disease, Egerton having a crisis in his illness in the middle of the month. She pronounced sentence of banishment on her sister. Thwarted, Edith protested to Hildegarde: 'I am dying to get back to my work at home of all kinds. After all, you might as well say a salmon would find the Blackwater damp, as say that sea air is bad for me. I was bred to it ...'[25] She dealt with the press reactions to the appearance of her new book *Stray-Aways* from London. Edith did not return to Drishane until 22 December, for Christmas celebrations with a family that had been ravaged by illness. Hildegarde's children were not allowed home this Christmas, for fear of catching the infection from their father, as Egerton could not throw off the disease.

With the distraction of political and military chaos in Ireland, it was not until the early 1920s were well under way that readers became familiar with the idea that, though Violet Martin had died, there were still novels appearing under the names of Somerville and Ross. Charlie Graves had been introduced to Martin by Mollie Helps long ago in August 1889, immediately after which he had written the *Spectator* review of *An Irish Cousin*. He was to remain a staunch supporter and friend of Somerville and Ross for over fifty years, and was instrumental, with Edmund Yates, first in bringing their writing before the public and then in keeping it there. From the time of their first novel, there had been controversy as to how two authors could write one harmonious text. When Charlie Graves first met Martin, 'she expressed her relief that he was the only writer who had not been inquisitive as to their method, and then with engaging inconsistency described [their] conversational preliminaries, adding that what they laughed over together generally came out right. In regard to reproducing dialect, in which they are admittedly unsurpassed, they from the first discarded phonetic spelling and arrived at the conclusion that the root of the matter lay in the idiomatic phrase and the mental attitude.'[26]

Graves, like everyone else, assumed that novel-writing was a closed chapter in the life of the surviving partner, and other reviewers openly speculated that Miss Somerville would now return to her first love, painting and illustrating. The publication of *Irish Memories* in 1917 had delighted Graves, as a 'truly noble tribute to the intrepid and magnanimous spirit of her "perfect comrade"'; he congratulated her on the 'exquisite literary skill shown in the portraiture. Had Martin Ross been the survivor she could not have done it better'; but, again like everyone else, he did not foresee that Somerville would carry on writing novels. The *Times Literary Supplement*, reviewing *Irish Memories*, said 'It is sad to look on the title page ... and sorrowful to realise that it is the last on which we shall see the joyous names of Somerville and Ross coupled together.' The publication of *Mount Music* in 1919 caused astonishment and in some quarters dismay; the literary critic Hilary Robinson singled it out as a disaster – 'the most self-indulgent prose they ever wrote'[27] – but there are good things in it, in the character of Dr Mangan and a fascinating study of a gentry convert to Catholicism, who wishes to join the new Irish nation, and becomes a nationalist candidate. The next attempt at a Somerville and Ross novel was to be more successful. The book that Edith wrote between May 1920 and March 1921, *An Enthusiast*, takes for its subject the immediate events in her district with Sinn Fein and Black and Tan violence, during a time when the Skibbereen court house and the police barracks were destroyed. In the novels written after Martin's death, there is a fiery immediacy and a loss of the impartiality and high finish of the earlier books, which, apart from *Naboth's Vineyard*, took a stance more detached and from a safe chronological distance. Unionist bigotry in *An Enthusiast*, published in 1921, is presented horribly through women characters like old Mrs Palliser: the author was in no way a believer in the superior sensibilities of all women. Woven into the book are events from Edith's own experiences at this time, including telegrams she sent to Drishane to organise her return from Lismore.

On the night of 11 December 1920, enraged by the successes of a flying column of Cork IRA men, Black and Tans and Auxiliaries had burned the centre of the city of Cork. As a symbol of their triumph, the British troops who had carried out this act pinned burned corks in their caps. Refugees from the city fled into the countryside as far as Mallow. Edith never forgot her horror at the sight of the black ruination of fine old familiar buildings when she returned from England through the city on 16 December, having been met by Ethel and Jim Penrose, with whom she then stayed for a week at Lismore. Her sympathy with the Irish position was already clear in a letter to Hildegarde of 2 December:

> I think it would be a sound diplomatic move if you gave out that I had become a Sinn Feiner! and I very nearly am one. I am so *sick* of the one-sidedness of Irish Unionists, slurring over reprisals, and saying that the ambushed lorries are acts of assassination. I can repudiate the horrible Dublin slaughter, but as the S.F s say they are the IRA army, and have a staff, and officers, and are to be 'interned' in future when caught, the fights with the lorries are acts of war and *as such* legitimate. The Black and Tans here pulled men out of bed and shot them, exactly as was done in Dublin and only that the S.Fs began it, it would be an even thing in the matter of crime ...

On 5 January 1921 Edith noted in her diary: 'Heard from E[thel S[myth] proposing self-denying ordinance of only writing once a week.' For a while this left Edith free to keep writing at her novel in progress which incorporates some unused material from the unpublished complete manuscript of *A Man of the People* written before Martin's death. The spate of letters from Ethel soon built up again, however. The medium Jem Barlow helped Edith with sittings to receive 'automatic writing with M[artin]', and other manifestations. At this time Edith slept for only a few hours through the night before being woken by the pain in her crippled leg. As a medium, Jem linked up with all the Castletownshend dead in Martin's company; she now showed herself to be to be a conduit not only of communications but also of healing power sent by the sympathetic dead. Egerton and his Uncle Kendal had both been practitioners of Mesmer's healing treatment of patients by touch; this would prove to be effective even after the physical death of Egerton and Kendal, who had died in 1919. At a sitting with Jem on 18 January: 'Uncle Kendal came, and said he would "put his finger on me" [I] think he must have as I slept all night for the first time for six months.'[28] This showed an undoubtedly positive reaction to male touch, even if dreamed. Apart from her pain, she must have found sleep difficult with the disturbed state of the neighbourhood, where murders were taking place. It was not uncommon to hear shooting at night.

Ethel Smyth lectured Edith long and hard for not condemning the rebels, 'your unspeakable countrymen', as she called them, and it is from Edith's letters that try to explain to Ethel why the Irish were in armed rebellion that we realise she is carrying in her memory the failures of England in dealing with Ireland from the period of Charles Kendal Bushe:

> I half think about writing an article about the absurdity, if it were nothing else, of grinding and crushing Ireland to death. Oh yes, I admit the assassinations, but I still cannot see why the Irish should not wish for freedom as they have wished and struggled for it since Henry II's time. If the English smash us to pulp, you will have nothing left to laugh at (yes, *you* and all the good and well-intentioned people who think they know what is best for Ireland) ... In all these centuries of disaffection and disappointment one simple thing has never been tried – giving Ireland what she asks for. If I said I wanted to go hunting, I shouldn't be consoled for a refusal by being given a ticket for a Sunday concert at the Albert Hall.[29]

In February the reviews of *Stray-Aways* started appearing, beginning with *Punch* and the *Saturday Review*. On the 5th she noted that she had finished the first draft of her novel *An Enthusiast* and had begun a clean copy. By 3 March she had clean copied 50,000 words. Whatever the wrecked state of her body, her lifelong efficiency as a copyist did not falter until the very end. From her letters to the American Elizabeth Hudson, whom she met at the Kenmares', we learn that Edith delighted in the company of younger people, but after her Sicily trip she was forced to take stock of the physical symptoms of her own increasing age. Some of her contemporaries like Jim Penrose and Percy and Eddy Aylmer kept as fit as could be, and were grand specimens of healthy country types, but her long-time suitor Herbert Greene had sunk into decay. She was enraged by his letting himself go, as he had once been a hearty walker and an even keener oarsman. At the outbreak of World War One, Herbert had joined the Home Guard and sent a pathetic photograph of himself in uniform to Edith. As a suitor who had been rejected over many years, the sending of this photograph might indicate that Herbert had been made aware, no matter how many decades past, that Edith showed a preference for men in uniform. Herbert, the dry and dusty don in embryo, had been an onlooker at those wild goings-on of the summers 1879–81 when all the excitement was master-minded by a jolly officer of the Hampshire Regiment. Edith described Herbert at a tea party in Dublin in a letter to Hildegarde in March 1921:

> Herbert came also. It is disastrous that he now has completely adopted the role of conventional dotard, and looks the part only too well, with a blue nose and an unkempt beard. I am humiliated at thinking he is a contemporary! He said Percy and Eddy had asked him and Sylvia to dinner at some smart place, and he was quite sure the world regarded Percy and Eddy as being his and Sylvia's children! How grateful Sylvia would be at this assumption! As a matter of fact he looks like Eddy's grandfather and has adopted a sort of senile smile that enhances the illusion.

Herbert was crowing over the fact that he was going to wear to an imminent family wedding the same frock coat that his father had worn before him. Edith was deeply thankful to be unable to attend this: 'these weddings have now become Resurrection Pies at wh. decaying cousins rise up in judgement against one, and bring home the fact of the Superfluity of the Veteran on the Stage.'[30] On 6 March Edith became involved in a wrangle over Boyle's tenancy of Uncle Kendal's old house, Cosheen, which now belonged to Egerton and Hildegarde. Boyle's wife Mab maintained that their tenancy was 'conditional on the state of Ireland'. Mab and Boyle lived with the tightest economy, putting the comfort and education of their four children before their own needs, and Mab in particular felt that the deteriorating economic and political situation in Ireland justified giving up their CT house. Edith wrote to her sister: 'if they are right in this ... I am afraid they are justified in wanting to back out, as no-one in their senses would come to live here now. It is even ludicrous. No bridges, no posts, the only attraction being (or the greatest one you have to offer) being that a sentry walks up and down your avenue to keep away murderers and incendiaries! (I shake with laughter when writing this, it is so absurd and so true) ...'

She had a hope that Lloyd George would find some formula: 'Let us hope, and not hope hopelessly, but *dynamically and hard!*' Boyle had thought of sub-letting his lease, but this would have been difficult in the circumstances. Edith's letter closes with a remark that shows us that the Somerville brothers had found in their beleaguered situation in Ireland a use for skills learned in World War One: 'Don't think I don't sympathise with you over Cosheen, because I cannot allow that the private sandbag battery is a very reassuring feature to the nervous tenant ...'[31]

Drishane was raided for horses three days later. The inside knowledge that the raiders showed of the workings of the house, and of the ineffectual nature of its Master, tell of the confidence that Cork Republicans had in their Western stronghold: 'Two young men came to the yard this morning at about seven.

Opened all doors, (shutting them again) and walked about. Katie heard them and put out her head and asked what they wanted. "We want the Boss." – "Do you mean Colonel Somerville?" – "No. Mike Hurley." – "He's at home." They were civil spoken, one smartly dressed (Kate said 'stylish'), the other 'rough-like'. They went down to Mike's and said he must come up with them and give them a horse! Mike begged them not to take Tara. They agreed to let him choose, but they *must* have one (a revolver enforced all this). So he gave them poor little Deirdre (of the Sorrows) *I told you* it was an unlucky name! The men gave Mike a paper ('This horse will be back in a few days') they said they were sorry and didn't like having to do it "but they had to".' Edith was worried that this theft would further upset Boyle and his wife. Mab in particular was nervous at the prospect of armed violence against the Anglo-Irish. 'This last "outrage" will upset Boyle and Mab still more, and no wonder! ... It is sickening to think what secret societies and bad handling has brought this poor country to.' Mab had been badly affected by nervous strain during the war when Boyle was on Atlantic convoy duty and London was under attack from the air. Edith thought that she had suffered then a type of 'shell-shock', and after the war Mab never quite recovered her previous calm equilibrium. Boyle explained to Edith that during the war Mab's pluck 'in actual danger to be faced, is absolute. But the possible, impending peril is what gets her down. The air raids got on her nerves so appallingly for that reason ...We *must* try and realise what the accounts of this country are, and what the impression to nervous people – or any people, really – in England must be...'[32]

Notebook 14 gives us a footnote on the fate of Deirdre at this time. The Irishmen who had served in World War One, some of them, passed into the ranks of IRA officers. The officer commanding the British garrison in Skibbereen, Colonel Percy Hudson, sent a message to Edith via Canon Madden who said, 'they know about Miss S's mare, she is six miles north of Leap. The Commandant of the IRA Flying Squadron has her – a very nice fellow, an MC. [He had been decorated as a British soldier, with the Military Cross] I have had letters from him.' This seems to suggest a working and integrated command and control structure in the IRA at the time, which was careful of public opinion. The Free State forces also took as officers men who had served previously with the British. Cameron, supported by Edith, was to propose that Free State officers be entered as members of the Cork County Club, in order to facilitate its survival and social transition. This was a very good idea, if the remaining Anglo-Irish and Free State officer class were to integrate, but it went unheeded, and the club did not survive.

On 18 March Edith crossed to London, and after a weekend with Ethel Smyth at Coign, went to see Mr Longman who 'was low about trade prospects. Said things never looked so black'. A week later Ethel Smyth took her to meet

'Lady Troubridge and Radcliffe Hall'. Her diary comment was: 'Latter in bed. Lady Troubridge young and nice looking. Talked psychic things.' On 1 April, Sylvia Townshend Gorges telephoned her at Coign to tell her that Union Hall had been burned down during the night, old Colonel Spaight and his wife being turned out of their beds at midnight 'and the house rifled and burnt'. Beginning to lose some of her sympathy with Sinn Fein, Edith worried about Drishane, but did not rush back. On the next day she dined at Fisher's Hill and had a séance with Mrs Sidgwick and her brother Gerald Balfour ('a strange lovely being', as she described him in her diary account of it). At the seance, a Miss Johnson and Mrs Sidgwick, who were from the sceptical wing of the Society for Psychical Research, were in top form as observers of the phenomena. They 'disbelieve everything and bore through evidence like weavils through a biscuit. Very enraging but interesting.' Mrs Sidgwick and Miss Johnson were referred to thereafter as the 'Weavils'. On 7 April Edith eventually returned to Cork.

CT was peaceful, and nothing had happened to the house. There were some new trenches cut in roads, but inhabitants were getting used to making their own circuitous safe routes. Reassured, Edith went back to London in three weeks to sign her agreement with Longmans for *An Enthusiast* and to be paid £400 down. On 3 May she sold to Mr Blackwood of *Blackwood's Magazine* her two articles called 'Kerry I and II' at this stage. They later re-appeared as two chapters of her memoir *Wheeltracks* as 'In Kerry' and 'The Kerry Beagles'. She was doing well as a writer of newspaper pieces. Bruce Richmond of *The Times*, who used to contact Martin to order work from the pair, now gave Edith work and valued it highly. He commissioned her to write an article 'about Whyte Melville, and others' for the TLS. At the beginning of June she went up to stay with Horace Plunkett at Kilteragh, meeting Lennox Robinson at dinner there. She wrote her 3,000-word Whyte Melville article between 6 and 9 June; on the 18th it was printed: 'My Whyte Melville leading article in this week's Lit Sup … an agreeable surprise.' The stress of waiting for night raids and burnings increased. Strict concentration on work helped to insulate Edith from the nervous strain that had overcome Mab, and that had overcome Edith herself in the summer of 1915. The Skibbereen courthouse was burned down on the night of 9 June and on the last night of the month the Pooles' house Mayfield near Bandon was burned to the ground. Its mistress, Edith's first cousin Grace Somerville Poole, and her sister Bess were quicker and more daring than others caught in the same trap. With the building on fire they brought up and loaded two cartloads of furniture and family portraits, portraits that survived to illustrate Rosemary ffolliott's *Pooles of Mayfield* of 1958.[33]

Edith's fine horse Deirdre had been taken, but at the end of May she had escaped from her captors and returned to Drishane with a sure homing instinct.

'She had walked home through Skib alone and then jumped her way to the chapel and so on to Drishane,' she told Hildegarde. But on 7 June she was taken yet again, and old Sampson on the 17th. Ethel Smyth's letters were a lifeline in these times. It was in some ways easier for their relationship to proceed on paper than in the flesh. Louise Collis wrote of Ethel: 'It was above all Edith's letters that endeared her to her.'[34] But Edith actually enjoyed the ferocity of their disagreements in person: 'Oh why aren't you here to fight me. It is so dull scrapping on paper and so enraging to both combatants.' This reminds us that her relationship with Martin was not all sweetness and light, but verbally lively, as they wrangled, and enjoyed wrangling. Castle Barnard was burned to the ground on the night of the 21st and Lord Bandon was 'missing and probably kidnapped'. Marking time, Hildegarde and Egerton often played croquet. On Midsummer's Eve Hildegarde's diary has an entry that shows the sisters' determination to keep on going in their customary way. They, and no-one else in sight, kept up a traditional rite: 'After dinner Jem, Edith and I went up to Balinafrin and lit fires to Baal.'

In July, when Edith began to clean copy her memoir of her Sicily trip, the reviews of An Enthusiast began, and she was particularly pleased with the Sunday Times review of the 14th. The novel was topical. Front pages of the English newspapers at this time listed the Anglo-Irish houses lost by burning; there was no certainty that anyone would escape. In CT on 1 July the Castle demesne woods had been set on fire, and on the same day that Egerton received a threatening unsigned letter. But the brave, unstoppable Ethel Smyth arrived on the 15th, bringing with her an enjoyable bone of contention; she had given Edith a copy of Maurice Baring's novel Passing By and they spent days arguing over it. Edith wrote in her diary after an evening of heated debate: 'Fought over Maurice's book all evening. Find it tres sec. ES adores it.' There were guests at dinner that night, five officers of the Sherwood Foresters from the barracks at Skibbereen. Ethel and Edith could not stop arguing over Passing By even when they went out to dine days later: 'Dined at Glen B. Fought over Passing By. H agreeing with me to E's fury.' However fiercely they might fight in private, Ethel remained a staunch admirer and publicist of Edith's work, and it was Ethel who wrote an 'especially nice' review of An Enthusiast for Country Life. Edith was proved wrong in her insistence that the Irish irregular troops were a disciplined and controlled military force who would never shoot women, when Mrs Lindsay was shot dead at the end of the month, for informing on the planned IRA ambush at Dripsey. It was believed that she was attempting to prevent bloodshed, in co-operation with the local priest. In August Edith went temporarily to Ethel Penrose at Lismore, where, in her own private sitting room, she wrote up 'Sicily'. She had no intention of leaving CT, but the auction at the

Castle on 17 August signalled a major retreat to the safety of the English West Country for the Townshends.

Deep in the Irish 'Troubles', Edith wrote her memoir of the Sicily trip of the year before. Her humour and style show no flagging; she had needed them both to endure the rigours of the Sicily trip. With her taste for authentic local colour, Ethel liked to stay in crudely appointed guesthouses, but Edith learned to dig her heels in and simply say, 'Death first'. In Syracuse they had come to a hotel where two very old barefooted and hunchbacked women, far too old still to be in service, had been called to attend on Edith and Ethel, one for each of them. A description of the hotel, with a grand exterior and courtyard with an open staircase, plays the old Somerville and Ross trick of anti-climax:

> It was a beautiful staircase, all of marble, with pillared arches, through which we looked down into the foliage of the courtyard and up into the hot, blue sky. A palatially planned, marble-paved passage led to our rooms. These also had the grand air, and were very lofty, with handsome tiled floors, and gorgeous chandeliers for electric light. With this effort, however, the grandeur failed. A sofa, with a broken leg, lay, like a crippled dachshund, in one corner. On an iron tripod was a small tin basin, on a shelf was a wine bottle full of water. Upon an intimidating wooden bed was a pair of trousers, that appeared to indicate very hasty flight on the part of its last occupant; if the danger had been fire it seemed regrettable that the trousers had escaped the fate to which they had apparently been abandoned. The hunchback, however, with a single generous gesture, removed them with the bedding. For my part I regarded the trousers with envy; they were not going to spend the night on the wooden bed, as I was.[35]

Back in CT, Edith seemed unrepentant in her support for the Irish cause, when she was approached by fund-raisers for the IRA and contributed. Hildegarde wrote in her diary: 'The IRA went round asking for money to defray election expenses, Edith gave them ten shillings.' At this time Hildegarde was beginning to be distracted by her husband's state of health. The Castletownshend typhoid epidemic of November 1920 had repercussions for many months, and Egerton in particular – who was being treated by a London chest specialist – could not throw off what seemed to be an infection of his lungs and throat. His chest was X-rayed in May 1921. After the harvest, and the Cork Show on 6 and 7 September, when Edith went to stay at Killarney with the Kenmares, he and Hildegarde went to Aix for September in the hope of improving his health, but he was to return in just the same obvious poor condition. Before the sisters went their separate ways, they had to arrange housing for the unmarried daughters of Dr Jim Somerville – Nelly and Mimi. Park Cottage had been raided and threatened with burning. Utterly horrified, the family had sold out instantly, 'lock, stock and barrel'. From Killarney, Edith wrote to tell them that she was a fellow guest of the daughter of the Duchess of St Albans, Lady Kitty Lambton, 'a *mad* [keen] Sinn Feiner'. After one day of Lady Kitty's easy company she wrote again: 'her S.F-ism is moderate (not much worse than mine!)'.[36]

Stephen Gwynn wrote a thoroughgoing appreciation of Somerville and Ross in the *Edinburgh Review* of October 1921. He commented on the revolution in political thought that had taken place in Edith's mind in writing *Mount Music* and *An Enthusiast*. He is interested in the character of Larry Coppinger, gentry but a Catholic convert, who marries Christian Talbot Lowry in a mixed marriage:

> One may take Miss Somerville as suggesting that in the younger generation there is a growing tendency to tolerate such vagaries. Christian does not refuse to be Larry's wife because he has stood for Parliament as a Nationalist, and his friend, no less a person than the local MFH, is said to have backed his canvass. So far so good. But Miss Somerville has not tackled the problems whose existence she indicates. Her Doctor Mangan is a powerful study of such a man as may be displacing the old landed proprietors; and they will not all get drowned in the nick of time to make things pleasant, as Dr Mangan was considerate enough to do. Again Larry and Christian get married, but we are not told how the difficulty with his church about a mixed marriage is circumvented. If Miss Somerville had faced things with the sort of ruthlessness which we find in 'The Real Charlotte' she would have let Larry become the husband of Dr Mangan's daughter and then followed his evolution.

Gwynn then passes on to discuss *An Enthusiast*, seeing its hero Dan Palliser, returned from the war with an MC and determined to make a go of his lands, as a truly drawn Irish type set alongside the idealistic Sinn Feiner, Eugene Cashen, 'whose honesty and will to succeed she can perceive'. Frustrated and futile, Dan dies in an attack by gunmen on his home. Of these two novels, Gwynn writes: 'These books are documents ... because they show how far the minds of Miss Somerville and her comrade were modified by the social revolution which was in progress through their whole lives.' When next Edith wrote a novel, *The Big House of Inver* in 1925, she took a step away from the present to set her story in the first decade of the century. After this novel she went further into the past, and back to the times of her own youth. Among their books Gwynn places *The Real Charlotte* highest: 'the best novel ever written about Ireland; ... it is the only book of theirs where sex-psychology is boldly handled. They make us feel how big, how ugly and how dangerous a force sex is in Charlotte who desires love none the less because she is physically repulsive.' Gwynn was the only Irish Nationalist reviewer to discuss the writers with such approval and so seriously at this time.

Hildegarde and Egerton were still in London, getting ready for a trip abroad to Alassio for Egerton's health again, when their son Nevill with a friend was abducted by Republicans in Cork on 3 October. Nevill, twenty years old, was a keen violinist who played Irish airs and dance music and attended *feiseanna* in his vacations, so that fortunately he was thus known to a Nationalist musical circle in Cork. Nevill had once seen the IRA leader Tom Barry at one of these *feiseanna*, but he did not make any mental connection between Irish musical culture and armed Irish separatists, or realise that a musician might also be a gunman who might shoot British soldiers, or land-lords. It seemed as though the younger CT generation, like Edith and Martin, also thought they could convincingly 'pass' in Irish company. Chiefly thanks to Nevill's coolness and the fact that one of their captors knew him, they were released after questioning and returned home, thankful to be alive. Nevill did not allow this to shake his faith in Irish people, but a similar incident in Dublin, when Boyle's son Raymond Somerville – the chosen heir of Drishane – was held by Republicans, struck its victim with an ineradicable horror of Ireland: a horror that was to be compounded by his father's murder.

In London, Egerton and Hildegarde attended a concert where they met Ethel Smyth; not feeling up to travelling, they moved to see Jack at Kneller Hall from where, on 8 October, Hildegarde wrote to Edith that Egerton was 'slack' but appeared to be getting better, although he was haemorraging slightly from the throat. Egerton's system collapsed on the following day. On the 10th, a telegram came to Edith from Jack: 'Egerton died yesterday afternoon'. Cameron and Edith packed and started immediately, 'stunned by a loss as unexpected as crushing'. Jack took charge at Kneller Hall, and arranged for temporary burial for Egerton there at Twickenham, judging the situation in Cork to be too unsafe to take him home. Coghills and Somervilles descended on Kneller Hall for the funeral on the 12th, and here Edith saw her beloved cousin Claude Coghill, Egerton's brother and her 'best playboy', for the last time. Hildegarde, whose own health now broke down, was then taken to Alassio where she spent Christmas with her children, and two of Dr Jim's daughters. Here the young did their best to cheer and comfort Hildegarde. The Irish party danced four-handed reels and jigs to Nevill's playing, Nelly Somerville teaching K the footwork with great success. Hildegarde, shattered, was neither sleeping nor eating. 'My first christmas away from home since 1881', she wrote in her diary. Before coming back to CT from Egerton's funeral, Edith saw Pinker to discuss with him the conversion of the RM into a play or film.

Hildegarde was out of Ireland when the political rainbow coloration of the Drishane Somerville siblings changed by a few shades as Cameron announced that he, too, had become a Sinn Feiner. It is easy to forget that numbers of Anglo-Irish people had been happy to label themselves as 'nationalist' or 'Sinn Fein' before the Irish Civil War of 1922–3 and some stuck with it regardless. The Home Rule objective of Irish independence while remaining under the 'Crown' was rather elastic in the case of those who thought of England and Ireland as a joint kingdom, with two crowns. To this cast of mind one should not be subsidiary to the other, as Ireland's was the older kingdom and the older civilisation. Some Nationalist proposals made chess-like diversionary moves with a puppet king; for example, Arthur Griffith, impressed by the case of Hungary and dual monarchy, wanted to offer the Crown of Ireland to a chosen member of the Austro-Hungarian royal family.[37] The Anglo-Irish would hardly be capable of such far-stretched elasticity. Sir Horace Plunkett represented a quite numerous type among the landed gentry, and we have seen that both Edith and Martin had already given allegiance to him. Plunkett founded the Irish Dominion League in 1919, but became a Free State Senator in 1922.

Both Boyle and Edith had described themselves as Nationalist, in that they thought Ireland a nation perfectly capable of self-government, and Westminster utterly incompetent in Ireland. The later sticking point for them both was the discarding of the oath of allegiance, to a king of the joint kingdoms. A letter to Hildegarde from Edith of 7 December 1921 describes Cameron's political transformation, which came in a reaction to a telegram from Boyle in London: 'Peace with Sinn Fein! God Save Ireland! ... The Chimp has now become an enthusiastic Sinn Feiner (having last summer been fighting tooth and nail with Boyle, as became a hot Ulsterian loyalist). I cannot account for the conversion, save that it has come on at a gallop since he discovered that Bertie Collins was a Sinn Fein policeman. At tea at Glen Barrahane, when Cameron trumpetted Boyle's telegram "God Save Ireland" etc. Mary snapped "I'm sure I hope he won't!" Mercifully tea and the Maddens supervened and the combat died down. They are both very silly and childish ... Men are singular beings I am glad I am not one of them.' Mary, Hugh's wife, like Hugh himself, was a diehard Unionist. The Treaty proved unacceptable to the Republicans, and caused a split that descended into the Irish Civil War. The Nationalist forces began to range up on two sides, the pro-Treaty Free State troops versus the Republicans.

As soon as Ethel Smyth made friends with Edith, she had taken over as her publicity manager, and with her contacts gave Edith tremendous help in showing her art work in London successfully. It was inevitable that the domineering Ethel would spread into all areas of Edith's life – and, networking from art into literature, that she would eventually come into conflict with Edith's literary agent Pinker. Edith was having difficulty in detaching herself from Pinker politely, and Pinker was quite clever enough not to lose this particular author, but he had to fight off Ethel. Muriel Currey's notes to her transcripts of Somerville diaries reveal that, by December of 1921, 'It is now obvious that the row with Pinker was brought about by E.S. who had a passion for quarrelling with people.' The particular row was over Pinker's claim of too large a share of any monies that might accrue from the proposed film or stage version of the RM. At the end of December, when Edith was making pastel designs for scenery, she 'Heard from Pinker announcing that he claimed £52.10 shillings for withdrawal of Dramatic Rights from him.' Ethel was delighted. The scenery designs give support to the theory that the Townshends and their Castle provided a major inspiration for the fictional demesne of Mrs Knox. Edith 'went to observe the Castle by moonlight for [the] scene at Aussolas.'[38] The peculiarly unreconstructed nature of Irish Big House domestic economy at this time is well brought out by a letter from Edith to her sister on the 28th: 'Ethel agrees with me that it is a wicked extravagance to have five women to attend to two people.'

The RM play was called *Flurry's Wedding*, and Edith worked at the script over Christmas and into the New Year. She wrote to her cousin Charlotte, Mrs George Bernard Shaw, to tell her about the play, and Charlotte had written back asking to read it, and to pass it on to GBS himself. At Drishane on 10 January 1922, Edith noted in her diary that she had heard from E.S. and 'wrote her a line' in response, never foreseeing her violence and impetuous reactions. Ethel had visited Edith's brother Boyle in London, to fulminate against Pinker's inability to represent Edith's interests with theatrical producers. Brother Cameron reported back to sister: 'She had been at Boyle's who said she was going out with a tomahawk to kill Pinker.' Wanting to discard him completely, Edith tried to discover how they had acquired Pinker in the first place. Her diary entry for 15 January gives: 'Hunted up old diaries to try and find the genesis of Pinker. Have failed – so far.' Edith took a lot of trouble to keep Hildegarde up to date in Alassio, and in a letter of 12 January identifies for her the coming men in Ireland, the 'tweenies':

> I think Griffith and Collins will make good, if only, *only*, they would put up men of education and integrity at the next election instead of these blathering asses. Men like O'Meara [doctor] and Gargan [bank manager] and Jasper Wolfe [solicitor] (since, I suppose, gentlemen will be barred – and the tweenies are really far cleverer than the Chimp and Charlie Morgan and you and me).

The play script had reached the Shaws and been read by both of them: her reaction was favourable, but his not. GBS saw the RM succeeding as radio rather than theatre, its humour being too broad for actual representation on stage. He sent a thoughtful and blunt criticism of the script on 20 January.

Like many storytellers and novelists of genius, you have no respect for the theatre and no knowledge of its limitations. Your imagination does not work in terms of the stage and its audience. You have always amused us by telling us stories about people whom we have never seen, and do not want to see, and about events which would be extremely alarming and disagreeable if we actually witnessed them ...

... You have not the double consciousness of the skilled playwright, who sees every incident with one eye in its natural light, and with the other as an effective stage contrivance.

But this is mere mechanism. Much more serious is your neglect of the cardinal fact that the stage greatly heightens the reality of the persons represented on it. It makes the *dramatis personae* not only more real than they are in the story, but more real than they are in life. Consequently you can bear incidents in stories, and in the life of your neighbours, which would revolt you in the theatre. Apply this to your play. As far as it has any thread at all it deals with the marriage of Flurry and Sally. That is to say, it proposes to entertain the spectators with the marriage of a decent young lady to a blackguardly horse thief, dirty and disorderly when not dressed up for some special occasion, unable to learn an honest living, and in no way distinguishable in culture, in morals, in interests, or in decency of language from the poorer rascals whom he orders about by virtue of the social position which he disgraces ...

You see, the play is abominably immoral at root. All through you are asking the audience to laugh at dirt, worthlessness, dishonesty and mischief for their own sakes. Also, you write like a lady in the worse sense of the word: that is, it never seems to occur to you that poor people are human beings. They are simply figures of fun to you ... The marriage of Flurry Knox to a gentlewoman might make a subject for Strindberg: it is not a subject nowadays for pleasantry ...you are wholly occupied with your story, and have no sense of its living atmosphere. That is quite fatal, not only in its direct effect, but because it enables you to go on and on without noticing that the people on the stage have no real humanity, and are mere mouthpieces for occasional funny remarks ...

I must not keep on lecturing and abusing you; but you had better get it straight between the eyes from me now than go through a long tragedy of hope deferred and final disappointment. I do not think there is any use your trying the theatre at all whilst you are in your present attitude towards it. You have been very badly brought up in some ways, as all we Irish people have been: we have trained ourselves to bear the dirt and ignorance and poverty of our unfortunate country by two villainous drugs: drink and derision ... Until you get away from all that ... stick to your pen and let the stage alone.

This, of course, is only my opinion; it can prevail with you only as far as you feel guilty ... Still, there is my opinion for what it is worth. Forgive me if you can.[39]

Edith's reaction to this letter, which would have destroyed a lesser woman, was quite straightforward and logical. She was astonished at Shaw's taking Flurry to heart: 'the play was *pour rire* and no one before has ever taken Flurry seriously as a degenerate and immoral horse thief', she expostulated to Ethel Smyth. Her own family contained the Flurry type within it; had not the English Emmie Sykes fallen for one, Edith's brother Aylmer Somerville, Drishane would never have staggered through all the troubles that befell it. Even to his earliest biographers, Shaw obviously had phobias about what he saw as deficiencies in the Irish character, and the tricky but attractive Flurry seemed to activate his own sexual hangups. Shaw longed for the time when 'life will be much happier and free from the revulsions of sex, which will become less tyrannous and finally have its reproductive function fulfilled in a less unpresentable way.'[40] Accepting his authoritative advice on her play, Edith wrote to Hildegarde about Shaw's letter: 'I am sorry to say he does worse than criticize – He absolutely condemns and gives what seem like unfortunately good reasons for condemnation ... In fact, if he is right, the play is hopeless. He ends his letter – which is kind and straightforward, and *not in the very least* offensive or rude – by saying that the oldest theatre-men make mistakes and are proved wrong by events, but he gives me his opinion. He can't do more and I am very grateful to him for being honest ... Anyhow it hasn't wasted much time, and was interesting to do.'[41]

To Shaw himself Edith wrote a letter of thanks: 'Your long letter came yesterday, and I have read it several times and each time with a deeper sense of gratitude to you for having taken so much trouble and written me such a valuable exposition of the Art of the Theatre. It is quite true that you *have* hit me pretty hard and straight between the eyes, but I know that the wounds of a friend are faithful ...on the matter of my characters. We may be very immoral Irish people, but we are all very much attached to Flurry and think he would make an excellent husband! ... please believe that I am *most sincerely* grateful to you and deeply recognise the value of all you say, as well as your great kindness in saying it to one who has "rushed in" where she should have feared to tread.'[42]

Edith began to cut the script at Shaw's suggestion. Pinker eased the situation by going to New York on business. Here he caught pneumonia and died. His death notice in *The Times* was read by Edith in Drishane on 4 February. For all her long connection, and her smooth, apparently personal way with thanks and generosity, which we can see in the easy tone of her letters to him, he was not a friend, only a necessary business aide. With that detached crushing coldness that Ethel Smyth was too long in apprehending, she wrote in her diary: 'Am relieved to think that the impending row with him has thus been averted.' She was able to detach herself from Pinker's son Eric, the successor in the agency, with little difficulty.

She had crossed to England again on 6 February to be with GBS and his wife Charlotte, at Ayot St Lawrence. Here further re-shaping of the script took place; with the new version she then went on to Ethel Smyth's sister's house, Hill Hall at Theyden Bois, where she read it aloud. In spite of all the re-working and criticism by experienced hands, when she sent the script to Nigel Playfair at the Lyric Theatre, Hammersmith, he did not like it and turned it down 'unconditionally'. Not too down-hearted, she set about another re-write. On 24 March she wrote to Hildegarde describing a tea party at the Ritz at which she met Admiral Adare, a cousin of Martin's friend Nora Tracey: 'He is an appallingly, quietly implacable Ulsterman, who would – I *almost* believe – justify this last dreadful slaughter of a whole family in Belfast. He said: "You know I'm a Die-hard". I said that *we* in the South would be the ones who would die hard if they break the treaty. I have never before met a genuine Die-hard, and I don't want to meet any more. It was rather awful to see a charming, gentle-mannered creature so fanatically implacable. Even horrible ...'[43]

Edith met up with Lady Kenmare, who gave her the news from Kerry. There had been a strike by farm workers on the Kenmare estate, who had staged a mass walk-out, leaving the animals in their care to suffer. Edith was pleased at the efficiency of the Dáil officials who came to arbitrate: they 'were *excellent*. Having gone into all details, they summoned the strikers and gave them a regular blowing up and said they were the best treated men in Ireland and hadn't a leg to stand on! And they have now gone back to work – ungrateful brutes – but pardon was practically compulsory (tho' flogging is too good for men who could leave cows unmilked for 24 hours and horses and pigs unfed or watered for 2 days!).'[44]

Edith's diary shows that she still revelled in the social life that she experienced when she was 'tied to the chariot wheels' of Ethel Smyth. On 30 March she attended the opening of Ethel's *Bosun's Mate* and went to the celebratory dinner at the Ritz afterwards. Here she talked to Lord French about Uncle

Kendal, who had been a friend when they were in the Army together, and was placed beside Maurice Baring ('very pleasant') at the table, who was much taken with *An Enthusiast*. Having been worried about the reception of the book by Catholics, she had been cheered by a long letter from Bertie Windle from Canada, who had also read it: 'Well my dear twin I congratulate you on this book ... no question it will live for it is a living picture of a time and as such it becomes history.' Bertie was naturally still bitter about his deposition from the university in Cork three years before; this is reflected in his comments on Edith's fine descriptions of the Irish landscape: 'why should every prospect please and only man be vile ...'[45]

She returned to CT on 11 April, where, on the 16th, she had tea with Jem Barlow and did automatic writing for 'the first time for exactly five months'. This was a new development. Martin's niece Muriel Currey had an interest in the timing of the phases of Edith's own automatic writing in pursuit of a publishable text, compared to the short writing that eventually she did every day as a form of remembrance, which she could do without a medium present. It was rare for her not to enter three or four lines, as a daily discipline, sometimes expanding into a rambling remembrance of a shared experience. But mostly they are formulaic, repeated over and over again, and resemble shouted greetings between friends who pass one another on either side of a congested road. Ethel Smyth looked askance at these writings when they were received in her home at Woking, and had conceived the idea that she was in competition for Edith's attention with a powerful ghost. When Edith was travelling with friends, or staying with her brothers in London, there was no extensive automatic writing, but when she returned to life at Drishane and a routine of work in the Studio, automatic writing became a natural exercise in that place. It was a way of providing the habitual counterbalancing voice, without which Edith felt unable to write at all. On 23 April Edith wrote with Jem again in the Studio: 'M. having impressed on Jem that she wanted to do so. Very much better than last time.'

At the end of April she began a list in her diary of the eighteen country houses in the neighbourhood burnt or abandoned. As Protestant landlords had been murdered, it was thought that Cameron's life was in such danger that he was persuaded by his sister to go to Switzerland and join Hildegarde. Forgetting Mrs Lindsay, Edith persisted in believing that the Republicans would not deliberately shoot women. She and Hildegarde began to write to each other in 'dog French' as their mail was intercepted. On 16 May, in the sisters' first letter in 'dog French', Edith told Hildegarde that Maurice Townshend of the Castle, then living at Shepperton, had been threatened. Raiders had come to Shepperton House looking for arms. When Maurice told them there were none in the house, the raiders told him at gunpoint to go down on his knees and swear that there were none. Here Maurice on the spur of the moment did a very bold thing: he made a savage joke. As he went on to his knees, he said: 'Can't I tell a lie as well on my knees as I can standing up?' He had found the right tone for the unusual Irish social occasion, and survived.[46]

When Cameron had gone the raiders became bolder. On 5 May Glen Barrahane was entered and Egerton's studio sacked. Refusing to show to the village that she was in any way alarmed, Edith carried on as usual and painted out of doors, in the bluebell woods. Her spirits were high, her humour unaffected. She had been left the extra duty of walking Cameron's dog, Elgar. She wrote to Hildegarde on the 16th: 'Tell Cameron that if he finds Elgar like a pillowcase filled with at least 600 lbs of tea, it won't be my fault. She *won't* come for walks unless I drag her till I think her head will come off...nothing will get her to move as fast as an invalid slug. She may be a great musician but she is a very bad accompanist.'

Undeterred by the state of the country, Ethel Smyth appeared for a 'holiday' on 19 May. She found Drishane an excellent place to work, for no-one could interrupt her here. She carried with her the early drafts of her *Fête Galante*, on which she worked while Edith wrote at her play. They talked and argued when they took breaks from work to drive in the trap or walk. Ethel left on 1 June. While travelling on the journey back she picked up some information about anti-Irish prejudice. The moment she got home, always thrilled by controversy and contradiction, she wrote to Edith 'to say Irish plays and players were in black books in England and quite out of favour'. With Hildegarde still recuperating in Switzerland and Cameron packed off to safety with her, Edith spent the month of June running the farm and making all safe. She feared a coming battle between the two parties in the army of Ireland during which the Big Houses would become fortresses for one or the other party, a premonition in which she was proved right. Assisted by her right-hand-woman Mrs Kisby, one of Edith's first moves was to select all of Egerton's best canvases and hide them, sandwiched between rugs and carpets, on the locked dining room floor of Glen Barrahane. She collected the most precious Coghill items, like Nevill Coghill's Zulu War VC, and hid them in her Studio.[47] She sold some cows, and in a development that was to prove valuable to them in the imminent desert crossing for Ireland's farmers, Edith was contacted by the Rineen Creamery for milk supplies.

Less hardy CT residents were not digging in; they were moving out, she told Hildegarde: 'Percy wrote to me this morning saying that he is going to clear out and "shut up" Red House until (if ever) better times come. A bad loss in all ways. Comprehensible, but, I think, rather narrow minded. But you can't deny the sense of it, and in his case, the justification. Not for us, our duty is here. I am sure of that. We owe Ireland nearly 300 good years and must try and "stick it" and hope for luck.' Sylvia Townshend Gorges, too, wanted to go, and put Tally Ho up for rent. It was the time of year when Edith and Egerton had customarily painted outdoors together. Oppressed by memories, Edith wrote to Hildegarde, who had started automatic writing with her sister's encouragement: 'If Egerton gives you any message for me I know you will give it to me. Tell him I miss him, now in this time of painting *more* than I can say. Going in on Sunday after church to see his sketch of the moment, and showing him mine. Well. My love to him, and to you, Your loving Edith.'[48] Making her own stretchers, Edith was painting on the backs of the old Glen B sea charts, made of linen, and was delighted with the working surface.

Hildegarde's assets were being stripped bare for death duties on Egerton's estate; in future, her income from letting Glen Barrahane was to be of the greatest importance to her, and the success of her herd. On the 16th she wrote to tell her sister that the Aylmer brothers were emptying the Red House: 'Mr Madden says that he thinks this resolve, which is quite against Eddy's wishes, is the result of typhoid ... Percy's isn't *personal* panic ... he assures us that his heart is breaking, but as Isobel [Mrs Chavasse] said, with great determination, he's breaking it himself.' Later in the month Edith was approached by a villager wanting to buy back family lands. As it was necessary to keep this to themselves, and letters were being opened before reaching their destination, she used French to write to Hildegarde: 'Il m'avait donne une grande histoire ... et qu'il veut bien reprendre "la terraine de ces ancêtres!" ... il disait que *cette* maison [Drishane] serait brûlee il y a longtemps si ses parens et amis ne l'avaient pas "protégée". C'est tres probable. ... [he offered a sum] Qu'en pense tu? ... J'aime bien ce viellard, et s'il faut vendre, je veux bien lui donner le préférence.'[49] In her absence the bull that only Hildegarde could manage, Dutch Count, was grumpily misbehaving, and had killed a calf: 'Barter said it was "in jelly, all its bones broken".'

On election day, 16 June, which was 'peaceable, friendly and orderly', Edith had been pleased to see no hint of intimidation or coercion. She wrote in the evening to Hildegarde to persuade her to persist in trying to communicate with Egerton. It is clear from this letter that, for success, the presence of Jem Barlow as a medium was very necessary. Edith on her own could not succeed in receiving words direct from Martin: 'Sometimes, but only in isolated sentences M can write alone with me, automatically; she [M] has constantly implored me to "believe" and not distrust as it increases the difficulty so much. Often the "gibberish" or unreadable writing is the result of *her* failure to concentrate. I fancy it is a difficult affair, more so, practically, for them than it is, morally, for us.'

On 27 June Hildegarde first invented the dog-French word for overdraft: 'sur-courant d'air'. Edith replied: 'This is your masterpiece, and, in having

grasped your meaning, I think I proved myself worthy of it.' In the same letter
Edith characterises herself, justly, as 'La Reine de Stopgaps'. Royal Navy destroyers
began to patrol the coast to give support to isolated and endangered Protestant
landlords. Edith's brother, Admiral Hugh Somerville, was appointed the senior
officer commanding at Haulbowline naval base, the last to serve in that post
before it was transferred to Free State control. The destroyers took mails and
landed parties of men to patrol and protect houses where necessary. Ship to
shore signals ensured that any emergency on land could be dealt with quickly.
Ethel Smyth was safely away again and back in England when what Edith
called 'The battle of Skib' began on 3 July. Sixty Free State troops in the police
barracks were attacked by 'three or four regiments of Republicans, I stayed
about the place all day waiting for possible refugees wanting shelter.' A Republican
garrison was set up in the Castletownshend coastguard station. Edith wrote to
Hildegarde via Hugh's destroyer: 'So far all is peace here, our Republican garrison
are kept in order by Conny Buckley, and are very civil to Hal [Chavasse], with
whom they are constantly in touch over Glen B. Conny (our shield and Buckley-
er) has been promoted to Lissard [seat of The O'Donovan] but he still bosses
the gang here. As Boyle said "These IRA boys here are 'On the Fencibles'" and,
I think, harmless. I only hope they will not be removed, as the Skibbereen
invading gang are brutes from Kerry and Limerick, devoid of decency or
honesty.'[50] This letter shows that an important and logical move had been made
by the Republican command in moving men from Kerry to Cork and vice versa,
so that the problems arising out of sympathy between tenants or servants and
their old employers were thus avoided – attacks on unknown persons in
unknown houses presenting fewer crises over recognition and betrayal.

Edith went in to her bank in Skibbereen and was shown over the damaged
town by her bank manager, Mr Gargan. A neighbour, also at the bank, Miss
Ogilvy, who was 'black with rage', was infuriated: 'The scum of the earth! They
have the town swept! Grocers, drapers, *every* shop, looted and nothing paid
for!' But Edith knew from Mrs Twomey, a refugee from the West in CT with
relatives, that Skibbereen had escaped lightly compared to Limerick, which had
been 'pillaged', with much loss of life: 'Mrs Twomey said that a poor little nun
who had just come back from Ypres, was shot dead on her own doorstep
(unintentionally) and nine or ten men were killed in her own street.' Edith
explained to Hildegarde that the violence done in the name of the Republicans
was causing such revulsion that ordinary people were hastily coming to terms
with the Free State: 'One good thing that these blackguards have done is that
they have turned all waverers into firm Free Staters.'[51]

In June, Edith heard that more horse raids were being made by the
Republicans, and she had to hide her valuable mare Tara at the back of the

Mall House. Mike was able to get Tara safely away to England later in the month. On 6 July Cameron was dropped back in CT by a destroyer, but this was far too soon to be safe, as he was thus in the village when a major Republican attack took place on 31 July. Edith described this dreadful day in a long and vivid letter to Hildegarde that was copied by many members of her family:

> During the night of the thirtieth large motors with about a dozen IRA came to re-inforce the seven men at the coastguard station. After breakfast today we were told that all the workmen and farmers, etc. from the country round had been 'commandeered' to help to destroy the ferry boat quay, 'Sir Joscelyn's Quay' and the Castle Bathing house landing place.
>
> (This explained why three of the men went to the farm two days ago and took cross cut saws, crowbars and pickaxes.) The idea being to prevent Free State troops from landing – as if this could prevent them! Hearing that boats were being taken Cameron went down at once to put mine in safety, and I followed and told Johnny Leary to do the same with yours. Hal telephoned to Cam to come and put gravel that had recently been landed on Ferry Quay into safety (It is for the waterworks [filterbed]). When Cameron got there, three IRA with loaded rifles were on guard over the workers; at intervals others marched in with more 'pressed' workers. At the Castle bathing house more IRA, under command of 'Captain Z' were superintending the destruction of the sea wall (facing east) and two of the small elm trees were being cut down 'to block boats coming alongside' which boats never do! It was intended to cut the whole row of trees. A good deal of the end of the Ferry pier had been destroyed and was being thrown in the water when a boat was seen coming at full speed. In it was the little R.C. curate, Father Lambe. As soon as he was in shouting distance, he began to denounce the destroyers. 'Stop that Devil's work! You have ruined the land, breaking roads and bridges! You shall not ruin the sea! My people shall not starve!'
>
> Before the boat was alongside, he leapt ashore, dashed up the slip and sprang like a wildcat at the throat of the biggest of the three armed guards. Father L. is a little fellow, aged about 30, in height *at most* 5ft 5ins; he looks less than 10 stone but he is tremendously wiry and athletic. The man he attacked went down like a ninepin. He was a big, lubberly boy of 19, and while Father Lambe tore at his rifle to get it from him, he lay on the ground, feebly protesting 'No Father! No Father!' One of the guards rushed to the Castle to summon their leader, the other rushed to the Coastguard Station to bring up the rest of the gang. Father L. transfigured by passion, with a dead white face and his very big, light blue

eyes blazing, ordered the wreckers to throw down their tools and go home at once. Then he caught the second in command, a burly young fellow by the throat and dashed his head against the wall, and, in the narrow lane leading to the street he met the big 'Captain' (a huge young man) and stormed abuse and denunciation of the wickedness they were committing. Meanwhile the wretched workers, thankful for release, hurried away up the hill and gathered in a knot outside J.H's public house. It was at this point that I arrived with Jem Barlow at the Two Trees. Just as she and I got there, two IRA dashed past at full speed on their way to the CG Station. A crowd of village people were standing at the Two Trees and in highest excitement they told us that 'the priest had stopped the work and was below'. ... in about three or four minutes we heard rifle shots from the CG Station and then we saw about a dozen IRA running along the Mall, one of them firing his rifle into the air every few yards. When they got to the corner and saw the group of workers standing at H's door they began to yell imprecations and filthy names 'Go back ye - ! Go back to your work ye -- !' The group fled down the hill again, the IRA howling after them, running as fast as they could, I saw a little sickly boy of about 15 or 16 (who had come to me to demand my pony and trap the night before and hadn't got it) racing and howling with them.

They had got about half way down the hill when I saw a little bare headed black figure dash round the corner by the schoolhouse and charge up the hill into the teeth of the oncoming crowd. The fleeing workers checked their flight, separating, and leaving the Priest face to face with the IRA pursuers. He charged on shouting, and to our incredulous amazement, the twelve armed men turned as one and bolted back up the hill! They fled into the public house and the little Priest turned and bolted in after them like a terrier after rabbits (I have since heard that he rushed upstairs and caught 2 of them in Mrs H's bedroom and there and then smashed their rifles!) in what seemed less than a minute we saw him burst out of the house with a rifle in his hand. Big Jim Z had got up by this time and forced his way thro' the throng and faced him. Father L. swung his fist round and with a jump caught him heavily on the side of the head. Jim Z made no return. Then the Priest broke through the encircling people into the middle of the road. He tore the cartridges out of the magazine of the rifle and then catching it by the barrel he whirled it over his head and with a few furious blows he smashed the stock and lock on the road and bent the barrels – no one dared go near him, He was like a creature possessed – this ended the fighting. They all trooped off, Father L in the middle of them, to the CG Station. In about an hour we got a message that Father Lambe had gathered a dozen or so of the decent men of the parish to back him and was going to burn down the Station! We knew this would mean the inevitable occupation of Glen Barrahane and Cosheen and I hurried down to protest. We found a big pow-wow proceeding down at Cosheen gate. As we came up Jim Brown said 'I object to the presence of Colonel Somerville!' The priest said 'I don't want Colonel Somerville or any other Colonels here! This is *my* business!' C and I retired at once. Afterwards we heard what had happened. Father L. had begun by marching with his own party into the guardroom and seizing 4 rifles. He said 'Now. If you won't listen to me and obey me I'll shoot one of you. You can shoot me then if you like but I'll shoot one of you first.' He pulled out his watch. 'I'll give you five minutes to make up your minds to quit this place ... if you won't do it, I'll shoot!'[52]

Edith's admiration for Father Lambe never faltered; in the years that followed they were to become good friends. Catholic priests were forbidden to take part in any political acts, and so for his pains on this day he was transferred to a remote parish, Sherkin Island, off Baltimore. He did not lose touch with his old parish, often re-visited, and returned to it as parish priest at the end of his working life. He was to spend so much time with Edith in her last months, in fact, rallying her and telling her stories to amuse her, that her sister and her niece Katharine Coghill in particular began to fear that Edith would convert to Catholicism under his influence. He did have a great influence over all the residents of Castletownshend as a result of his bravery. Edith's account of his action ends: 'They gave in. They all promised "to give up politics" (this was how it was told to me) and to go to their homes. And they went ...'

Despite Father Lambe, marauding Republicans from other areas continued to make bold raids in the village. According to her diary, on 4 August Edith and Jem were playing croquet at Drishane when two young men with guns appeared on the lawn beside them: 'two of the "Army" came and demanded my pony. Had to let him go.' To Hildegarde and Edith the situation seemed only capable of deterioration: more and more precious belongings were sent off by destroyer to be stored by Hugh in the Naval quarters at Haulbowline. On 8 August the CT coastguard station was burned to the ground, and that night there was a fierce battle: 'Firing, apparently near Lissard, began at dark and is going on now.' The Royal Navy destroyers took mails and delivered them, and some emergency passengers. On a letter from Edith to Boyle on 12 August 1922 Hugh has written across the top: 'This came open for us to read. "Classic" is running so you can come over easy. Thanks for your letter, love to Mab. Yours,

Hugh.' Edith wrote below to Boyle explaining that they were all getting accustomed to the 'Tristan da Cunha existence' and describing some of the acts of destruction carried out by the Republicans: 'We all now regard the Free State troops as our saviours ... the hope is that a great many ex-officers have volunteered, and a leaven of gentlemen may save the lump. I am afraid I will never again have the feeling for Ireland that I once had. The cruelties and barbarisms of the Republicans match the Russians and Germans. I couldn't have believed that Irishmen would have behaved as they have. Thank God, we only know of these things by hearsay, but the horrors that have taken place elsewhere while these *gorilla* (not guerilla) troops have been in power make one ashamed to call oneself Irish.'[53] This was not an admission that Edith would make to Ethel Smyth, for throughout this period she upheld the independent Irish cause against Ethel's intemperate attacks. We can hardly be surprised at the change of spelling from 'guerilla' to 'gorilla', for after Deirdre's first escape when she was taken for the second time, Notebook 10 tells us of her death and that her back was broken by unskilled rough-riders continually putting the strong little mare over high fences.

Edith was relieved that they were able to keep paying the wages of the men from the dairy income. Cameron was now the chairman of the Skibbereen branch of the Farmers' Union, and more moderate nationalists were keen to incorporate him into the workings of local affairs, almost as though he had been taking notes to study for the part of Dan Palliser in *An Enthusiast*. On 22 August when Cameron was in Skibbereen with Edith, he was taken to meet Michael Collins. Edith described the meeting to Hildegarde on the 24 August, after Collins had been assassinated:

> I need hardly say how shattered every person and thing is by the murder of Michael Collins. C and I, by curious chance, had just driven into Skib., when an armoured car came tearing up the main Street, followed by a huge motor full of F.S. troops, and then 2 smaller cars. We went on up Bridge Street and saw the cortege pulled up at the Eldon, and just then met Mrs Gargan who said 'Michael Collins has just come to town! He's in at the Eldon [Hotel], and Joe is there!' (of course 'Joe' is always at the heart of the situation). I was *dying* to go in myself to see the creature, but I heroically refrained and sent C in instead. Callaghan the schoolteacher and Sheehy [editor, *Cork County Eagle*] were there and they instantly introduced C as a friend of the Free State. C was very favourably impressed. He said Collins had a sincere look, and a straightforward manner and spoke sensibly and simply saying it would be 2 months before the country was quiet. I had a brief sight of him as they

whirled away and thought him a fine looking man and he looked pleasant and pleased by the ridiculous squeals and yells that was the best Skib. could raise in the way of a cheer. I expect you know – or will know – more than we as to the details of his murder. I hear that he was to have met de V. today at Kinsale, and they were to have patched up a peace. If this is true then MC was less sincere than he looked.

Lismore Castle and Strancally went up in flames, like Mitchelstown and Aghada; a rare letter survives that was written by Edith to her Twin Ethel Penrose from the end of August 1922, deploring the burnings, and sending a signal of support and solidarity. As the Devonshires' agents, Ethel and Jimmy were in their persons prime targets for attack: 'The Republicans in burning houses have also burned their boats, and are more hated than Cromwell was! They couldn't have taken a better way of booming the Free State!' Edith told Ethel how she was managing. She had a much loved workman at this time, a carpenter called Swaddling with beautiful manners; he was about the place keeping her in good heart, and there were regular visits from the 'tweenies'. Mr Gargan of the Bank came to tea, 'and for an optimistic man, was distinctly blue. Michael Collins was a real loss, he says, apart from being a fetish, he was able and sincere. He died like a man, anyhow. Mr Gargan says Alderman Cosgrove is a good man and unprejudiced and ready to use the best tool regardless of its religion or politics ... When (or if) you ever write to me again you might give me an idea of your plans for the winter – I would *not* advise this place Good bye my dear – good luck – tell me how you are when you write – much love – ever thy Twin.'[54]

The empty Glen Barrahane was ransacked on 8 September. Not admitting outwardly that she was distracted, Edith worked at the manuscript of her second memoir, *Wheeltracks*. Both mistress and groom decided to chance their arms when Mike heroically succeeded in taking a horse to Cork and shipping her to England. Edith wrote to Hildegarde on the 14th: '... things go storming on. Free Staters up one day, Rebels the next ... I have had a most *straining* three days since Sunday when Mike and Lady Day [a young mare] set forth by road to Cork. No word from him was possible, but I am thankful to say at 10 o'clock last night he walked in! He had had an appalling time. Arrested as a Republican by Free Staters in Bandon – only by chance found a man to bail him out and rescue the mare – Then narrowly escaped Repubs. between Bandon and Cork and had to ford rivers and jump fallen trees, and scramble in and out of trenches, or cross country with this *quarter*-trained little mare! ... He has just been talking to me, with absolute horror he says we have *no* idea here of the conditions in this county in this comparatively quiet place, of what it is like

from Bandon onwards. "Desperate, Miss, Desperate!" Shootings, robbings –
Horses worth £300 stolen and battered about, and sold anywhere and anyhow
– well – It is no good ullagoning [bewailing] – we must go on in faith.'

On 29 September there was an attempted raid on Drishane by armed men,
but Cameron spoke to them from an upper window and they did not breach the
lower shuttered ones. Cameron then signalled to the destroyer from Edith's
room, and men came up to the house via the Dutchman's Cove in about fifteen
minutes. Edith telephoned Seafield but got no answer. There was no answer
because the Chavasses were being raided at gunpoint at the time. Later in the
night, at about three in the morning Edith was woken by a thump. She picked
up her hunting crop and crept to Cameron's room. He was not in his bed. She
then heard someone coming up the main staircase towards her. 'I whistled very
softly and Cameron answered (it was pitch dark) "It's all right" The destroyer
lookout had seen what he had taken for an alarm light from Drishane and some
men had come up to check that Cameron was all right. They had broken in
through the greenhouse door, making the thump that had woken Edith.

Edith described the scene to Hildegarde by letter, and stressed the effectiveness
of the destroyers offshore as a safety measure. 'I may here say that men are so
deadly afraid of admitting anxiety "No panic, please!" that they neglect obvious
precautions. Only that I had *charged* Cameron to explain to this new destroyer
("Leamington") our system of signals, when he went to call, he wouldn't have
done so, and it was *my* suggestion (with the "Newark") that we could and
should have a code of signalling, and that they should anchor in view of our
windows. I have no doubt this was considered suitably ladylike nervousness! It
was mere common sense as has since been proved ... It is on a par with the way
that almost any man will wander miles out of his way in London rather than
ask for information ...'[55]

On 4 October she heard from Frances Perkins in London that Kinkie had
recovered from a serious operation: 'I have been thinking of Kinkie every day
and longing to have news of her and it was an immense relief to hear that her
trouble was over and well over.' Edith went on to explain that all letters were
read by the censors and how difficult their isolation was to bear: 'we are kept
socially alive by the necessity of being civil to the Destroyers (I don't mean the
home-grown ones – the R.N. variety ...' The CT village shops were raided on 5
October. On the 18th, Edith wrote to Hildegarde to tell her that another batch
of possessions had been safely got off to the destroyer from Dutchman's Cove,
by herself and Mrs Kisby and a donkey cart on land and Hugh waterborne in a
tender. 'Such a job!' They had been accompanied by Cameron: 'Chimpan so
reactionary and difficulty-making that I was ready to slaughter him. He is more
devoid of initiative than any old snail – He can't suggest, and in consequence

tries to keep his end up by hindering (his hinder end!) O for one hour of Boyle or Jack or yourself!' She insists that Hildegarde should not think of returning to Glen Barrahane as yet, as there was 'no need to have more in the Soup than is necessary.'

While Hildegarde was away, Edith kept her informed on the running of their joint farm. It was under control: all the corn was brought in safe, there were twenty 'infant pigs' that were sold to the destroyer cooks for £7. 11 shillings apiece according to weight. Edith had given the go-ahead to convert the old hound kennels into a piggery. The creamery had brought in £22 for the month. Nelson's sales of *Mount Music* in a two-shilling edition to her relief brought Edith £150, 'and I am almost out of overdraft!' Thieves and armed burglars roamed the district in the wake of Republican and Free State troops: 'the rather hopeless thing is the endless ties binding the two parties together – brothers, cousins, etc. also the want of discipline resulting from the utter commonness of the officers. However, I think there *is* a certain improvement and you can assure all the old diehards, beginning with that pea green irreconcilable, Master Jack, that nothing would induce me to let you come if I thought there was the faintest personal danger'.

Her diary on 3 November records her work at a chapter on Irish hunting for a book called *Ireland a Nation*: this was a volume that was originally to have been sponsored by the Free State, an arrangement that fell through.[56] The disturbed state of the countryside, with bridges and roads damaged and unusable, meant that there could be no official movement or traffic in livestock. Other Holstein/Friesian breeders like Marion Gubbins at Dunkettle were in the same predicament as the sisters with their herd, for want of fresh bulls. They were forced to keep breeding from Classmate. The Ponsonbys' Castlemartyr herd manager made an abortive attempt to exchange their bull with Classmate. One of the CT heifers, a close relation of Classmate, was put to him but, Edith told Hildegarde, 'didn't hold to him, (wh. is said to be the result of too close relationship, amazing tho' it seems) and I could *not* sanction alliances with cad-bulls – better that they should take the veil. We have sold about £100 of meat and potatoes to the ships ...' Few tenants were to be found now, and gentry households ran on the tightest economy using the most basic household equipment. All the silver of Drishane and Glen Barrahane was stored in plate-chests with the Navy. The Coghill family was in turmoil with legal difficulties over the complications of the entail after Egerton's death, and these now became more complex. Less than a year later, his brother Claude Coghill suddenly died at Athboy: 'It is too sad to think of Joe, the best play-boy in the world, out of it.' After telling Hildegarde that she often recalled 'his delightful absurdities', almost her next thought was to induce his widow Maud to take the Mall

House, but Maud stayed in Meath; she had £800 a year and a mind of her own.[57]

At the beginning of 1923, Bertie Windle sent his Dictionary of National Biography article on Martin to Edith for her approval. She didn't like it and re-wrote it, writing to the DNB editor to explain what she was doing.[58] She was completing *Wheeltracks*, intending to take the MS with her to Mr Longman in March. Over the years, the sisters moved back and forth across the channel separately, trying to arrange their trips so that there was always one of them in charge of the farm. A letter to Hildegarde of 13 January asked her if, when she returned from Switzerland, she would take Boyle and Mab at Glen B in the autumn: 'Cameron is fearfully keen that if Raymond is to succeed him he should not do so as an almost total stranger to the place and people (as he is now) and a stranger who, after his horrible Dublin experiences, most likely hates Ireland!' This was in fact the case, though it was many years before Raymond was able to say so. Cameron had placed Raymond in his own regiment, the King's Own Lancaster, in which he served through the war from his twenty-first to his twenty-fifth year, winning an MC. He retired from the army having been badly wounded.

There was an added difficulty in that since his retirement Cameron, installed as Master of Drishane, had adapted in an over-positive manner to being in charge of it rather than Kneller Hall. This affected his behaviour towards his brothers, with whom he had been accustomed to dealing only on light-hearted leaves for half a century. Edith wrote to Hildegarde on 22 January: 'It seems to me that there is considerable danger in leaving Cameron and Jack alone here with no-one to mitigate their *a deux*-ness ... Cameron gets very dictatorial and silly with his younger brothers (I have known it with Boyle) and he and Jack are such good friends that it would be a great pity, as a row would never be quite got over. Either you or I could avert this, so I trust that it may be possible for one of us to be here. If you mention this, do so on a separate sheet.' Edith thought of Hildegarde as the best type of buffer-state, 'better than I, being bigger and kinder.' Edith was careful in handling 'personalities'; she told Hildegarde at this time, for example, about Ethel Smyth: 'don't bring her to your present hostess as they do *not* amalgamato ...' Jack had succeeded Cameron as commandant of the Army School of Music at Kneller Hall, and at this stage they were referred to as 'the past and present Commandants'.

Edith found herself keeping a watch on her eldest brother's activities. Cameron, 'very shuffling and secret', had gone behind Edith's back and sold all the larches in kennel wood to a dealer, Grady, who had rooked him. 'If only he hadn't been born on a Friday and was a little less "loving and giving" it would have been so much better for him!' Her own decisiveness was quite unabated.

Her letters to Hildegarde show how the entry on Martin Ross that appeared under Bertram Windle's name in the *Dictionary of National Biography* was recast. He had sent his 800-word draft to Edith on 8 January 1923. 'He was short on facts and engulphed her in a "Whirlpool of Relations" and left her out. Worked at it all day, and wrote another one, using all of his that was to the point,' she wrote in her diary.

On 1 February Marion Gubbins and Hildegarde after many years of service were elected to the committee of the Munster Show, having been proposed by Cameron and Edith, only as a form of protest, not expecting them to succeed. Edith had not expected the electors to 'have so much sense'. The fox terriers of Glen Barrahane and Drishane, fixated on the sisters as they were, unhesitatingly gave birth in their adoptive mother's bed depending on which sister was away. Quite unexpectedly, a new litter of Folly's puppies had to be cared for, so Edith delayed going to her publisher in London. There was much to discuss: on the 2nd, 'Heard from Mr Longman suggesting an edition de luxe of our books'. The 15-volume edition was to cost 10 guineas. The manuscript of *Wheeltracks* was ready, finished on 6 February. She waited for Hildegarde to return and replace her as dog over-Mother: 'the poor little doglings – to whom you must be as a nursing mother – They cleave to me by day and night.' This comfortable familiarity with the process of reproduction gained through dogs and the home farm proved an unexpected boon. Breeding animals were keeping the sisters off the rocks of bankruptcy. They were astonished at the success of their pig-breeding scheme which earned them at this point £60 a month: 'I only wish we had started when I had to sell the poor hounds.'[59] After Egerton's death, the sisters grew closer together as a unit running the farm, with Cameron, only a nominal partner in it, more concerned with the grounds and gardening than with heavy agriculture.

It is curious to see how Ethel Smyth tried to place herself in relation to the sisters. At first she made the ill-judged move of talking about them to each other, then reporting back to the other sister. We find repercussions such as this from Edith to Hildegarde of 14 February 1923: '*Slanderer*! You told E.S. I spoilt the puppies and that they were selfish and venal! Liar *and* slanderer! They are far better little dogs than Folly who is a complete "eye-service dog", greedy, self-seeking and secretly wicked.' What was more, Hildegarde's Folly had bitten Edith's Taspy in the throat; but Ethel would never divide and conquer the sisterhood. Leaving Hildegarde in charge, Edith was in London from 2 March. She dealt with Mr Longman, stayed with Ethel and dined with the Asquiths on the 14th, meeting at this exclusive politician's dinner Oswald and Cynthia Mosley, who were, she thought 'the only white people' there. On the next day Lady Kenmare arranged a luncheon for her to meet Eddy Marsh, Edmund

Gosse and Desmond MacCarthy, all 'highly agreeable'. As a replacement for
Pinker, she now took advice from Mr Thring at the Society of Authors. She was
back in CT on the 20th. A week later, in preparation for the change of hands to
Free State naval ratings at Haulbowline, the destroyer Seawolf 'dumped Glen B
and Drishane plate chests' back where they came from. On 6 February Edith
wrote to her sister that Sir Horace Plunkett's house at Kilteragh was burned:
'Poor Sir Horace's lovely house has been my last straw on an already swollen
hump. Of all the men in Ireland to attack! The only one in all Ireland's history
to do her any real practical service!' After this Sir Horace left Ireland.

On 1 April Admiral Hugh Somerville stood down as the last British naval
officer commanding at Haulbowline, which then passed into the hands of the
Irish Free State. The destroyers offshore were dismissed from their Irish coastal
stations. As upright and courageous as his brother Boyle, Hugh had coolly gone
out in a launch to dismantle a boom and blockade of the sea entry to Castlehaven,
being shot at throughout the operation. Back in CT the inhabitants of Drishane
and Glen Barrahane hardly knew what to expect next, now bereft of their
friendly destroyers and quite unable to believe that there would ever be a Free
State alternative to the British Navy. On 2 April, 'Two "Republicans" came and
demanded "dog tax"! Nevill saw them and had to pay four shillings each dog,
to save them from being shot – as was done to Cobbler, Beamish's dog, when he
would not pay.'[60] During the month Edith made selections from her forthcoming memoir for printing in *Time and Tide*, a remunerative form of advance
publicity. Her relationship with Ethel Smyth had passed through its stormiest
period and had settled into a friendship; Louise Collis describes this friendship
as coming with Ethel's realisation that Edith was incapable of altering her
profound belief that love was 'elevated and purified, rather than diminished, by
the absence of sexual expression and Ethel could not persuade her otherwise'.[61]
A stray letter survives from Edith to Ethel written on 7 April 1923: 'You are
absolutely free of family ties. Your family and you love each other, I know,
probably as much as we and ours do but you ... need only consider yourself,
your work, your artistic engagements. You are not tied up with your people in
a hundred little ways (which you may not believe in, but which nevertheless
exist, and are far more intricate and binding than the big ones). You have a
house of your own and are beholden in no way to anyone. It is a splendid
position and I often wish it were mine. But it never was, nor ever will be, so
there is no use talking about it. And I'm inured now to my limitations and don't
often feel they are hampering. But they are.'

The most obvious limitation of her position was that Edith was intricately
bound to Drishane and her brothers by financing its survival. The maintenance
of the house swallowed money at an astonishing rate. No matter how large the

sums are that come in advances and are recorded in the diary, in no time her bank book reminds her that she has about £10 in her account. On 28 April Longmans sent a £400 advance for *Wheeltracks*, so that she felt free to travel, and went back to London on 7 May. She was with Sissy and Hugh Cholmondeley at Edstaston at the end of the month, and returned to London for a *Time and Tide* lunch with Lady Rhondda where she met, and enjoyed the company of, Miss Chris[topher] St John. 'Miss St John' had abandoned her given name of Christabel Marshall for her pseudonym as a writer. Edith went on then to dine at the Laverys, where she ended up with a fascinating companion: 'talked spiritualism with Austen Chamberlain', but gives no further details. The Laverys were thinking of coming to paint in CT, and made enquiries about a holiday let. Edith was back there by mid-July. The family had decided that the country was calm enough to bring Egerton's body back from temporary burial in Twickenham cemetery near Kneller Hall. On the 19th Edith wrote to Ethel Smyth: 'What Uncle Kendal has called Egerton's "old cloak" was put in the church yard on Sunday. The fact that this was done has given enormous pleasure. The whole county came to the funeral, and all the men competed for the privilege of putting a shoulder to the coffin, for even a few steps. It shows that the "class-animosity" has not gone very deep here, at all events. The 3 boys were home for it. H did not go. It was a big trial for her, but – in a way that I can understand – it has brought her peace.'[62]

In this summer the Morrises' house at Spiddal was burned. There were only two servants there when a group of Republicans arrived and poured petrol all over the hall and staircase, methodically smashing the lower windows to create a fierce updraught. Given ten minutes, the cook saved her cooking utensils, the laundrymaid her linen. The great library of Irish books and Lord Killanin's gold collar of Ss as lord chief justice of Ireland, which was displayed in it, were destroyed with everything else. Martin Morris, Martin's favourite, left Ireland to die 'in exile' in England in 1927, while the rest of the family settled in France.[63] Still disregarding all dangers, Ethel Smyth came over on 12 September for a fortnight. Reviews of the memoir *Wheeltracks* started to appear at the end of the month. Edith's writing was beginning to be noticed and appreciated in Ireland by sympathetic reviewers, who realised also that her memoirs were valuable as vivid social history. In mid-October Edith was astonished by a review in a prominent Nationalist newspaper: 'very friendly review of *Wheeltracks* in the *Freeman's Journal*. Unprecedented.'

She went over to London to see Longman on 13 October, and stayed with Mary Hunter while she organised Walker's Gallery plan for her next exhibition in the David Cox Room. She was back in CT on the 24th. Still using dog-French in her diary, as she did in letters to Hildegarde, in October and

November the sisters made a decision to trim the amount of land they farmed. They had a new bank manager, Mr Jones of the Bank of Ireland: 'His bank is taking over our entire debt which now amounts to "cinq milles" but it is well secured.' Then on 21 November she recorded the sale of the demesne farm, without the Round O and the Big Lawn, to a Mr Salter for 'deux milles deux cents livres. A relief and a grief.' There was an immediate distraction from grief, as Ethel had organised the publicity for her picture exhibition at Walker's, deliberately arranged to take advantage of the Christmas market. Edith crossed to London to hang her pictures on 27 November; opening day was 4 December. She wrote to tell Hildegarde, in Dinard, of a visit to the exhibition by one of the most successful painters of the day:

> Sir John Lavery came down to the Gallery yesterday morning – He was very interesting, as he was not at all indiscriminate in commendation. He fixed instantly on 'Dinny Donovan's' and said 'I like your pigment' – which means colour and the way it is laid on. He made no secret of being struck and surprised, and – I need hardly say – picked out all the best ones. Of some he said the colour was 'delicious', and he said they would 'ripen' and improve in colour as the paint was so fresh and well put on! All this was highly gratifying as you may believe, and he left with congratulations and assurances that he had been most interested and would have been sorry to have missed it, specially as he didn't know the South of Ireland. It was really very nice of him to come, and then to speak his mind as man to man.[64]

Less worried about her finances, she was back in CT on 21 December, having sold 446 guineas' worth of paintings. Though Ethel Smyth remained a good friend, by now it seems that she had abandoned hopes of converting Edith to being her lover. She had become irritated by Edith's failure to put Ethel at the top of her list, and began to criticise her for other failings (her inability to keep to any fixed plans, for example), writing to her on 19 February 1923: 'as well fight a feather bed as try and make an impression on an utterly fluid character.' Louise Collis remarks on the fact that Edith gradually ceased 'to occupy first place' in Ethel's affections and makes a pertinent comment that 'Edith, who had always been astonished and slightly embarrassed by her election to it, seems to have taken a lower room with the humility characteristic of her'. Neither did she did resent in the least Ethel's transference of her affections to Virginia Woolf. But, had Edith read it, she would have resented Ethel's description of her in a letter to Virginia: 'The real inwardness of that connection has worn itself out owing to automatic writing, though I ask myself if that is not a symptom of arrested growth that was pre-ordained ... I often think how her real bent was painting and how she took to writing because of her cousin who was the real writer. But Edith is so competent that she could not help becoming a good writer too, carried no doubt, by the cousin.'[65]

This is a patronising analysis, ignoring plain facts: as an invalid who worked slowly and for long periods not at all, Martin as a fiction writer was plainly 'carried' by her more energetic partner. Edith had written excellent letters and published stylish work before co-operating with Martin, and their sole, stated, object in commencing and carrying on writing together was financial, as together they produced work that was more saleable than either could produce alone. At various points of need they carried each other through bad patches. Edith was more successful as a writer than as a painter. We know more now about the events of the Martins' first stay in CT in 1886, and how their association came about. Clearly Martin at first battened on to being *persona grata* with the Coghills as a better option than life with Mama, and only after having made this judgement did she attach herself to Edith. If their handwritings are any guide as to which personality was dependent, following Ethel Smyth's analysis we might expect Edith's hand to mimic Martin's. But it was Martin's handwriting that altered, in its fast current form becoming almost indistinguishable from Edith's after years of work together. Only the secondary 'r' of Martin's hand remains an infallible indicator that she was holding the pen. Because Ethel Smyth is a large figure on the scene, her ignorant opinionatedness on the subject of Edith Somerville has seeped in many directions: but her opinions are those of an outsider quite unfamiliar with the position of single women in Anglo-Ireland and should not be allowed to overlay the less well-known but comprehensive evidence of Irish sources from the home front.

Edith started 1924 on bad terms with Mr Longman. Giving her no warning, he had made a second edition of *Wheeltracks*, without incorporating the author's corrections. She was further annoyed by very poor prices for beasts at the farm auction. Automatically written dialogue with Martin was a calming influence. Miss Barlow was encouraged to become more ambitious in her mediumship. On 20 January, Jem prepared the Drishane spiritualist circle to attempt a 'visualisation' of Martin; why this was attempted at all is not known. Edith comforted Hildegarde by assuring her sister that Egerton '*is* there though you cannot see him' and that this inner understanding of continued companionship depended on their own faith and love. In her own case, this mechanism, that gave a voice to the dead, was very efficient. With the aid of automatic writing Edith was able to formulate a dramatic plot, inspired by an old letter of Martin's (quoted on pages 260–1). By early February she was immersed in a long novel which was to become *The Big House of Inver*, one of the most powerful of her books. On the 16th the circle of sitters began their experiment in Drishane to bring about a materialisation of Martin. They sat in complete silence in the library, while Cameron played Brahms in the drawing room. Hildegarde and Jem both thought they saw a change in the light where they were expecting to see Martin, sitting in the chair in which she used to write. Edith did not. They continued this experiment for half an hour every day for a week with no success. The period of experiment ended when Edith went to London on 5 March. The day before she left, in tidying her papers she discovered, to her relief: 'I am now on the right side of my bank account by £2.'[66]

Edith was preparing to go abroad for a spa cure with Ethel Smyth, still a boon companion despite all, and her passport had lapsed. In London she went to war with the Passport Office, who could not decide what nationality she was: 'I am a citizen of *nowhere* thanks to having been born in Corfu!' She went to the morning dress rehearsal of Ethel Smyth's *Mass* at the Queen's Hall, followed by the actual performance in the afternoon of 8 March. On the next day she left with Ethel, who was suffering from arthritis, both to take a cure at Dax. Their consultant was Doctor Lavielle; they both took mud baths and douches and both felt 'wretched'. They went back to Coign on 1 April, not much better for the treatment, Edith being still unable to walk. Ethel bath-chaired her about, pleased to be allowed to be of service. The tone of Edith's happiest letters to Ethel Smyth is caught at its shining best in an April Fool's day extravaganza purporting to be a letter from Adrian Boult in Massachusetts. Nevill Coghill recalled this spoof in a memoir of his aunt, and he confirms that it was written by Edith in a convincing imitation of Boult's own handwriting, which was known to Ethel. Apparently composed on 15 March 1924, and typical of Edith's drollery, it cuts horribly near to the bone.

> Dear Dame Ethel
> You will be surprised to see my present address. I regret it. I regret many things, but few more than that I should have been obliged – if I am to preserve the integrity of my artistic conscience – to fly from England.
>
> The fact is that I cannot face the prospect of having again to conduct your Mass in D (Pregnant initial! That so often stands for what is unspeakable!)
>
> I have hitherto ignored your inept pilferings from Bach, Beethoven and Brahms – those three Bees who have so long adorned your bonnet – but I can no longer conceal from you the horror and resentment you have aroused in me by your deliberate plagiarism, *en masse*, in *your* mass, of the greatest Masster of our own or any other day – It is almost superfluous to say that I allude to Sir Edward Elgar.

Your artful and artificial violence has hitherto blinded – or should I say deafened? – me to your shameless dishonesty with regard to the Maestro's inspirations. I can make allowance for the lack of originality that is natural in a Woman Composer, but my forebearance has its limits, and I can no longer shut my eyes to what I regret I can only call Pillage, appropriate to the venal composer of 'The Wreckers'.

It may interest you to know that on arrival in this state (whose name unfortunately awakes very painful remembrances) I was received by the Massed Jazz Bands of this great country, who greeted me with a magnificent rendering of the beautiful, and in this connection *prophetic* air 'Mass is in de cold, cold ground!'

The significance of this was not lost upon me. More than ever I felt that I had been well advised in living up to my name and doing

A. Boult

April 1, 1924.

Nevill's memoir tells us that: 'My Aunt was present when Ethel received this outrageous letter, and thought she was going to have a fit, until it dawned on her it was a hoax. Then she shouted out "Edith!" Such are the gambols of the great.'[67] It is highly significant that in her 'gambolling' Edith was quite capable of replicating other people's handwriting, just as she could their voices. Whether conscious or not, her own contribution to the apparent validity of automatic writings received in the 'authentic and unmistakeable' handwritings of the dead must be a possibility. Watching Adrian Boult conduct Ethel's Mass in January Edith had been very taken with him, describing him to Hildegarde in horsey terms: 'His figure is so good and his action charming'.

Edy Craig, Gordon Craig's daughter, and her partner Christopher St John (Christabel Marshall), came to Coign on 5 April to hear Edith read *Flurry's Wedding* and give their opinion. 'They were a pleasant and kind audience.' Then Edy Craig worked with Edith at a change of scene for the fourth act 'to simplify stage work'. Discussing the casting of the play with her nephew Nevill Coghill about this time, she wrote to him: 'If only your Uncle Aylmer were available to play Flurry Knox – the Half-Sir is not an easy part to play.' With much difficulty she travelled back to CT on 9 April, and immersed herself in the writing of her new novel 'Inver', distracted by pain in her legs. As light relief, in early May she read the script of the communications made to the medium Mrs Travers Smith, who had sittings with Yeats at this period, from 'Oscar Wilde'. Edith thought them 'very remarkable and unanswerable (in spite of old Richet's theory of "cryptothesia").'[68] Edith followed all the scientific and pseudo-scientific theorising about mediumship in the journal *Light* and argued vigorously and enjoyably with Ethel Smyth in this field also.

She made an inspection of her horses on 13 May with Mike, who took more work upon himself while Edith was crippled. She had in her stables then Dan Russel, 4 years old, the un-gelded Marquis, 3, Brian Boru, 2, and the pony, 5. Any remaining gentry in the countryside seem to have been fallen upon as fair game by rogues. Hildegarde and Edith were making a quiet tour of inspection of their farm 'and found Jack Hennessy stealing litter! Having last week found that Curly Leary had stolen 60 loads of stones from my quarry.' Apart from feeling betrayed, Hildegarde was becoming severely depressed by the farm overdraft. But a sale of heifers on 17 June lifted their spirits, as the price was better. They made £240, about £14.10s. per animal 'which is thought very good'. At the end of the month Boyle, now retired from the Navy, with his family moved into Uncle Kendal's old house for good. In spirit form, Uncle Kendal expressed indignation 'at Boyle's changing from Cosheen back to the old name "The Point House".'[69]

In July Sir Arthur Quiller Couch, 'Q', wrote to Edith to arrange for 'An Outpost of Ireland', Martin's piece on Aran from 1894, to be included in *The Oxford Book of English Prose*. Then the 'wave' of summer visitors flooded in, and the manuscript of 'Inver' was put aside. At odd moments of free time Edith worked in snatches in the Studio on the design, inspired by interlace from the Book of Kells, for the mosaic floor for the church apse of St Barrahane's that was to be executed by the London firm of Rust.[70] At least the visitors were made use of, as they found themselves called upon to contribute to the Irish Jubilee Nurse's Endowment Fund that was presided over by Lady Kenmare. On 29 August Ethel Smyth arrived: 'She compelled me to read the book to her.' Edith had written twelve chapters; these she had read out aloud by the following day: 'ES approves' she wrote with relief in her diary. Ethel and Edith did regular long daily walks as part of their health regime. On 6 September the two women went over to a house party at the Kenmares'. Edith must have felt optimistic about livestock farming, as while she was over in Kerry she bought a dozen bullocks at a fair with the help of the Kenmares' steward, Lynne, for £92.10s.

She found a 'very favourable' eulogistic entry about herself in *Time and Tide* at the beginning of October as part of a series on 'Powers and Personalities'. It was clear that despite incessant hard work on the farm and payment and recognition for her steadily published literary output, any profits she might have made were swallowed instantly by the farm or house, the former of which the sisters adamantly refused to give up and thus put their men out of work. Mr Longman wrote on 9 October with a cheque for £67.10s. from a 2/6 Harraps edition of the old RM. On the 11th she wrote in her diary: 'Got my Bank book and found that the recent douceur from Harraps does no more than staunch the wound.' She wrote endless appeals for the Jubilee Nurses fund for Lady Kenmare. Longman's offered her ten guineas to design a jacket for a collected edition of Father Sheehan's works. Unfortunately as she found his books detestable ('dull, turgid, besides being propaganda of the worst sort'), she turned the commission down: 'my conscience wouldn't let me have anything to do with them.' The month of December in her diary after Martin's death in 1915 was always marked as 'this time of remembrance', and in 1924 on the day of Martin's death she had a sitting with Jem: 'a satisfaction on this day of remembrance' to help with a difficult section of 'Inver'.

Neither sister was really prepared for the 'shattering' overdraft statement of £3,600 that came on 10 January 1925, for the farm – 'not personal, though that isn't particularly healthy either'. Visitors relieved the gloom. The Protestant Nationalist and MP Stephen Gwynn, who had written so appreciatively of Somerville and Ross in 1900, arrived to stay with her on 12 February. He was one of those men that Edith took to immediately, and they talked unstoppably. 'Gwynn arrived, pleasant and "like an old shoe",' her diary noted. He wanted her to persuade Lady Kenmare to change the name of the Nurses Fund, and to remove the word 'Jubilee' on account of its unfortunate associations. She wrote to Lady Kenmare as a result suggesting 'War Memorial Nurses', but to no avail. They lost another of their eleven Kerry bullocks, which they had taken out to Horse Island, possibly to marauding rogues: 'Our sixth loss in twelve months'. 'Inver' was not proving easy to write: 'High pressure and very difficult'. No method of earning income was untried. She went over to the proprietors of the Eccles Hotel at Glen Garriff to give them a set of drawings and watercolours on sale or return to hang in the library. Avoiding the local marts, the sisters arranged to ship twelve in-calf heifers to a sale in Reading to see if they could get a better price in England.

In March, with other agrarian reformers, they became embroiled in a country-wide struggle with the government, which wanted to forbid all breeds of cattle except shorthorns, Angus and Kerries. Edith re-wrote for Bulmer Hobson his Irish Agricultural Organisation Society manifesto against this course of action, as it was 'injudiciously ferocious against the Government'. It had been a waste of money shipping their cattle to England. Their heifers at Reading sold for £187, 'a wretched price, could have done better in Skib.' Although it had been a much-interrupted struggle, she finished the first draft of 'Inver' in thirty-six chapters. Hildegarde went to Dax for a cure on 28 March; the sisters had arranged a new and improved system of farm record books, and as a result Edith wrote in her diary: 'I received, with fitting awe, the fateful books of office and full instructions (which I trust I shall be able to observe).'

In May Edith showed three pictures at the Lyceum Club's exhibition at Gieve's Gallery. 'The Times lauds them as "passionate Irish landscapes". One is of Taormina, and another one of the Slipper's ABC drawings "G is for Geese"! Very passionate.' The third was in fact an Irish landscape, painted in Kerry. On 30 May, proud and all unawares, Mr Longman sent Edith the history of his firm and its publications. Strangely, there was no mention in it of one of Longman's most reliable sellers, Somerville and Ross. Immediately Edith sent a 'sassoferrara' [a Buddh word for an explosion of rage]. It may well be that this gaffe of Longmans finally caused her to cut the long connection with the firm.[71] She had been considering it since the time of the *Brown Bog* fiasco. She went to London on 9 June and started a round of visits to other publishers, starting with Heinemanns. With the typescript of her book to correct, she went to stay with Ethel Smyth for a long weekend, Ethel re-checking the typescript as Edith completed the sheets. She left a copy of the script with Theodore Bayard, whom she called Sprattino, at Heinemanns, before returning to CT and the harvest on 24 June.

In this June she was paid £67.10s. for a Harrap edition of *In Mr Knox's Country* and was thus enabled to pay Dr O'Meara's cumulative bill: 'not excessive £13.10 shillings (!) for six years.' On top of the farm work she read proofs of the new edition of *Irish Memories*. She went ahead with a transfer to Heinemanns. The Bank of Ireland was now spreading its wings, and officials called 'Recoverers' were trying to put order on income tax returns. 'Sent all my income tax muddles to Radcliffe, the new Bank of Ireland Recoverer (the last having bolted with all he could recover!)' The sisters went to the Dublin Horse Show on 31 July and sold Dan Russel for £180 – 'not enough but we will have to take half a loaf and Dan will have a very good home.' With the harvest and shows safely over, she went to the French spa of Luchon in Poitou with Ethel Smyth on 10 August for a new course of treatment. They both wrote fierce complaints of the sufferings caused by their treatment, but still managed to see quite a lot of medieval churches. From Luchon, Edith wrote to Hildegarde to complain also of the heat and expensiveness of the place, as it was more fashionable than Dax (it was three times more expensive). Edith had heard that Lord Kenmare was selling out of his land at Killarney: 'I am *awfully* sorry, I know how deeply he will feel it but it has been forced on him ...' Edith had heard, too, of a dangerous incident in the yard when Hildegarde had faced down an angry bull: 'you show foolhardy courage in standing with Rigo –, *a dog*! in the awful path of Castlehaven Pict! I wonder he didn't smash you both. What a pity Dutch Count's sons are such demons, just like himself. I should love to have seen the brute, but *not* from your point of view.'[72]

The travellers were back in London on 1 September and Edith saw Heinemann's C.S. Evans about co-publishing with the American firm of Doubleday and Page. Business over, she went to stay with the Woodhouses at Nether Lypiatt Manor in Gloucestershire, from where she attended a performance of Ethel's Mass in Gloucester Cathedral. There was obviously some element of the child-like or innocent in Edith's appearance. The super-sophisticated Violet Woodhouse responded to Edith, then aged sixty-seven, as though she were some kind of waif or orphan. Edith wrote to Hildegarde to describe the harpsichord playing of Violet:

> Violet W gave us an enchanting evening of Bach, Scarlatti, Couperin, etc. She is perfect, both as artist and as thing to look at, and I adore the delicate refinement of the harpsichord (for which this music was written) and the almost fierce reserve of strength that it can produce on occasion. Violet is a most charming creature and the kindest hostess. She came into my room last night with an open tin of Brand's beef jelly and said she knew I wasn't eating enough, and I was looking *pale* (!!!) (such a compliment!) and that I must eat it *all* before I got into bed. I needn't say I didn't do this, but I ate a good bit and I must admit I slept better last night than I had done for some time and feel much fitter today ...
>
> I shall not die happy 'til you hear her play. It is one of the few things in music that seem to me to be entirely flawless ...[73]

Edith seems to have been unaware that even a superstar of the musical firmament, like Violet Woodhouse, rated her in return as a literary superstar. Woodhouse was, most unexpectedly, a devoted fan of the RM series. Edith had spent quite a lot of time at Lypiatt in bed, nursing her leg, and writing. Ink stains on her red silk coverlet were preserved as a 'badge of honour, to be pointed out to subsequent guests as proof that they had been placed in the same bedroom in which the famous author had once slept'.[74] Returning the compliment by being concerned for her hostess's health and well-being, Edith gave Violet as a parting gift a recipe for an old Irish remedy for rheumatism.

When she got back to CT on 11 September she found that the crowds of visitors that so hampered her working were still there. Instantly she went away again to stay with the Kenmares. Lord Kenmare, a most generous admirer, gave Edith a pony and trap to take her about painting wherever she liked, as a gift. The pony was a very handsome one, Dido, and the harness and trap of the best. In the evenings she and Lady Kenmare wrote letters for the Nurses' Fund, still called 'Jubilee'. 'Elizabeth and I walked about the town and paid a visit to a bed-ridden old fiddler. Again I was struck by the diction of these Kerry people – so much more poetical than ours.' Edith was on tenterhooks when Heinemann sent an advance copy of *The Big House of Inver* to Lady Kenmare. She read it at the gallop, her reaction 'highly favourable' mid way, then at the end '*much pleased*'. When Edith got back to Drishane on 16 October the reviews started

to come in: 'Gorgeous review of Big House in TLS. ES wired to tell me of it.'
She had a 'wonderful' letter from Maurice Baring about the book and a good
notice in the *Observer*. [75]

*The Big House of Inver* concerns the ruin of the family of Prendeville
through legal and illegal unions between Anglo-Irish and Irish. As in *An Irish
Cousin*, the custom of gentry men fathering children on servants or the women
of their estate workers is central to the plot. This was not a melodramatic
invention of the authors; because of it the Yelverton family had lost its social
position, wealth and lands. Shane Leslie, in his memoir, *The Film of Memory*,
published in 1938, refers also to this custom:

> How far the blood of the gentry and the peasantry mingled in the old
> days cannot be accurately decided. There are few old families which have
> not more than foster-relations in the mountains. Until the barrier of
> religion arrived, the Irish women absorbed the sons of the invaders, and
> out of their marriage arose the medieval Irish nation with Celtic blood
> and Anglo-Norman names. The Penal Laws made the intermarriage of
> Catholic and Protestant a felony and social degradation. All romance and
> interbreeding became secret. In the eighteenth century the illegitimates
> (they were called by-blows) hung around the big house, and it was
> considered bad taste for a visitor to ask the name of any young man
> about the place ... When the old age pensions were first awarded I
> remember a handsome old crone like Lady Macbeth demanding her
> pittance with pathetic indignation. 'If I had my rights I would be better
> than any of you.' The lawyer whispered to me that she came from Lord
> Roden's stock and indeed her big-boned nose and silvery hair would have
> done credit to any earldom. [76]

The handsome old crone of illegitimate descent in *The Big House of Inver*
is Shibby Pindy, whose name is a mutated form of Isabella Prendeville. The
daughter of Captain Prendeville who lives with him in a tower house close to
the wreck of the family's splendid mansion, she attempts to save the main house
and an inheritance for her legitimate half-brother, Kit, yet another beautiful
blue-eyed horseman, spoilt and selfish. Shibby's attempts to thwart fate fail. The
Captain sells the family house behind her back. Though he has a chance to
marry well and thereby keep his house, Kit gets a child on a village girl and goes
to America. The interaction of social classes is sharply observed, and the
euphemisms and avoidances that make it socially possible for the Captain's
legitimate and illegitimate children to live together in the same dwelling betray
an author well versed in the concealing power of make-believe. It was a roaring

success with readers. Again Edith imaginatively utilises the setting of the Yelvertons' Belle Isle; it, and not Tyrone House, which was also used for architectural detail, has a nearby Cromwellian tower which was in Edith's time there used for partying and luncheons.

The money that came in from *The Big House of Inver* immediately disappeared on repairs and debts. The Studio was invaded by workmen who seemed to be rebuilding it entirely. Edith had to write many letters about the new book, commenting in her diary that 'Hildegarde says, truly, that publishing a book is worse than having a baby'. It was in the list of Heinemann's six bestsellers: it sold 8,141 copies in six weeks. In a BBC review it was featured as one of the two best books of the season. Horace Plunkett wrote from his new home at Weybridge in Surrey to congratulate her, and sent an enclosure.[77] He was one of a number of men who sent information on psychic phenomena to Edith. He enclosed a letter to him from his friend Richard Preston, brother of Lord Gormanston. The family house was famous for its 'spectral' foxes that appeared around the house at the death of each Lord Gormanston. Richard Preston's letter concerned the death of his brother the week previously and described 'how the foxes had come and barked round Gormanston when his brother's body was brought there last week.' What governed the precise timing of their regular demonstration was difficult to discover, but happen it did: Martin's sister Edith had written to tell Martin about the foxes that had appeared at the death of the previous Lord in 1907.

Edith began the new year of 1926 by going over to Killarney and working with Lady Kenmare on the Nurses' Fund. She was then distracted from work by Mary Hunter, Ethel Smyth's sister, who asked her to stay with her in London in order to see the exhibition of Sargent's work at the Academy. This was an offer 'Too attractive to refuse'. Before she left she totted up her own personal collections for the Nurses' Fund at £321. Her diary records her reactions to the London sights. At the Academy there were 600 pictures in Sargent's exhibition - 'A noble and marvellous show. The water colours a revelation ...' She went to the exhibition again on the following day. On the 23rd she attended a performance of *Juno and the Paycock* acted by the Irish Players: 'Acted to perfection. The first act's enchanting comedy, the last a sordid tragedy, scene a Dublin tenement house, time, 1922. Felt shattered. Eliz. [Lady Kenmare], ES and I went behind and talked to delightful Sara Allgood and her sister Maire O'Neill.' On the next day, when she was wearing one of her own designs of an eye-catching blue dress with inset panels of embroidery, she met George Moore again at a dinner of Mrs Hunter's in Richmond: 'didn't like the drowsy old wasp, even though he said to me "What a pretty Dress!"' She went to Heinemann, had lunches with Baring and the Kenmares, saw the Penroses, then

began to think of her play again. As soon as she got back to CT, she made a
third version and sent it off to be typed. The typed version then went to the
great Abbey Theatre actress Sara Allgood to see if she could place it, but she too
failed. Bridge, séances and worrying at the farm occupied her until she went to
London on 8 April to take a painting holiday with Kinkie at Burgos. Out of this
holiday she wrote the section 'Spanish Impressions', published in book form in
*Happy Days* (1946). Coming home on 3 May, she ran straight into the chaotic
gridlock of the General Strike, but made it back to Dublin by the 7th, helped on
her way by all the volunteers who came forward as strike-breakers to keep
transport running.

Back in Drishane she got the official report of the establishment and
funding of the Irish Jubilee Nurses on 4 June: 'Elizabeth Kenmare has now got
and invested £30,000, so nurses are safe.' She wrote her piece on Spain. Ethel
Smyth turned up at the end of June, bringing with her the manuscript of her
*Three Legged Tour in Greece* to complete. The hot-line from Edith's remote
corner of West Cork to the centres of the great world of British publishing was
astonishingly efficient. On 9 July, 'Blackwood's (Edinburgh) sent proofs of
"Some Spanish Impressions", [I] corrected and returned them. Quick work as I
only sent the typescript off on July 3rd.' On the next day a letter informed her
that Mr Longman had decided to publish *Flurry's Wedding* and he sent a
specimen page with suggested agreement. Then a wrangle developed over
American rights, and he withdrew. The play was very ill-fated.

The summer invasion built up and up. On 4 August she entered in her
diary: 'Fourteen people in all came to CT today, ten dined here.' On the 6th she
heard from Mr Longman 'renouncing *Flurry's Wedding* because of US dramatic
rights.' Then there was a charity Bazaar that raised £115 and a tea party for
eighteen. On top of all Mrs Anstey, a Somerville and Ross fan who had become
a friend through Ethel Smyth and who was stone deaf, arrived with her maid:
'She in high spirits and full of talk to which we labouringly replied on paper.'
Later, Edith was to write: 'a more impassioned Queen of Sheba never came here
…' Mrs Anstey insisted on paying for a great many gifts, and her generosity was
to become embarrassing. She was taken to the church to measure the altar for
the frontal that she was giving 'in Martin's memory'.[78] For twelve days Edith
had no time to call her own: 'Did nothing much, cares of hospitality absorbing
all energies.'

It was not until 12 October that she was able to start on what she called in
her diary 'Book': the novel that was later entitled *French Leave*. At last the Irish
government sent compensation, through the family solicitor Travers Wolfe, for
Edith's stolen horses Deirdre and Finbarr, the sum of £100. She was not writing
with her usual impetus. On the 27th she had written only seven pages: 'a slow

struggle so far'. On 2 November she was shocked by a telegram from Frances [Perkins] Cameron: 'Kinkie passed away, quietly, at Fareham yesterday. Heart failure and cerebral haemorrhage,' and commented in her diary: 'There never was a more faithful and devoted friend than Kinkie, whose allegiance has never wavered since I met her in Paris thirty two years ago.' Only seven months before, Kinkie had been fit for the Spanish railways and painting treks in the mountains.

In November a local branch of the nursing association was set up in Castlehaven Parish. A major donation of £2,000 had been left to the fund at the death of Edith's Aunt Henrietta, sister of T.H. Somerville.[79] It was no surprise that Edith was president and Hildegarde vice-president. A nurse was provided by the Jubilee Institution in Dublin, and appointed. Jem had been away and came back on 20 December: 'she came to tea and wrote with me afterwards. Force and currents pretty good,' the diary records. Nurse McCurdy arrived at the beginning of January 1927. The sisters 'sent out 28 invitations to farmers' ladies to come to tea to meet Nurse McCurdy'. The tea party came off on 28 January, when 21 of the 28 were able to come. The weather was foul, and Edith wrote on at her novel, with the alleviation of bridge in the evenings. By mid-February she had written about 40,000 words, 'not much more than half'. She went to stay with Caz Anstey before Nevill's wedding on 25 March, being motored to Oxford in Mrs Anstey's motor car. Mrs Anstey was a hostess who plied her guests with entertainments, so that while in London Edith was treated to Gerald du Maurier in 'Interference' and Edith Evans in 'The Beaux' Stratagem'.

Edith's diary shows a talent for procrastination. Back in CT, she avoided tackling her slow-going novel by planning and booking a room for an exhibition at Walker's Gallery for December. She also found a completely absorbing book to read – *The Revolt in the Desert*. 'Finished with deep regret [T.E.] Lawrence's gorgeous book ... a great artist as well as soldier.' With the help of Jem she did some more chapters, reaching 60,000 words by the end of May. In June the altar frontal commissioned by Mrs Anstey came from the Egan workshops in Cork - 'most beautifully worked and looks very well.' On 11 June 'Jem had tea with me and in honour of Martin's birthday we wrote.' Mrs Anstey had asked Gerald du Maurier if he would read *Flurry's Wedding* and he had answered 'delighted to read play', but he, too, had rejected it by 12 July. She finished her slow-starting book on 11 August, with a total of 84,000 words; it was written fitfully over a period of ten months. The manuscript went off to Heinemann on the 16th, and three days later he replied accepting it.

When she signed an agreement with him on 17 September, the title was still not fixed, the manuscript having been sent with some suggested ones. It was changed to *French Leave* on 3 October. Meanwhile the Hitchcock edition de luxe of the works of Somerville and Ross was being prepared for press in America. This opulent edition was to connect Edith with a new and opulent public, and thus with a new source of income. On the 12th Edith had both the proofs of the new novel and the proofs of her invitation for her Walker's show, entitled 'Some Irish Yesterdays'. She crossed to London to stay with Mrs Anstey on 22 October, finding at her flat, on her return from a tour of friends, a pile of 600 papers for her to sign as her signature was to be pasted in to each copy of the American edition de luxe. She found she could write 200 in two hours. On 20 November she sent out the invitations for her show. There was an entirely new development: knowing that she was in London, the BBC approached her to make some readings from the RM. She went to the BBC office on Savoy Hill, and her diary notes: 'Miss Hilda Matheson and a young man named Brennan "tried my voice" ie I read to them a part of "When I first met Dr Hickey". They declared it was allright and booked me for December 12th.'[80]

Her Walker's show opened on 1 December and by the 3rd she had sold 204 guineas' worth. At the opening she wore a green dress of her own design, again with oriental embroidery set into panels. She went every day to Walker's and was dined and lunched incessantly. Her diary gives the details of her BBC début on the 12th: 'Hilda Matheson dined here and taxied me to the BBC. Read my piece.' She read *The House of Fahy*, a well-known trial piece for any dramatic reader. Then she went down to Coign to see Ethel for a few days; here Hildegarde telephoned her: 'They listened at Willy Casey's [pub] and didn't know my voice until I abused Maria when the familiar words "You brute" stirred recognition.' She packed up at the Gallery and returned home on 22 December. She found herself on New Year's Eve correcting very bad proofs from Faber for an omnibus edition of the RM. She sent them off and 'Sent the Bank £120 to the Farm Account, leaving me with £23 to face the coming year.'

Muriel Currey begins her transcript of the year 1928 with the remark: 'The decrease in the exchange of letters with Ethel Smyth is very marked, also of visits to Coign.' Ethel's attention had wandered elsewhere, and this might have been something of a relief to Edith. At CT Hildegarde needed all of her sister's support. On 7 January Edith wrote in her diary: 'Walked with H., she is in black depression re farm and awful overdraft.' *French Leave* was published on 2 February. Edith was in London when the *Times* and the *Spectator* reviews appeared on the 10th. She learned from Eugene Connett that the American edition de luxe had sold 10,000 dollars worth. She had tea with Katie Currey who told Edith about Martin's niece Barbara in India. She had been formally introduced to the Maharajah Bikaneer at a court function. He had been told by an aide that Barbara was a niece of Ross, of Somerville and Ross. As Barbara rose from her curtsey, the Maharajah said, quoting from 'The House of Fahy':

'At that juncture Maria joined me, she had the cockatoo in her mouth.' He, too, was one of the many who chose *The House of Fahy* above all the RM stories. Edith was beginning to show intolerance of experimental painters; on this trip to London, she went to see an exhibition of Sickert's paintings, at which she did not respond to his range of dark colours: 'most abominable'.

*French Leave* is a novel in which the heroine, after studying art in Paris with the intention of being an independent artist, gives up her ambition in order to marry young Lord Corran. On 13 February Edith replied to Hildegarde, who, having given criticism on the drafts, had written to say how much she had enjoyed the final version of *French Leave*: 'I have, so far, had an A1 press – the only faint crabber being "The Outlook" – It is typical that they pick out for disapproval the one part that is word for word almost founded on fact! Viz Paris. *Private*. I never told you that Ethel S, who had read the proofs, shook her head, and disliked it, and obviously kept back more dislike, even, than she expressed – so that I felt very low.' It is possible that the novel, set in 1884, the year before Barry died in Egypt, represents an attempt by Edith to make a fictional version of life as it might have turned out for her had Barry lived and their relationship clarified, and to make a demonstration to Ethel on her feelings about workable relationships between men and women. The novel contains a portrait of Martin, as the mother of the heroine, Patricia Kirwen, who is in large part Edith herself. It is a vivid and lifelike portrait, far removed from the idealised Martin of *Irish Memories*. It is also reminiscent of the dislocation between Edith's actual perceptions and ideality that we find in her critical opinion of Mrs Anstey, given in a letter to Hildegarde, compared to the fulsome aggrandisement of her obituary for the same woman.[81] Clearly Edith was well able to hide her own feelings completely behind a front of compliant and urbane manners. In *French Leave* Lady Kirwen is given Martin's smothered laughter, her enjoyment of woodwork, her moments of absent-mindedness, her short sight and her appearance:

> Lady Kirwen [was] one of those unexpected little ladies who, in a former incarnation, might have been a carpenter, and in a future one might develop into an architect … She was short and spare ('My size dates me,' she was accustomed to say; 'I'm a dump. All my contemporaries are dumps') with a thin, weather-beaten face and slightly prominent teeth. All that remained of the looks that she had once possessed (or Sir Ingram would not, certainly, have married her) were her soft, short-sighted brown eyes, a charming smile, and a light figure … and she was deeply ashamed of being still the victim of that infirmity of laughter which in French is well called *fou rire*, that can overwhelm at any moment, and is as unpredictable as it is shattering.[82]

Of all the novels, *French Leave* has the most financial detail about Edith's fight to get art training in the 1880s; for those interested in women's education it is worth reading for this alone. We also gather from it the intensity of sheer rage that rose in Edith when she realised the proportion of money spent on her brothers' education, at the expense, as she saw it, of hers. Chapter VI opens: 'In the eighties of the nineteenth century it can hardly be denied that daughters were at a discount. Like the dogs, cited in that Canaanitish woman's magnificent effort of special pleading, they were permitted to eat of the crumbs that fell from their brothers' tables; if no crumbs fell, the daughters went unfed.' Cameron Somerville may have had unhappy memories of a youth in which he had to compete strenuously with his elder sister. In Chapter VII the situation of the heroine Patricia's younger brother Gilbert is compared to hers, which was bound by 'senseless limitations by which she had found herself hedged in ever since she left the schoolroom. There, making every allowance for her three and a half years seniority, she knew that she had been a better man than Gilbert; year for year she had beaten him on all points; but now it seemed as if each year widened his freedom and narrowed hers, quite irrespective of their powers or capacities. Patricia was not the only girl who in those far back years was dashing herself against the bars of her cage, but she was certain ... that in no cage were the bars so strong and so close together as in that which enclosed her, of which her father kept the key.'

By 1928 for women much had changed, but not everything. Edith had been to a concert of Ethel's music after which she had attended the party in Ethel's honour at the Welbeck Palace Hotel, where among the guests: 'I met Mrs Pankhurst, and we fell into each other's arms (Martin and I had been her Stewardesses in Cork long ago). We spoke of the bother and need of handbags, and I said the only valid reason for not giving women votes was their submitting to dressmakers in abolishing pockets. Mrs P said in a small voice – "*I* haven't got a pocket!" I replied in a still smaller "Nor have I".'[83] Mrs Pankhurst was like Edith and Mrs Fawcett in believing in the importance to women of their kind of dressing well in public, to demonstrate that suffragist leaders were not, as cartoons would have it, hideous frumps who were unladylike societal outcasts. She was born, like Edith, in 1858, and died later in this year. The feminist classic Charlotte Perkins Gilman's *Herland*, written before 1916, has an all-female society, reproducing their kind by parthenogenesis, who wear especially designed clothes with multiple concealed pockets; evidently the pocket question for independent women was a deep and possibly marsupial one.[84]

There were further 'good and abundant' notices of *French Leave*. Edith went about her business in London; two diary entries a few days apart show her line of attack. It seemed that Longmans still had to give leave before other publishers could issue the work of Somerville and Ross. On 23 February she went to '1. Longmans, nothing doing. 2. Saw Mr Frere Reeves, 2nd edition to *French Leave* coming, 3. Faber and Gwyer, saw young de la Mare [who had just brought out an Omnibus RM]. Suggested a complete edition.' 'Young de la Mare' was the poet Walter de la Mare's son. Four days later she returned to the attack: 'Took "edition" to Mr de la Mare. Then saw Mr Bayard and Evans [at Heinemann] Both keen for a collected edition. (But old dog in the manger Charles Longman won't agree I'm sure).'

America was presenting itself as a prime market for her Irish hunters. Back at Drishane at the beginning of March she learned from Mrs Hitchcock in America that her horse Brian Boru, which Mrs Hitchcock had bought from Edith for £600, had been sold on to Sonny Whitney for £1,000.[85] Full of plans for the golden future in horse-coping, she was suddenly brought up short by the death of one of her brothers. On the 12th Aylmer Somerville died in his sleep at the Red House. He had come back to CT in poor health for the last two years of his life. Edith later told her niece K that he had 'smoked himself to death'; he was only sixty-three and exceptional in that family of long-lived brothers and sisters. As an outstandingly successful Master of the West Carbery Hunt and a noted rider at horse races for so many years, Aylmer was well liked by his countrymen. Cameron, who had been away at the time, wrote to Rose Cameron Bingham: 'No-one was so *adored* by the people ... I did not go over for the funeral. Boyle tells me that they carried him round from the Red House through the [Castle] Demesne – and as every man in the whole Barony – and some from far beyond Skibbereen – wanted to help to carry him, they had to change bearers every 20 yards or so, so that all might have helped! "He was ever a hero to us" one old man said to Edith.'[86] On the day of his funeral on the 14th his sisters made his coffin wreath, a horseshoe-shape in violets. He joined the band 'over the border'. Only five days after his death Aylmer was communicating through Martin, who acted as 'control' for the family party of those who had 'crossed over'.

On the 28th, Edith had 'a charming letter from Mr Charles Longman who is retiring from Paternoster Row' which seemed to suggest that Longmans would let her leave them. Mrs Anstey wrote and 'insisted' that she paid for a portrait of Edith to be painted by the artist John Crealock. Mesmerised by generosity, Edith 'Wrote and submitted'. On 3 April Charles Longman repented of his kindness of the week before and wrote anew to insist that his firm 'would never give up our copyrights'. America signalled approval again when Houghton and Mifflin took *French Leave* for an American edition. At the Good Friday service in the church of St Barrahane's the new Lenten frontal was displayed for the first time. It was of purple poplin worked in silver, with some of Jem's 'healing' crystals worked into the representation of the 'De Burgo Chalice'.[87] On the central panel was embroidered 'Given by C.A.A. and E.Œ.S. to the dear memory of Martin Ross'.

Edith had a letter from the BBC on 14 April that confirmed the success of her debut as a radio performer. They offered her a fifty-minute slot on 1 May reading 'Philippa's Foxhunt' for a fee of 25 guineas. She went over to Caz Anstey's on 19 April. In the way that Ethel Smyth had found so irritating, the family was always around her in close formation. In London Boyle appeared and accompanied her to the BBC Savoy Hill studio and sat with her while she read. At Mrs Anstey's, which was used as a stopping-off place by her cousin Cissie Cholmondely, she found and borrowed Cissie's hunting habit, and wore it to have her portrait painted by John Crealock. On 3 May she wrote in her diary: 'Went to the studio and the picture is said to be finished (Rather flattered, over-sweetened, character lost, but well painted) Boyle, Mab and Mrs Anstey came to see it and liked it. The background is nice.' On the 15th, she made personal contact with her first biographer, the spiritualist medium Geraldine Cummins, whom she had met briefly before in Cork through the MWFL. 'Went to Miss Cummins early and had good writing with her.' In June the American money from the Hitchcock edition started to come in: 624 dollars on the 18th, followed by 433 dollars less than a month later; it was much needed.

At the Cork Agricultural Show on 27 June, the sisters reached the peak of their achievement with their Friesian cattle when their bull got 1st, and Alma III 3rd. Geraldine Cummins made her first stay at Drishane, 28–30 July, and was a success as a guest and amanuensis. With her Edith produced much longer and more complex scripts than with Jem. On 13 August Edith noted that Katherine Tynan had given her another favourable review for *French Leave*, and it was still selling well. Longing to be intimate with Edith, Mrs Anstey came for even longer this summer, arriving on 3 August and not leaving until 8 September; she insisted on contributing to expenses and so in effect was a 'p.g.'. On the 15th Edith wrote to congratulate Ethel Smyth on the success of her Mass at the Three Choirs Festival at Gloucester, as Ethel had written to her describing it. There had been no mention of her in Edith's diary since May 31st.

Edith wrote to Hildegarde on 5 November to explain that Mrs Anstey was trying to force herself on Drishane as a permanent paying guest, to her horror: 'I couldn't undertake any work unless I was alone (of course I don't count you or Cameron) Mrs A is *really* a little mad, otherwise I am sure she wouldn't be forcing herself down my throat like this. I have *never* encouraged her flop [fixation on Edith]. It bored me far too much. This sounds ungrateful but I have *not* failed in pity and consideration and gratitude, but this dementia is getting too much, and seems to get worse, no matter how unforthcoming I am.' When we compare the tone of this comment to her obituary notice for the same woman the contrast is considerable. A heavy layer of Christian charity and optimism colours all her memorialising. Despite the seeming sophistication and worldliness of her mother's family, her religious upbringing had been strict, and was ineradicable. As she grew older, her moral sensitivities grew keener. She preferred not to know about the faintly improper love lives of the rich bachelor brothers Percy and Eddy Aylmer, who were enthusiastic womanisers, and neither of whom married. She once felt sorry for a pretty woman guest, Molly French, who had just come to Percy's eager attention because 'Percy has a terribly slaughtering way with him'.[88] Edith refused to be slaughtered, but she could still be charmed by men, to the very end of her life.

Slowly during the winter the sisters drew away from the edge of financial despair. Edith's portrait – paid for by Mrs Anstey – arrived, and Hildegarde did not like it. It was hung and looked at critically for some weeks. On the last day of the year Edith could stand it no more; quite unabashed she recorded in her diary the overpainting of another artist's work: 'Began to try and make Crealock's portrait of me more like. Obliterated rose-bud mouth and lowered hat.' On 2 January 1929 she decided that it would do: 'Had committee re portrait who all approved of alterations and could suggest no more.' She went to London for treatment with a homeopathic practitioner called Perks on 4 January, and stayed with Mrs Anstey while she spent two weeks framing and preparing pictures for her forthcoming New York show, which both she and Hildegarde were to attend. They trusted Richard Helen to cope with the farm in their absence. Edith despatched £700 worth of pictures to America on 30 January and booked tickets for herself and Hildegarde at £38 each. Then she went back to CT. Seeing no other way out of her financial problems, Hildegarde had faced up to the sale of her personal farm Farrandeligeen. Edith's diary entry for 2 February is: 'Hildegarde signed away Farrandeligeen to William Driscoll, and has to give him a fistful of grass and put the fire out in final ratification.' This ritual they eventually carried out on the 14th: 'Walked with Jem and H.to Farrandeligeen. Met the proprietor ... and H formally gave him a handful of grass – a custom 6–700 years old.'

To fortify the sisters for their coming journey Jem received messages from Martin: 'all your faithful band from over the Border want you to feel that they are ever present and powerful'. Hildegarde and Edith went on board the *Cedric* at Cobh on 17 February at ten in the morning. They stayed on deck until 1.30 in order to see the bonfire that was being tended by the 'faithful' brothers Richard and David Whoolley on the CT Harbour edge, when the liner bore away from sight of land to the open ocean. The trees around Drishane were then the last that the traveller could see from shipboard en route to America.

Edith settled down to read a choice book: 'Finished Elizabeth Bowen's *The Last September*. Remarkably clever and terribly founded on fact.' The sisters both found ship life 'entirely abhorrent'. They got in to Boston Harbour at nine o'clock in the evening on 24 February, after a rough and cold seven-day passage.

They were plunged straight away into American high society and a luxurious life, at first staying with a Mrs Sage at her Park Avenue flat. Edith went to Ackermann's to see the gallery where her exhibition was to be held. The Hitchcock edition de luxe being sold out, it had instantly become a desirable rare item and its price shot up from 50 to 175 dollars. Edith was interviewed at Mrs Sage's by the editor of American *Vogue*, Mrs Carmel Snow, on the 27th. At lunches and dinners at which they were the guests of honour Edith and Hildegarde met an endless parade of wealthy Americans who hunted – Peabodys, Whitneys, Morgans and others. After New York they went to Aiken, South Carolina, to stay with the Hitchcocks. Here they attended hunts, races and steeplechases as guests of honour. After the exhibition in the Hitchcock's squash court and so many introductions that her 'head reeled' Edith lost her voice. By 21 March they had moved on to Virginia.

Huge numbers of people came up to Edith at parties to say that they had read 'all her books'. Edith commented in her diary: 'Very amazing, judging by Longmans accounts one copy must have gone round Virginia.' They were back in New York on 7 April. On the next day she lodged 2,050 dollars, 'the spoils of Aiken'. Edith was engaged to read 'Philippa's Foxhunt' at the Colony Club, in a very large room with about 150 people in it. Hildegarde stationed herself at the back and 'coughed menacingly' when Edith's voice showed signs of becoming inaudible. After Hildegarde had left to stay with other friends, a parlourmaid of hers, who had worked for her thirty years before, turned up at this reading and came to Edith: 'She nearly cried with joy, and asked after "Miss Hildegarde and Masters Jack and Hugh" etc. It was most touching to see how she remembered and loved all of us, – and I had forgotten her existence! I must ask Jeremiah [Driscoll] about her, she was very well dressed and seemed very happy and comfortable.' Edith wrote this to Hildegarde in the train from Boston to Philadelphia. Her New York Show opened on 10 April. A week later she had sold 4,250 dollars worth. High society couldn't have enough of the sisters. They were taken to have tea with Mrs Roosevelt, and to dine with the president of Yale and 'apparently all the Professors and their wives.' In Boston, Edith gave a reading of 'The House of Fahy' and was then persuaded to read 'Poisson d'Avril' and the 'House of Fahy' at the Cosmopolitan Club. She commented: 'My mouth stretched permanently to servile grin.' A Boston paper published a long article about her with a ghastly photograph, in which she obviously had not had time to compose her face: 'an *appalling* portrait of me. I didn't think I was so hideous ...' She had a heavenly break with Mrs Sears at her house, where she was allowed to inspect closely the Sargents and Monets. Her last lunch and reading was at the English Speaking Union where she read 'When I First Met Dr Hickey' and part of 'Alsatia'. On 3 May she went back to Ackermann's and converted her money from all sales back into sterling: a total of £1,221 deducting expenses. It had been an exhausting but worthwhile couple of months.

They embarked to return on 4 May and docked at Cobh on the 11th, seeing Cameron with Taspy in his arms waiting at the bottom of the gangplank. In their absence a serious war had broken out between Mrs Anstey and Ethel Smyth, who both felt that they owned Edith. But more immediately deserving of their attention was the making up of the record books from the notes made by Richard Helen. 'Am now making up 12 weeks of dairy milk records "no laughing joke at all".' According to her diary on 20 May Edith 'went through masses of old letters from myself to Martin, mostly re hunting, with a view to Fanny Fitz's possible adventures. Wrestled rather vainly with preliminaries of book, but M encourages me to stick to it. Enormous diatribes from ES and Caz re America.' Fanny Fitz had been a character invented for two consecutive stories in *All On the Irish Shore* of 1906. Her adventures could have been developed into a series like the RM, but nothing came of this proposal, made by Martin through automatic writing. It is quite revealing that Edith wades through her letters to Martin, many of which fell by the wayside as only a small proportion of them survive, and encapsulates the whole lot as 'mostly re hunting'. There are indeed long descriptions of a great number of hunts, but they are not outweighed by the doings of their relatives and friends. Edith's eye in scanning the letters obviously leapt from hunt to hunt.

Critical letters came from Ethel Smyth that tried to explain to Edith that she should not be deluded by the flattery of her recent American hosts. They are described in Edith's diary as: 'More diatribes from ES as to the perfidious flattery of "innocent and unpsychological" foreigners by Americans.' Edith refused to get cross and allowed herself to be absorbed by the maintenance of farm and livestock. June disappeared in preparations for the Cork Show, and as soon as it was over Mrs Anstey arrived on the 28th. On the following day Edith coolly noted that she had a letter from Ethel Smyth: 'Now madly in love with Elizabeth and her Swiss garden'.[89] Ethel seems to have been deliberately punishing Edith by praising women who could respond in a way that satisfied Ethel's sexual vanity, as she was to do later, in Drishane itself, by falling for Sylvia Warren. A large part of the American money disappeared on a renovation of the Gate House at the bottom of the village street, which was added to the portfolio of letting houses. The weather was fickle and the hay

came in, but in sections. The day of the Skibbereen Show and the day of Mrs
Anstey's departure were one and the same, 24 July. There was triumph for the
horses, Scortha got 1st in the 3year olds, Flurry Knox 2nd and 'the cattle and a
boar also did well, so sleekness prevailed'. On the rentals front, the Gate House
[later the White House] was being prepared for tenants who arrived on 17
August. The Archbishop of Dublin was a guest at the Castle, so that the sisters
put in a lot of time perfecting the choral singing at services on his behalf. There
were so many musical young in the village that they mustered a creditable choir.
Perhaps hurt by Ethel's cruel childishness, and regretfully withdrawing from a
friendship that had been very important to her, Edith was half-heartedly
working at a manuscript called 'Impressions', which was later to become the
book *The States through Irish Eyes*.

In October she read Vera Brittain's book on marriage – 'a very outspoken
and prophetic little book, called "Halcyon" … on the future of marriage, monoga-
mous or otherwise,' which may have set her thinking about her own essay on
marriage, 'For Richer for Poorer', which was written in the Spring three years
later. In the Studio the whole of this autumn was dominated by hand-colouring
a set of sporting drawings in an edition of 500 for Eugene Connet in America.
On 8 November, Hildegarde completed the farm accounts: takings April 1927
– April 1928 were roughly £1,116. 14s. 8d., expenses £1050. 17s. 1d., 'so with
overdraft percentages, the two come level and no income tax is payable.' Only
just breaking even, the Somerville sisters appeared to be running the Drishane
farm simply for the pleasure of keeping it in the family and giving employment
to men they liked and respected. Their bank manager did not conceal from
them his disgust at their 'sentimentality' in doing this, but they were to soldier
on in this parlous financial state for more than fifteen years. Letting houses,
taking paying guests and training up horses, combined with income from part-
time writing and painting, just managed to keep things going. By 1930 Edith
had more time for writing as Ethel Smyth had faded as a correspondent. It was
very rare for Edith to comment on the nature of Ethel's letters to her, but on
7 January she entered in her diary: 'Violent letter from E.S. by second post –
quite unjustified and very unexpected. The result apparently of illness and
overstrain.' This was a sign that Edith was being off-loaded as an intimate and
had reached the status of an old familiar friend, on whom Ethel took out her
rage. All was 'calm again' by the 10th in the Smyth/Somerville correspondence.
They maintained their friendship on a certain level, still travelled abroad
together now and then, but passion had been put aside, to Edith's relief and
Ethel's regret.

CHAPTER 9

# Last books: America, Ireland and a bad time for farming

His gentle, charming, playful spirit can seldom have felt itself at home in that fierce amazing inconsistent century, when the height of intellectual civilisation could exist undisturbed by, almost, it would seem, unaware of the barbarism, the ignorance and the brutality that smouldered beneath it, soon to flame into revolution. An age when ladies and gentlemen spent hours over their hair-dressing and did not take baths; when a dozen young men could shut themselves up for a week, with a hogshead of claret, a piper, a fiddler, and the carcase of a cow ... ; when Religion and Justice saw, with tranquil acceptance, prostitutes burned at the stake by the men who had made them what they were.

An Incorruptible Irishman (1932), 'An account of
Chief Justice Charles Kendal Bushe, 1767–1843'

During the 1930s, in her writing Edith retired further upon the family past; her interpretation of it was, like that above and unusually for her class, always concerned with the position of women within it. Her vision of society was not class-bound, prostitution not unmentionable. In this decade firstly she produced the vivid biography of her ancestor Charles Kendal Bushe, 'The Chief', then a volume of essays, two anthologies, and finally at the age of eighty her last novel, *Sarah's Youth* (1938), set in the early years of the century. Dwelling on the past, and fixing in prose the good times and good people that were gone, would have given her release from the family worries and duties that lay heavily upon both the Somerville sisters. Neither of them realised the depths of the young and right-wing Sir Patrick's disenchantment with Ireland, which he concealed from them, or that the coming change from Irish Free State to Republic of Ireland would cause him to make the decision to cut and run from the country the moment that both sisters were dead. Perhaps governed by more than half a lifetime of travelling home to his mother at Glen B, he eventually chose a home in England at Lydney in Gloucestershire that was within range of

Bristol, and of the route home by the 'Bristol Boat' to Cork. As small boys the Coghills began travelling this route to their schooling at Haileybury.

The Somerville sisters hoped that Paddy would marry an Anglo-Irish girl and settle in Glen B. It was a shock to them to discover that he chose otherwise. On 15 January 1930 Sir Patrick Coghill's engagement to Miss Nina Shepstone was announced in the *The Times*, causing despair all round the family as the girl had not been liked when Paddy had brought her to CT for inspection by his mother, his godmother-aunt and the tribe. Miss Shepstone seems to have been a light-hearted socialite who might have been out of her depth among the farming and hunting Amazons of CT, or disliked them in return. The breed of 'flapper' still thrived despite the advances in education and opportunities for girls. Edith began to realise the momentous changes that the women's movement had wrought in the space of twenty years when Ethel wrote to her on 1 February, sending a programme for the unveiling ceremony of Mrs Pankhurst's memorial statue in London and describing the scene. There was, she wrote, 'a Police Band, and the traffic stopped for the "Procession" to go through London. Twenty years ago she and her following stopped the traffic, fighting the police and being dragged to prison.'[1] What was more, Ethel conducted the same Police Band in playing her suffrage anthem, 'March of the Women'. Ethel was less interested in Edith since she had fallen in love with Virginia Woolf, who was part admiring, part horrified. She told her nephew Quentin Bell, 'An old woman of 71 has fallen in love with me. It is at once hideous and melancholy-sad. It is like being caught by a giant crab.'[2]

The whole of early March had been disrupted by the severe illness of the small dogs Taspy and Prinkie, which only Prinkie survived. Mike, Hildegarde, Edith and Dr Hodson had sat up on night shifts nursing them. With her doctor's kitbag ever at the ready, Dr Hodson had chloroformed Taspy when severe fits had started. Although she had officially retired from practice, Dr Hodson was in action again on the night of Toby Coghill's birth at Glen Barrahane on 26 March. Sylvia Lovera remembered the night when the house generator had failed and Betty Coghill, 'Mrs Ambrose', had gone into labour in dim candle-light with no sign of the doctor from Skibbereen. The weather was foul: 'a message was sent to Drishane where Dr Hodson was with D [Edith] ... she was a retired doctor and lived at the Mall House – she rode and hunted and had a small surgery for locals and two very elegant English maids ... Both D and Dr Hodson were pretty old then - however they both put on incredible old tweed coats and hats and set forth down the avenue - I met them and D said "My dear a more reluctant Mrs Gamp never set forth".'[3] But, quite unperturbed, Dr Hodson delivered a baby boy who grew up to be entirely worthy of his saviours.

Despite the disruptions Edith had been able to send off twelve chapters of her American memoir to Houghton and Mifflin in Boston by the end of February and was pleased with the finished version of her *New Statesman* article on Surtees, 'Cer-tes, a classic', which arrived at Drishane on 20 March. She felt ready for a holiday, and went to stay with Mrs Anstey on 3 April. Edith's wide openness to change on the women's liberation front contrasts oddly with her rigid conservatism in art, which is perhaps a legacy of her sporadic art education in the 1880s, which she was so grateful to get. Her diary comments on the exhibitions she saw during her spring travelling in this year show no understanding whatever of the modern movement. Such had been her fight to get training that she remained locked in love with the favoured painters of her student days. In April Edith was to go to Paris for three weeks with Dr Hodson, who had at first taken the Mall House in CT for vacations, but who eventually took permanent root. Dr Hodson being a keen amateur painter, and suffragist, Edith felt completely at home with her and travelled abroad with her more than once.

While in London, en route to Paris, Edith went to the Leicester Galleries to see works by Berthe Morisot and Winifred Nicholson. Like a huffy old reactionary, she wrote in her diary: 'The former indisputable, tho' not attractive (save a few) Mrs Nicholson filthy in colour and technique, and *no* drawing. Sluttish the only word. After lunch went to see ... some wonderful Zoffanys and Stubbs, the greatest contrast imaginable.' In London she also took the opportunity to sign an agreement with a representative of the Boston publisher Houghton Mifflin, Roger Scaife, who was in London at the time. In manuscript form *The States through Irish Eyes* was without its title at this early stage; it features in Edith's diary simply as 'Cruise' after 'Impressions' was abandoned. She met up with the increasingly deaf Ethel Smyth at a lunch party hosted by Lady Stanley: 'Ethel in great heart, and roaring like a lion, and with answering yells from her hostess – the row was terrific, but entertaining.' Hard on the heels of the lunch party Drs Coghill and Hodson appeared for tea, and 'much talk' on the coming expedition abroad.

Edith and Eleanor Hodson arrived in Paris on 7 April. They both attended classes at Délécluse and Colarossi where Edith became aware of a lack in her old reserves of stamina. Feeling her age, she wrote to Elizabeth Hudson that she 'felt like Rip van Winkle' returning to her old Paris Studio life: 'I haven't quite forgotten how to draw and I'm sure a good rub-up will do me good.'[4] On 14 April Edith went with Eleanor back to Eugene Délécluse's studio and wrote in her diary: 'Found the little man there – haggard and war-worn, he was one of the 5 who came out alive, out of 250 in a sally at Verdun.' Her old painting companion Mabel Royds turned up to join them on the 21st and immediately plunged back into Paris Studio life. On the next day Edith's diary entry was: 'Royds and I went to Colarossi's and drew *les nus* till fed.' When Edith was not at the studio she worked in her room at the clean copying of the 'Cruise' manuscript: evidently she still had the capacity to switch effortlessly from writing to painting and drawing and back again instantly. On the 24th she entered in her diary: 'Have done 4 (or more) good length chapters since April 9th – being able to do four times as much in this quiet little town than in the excited rush of life in CT.' In high good humour she bought in the *Bon Marché* two 'hightum and tightum' hats.

Mabel Royds had a taste for the modern painters and tried to convert Edith to an understanding, at least, of their aims. It is easy to forget that these two eager aesthetes were in their early seventies at this stage. Edith's diary records the indefatigable Royds' wasted efforts. On 1 May she went with Royds to the 'Independents' exhibition in the Boulevard Raspail, but she was horror-struck: 'Almost incredibly childish, absurd, and in some cases, obscene. Regretted the 5 francs it had cost to go in.' Not to be deterred, Royds then took Edith to view André L'Hote's studio. He was a cubist (or, as Edith would have it, a 'Cubeast') and the chosen master of the Irish artists Evie Hone and Mainie Jellett. There was no alteration in the negativity of Edith's reaction: ' ... proportions all blocked in angles ... a "finished" work of his (Woman in Bed) perfectly hideous – was *not* impressed by any work.' Still hopeful, Royds then took Edith to the Luxembourg Musée: 'She extorted admiration from me for one Gauguin (colour only) and one Pissaro – a very dark and successful sea picture.' Appreciation of Edith's landscape painting has begun to grow since her death. Three of her canvases were shown at the National Gallery of Ireland exhibition, *The Irish Impressionists* of 1984. In her *Sunday Times* review of this exhibition, Marina Vaizey wrote: 'It is the women who are a surprise: Mary Swanzy, May Guinness, Grace Henry, Edith Somerville: robust and interesting ...'

However out of fashion and unwanted Edith might have felt her painting to be, her horse-business flourished mightily in her absence. On 1 May she had the excellent news that her horse Scortha had been sold by a dealer to an American buyer for £500. Edith was back in London staying in Jack's flat a week later, when Ethel Smyth pressed on her a copy of Virginia Woolf's *A Room of One's Own*, which she found 'admirable', before moving on to the novel *To the Lighthouse*. In her diary there is a wry entry that shows how aware Edith was of Ethel's turbulent passions, now safely directed elsewhere: 'E.S. full of Virginia Woolf and her books – vice Elizabeth, Lady Russell [author of *Elizabeth and her German Garden*], who has gone a bit back in the betting.'[5] Though she laughed at Ethel for her consuming passions, broadcast to her friends, Edith never lost her admiration and liking for her. The pencil drawing of Ethel by

Sargent hung over Edith's easy chair to the end. On the 7th the happy news arrived that Paddy had broken off his engagement, 'unregretted' as Edith noted in her diary. As a reliable sign of her rising good humour, for Mike had sent more news of the selling of her trainee horse Scortha and promising prospects, she then bought in Woodrow's two more hats.

Mrs Anstey came to Drishane for a summer vacation on 20 July, and came in for all the excitement of the Skibbereen Show, where Edith picked up a mare. 'Prowled and spotted a quite nice chestnut filly and after the ritual haggle (Mike the operator, I was sent away) she was bought for £36.' The Annual Church Funds Bazaar, to which Edith still gave what she called her 'dirts' – which were quickly produced paintings for charity events – was on 12 August. She was tidying the old letters in the Studio in order to assemble the material relating to Charles Kendal Bushe. While ordering his letters, she found a bundle of old Martin letters and sent them on to Martin's nephew Jasper. For her late summer vacation she went for the first time to Eastern Europe, to visit Aylmer's daughter Gilla, her husband Max and her in-laws, the Lobkowicz family, in Czechoslovakia. She travelled with Jack for company. Her diary entries are brief, as she was working on Bushe papers en route. They left London on 26 August to travel through Belgium and Germany to the Lobkowicz castle at Eisenberg. Gilla's husband Max collected them from the train at Carlsbad. On the 31st Gilla and Max took them on to another family seat at Jeziri on the border of Saxony. Edith was carrying in her luggage her manuscript notes and old family letters for her book on Charles Kendal Bushe and worked on them throughout this trip. She seems to have worked on her papers single-mindedly, as, although she comments in her diary on the magnificence and huge scale of the scenery, she did not paint.

On her return to England on 11 September she went down to Eastbourne to interview Charlie Harris, who was the son of Aunt Maria, 'the Chief's youngest daughter'.[6] Before returning to CT she had to research as much as she could for her biography, but she still socialised, and in London she met up with the new generation of lady doctors. Hebe Coghill, Joe's daughter, had followed in her Aunt Violet's footsteps and qualified as a medical practitioner. Like Violet, too, who travelled with Dr Lina O'Connor, in her free time she travelled about with a colleague, Dr Ethel Dowling. Edith also spent a weekend with Cissie and Hugh Cholmondeley at Edstaston. She got back home on 22 September only to find that Prinkie, damaged by the illness of earlier in the year that had killed Taspy, had died the day before: 'No use trying to say what I feel about the little thing, whose shrieks of welcome I've been looking forward to ever since I left home. My room a lonesome place now.'[7]

But in late October a guest arrived who cheered her spirits, her old friend and fellow oarswoman Loo Loo Plunket, bringing with her a load of Bushe and

Plunket family papers. Some of these had come from old Kate Plunket, then 109 years old, at Ballymascanlon House in Louth. Edith's diary noted: 'She will be 110 next month, and as a little child of five years old sat on Sir Walter Scott's knee when he was staying with her father, the first Lord Plunket at Old Connaught [Bray].' She started to work on these papers immediately, entering in her diary on 17 October: 'Bushe-whacked through jungles of old letters brought by Loo Loo'. She gained some historical and chronological aid from Dr O'Meara, who was always a reliable source for relevant background reading. He provided from his extensive library the one volume of the eight-volume set of *Lives of Illustrious Irishmen* by James Wills that covered the life and career of Charles Kendal Bushe.[8] James Wills, known as 'Jimty', had been the father of Willy Wills, the playwright and first patron of Violet Martin, and was even more eccentric than his son. The DNB remarked on his absent-mindedness, giving as an example of his behaviour the fact that he had once boiled his watch 'in mistake for an egg', but as a biographer he functioned perfectly well.

Still not ready to write, Edith returned to London on 14 November, staying with Mrs Anstey. She worked at the British Museum Library, starting with a thorough reading-through of the Dublin newspapers of 1800, the year of the Union debate. She tracked down there a rare copy of Shiel's *Sketches of the Irish Bar*. She had some socialising, visiting the Arrans at Thoby Priory with Jem Barlow. Jem had come to London for one of her 'crystal shows', which took place on 27 November. The wearing of 'healing' crystals had obviously caught on in some quarters of the upper classes. At a tea and crystals convention for sixty people, rather like a New Age Tupperware party, Edith met the Mayos, the Kenmares and the Arrans. She was congratulated on her latest book: the whole of the special edition of *The States through Irish Eyes* had been sold, and 1,000 of the ordinary edition. Edith spent her last weekend of the 6/7 December down at Coign with Ethel Smyth and her enormous dog, who was the only item of real interest recorded in her diary: 'Pan grown into a bear as big as a cow.' She arrived back in Drishane on the 8th, and cast about for an opening to her new manuscript. Soon Eleanor Hodson arrived for the Christmas holidays on the 15th, staying as a guest in Drishane. It was fifty years since Jim and Ethel had married in CT on the last day of 1880. 'We wired to Jim and Ethel. All our love to the Golden couple. Coghills and Somervilles.' The book was in slow progress, on 23 December Edith noted: 'Began work at the Chief, finding the preliminaries very difficult.' Stimulation came from automatic writing: she had some sittings with Geraldine Cummins who received automatic scripts from Bushe, some of which Edith was to incorporate into her biography of him.

The new year opened with a 'flu epidemic in the village. On 27 January 1931 Sylvia Warren sent Edith an American review of *The States through Irish*

*Eyes*; she was particularly pleased with one sentence of it: 'The first English author who didn't look at America down a long cold nose.' In her manuscript draft on Charles Kendal Bushe she 'Worked in considerable dubiety as to what to use of the Bushe-Cummins correspondence.'[9] The demands of the material world bothered her. Castletownshend main street was clogged with builders' impedimenta again, this time at the bottom of the hill. In February a local builder began an overhaul of the range of buildings by the Coal Quay known as 'The Stores'. On the 6th Edith went down and talked to the builder, Will Casey: 'He showed me vast recesses at the back of the building, caves, cellars, what he called "a dungeon" and a lime-kiln (the only one in West Cork) Our gt gt gt grandfather's smuggling must have been on a gt gt gt grand scale.'[10]

Later that month, on the 14th, there was an article about Somerville and Ross in the *Cork Examiner*, that Edith described in her diary as an 'Unexpected panegyric ... the Prophets having honour at home.' Honour, however, was intangible compared to income. So low in funds was Edith that she was too embarrassed to explain to Caz Anstey that she could not go to London as often as she used to, as she couldn't afford the fare. But she had promised to attend Ethel Smyth's opening night of her new opera, and some financial leeway was arranged. At the end of the month she was in London for the opening, staying with Caz at her flat in Beaufort Gardens, for the premiere of *The Prison*, to which she went with Dr Violet Coghill. Muriel Currey noticed that Edith 'received it with modified enthusiasm'. Her diary entry was: 'Music complicated and imitative. She had a great reception ...' But her comments to Hildegarde are most pointed: 'I did not greatly enjoy The Prison ... funereal of the most ebony black ... [it is] vulgar to have dawn signalled by sparrows chirrupping and a bugler blowing the Last Post for close of day ... Violet, who had been cutting corpses up all day, felt she would have liked a little more gaiety.'[11] Violet was now a distinguished demonstrator of anatomy, and trained young women doctors.

Edith visited and interviewed more relatives of Charles Kendal Bushe, but found time, with her cousin Rose Cameron Bingham, to have a sitting with the medium Eileen Garrett. She met Cicely Hamilton at lunch with Ethel Smyth and, her diary noted 'liked CH very much, most agreeable and unaffected and interesting plain looks'. She was back in CT on 18 March. Such were the difficulties in farming that, with the advice of Richard Helen, their assistant manager, they decided to sell some of their Friesians in order to concentrate on pigs and horses. At Marsh's auctioneers their twelve cows sold for £240. Pigs were then bought in. At the end of April Edith met Mrs Anstey at Bath where they both had treatment for rheumatism. When she came back to CT on 13 May, she was walking easily, though she had loathed the strict regime of her treatment. She returned to her 'Bushe whacking', visited the houses associated with him, Kilfane and Kilmurry, and researched in the library at King's Inns in Dublin.

In June there were more good reviews of *The States through Irish Eyes*, part of which is set among rich landed Americans who hunted, but Muriel Currey noted in her transcript that 'most of the writers seem annoyed that there should be USA Ladies and Gents.' American society was something of an unknown quantity then, with a general assumption that they were all egalitarian republicans. As she was less lame, and not writing well, Edith accepted more invitations. It was widely known that she was a lover of horses, so that wherever she went, her hosts would show her any particularly remarkable horse in their neighbourhood. When she was staying near Mount Juliet in June, she was taken by Dermot MacCalmont's head groom, Ruttle, to see a legendary racehorse, The Tetrarch. In her diary she entered: 'Aged 20, a hollow-backed wreck, in a paddock, but his legs as fresh as ever. Almost white and his head still beautiful.' The writing of her biography faltered in its pace. In August she almost had writer's block over the 'very difficult place' in her CKB book dealing with the period of the Union Debates. She was reading W.H. Lecky's *Leaders of Public Opinion in Ireland* for inspiration, but the summer invasion had cast its usual blight.

On 25 June Mrs Anstey arrived at Drishane and Archbishop Gregg and his wife moved into Glen B as holiday tenants. The Choir was put on its mettle for the ecclesiastical grandee. Huge numbers of people turned up for a tennis tournament, in which the Archbishop played. In combination with Hildegarde in the mixed doubles he was unbeatable. Later on they crowded in for the Regatta, and only started to depart after the first week of September. Charles Kendal Bushe was not getting much attention; but on 17 September Geraldine Cummins arrived with a lifeline from CKB himself: 'Wrote with GC in the Studio. Very successful. The Chief interested and interesting.'[12] Geraldine stayed for a week, and her automatic scripts did away with Edith's writer's block. Edith now made use of two mediums.

At the beginning of October, Edith read aloud to Jem Barlow and an attendant Martin the draft text of her biography, which now incorporated 'detail' furnished by Cummins' automatic communications from Bushe. On the 12th she went off to London, mainly for a performance of Ethel's opera *The Wreckers*. Someone had at last had an effect, short-term only, on Ethel's dress sense. The opera was a mixed experience: 'Very well staged and well put on, crowds effective, and the principals screamed and yelled convincingly. Orchestral parts, overture and interlude very fine and the only part I really enjoyed. Great enthusiasm at the end and ES got up on the stage. She looked nice and very well dressed and was tremendously applauded. I am now definitely certain that I don't like opera – at least good opera, as my Mother said of poetry.'

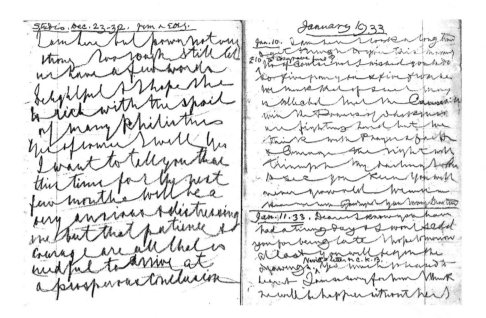

15 Automatic writing was Edith's link with her writing partner, and the means by which she contrived to continue to write for decades after Martin Ross's death. These scripts, from 1932–3, are now held at Queen's University Belfast.

On 25 October, with the coming Irish election a heated topic of conversation everywhere she went, Edith discussed a new name in Irish politics with a fellow guest at a dinner with Mrs Hunter at Hill Hall: 'Talked to Lord Balfour about Cosgrave and Ireland. He said that as Chief Secretary there he was disliked, though he introduced the Land Bill, while his brother was popular though he brought in Coercion. The present coercion measures in Ireland only equalled by the power exercised by the Ogpu in Russia,' she wrote in her diary. OGPU was the name of Stalin's secret police. Edith's idea of what constituted the sort of 'tweenie' who was going to save and remake Ireland had expanded to include revolutionaries: President Cosgrave had served in the Easter Rising at the South Dublin Union under Eamonn Ceannt. His death sentence commuted to penal servitude for life, he was held among the prisoners at Frongoch POW Camp in North Wales until his release in January 1917. He was a politician of great ability and subtlety with an understanding of the complicated composite nature of the Irish vote, and an idea of utilising the residual power and goodwill of what remained of the gentry class, now established in the professions, or farming and stockbreeding on the lands that remained to them. A member of the first Dáil Eireann and supporter of the 1921 Treaty, he became acting chairman of the Provisional Government on the death of Griffith and in October 1922 became president of the Executive Council of the Free State. Edith was to give him her full support.

She was back in Drishane on the 28th. In November she invested in two young horses, a black colt called 'The Chief', and a chestnut named in memory of her stolen and lost Finnbar. The *Spectator* wrote to her to ask her to contribute to a series of articles in support of Cosgrave and his government. Knowing well, she thought, what the alternative to Cosgrave would be, she wrote the article 'The Re-Creators' over Christmas and sent it off on 6 January. It was published on the 23rd. Yeats' article in the same series followed hers a week later. On 2 February at a sitting with Jem at which she received automatic writing, she learned: 'The Chief helping Cosgrave as much as possible'. Over the same period Edith felt she had finally found a satisfactory way to weld all her Bushe material together. She wrote hoping that the book would find a market, and in triumph at having finished it, to Geraldine Cummins in London on 4 February:

> I've 'The Chief' off my hands at last, and I'm having a busman's holiday writing letters. A terrible heap of them had piled up against me … People say there is to be a boom in Ireland and Irish affairs, and all Irish America is expected to be in Dublin and Cork next summer [for the Eucharistic Congress]. They are erecting an altar in St Stephen's Green [Dublin] that is to be a hundred feet high, and it is said it is being guarded day and night to keep 'Communists' from blowing it up. That, however, might have its bright side …
>
> I forgot if I told you to look out for a little article that I was asked to write for the 'Spectator' for January 23rd about the election. Mr W.B. Yeats has done the second … The speechifying is in full swing now – (poor wretches) and the elections are on the 16th. So I shall not go to London before that, of course, as every vote is wanted when one remembers the flood of ignorant and senseless boys and girls who have been given the vote.'[13]

During January she had helped the editor of the *Cork County Eagle*, Patrick Sheehy, by writing political 'squibs' in support of Cosgrave's general election campaign against de Valera. However, de Valera won the general election, his party Fianna Fáil winning 72 seats, though he did not have an overall majority. The success of the Republicans in Ireland struck a chill into the British public, who might have had hopes of Cosgrave and his gradualism, but had none of de Valera. Imbued with the opinions of the farming society of rural West Cork,

Edith remained mystified at the attraction of de Valera for the voters. She knew the farming community and trusted too much that the low opinion of de Valera prevalent in this class was more widespread than it actually was. His policies were wrecking Irish agriculture. In Notebook 10 Edith recorded farmers talking at Clonakilty Junction in 1933: 'Ah he's a dam' fool of a man! Professors and teachers are the most ignorant narra' minded people in the world. They have plenty to eat and they know nothing. He never saw a field til he came out of University, and what does the like of him know of turf – or anything else?'

On 8 February 1932 the Provost of Trinity College, Dublin, E.J. Gwynn, wrote to ask Edith if she would accept an honorary degree of Doctor of Letters. She accepted and her robes were ordered. Edith went to London on 3 March to stay with Caz Anstey; from her flat she wrote to Hildegarde: 'I am working hard at an index for my book, but, in the present state of just hatred and contempt of Ireland I am afraid no-one will look at it and I don't blame them. The Sylvias have been here for tea. Young Sylvia [Townshend Gorges Lovera] said that the *loathing* for Ireland among the people she met in Plymouth can't be expressed .. *All* tarred with the same Republican brush – But I suppose that is inevitable – The most hopeful feature of the case is the certain disaster of the Eucharistic Congress – That *may* open their eyes.'[14] But the Eucharistic Congress, which was indeed a test of the new State's organisational powers, was to be a shining success. Quite different eyes from those that Edith had envisaged were opened.

She saw a specialist in London about her lameness and started a new course of treatment. On 2 April she attended a debate about spiritualism in the Queen's Hall organised by Mrs Dawson Scott in which she did not participate though she sat on the platform, as a token, with other prominent believers. There was a widespread reaction in the press, and Rose Macaulay attacked the subject with venom in *Time and Tide*. Thinking over how to respond to this attack in a calm and measured way, Edith returned to Drishane on the following day. She had a letter from Ethel Smyth, who had been sent a script of her biography to read, 'abusing me for over use of quotations in my books. I could retaliate as to the same fact (if it is a fact) in her music!' Twelve copies of the printed book arrived at Drishane. Boyle had always taken an interest in her book jacket designs and had collaborated with Edith on the design of the cover of the first edition of *An Irish Cousin*. Apparently he had collaborated again: 'It looks very well done and Boyle's and my dust jacket is most successful. Had remorseful postcards from E.S.'[15]

The May reviews of *An Incorruptible Irishman* were good, 'even the Irish ones'. To Edith's scorn and amusement, with bland casualness and a typically contemptuous English misreading, Harrod's advertised it as 'The Incorrigible Irishman'. Charlie Graves wrote a long, approving article about the book in the *Guardian* on the 24th. During June Edith was made to practise wearing her TCD doctoral robes by Hildegarde, so that she became accustomed to moving around in them; they were very heavy and made her hot and uncomfortable. She was generally irritable. There had been a critical review on the 12th in *Time and Tide* by Stephen Gwynn, 'rather nasty', to which Geraldine Cummins responded in a letter published on the 25th. On 15 June she had a cheering letter from Ethel Smyth sending a quotation from the just-published diaries of Arnold Bennet, in which Ethel had immediately spotted the laudatory reference to *The Silver Fox* in his entry for 1 February, 1898. But four days later her diary shows that Edith sent a formal letter to complain to *Time and Tide* about Rose Macaulay's 'offensive notes in which she asserted that spiritualism was a mixture of fraud and hysterics'.

She went up to Dublin for the university ceremony on 29 June 1932 in which she was awarded her honorary doctorate from Trinity College Dublin. She had accepted the degree on condition that Martin's name should be associated with hers during the conferring, as the literary firm of Somerville and Ross was still at work. Sir Robert Tate was the University Orator at this time, and a man of rare sensitivity. In his Latin oration he skilfully skirted the problem raised by the continued literary career of a woman who had ceased to breathe at a quarter to eight in the morning of 21 December 1915. Herbert made an elegant translation of Sir Robert's flowery address to the congregation for Edith, sent on 18 July:

> I recall with veneration to your memory the cousin associated with her in so many works, whom living she loved more than the light of day, and whom, now that she is taken from her sight, she cherishes with no less love than if she were present and helping. Therefore, not only this island of ours, but the greater Ireland, scattered over either half of the world, will confess, and gladly, that for no woman's brow could our academic wreath more worthily be woven.[16]

Hildegarde made sure with safety pins that the robes stayed put, and there was no mishap during the manoeuvres of the ceremony. The part of the day that gave Edith most delight was the singing of the Trinity College Choir after the celebratory dinner in the Dining Hall.[17] In a press photograph taken of Edith in her doctoral robes, she rests her hand on her new volume beside her, *An Incorruptible Irishman*. She was proud of her doctorate, and it can hardly be maintained that it was undeserved. She knew that she had been highly placed when she sat her Trinity examinations in 1878, and that she could have taken a degree course with no difficulty had she been born a generation later and had finances not been prohibitive. Though it was not the done thing in academic circles, from now on she asked that she should be addressed formally in society as 'Doctor', and by her correspondents. It must have been an enormous pleasure to her to be on equal terms of address with those women whose company she so enjoyed – Doctors Coghill, Hodson and O'Connor.

Summertime began to fragment into disparate pieces in its usual way, preventing steady writing work. Finances were low again. Back at Drishane on 30 June she found stacks of congratulatory letters, and telegrams from Sylvia Warren about the feats of one of Edith's horses exported to America, Nora Creina, who had taken 1st in a Hunter Novice Class of twenty-eight. On 1 July Edith's letter taking issue with Rose Macaulay's damning definition of spiritualism in her 'Notes on the Way' article of the previous issue was published in *Time and Tide*. The difficulties of keeping her own personal account at the bank separate from the farm account did not decrease. Three days later she wrote in her diary: 'Found with considerable dismay that the half yearly extortion of interest on the farm overdraft had been taken from my account viz. £70.' Kind letters gave consolation: on 5 July Lady Rhondda wrote to Edith to give her approval of the letter disputing Rose Macaulay's piece on spiritualism; Provost Gwynn wrote to her to thank her for the copy of *An Incorruptible Irishman* that she had given him 'and reverting to the "Real Charlotte" – the only one of our books the Dublin intelligentsia seems to have read (with the RM).'[18] Further consolation, now without a personal dog of her own, came when she was given another nine-weeks-old fox terrier, and started to train her under the old family dog-name of Cozy, being the fifth in that line. Then, inexorably, the summer 'wave' of visitors began to rise.

Young Sylvia remembered an event from this summer which shows that, despite her age, Edith still understood young men on the Buddh 'egg' scale from the point of view of a 'squaw'. Sylvia wrote: 'I would think that she took on the whole a lot of interest in the young – and their goings on and sayings – I can see her absorbing and considering some bit of nonsense with a sort of half smile – One afternoon I walked home alone from a vast picnic in Horse Island sound ... – and I found D standing outside Drishane hall door saying that 5 American young men had unexpectedly arrived on bikes from Cork "touring" – They were sons mostly of friends and admirers of D's and had just turned up at Drishane, and she said they must be asked to stay the night and I was to rush round houses and see who could put them up'. This was no small feat as the village was crowded out, but Sylvia managed to book beds here there and everywhere, including one in her mother's Tally Ho, and reported back to D: 'When I got back the drinks were in full swing in the drawing room. I had not so far seen any of them and D said creep in and we will look at them through a slit in the screen and as you have been to all the trouble making arrangements you can choose your young man. So we both peered through the hole and I said "I'll have that one." and D said "Let's have another look". He turned out to be a certain Johnny Holloway ... very nice, very strong and very useful – next morning he hauled up a boat for me and mended a Seahorse outboard which had so far defeated everyone else ...'[19]

The Greggs were back at Glen B. The Regatta and Church Bazaar took up all the sisters' time, and Edith did not get forward with any formulation of her next book. By 23 August she had finished a piece that later became a chapter of *Maria and Some Other Dogs* – 'In Praise of Ladies' – that is to say, lady dogs, whom she prized for being more biddable and stable and for not suffering from the bad behaviour of male dogs when they were wandering over the countryside 'on the ramp'. Doing the farm accounts, Hildegarde and Edith noticed now a steep and disastrous fall in the price of heifers and pigs. On 18 September, Edith's diary records that the sisters 'went to the farm and had the painful task of telling the men that we had to cut down wages or shut down farming'. On the next day Edith had to do the same to the men of the stables: 'Had the painful duty of warning Mike and Pat that wages must be cut down or the stable shut down.'

W.B. Yeats wrote to her on 21 September, mis-spelling her name as he could not help doing, asking her to join the Irish Academy of Letters. Edith and the scholar Helen Waddell were the only two Irish women to accept. In the most charming way Æ (George Russell) wrote to apologise for Yeats on 1 October explaining his 'absence of mind and mistakes in ordinary affairs, while intellectually, his mind was the most brilliant he had ever known'. Farm finances were going from bad to worse; by early November they were in deep trouble, for they were being offered 7 shillings for pigs instead of the normal 30. It was best to kill their pigs and sell the carcasses in the village, as it was too expensive to feed them. The sisters were ill with anxiety over the farm overdraft, which had gone over the limit. Edith was writing a collection of essays, *The Smile and the Tear*, knowing that publishers were in a financial downturn as well.

Early in December of 1932, Edith began to worry about the health of her brother Boyle; writing later to Hildegarde for advice she explained that he 'looks not a bit well. Rather thin and a bad colour.' Boyle flew off the handle at anyone presuming to give him advice, and the situation required delicate handling. This was Hildegarde's speciality. Edith was enraged at the economies, described as 'privations they were inflicting upon themselves – quite needlessly', that Boyle and Mab practised, suspecting that they were 'dining on poached eggs'. Boyle was sitting up late at night completing his book on Commodore

Anson's world voyage, published by Heinemann in 1934. He was having 'nerve attacks'. Edith explained to her sister: 'It is this maniac, *short-sighted* economy that brought on that 5th nerve attack, and he looks to me ready for another at the smallest provocation ... you know Boyle's intemperate yells if one protests, so I've said nothing to him.'[20] But she did write to their youngest, most vocal son Michael for help with his headstrong parents in bringing them to reason.

In the same month Jack started a campaign to make Edith face up to the organisation of a pension; he had volunteered to approach the Royal Literary Fund (RLF) on her behalf. She wrote to Hildegarde: 'I've written to him and said go ahead, but I stipulate that the plea must be made on the Irish breakdown. If I hadn't, since 1920, had to put practically all I earned into the farm, I could have invested nearly £2,000 and have had enough to live on – I have a thousand pounds worth of horses now, that aren't worth ten shillings.'[21] The draft of her application to the RLF has survived. She explained that she had invested in a house and the farm, from 1901, 'believing that, with cattle and horse breeding, the farm would support me when literature would no longer do so'. This is firm evidence that Edith believed the invalid Martin would not recover from the effects of her fall of 1898, thus putting an end to steady substantial income from literature. Farming and house letting were taken up long before Martin's death in 1915. After describing the effects of the Civil War, she explained, 'Had we dismissed our workmen they and their families would have starved and our stock ... would have had to be destroyed.' Having given an account of her losses, she continued: 'in this difficulty I devoted, as far as was possible, all my earnings to keeping the farm going, but it was impossible to do this without a very heavy overdraft ... this last disastrous year of Mr de Valera's government has brought to me, as to very many others, what is very little short of ruin. It is impossible to sell the farm and thus pay off the Bank as there is no sale for land or indeed anything else at present ... my assets, as well as what may be called the corpse of my farm – [are] 4 young horses that are a great expense and are at present unsaleable ... my present difficulties are wholly attributable to the state of my country.' At the end of her 1932 diary she wrote: 'The outlook, political and financial – especially the latter personally – about as dark as it can be.' Beginning her new diary she wrote of the overdraft 'like a thundercloud over our heads.'

To Edith's distress, on 19 January 1933 for financial reasons Longman turned down *The Smile and the Tear*. Writing to Hildegarde in Dublin a week later, Edith has made no headway with the problem of Boyle, who had been inoculated against the 'flu in preparation for a return to London, a London with a severe 'flu epidemic: 'He doesn't look a bit too well and ought *not* to be going into an infected place like London. Change to the South of France or a sea voyage is what he wants. It is no use talking – Mab suffocates one with a cloud of words and he becomes violent. Such a pair!' De Valera had called a general election again in January 1933 in order to strengthen his position. Jack was intensely worried about his sisters, and ready to have them live with him in London. He wrote to Edith on the 4th: 'If by any evil chance de V were to get in with an independent majority I don't see how any of you could go on living in the country. I don't think you need be afraid of MacDermot splitting the Pro-Treaty vote. He's not such a fool.' MacDermot was a politician in a new Irish party of great interest at this time.[22] Hildegarde was sending the newspapers from Dublin with the latest election news; on 3 January 1933 Edith wrote to her sister to express her feelings about Frank MacDermot of the breakaway National Centre Party: 'I fear Mac Dermot is going to be no exception to the jealousy and self-seekingness of all – or *most* – politicians. It is sickening – like the Generals in the South African War, each playing for his own hand and sacrificing his country. I had hoped that McD's being a gentleman *might* have helped. Baldwin and Mrs Pankhurst are the only two people big enough to have put themselves aside for the public good. Cosgrave is calling out for money. I wonder if men, like old Joe Leycester, who have plenty, will realise that this is their last chance. I am afraid we can do nothing being Prods and gentry and paupers, three damning drawbacks and we've no money to give.'

Others of the remaining gentry had concluded that there was no 'last chance'. Edith noted in letters and her diaries in this period several Big House auctions, their owners accepting what they saw as inevitable: that the coming of de Valera into power marked the end for them. On 26 January Edith wrote to Hildegarde: 'We are *most* grateful for your Irish Times. It always has later news than the [Cork] Examiner, and gives a far better general survey. It now looks as if the three parties, C[lann] na G[ael], Centre, and Independents (and possibly some of Labour) may – as Pro-Treaty – out number F[ianna] F[áil]. But if deV[alera] *can*, as the largest single party, stick, he surely will.'

On 10 February all of Jack's string-pulling finally had an effect: 'wonderful and very unexpected news that the Royal Literary Society has voted me a donation of £300 ... they have "to the fainting squadrons brought relief" at a moment when it was badly wanted'.[23] There was further good financial news on the 24th when she had an acceptance from E.V. Lucas at Methuen for *The Smile and the Tear* 'and to publish for Xmas as I suggested.' Methuen's had published *Dan Russel the Fox* in 1911; they were also the publishers of the scientist Sir Oliver Lodge, whose hard-headed, but accepting, approach to automatic writing and spiritualism pleased Edith.[24] At the beginning of March she went up to Dublin to celebrate her election as founder member of the Irish Academy of Letters at a grand Irish Academy Dinner. She stayed with the

Greenes on St. Stephen's Green, and met Yeats there at a Sunday luncheon party, describing him on the following day to Hildegarde:

> Yeats is a huge man, more like a big country-gent than the typical poet (which I had believed him to be). A brown, healthy, good looking face and charming wavy grey hair, (*not* long hair). Very interesting talker, though at moments he fell into abstraction. A nice voice, decided Dublin tone, (rather reminding me of GBS's) and *no* assumption of high-brow or stuffed- shirt-ness ... [James Stephens] and Yeats began, at lunch, to discuss de Valera, and I grieve to say, they both seem to have been subjugated by his abominable charm. Olive [Guthrie] backed me up in describing the ruin he was bringing on farmers, but both these poets were only concerned with the brute's personality, and kept re-iterating that he was sincere, and a gentleman, and a patriot and neither of them cared tuppence for the people to whom he has brought starvation. I must admit they were very interesting and quite temperate and well mannered and obviously they knew *nothing* about why wheat couldn't be grown on the Killarney mountains, or cattle sold at profit for pence apiece'[25]

Lady Leslie, also at the lunch, weighed in on the side of Olive and Edith: 'She has been living *marooned* at Glaslough – the strike and the snow combining for entire isolation.' Edith had been worried about meeting Dublin literati at the Irish Academy Dinner, but having met Yeats and Stephens, and liked them, she felt much happier at the prospect. The Dinner itself was described in a letter to Cameron on the seventh. She was the only woman of the company and alone among them had opted to wear academic robes. She was collected and escorted by Lennox Robinson in a hired car to Jammet's Restaurant, and sailed with him through the lower dining room diners, in her red and blue 'Solomonian' robes, to the private dining room on the upper floor. 'No politics were talked, as far as I could hear anyhow – Professor Starkie sat opposite to me and was very interesting, telling me, across the table, about his experiences with Hungarian gypsies[26] ... Mr Robinson sent around a half bottle of champagne with a card "From one West Corker to another" (and when I tried to pay my five bob for the dinner said it was paid – which really was distressing as I know he isn't well off.' After the proposing of toasts and when all the men had stood up to drink Edith's health, they stayed standing and circulated so that they could all take turns in sitting beside Edith and talking to her: 'Various of the men came round and took turns to sit beside me and talk and be polite. I must say I was astonished, as I had never thought they knew anything of our books. A rather attractive young rebel, Frank O'Connor, from County Cork, talked to me for a long time. He had been *out* with the Sinn Feiners, and *in*, in prison! He had a good brogue and said his only education had been up to the 4th book in the National School! But he had excellent manners and was a most interesting talker. Another strange being, Peadar O'Donnell, came up, and said he was a Communist. I said I hoped he'd go to Russia. He said he meant to do so and promised to write a book about it and said he would send me a copy. I hope he will ... I think they were very much pleased that I should have come.'[27]

Hildegarde was sent a description of an afternoon tea party on the next day at Professor Starkie's, who clearly quickly collected good conversationalists when he met them. Edith's observation that the biography of Charles Kendal Bushe had connected Somerville and Ross with an old order in Ireland that had positive significance for moderate nationalists was astute; the party had been 'A great crush. I was introduced to a lot of people among them Lady Glenavy – youngish and good looking who made me many civil speeches. I fancy 'The Chief' has been very much read, and has put up my stock among these rather exclusively *Irish* Dublin people ... Olive introduced me to Mr and Mrs McNeill. I like them both very much. He felt like a gentleman and looks the image of old Mr Purdon RM. Very quiet dry voice – devoid of swagger.'

James McNeill was an Ulster Catholic educated at Belvedere and Emmanuel College, Cambridge, and brother of the great Irish scholar and revolutionary Eoin McNeill. He had been an Indian and Irish civil servant who joined de Valera's political movement in 1916; he helped to draft the Irish Free State constitution. He was Irish high commissioner in London, 1923–8, but at the time that Edith met him had recently been forcibly retired from the post of governor general of the Irish Free State, de Valera being strong enough now to discard what was seen as an outdated symbol of irrelevant British monarchy. De Valera had made thoughtful and diplomatic choices for those men like McNeill who had served in the intermediary group working at the difficult interface between England and Ireland. But in 1933, when he regained power with a working majority, he felt he could dispense with a governor general. This triggered, in part, the 'economic war', that was financially disastrous for Ireland, when the British imposed economic restrictions in retaliation.

Through the Kenmares Edith had made friends with a wide circle of independent American women, like the impressionist Ruth Draper and her friend Elizabeth Hudson. In March 1933 Elizabeth Hudson's partner Dorothy Sturges died; Edith delayed writing a letter of sympathy, but finally wrote from London on 26 March. The tone is that of her letters of sympathy to Kinkie or Hildegarde, to whom she also recommended spiritualism when close friends or family died. It is clear that Edith was describing friendship, innocent of any sexual interpretation:

Dear Elizabeth, I know only too well what you suffer. I don't believe that there is any grief that cuts so deep. The love of such a friend is the purest, and most unselfish, and most faithful of any love. There is none other like it. I have proved it and lost it and found it again. It was not really lost – only clouded for a time by my ignorance of what the true conditions were. For six months everything was dark for me. I'm sure it is so for you now. But then, in a mercy, light came. Nothing can really make up to one for what one has lost, but there can be, and there is, a very wonderful alleviation for both the one who has gone and the one who is left. I believe that Dorothy is feeling the loss of you as much as you feel her loss. It is inevitable. Even now, after all these years, for us both, the loneliness hits hard. But I do hope and believe that presently you will have the same mercy granted to you as has been granted to me. It needs patience, and determination, and faith, but I believe you will find these. Faith is the hardest. It took me three months (after the first ray of hope had come to me) to get a word, real and unmistakeable, from my cousin – but it came at last.[28]

Edith went to London to Caz Anstey on 8 March and made her arrangements with Methuens. At a grand St Patrick's Day luncheon at Mrs Crawshay's she met Shane Leslie, Lord and Lady Lansdowne and Sir Ernest Budge, the Egyptologist. The last turned out to be a surprising fan of the RM. He 'said that Sam Weller, Captain Cuttle and Flurry Knox were the three great characters of comic fiction'.[29] In the evening Caz took her to see O'Casey's *Plough and the Stars*. Dublin, the setting for O'Casey's play, remained very much a foreign place to the Anglo-Irish of West Cork, as they usually travelled Cork – Bristol – London and mostly kept a distance from it except for the Horse Show and shopping. Edith's description of the play, her own and the audience reaction, is a piece of reportage of a valuable immediacy: 'Maire O'Neill and Fred Sinclair the stars, but all acted well. A *horrid* play. Grimy, ugly, hateful. Dublin roaring raucous voices. Most of the characters drunk most of the time. Was glad when it was over, ending in death and destruction and incessant appeals to God at which most of the audience laughed.'[30] Edith remained all her life a strictly brought-up Christian, and despite her enjoyment of rather outré people, blasphemy shocked her to the core. She would simply leave the scene if she found herself in the presence of a blasphemer; and she once calmly left the room when George Moore had tried on a leery tale to see if he could shock her.

She was back in Drishane on 31 March, when she settled down to write her views on a subject that Martin Ross had covered at the beginning of her writing career in the article 'In Sickness and In Health'.[31] It is interesting to compare the detached, hard-bitten tone of both pieces. Curiously, Tom Connell the Drishane coachman features in Edith's. Taking a long view, and a dispassionate one, Edith wrote an extra chapter to *The Smile and the Tear*, on the subject of marriage entitled 'For Richer for Poorer'. She helped Hildegarde to do the income tax returns for the farm: 'the farm lost about £160 during last year. Under the present Government it will lose considerably more this year,' she wrote in her diary, which also reveals that she nominated Shane Leslie for the Irish Academy of Letters, having liked him more than Martin had. By mid-May Sylvia Warren had again come to the rescue by asking for two horses, Run o' Luck and Rayleen, to be shipped to her for sale in America, and asking Edith to train on a filly that Sylvia had bought in Meath. Edith was very pleased and excited at the birth of a fine-looking thoroughbred colt to her mare Loureen, by Sirrah, who belonged to 'one Hurley at Glanmire'. Geraldine Cummins arrived at the end of the month for a fortnight's rest and collaboration with Edith although much of her time was taken up with the documentation and preparation of the shipping of her two horses. Edith finished reading *Twenty Years A-Growing* by Maurice O'Sullivan – 'a Blasket Island boy. Written in Irish and well translated into Anglo-Irish idiom. A very remarkable book – a work of – apparently – unconscious art. Devoid of humour, full of feeling for beauty ...'

At the end of June an American couple in the diplomatic service, David Gray and his wife, came to stay in CT for the first time. Through their interest in spiritualism they were friends of Cummins, who had told them of the spiritual and worldly attractions of the village. He was the American minister to Ireland and a successful playwright, and he had come to West Cork in search of peace to write a novel. He had written the introduction to Cummins' book *The Road to Immortality*, published in 1932. At this time Edith was adapting an RM story for the stage with the occasional help of Cummins, 'the faithful little Geraldine', who was then based in Cork.[32] Hildegarde was away and the business of socially receiving and tidying up after a series of tenants fell upon Edith, who wrote to her sister on the 22nd: 'It *maddens* me having to leave my play just when I am interested! But it isn't your fault, only my abominable luck, and all my life has been the same, and the same for Martin. How we ever did *anything* I don't know. It is the infernal want of money makes these chores compulsory.'

Drawn by Edith's sympathy and understanding after the loss of her partner, the American Elizabeth Hudson stayed in Drishane in July 1933, arriving on the 12th, when much was to do about the Somerville and Ross bibliography, begun at Hudson's instigation. By August its publisher A.J.A. Symons was beginning to take an intrusive part in the organising of the volume. He antagonised Edith by insisting on a fulsome biographical blurb that Edith refused to countenance.

She was dead set against anything that smacked of 'self-advertising'. All through the summer Edith worked fitfully on her stage adaptation. In September, to Edith's regret, Geraldine had to leave to work in England. Edith explained to Hildegarde: 'She is the ideal "old shoe" and sits in faithful and comfortable silence at the table in the Studio and I don't really feel that anyone is there! She loves being here, I think, as she can do her own work undisturbed, which is impossible for her at her home, where chores are laid upon her all the time.' Caz Anstey was forever importuning Edith to visit her, or at least to write, and Edith became irritated: 'She doesn't remember that I am swamped in letters of *all* sorts, that *must* be dealt with, apart from every possible house, farm and stable interruption and social devilments – I live in a state of perpetual frustration and only that Martin urges me on to try and write I should give up in despair. About a week of 'seeing off' days during last month. Hanging about until 12 o'clock when, with thankfulness, I see Jerome [the chauffeur] arrive!'[33] The agricultural market in stock was not improving: on 18 July the sisters sold an £18 heifer for £8.15s. Not everything was ill-fated: the horses left for America on the 25th and the next day at the Cork Show the beloved Finbarr got a 1st.

Edith went up to Dublin for the Horse Show, and on 9 August her diary notes that she attended a meeting of the Irish Academy at the Peacock Theatre: 'Yeats in the chair. The only comparatively white one. Nothing much done save a protest against censors stopping G.B.S.'s "Black Girl in search of her God".' Then she had to get back to Drishane to welcome Mrs Anstey on 11 August. Crowds of relations filled the village. On the 18th a visiting family, the Williams, 'brought Mrs Cameron – i.e. – Elizabeth Bowen to see me. Very agreeable, good-looking and clever.' At a tennis party on the 23rd there were sixty-five people, while the sisters tried at the same time to oversee the threshing, which had been delayed by the weather. On 25 August an advance printing of her essay on marriage 'For Richer for Poorer' came in the *Cornhill Magazine* for September, for which she was paid 11 guineas. The CT Regatta this year was attended by some marine biologists working at Lough Ine – Professors Julian Huxley, Neal and Renouf. Jack went down and dined on Sergeant Sullivan's yacht *Ailsa* that was in for the Regatta, and after dinner brought his host up to meet Edith. Serjeant Sullivan, who remembered her and Martin in court taking notes from forty years back, was a 'great talker and interesting. Loathes Lloyd George and said he had seen letters from Ll.G to the Dublin murder gang, bargaining for his life, while announcing publicly that England would suppress and crush all rebels.'[34]

Financial relief was at hand. A cable came from Sylvia Warren on 8 September with an offer of 1,500 dollars for the mare Rayleen, which Edith thankfully accepted, writing in her diary: 'Wonderful these hard times.' Ten days later Mrs Anstey left, the 'summer exodus nearly complete'. *The Smile and the Tear* was published to good reviews early in October, the ever-faithful Charlie Graves giving 'a first rate notice in Punch'. On release the book sold 700 copies in two days, and had sold 1070 copies by 8 November. During this month, after doing some accounts, and impressed by Sylvia Warren's sales, Edith concocted another plan. She was going to use Cameron's land and raise horses on it for sale in the USA. She had put about £2,000 into the farm and had lost £350 in her investment of leasing the White House, which had not proved an economic success. Undeterred, she wrote optimistically to Hildegarde, who was in America: 'just now I have £400 clear and no debts, and I have three good horses to sell in the Spring, so that I could risk trying this scheme'. Her optimism was inspired by what she felt to be a coming change in the political situation. Earlier in the same letter she had written: 'everyone says the times *must* improve (and even Dev now talks about a settlement of the economic war – which *he* will not bring about, but he may go out [of power] over it) ...'

Edith planned to use the Big Lawn for horses, but to dedicate the income from Cross Street rents, the Stores and the White House, to paying off their loan debt to Percy Aylmer. She had already made the decision to leave her property to her godson, Patrick Coghill. She envisaged, rightly, that the time would come when it would be valuable. She was determined as well that Drishane should not be rendered landless: 'It seems to me that the only alternative for Cameron would be to sell *everything* up to the croquet ground, and the flower garden, which would be quite horrible for us all, from every point of view ... I know it is a bit of a gamble for me, but it seems the only plan by which the land can be used to advantage (short of making Drishane a villa residence). I think between horses and pigs, I could pay the men and the rates, and would chance *making* money, and you would be free of personal anxiety, as the houses and the Round O are fairly safe to bring in about £60 – or possibly more and I would be responsible for the rest of the debt to Percy.'[35]

By December of this year Elizabeth Hudson was trying to learn how to receive automatic writing from her deceased friend Dorothy Sturges, but she was finding it difficult to break out of a peculiarly helpless grief. She wrote to Edith for advice, diffidently apologising for troubling Edith with trivial queries, and received in the reply the encouragement: 'I love you to ask my help. It will never be refused. "Trivial" is not the word. The love for helpless things is never trivial.'[36] We do not know how Elizabeth Hudson felt about being classified as a 'helpless thing' by the lifelong minister to lame ducks. The RM play *Flurry's Wedding* was on the stocks again and early in January 1934, a copy of the typescript was sent to the Gate Theatre in Dublin, as Edith had met Michael Mc Liammoir and liked him; she told Geraldine Cummins: 'I have met the young man who runs it [The Gate]. He was very civil and full of my books – but unless "Flurry" possibly, there's no part in it for him. He might be disposed to give it a try-out ...' But as with every other manager to whom it was sent, the play did not find favour. *The Smile and the Tear* was proving a steady seller. The second edition had sold 1,200 by 4 January. At the end of the month Edith went horse-coping and bought a beautiful colt, 'King Cormac', for £65. She was surprised on 10 February to receive from Durrants, the press cuttings agency to which she subscribed, an account of a broadcast by Maurice Healy 'in the course of which he gave Martin and me "though alien in religion and politics" great applause for faithful characterisation of the Irish people'. [37]

Early in April Jack's son Tony became dangerously ill, with a form of brain fever, and Edith tried to organise through Geraldine Cummins the provision of spiritual aid to him. Like their later refusal to sense the imminent eruption of World War Two, Geraldine's spirits indicated a recovery for the boy (who was to die later in the year). But nothing could affect Edith's firm belief that she was aided by the dead Martin. The incontrovertible evidence, she felt, was that their writing continued, which it could not have done had she been alone. Writing seemed to be a necessary mechanism to keep Edith's personal show on the road. Financially it would have been better to give up writing and enlarge her stables. Finbarr, Filigree and the Chief went off to Sylvia Warren in America, arriving on 16 April. Finbarr was the first to be bid for at 1,800 dollars. Riders not readers were now the economic mainstay. Illustrative sections of the prose work of Somerville and Ross, as classic authors of the past, were being anthologised wholesale. Young editors were unaware that the authors were still in business or had published work on their own account as well as together. In mid-May Edith was sent three volumes of anthology by Longmans: 'Was annoyed to find that my name was given as "part author" of "At the River's Edge". The most beautiful piece of prose in the English language and Martin's work only.'[38]

It seemed impossible to get out of debt. Money was in shorter and shorter supply when in mid-1934 Edith struck upon the idea of selling Somerville and Ross manuscripts. The London dealers Maggs Brothers had written to Edith with a particular request from an anonymous buyer to purchase the original manuscripts of *Some Experiences of an Irish R.M.* It took some months of searching before she remembered that she had given the original manuscripts of the first set of stories to a Red Cross fund raising sale during the war.[39] These have never surfaced since. Four more months were to pass before she rooted about, found other manuscripts and took them over to Maggs. In mid-June she went to London and stayed with Caz Anstey while she worked in the British Museum at an anthology of hunting poems. She discussed her stage play 'Flurry's Wedding' with Tyrone Guthrie and his wife. She described this meeting to Hildegarde: 'I dined with the Guthries last night (and fell in love with them both) ... too many scenes, needs compression ... He said the dialogue and the characters are *brilliant* but "no manager could put it on the stage in its present form" ... but it can be put right, and there *is* money in it'. Although she was in London and immersed in society and literary plans, her thoughts were never far from her horses. Edith never missed the Cork Show if she could help it and this letter ends: 'I must write to Marion Gubbins and ask for a bed (unless you want one?) The Show is this day fortnight Thursday 28th.'[40]

Sylvia Warren was at Glen B on a horse-coping trip. She and Edith, on her return to CT, motored about looking at horses. In August the annual invasion swamped out any possibility of literary work as usual. The Archbishop, the Regatta, the Bazaar – all the regular fixtures. September opened well: Sylvia Warren had sold The Chief for 2,500 dollars. This converted to £497.10s. 3d. 'A wonderful achievement and water in the desert,' Edith's diary records with relief. In London Jack was distraught over the continuing severe illness of his son Tony, and Edith was trying to discover through automatic writing what the hopes were for his survival. On 21 September Edith had 'a crushing letter from poor Jack. All hope for Tony gone. All the psychic messages "mistaken". This terrible illness has conquered.' Tony died three days later. She sent the automatic scripts, received after his death through Cummins, on to Jack to comfort him. She was soon to see him herself in London.

Having at last found some RM manuscripts, Edith went across to Caz Anstey's on 18 October, carrying her old manuscripts and illustrations. She had no idea how valuable the manuscripts were, and a letter to Geraldine Cummins describes her astonishment at such an unexpected turn in her fortunes: 'I must tell you the final result of my deal with Maggs Bros. I brought some drawings and the scripts of *Further Experiences of an Irish R M* and *In Mr Knox's Country*, and laid them on the table for Mr Maggs, in his palatial shop [in Conduit Street]. He noted that I had brought some additional stuff, and said he would telephone his client – *in Lausanne* if I didn't mind waiting. I said graciously that I didn't, and in about ten minutes he returned to offer me £1,350! You may not be surprised to hear that I accepted – and the farm overdraft proceeded to dance jigs of joy! – It was really great and very unexpected luck, and it was by the Mercy of Providence that they didn't ask me to name a price! The client is Comte de Suzannet, who has the finest collection of this rubbish of this sort in Europe!'[41] She made sure that Paddy dealt with most of this sum within England, investing it in London, so that it never got into the Irish economy: 'I don't want to give a quarter of it to Dev.' Paddy inherited this large sum in shares on her death. She disbursed some of the Maggs windfall round the family to where it was needed most. She visited Ethel Smyth, now terribly deaf and going lame, heard Menuhin play at the Albert Hall and saw Peter Davies, who was publishing her hunting anthology *Notes of the Horn*. When she travelled back to Drishane on 1 November she brought with her a spaniel puppy for Cameron. Apparently none of the brothers and sisters could exist without a personal dog; as a result when they were all together there was a large miscellaneous pack in attendance on them, and the super-refined Grays, especially, found this all too much for inhalation. Two new horses were bought in with manuscript money, and a good wireless

In CT there was not a shred of the old gentry/tenant relationship left. At the end of the year the sisters began to suffer noticeably from the depredations of goats, belonging to some of their local neighbours, who were allowed to roam free and raid the sisters' lands. Edith checked with the family solicitor to see if there was any way of discouraging these depredations, but did not get much help, she told Hildegarde: 'Wolfe said trespass had *no* proper laws, and such as there are date from Queen Elizabeth's time. If we could poison something that goats eat, such as underclothes and tobacco tins, that didn't appeal to cattle or horses we might do some good ... Margaret Keohane's baby arrived last night. A daughter. Faint disappointment as to sex but Mrs Kisby says Margaret didn't mind, and I think its less likely to drink and go mad.'[42]

Hildegarde started the year 1935 by falling ill. She thought of going off to Switzerland to recover her health, but Edith (to no avail) disapproved of her going to a cold place. With some of the remains of her manuscript money Edith offered £20 to send her South: 'When Martin was really ill and bronchitic in 1911, at Mab's, I whirled her down South (Amelie) and it was amazing how soon she began to pick up. Remember Eddy [Aylmer] killed himself in Switzerland.'[43] By February Boyle had joined the invalids and took to his bed at his house, The Point, off the Mall and on the shore below Glen B. When Edith had any spare cash to 'put away' she read the financial pages to see what might be a good speculation. She noticed: 'Baird Television shares available ...They might be worth thinking about' – but did not act upon the thought.

Ethel Smyth enjoyed writing her memoirs, in which she did not show discretion. Edith wrote to Hildegarde at St Cergue, high above Lac Leman: 'She said to me she meant to publish some of my letters! Which terrified me and I've today written to her, very firmly, and said that she and I had very different ideas about publicity and that I must stipulate that *none* of my writings should be included in her book without my seeing them and giving express permission that she might use them. She is such a rash creature! I believe one of her sections is to be about her stay in Egypt, and no doubt she will give a minute account of her friend the hermaphrodite! You are my literary executor, and if I die before the book comes out, you must see that nothing of mine is printed without your permission.' Later in the month she sent Hildegarde money: 'You *really* needn't thank me for the cheque … In the first place, it was a great and very unusual joy to be *able* to send it and not feel a ha'penny the poorer. In the second, I know you would have done exactly the same, and you and Egerton very often *did*, when Martin and I were starving on the Parish!'[44]

While Hildegarde was abroad she visited Comte de Suzannet in Lausanne, and was shown into his library. Here, to her amazement, she saw displayed on a table a three-volume first edition of *The Real Charlotte* of 1894, inscribed 'For Hildegarde from Edith'; there was 'complete bewilderment as to how and when and by whom they were stolen. The Comte bought them from Maggs and gave £35 for them. Who was the thief?'[45] To his sisters' relief, Boyle was on the mend by mid-February. Edith could not offer to send him away for a cure as her period of financial well-being thanks to the sale of manuscripts did not last very long: 'I've got to try and save money to send the horses to the USA they will cost £400 by the time they are – or aren't – sold, and my MSS money is melting fast. However, I've invested £1,200 out of my reach which is something to the good, anyway.'[46] This was the sum that remained safely in shares in London, to be inherited by her godson Paddy untouched by the Irish authorities in 1950. But the horse trade remained a regular standby, and Sylvia Warren cabled that Don Juan was sold for 1,800 dollars on 23 April. Early in May, and recorded in her diary, Edith transferred £100 to 'the wretched farm overdraft. Was accused of sentimentalism by Mr French [bank manager] because we hesitate to close down the farm and sack our men.' March had brought an awful request from the principal of Alexandra College to give a speech there, as a distinguished old girl, on 25 May, 'A proposition that strikes a chill to my stomach.' She went up to Dublin for the Alexandra ordeal, so nervous that she could touch none of the grand tea that was laid on beforehand. She said a few words to the girls before reading to them her fairy story 'Little Red Riding Hood in Kerry'.[47] Rose Marie Townshend, then a girl at Alexandra, was of great assistance to her in being a familiar friendly face and in being so pleased to own her as a distinguished relative.

In the same month, Cicely Hamilton wrote to arrange a stay at Drishane: 'I imagine she proposes to learn all about Ireland in a fortnight and write a book – such as the excellent ones she has done of Germany and France – Explaining the Irish situation. God help her!' She arrived on the 28th. In manner and appearance she was of the same type as Ethel Smyth. Writing to Hildegarde two days later, Edith described her as: 'a most pleasant and agreeable woman (much adored by the Chimp) who does his best to walk her off her stout legs … Miss H is curiously like Ethel Smyth – Voice, manner, even look – *Very* clever and evidently a first rate journalist. She is entirely sound about Dev and not inclined to be led about in blinkers by anyone.' Edith had been without dogs for a short while after the deaths of Prinkie and Taspy. But they were back: as well as Cozy she had Nancy, who was given to her by the writer Donn Byrne: 'I wish I had never yielded to Mike and started dogs again (but I should be miserable without them) ...' When both sisters were away, a rare event that was about to happen, their combined dogs were looked after as a pack by Mike. Travelling alone, a thing she hated and did very rarely, Edith met up with Hildegarde in June at Aix le Bains, the family favourite for soaking away 'Aches and Pains'. For reading on her journey she had been loaned Rebecca West's *Harsh Voice* and disliked it. Her criticism was sent on to Hildegarde: 'It imitates Henry James – or is of his school – and there is a sort of angel-prostitute, who, out of love, calls her lover (another woman's husband of course) "a lousy bastard" but saves him from starvation, and he sobs alternatively over her and his wife, and is the finest kind of American he-man ... I picked up an English novel by Theodora Benson. Very smartly written, and terribly up-to-date, and (I admit) amusing reading; but I'm getting rather sick of lice and bastards and English Bright Young People.'[48]

In Castletownshend she had left behind a worry in the shape of Boyle, who had become ill again, but refused to see a doctor. After the sisters had separated, we hear of Boyle in a letter of 19 June: 'The account Boyle gives of himself is *wretched*. I agree with you that he ought to try Perks [a homeopathist]. He is very obstinate and silly and tempestuous, but I'm going to have a shot at him.' Edith was keenly aware that Boyle and Mab at the Point kept themselves short in order to provide the best for their children, and she knew that Boyle in his retirement in CT avoided dentists' and opticians' bills by carrying on year after year without treatment for himself. On 22 June Edith posted ten pounds to Boyle 'to bribe him to go to Perks' she explained to Hildegarde. Yet another stalwart of the parish was brought low by illness; the daughter of old Canon Madden, Elizabeth Madden, was diagnosed as having, like her father, Bright's Disease. Edith's reaction to this news reminds us of the clinical severity of her views on long-drawn-out crippling illness: 'I can't get that poor plucky creature out of my mind! How far better for her to have died, and not flap along with a broken wing for the rest of her life!'[49]

Quite often in the summer there were timing collisions between tenants, paying guests and honorary guests. Elizabeth Hudson stayed in Glen B briefly in July, after some confusion between the sisters over where she was to sleep: 'I don't know what your bedding out (or in) scheme is,' Edith complained. 'You seem to have made a sort of jig-saw puzzle letting of Glen B! I fail to grasp its intricacies but I congratulate you on achieving something.' The income from Glen B lettings was all-important to Hildegarde, who never really understood herself to have untangled the Coghill family's financial affairs after Egerton and

Joe's deaths. It was a relief that her sons Paddy and Nevill were self-sufficient with incomes from their careers: Paddy in the Army (by 1938 he commanded the Hertfordshire Yeomanry), and Nevill teaching at Oxford University. After taking his first class degree in English in 1923, Nevill had become Fellow and Librarian of Exeter College. The congestion in CT this summer was so great that beds had to be shared. The young noticed that the sisters were ageing; now much less mobile, Edith was crippled by her arthritic hip, and had to have painkilling injections given directly into it by the district nurse.

As if she were standing in for Constance Bushe, Edith was quite happy in her old age to act as a mentor to much younger women, as she did for Elizabeth Hudson and her nieces Katharine and Diana, who was her god-daughter. She liked sparky and independent young women, the types she called 'street urchins', 'rogues' or 'buccaneers' who were shortly to go to war. She remained to them all a revered fixture, and was quite formally a benign mother figure. However, her letters to Elizabeth, or 'Huz' – short for Hudson – are remarkably frank in some ways. Edith was adamant that she did not want any luxurious production of the RM when he was given an American edition: 'Nothing would induce me to agree to the account-book style of binding. I'm afraid my drawings are hopelessly matter-of-fact and *un*-stylised, but so is the writing, so they suit one another. I think this fantastic over-production only makes a book unreadable, and I *want* it to be for good sensible hunting people, and not for super-civilized cranks and collector-fiends like you!' In the same letter of 6 October 1935, Edith explained her difficulties in overcoming her lameness, which was a terrible hindrance to her in overseeing any farm work: 'it is a very slow business and I am not patient. I said this to Martin the other night and she replied, unfeelingly: "No, you never were!" The letter ends with a scathing criticism of an unknown author, whom we now know as Molly Keane, a criticism that makes us realise the gulf that lay between Edith's upbringing as a girl in the 1860s and Molly's, fifty years later:

'Roger Scaife [of Houghton Mifflin in Boston] sent me a book called "Full House" by one M.J. Farrell, and asked my opinion on it! Hildegarde and I read it and I can hardly express how we loathed it. Ladies and Gents talk like people in Dublin slums, and one of its main topics is the state of dog's internal affairs! The brutal woman is undeniably clever. I think she must have been a governess in a very fast house, and tries to be more indecent than her employers.'[50] Sylvia Warren continued to be a very successful horse dealer. No sooner had the horse Palmist arrived on the dock in America than he was sold for 1,700 dollars. Edith had by this time shipped so many horses to America that she had made a personal friend of the United States consul in Cork, who helped her with the paperwork and formalities. There is so much detail on horse-coping in the diary at this juncture that it seems it would have been much simpler financially for Edith to invest all her energies in that. She needed the conviction that Martin was writing with her in order to keep at writing at all. On 3 December Edith recorded in her diary: 'Wrote a little. M. very insistent on sticking to it. 20 years ago tonight since that terrible night journey to Glen Vera' when Hildegarde and Edith had taken Martin to the Cork nursing home in which she died. According to Edith, Martin had written that the years since her death, for her, 'were like an evening past' but Edith added, 'Not so for others. For one it is ten years of years.'

Edith thought that the new Irish government managed to do some things right. She was pleased that Dublin had 'behaved decently' at the death of King George V, on 20 January 1936, in flying flags at half-mast. Ireland was under close observation 'taking her place among the nations of the world' and statesmanlike international formalities and ceremonials were to be expected of her. On the other hand in the same month Edith was incensed over the Irish government's determination to eradicate cattle, and their breeding, from Irish agriculture. This was a policy of the Minister of Agriculture (James Ryan) who 'now actually says they hope to clear Ireland of cattle – as if they were vermin!' Edith speculated to Hildegarde on 6 January that this was simply, and short-sightedly, to deprive England of supplies. The day before, six of their cattle were sold at Marsh's for £27: 'Thanks to the beneficent rule of the Dago [de Valera]. In happier times they would have fetched about £70.' 'The Dago' was a not uncommon term of disparagement for de Valera. Methuen's took the book over which she had struggled for so long during the autumn, *The Sweet Cry of Hounds*. She had five horses and one pony in hand. Cameron and Edith had listened to the proclamation of the new king on the radio on the 23rd: 'It is wonderfully impressive – and then one thinks of this rotten little fag-end of a country trying to substitute a Dago adventurer for the King! ... Did Cameron tell you that the "Irish Free Press" never mentioned the King's death on their posters and reserved the biggest letters for a row at a coursing match!'[51]

The same letter of 6 January describes a burial in the old Castlehaven graveyard, near the Somerville family vault. It was hardly surprising that live Somervilles had the horrors at the thought of being buried there. It was on a patch of ground being encroached by the sea, and at times went under the waves at high tide. Sometimes fresh burials had been washed out in storms. Jerry Hayes was buried there during a huge south-easterly gale. The grave had been dug the day before and had to be baled out of salt water. As the bearers carried the coffin down to the graveyard, waves broke over them from the strand. Out of the weather, all was well in the stables. Safe under cover Edith had in hand two excellent new horses, Rory O'More and Moireen Rue. Moireen was a mare, 'the greatest darling I've ever seen. Quite lovely.' The daughter of Martin's sister Geraldine, Eileen Hewson, was staying at Drishane. With her hosts she was playing backgammon, bridge, and doing crosswords, 'so the humble pleasures of the poor are hers.' Cameron had to attend a gathering of the British Legion for all County Cork in the city, so he went to stay with the Gubbins for the duration. Edith was irritated by Eileen, and by Caz Anstey and her continual stream of generosities: 'Caz has the great fault of trying to impress what she thinks are kindnesses of hers, and of rubbing in her presents etc. It is very bad form, and is where her de Fonblanque blood fails her.'[52] Guests arriving in this month told Edith that as they came through customs, they were charged 'huge sums' of import duty for the clothes they were standing in as they were of British manufacture. When the sisters crossed the Irish channel, they made sure they were wearing clothing with the labels of their Cork dressmaker, Gleeson.

In February, Geraldine Cummins moved in for a month to work on a typescript with Edith, on another attempt at 'Flurry's Wedding', the stage setting of part of the RM. On the first of the month Edith was delighted to hear that Sylvia Townshend Gorges was to marry her Italian count. Clemente Lovera di Maria did not at that stage speak English at all well, and it is a sign that Edith's spoken French remained in good order from her student days that she and Clemente habitually spoke French together. Clemente, from Northern Italy, was fair-haired, blue-eyed and extremely good-looking. 'What a lovely young man you have, Sylvia! Very different from my old show of a husband!' said a CT lady, recorded by Edith in Notebook 10 under 'Matrimonial'. In a letter to Hildegarde the more liberal Edith makes a comment on possible conversion to Catholicism for Sylvia that must have firmly lodged in her sister's mind, as when Edith herself was dying Hildegarde's chief worry was that Father Lambe would convert her at the last moment: 'I think she [Sylvia] ought to be happy with him, as she must know him thoroughly and he has been wonderfully faithful. I suppose she won't change religion to please her mother-in-law and the Pope? If she could it would simplify things very much, and except for being bossed by the priests, there really are no *fundamental* differences to be got over.'[53] Sylvia and Clemente became great friends of Father Lambe and used to visit him on Sherkin.

Edith had made sufficient headway in explaining to Boyle and Mab that they must not neglect simple precautions in their own health. Mab had been very much out of sorts with, as it turned out, digestive trouble caused by rotting teeth. On 4 February Edith triumphantly told Hildegarde that the Skibbereen dentists Hackett and Molony had gone to The Point with ether and their instruments and removed five of Mab's teeth. Boyle had to look after her as an invalid, and watched her diet carefully as she did not want to eat anything at all. He himself was not in the best of tempers through eyestrain headaches caused by the completion of his book *Will Mariner*, to be published by Faber in

October. Edith was concerned as well over Geraldine's health, telling her sister that she was: 'as thin as a rake and pale yellow – [but] she is beginning to pick up ... I think she is persistently overworked at the psychic business and is too gentle and yielding to refuse.'[54] On the last day of February Geraldine talked to Boyle and made her farewells before leaving for London. She talked to him about the progress of his book, and he told her that he was 'tormented by interruptions from young men of the locality who came to ask him to write letters recommending them as candidates for the Royal Navy ... He said with a laugh that he had a feeling he would never get his book finished.'[55] Edith knew that he had more than one anonymous letter warning him to stop making these recommendations.

On 10 March Edith went again to London to Mrs Anstey, to have heat treatment for her lame leg. She saw a lot of the Kenmares and visited a masseuse who blamed Edith's long years of side-saddle riding for the wrecked state of her legs. 'They were worth it, anyhow!' she insisted to Hildegarde.[56] At a tea party she met Ethel Smyth who regaled her with stories of her work in progress, the memoir *As Time Went On*. Ethel shouted at Edith, '*You* come into it!' which Edith found a 'really alarming thought'. On the 23rd she wrote to tell her sister, who was immersed in the care of two large pig litters, that she had found just the consultant for Boyle's eyes. On the night of 24 March, at The Point House, just as in the rest of the CT Big Houses, Boyle and Mab prepared and served their own evening meal, because all the servants in the place were at an entertainment in the Village Hall. It was dark. As they cleared up after their meal a car drove to the end of The Point avenue and they heard the footsteps of some people come to their main door. Holding an oil lamp, Boyle went and opened it. In her kitchen Mab heard voices; a man asked Boyle if he was Mr Somerville, and on his confirming that he was Admiral Somerville, he was shot several times and once through the heart. He died instantly, falling with the lamp, its glass smashing.

Crying out, Mab ran into the hall carrying another lamp. The gunman shot at her but only extinguished the lamp, smashing the lamp glass while the bullets buried themselves in the woodwork of the hall doorway and in the plastered wall by her head. She heard the gunmen run back to their car and drive off. Mab did not know if Boyle was dead or badly wounded. Having heard the car drive away, she left him, thinking it safe to run in the dark down the Point avenue and up the Mall to Boyle's brother Hugh Somerville at Malmaison, along the route that the murderers had driven. Hugh then drove in his car with her to Drishane. At Drishane, Hildegarde, Cameron and Sylvia were dining. Hugh left Mab with them and tore off to the police barracks in Skibbereen. Hildegarde's first thought was that the assassins really wanted Cameron, and

that they might still be in the village. Cameron was the senior officer commanding at the Remembrance Day ceremonies in Skibbereen, and the head of
the family. Telling them to bar the doors and shutters behind her, she left Sylvia
with Cameron, for her uppermost thought was still that Cameron was the
intended target, and might yet be shot. She walked back to The Point with
Mab, where they waited with Boyle's body until Hugh came to them with the
police. Hildegarde confirmed that Boyle was dead.

The assassins had entered the village by car, and had in fact driven out of it
by the time Hildegarde was hurrying down to The Point with Mab. The account
above is that of Sylvia Lovera who was dining that evening in Drishane.[57]
Edith's diary records that Jack telephoned her in London at Mrs Anstey's at
nine o'clock on the morning of the 25th: 'He had read in the Times that Boyle
had been murdered. Last night men came to the Point about 9. Boyle and Mab
were in the dining room. She heard steps in the yard. Then a man came to the
hall door. The man said "Are you Mr Somerville?" Boyle said "I am Admiral
Somerville" thereupon the man shot him through the heart. The Doctor says
death was instantaneous. The man fired some more shots. Mab rushed out with
a lamp (she had been in the inside place, washing something) but the lamp went
out and the man or men bolted down the avenue. It was pitch dark, their
confederate was waiting at the gate with a motor. It was heard coming and
going in the village, at speed. All is incredible and beyond expression.'

When the BBC recorded an interview with Boyle's surviving children in
Diana Somerville's home near Oxford in 1987, for their radio feature
programme 'The Irish Cousins', they were resigned in talking of their father's
murder. Diana said that Edith had not altered her views of Irish people as a
result of it: 'she didn't think that these people [the murderers] represented the
real Ireland – indeed she was right – the village reaction to it was terrific, and
when we arrived the next day all the curtains in the village were drawn. At my
father's funeral it was a long step from our house to the CT church and then up
very steep stone steps but the village men insisted six of them in turn to carry
the coffin all down the village street. They were Roman Catholics of course and
they all stood outside during the service.'

Nevill remembered that the murder was denounced from every altar in
Ireland on the following Sunday, and he, too, like his aunt, did not allow this
horrible and unnecessary brutality to change his view of Irish people.[58] It is not
clear who, in the IRA, authorised Boyle's murder, or whether it was an escapade
by an independent. Had they understood the differences between the Somerville
brothers, or Boyle's Nationalist political beliefs, or his Anglo-Catholicism,
might they have chosen another brother to execute in their demonstration to de
Valera that they still existed? Now that the identity of the killer is apparently

known, and photographs of the Colt used by him have been published in the newspapers of February 2000, it is only an ironic footnote that Boyle was as involved in the study of Irish language and history as it was possible to be.[59] He had long complained of the frequency with which his work was interrupted by boys wishing for his recommendation to the Navy – the supposed reason given for his execution. A cardboard placard with a typed message was left on his body. Knowing that Boyle felt that to refuse to write such recommendations would have been a failure of neighbourliness, Edith was to make an oblique reference to this on Boyle's memorial. If Hildegarde's own description of this night in the Coghill papers is correct, the assassins were certainly not local men, as some still believe, because she describes the message on Boyle's body as objecting to his recommendations to the Army for local boys, which Cameron had done, rather than to the Navy.[60]

On 8 and 18 April two newspaper tributes to Boyle appeared, one furious and the other calm. In the *Irish Press* the American diplomat David Gray wrote: 'It happens that I knew Admiral Somerville. No Irishman of Unionist stock and naval career could have accepted the Treaty Status more loyally or with greater hope for its success. He was a profound student of Irish history and of Irish archaeology. It was from his lips that, as an American student of Ireland, I first heard details of the barbarities of Cromwell's captains in West Cork, recounted with an indignation so passionate that old Irish wrongs became to me living things ... It is true that he interested himself to procure certain enlistments of Irish boys in the British Navy, but I know that his motive in doing so was compassion for the parents of sons for whom there appeared to be no other steady employment ... I know that loyal as he was to his service he did this for Irish people not the British Navy ... I have known no man of so noble a nature or with so generous and vital sympathies. Yet some half-witted, cruel-hearted ruffian with a gun, profaning the name of Irish freedom, has robbed Ireland of such a son, and dishonoured his country to the utmost of his capacity in the eyes of the world.' The second tribute in verse, from *The Irish Times*, was from George Duggan, the Irish civil servant, who had known Boyle when he worked in the Admiralty before his appointment to the Free State administration. He had known of Boyle's chartmaking work, and his book *The Chartmakers*. Of five quatrains, the third and last run:

The watch was over. You came home to rest,
Books, friends and kinsmen by you. At your door
The broken waters of the bay kept fresh
The memory of the sea.
. . . . . . . The coward blow

That quenched the light, when the first spring airs crept
From the restless ocean, left undimmed a star
For men to steer by.

Working through May, Edith immediately took over Boyle's work on *Will Mariner*, prepared it for a reader and later proofread it. Taking the manuscript with her, she went to Caz Anstey's to stay during further treatment for her lameness in London. She met up with the Kenmares and Ethel Smyth, and finished the work on *Will Mariner* before she returned to Drishane on 3 June. The book was accepted by Faber on the 13th. In mid-May Edith had the news that Sylvia Warren had repeated her success of selling a hunter on his arrival at the dock, with King Cormac, who was sold for 3,000 dollars – 'A great price, but he is a lovely horse,' her diary notes. Sylvia Warren urged Edith to take a holiday in America to alleviate her grief. Probably Edith was unable to face the thought of the coming winter without Boyle's company, and as a result accepted the offer of another trip to America as a welcome distraction. Sylvia Warren spent the summer travelling through Ireland on a horse-buying trip, returning to CT on 30 June. She was to take Edith back to America with her, and Edith's niece K was to accompany her aunt as minder.

Elizabeth Hudson seemed to have a talent for putting her foot in it. Her charm must have been considerable to survive with such a super-critical mentor. By the middle of 1936 Hudson had persuaded Edith to allow her to produce and publish a previously shelved bibliography of the works of Somerville and Ross. Hudson attempted to write a foreword, and sent it to Edith for comments. Edith wrote, with a careful preliminary buttering: 'In your very charmingly written foreword you say: "Somerville and Ross belong to a small group, chroniclers of their time, Maria Edgeworth, *Charles Lever*" – well, I *must* tell you that nothing enraged us more than being accused of the "rollicking humour of Lever"! I'm not denying his excellence but we were *not* of his school, and I hope you don't mind that I have substituted Jane Austen's name for Lever's. She also was "a chronicler of her time" and being a woman it seems suitable to bracket her with Maria Edgeworth *and* ourselves! ... I do hope you will forgive this liberty. It was a literary friend of mine who resented the mention of Lever, and reminded me that we repudiated him as a Blood-brother! Which is perfectly true.'[61]

On 13 August for the first time, more than four months after the event, de Valera mentioned Boyle's murder in an electioneering speech. In her diary Edith wrote that he had 'condemned, for the first time, Boyle's murder by IRA gangsters'. This might indicate that the vigorous but diplomatic U.S. minister David Gray had been effective in his representations to the Irish Government. He had written a powerfully expressed plea, published as a letter in *The Irish*

*Press* on 18 April, 'reproaching the Irish Government for showing no interest – either in denouncing the crime or offering a reward for the detection of the murderers.' But there was a break in relations between Fianna Fáil and the IRA. Unknown to Edith, the IRA had been declared an illegal organisation on 18 June, and its chief of staff, Maurice Twomey, had been arrested. Anglo-American and Irish-American relations were in a delicate stage of development that may have precipitated this.

Edith travelled with K back to America in mid-September to stay with Sylvia Warren at her home in River Bend, Dover, Massachusetts. On the journey she tried to read Winifred Holtby's *West Riding*, then gave up on it and attempted *Testament of Youth* by Vera Brittain with no more success. By 22 September she wrote in her diary: 'Am tired of these women without the faintest sense of humour, who turn themselves inside out for the public.' Muriel Currey intervenes in her transcript here: 'I used to know these two very earnest young women, very "modern", certainly no-one ever had less sense of humour – "Life is real, life is earnest".' From the horse dealing point of view this trip was as successful as the last, but in human terms it was a trial. Almost as soon as she arrived she began to suffer from phlebitis in her left leg. It was also difficult for her socially as she was expected to shine at social events while the news of home that reached her while she was in America was profoundly depressing. Hildegarde wrote that Jack's wife Vera had 'lost her wits'. Edith wrote back in that brutally unfeeling tone that had surfaced at Martin's death: 'Oh *poor* Jack! He really is angelic not to knock her on the head – (and the best thing for the poor creature, too) ...'[62]

An auction was being arranged at The Point, as Mab had moved perma-nently out of Ireland to Oxford, to be with two of her children who lived there, Diana and Raymond. Although the unavoidable truth did not emerge until 1939, Raymond, Boyle's eldest son and Cameron's heir, had been shocked past recovery out of his affection for Ireland. Many like him were to opt to leave Ireland, and even to cease visiting it on their parents' death. Old family ties with Ireland were undone in increasing numbers. Ethel Penrose had lost her husband of fifty-six years. Jim had been an outdoor man all his life and could not adjust to taking care of his health by avoiding harsh weather. Even in old age he still went out in all weathers, got soaked and let his clothes dry on him. By the mid-1930s he had breathing difficulties from repeated lung infections, and his huge frame had become gaunt. Ethel cabled through the news of his death to Edith in River Bend on 10 October. After cabling back, Edith immediately wrote to Hildegarde and simultaneously thought of the possibility of Ethel returning to CT, to Boyle's old home: 'However much she must have known that Jim's hold on life was a light one, it will be a terrible shock to her to find that he has had to leave her, even tho' she may be thankful for such an easy crossing ... I wonder what she will do? and Judith? I don't suppose she would think of coming to the Point? Yet I think she might be happier there than in London ... Ethel once said to me how she wished it had been possible for her and Jim to live in CT ...' Jim Penrose had taught Edith to row and shoot when she was a young girl, and like her Somerville Grandfather and Egerton, he was a man who liked the company of women in what had been thought to be male-only preserves. Edith wrote to Hildegarde again five days later: 'What a mercy that Jim's death was not during one of those breathless attacks, but peaceful, in sleep. He was a splendid fellow, so handsome and big and clever, and modest, and the very nicest most unselfish man possible to exist.'[63] But Ethel never thought of coming back: she, like Raymond, had given up on Ireland. Her children and grandchildren drew her to England.

Two books came out and were reviewed in Britain while Edith was still in America. *The Sweet Cry of Hounds* had a friendly review in *The Observer* on 15 October, and two days later Boyle's book *Will Mariner* was reviewed in the *Times Literary Supplement*. On the 17th K, who had been in New York, arrived to help nurse her suddenly crippled aunt, who regretted being persuaded to travel to America. 'I was right in refusing to go, tho' that I should have been *felled* in this way never entered my head,' she wrote to Hildegarde. Brought low at last by the hopeless prices, Marion Gubbins of the Hermitage and Dunkettle had to have a sale of her cattle, which Hildegarde was to attend, and Edith instructed her sister: 'I hope you buy a heifer as well as a bull'. After the Gubbins sale, River Bend folk were astonished to hear of the prices of pedigree cattle: 'I've told people here of Marion's lovely cattle going at an average of £10 – when here one rotten little Guernsey fetched £1,000!'[64] After being treated magnificently as an invalid by her kind American hosts she tottered back to Drishane on the last day of November, only to find herself burdened with a house guest with whom she was incompatible: Eileen Hewson was back. She had been imported hopefully by Hildegarde as an amusing companion for Edith, for after all she was Martin's niece, but she was not simpatico. There was a niece of Martin's who was simpatico, and this was Muriel Currey, who had a resemblance to Edith and a similar sense of humour. She, but not Eileen, was sent presents of £25 to celebrate Martin's birthday. In writing to Hildegarde to express her lack of desire for the company of Eileen, Edith incidentally defined what she did like in a companion: 'I beg you to believe that in future I infinitely prefer solitude, (unless I have a creature like Geraldine, who is *always* reading and writing and taking the dogs out walking). I must say that poor Eileen did try to take them, but they despised her and ran home at once.'[65]

On 21 December Percy Aylmer died at his home in North Wales, and as a result an interesting financial situation arose that took some time to come out in the open, a situation that might have turned quite disastrous for the sisters. All remained quiet over the festive season. Somehow, and with the aid of special handrails, Edith pulled herself up into the organ loft and played the organ in church on Christmas Day, but she was badly hampered by what she called 'My vile body'. Mike had started to drive her everywhere in the trap, and in it she went out for daily airings. She longed for the festive season to be over: 'It demands robust health and entire leg-power.' After Percy Aylmer died, his lawyer Mr Luxmoore became very interested in a loan of £2,000 he had made to the sisters when they badly needed it. Percy meant them to have it as a gift, but out of politeness described it as a loan, and he gave them a bond recording the particulars. 'I am so deeply thankful that when I offered Percy to pay off £1,000 (when I had that Count Suzannet money) – he wouldn't let me!'[66] Unknowing, Percy's executors posted to the sisters a sealed envelope that Percy had addressed to them. In it was their bond to him over the loan, with a note to them telling them to burn it. Edith wrote in her diary: 'Unspeakable relief. Percy also left H and me £100 each. Tried to thank him, Martin taking the message.' She ended her 1936 diary with: 'Felt very wretched lame and stiff. Glad to think this dark and disastrous year is over.'

By 20 January 1937 Edith had tidied things up drastically by burning the bond, deciding that 'it was safer to destroy it' and say nothing. Mr Luxmoore retired baffled. 'I can't see that there is any legal proof that we ever had it. Now that the Bond is burnt – by Percy's order. He gave the money to pay our debt at the Bank, and we never had it at all.'[67] Although Eileen Hewson had failed to engage Edith's affections, she did make an impression elsewhere: 'Eileen and Cameron are a shining success. They talk seriously and instructively and even do crosswords! He bows to her, making a face like a super-intelligent dog at her and she responds with an absolutely imperial accent, and they cap each other's experiences of travel all over the world. It is beautiful. Don't think I'm sour or disagreeable. I'm not in the least – I'm very fond of them both and *thankful* they click so perfectly – but I can't help being entertained …'[68] Muriel Currey notes in her diary transcript: 'She was trying to write every morning but Sylvia Warren was now turning her into a house agent for American summer tenants.' On 16 January Edith found herself 'able to walk to the kitchen garden without severe suffering. My first pedestrian expedition since October 8th.' On the 20th she had the perturbing news from Arthur Symons that her bibliography was to be published 'in a party' with Baron Corvo's *Meleager* and Beardsley's letters. 'What an odd party,' Muriel commented, and Edith herself puzzled in her diary: 'Why I can't imagine.'

Under orders from Mab in Oxford, Edith had to put order on Boyle's papers in mid-January: 'Went to Boyle's studio and was heart-rent looking at all his many interests and works – maps and books and papers innumerable.' All around his studio were pinned copies of maps and charts from his first book *The Chartmakers* (1928). His books and journals on Irish archaeology and the Irish language were to the fore since his return to Ireland. As a linguist he had studied the languages of Polynesia and published a dictionary of them; on retiring home, his attention turned to Irish, ancient and modern. His youngest son Michael remembered his word-slips scattered about. By April everything in The Point had to be sorted and moved; the house had been let to Boyle and Mab unfurnished and it was now to be re-let. Mab asked if her special things and Boyle's from The Point could be stored at Drishane and on 1 May Edith wrote to Hildegarde: 'The Point advances and the Studio is ready to receive the first van-load'. Edith's Studio became a kind of dumping ground for material waiting to be sent off to other places. It seems that some of Mab's furniture, never sent for, contained part of Boyle's papers, as some of Edith's letters to him still remain in the Drishane House manuscript collection. In a similar way Sir Patrick Coghill used Edith's Studio as his den and general dump after he had rented part of Drishane and let Glen B go downhill.

Circumstances were even in the 1930s conspiring to make any biographical study of Somerville and Ross a trial of endurance in a manuscript maze. Edith's first biographer, Geraldine Cummins, working in the early 1950s, made much of her own letters and relationship with Somerville and recoiled from the maze, though she rightly saw the importance of the photographs of Edith Somerville as an actress in the 1870s and 1880s. For many years Geraldine Cummins has been to biographers of Edith Somerville an unknown quantity difficult to define. She was disliked as a charlatan by the succeeding Mistress of Drishane, Moira, Mrs Desmond Somerville, who felt that Edith was too childishly susceptible to fraudulent mediums, quack cures and 'alternative' doctors.[69] Unlike her successor, Edith had been brought up thinking that mediumship was the most natural thing in the world by her mother's generation, and she was a convinced practitioner of what would be called today 'sympathetic magic'. However, Geraldine's fees for sittings represented her income. What these fees were is not entered in the Somerville diaries. We know that they were charged, as there is one reference in Edith's diary to a free sitting on 5 June in this year: 'After tea Geraldine *gave* Martin and me a sitting. She went into a deep trance and M. discussed the book and its possibilities. Marvellous privilege!' The book was the last novel, *Sarah's Youth*. Edith believed in Geraldine because it was necessary and practical; the comforting assurance of the continued spiritual existence of Martin, Boyle and Ethel made going on without them possible, and joining them again inevitable. The overlap with orthodox Christian beliefs on resurrection, the survival of the personality after death, was more encouraging to her than not. So much curbed emotion was invested in her belief that it clouded Edith's critical judgement, a faculty that in other respects was over-active. A feature of Cummins' own handwriting, a decorative loop at the entry into an ascender downstroke, is also seen in her automatic scripts, which would seem to indicate a certain consciousness on the part of the medium.[70] The Cummins scripts, claiming to represent, for example, the voice of Shaw after death, bear very little examination now. Cummins was a clever and sympathetic woman from a distinguished Cork medical family; how far she was conscious of deliberate fabrication in order to 'heal' her clients must be left for her biographer to discover.

Edith was again accused of 'sentimentalism' in keeping on her farmhands by Mr French at the bank when she went to him to deposit large sums sent over by Sylvia Warren for a good bunch of horses that all sold the moment they arrived in America. At the beginning of July she cancelled her subscription to *Time and Tide* because 'It is turning "Left" and published a disgusting story a short time ago.'[71] The Americans started to come earlier in the summer than the returning family members, and the village started to fill with them in the first week in July. In simple good taste Edith designed a memorial for Boyle in the shape of a stone seat at the gate of Drishane 'for the use of the people of the village'. Under Boyle's name it had an inscription in fine uncial letters 'cómarsa mait', meaning good neighbour, the Irish letters drawn for her by R. Motherway of Skibbereen, and cut by Seamus Murphy. It was not ready for installation until the end of the year.

After the harvest in 1937 Cameron and Hildegarde went away on an extended round of visiting in the late summer. Elizabeth Hudson was still struggling with A.J.A. Symons and the Somerville and Ross bibliography. For some unknown reason Edith and Elizabeth called him 'Alphonse'. After her summer stay in CT, Elizabeth carried on to London to deal with him. Edith speculated in a letter to her on 17 September: 'I believe he will ask you to fly with him, now that he has got clear of the other lady. I'm afraid he is – (as Edmund Gosse said to me of William Black) 'a Roguey-Poguey'. But don't fly with him unless he promises to put in those two drawings. You might point out that few bibliographies give him such a chance!' Fulsome thanks were sent to her from Mike for a handsome tip that Elizabeth gave him as she left. Edith chaffed her: 'He seems to have cherished a guilty passion for you, like Alphonse.'[72]

The effect on remaining Irish landlords, who were tempted to sit out the difficulties, of de Valera coming into power in 1932 was clearly apparent five years later. Under the careful gradualist Cosgrave there might have been hope. By 1937, estates that were not redistributed had become derelict, their owners having fled and abandoned them. On 14 October a keen reader of Somerville and Ross, the writer Ruth Duffin, wrote to Edith sending a clipping from a Leitrim newspaper. 'I never read a bit of racy Irish speech without thinking of you and Martin Ross,' she wrote. The clipping concerned the efforts of Leitrim County Council to trace the onetime landlord of a now derelict estate, Lord Massy. He owed £41 arrears of rates. The solicitor involved, Mr Henry McMorrow, was quoted as saying, 'At the present time the place was so derelict it would give neuralgia to a snipe.' Ruth Duffin commented: 'You may like to have proof that our people have not yet been chilled into uniformity by the BBC.'[73]

There were great changes to be faced by painters of the old guard like Edith, for by this time modern art was being shown and painted in Ireland, for appreciative buyers. Edith wrote to Elizabeth Hudson, who kept an eye on things in America for her, strongly objecting to the suggestion that any of her paintings, left in New York for sale, be exhibited with some of the younger Irish painters whose work she disliked; but she was too late. They were in fact exhibited at Mrs Cornelius J. Sullivan's Gallery in New York in a mixed exhibition of old and new Irish painters in January 1938. At the age of eighty Edith harked back to what she had loved as a young woman student and remembered Nathaniel Hone, whose work represented the 'old' alongside hers in New York: 'He was a *great* painter and was never properly known or appreciated. I've seen a number of his paintings and he was a master. I do not know why he does not seem to have exhibited, and lived – I believe – a sort of Recluse life. He was one of the Barbizon School, and I think he studied there. I hate anything I have seen of Jack Yeats. I know nothing of the other two – Reid and McGuinness. Humbert Craig is, *I* think, the best of the Dublin artists and has done some lovely things. Keating is rather brutal, but strong and exciting.'[74]

There was a novel on the stocks again, *Sarah's Youth*, at which Edith wrote regularly. Hildegarde was in England visiting her children when Edith wrote to her on 13 November: 'Cameron will be back about the 16th ... I trust you and Paddy will be here then ... I shall have had three months of single-handed effort of all sorts and one of solitude! I shall be thankful to see a white man's footprint on the studio steps!' Edith's solitude had not been complete. Ethel Penrose had stayed and broken to her the news that she was going to live in England where her children had settled, in Hampshire. Edith complained to Hildegarde: 'I'll bet none of her beastly children can feed her as Mrs Kisby did, and the English climate, all fogs and rain, is the worst in the world for her. I shall miss her horribly.' The BBC had broadcast a reading of *Poisson d'Avril* which had been read, in Edith's opinion, by an actor with a 'foul Dublin cad-voice'. The owner of the voice was the actor Dennis Johnson. She described her cross letter to the BBC with the expressive Buddh word 'A sassoferrara', meaning a ferocious blowing-up.

December saw the death of Jack's difficult wife, Vera Aston Key, who had never recovered from the death in 1934 of her even more difficult son Anthony. Edith was nothing but relieved: she had already suggested to Hildegarde that Vera should have been put down like a damaged animal. 'A more disastrous marriage could hardly be imagined than poor Jack's – he, who was worthy of the nicest wife who could be found.'[75] Here, again, is a clear indicator that Edith was certainly not a female supremacist, who supported women right or wrong: rather she loved certain personalities no matter what their sex. She and Cameron celebrated Christmas without Hildegarde. Once he was home again Cameron became fascinated by de Valera's attempts to circumvent the rulings of the Boundary Commission, which had divided the Protestant North from the Catholic South regardless of controversial areas of mixed population. She wrote to Hildegarde on the 30th: 'You've seen, of course, this impudent assumption of dominion over *all* Ireland ("Erry" – Thus that great linguist, the Chimp, declares it should be pronounced) the North has, however, left the matter in no uncertainty and even the callous – or cowardly English Government has given Dev a bit of a rap over the knuckles. It is all such eye wash. Dev knows he daren't risk the return of all the Irish out of good employment and old age pensions in England ...'

With Mr O'Connell the mason, Michael Brien rebuilt the wall at the Drishane gate to incorporate the stonework of Boyle's memorial in the first week of January 1938. After this was finished, Edith employed him as a roofer to repair damaged slating and generally refurbish those houses that she managed as a rentier – Tally Ho, the White House, her own Mall House and Glen B. She explained to the still absent Hildegarde in mid-January that 'the USA must have first refusal' as tenants: they were wealthier and most reliable. On the 13th Evelyn Chavasse came to say goodbye before he left to take up service on board the Royal Navy flagship HMS *Norfolk* in Bombay, 'which seems to be manned by CT boys. David T., Arthur Leary, Jacky Lovell and now Evelyn! Eveline is not going out. Too expensive, so she and the *enormous* Gervaise [the Chavasse baby] stay with Hal for two years.'[76] On the same day she finished the last chapter of her novel.

Her old hunting companions, like herself becoming crocks, tried to move away to more favourable climes in which to be invalids. Charlie Morgan (of Bunalun), 'a wonderful old sport ... now says he will sell Bunalun and go and live in Valparaiso – (as if he *could* leave Skibbereen! ) ...' Christine Morrough left Innisbeg and came to settle in CT: 'she is a true Morrough, but, on the whole, I think she tells the truth, even though *in excelsis*. And she has very nice manners.'[77] She took The White House at £35 per annum. At the end of the month a terrible storm – the worst since the 'Big Wind' of 1839 – brought down telegraph wires and trees, one falling on the Studio and blocking the outside stair-access. It was a great irritation to Edith in that it 'takes Michael Brien away from me', as her slater was required here, there and everywhere in the neighbourhood to repair the damage of this storm. Slowly the fallen trees were sawn up and burned. Confined to the Studio, she kept an eye on reviews and caught up with more personal correspondence. She was proved right in her fears about a book on Maurice Baring by Ethel Smyth. It was reviewed very badly. Edith had feared that in trying to popularise Baring's books in her own crashing way, Ethel Smyth would 'kill them stone dead'.[78] The reviews were awful, she told Hildegarde: 'I pity Maurice from the bottom of my heart. I should go mad if she did it to me – and she would, for tuppence ... her super-praise has antagonised reviewers and I'm not surprised.'[79] The reviewer Desmond MacCarthy found it difficult to write his review and wrote to a friend that the work was like 'that of a bull in a china shop, but a bull with an intense love of china'.[80] A small change was worked in the village: on 13 March Edith was glad to see, she wrote in her diary, 'several men sitting on the Admiral's seat after church'.

On 25 May Edith wrote in her diary: 'Heard, with deep regret, that Dr O'Meara died this morning. He has been going blind and has been ill for a long time.' He had been the family doctor for forty years, and had been in attendance at the death of Edith's mother in 1895. In the early summer, still terribly unsettled, Hildegarde went on holiday to the Haute Savoie; more and more the sisters had to rely on their men to run the farm – but they, too, were getting on – their stalwart Richard Helen was approaching seventy. There was another difficulty in keeping the farm records, as Edith began to face the ruination of her handwriting, caused by arthritis in her hands. She kept dreaming back to the schoolroom days when her mother kept driving her to calligraphic perfection. Her mother's voice echoed in her head, saying: 'Failure! Begin again!' Remembering the voices of the dead so clearly that they could be mimicked years after the speaker's death was an inherited characteristic of some of Edith's nephews and nieces. In the 1980s both Claude Chavasse and Sylvia Lovera di Maria were able to speak on request in the tones of Edith and Hildegarde.[81] This kind of aural imprinting would have an effect on the readiness of the mind to function as a receiver of automatic writing. With her spiritualism, her farming and the book trade, Edith's life was a curious mixture of the most bizarre and the tediously mundane. She wrote to Hildegarde, for example, to tell her of developments on the Colthurst estate. Sir George Colthurst had refused to exhibit the Blarney stone in America for eight months, despite being offered £100,000; by keeping his stone at home 'he makes £500 a year from tourists'.

The tales about the provenance of the Blarney stone seem to relate to those origin myths cultivated by the British Israelites who had dug up the royal site at Tara expecting to find the Ark of the Covenant. Edith continued: 'Its story is that it was brought to England by the Prophet Jeremiah together with his three daughters. One of them married the King of Scotland and took half the stone (on which Jacob slept) to Scone and it is now in Westminster Abbey; the other two Misses Jeremiah married the North and South Kings of Ireland, and the Southern Queen brought the other half of the stone to Blarney. Why it imparts the gift of Agreeability is not known. Certainly it did not come from Jeremiah.'[82]

With a sudden heart attack, Ethel Penrose died on 1 June 1938. In her diary Edith wrote, 'My first and ever faithful friend', and in a letter to Geraldine Cummins on the next day: 'She was a very wonderful and delightful person, she was my first and – with Martin Ross – my dearest friend. Let me die the death of the righteous, and may my last end be like hers ...'[83] Hildegarde came back and the sisters changed duties. Taking with her the manuscript of her novel *Sarah's Youth*, she crossed for medical treatment to London in June, staying with Jack at Iverna Court. She went to see Caz Anstey, who was dying. Although Caz was shockingly thin, Edith wrote to Hildegarde, 'Her spirit is undefeated as ever', and on seeing Edith she was 'full of talk'.[84] Back on the farm Hildegarde had the ill luck of one of the cows falling sick with red murrain, a dangerous form of plague in cattle, but she coped. Hildegarde's daughter K, who had taken a job in London, was detailed to drive her aunt about, which she did 'in the most devoted way. She is very successful with Susan [the housekeeper] and Jack. I think she is happy and satisfied.'[85] She wrote to Drishane from Jack's on 24 June: 'Mr Longman has just rung me up to say they will be glad to publish Sarah, so that's allright. I'm to see him to fight over terms on Monday (Be praying for me) ... I dined with Mab last night and Daisy Morrough was there and Super-Daisy "My Kidneys! Agony!"' Always entertaining company, Daisy Morrough had a theatrically exaggerated manner of speaking that was much imitated. Longmans aimed to put the new novel on the Christmas market. She met Ethel Smyth 'looking well with an ear machine and the most appalling clothes. But in great spirits and full of Virginia Woolf's remarkable book "Three Guineas".'[86]

Like Ethel Penrose, Mrs Anstey was given a quick death, on 18 June. Edith wrote a fulsome obituary tribute, published in *The Times* on the 23rd, for which her relatives were deeply grateful and 'very much pleased'. Caz had been quite a trying person in some ways, but only Hildegarde ever heard any complaints. Telling her about the obituary Edith wrote: 'I felt every word of it – and the more the days pass, the more her loss and the loss of Ethel, is borne in, and hurts. I am truly thankful I had the long, gay, jolly drive with her on

Sunday, when she was like herself, full of questions about everyone and dogs and horses.' To the sisters' irritation, Dev had won an election again: 'How *amazing* that Dev should have swept these idiot electors! I begin to think our people are the stupidest in the world – *Maddening* – ...'[87] Edith caught a chill and took to bed in Iverna Court. Here she was visited by Aylmer's daughter by his first marriage, Gilla. She was by then married to her second husband Max Lobkowicz, who was at that stage a counsellor at the Czech legation. Describing this visit to Hildegarde we hear for the first time of the possibility of another war:

> Gilla says the 'checks' *will* fight. The Germans only have war materials to last fifteen days. The Czechs can hold them for that time, and then France, England and Russia will come in and finish them off. She says Goering and Goebbels are the danger, and they squeeze Hitler. Nazi aeroplanes have been *constantly* reconnoitring over Prague ...[88]

When Edith got back to Drishane on 6 July, Hildegarde was able to take off with Nevill when, together, they went to Aix via Chartres. Edith wrote to Christopher Anstey to thank him for posting to her all of her letters to Caz – 'A terrific bundle for which the fire is indicated', noted the diary. Some of the papers that had come up to Edith's Studio from Boyle's were the Somerville genealogical papers that both he and she had accumulated over forty years. She began to work on these on 26 July, shaping what was to become the *Somerville Family Records*. The usual Bazaar, Regatta, Archbishop and choir doings absorbed most of her time. It was not until 13 September that she entered in her diary: 'Began to try and write some sort of Somerville memoir.' Increasingly worried about her sister, in mid-September Edith wrote to Hildegarde in France: 'The War news is terrifying, and looks as if fighting was almost inevitable. I hope you and Nevill will take flight if things look any worse ...' Her novel *Sarah's Youth* was published in October to bad reviews, it being a book from another era and unpalatable to modern reviewers who found it 'innocuous'. Nevertheless it was selling well. Edith thought that the reviewers were disappointed 'at our omission of lavatories and their uses, of immorality in all its degrees and of obstetrics. The two last really successful books were devoted to confinements in all their details. One written by an ex-hospital nurse (so quite reliable) the other by a man.'[89]

*Sarah's Youth* is full of interest to the biographer in its themes. It is set in 1928. Yet again we have a cross-class union when the tomboy heroine Sarah Heritage Dixon falls in love with a blacksmith's son, Tim Kavanagh, another of the blue-eyed, fair and athletic horsemen that seem an irresistible subject to the writer. Like John Michael Fitzsymons in *Dan Russel the Fox*, he betters himself by education, but with more success, as Tim becomes a vet. Not simply an autobiographical creation, the heroine is a composite inspired by a group of wild girls at CT. Violet Coghill was every bit as adventurous as Edith and it was her overweight sister Beatrice Coghill who had a dangerous adventure, like that in *Sarah's Youth*, on horseback in Uncle Kendal's breeches. It is possible that Edith has used her niece Diana as a physical model for Sarah. She rides astride, a thing that appalled Edith in fact, though she became used to seeing Sylvia Warren and Diana riding in breeches. She used characteristics of Marian Gubbins and Hildegarde in her portrait of the six-foot huntress Miss Mary Lorimer MFH. Though the novel is set in a time after women had the vote, in it we have a father who attempts to use his daughter Sarah as security for a loan, offering her to a cousin, Richard Nolan, in marriage. The loan was necessary to pay off the mother of an illegitimate child fathered by Captain Heritage, Sarah's father, when he was a young man in the army.

The theme of the Sarah/Tim connection is so persistent, mirroring the Katherine Rowan/John Michael Fitzsymons union of *Dan Russel the Fox*, that there may be some relation to a teenage fixation of Edith's on her father's handsome coachman, Tom Connell. He certainly stuck in her mind, featuring twice in her rememberings in *Notions in Garrison*. Such cross-class attachments were certainly drummed out of her, maybe to the effect that she was bitterly censorious ever after of women who did marry across class boundaries. Her much later close – but entirely formal – relationship with her huntsman Mike Hurley did raise some eyebrows. Sarah takes most of the book to come to her senses: 'What was it she had heard Miss Mary say to a visitor who had told her some story about a girl, a daughter of some grand friends of hers, who wanted to marry a Hunt servant? "Wretched girl!" Miss Mary had said. "It means a lifetime of misery for them both!" And Mrs Dryburgh had said: "To marry out of one's own class! There's no greater mistake in the world!" Sarah had turned away lest the ladies should see the colour which had risen to her cheeks. But her temper had risen too. Be hanged to them! They didn't know Tim. He was going to be of her own class! Anyway, it was no business of theirs!'[90] It would seem that Edith when young had lived too long uncurbed under her grandfather's protection, so that she did not understand until perhaps her late teens the nature of the cage in which she was trapped. Yet again, the book ends with the suggestion that Bobby Dryburgh, a Barry Yelverton-like figure, will marry Sarah so that they could devote themselves to the survival of the Dryburghs in Ireland.

There were advantages to living in a make-believe world. Edith had invested so much in the belief that Hildegarde's home Glen Barrahane and her home Drishane would be inhabited and inherited by the children of Egerton and Boyle or Aylmer that it was best that the future was hidden from her. She still enjoyed her adventures as a horse-coper. On 1 November she went to East Cork in a motor to Jim Barry's where she bought a four-year old bay, 'very breedy-looking and a charming mover'; on the way back she called in at Dunkettle for tea with Marion Gubbins: 'She is terribly crippled and can hardly move, but was like herself and full of talk, but it was sad to see that splendid creature brought so low.'[91] Funded by Edith's bequest from Mrs Anstey, a new bathroom was being constructed off her bedroom, and Edith very much enjoyed the company of the plumber. Muriel Currey comments on the diary entry of 29 November: 'Twin excitements of Mike returning with a horse he had bought, and the plumber arriving from Bandon. When not distracted by the charms of either, she went on with her researches in very dull family letters.' Edith heard from Charlie Graves again on 13 December. His letter told her that he had written the one good review of *Sarah's Youth*, in *Punch*.

Edith's diary records that Daphne du Maurier wrote 'a fan letter of the deepest dye! Very much pleased with "All on the Irish Shore" which I had told Longmans to send her.' When Edith wrote to offer her another book she asked for *Irish Memories*. Elizabeth Hudson did not seem to be making much headway with her automatic writing, and the effect of this was to increase her reliance on Edith, who did not have time for long replies, by letter. Another outpouring of emotion came to Edith from America in the New Year as a result of Elizabeth's dog dying. Edith replied on 16 January 1939:

> Dearest Huz, It is so wonderful to feel that Age needn't make any difference where hearts are concerned, and that your love for me, and mine for you take no heed of such a spoil sport! But I'm truly grieved for you over the loss of Magnus. I know, in quite a peculiar way, there is something in the whole-souled, trusting devotion of a dog, that goes deeper into one's heart than one can easily express. It is something to remember that we shall find them again at 'some golden glittering corner', waiting for us.

During February and March she wrestled to make sense of the Cameron/ Somerville marriages for her genealogical work. On 20 March she heard that Gilla with her husband Max and their three boys had escaped from Prague. Gilla was in Brussels when she was told to get Max and her boys out of Prague with all speed. She wired to them and they flew out at mid-day. Hitler entered Prague eight hours later. There was a welcome distraction in June when Edith made a new acquaintance, a relation of old friends, who was a descendant of Daniel O'Connell's. He lived in a house that he had rebuilt after it had been burned down in the Troubles; charmed, Edith wrote to describe him to Hildegarde:

'I went, by invitation, to Donal O'Connell's on Thursday to see his horses. I brought Mike, and compelled Cameron to come too – for civility's sake, and so that we can ask Donal (with whom I am rather in love) to come here ... Donal has some lovely furniture and interesting things and pictures. He said that the Sinn Feiners burned a priceless scrapbook, containing letters to the Liberator from every big man in Europe, including Napoleon.'[92]

Cameron had been elected a member of the local council, a gesture of peacemaking that pleased Edith enormously: 'Cameron has just gone in to his meeting. He adores them all more and more and his cup of happiness brimmed over when the beloved Paddy Mahony's tender for making the equally beloved bandstand was accepted. If you had seen him (as I did) enveloping "Jacky Dunny" in a vast caress – to explain that he wanted a motor to Skib – you would have realised (as I do) how much nicer and kinder he is than you and I.' Geraldine Cummins, recovered from a serious operation, was about Drishane this summer: 'looking better and seems in good heart. She has a regrettable effect on Cameron who becomes appallingly instructive, and pontificates about Japan ... and Geraldine listens with slavish and entirely artificial interest. I pity her, but she brings it on herself ...'[93]

On 18 July Sylvia Warren arrived, to be followed by Ethel Smyth three days later; all work on the family tree was given up, and socialising became a sore trial, as both guests were deaf and not very patient. On the 22nd a wire came from Roland Bryce at Garinish, 'The President wishes to have the honour of calling on you'. This event was rather a success. According to Edith's diary, there were two detectives, an ADC, Douglas Hyde and his daughter Mrs Sealy: 'All were very civil and pleasant, the old President even adoring, hugging H and me at every opportunity. Took them to the Studio where they seemed to know something about painting (Mrs Sealy paints). Gave the President "The Smile and the Tear" and in all love we parted.' Left to themselves for a while, Ethel fell for Sylvia. On 1 August Edith entered 'Terrible noise at tea. The ear trumpets in full blast. E.S. having developed a violent flop for Sylvia ["Crush" is the American equivalent] loses no opportunity of declaring her passion at haute voix.'

The Regatta started on 27 August. All of the calming communications from the spirit world denying that war was about to break out were proved false when on 1 September Edith wrote in her diary: 'This morning the German army broke into Poland and War began. All the hopeful spirit messages mistaken and their confidence in the White Powers misplaced.' Edith found Ireland's position during the Second World War puzzling. Many Irishmen went across to England to serve in the armed forces, and smaller, but significant, numbers of Englishmen who did not wish to do so came to neutral Ireland. She wrote to Jack on 8 September: 'We are ordered to blacken our windows ... and we have done so – But *why* if we are 'neutral' and are secure from attack? Also letters are believed to be censored – Again, Why? The Reich Embassy remains in Dublin ... Dev is having it both ways out of swagger that "Eire" has no connection with England, and funk in case we are bombed! We – we neutrals, are starting a Red Cross bandage making etc show in Skib and hope to get Red Cross lectures started. But why the DEV are we called neutrals?'

The income from horses and America had helped to trim the farm loan.[94] On 14 October Edith heard from Mr French that he would accept her securities, her untouched shares, against the farm debt 'which is now £700'. Many of the tenants who stayed in Castletownshend houses on vacations were military men on leave. There was general disgust at Chamberlain: 'I *can't* understand Chamberlain and the rest taking these Japanese abominable insults with gentle protests. No wonder Goebbels is putting out his foul tongue at England, Major Lomer could hardly speak of it he was so angry ...' In a letter to Jack on 24 November she berated him for his jingoism: 'I am a militant Pacifist, and loathe and despise the prehistoric bloodybones folly of War, which never settles anything. Look at Europe now, after "The War to End War". However I can't fight you now. Come home for Christmas and we can fight comfortably.'

Edith was in need of Jack's support and sense, as Cameron had put in train sales of lands that she was dead set against: 'I've no time now to go into the large question of Cameron's overdraft (he may have written to you). W.G. Wood [Auctioneer] came and "walked the land" and valued it at between six and seven hundred – I became desperate at the family disgrace. Our name on the posters, selling the family acres! I found Cameron and Wood on their knees over the Ordnance Survey Map on the floor and I "touched Wood" (for luck!) and secretly put a letter in his pocket saying to do no advertising till I saw him again – (I wanted Cameron to have an un-influenced deal, and to make up his mind not knowing I was involved) Well the end of it is I have made up my mind to sell out enough [shares], and I hope I shan't lose a lot but I shall have a quiet mind ...' Her diary shows that she was still speculating in horses as a new colt, Angus Oge, 'arrived in torrents of rain looking like a drowned rat (but a very pretty rat)'. He was the grandson of Gay Crusader, the Derby winner. Mr Wood and Cameron came to an accommodation with Edith. On 1 December she wrote to Jack: 'You have made no comment on my dashing purchase of the Family Acres! ... the family face will not be blackened by, among other things, by the inevitable discharge and the throwing out of work of 3, if not 4 good decent men ...'

When Claude Chavasse and Paddy and Nevill Coghill had been boys at Haileybury, they had come under the spell of the brilliant classics master W.J. Farrell, who had served in the first World War in the Royal Field Artillery, Special Reserve, in the same regiment alongside the boys as soon as they had left school. When the Second World War approached, Jerome Farrell decided to move back to Ireland. Another Farrell, but a married man with a family, was also moving to the village. Both were Catholics. Edith wrote to Jack: 'No further news from Mr Farrell, who with wife and daughter, is coming here next week to look at Tally Ho! We hear they are charming people, Irish, and well-bred, the only crab being that we fear they must be RC (Gormanston grandfather) and so can't sing in church (they will probably be prima-donnas and first tenor *wasted* on the chapel!).' Toby Coghill remembered all his life the shock he experienced as a schoolboy at a party in Jerome Farrell's [now Acacia Cottage] when he heard Mr Farrell and Father Lambe having an animated conversation in a language he could not quite identify. It was Latin, the language of the Catholic Church at that time.[95]

Sir Patrick in later life was frequently questioned about the Castletownshend attitude to Catholics. He was quite bewildered at the thought of any overt antagonism between the two religions, and puzzled by the assumption that the McRory family of the RM stories were a Catholic family being sent up by Somerville and Ross for their *nouveau riche* bad taste. Such middle-class social climbers were distasteful, but rare in those days: he thought that the MacRorys were Non-Conformists. In one of the RM stories they all turn up at a Harvest Festival service to general astonishment. Sir Patrick wrote to Professor John Cronin to explain that Anglo-Irishmen who went to English public schools like Haileybury might be Catholic or Protestant, and some of their masters, like Jerome Farrell, were Catholic themselves. Others went to the great English Catholic public schools:

> I knew three families in County Cork who went to Downside – one of the best schools in England. There were five boys of my age, who were very good friends – All joined the Army as regulars, and two of them before the war started in 1914 ...
>
> ... from 1896 onwards we loved our Doctor O'Meara, from the moment I was born. His two sons became doctors too – both of them very good friends with us ... There were no social climbers at that time. Now for the MacRorys – I wonder whether the McRorys were Catholic – I never thought they were. Catholics rarely came to a Protestant church, only perhaps, for a funeral. But quite often Methodists or any sort of Dissenters could arrive at a Harvest Festival.[96]

By Monday 4 December 1939 Somerville landholdings had been re-shaped. Outlying portions were let go, but the core was retained. Edith wrote to Jack: 'Cameron has sold Horse Island today, to Dan Collins of Trahartha – £100 – quite a fair price, for both parties – and now poor Cam is fairly up in the bottle – long may he keep so! We've done our best for him!' Edith was now eighty-one years old; over her lifetime she had written millions of words. She began to show the first signs of losing her excellent memory, for on 22 December she read *Mount Music* 'and failed to recognise that a single word was mine'.[97]

# CHAPTER 10

# 'Eighty years of unbroken love and good fellowship. I thank God for them.'

… [I] never thought I would have to end a good active hard working
life dying like a worn out old horse in the corner of a field.
Edith Somerville, her last diary entry in her own hand,
12 September 1948

GRADUALLY THE Hudson/Somerville letters became less frequent; but a letter survives from 1 January 1940. Elizabeth and Edith had both read and discussed a new novel called *Under the Wind* by Mrs Agnes Keith. Edith's criticism of it reveals her own physical fastidiousness. She had found the physical details as revolting as the lack of reticence. As ever she fell back on an anecdote: 'It is all very well to talk about Nature, but, (to quote an essay on Pigs by a very small cousin) "Pigs is durty things" and so is Nature.' The end of Edith's letter was an attempt to explain why she did not have time to write very often, or at any length, 'not to her or to anyone' because 'I'm half mad with frustration about my work, and am going to get into trouble all round. *But I don't care.* With this declaration of Artistic Inderbloodypendence (I learned this nice word from my nice brother-in-law long ago) I will cease. Only adding much love and all blessings from Edith.' She was eighty-two years old, still excited by painting, and still connected in her mind the subject of painting with Egerton who had enabled her to become a painter herself. She was writing sections of what became *Notions in Garrison*, a collection of pieces that includes a loving study of her brother Boyle.

Even before it gathered momentum, the war had drastically affected livestock prices. At the end of the previous November her diary had recorded a plummeting market in horse sales: 'Horses are now being given away practically. A thoroughbred mare and foal went for 2 guineas at one of Goff's sales in Dublin, and the horse that won the Irish Grand National was bought by Hyde for £9' and much had happened on the landward front. Edith had stepped in, paid Cameron's debts and saved Drishane lands. On 9 December 1939, she had been to do business with her solicitor Boland in Skibbereen where he showed her a deed of gift of Charles II to the first Becher 'Adventurer': 'He had fifty miles of country. Now they haven't one acre.' The next day Edith 'Told Mike and Richard I had got the land. Needless to say they knew all about it.' On 2 January 1940 she entered in her diary: 'The deed of sale of Drishane and Farrandau from Cameron to me is signed.' Less than a decade later the land had slipped back into the possession of the Drishane heir, and Edith's intervention – at great cost to her – became a forgotten detail. She never criticised her brother Cameron outside letters to Martin or Hildegarde, and she preserved silence on his ill-managed financial affairs after his death.

The war years at Drishane were made bearable by the fact that Drishane lands had their own peat diggings, the peat being 'hard and slow-burning'. At least, warmth was not a difficulty, but the lack of paraffin meant that the household rose and retired to bed according to daylight hours. Tea and coffee and items like Edith's particular face powder from the Army and Navy Stores were brought over by the young on leave. It was this last Anglo-Irish generation who learned to change skins on the Irish sea crossing; their service greatcoats had regimental buttons that could be removed by sliding off the backing split-rings. Once on board a ferry it became second nature to sit down, take off their buttons, tie them up in a handkerchief, and 'stow them'.[1]

The bibliography of the works of Somerville and Ross that Elizabeth Hudson had slaved over for so long was being printed at the Chiswick Press under the supervision of A.J.A. Symons, whom both Edith and Elizabeth had come to detest for his grandiose, vague and unbusinesslike ways. Almost on the brink of publication, Symons delivered a costing far above that originally agreed upon. Edith wired to the Chiswick Press: 'Defer Publication', and Elizabeth became embroiled in a painful wrangle over finances. Edith refused to allow her to meet the costs herself as the Hudsons were in financial straits of their own, and Edith, writing to explain why she could not contribute, gives another account of her Drishane land purchase. The bibliography was not published until September 1942, after Cameron's death.

> ... Finally I must say that I have not got the money at the moment and shall not have it until the War is over and I can sell a horse or two. At this moment, thanks to Adolf, I have three eating their heads off, and not the faintest chance of selling any one of them. I must further confess to you that I have had to spend a very big lump of my savings in order to save some of the family acres, which Cameron had determined to sell to *anyone who would buy them*, including all our farm buildings etc.etc..

He had got himself into difficulties (I needn't say this is strictly between you and me) and got a valuer down and arranged for the land to be advertised in the local papers as for sale to anyone who would buy it. This would have meant H and I giving up entirely (we had been C's tenants) and our four excellent workmen being thrown out of work, with little or no prospect of work elsewhere, at the beginning of winter. So I rose up and found that I could, more or less, meet the price (thanks to a complaisant Bank and fair securities) and the land is now mine, and H and I are carrying on as well as we can. But for this I could easily have done as I said and gone shares in producing the Bib.[liography] – but as *all* securities are down to below zero, I would rather not sell, at a considerable loss, in order to produce our poor book at what I feel to be the worst possible moment ...[2]

With her diary entries, and her letter to Jack, this letter to Elizabeth Hudson is important evidence remaining as to Edith's Drishane lands purchase, behind the scenes, in 1940. When Cameron died, his will of 1936, made before anyone knew that he was effectively bankrupt, was unchanged and his misfortune tidied away.[3]

On 13 April the Comte de Suzannet, having bought the business correspondence between Pinker and Somerville and Ross at the sale of Pinker's papers, wrote to Edith to ask her advice on where this should be placed after his death.[4] She requested that it be given to Trinity College Dublin. Sensibly, considering what was about to happen regarding the inheritance of Drishane, she did not envisage any archive of her papers surviving there. She thought her heir and literary executor would consider it 'a burden', and would prefer to sell it into the care of an academic institution; but the chosen Somerville heir, Raymond Somerville, now repudiated Ireland, as his Coghill cousins were to do later. Behind the scenes, during 1939, Boyle's son Raymond, unable to face his inheritance and all it entailed, had decided to make an arrangement with his first cousin Desmond, son of Aylmer, to whom he transferred it. Raymond had a future in Oxford, where he acted at the Oxford Playhouse. The future at Drishane was uncertain. On 18 May Longman's sent Edith her royalties of £61 ('not bad considering all things') and she discovered that Penguin had sold 75,000 paperback RMs. She found some well-buried first drafts of RM stories to send to Hugh Walpole who was organising a Red Cross Sale including 'The Man Who Came to Buy Apples'. The news broadcasts on the radio became the focus of everyone's attention.

Their American friends wanted the sisters to stay with them in America until the war was over. On 4 June Sylvia Warren wrote: 'renewing the generous offer to take us all in! But even if we could leave everything and pay £70 apiece for passage, there are now no steamers, the last two having been packed with flying Americans.' The Grays – still in post in Ireland – came to the village on the 8th. Edith went to Canon Madden to tell him 'of the arrest of the Reverend Billy Pearson who was taken to the prison in Cork because the Civic Guard said he had a head shaped like a German. The Canon enchanted.' At the Skibbereen Show, Edith got 1st with Rathmore and a 2nd with Cleona. On 5 July Ethel Smyth wrote, childishly, to tell Edith that she had given her author's copy of her latest book to Sylvia Warren, rather than to Edith. This was a result of Ethel's current 'violent flop' on Sylvia, as Edith called it in her diary.

Great inroads had been made into Edith's share holdings, untouched for so long. Muriel Currey had noted previously that on 27 November 1939 'She raised money [by selling all her United Steel shares] to cancel Cameron's overdraft and prevent the estate being sold by the Bank.' It was not until the middle of 1940 that she comprehended the long-term effects of his disaster upon her; on 7 August she wrote: 'Cameron's financial affairs very complicated and unpleasant and have unpleasant reactions on me.' She had decided to cash in a large proportion of her shares through her Dublin stockbroker Solomons. She must have been one of the very last Anglo-Irish to be in a financial position to hold on to family lands, and to have the fervent wish to do so. The very land deeds of once grand Anglo-Irish families had become museum-pieces, or mere curiosities displayed in the offices of country solicitors like Travers Wolfe in Skibbereen.

This summer was the hottest and longest summer anyone could remember. Fires broke out spontaneously and watchmen were employed to guard hayricks. The first wet day was on 12 September. By now, through the good offices of all the Americans to whom Edith had sold hunters, Hildegarde's grandchildren Toby and Faith were safely in America, having been followed by their Czech cousins: 'Sylvia Warren is now a professional Baby Farmer – and horse coping is no more'. She had taken in the three Lobkowicz boys. To distract herself from the war, Edith immersed herself in the completion of the Somerville family records: 'After all if I don't [publish] no one else will, and all Boyle's and my work will go for nothing and moulder in a cupboard.' Guys of Cork contracted with her to print the records for a very reasonable sum. She began to arrange her legacies, and sent Hildegarde, when she was in Dublin, to meet Dr Praeger and Professor Macalister in order to leave to the Royal Society of Antiquaries in Ireland her paintings of Stone Age monuments in her neighbourhood, entitled 'The Altar' and 'The Druid Circle'. In London Jack had become an air raid warden: 'I wish Jack would write and say how he is. These constant raids must exhaust him and he never will spare himself.'[5]

Imperceptibly the running of the village began to take a different direction; as Cameron was the head man, and he was no longer a Unionist, this led to some difficulties with Hugh and his wife Mary, who remained diehards. After church one day, 'Mary fell upon Cameron to demand why we hadn't done the "God Save" – She is so d----d loyal.'[6] The family was breaking out into all kinds of non-Unionist activities. Edith's Townshend cousin, Sylvia, the daughter of Sylvia Townshend who had been Mrs Gorges, had married her Italian count, Clemente Lovera di Maria. To Edith's fury, Clemente had been interned as an 'enemy alien' in a prisoner of war camp in Wales near Llandudno. Sylvia followed him and took lodgings nearby in order to visit him. Edith began a great campaign to get him out and wrote tirelessly at letters on his behalf. Edith, Cameron and Hildegarde were rivetted to their Philco radio at news broadcasts, knowing precisely where all their nephews were stationed.

The new year of 1941 opened with a paraffin shortage, and Drishane laid in a stock of candles. Edith still had the habit of a rhythm of writing daily. She was completing *Notions in Garrison* in the daylight hours, and her imagination was in good health. In Chapter IV, 'Some Ghost Stories' is a strange and evocative passage concerning the ghost of a gentry woman called Harriet, who had fallen in love with the handsome family coachman, and married him secretly. Her brothers, furious at her choice, killed the coachman and disposed of his body. Harriet flees and dies in penury, but her ghost walks her father's house. In the coachman's old room, every year on the day of his death a fire bursts into flame on the empty hearth. This story has several echoes of fictions and facts from Edith's own life: the literary association of sexual love with fire and its capacity to spring back into life from apparent death, and the configuration of a handsome coachman admired by the daughter of the house, to family disapproval, that occurred in fact at Drishane in the mid-eighties when Tom Connell was in the Somervilles' service.

At the end of January, Edith 'Wrote to Mr R.G. Longman to condole over the bombing of Paternoster Row which is said to be in ruins.'[7] It was to be some time before Edith found out the fate of stocks of the Somerville and Ross volumes stored there. In March 1941 Edith mentioned in passing in a letter to Hildegarde that Cameron had been out of sorts, to the extent that he had not played the piano. To pass up on his daily practice was a most unusual event: '*nothing* would induce him to go into the drawing room as it was so cold. However, I dare say he will change with the weather.'[8] Lady Kenmare wrote to Edith on 21 April 'about Ethel Smyth, who has nearly gone out of her mind in consequence of poor Virginia Woolf's suicide. She (VW) had recurring attacks of brain trouble and thinking another was coming on, drowned herself. The most brilliant writer and a very beautiful creature. Betty Balfour said Ethel adored V and is terribly broken ...'[9] Methuen's accepted *Notions in Garrison* and co-signed the agreement on 26 May. It was in mid-June that she heard from

Mr Longman 'that all the Somerville and Ross books perished with Paternoster Row, except Irish Memories and Sarah's Youth.' On the 17th she went to Dublin with Geraldine Cummins to stay with the Grays in Dublin. Here she visited Douglas Hyde at Aras an Uachtarain and talked to him, with great enjoyment, for twenty minutes. A visit to Jack Yeats in his studio was not so successful: 'Didn't like his work and had to sacrifice truth to politeness'.[10] Her diary shows her increasing irritation at her own infirmities. Her 27 June entry is: 'My mind is like a motor engine in a broken, useless chassis.'

She wrote to Maurice Baring on 5 July to tell him the fate of Longman's stock of her books, 'utterly destroyed in Paternoster Row! No more royalties, and, as the poet says, "O, the difference to me!" I am afraid I shall have died in the workhouse long before Longman's reprint – if they ever do …' A letter to Hildegarde of 18 July 1941 mentions that Edith was making out the acreages of her own farm, Farrandau, and the Drishane Home Farm fields for their solicitor, which should date the final legal transfer of lands from Cameron to Edith. The Cork Agricultural Show was abandoned this year on account of 'The Emergency', which was the Irish euphemism for the war. The page proofs of her book *Notions in Garrison* came early in August, very well printed with hardly any mistakes. In September A.J.A. Symons died: 'no doubt the unfortunate bibliography will be buried with him.'

It had been in March 1941 that Cam's face had swollen up and he had stopped playing the piano. The doctor had treated him for dermatitis with ointments and dressings. But, Edith wrote to Hildegarde, 'I feel that these outside sloppings and greasings do not touch the root of the trouble'. The District Nurse now based in CT took Cameron under her care. The Irish Customs devised new means of punishing their remaining gentry and began to charge even larger sums to travellers who were 'importing' English-made clothes. Again Edith and Hildegarde made sure that they at least had their dressmakers' labels saying 'Gleeson, Cork' in whatever they were wearing if they crossed the channel. K came on leave from her duties in the WAAF. Much excitement was caused by a letter from Hugh's son Nugent, in the RNVR like Nevill, in which he described how his flotilla brought down 'a Dornier and a Heinkel' that had made four attacks at mast height on Nugent's ship: 'tho badly wounded he fought his ship till he collapsed and tho' she was also badly hit, he brought her, and his flotilla, home safe.'[11]

Edith sent to the Army and Navy Stores, for Hildegarde or K to collect necessities like typewriter ribbons and 'little tins of "Fuller's Earth Cream" (I can do without lipstick, but this is indispensable for my complexion) …'[12] Edith's face had become weatherbeaten, and she wished to conceal the redness of her cheeks. This she did so successfully with Fuller's preparation that

Nugent's daughter Clodagh, who met Edith when she was ten years old, marvelled at the fineness of her skin. Clodagh was very conscious that she was meeting 'a great lady' and retained in her mind the initial strong impression of sparkling eyes, shining white hair and fine skin.[13]

Cameron's skin did not improve. Edith did her utmost to ensure his diet was of the best, and encouraged his friends to call and entertain him with talk. Many enquiries about Cameron's health came from the Skibbereen branch of the British Legion, which organised the Remembrance Day ceremonies, over which Cameron presided. Edith was gloomily conscious of her little dog Nancy being in very low spirits after Cozy had been put down. She explained to Hildegarde that in automatic writing Martin assured her that Cozy was 'Lord of all she surveys, and I am her slave' – but I won't get another little dog, only to break my heart someday (or hers) ...' In July Paddy came home on leave, complaining to Edith before he left that each time he had to leave CT he hated leaving it more. From Paddy's own later memoir we discover that in saying this he was dissembling merely to please his godmother. She, just as much as her sister, longed for him to marry and settle down at Glen B after the war.

A government valuation survey in that month forced her to make a careful measurement of the acreage of her lands. Elizabeth Hudson wrote from France where she worked as a volunteer nurse. She was exhausted and ill, but Edith tried to persuade her to take leave – without success. The letters that came to Drishane made its inhabitants feel all the more stultified. She wrote to Maurice Baring, having forgotten that she had already told him of her loss at Longman's, on 9 October 1941:

> We are all very quiet and peaceful and dull. All the young ones are away, making themselves Nationally useful, or so they hope. The rest of us can't get out ... and if we did we couldn't get back again, so we are compulsorily useless, and I enjoy it very much, and am having time for painting – (so much more enjoyable than book-writing) ... I was glad to hear that Heinemanns [Baring's publisher] had escaped destruction. I heard from Mr Longman that *all* my and Martin Ross's books – save only *Irish Memories* and *Sarah's Youth* – are in ashes. He said (very non-committally) that some of them might be reprinted, and rise again, but I may paraphrase Flurry Knox and say I'm afraid a person would be a long time looking at a Phoenix before he thought of the Authors of An Irish RM. It is a bad business for me ...

On 5 November Brinsley Macnamara wrote to Edith to tell her that she had been awarded the Gregory Medal by the Irish Academy of Letters. She found out later that this had been at the instigation of Sean O'Faolain, who was a devotee of *The Real Charlotte*.[14] Becoming too ill to be looked after at home, Cameron went to Dr Welply's nursing home in Bandon where he was under the care of Dr Welply and Dr Hegarty. Cameron took his Philco radio with him to keep up with the war news, which was disastrous; *Ark Royal* had been sunk. Edith wrote to Cameron in between hospital visits; they were both intrigued by the personality of Hitler, which was a fraught subject of discussion. Edith 'can't believe Hitler bonkers ... ones always hearing (what seem to me improbable) stories of his biting the carpet ...' On 12 November Edith wrote to him: 'I expect you have seen the Examiner this morning. I am truly grieved to see by it that Lord Kenmare has just died. He was 80. She is just Hildegarde's age. I've *never* known a more devoted and happily married couple. I can't bear to think of her grief ...'

The doctors were preparing to operate on Cameron, but he caught a cold and the operation was postponed on 18 November. Edith did not apparently realise that to keep writing to him about friends who were dying might be lowering. She next wrote about her old friend and painting companion Mabel Royds Lumsden, who had been rushed into hospital with a clot on her brain. Archbishop Barton's wife had written to Edith knowing of their great friendship, or perhaps because she had opened Edith's last letter to Mabel. 'Mrs Barton knew that Mabel – whom she loved – was a great friend of mine. She is the last – or nearly – of my painting pals and the one I was most fond of – I wrote to her only last week and fear she can't have got the letter. She and Elizabeth Yeatherd – two of the very best, both gone from us.'[15]

In other ways Edith was more sensitive, as she sent in to Cameron his patience cards and a board, and his little folding table for writing on. She thought he had caught a cold through carelessness: 'Do avoid draughts in future – you have been a hothouse plant for too long to be able to stand them.'[16] Cameron had missed the Armistice Day celebrations in Skibbereeen on 11 November for the first time, and members of the British Legion were alarmed. On the 21st Edith wrote about Hildegarde meeting one of them who 'told Hildegarde he could hardly get through the streets "for the men of the Legion that were asking for the Colonel." You will have to give them drinks all round when you return.'

Various items of news were forwarded to Cameron as he continued to suffer from his cold. Hugh and Mary at Malmaison had installed electric light at a cost of £135, and were delighted with it. In the cold weather a helpfully heated discussion flared up as to the relative powers of the Aga stove at Drishane and the Esse at Glen B. But at last in Bandon on the 25th the doctors pounced. They telephoned Drishane to say that the operation had been 'satisfactory'. Yet another letter arrived from Edith that did not avoid the subject of death: 'Yes, my dear "Royds", Mabel Lumsden, is going just as Martin went. A tumour on the brain. I am *deeply* sorry – She was one of the nicest people I've ever known and her poor husband is *broken* by her loss.'[17] On the 27th Dr Welply telephoned to say that Cameron was 'well over' his operation. The sisters' spirits began to rise in the hope that Cameron would be home with them for Christmas. Rose Cameron Bingham had been writing 'volumes' to Cameron to cheer him, and Edith had sent in *Wheeltracks*, which he had been reading with pleasure. Nevill had sent a poem to Edith to congratulate her on receiving the Gregory Medal – 'the first time on record that an Aunt has had a poem written to her, *as an Aunt*.'[18]

In her diary on 7 December she made an entry that reminds us of the influence of Herbert Greene, who was given to peppering his talk with Latin tags, some of which, like the everlasting 'Res angusta domi', stayed with Edith all her life: 'Had my bath in moonlight. Last time this happened I was going cubbing. Eheu fugaces. Times were better then.' On his last leave Paddy had told her a delightful story about one of his fellow officers in Syria that she passed on to Maurice Baring, staying with the Lovats in the Highlands, to cheer him up on his sick bed. Baring was depressed as he had a form of *paralysis agitans* that prevented him from writing. 'An officer managed to get himself smuggled home in a Service plane without leave. He had a week at home, and was smuggled back again, and all was well. But, in due course, his wife proceeded to have a baby. And what can they do about it? Either he or she are "for it". We've heard no more ...'

The sisters were again required by another official government demand to make out acreages of their holdings for taxes. This absorbed them until 12 December when Dr Hegarty told them that Cameron was 'going on excellently'; he was sitting up and writing. By the 18th he had walked the length of the corridor outside his room, and had written to Edith worrying about the cost of his treatment. Although he knew that she had prevented the sale of Drishane lands by buying off his debts, he did not know if there was anything left to pay for his medical treatment. Edith's reply, her last letter to her eldest brother, was reassuring: 'Jack's subsidy will help you a good deal, and Hildegarde and I will supplement according to our humble means, so it won't really cost too much.'[19] It was arranged to collect Cameron from Bandon on the 22nd for Christmas.

Nurse Walsh was in attendance on Cameron in his sick bed at home when his heir and nephew Desmond arrived from his regiment in the North of Ireland on 1 January 1942. During the fortnight that Desmond was there he talked over the difficulties of his inheritance and reached an understanding, noted in her diary, with Edith. In the afternoons Edith sat with Cameron at his bedside and noticed his increasing breathlessness. Dr Hegarty came out to Drishane to examine him on the 5th and 'was *not* satisfied with him'; the next day an oxygen cylinder arrived to help Cam with his breathing. Hildegarde and Edith wired to Jack to suggest his coming. He was with them on the 10th. Two days later, Edith entered in her diary: 'Had a talk with Desmond. Settled to transfer the land that I now own to him. He wants to keep it as long as he can and proposes to indemnify me with a yearly subsidy.' On the 13th Desmond returned to Belfast. Jack was a tower of strength; he tackled the maze of Cameron's financial affairs and, on the 16th, Edith noted: 'went to see Mr Poole of the Provincial Bank on Cam's behalf. The War has left him and me on the rocks.' Edith was unable to sleep during this period of Cam's last days 'owing to very deep and considerable financial anxiety which is shared with C., and seems, for both of us, to be an insoluble trouble.' On the 22nd a great parcel of provisions arrived from Sylvia Warren in America: 'They are the kindest people in the world, over there.'

From Belfast Desmond wrote a formal letter to Edith on 29 January making the financial arrangements for running Drishane as a combined household. He said that he would be grateful to have the Drishane land, if Edith would execute a deed of gift, and that he was grateful to her for saving so much of the old property for Drishane.[20] By this time Cameron had become 'terribly weak and breathless' and he was now showing symptoms of dropsy. On the same day, at Jack's insistence, Edith applied for a Civil List pension; then on the morning of the 30th, Nurse Ward, the night nurse, came early to Hildegarde and Edith to tell them that Cam had died peacefully in his sleep at ten to six. Desmond was wired immediately but he could not get leave for a fortnight. The C.O. of Cameron's old King's Own Lancaster Regiment was among the first to telegram regrets and sympathy. In her diary that day Edith wrote: 'He was my earliest friend and his love has never failed me for eighty two years. Grief almost forgotten in thankfulness that he has no more to suffer and has escaped.' On the day of Cameron's death, Desmond wrote to Edith to explain that he could not come immediately because of pressure of work. In agreement with his aunt he was glad that Cameron had been painlessly 'released from the burden of life' and he told her that he had written to Boland to do the necessary business. He was proud that Cameron had seen fit to leave Drishane to him and hoped that he would be a worthy successor, attaining Cameron's credit in the locality.[21] Desmond was unaware of the irony in his use of the word 'credit', or of any double standard in his attitude to the sons and daughters of the house.

Mike collected twenty men to carry the coffin in relays to the church. Claude Chavasse came down from Mallow and took part of the service with Chancellor Madden. The funeral brought Edith very low: 'If I could have gone away with C it would have saved a great deal of trouble,' she wrote in her diary, but nevertheless she kept on detailing the succession of events. After the funeral, 'H and I drove West and anxiously discussed the problem of Mike's future.' On 6 February Hildegarde was cheered by a happy letter from Paddy who had been appointed vice consul at Adana in Asia Minor. Jack kept plugging away at Cameron's financial affairs and finally got somewhere: 'Jack saw Mr Poole of the Provincial Bank and poor C's affairs more or less on a basis.' Jack was back in London on the 25th from where he sent Edith money to tide her over, and a proposal of financial aid. It was needed: on that same day Mike had to sell at Bandon Fair one of Edith's finest horses, Slaney, for £14. 15 shillings. 'A lovely mare, but too much blood! they only were buying "hairy horses" for work. She cost £50 three years ago, and has cost another £50 since. Another result of the war which has done so much damage.'

She was, in consequence, that much easier to persuade to accept a donation from Jack of £10 a month. He wrote to her: 'If the boot was on the other leg you'd be doing the same for me – probably more, so *please* don't say another word about it.'²² In October 1942, Desmond and Moira spent their leave at Drishane. Until he left the Army, they would only appear for a few weeks' leave each year. Some of Edith's diary entries in 1942 give an inkling that there might be difficulties ahead when they took up residence in Drishane permanently. 'I gave Desmond my painting of Lough Quitan, Kerry, and we turned to and hung it, and re-hung others, in the ante-room, a slow and disputatious job, Moira being Senior Wrangler! But all went well and the pictures look nice.' On that same leave it was Moira's fifty-first birthday, and there were seventeen guests at a party in her honour; Edith wrote in her diary: 'I stoked the dining room fire and did other useful things and bore the position of deposed monarch with (I hope) great fortitude.'

Maurice Baring wrote to sympathise with the loss of Cameron, and Edith's response explains why he had not heard from her for months.

> ... I would have told you that we had lost Cameron (January 30th) but I've been rather ill ever since and could hardly write letters. He was the best and most devoted brother in the world and we *can't* get used to doing without him ... This has been a dark year for us and we've only just heard that a young sailor nephew, Philip, has been 'killed by enemy action'. He had commanded a destroyer, and came safe through the furnace of Crete, and had won three decorations. He had only just been promoted Commander when the telegram came. His father (my brother Hugh) and mother adored him. He was a charming boy – you mustn't try to write to me, I know I have your sympathy. So many are in trouble. I have had the saddest letters from dear Elizabeth [Lady Kenmare]...

I have had a horrible time with an inflammation of the nerves, which was the result of the strain and misery of Cameron's illness ... [shingles] involves as much pain to the square inch as one can easily stand. And misfortunes seldom come singly (or should I say shingly?) I've had a good deal of rheumatism to compete with. I've taken to reading – quite a new amusement for me, who have read nothing but newspapers since the War began and I have started on a course of Trollope (I believe I was allowed to read him when I was 15 and he was coming out in the *Cornhill*) I found that I enjoyed 'Barchester Towers' very much, but I resent his habit of retiring to a slight eminence and thence reviewing his people – like blind mice – 'see how they run'! I think it puts one off.[23]

Her desire to shield Cameron from embarrassment meant that she paid out hundreds of pounds to pay his debts, and keep the family home surrounded by its lands, secretly, to prevent any loss of face for him. In her generosity to him, she did not consider her own future position, apart from ensuring that Drishane remained a functioning landholding and did not sink to the level of what she described as a landless *cottage ornée*. Her nephew Desmond Somerville, who inherited Drishane and its lands, was enabled to keep living there by farming the lands that Edith had preserved for him. But farming at this point was not a bright prospect. Edith sold her cob Cleona, who had cost £35 three years previously, for £15, to Mike's disgust: 'Mike scandalised, very properly, but horses are down and out' she wrote in her diary. To her amazement on 19 May she received in the mail page proofs from the Chiswick Press of the Somerville and Ross bibliography that she had long presumed dead and gone, and began to correct them. All through this summer she was hampered by shingles and had passed the post of church organist over to Hildegarde. At last on 13 September, she wrote in her diary: 'I drove to church and played, first time since February 22nd.' She was sorting Cameron's papers and was astonished to discover that he appeared to have kept every letter that she had ever written to him. The market for stock began to improve, and Richard Helen was managing to sell heifers at a reasonable price compared to horses. The sisters were delighted in October when Jack announced that he was to marry again, to Mildred MacCheane, who became a favourite with them both. When the Comte de Suzannet wrote to Edith on 7 October to ask if she would like to decide to whom he should leave his by now extensive collection of Somerville and Ross manuscripts, she again asked that he leave them to Trinity College Dublin. She already saw that the future of her papers might cause difficulties for her family. She did not want there to be an archive in Drishane, as she saw the keeping and organising of it as a 'burden' on nephews who would find it irksome.[24]

Edith was beginning to be more mobile, walking about the farm and inspecting stock with Richard and Hildegarde. On 2 November 'the child of many delays and disappointments', the Bibliography, arrived, and was good to look at: 'The Chiswick Press have done it extremely well.' A gleam of hope for the horse-coper came at the end of the year when the Ministry of Agriculture, which had been forbidding the export of her hunter Angus Oge, for whom she had a buyer in America, relented. In thanks Edith sent a gift to the Minister of Agriculture Dr Ryan in the form of a signed copy of the omnibus edition of the RM. Her old friend Ethel Smyth was failing, her once acute memory slipping away. But she had flashes of understanding, and still sometimes wrote to Edith. Showing her highly trained capacity for blocking out unwanted memories, Edith wrote: 'Ever since I met her in Killarney in 1919, she has been a devoted and faithful friend and our friendship has been unclouded by any storm or misunderstanding.' She began to write, slowly and in careful sections, the book of essays *Happy Days*. On long reins, Mike began to train the hunter that Edith had bred, the superb-looking Dragonfly, closely watched by Edith. She wrote to Longman's to try and organise for the reissue of the blitzed books, to be told that they would not stand in her way if she wished to transfer to Faber, but nothing could be done until after the end of the war.

Hildegarde and Edith went to the Skibbereen Show to see Mike take 1st with Dragonfly. Thomas McGreevy, director of the National Gallery, and a friend of Geraldine Cummins, came down to CT to choose three of Edith's pictures for the Irish Exhibition of Living Art to be held in the National College of Art in Dublin. Among them was the painting 'Baltimore' which the art critic of the *Irish Times*, in a review of the exhibition, described as 'one of the outstanding paintings'. The publishing house of Dent had been writing to her to suggest an 'Everyman' single-volume précis of all the RM stories – at which she was so cross, at the 'disembowelment', that she told them to go away. But they wrote back hastily and politely, explaining that they had many requests for volumes of her work to be 'Everyman'd', and offered her £150 advance on a single volume of complete 'Some' and 'Further' RM stories, which she accepted. This involved her in writing a new RM foreword, which filled up her writing time until the turn of the year. Her fox terrier Nancy was very ill; typically Edith was entering Nancy's condition in the diary every day, rather than her own. Deficiencies were taking their toll on animals and humans. The sisters' diet must have been very poor during the war, as their skin broke out in boils and rashes.

There was a bright spot to open 1944. Katharine became engaged to Terence Johnston, from a Northern Ireland family, and her wedding was on 19 January. Edith was too ill to play the organ at the church service, but to everyone's amazement she got herself out of bed and dressed for the wedding party at Glen B afterwards. She had concocted a sensational hat, swathing an old one in green satin and decorating it with a stuffed seagull with outspread wings. When she walked through the door into the party, the first person with whom she had eye contact was the unfortunate Claude Chavasse, who could not think what to say. Eventually he managed, 'Cousin Edith! What a ... what a ... wonderful hat.' 'Yes,' she said snappishly, 'I look like an Air Vice Marshall in heaven.'[25] At the end of January she had to let Nancy go. The dog was first given morphia. 'I sat with her for an hour and a half while she sank into her last sleep. Then Mike and Major Roberts gave the chloroform. My darling little Nancy.' On the following day she 'did not go out, was very lame and wretched, and wherever I go I feel that little thing at my heels. Then I look down and know I've lost her until I get to the other side of death.' Now Edith's diary is taken over by obituaries. In May, both Ethel Smyth and Elizabeth Kenmare died. Edith sent off an appreciation of Ethel to *The Times*. In her diary she wrote of Ethel: 'She was 86, born on St George's Day, 1858, ten days before me. She was a splendid creature. I am thankful to have known and loved her and to have been loved by her' and of Elizabeth Kenmare simply: 'I shall never know another creature in all ways as perfect as she.' She acted upon her feeling that her letters to Ethel were too personal to survive. Edith asked Christopher St John, who was Ethel Smyth's literary executor, to send back the letters she had written to Ethel.

Hildegarde and Edith sat and read their way through her letters to Cameron, getting great amusement from the oddity of the personalities of their younger selves. Quoting Walter Savage Landor, Edith wrote, 'Until Martin came my sense of humour was very undeveloped, but I was a light hearted girl "who warmed both hands before the fire of life"...' [26] When David and Maude Gray visited them in June, they brought with them the latest word on Boyle's death from the diplomatic circuit. They were told: 'It is said that the Nazies inspired Tom Barry to arrange the murder of Boyle as he was doing too much for the British Navy.'[27] The farm gave them occupation and distraction. The harvest was good in this year – 'our oats the best in the county'. During October she made a copy of the portrait of the Countess of Desmond, an ancestress she claimed through the Townshends, from the original at the Castle; this alone was what she eventually chose to leave to Desmond in her last will. In it, clause 4, subclause iii, she asked 'that this picture be henceforth deemed a Somerville heirloom'. By this route it joined two other ancestors that Edith had painted. Very attentive to his sisters, Jack acted as agent for Edith in London and was very quick to descend upon the BBC when they made an unauthorised broadcast of one of the most successful RM stories, 'Lisheen Races Second Hand'.

Time began to take its toll on their farm hands. In the spring of 1945 Richard Helen came to the sisters to explain that his rheumatism was now so severe that he could no longer plough for them. Hildegarde recorded this as a 'bad blow for us' in her diary, but she does not dwell on her own difficulties. The choir and the organ playing in the church became a problem, as the sisters had shared the dual duty for sixty years without any serious apprentices. Now Edith, up in the organ loft, was too blind to see the music, and Hildegarde, down in the choir, was too deaf to hear when to come in. Hildegarde wrote in her diary: 'For the first time in years no music in church. I sat in the Coghill pew and thought of old times and packed choirs and Egerton's lovely bass ...'[28] An oculist in Cork after an examination told Edith that nothing could be done to help her see the music. She was working at the essays that were published in *Happy Days*, in the Drishane dining room, as she had to give up her fire in the Studio, such was the shortage of turf. Though they were becoming increasingly decrepit, the sisters still functioned efficiently at jobs they had carried out for decades. Hildegarde still earned income from her flower farming. In her diary on 22 February she wrote: 'I went down and packed 46 bunches of Daffs and 5 bunches of jonquils and sent them off to Dublin market ...' Edith had more difficulty in sending off her products. As the Irish government strictly regulated the passage of Irish material to Britain through the mails, on 16 April Edith had to write to the Chief Controller of Censorship in Dublin to ask for official permission to post her essays to Longman's.

There was an influx of family. Boyle's son Michael arrived with his wife and children. He had married Barbara, the novelist daughter of Archbishop Gregg. Remembering her own nursery diet of tea, bread and slops with the occasional top of Grandpapa's boiled egg, Edith recorded her astonishment at the amount their little girl ate: 'I will record the difference in the present day feeding of children, and myself when young. Little Christine aged 8, eats as much for breakfast as a man. Coffee, sausage, bacon, egg, marmalade, a large piece of hot brown bread. Cameron and I had boiled bread and milk (in the nursery) later (in the dining room) cold milk, brown bread and butter, and the tops of Grandpapa's and Papa's eggs. I have been impelled to this note by seeing a little girl eating as much as her father's considerable appetite demands.'[29] On 8 May they listened to the voice of Churchill making the announcement of peace on the radio. 'H. had a few signalling flags hung on the gate of Glen B. A Guard was sent to take them down "This is a neutral country!" De Valera went formally to the German legation in Dublin to condole on the "death of Herr Hitler"! Poor Eire, made the laughing stock of the world.'[30] The following day Hildegarde put up the signalling flags again, this time without interference. 'The Hun Legation has had to leave Dublin and Hitler is said "not to be dead but in the County Clare".'

By 12 May Edith was getting up a head of steam over press censorship. 'No Irish paper has mentioned the concentration camp horrors. The Southern Star has never mentioned the War 'til today, when it had pictures of Churchill, Hitler, and Himmler side by side, suggesting their equal importance. Fresh horrors of an even more awful concentration camp are now coming out, and the kindly, decent Irish people are kept in ignorance and their sympathy suppressed, out of sheer hatred of England and America.' On 21 June Edith wrote in her diary, 'Desmond and Moira entered into permanent residence.' Sir Patrick Coghill, still 'Paddy' to his family, returned from Syria after VJ Day to find Hildegarde in Glen B with Ambrose and Betty, Biddy, Mrs Brian Somerville, and her children Andrew and Jennifer: 'What Mother and D must have endured during the War can hardly be imagined, especially in their loneliness after Uncle Cameron had gone ... the strain of living in such conditions had told heavily on the old ladies ... I had said good bye to Mother in June 1941 on Mallow Station and I did not see her again until late August 1945 – four very long years and a pang went through me when I saw how much she had aged in that time ...'[31] The young of the family began to discuss the future for the sisters, who carried on unaware. Longman's were designing the illustrations and text layout of *Happy Days*. There was a flurry of fruitless correspondence between Edith and George Bernard Shaw at this point about the disposition of Charlotte Shaw's bequest, which Edith had hoped might benefit the Irish art world. Simply because there was no-one else Edith continued to play the organ at services, from memory; her arms remained strong enough, and she was able to pull herself about and up into the organ loft with the aid of handholds.

It was time to face facts. At a meeting about the future of the farm on 18 November, with Desmond, Richard Helen and John Connell, it was decided to close down in the next spring, putting in the usual crops in order not to incur the penalty involved by insufficient cultivation. Major changes were set in motion behind the scenes, once the sisters' retirement was agreed upon. In the following year, Edith and Hildegarde moved to Tally Ho, on the main street of Castletownshend to set up home together. This was arranged through the generosity of Hildegarde's son Sir Patrick, and the ostensible reason was that the dwelling, with major apartments and bathroom on the ground floor, was safer and easier than Drishane for the increasingly crippled Edith, who needed easy access to a bathroom from her studio. In public a tactful silence was kept on this subject by the sisters, but Martin's niece Muriel Currey, in her extracts from Edith's diaries, includes her own comments in which she throws tact to the winds. It was a fact that Desmond's wife Moira Somerville did not get along with Edith or Hildegarde and vice versa.

Tactfulness was a skill of the elder generation, and Edith never complained to her godson of her dislike of leaving Drishane, or of the manner in which her leaving was manoeuvred. The Coghill brothers seemed to have played an ignoble part, leaving Moira to do the cruel deed, that of insisting upon her removal, which they could not do themselves. By this short-sighted move Edith's papers were to be decimated, and the remainder divided at sales and scattered. On 29 November Hildegarde entered in her diary her concern at Edith's uncomfortable situation: 'Edith low about her position at Drishane and would like to be on her own somewhere ...' It is unlikely that Edith seriously considered leaving her home at this point, but it is interesting that she mentioned the possibility to her sister at this time. They had a larger worry in the fate of their herd. It was with the greatest regret that the sisters had decided to give up their Friesians. Hildegarde was becoming increasingly deaf and forgetful, and Edith, who was the more physically infirm, but mentally alert as ever, found her sister's failing memory heartbreaking. She wrote regularly to her godson Patrick with accounts of his mother's health, and in one of these letters, also on 29 November, we see how Edith's land, paid for with her literary earnings in shares, was silently subsumed back into family ownership.

> ... [H. is] really very well, save for this hateful deafness ... she is very bad about giving her attention to a speaker, and still worse about trying to use the machine that Nevill sent her! ... She has just done a wonderful job o' work and *listed* all our Friesians in view of our proposed retirement from business. I shall miss the interest that the farm has always been to us (and specially to her, the *Friesians*) ... I'm deciding to sell my farm – Farrandau, as 'shreds and patches' are no use, and I'm keeping on Joe Kingston and Mick Minnehane (whose holdings are south of the road) I don't know what Desmond will do with what is left of the land – and I don't think he does either! Boland [solicitor] made some muddle over what I intended to give Desmond, and seems to have over-stated the case, and included *all* that was left of what I got from Uncle Cameron! However it doesn't make much difference now ...

Eoin O'Mahony had written to her first about being the guest of honour at a Cork dinner for Dean Swift on 22 October, She turned this down, pleading infirmity and blaming Ann O'Domini. He took a second line of attack, through Hildegarde, with better success. On St Andrew's Day, 30 November, she had been persuaded after all to be the guest of honour at the lunch on the day of the celebrations of the bi-centenary of Dean Swift's birthday. The lunch seems to have been organised by Eoin O'Mahony and the Cork University Philosophical

Society more as a tribute to Edith Somerville than to the Dean, as he was hardly mentioned in the luncheon celebrations; the Dean's turn came in the afternoon lecture. Muriel Currey was astonished at Eoin O'Mahony's powers of persuasion as 'to the last moment she was protesting she was to ill to go'. In the event she enjoyed it enormously, and wrote to describe it to Geraldine in London: 'If only you had been at home how much *Eoin*, my "devoted Eoin" in all his letters, and I would have rejoiced! ... He really organized the whole affair most wonderfully. There must have been nearly 70 guests at the lunch in the Metropole. The hall there was humming with them when we arrived. A charming youth [the young Ralph Sutton] advanced upon me with a huge bouquet of lovely chrysanthemums and streamers of blue satin ribbon, and then, in pomp, on Eoin's arm, I was swept into the dining room in which were two very long tables with a third heading them. At this Eoin, I, Elizabeth Bowen, Hildegarde and a very nice and agreeable Canon Sheehan were established ... I commend to your notice Eoin's most successful Menus. They made everyone start laughing and talking. They were really a brilliant idea and very well carried out ...'[32] The organisation of this celebration with such careful choice of suitable flowers, colours and food indicates a great deal of behind-the-scenes planning and conferring that was carried out between Hildegarde and Eoin O'Mahony; they still achieved complete surprise and pleasure. Edith had imagined herself as an onlooker at a ceremony and panegyrics for Swift, whereas in fact he was the front behind which her surprise was hidden.

The Menu, to Somerville and Ross afficionados, can still raise outright laughter. It is clever in its *double entendres* and its subtle intertwining of the chronology of the books with the biographical circumstance of the writers.

Clear Silver Fox
Thick Irish RM
Sole Flurry Knox
Plaice Dan Russel
Roast Beef Martin Ross
Sauce Charles Kendal Bushe (*An Incorruptible Irishman*)
Kidney Stray-Aways
Mushrooms All on the Irish Shore
Cold Meat and Salad
West Carbery Foxhounds
Real Charlotte Russe
Bombe Big House of Inver
Surprise Mount Music
Coffee Irish Academy of Letters.

After lunch, and a speech on the work of Somerville and Ross by Eoin O'Mahony, Edith stood up and spoke for six minutes in response in smiling good humour. She was then taken to the university Lecture Hall where she took the chair while Judge Flood gave a lecture on Swift. She signed dozens of signatures on menus at the following grand tea in the university, and was driven back home, happy. She had been quite wrong in her fears, confided to her diary, that 'I only hope I won't be dead before Jerome brings home what is left of us.' But in fact her body was malfunctioning, and Hildegarde knew of her increasing unhappiness at Drishane, writing in her diary on 6 December: 'She is getting very restive and conditions unpleasant for her.' At the very end of the year Edith had some kind of seizure that disabled her writing hand. Doctor Burke said there had been a failure in circulation, and only gradually was she able to control a pen again. By 9 January 1946 her writing was more or less legible, but a ruin.

In Drishane, when Desmond Somerville had returned from army service in the summer of 1945, it was immediately clear to the Coghill brothers that personal relationships were too difficult with a resident mistress long past retirement age and a young one in waiting who were none too pleased to be sharing the same position; the elder particularly was irked by the overtly controlling manner of the younger. Hildegarde was disturbed by Moira's fluctuations in manner towards Edith; she disliked any mention of Edith's painting or writing. There must have been much discussion behind the scenes among the younger generation. It took a great deal of persuasion even to make Edith entertain the prospect of a move; she wrote to Paddy on 1 February:

> I want to thank you very much, my dear Godson, for your most kind and faithfull thought for me. I haven't seen your mother today and we have not had time to talk over your suggestions. I need not tell you that she is more to me than anyone else in the world, and your thought of our being together in Tally Ho is a very delightful one, but there is a great deal to be considered and until she and I have gone into it thoroughly I don't like to say anything definite, but I am afraid there is a great deal involved in my uprooting myself, – difficulties that I won't go into now, and one unfortunate fact that on May 2nd, I shall be 88, which is a bad age for transplanting and might involve the waste of a great deal of money.

By 25 February, the sale of the herd had been organised. In her diary Edith entered: 'All Friesians to Marsh's yard for sale tomorrow. H and I have been keeping them for about 20 years [actually since 1910], through good and evil report, through fair and foul weather, and now at last we are beaten by the cost of wages, more than £100 p.a. for *each man* and we can't face it any longer. All the work has – during the last years – come on H and she has bravely stood to it and for it, but now we have to haul down the Black and White flag, Hail and Farewell – from Elsa to Castlehaven Candid.' On the following day the sisters were consoled by 'wonderfully high' prices, the herd selling for 1,100 guineas, 'rather better than half the debt which has been crippling us since that disastrous and ruining "Irish Treaty".' Rose Marie Salter Townshend moved back into the Castle with her family on 9 March; showing a grit and application very like her cousin Edith's, she came back into her own with enduring success. She was beginning again, but the Somerville sisters were closing down. On 22 March there was a second auction of farm goods and gear, 'the final and culminating sale of all that now remains of our nearly thirty years as farmers'. On the next day Hildegarde went to their bank manager and wiped out their debt. Neither sister knew how to take the open cheerfulness of people who were pleased by their successful sales, when they were 'warmly congratulated for what, for both of us, is called a release, but is a grief and an unavoidable defeat'. The worst came on 26 March when they had to pay off their men: 'The three men Richard [Helen], John Connell and Dinny Crowley, came for a formal farewell, gave them respectively £25, £15 and £10, and after their withdrawal, our tears.'

They began to take stock of their papers. Edith donated to the library of University College, Cork, further books to supplement those they already had. At Glen B, Hildegarde felt compelled, like Edith at Drishane, to tidy up and destroy papers, which she burned in the schoolroom fireplace; they had come to think of their papers as 'rubbish'. In May she helped Nevill to put order on Edith's literary papers, in preparation for a sale of MSS at Sothebys. His catalogue remains a precious resource for researchers. Of the younger generation he was the closest to Edith, and the most knowledgeable and understanding eye to assess the joint writings, which are a dangerous minefield for even experienced palaeographers. Edith's miscellany *Happy Days* came out at the end of May. It was reviewed in *Punch* by a writer who thought Somerville and Ross were both dead. In her diary Edith noted: 'Wrote to him or her and said we were not dead at all.' During June she was trying to write an article about joint-writing for David Marcus, the editor of the new journal *Irish Writing*. The request, which came through the agency of Geraldine Cummins, caused her to think anew about how she and Martin had written together, given their circumstances: 'read our old diaries. Was astounded by the account in both my diaries and Martin's of entire want of method and system. All our writing done in casual scraps. We had no consideration for ourselves and still less did anyone show for us. How the RC was written it is quite impossible to imagine. I feel it can never be believed or understood if I try to set it out.'

The article was headed 'Two of a Trade', and although Geraldine told Edith that it was 'a thoroughly Irish masterpiece of evasion', the piece is of real interest. Edith acknowledges that the fact of Willy Wills and Aunt Louisa having made money from a 'Shilling Shocker' was an element in their decision to write: 'But, as a matter of history, it must be admitted that it was originally our mothers who incited Martin Ross and me to the first writing that we did together ... they it was who decreed to us the responsible task of compiling a Dictionary of the Family Language, and so set our feet in the path of Literature.' Here again we have a tidying up of reality; Edith had begun the Dictionary with Ethel, on Ethel's invention of the term 'Buddh'. Their mothers may well have encouraged them to complete the second version of the Dictionary in 1886/7, but it had been begun in a first version in 1885, before Martin had met her CT cousins. In *Two of a Trade* Edith goes on '...we had acquired a sort of reputation as letter writers, and in those days there was no question, mothers *had* to be obeyed! Also it may be said that we had discovered in one another a very similar outlook in literary and artistic matters, and this task was not without appeal.'

Encouraged by the family approval of the Dictionary 'and being as impecunious as is the normal condition of young hussies, we decided that we would emulate Aunt Louisa and Willy Wills ... Martin Ross, though four years younger than I, was far better equipped than I was for a literary enterprise. She had recently flung herself into the study of Carlyle, and had been so impressed by his sledge-hammer style that in respectful and passable imitation of it, she had written some essays about Galway that had been warmly accepted by Edmund Yates ... Carlyle was forgotten in the excitement of devising a plot for the coming "Shocker".'

According to 'Two of a Trade' they found that their cousins objected to them writing together, saying that their work was a pointless waste of time, foolhardy and conceited, and the 'Shockers ... found themselves the victims of a kind of inverted Boycott, a determination to pursue them to any retreat in order to compel them to take part in the sport of the moment'. Edith acknowledges in this article that Martin made 'a more subtle and recondite' choice of words, and had a more poetic style than her own, which she felt to be influenced by her training as a painter. When they worked together, she wrote, 'there had been long spaces of silence, both grappling with the same intangible idea. Sometimes the compelling creative urge would come on both, and we would try to reconcile the two impulses, searching for a form into which best to cast them – one releasing it, perhaps as a cloudy suggestion, to be caught up by the other, and given form and colour, then to float away in a flash of certainty, a completed sentence ...' This description tallies very well with Nevill's account of the stages of their creative process made for the BBC programme celebrating Edith's ninetieth birthday.[33]

A second edition of *Happy Days* was brought out on 4 July. In her diary entry on the 8th she went out with Mike for an evening run in the trap drawn by 'old Billy full of going – pulling and rushing his hills. He is 25 or 26 and looks as young as ever.' But only nine days later she entered: 'My poor old Billy fell with Mike and broke both knees on rough broken stones. A terrible loss to me. Mike in deep grief.' Mike had to go to Bandon Fair and get her a replacement; Hildegarde was deeply alarmed when she was driven by Edith, whose grip on the reins was now not certain, in the trap with the new horse, which was not steady. By 17 August Longman's had sold 4,500 *Happy Days* and were printing another 4,000. The money arrived from the Sotheby's sale of Edith's literary manuscripts, and, Hildegarde recorded in her diary on 31 July, 'D at once dealt out huge cheques to me, Hugh, Jack, Desmond.' Edith was still reading new writers with interest. In September she was sent a copy of the Irish literary journal *The Bell* and was impressed by the writing: 'Read an article by Sean O'Faolain describing a wake and was impressed by it. It is like a strong water colour, painted on very rough paper.'

Hildegarde's youngest son Ambrose's amiable wife Betty was able to talk to Edith easily, and discussed the painful subject of the move to Tally Ho with her; she was probably carefully chosen for this post of emissary and smoother-out of difficulties. A sign that Edith was at ease with her was the gift of a painting, 'Baltimore headland and the Kedges in a break in the clouds that I was lucky enough to catch on the hop'. Early in October Edith started to sort papers, many of which – 'the letters of dear, delightful people' – she destroyed in order to reduce their mass. The fact that Patrick had come to the conclusion that he could not keep up Glen B and was going to let it go was obscured by the drama of Edith's removal from her kingdom, and, overlooking the cruelty, the unsympathetic young told themselves that it was all for the best. Muriel Currey comments in her transcript of the diaries at this point: 'For some time it had been clear that the joint household had not been a success and as H wished to leave Glen B it had been decided that she and D should join forces at Tally Ho.' Hildegarde no more wished to leave her home than Edith did. On the morning of her birthday, 1 August, she burst into tears at the Glen B breakfast table, knowing that it was her last to be celebrated there.

By this time Sir Patrick had won his objective, with the aid of Moira, and had organised the removal company Nat. Ross to transfer the great mass of remaining papers and belongings from Drishane and Glen B to their new home nearby. Edith complained of the hurry – 'only a fortnight more sorting and packing' and made sure that Patrick knew how dire was this late upheaval in her life: 'for no-one in the world but your mother and you would I have stirred out of Drishane'; her papers were to be stored in three great presses in Tally Ho. On 17 October she wrote to Jack: 'I went down to Tally Ho, after tea, and surveyed the 2 rooms that I am to have. I won't bore you with details. I cannot say that they compare well with my beloved old rooms here, but they have, at least, the merit of no stairs, and I'm now so awfully lame that this is really a boon.' She made clear in a following letter that the upheaval was actually worse for Hildegarde: 'No-one but myself knows how much I detest turning out of the Studio (*and* my bedroom) and I most fervently wish that poor Hildegarde, who is, I know, quite as miserable as I am about it (if not more, as she is less vocal than I am) had been left to die in peace at Glen B and I at Drishane, in spite of the stairs.' On the 20th Hildegarde wrote in her diary, 'Alas! My last big party at Glen B.' Her daughter K was with her through this trying period, 'a great help and comfort'.

At Drishane Edith was irritated by the sensation of a great clearing-out of the house taking place all round her. She discovered that Moira had thrown into the ashbin all the copies of the antique *Quarterly Reviews* and took them out again to store them in the Studio ready for removal. Sylvia Lovera also was alert to the fact that things were being put in the ashbin at Drishane that she felt should not have been, and she silently rescued material that eventually came to safety in her flat at the top of the Red House.[34] Hildegarde and K came up to Drishane on 2 November to discuss the move, the 'exhausting future and all its complicated movings – I try to feel – like riding home in the dark after a long day's hunting – the finish must come sooner or later and may be less exhausting and hateful than we expect ...' The move of belongings began three days later, Muriel Currey commenting: 'Certainly no-one was less complaining. She had left the home in which she had lived all her long life, and there is not one word of self-pity in the diary.' We learn something of Edith's capacity to hide her feelings and pretend amiable co-operation from Sir Patrick's bland account in his memoir: 'Although it must have been a terrible wrench leaving Drishane, I never heard a syllable of complaint – or indeed any reference at all. Perhaps some sorrows are too deep for words.'

On removal day itself, 16 November 1946, Edith wrote to Hamilton Townshend's wife Rhoda: 'My Studio looks like an Auction Room in delirium tremens ... It is a terrible thing to have to tear up about eighty years by the roots. But the worst is now over and I am in hopes that once H and I are reconciled to the Widow's Almshouse, we shall not mind it too much.' To Sir Patrick himself in a letter on the same day she was less morose: 'The transit of the two Venuses has been well and happily accomplished', and she wrote to him 'to thank you for all you have done for me, and to tell you what a wonderful

pleasure it is for me to find myself again under the same roof with your mother.'
Hildegarde wrote in her diary on the 20th: 'Left Glen B I fear for good and
came down to Tally Ho. K came to help ...' On 21 November, in a letter to Jack
from Edith, it was clear that the removal was protracted and that Desmond
Somerville had no notion then of the value of the papers that Edith felt forced
to decimate by burning: 'Desmond comes in, howls at the heaps of "boj"
[rubbish] on tables and sofas and floors and says pitilessly "Well, I should burn
all this stuff!" But he and Moira are entirely unartistic, their ideals being the
flawless Barrack Square, and the perfect Private Hotel which looks as though
the foot of man or woman had never defiled its chaste carpets. H and I are only
longing for you and she [Jack's second wife Mildred] to come over and see us in
our nostalgic untidiness.'

Hildegarde and Edith adjusted to their new dwelling. The winter weather
had been appalling until the beginning of April, when Mike started to take
Edith for drives in the trap again. But even this pleasure was lost to her when
on 29 May she had a smashing fall in her bathroom, having had a slight stroke.
Nurse Eileen O'Riordan came to care for her. In Tally Ho, Nurse O'Riordan
slept in the room beside her patient's, and by 12 August Edith could hobble
straight out of a French window to Mike and the pony trap. She had the
company of Hildegarde and Betty, Mrs Ambrose Coghill; her trusted maid
Philomena was still with her, she told Jack: 'I should be *sunk* without the
faithful Philomena. I'm too old to have been transplanted and my roots have
resented being uprooted. However "This too will pass".' On 1 August 1947 she
wrote to Hildegarde for her birthday when she was away with her daughter K
at Wild Forest in County Down :

> I pray you will have as many more happies as you like, all made equally
> happy with the cream of the *Young Entry* in your grandchildren beside
> you, as now – you may be proud of them – I'm sure you are! even I, a
> humble and far from great Aunt – take pride and glory out of them. You
> and I have had 80 years of unbroken love and good fellowship. I thank
> God for them. Love from Edith.

She was writing *Maria and Some Other Dogs*, with the aid of Geraldine
who typed the text. Longman's reprinted *Happy Days* again. She was still
reading with pleasure; Nevill saw to her supplies of books. Having asked for a
copy of her fellow Irish Academician Helen Waddell's book *The Wandering
Scholars*, she was delighted by it. On 17 February 1948 Geoffrey Cumberlege
of Oxford University Press wrote to her to tell her that *The Real Charlotte* was
to be published in the World's Classics series on 11 March. She was the only

living author to be included in the list. On 1 May, 90th birthday tributes started
to arrive, including one from David Cecil. On the next day, her birthday, the
BBC Third Programme broadcast a ninetieth birthday tribute, given by Nevill
Coghill. The script that he read from has survived:

> First I would like to say a little of these Ladies, as I have known them,
> Edith Somerville and Martin Ross ...
>
> When I was a boy I knew Martin Ross as well as any boy can know a
> grown-up who is also a genius and a woman. Her real name was Violet
> Martin, but we all called her 'Martin' ... she was slender, and graceful
> and intrepid; a lovely rider to hounds, in spite of her short sight, very
> dangerous to riders in our rough country. She was as kind as she was
> courageous; the delicate serenity of her manner was the first thing one
> noticed; yet it would dissolve in an instant into unquenchable laughter,
> for she had a shattering sense of humour and the gift of sudden wit.
> Vividness of perception, trenchant intelligence and easy grace, were the
> qualities of her life, as of her style. As she lived, she wrote, with unerring
> felicity of phrase and impulse. Courage, candour and affection blazed
> from her. Edith Somerville, her cousin, has the same flame of life;
> whatever she says has an edge to it, and is the delight of all who listen to
> her ... her landscapes are full of an inward sense of our wild scenery; her
> pen and pencil sketches of the people of Ireland are as idiomatic and
> truthful as the dialogue in her books. They have an equal mixture of wit
> and pathos ... [Nevill passed on to describe their books, and then
> reached the problem of explaining how they wrote together.] As a matter
> of fact they *talked* their stories and their characters and their every
> sentence into being ... the two imaginations became one, working with
> the equal harmony of two hands knitting a scarf. I have studied all their
> manuscripts closely; almost every entry is dated ... Delightful thumbnail
> sketches, evidently done like lightning while considering a point, decorate
> the margins here and there. I have found brief notes, two sentences long,
> containing the gist of a story, which in a later manuscript is expanded
> into a twenty-line synopsis, and later still into a full first draft, with
> corrections and insertions; then at last the fair copy, as sent to the printer.
> One can watch the creative process at work.

The intimacy of Nevill's tribute to both writers brought tears to Edith as she
listened in Tally Ho. She wrote in her diary: 'it couldn't have been more
gracefully written or in better or more well-bred taste. It lasted 25 minutes and
nearly broke my control.' More than anyone, Nevill knew the manuscript drafts

and understood their genesis. It is a great loss that he never had the time, as he
had hoped, to write a biography of his aunt, because of the prior claims of his
work at Oxford and his specialisation in Middle English. He was already well
known for his BBC broadcasts translating Chaucer and Langland, and for his
remarkable theatrical productions. An inspiring and much-loved teacher, he was
to be elected to the Merton Chair of English literature in 1957.

Edith's diary entries now became so illegible that she asked others to make
entries if she thought it important. She could still scrawl letters but couldn't
write small enough for a diary any more. Her last diary entry in her own hand is
on 12 September 1948: 'Nurse Eileen O'Riordan and I continue as before,
unchanged since May 1947, when I tripped up and haven't done a day's work
since, and never thought I would have to end a good active hard-working life
dying like a worn out old horse in a corner of a field'. Even so, she still exercised
an authority over her younger sister; Hildegarde was worried that Edith would
hear of her son Ambrose's divorce from Betty, the news of which she felt would be
an appalling shock. She wrote in her diary: 'I hope D won't hear of it. She is not so
well this last week. She sleeps most of the day and I do hope she may sleep away
and cross over in her sleep – she is suffering from intense irritation ... in patches
on her arms and shoulders – it really is worse than pain ...' Whatever useless state
her body was in, Edith could not give up the mental habits of a lifetime, and
organised her thoughts towards book production to the very end. Her last book
was *Maria and Some Other Dogs*, produced by Methuen, by the look of it still in
war economy mode, in July 1949. In it she included Martin's early piece 'The Dog
from Doone'. A copy of this volume was her last author's gift to Hildegarde; her
birthday letter, written on 31 July, shows, as do her letters to her godson Patrick
and her friend Elizabeth Hudson, a longing to be quit of her body and a care to
express her thanks to those whom she loved.

> Saturday July 31st 1949
> My dearest child, it is a long time since the August 1st when Miss Kerr
> (186?) told me 'It is a little girl! And now *your* nose will be put out of
> joint!' But it wasn't! I was only given a beloved companion! And now
> that I fear we're not likely to be given another of your birthdays together,
> I can only say that I have always loved you with the deep and peculiar
> love that goes only to a faithful and devoted sister. Paddy (if I'm not here)
> will give you 6 copies of *Maria* and the same of Scribner's new edition of
> the old Irish R.M. These are not my original presents, but I hope they
> will be useful to you. They will go to you with all my love (and more
> gratitude than I can express)
> Edith.

Father Lambe, a faithful visitor, was the person who gave Edith most pleasure with his company and good talk. Mike saw her every day. On the day of Edith's death, Saturday 8 October, Nurse, Philomena, Betty Coghill, K and Hildegarde were all about the house. In the afternoon, K took Hildegarde out for a drive, and Philomena and Betty were not in evidence. Only Nurse O'Riordan was with Edith as it came towards tea time, when Edith was dozing in bed. Nurse turned her back on her to go into the kitchen to prepare tea. Minutes later when she returned to the room Edith had had a heart attack. At this stage one, perhaps two, messages were sent out of Tally Ho. Father Lambe arrived first and it was he who was holding Edith and smoothing out the lines of pain on her face as, by her account, Moira Somerville ran into the room.[35] It is difficult to know what to make of Moira's own dramatised account of this scene. She claims to have snatched Edith's body from Father Lambe (whom she identifies as Doctor Burke) because Edith 'had never known a man's arms around her' and to have been with her when she died. Her story does not tally with a written account of Edith's death sent by Hildegarde to Rose Cameron Bingham, or with an account given by K Coghill to Gifford Lewis. The death certificate is signed by Nurse O'Riordan, who is correctly described as 'present at death', as she was the nearest to Edith at the time.

By night time Edith had been coffined. When Moira returned to Tally Ho in the evening, she found a wake in progress. She could hear the sound of Mike sobbing, over the sound of the prayers. To Desmond was allocated an immediate practical problem: the task of digging Edith's grave, alongside Martin's, deep enough. The grave-diggers had hit rock and Desmond had to procure explosives at short notice in order to blast away sufficient quantities with small charges of dynamite.[36] Great care had to be taken to avoid damaging the Clarke memorial windows, only feet away. Accounts of the funeral by members of the family failed to mention that there was a huge throng of attendants at the funeral, including Eoin O'Mahony, Sean O'Criadain and Anne Crookshank. Edith Somerville's face had been of a strong family 'type'. Professor Crookshank, a cousin, remembered the shock of seeing what she thought was her grandmother's photograph in the *Irish Times*, and, not understanding that it was related to the announcement of Edith's death, imagined that her grandmother was for some strange reason featured there.[37] K Coghill's account dwelled chiefly upon the behaviour of Mike. As the family walked away from the graveside, K became aware that Mike was rooted to the ground at the graveside, with tears streaming down his face. Too embarrassed to draw attention to him and his plight, she left him there.[38]

Rose Cameron Bingham, who had been telegrammed the news of Edith's death, wrote from Oban to Hildegarde to sympathise and had a detailed response on 26 January 1950. Hildegarde's unclouded memory of her sister's personality discounts all her curbed anger and irritable 'blorting': 'I do indeed miss her very much. I have had her all my life, and when I married Egerton we just moved into the Cottage, five minutes away from Drishane – Edith was a wonderful character. I have never known her cross or out of temper and she never abused anyone and made the best of everyone – and she was such a help to us in every way ... Edith had such an easy passing over – just slept and in her sleep had a slight heart attack and just passed over. Nurse was with her, who had been with her from the time she got ill – so did all that could be done – but it was what Edith had always wished for, to die in her sleep'.[39]

In Edith's will her largest bequest, of £100, was to Mike. There were smaller monetary bequests to certain nephews and nieces and faithful servants and to Doctor Burke. In Ireland she left just under a thousand pounds; before her death she had arranged with her heir Sir Patrick that he should charge all her funeral expenses to her Irish estate, to avoid touching his English inheritance. This was the sum she had invested in London to avoid paying tax to de Valera. Paddy submitted an itemised expenses sheet of over £200 to the Irish authorities, including Edith's nursing costs, against the Irish estate. As a result, the sum was reduced to slightly less than the amount needed for her bequests, but of course these were covered by the addition of the English money in shares. Amusing stories spread after Edith's death that she did not leave enough to cover her bequests. Geraldine Cummins 'quotes' this fact, and it has been unfortunately printed again in the Irish Manuscript Commission Catalogue of the Drishane papers. Edith's will is a public record freely available to the researcher, and shows that all of her bequests were covered, with a large residue to Sir Patrick. All of Edith's papers, manuscripts and copyrights went to her sister, and were to go after her sister's death to Sir Patrick and his brother Nevill. These had been moved to Tally Ho, where they were all catalogued and numbered by the brothers with Coghill Archive numbers. Over a long period, Muriel Currey made a 370-page typescript series of extracts from the diaries, only completing it on 8 April 1965. This typescript was read and annotated by K for verification. Muriel ended her work with a comment: 'Her generosity remained incredible – she seemed to regard money as simply something to be given away – and an overdraft so normal as something just to be ignored. How glad and proud I am to have known her all my life.'

Having let Glen B to Ralph Becher while the Rectory was being rebuilt for him, Paddy settled down at Tally Ho to life with his mother. He was quickly assailed by boredom, and was unable to comprehend what was required of him. He describes his feelings frankly in his memoir: 'By the following summer I was beginning to get a bit worried about Mother. She too at 83 was beginning to fail. All the housekeeping devolved upon me and I felt extremely inadequate to cope with any serious illness. So after much thought I approached Desmond and Moira, with a view to taking over part of Drishane and sharing expenses, which would help both our pockets. I should be saved from housekeeping chores, as in Moira I had not only a fully qualified nurse, but in every way a most admirable person to call on if Mother fell sick. Negotiations were smooth and brief and Mother and I moved up just before Christmas 1950.' Edith had been dead for just over a year. Paddy seems to have been unaware that the room given to his mother as her bedroom was her old room next to her sister's: 'in every way we were extremely comfortable. But spiritually it was not our house. Mother kept on saying that it was not the Drishane she knew. I knew very well that her whole heart was wrapped up in Glen B – which indeed she had "made" and irradiated with her own happy spirit. I realised she only tolerated Tally Ho, but I had hoped that she would have been really happy being back in Drishane. But she was, if not openly delighted at being there, at least content ...' Paddy took his mother out each day for a drive, and escorted her to social events, 'but after a year of this, I felt myself getting restless and bored. There was just nothing to do ...' He volunteered for the position of Organising Officer for a new 'Special Branch' of the Jordanian Police. 'So it came about that after lunch on March 17th 1952 I said "Goodbye" to Mother in our sitting room ... I shall always remember my last glimpse ... she was standing straight as a lance by the fire ...'

Hildegarde died on 6 March two years later. Paddy wrote from Amman to his brother Ambrose: 'How lucky we were in her. Looking back the miracle and mystery to me is how she kept the family going from 1921 till 1926. There was no money. Overdraft – the result of the War, our education, and increasing cost of living ... uncomplainingly she denied herself everything ... alas to no purpose as the second war finally killed any hope of us ever living in Glen B and Glen B was her creation ... I know no other home with such an atmosphere of love and welcome. I feel guilty that at the material time I was so selfishly concentrated on trying to make my own way in the world. I never realised Mother's achievement. Had her natural talents been really cultivated by a first class education – which could not be afforded – there is no knowing to what eminence she might have risen. But without that education she revealed her natural genius as a Mother and let us be humbly grateful.'[40]

When she died, Hildegarde's devoted Swiss servant Fanny Vickery put into her hands a replica of her wedding bouquet of myrtle. Later, the Coghill quilt, an embroidered cloth that Hildegarde had loved and had worn when playing the part of Cleopatra, was laid over her coffin in the church. Bridget O'Driscoll, who had been head housemaid at Glen B and later the Nannie of Hildegarde's youngest son Ambrose, wrote to him to commiserate. Ambrose had a personality of such charm that even in his forties she called him by his childhood compound name of 'Masterambrosedarling'. Bridget was by 1954 eighty-two herself, and had known her mistress all her life: 'I loved her. I can't realise she is gone ...' but she knew that K could not bear to come back: 'I am afraid her visits to CT are finished so all the family I loved are gone from CT.'[41] K feared, rightly, that her brother Paddy would soon shed the irksome burden of Glen B. At Hildegarde's death all the Somerville and Ross copyrights and papers came into the hands of Nevill and Sir Patrick as executors. The papers were stored in Hildegarde and Sir Patrick's quarters in Drishane.

Meanwhile Desmond Somerville had found it difficult to survive financially as a farmer. A later letter from K to Toby Coghill explains that Moira Somerville saw the difficulties then besetting them as a loss of 'luck' from the house. She had begun to work on a history of the Somervilles, using Edith and Boyle's research papers, and being a strong-minded woman had no qualms, very like Edith, about constructing versions of events to suit herself. From the extent of her notes and recollections, it is even possible that she thought of writing Edith's biography herself. K became very angry when she heard of Moira's appropriation and re-provenancing of a Townshend family possession, the famous 'Fairy Shoe' which Hildegarde had taken with her from Glen B to Tally Ho, then to Drishane from Christmas 1950 where it was with her until her death there. It was a beautifully made miniature shoe, not a child's, with marks of wear. K explained later to her nephew Toby:

> Paddy and Nevill are both non-believers and totally indifferent to the Fairy Shoe, so Paddy tends to forget everything about it. As you know, it was found in the Bantry mountains in 1835 by a peasant on his way to fetch a doctor to his sick wife. The peasant gave it to the Doctor (Armstrong), who left it to his daughter. She married a Townshend, and, in due course the shoe was inherited by her daughter Charlotte. I can remember as a small girl of perhaps five being taken by mother to see old (as she seemed to me) Miss Townshend when she lived in Wynnstay Gardens, to see the shoe. When she died in the mid twenties she left it to the Sylvias. Young Sylvia didn't like or want it, and, standing on the Glen B avenue one day she said so to me and asked if I thought Dabda [Hildegarde] would like it?' 'Yes, yes, yes!' I replied. So she handed it over at once and Dabda was enchanted with it and cherished it all her life. It made a lot of money for the District Nurse, as mother used to charge any visitor (I think it was half a crown) to see it, in order to raise money for the Nurse ... After Dabda died, the Shoe and any other bits and pieces of jewellery, silver etc. were sent to the Bank of Ireland in

Skibbereen, for safe keeping. Some time later, maybe six months or a year, Moira wrote to Paddy out in Amman, begging to be allowed to borrow back the shoe, as since it had left Drishane everything seemed to be going wrong and all the luck was gone. Not being fractionally interested in the shoe, Paddy wrote back *giving* her the shoe without asking anyone else what they thought of it – I would *gladly* have had it. I didn't know what he had done until months later when I heard that Moira was trying to make out that it had always belonged to the Somervilles ...[42]

The family saw no reason to prevent Geraldine Cummins from writing her very personal memoir of Edith, and it appeared in 1952. The Coghill brothers realised that their Somerville and Ross papers were 'treasure trove', unavailable to Cummins, but it seems that only the younger clearly perceived their value in literary terms rather than monetary. Nevill seemed to be the only one to remember that in 1925 Edith had asked for a sympathetic woman biographer to be chosen for her. Knowing of the Somerville and Ross link with Kipling, he had tried first to get the Kipling scholar and critic Dr Joyce Tompkins, but had failed, then secondly tried for Elizabeth Bowen, who was unavailable. When Sir Patrick returned from Jordan in 1956, he returned to Drishane, determined to sell out from Glen B and settle in England. In his memoir, his disgust at the new Irish Republic was undisguised: 'Having spent most of my life in England or serving the Crown, I intensely disliked living under the Irish Republican flag and Government. My visits to England gave me always great happiness and satisfaction and returning to Ireland was always accomplished with much the same reluctance one experienced when returning to school in one's younger days. One felt one was returning to futility, to a bogus 18th century civilization which was quite moribund, if not mummified, and what was worse, to boredom. Gradually Nevill came to think on similar lines ... by 1959 he felt he could not be cut off from the world of scholarship and reasonable proximity to a good library.'

So Nevill sold the Point House, and Sir Patrick Glen B. After much searching, Sir Patrick had found the ideal house at Lydney in Gloucestershire. He set about organising the sale of his assets to fund its purchase and fitting out. With what little he had decided to keep from a hundred and ten years of Coghill accumulation at Glen B, he moved to Savran House in September 1961. With Nevill, he was a conscientious literary executor. The RM remained a steady seller as Anglo-Irish classical farce. In 1966 a television company made a bid to acquire the rights to film the RM series; both brothers felt positive about this. Nevill had come into contact with film people through his work with Richard Burton and Elizabeth Taylor in filming *Doctor Faustus*, released in 1967. He put film acting work in the way of Ambrose, who had inherited the character of his Uncle Aylmer as horseman, charmer and ne'er-do-well. Just as Edith suggested Aylmer for the part of Flurry decades before, Nevill now suggested to his brother: 'I wonder if the thought has struck you that if the RM television series gets started, Ambrose might be considered for Flurry?'[43] Ambrose, magnificent in cavalry uniform, rode in the film version of *The Charge of the Light Brigade*, and in *Faustus*, naked and gilded, he played the cameo part of Avarice.

In the same year, accepting that they themselves would not write it, and being unable to persuade Elizabeth Bowen or David Cecil to undertake the research, Sir Patrick asked the biographer Maurice Collis to write a biography using the Somerville and Ross papers before the most important of them went up for sale at Sothebys. Knowing that Edith had expressed a hope to the Comte de Suzannet that her papers would be housed in Trinity College Dublin, the then Keeper of Manuscripts, William O'Sullivan, attempted to buy the Coghill Archive entire for Trinity; but Sir Patrick hoped to raise more through Sothebys, and so the collection was broken up. At the sale in 1968 the surviving correspondence between Edith and Martin went to the New York Public Library, and the diaries and most important literary notebooks to Queen's University Belfast. Sir Patrick gave to Trinity College Dublin the records of the West Carbery Hunt. Manuscript versions of the RM and the papers and letters of the Somerville and Ross literary agent James Pinker came via the Comte de Suzannet to this collection also. At some stage the trunk containing the collection made by Hildegarde at Edith's request in 1925 including Cameron's letters, plus other added genealogical material, had returned to Drishane and disappeared from view. As no papers of Edith's had been left to the owner of Drishane, and they had all been moved to Tally Ho in 1946, this 'lost' trunk, apparently forgotten by Sir Patrick and mourned by researchers, in effect created a biographer's block. It contained what remained of the records of the first third of Edith Somerville's life. Without this, in *The Irish Cousins* of 1970, Violet Powell made a very successful attempt to describe the lives of Somerville and Ross through their published works, and, at the behest of Sir Patrick Coghill and his sister K, Gifford Lewis made an alternative attempt using illustrative material in 1985.

All of Hildegarde's children were aghast at the 'mis-interpretation' of their aunt's character in what K described as 'Collis' dreadful book'.[44] As the years passed, it became clearer that the originally complete and coherent Somerville and Ross Coghill Archive had been irregularly re-distributed by Sir Patrick, without telling his siblings and heir, in a way that confused the sequences that

he himself had made so clearly in 1950. By 1980, when he authorised Gifford
Lewis to try to reorganise the sources so that they could be used for a better
new biography, to displace the Collis one, it seemed impossible to retrieve the
confusion. In 1995 a catalogue of the rediscovered Somerville and Ross material
in Drishane was published by the Irish Manuscripts Commission. More may re-
appear, but a great deal was lost by deliberate destruction, even after the
Somerville sisters destroyed what they deemed, or rather doomed, to be
superfluous letters in 1946. When Sir Patrick sold Glen Barrahane, he cleared it
and made a great bonfire of things he did not want to take with him to
England. His sister Katharine, who had forced herself to return to what she
knew would be a ghastly scene of destruction, saved the portrait of herself as
a child by Gabriel Nicolet from the top of the fire. Then she saved the Elliott
and Fry portrait of Edith on Bridget, with the hounds in the foreground, taken
when Martin, incapacitated by laughter, was trying to act as drover and make
them all look the same way; and last she saved Edith's ebony and silver crucifix.
The buyer of Glen Barrahane wanted a more convenient house and demolished
it to build anew.

# Conclusion

THOUGH EDITH, Hildegarde and Martin had spent so much of their lives
trying to improve and alter the status of women, it is not possible to say
that their efforts had any long-term effects within their family circles, or the
outer world. They remained in thrall to men. At the height of the women's
suffrage movement, numbers of women gained an education and a profession
through being promoted by a pro-suffrage male mentor; the hope that all men
would eventually see the benefit to society was illusory. The doctrine of 'separate
spheres' for men and women is again being reinforced by the increasing stress
laid upon male and female sexuality. This is a stress that encourages young men
and women to understand their relationships solely in sexual terms. It encourages young women to talk to one another about men, it encourages young men
to talk together about women, and it increases the distance between the sexes.
Best mates have a lasting, lifelong importance that lovers do not have; homosexuality, increasingly accepted, offers a relative stability; marriage has largely
lost its significant meaning. In the second half of the nineteenth century in
Castletownshend's Anglo-Irish community, which through genetic accident was
overwhelmingly female in the elder generation, it seemed that a different kind
of relationship between men and women could be developed. The Somerville
sisters had excellent relationships with their male first cousins, which were
direct, truthful, generous and lifelong. It was the wealth and sympathy of the
Aylmer brothers that supported and funded Edith's entry into book publishing
in 1885, and the sisters' entry into large-scale farming in 1918. They had
carried out – within the family circle – Edith's feminist exhortation: 'Every man,
consciously or unconsciously, judges women by the women he knows best, and
it rests with each of us to form that opinion.'[1] But if Edith and Hildegarde had
hoped that the Somerville and Coghill boys of the next generation were going
to grow up into liberated, paid-up members of the men's league for women's
suffrage like the Aylmer brothers or Egerton Coghill, they were to be disappointed. Edith was, she thought, close to her much-admired nephews Patrick,
Nevill and Raymond, all of whom – in their own ways – were to conceal their
true thoughts from her and to fail to communicate directly. After her death, Sir

Patrick was to pay so little heed to his godmother's expressed wishes, and was to so badly manage the Somerville and Ross Archive, that a thoroughly researched biography was made an impossibility for decades.

The novels, essays and short stories of Somerville and Ross are much concerned with the inter-relationship of the sexes, and how lasting marriage is achieved. They deal with familiar difficulties in the sexual relationship of men and women, and, as was only to be expected, in describing sexuality they took no bold step to compare with Kate O'Brien, in the next generation of Irish writers. Martin had shied away from what she called 'the central physical point of life', and left her partner to deal with the romantic themes of their novels. Often their heroines settle for the unexciting but steady suitor and discard the dangerous but sexually exciting alternative; Sally and Flurry Knox remained their only triumphant *mésalliance*. By the '30s and '40s, when she had reverted to writing of the Ireland of her teens and twenties, Edith had become hopelessly old-fashioned and out of date in the eyes of critics. This was a time when Kate O'Brien was writing of the rise of the new Irish 'Top People' as the Anglo-Irish lost their power; she was to write of homosexuality in *Land of Spices* (1941) and of lesbianism – indirectly in *Mary Lavelle* (1935) and directly in her *Flower of May* (1953) and *As Music and Splendour* (1958).

Although it seems that both Edith and Martin had considered marriage as a possibility, they concealed this as they were trained to conceal all sexual matters, and their natural talents provided them with an alternative route. And although they both made a cult of female friendship that networked this alternative route, this did not preclude close and admiring relationships with men. As they became older their moral sense grew stricter, and the tenets of their religion held them tighter. Unchanged from their parents' day, the chief sources of moral outrage and disgust remained bastardy and apostasy, or as Martin termed it, perversion. She had recoiled with suspicion and horror from *The Picture of Dorian Gray* and from the overt sexuality of *The Ballad of the Nun* in the first number of the *Yellow Book* in 1894. Both writers in their essays on marriage are hard-bitten, seemingly disappointed in romantic love. In her essay *In Sickness and in Health* (1890), written when she was twenty-seven, Martin wrote of peasant marriages in which: 'Love [was] the negligible quantity and attachment the rule. It is for us, more singly bent on happiness, to aim at rapture and foreknow disappointment.' Some bitter experience seems to inform her: 'It is romance that holds the two-edged sword, the sharp ecstasy and the severing scythe stroke, the expectancy and the disillusioning, the trance and the clearer vision.' The essay was written in the second fortnight of April at Glen Barrahane, during a year when she was very much taken with Warham St Leger, whom she failed to persuade to visit her at Ross in the late summer. She had formed an attachment to him by 1888.

The pragmatic marriages of the Cork country people that she knew also fascinated Edith. When she was eighty-five, in her essay *For Richer for Poorer* (1933), she wrote: 'these state alliances, founded though they may be on the commonplace of financial security, have a way of making for happiness that love matches do not invariably achieve, and one begins dispassionately to wonder if the Romantics and the Poets haven't been wrong all the time, and the stern, business-like parents right.' The essay closes with a re-set version of a quotation from a Drishane housemaid, taken down in December 1882, when Edith's relationship with Barry Avonmore had been put on hold. 'I think I will never be married. I'd love to be an ould maid. A single life is airy.' It shows an unusually extensive re-write. In the final version, made fifty years after it was first recorded, Edith fictionally describes herself in conversation with a widow who farms alone. 'I asked her whether she thought a married life or a single one was the happier. The reply was ... "once ye'd got over the disgrace of it, a single life'd be the more airy. But faith!" she added with a laugh, "if ye get marri'd, or if ye stay single, its aiqual which way it is, ye'll be sorry!"'

The effects of the 'cage' imposed on Edith by her class and family proved to be lifelong. She was unable to throw off the bonds and burst out of the cage like the Gore Booth sisters, Maud Gonne or Ethel Smyth. It is Elizabeth Bowen with whom she shared the intense love of home and family, and the impulse to chronicle the Anglo-Irish world in her memoirs. Perhaps because they had both seen that it was all over, Bowen could not bring herself to write Somerville's life in the early 1960s, when her remaining papers were still coherently organised and accessible. The 'cage' had naturally imprinted class awareness, the unembarrassed grading of human beings, from Judy O'Grady to the Colonel's lady, by their accent, clothes and manners. This may have been reprehensible, but the designation of peasant was not meant to be scornfully dismissive or derogatory; Somerville and Ross faithfully preserved and recorded speech, including that of the peasantry, with much less of the subsequent re-writing and 'improvement' of those Abbey Theatre play scripts that artfully aimed for 'PQ' or 'peasant quality'. Not too impressed by restrictions on familiarity with servants, they had both taken notice of their servants' and tenants' world, listened closely and participated in dialogue. The bent of their own humour led them to collect the speech that gave them such pleasure; it was not until they had begun to write descriptive articles for money that they thought of incorporating 'gems' of recorded speech, which Martin Ross first did in her article 'Cheops in Connemara' for *The World* in 1889, and Edith Somerville in her 'Mrs Maloney's Amateur Theatricals' for *Home Chimes* in 1885. The idea that they wrote of Ireland *de haut en bas* is beginning to be discarded, and even in Edith's lifetime there were Irish writers who acknowledged the quality of the

RM. In 1919 Robert Lynd wrote in *Ireland a Nation*: 'The Irish RM is no doubt merely the last and best of the books in the Lever-Lover tradition, but it is also a masterpiece which has caught the Irish accent with a genius as sure as Synge's or Lady Gregory's ...'

They are ranked now among Munster women writers, and some of their books are acknowledged as Irish classics. Edith Somerville's life was an unusual one, gauged from the evidence of her literary and artistic output, and when it is examined the same question arises that came into her mind when she surveyed her career for David Marcus and *Irish Writing* in June 1946. 'How?' Her writing was done in 'casual scraps' of time snatched from the beginnings and ends of a multitude of other occupations. The literary work shows the power of mind over matter and circumstance. Apart from earning the income that made it possible to keep up home life, writing and talking with Martin put order on thoughts, fixed them. Above all, what was desired was the right shaping of words: 'a flash of certainty, a completed sentence'. The feeling that their conversation would carry on, death not interposing much of a pause, one or both being dead, shows in the lack of attention that Edith paid to the final appearance of their tombstones side-by-side. Completely incongruous, a rough monolith and a standard-issue dressed stone stepped-cross, they remind us that, apart from their shared humour and their way with words, it was two very different women that were bound in undying friendship.

# *Notes*

INTRODUCTION

1 Elizabeth Bowen, *Bowenscourt* (London, 1942), afterword, p. 336.
2 Declan Kiberd, *Irish Classics* (London, 2001), pp 360–78.
3 Molly Keane, Foreword to *The Selected Letters of Somerville and Ross*, ed. G. Lewis (London, 1989) p. xxi.
4 Edith Somerville, *Wheeltracks* (London, 1924), p. 15.
5 Somerville and Ross, *All on the Irish Shore* (London, 1903) p. 108.
6 Somerville and Ross, *An Irish Cousin* (London, 1889), chapter XXI.
7 George Bernard Shaw to Edith Somerville, 18 January 1922. Originally in the Coghill Archive but now catalogued in the Drishane Archive. Printed in the IMC Catalogue, p. 194.
8 Violet Florence Martin. Her will, dated 29 March 1906, was witnessed by Egerton Coghill and Hugh Somerville at Glen Barrahane. Filed at Somerset House. Executor Edith Somerville.
9 Edith Anna Œnone Somerville. Paid her eldest brother's debts, December 1939. Will made, 18 April 1948 at Tally Ho. Codicil, 18 March 1949. Witnessed by Rhoda Townsend and Nesta Penrose-Fitzgerald. Executor Sir Patrick Coghill.
10 Violet Martin to Edith Somerville, 20 August 1889.
11 Edith Somerville to Cameron Somerville, 25 June 1908.
12 Ibid., 17 October 1897.
13 I.M. Lewis, *Ecstatic Religion: A Study of Shamanism and Spirit Possession* (London, 1989), p. 26.
14 Sir Patrick Coghill assisted G. Lewis as best he could in the late 1970s, locating the Buddh Dictionary, authorising the filming of the correspondence between Somerville and Ross by then at the New York Public Library, and sorting what remained of the Coghill Archive. However, unremembered by Sir Patrick, some of this Archive had remained at Drishane, and some had been returned there in 1968.
15 Lillian Faderman, *Surpassing the Love of Men* (London, 1985), pp 205–9.
16 Brenda Maddox, *George's Ghosts* (London), pp 37, 78. In a convincing analysis, Maddox sees such communication as motivated by the 'receiver' as a means of achieving ends that would otherwise be impossible.
17 D.G. Gifford, a WAAF during the war, serving in Central Records at Gloucester, confirmed that formal Discharges under KRACI Clause 11 were made out to WAAFs who had become pregnant, but not in the infrequent cases of lesbianism which were tolerated and dealt with informally.
18 The 1968 Sotheby's Catalogue for the sale of Somerville and Ross MSS comments on the misquotation of material by Collis. Some of these were corrected in G. Lewis, 1985.
19 Canon Claude Chavasse to Gifford Lewis, 28 April 1980.
20 Katherine Tynan, 'Exit, the Spirit of Laughter', *The New Witness*, 30 December 1915, p. 247.
21 Charles Graves, 'Novels of the Week', *The Spectator*, 25 November 1899.
22 George Bernard Shaw, *Heartbreak House* (London, 1919), pp 2, 3.

CHAPTER ONE

1 Edith Somerville to Jack Somerville, 4 August 1923.

2  Edith Somerville to Alice Kinkead, 9 December 1917.

3  J. Lawlor and W.H. Auden (eds), *To Nevill Coghill from Friends* (London, 1966), pp 14–21.

4  Ibid., p. 15.

5  W.H. Lecky, *Leaders of Public Opinion in Ireland* (London, 1912), vol. 1, p. 248.

6  Nancy Crampton Bushe to her son Charles Bushe, quoted by ECES in *Irish Memories*, p. 49.

7  ECES to HAC, 17 January 1933.

8  BLGI Coghill.

9  ECES, *An Incorruptible Irishman* (London, 1932), chapters I–V.

10  Ibid., pp 9–12.

11  Also in *Irish Memories*, pp 43–52.

12  Ibid., Appendix I, p. 338.

13  ECES to HAC, 16 June 1922.

14  Eoin O'Mahony reviewing R. ffolliott, *The Pooles of Mayfield* (Dublin, 1958) in the *Limerick Weekly Echo*, 11 July 1959.

15  Genealogical papers of BTS and ECES, IMC Catalogue 1.Y. 8a–11a.

16  Confirmed by separate research in G. Charles-Edwards, 'The descent of the Irish Somervilles', *Irish Genealogist* 5:6 (1979).

17  ECES, *Somerville Family Records* (Cork, 1940).

18  Major Seymour Clarke, *The Genealogy of the Martins of Ross* (privately printed, Aldershot, 1910). Coghill Archive.

19  ffolliott, *The Pooles of Mayfield*, p. 232.

20  Somerville and Ross, *Wheeltracks*, pp 1–7.

21  ffolliott, *The Pooles of Mayfield*, p. 233.

22  ECES to CFS, 12 November 1941.

23  Somerville and Ross, 'Great Uncle McCarthy', *Some Experiences of an Irish RM* (London, 1899), chapter I.

24  Mary erected a splendid memorial for her brother in Drumcondra Church. It has three life-size figures: Coghill robed as Chancellor of the Irish Exchequer, with Religion and Minerva.

25  Described in *Wheeltracks*, p. 181.

26  Ethel Coghill Penrose, *The Days of My Youth* (MS c.1937) typescript, pp 22–3.

27  VFM, 'The Martins of Ross', chapter I of *Irish Memories* (London, 1917) pp 4–6.

28  Ibid., p.13.

29  Ibid.

30  Geraldine Martin, Mrs Edward Hewson, quoted in *Irish Memories*, p. 100.

31  ECES, 'Two of a Trade', *Irish Writing*, 1, August 1946.

32  Claude Chavasse, interview with GL at Lemybrien, 19 March 1980.

33  ECES to HAC, 17 December 1927.

34  Somerville and Ross, *Stray-Aways* (London, 1920), chapter XV.

35  Somerville and Ross, *Irish Memories*, pp 69–70.

36  Somerville and Ross, *Wheeltracks*, p. 53.

37  Somerville and Ross, 'Great Uncle McCarthy', *Some Reminiscences of an Irish RM* (London, 1899), p. 4.

38  Edward McLysaght, *The Surnames of Ireland* (Dublin, 1978), p. 236.

39  ECES to ES, 17 July 1922.

CHAPTER TWO

1  Rose Barton, 1856–1929, studied under Paul Naftel in London in the late seventies and went to Paris in the early eighties to study under Henri Gervex. She was an accomplished watercolourist like her lifelong friend Mildred Anne Butler.

2  Alice Kinkead, c.1860–1922, portrait and landscape painter, showed at the RHA from 1897 and towards the end of her life at the Paris Salon. She studied with Edith Somerville in Paris at various times from 1895. She was also a silversmith.

3  Coghill Archive, MPC No.75.

4  Somerville and Ross, *Irish Memories* (London, 1917), p. 12.

5  Gifford Lewis, *Eva Gore Booth and Esther Roper* (London, 1989) pp 151–62.

6  Somerville and Ross, *Wheeltracks*, p. 268.

7  Ibid., p. 14.

8  Ethel Coghill Penrose, 'The Days of My Youth', unpublished MS written c.1937.

9  Claude Chavasse, interview with GL at Lemybrien, 19 March 1980.

10  Somerville and Ross, *Wheeltracks*, p. 21.

11  Nora Robertson, *Crowned Harp* (Dublin, 1960), p. 41.

12  Somerville and Ross, *Wheeltracks*, p. 19.

13  Somerville and Ross, *Notions in Garrison* (London, 1941), p. 36.

14  Adelaide Somerville to ECES undated, but May or June 1881.

15  Somerville and Ross, *Wheeltracks*, p. 59.

16  Ethel Coghill Penrose, *The Days of My Youth*, p. 17.

17  Ibid., p. 5.

18  Ibid., p. 6.

19 Ibid., p. 13.

20 Claude Chavasse, interview with GL at Lemybrien, 19 March 1980.

21 The diaries of EŒS, 1873–1948, were sold by Sir Patrick Coghill at the Sothebys sale of MSS on 9 July 1968 to Queen's University Belfast.

22 Somerville and Ross, *Buddh Dictionary* MS f.79; EŒS to CFS, 30 September 1879.

23 Particularly Katharine Coghill. Interview 3 with GL at Marston.

24 Penrose, *The Days of My Youth*, p. 17.

25 ECP to EŒS, 27 December 1877.

26 Somerville and Ross, 'Extra Mundane Communications', *Stray-Aways*, p. 276.

27 ffolliott, *The Pooles of Mayfield*, pp 25–6.

28 In the collection of his grand-daughter, Rosemary ffolliott.

29 Drishane Archive No. L.B. 657.a.

30 Mia Jellett to Thomas Hewitt Poole, MS collection of R. ffolliott.

31 ECP, *The Days of My Youth*, p. 10.

32 EŒS, *An Incorruptible Irishman* (London, 1932), pp 112–13.

33 Edith Somerville was to describe the Somerville connection with the Camerons in Somerville Family Records, p. 126.

34 It is vividly described by Maurice Healy in *The Old Munster Circuit*, pp 69–71.

35 EŒS to BTS, undated, January 1879.

36 EŒS to BTS, 2 March 1879.

37 EŒS to CFS, 30 April 1879.

38 EŒS to BTS, 11 May 1879.

39 ECP to EŒS, August 1879.

40 EŒS to BTS, 30 October 1879.

41 EŒS to CFS, 28 November 1879.

CHAPTER THREE

1 EŒS to CFS, 30 May 1880.

2 He had been a full Lieutenant in the Royal Hampshire Regiment since 20 February 1879.

3 EŒS to CFS, 29 August 1880.

4 Josephine had married George, the brother of Augustus de Morgan the mathematician. William de Morgan, the ceramicist and novelist, was the son of Augustus.

5 EŒS, *An Incorruptible Irishman*, pp 99–108.

6 EŒS to BTS, 27 November 1880.

7 ECP, *The Days of My Youth*, p. 4. '[CT] appears in *Naboth's Vineyard* in a very thin and palpable disguise.'

8 F.S.L. Lyons, *Ireland since the Famine* (London, 1973), p. 175; J. Waldron, *Maamtrasna: the Murders and the Mystery* (Dublin, 1992), p. 19.

9 EŒS to BTS 27, December 1880.

10 EŒS to CFS, 7 January 1881.

11 Lyons, *Ireland since the Famine*, pp 164–77.

12 EŒS Diary.

13 Gabriel Nicolet, 1856–1921. French portrait painter, watercolourist and pastellist. Exhibited Paris Salon, 1889; Exposition Universelle 1895 and 1900.

14 Somerville and Ross, *Irish Memories*, p. 113.

15 Irish Fine Art Society Catalogue, Cork, November 1881, numbers 4, 124, 130, 132.

16 ffolliott, *The Pooles of Mayfield*, p. 115.

17 ECP to EŒS, undated but marked 1881; and EŒS to BTS, 11 October 1881.

18 R.F. Foster, *Modern Ireland, 1600–1972* (London, 1988), pp 405–15.

19 Somerville and Ross, *Irish Memories*, p. 113.

20 Carl Sohn, 1845–1908. German. Well known as a portrait painter of European royalty.

21 Katharine Coghill Johnston: account of the personal jewellery of EŒS, recorded by GL. Her button box, containing oddments like the WCH cuff and tunic buttons, was at Savran House.

22 Somerville and Ross, *Irish Memories*, p. 113.

23 EŒS to CFS, 19 January 1910.

24 Somerville and Ross, *Irish Memories*, p. 91, and ES Diary.

25 Joan Weir, *Back Door to the Klondyke* (Erin, Ontario, 1988), p. 30. BLGI.

26 IFAS Catalogue, November 1883, numbers 117, 132 (The Little Goose Girl), 139.

27 EŒS MS Autobiography, QUB MS 6.2.

28 Buddh Dictionary, MS f.10.

29 Bouguereau, 1825–1905, dominated the Salon with Cabanel, keeping out the Impressionists, Manet and Cezanne. Exh. Salon 1849, Grand Prix de Rome 1850, Exposition Universelle 1855.

30 Somerville and Ross, *Irish Memories*, pp 113–21.

31 Ibid., p. 113.

32 Dagnan-Bouveret, 1852–1929, pupil of Gérome and Corot. Favourite portrait painter of the Parisian aristocracy, painted in Brittany. Exh. Salon 1876, Grand Prix Exposition Universelle 1889. Last exh. Salon in 1929.

33 Somerville and Ross, *Irish Memories*, p. 121.

34 ECES to CFS, 1 August 1884.

35 Egerton Coghill gave ECES a copy of *Tom Sawyer* in December 1876.

36 ECES to CFS, 23 December 1884.

37 Exceptions were Claude Chavasse and Elizabeth Somerville.

38 Surviving in her music stored in a box in the organ loft at St Barrahane's.

39 Made at Luchon, 30 August 1925. Attached to ECES to HAC, 2 September 1925.

40 Somerville and Ross, *Irish Memories*, p. 119. Gustave Courtois, 1853–1923. French. Exh. Salon 1878, 1880; l'Exposition Universelle, 1889; Salon de Société Nationale des Beaux-Arts, 1911 and 1914. Chevalier de la Légion d'Honneur.

41 Ibid., p. 116.

42 ECES to Adelaide Somerville, 22 March 1885.

43 Ibid., 1 April 1885.

44 ECES to CFS, undated (May 1885).

45 ECES to CFS, 26 April 1885.

46 ECES to CFS, 27 May 1885.

47 The sole surviving copy of the Buddh Dictionary is held in the Coghill Archive.

48 ECES Diary and a later comment to Elizabeth Hudson by letter, 6 October 1935.

49 ECES to CFS, 9 December 1885.

50 EPC, *The Days of My Youth*, pp 5–6: 'such giant broods … have their disadvantages.'

51 Left as a bequest in her will to a great-niece, it has since disappeared.

52 ECES Diary.

53 *Argosy* 1887, Summer Number, pp 66 ff

54 Buddh Dictionary, MS f.49.

CHAPTER FOUR

1 VFM, 'The Dog from Doone', *Stray-Aways*, pp 57 ff.

2 Daisy, Countess of Fingall, *Seventy Years Young* (London 1937, reprint Dublin, 1991), p. 321.

3 Violet Martin's diaries, 1875–1915, bar 1877 and 1881, were also sold to Queen's University Belfast. They are more patchily filled than those of ECES, particularly after her hunting accident of 1898 and subsequent illnesses.

4 ECES Diary.

5 The best-painted detail is the pince-nez, hanging on their cord on the habit-coat.

6 Based on a story of Cameron's, 'A Mule Ride in Trinidad'. Her drawings are dated Paris, 12 April 1886.

7 VFM to ECES, 14 and 15 August 1889.

8 ECES Diary, 6 March 1886.

9 QUB Somerville and Ross Papers. Sotheby's Catalogue No. 881.

10 VFM to ECES, 14 December 1886.

11 VFM to ECES, 28 March 1886; Maurice Healy, *The Old Munster Circuit*, p. 238.

12 Some of these sketches were published in *Irish Impressionists: Irish Artists in France and Belgium, 1850–1914*, pp 188–9.

13 Two photographs survive taken of the dancers at the Ball: a group, and a study of Martin, seated, with Jimmy Penrose dressed as a Roman. Illustrated in Lewis 1985, p. 61. In 1902 James Penrose, a talented raconteur, was the dedicatee of *A Patrick's Day Hunt* where he is named as 'Professor of Embroidery and Irish Point.'

14 Wills' letters to VFM passed to ECES on her death. They are now in QUB, Sotheby's Catalogue No. 919.

15 Aunt Louisa Greene was the sister of Thomas Greene who married Edith's Aunt Sylvia Coghill, 15 May 1856. She was thus also the aunt of Herbert Greene, Edith's suitor.

16 Somerville and Ross, *Irish Memories*, pp 132–3.

17 Ibid., p. 1.

18 Ibid., p. 125.

19 Sir Patrick Coghill, 'Somerville and Ross', *Hermathena* 79 (1952), pp 47–60.

20 ECES to CFS, 6 May 1886.

21 Ibid., 8 September 1886.

22 The Conservative ladies' 'Primrose League' created its 'Ladies Grand Council' in 1884, each local branch of the League being classified as a 'habitation'.

23 In the Buddh Dictionary, f. 62, and used often, e.g. 'I will say that Miss O[verweg] is a real staunch squaw', ECES to VFM, 2 March 1887.

24 Violet's Aunt Marion Martin was married to Arthur Bushe, fourth son of CKB. The Bray area is well observed in *The Real Charlotte*.

25 VFM to ECES, 18 March 1887.

26 ECES to VFM undated but headed 'Hell – April? 87 – Tuesday anyway'. She was at this stage living in the Hotel de la Haute Loire, Boulevarde d'Enfer.

27 Somerville and Ross, *Irish Memories*, p. 179.

28 Edith Martin married Cuthbert Dawson of the 2nd Dragoon Guards, 22 November 1882.

29 ECES to VFM, 11 March 1887 – a letter in which she regrets that Martin's work is published alongside 'pukey rubbish'.

30 ECES to BTS, 27 July 1887: 'It is a great comfort to me that Egerton and Mr Baxter like it very much and they don't say they like a thing unless they mean it.'

31 The over-riding drift of the code is concerned with the marriage market. 'Howling wolves' a noun meaning 'Young men of a dangerous attractiveness, the chaperone's natural foe' would have found it a useful key.

32 ECES to CFS, 10 August 1887.

33 The phrase was first used by VFM in describing Warham St Leger's reaction to *An Irish Cousin* (undated but 1889 fragment marked X in alphabetical sequence). He 'prophesies great things – for *me* not for you – the poor hack and amanuensis – thought it "so like the way I talk" – principally in words of four syllables ...'

34 Joan Weir, *Back Door to the Klondike*, pp 27–8.

35 Contorted facial expression was a speciality of her cartoon work.

36 ECES to VFM, 29 April 1888.

37 Buddh Dictionary, f. 42 and f. 68, 'wogging' was acting like a hussy, a dangerous and artful person.

38 ECES to VFM, 8 May 1888.

39 She sang sentimental Irish nationalist songs with feeling: see *Wheeltracks*, pp 68–9, 'in the teeth of English-bred cousins'.

40 ECES to VFM, 3 June 1888.

41 Warham St Leger, pensioner, aged 18, at Jesus College Cambridge 1868. Son of the deceased Rev. William Nassau St Leger. Attended Clergy Orphan School Canterbury. BA 1876. No death record in Britain has yet been found for him. He may have gone abroad for health reasons; there is no correspondence with VFM after 1895.

42 Maud Morris Wynne, *An Irishman and His Family: Lord Morris and Killanin* (London, 1937), p. 278.

43 Herbert Wilson Greene, 1857–1933, Fellow and Dean of Magdalen College, Oxford, 1888–1910. Greek scholar, worked on the revision of Liddell and Scott's Dictionary.

44 VFM to ECES, 26 July 1888.

45 VFM to ECES, 7 August 1888.

46 ECES to VFM, 5 August 1888.

47 In a now missing section of VFM to ECES, 17 August 1888.

48 VFM to ECES, 29 August 1888.

49 VFM to ECES, 7 August 1888.

50 VFM to ECES, undated but *c*.27 December 1888.

51 ECES to VFM, 27 December 1888.

52 Somerville and Ross, *Irish Memories*, p. 131.

53 Printed in full in *Selected Letters of Somerville and Ross* (London, 1989), pp 124–7.

54 Drishane Collection. Exhibition Catalogue 'Dr E Œ Somerville 1858–1949' for the exhibition at Drishane, 5–9 September 1984; catalogue number 29.

55 QUB Somerville and Ross Collection, Sotheby's Catalogue No. 881.

56 Hesketh Pearson, *Bernard Shaw* (London, 1942), p. 155.

57 VFM to ECES, 18 May 1889.

58 John Cronin, *Somerville and Ross* (Lewisburg, New Jersey, 1972), pp 92–3.

59 ECES to HAC, 9 May 1889.

60 TCD Pinker MS 4276.

61 VFM to ECES, 5 September 1889.

62 The pleasure was lifelong. We find in many letters from ECES to Alice Kinkead VFM referred to as 'Mr Ross'.

63 Sir William Gregory to Anna Selina Martin, 26 October 1889.

64 VFM to ECES, 16 September 1889.

65 Charles Graves, 1856–1944, Assistant editor of the *Spectator* 1899–1917; *Punch* staff writer, 1902–36. His publications included *Mr Punch's History of the Great War*, 1919.

66 TCD Somerville and Ross Collection, Pinker MSS, 25th July 1889; sub-editor of *The World* to VFM.

67 Ibid., 1 January 1890, Perry to ECES.

68 *Home Chimes*, 2 (2 May 1885) pp 408–12.

69 TCD Somerville and Ross Collection, Pinker MSS, 18 November 1889, Edmund Yates to VFM.

70 Ibid., 28 December 1889, E.Yates to VFM.

71 VFM to ECES, 20 August 1889.

72 BTS to ECES. 27 October 1889.

73 VFM to ECES, 13 September 1889.

74 VFM to ECES, undated fragment, X in the alphabetical sequence.

CHAPTER FIVE

1 TCD Somerville and Ross Collection, Pinker MSS 4276.36.

2 QUB Somerville and Ross Collection. Miscellaneous envelope marked by Sir Patrick Coghill as 'Newspaper Sources'.

3 Somerville and Ross, *Wheeltracks*, p. 75.

4 Payments are to be found listed in the diary Memoranda, and within entries.

5 QUB holds the original drawing, within the set of book illustrations.

6 EŒS to CFS, 11 July 1890.

7 EŒS to VFM, 26 July 1908.

8 Somerville and Ross, *Irish Memories*, p. 233.

9 Somerville and Ross, *Irish Memories*, p. 135.

10 VFM to EŒS, 18 September 1890. It seems Edith did not sell any shares until she had to pay her brother's debts in 1939.

11 VFM to EŒS, 24 September 1890.

12 Ibid. Marked K in the undated alphabetical sequence.

13 Nevill Coghill, Introduction to the 1946 Sotheby's Catalogue of Somerville and Ross MSS.

14 VFM to EŒS, 23 December 1890.

15 Somerville and Ross, *Irish Memories*, p. 152.

16 VFM to EŒS, 13 April 1890, printed Lewis 1989, pp 170–4.

17 Somerville and Ross, *Irish Memories*, p. 218.

18 *Daily Graphic*, 5 October 1891, in Coghill Archive, scrapbook of reviews.

19 The Oxford visit described in *Irish Memories*, p. 235 was not their first. The VFM Diary suggests that St Leger knew of her arrival at Kew from Oxford.

20 Photograph published in Lewis 1985, p. 148.

21 VFM to HAC, 12 December 1895.

22 Somerville and Ross, *Irish Memories*, pp 236–7.

23 Edmund Downey 1856–1937; Irish publisher of T.P. O'Connor, George Moore, A.P. Graves et al; published Charles Lever and wrote his biography; a Parnellite and Sinn Feiner.

24 *Beggars on Horseback* was published as a volume by Blackwoods in 1895. The original illustrations are at QUB.

25 Ibid., pp 170–2.

26 Coghill Archive photograph published in Lewis 1985, p. 198.

27 VFM Diary; Charles Fox Martin m. Lucy, d of R. Sherwood, c.1881.

28 The drowning of Quin in chapter 10 of *The Silver Fox*. Also mentioned in VFM to EŒS, 3 January 1884.

29 Somerville and Ross, *Irish Memories*, pp 240–1.

30 Undated, Coghill Archive review scrapbook.

31 EŒS to VFM, 25 November 1894; published Lewis 1989, pp 199–203.

32 A series of letters was written by VFM to EŒS from St Andrews: 16, 23, 29 January. Published in Lewis 1989.

33 Seventeen letters from St Leger to VFM survive in the QUB Somerville and Ross Collection. Sotheby's Catalogue No. 919.

34 Buddh word 'To hifle: v.i. denoting the energetic progress of one who has some definite object in view.'

35 VFM to EŒS, 29 January 1895. Quoted in part in *Irish Memories*, p. 354.

36 Founded in January of 1894, it ran until April 1897. It became celebrated mainly on account of Beardsley's illustrations.

37 VFM to EŒS, 11 March 1895.

38 'Pack' or 'Packy' is an abbreviated form of Patrick. This drawing was used on the cover and binding of the first edition of the first series of RM stories.

39 EŒS to Adelaide Somerville, 20 May 1895.

40 VFM quoted in *Irish Memories*, p. 192.

41 VFM to HAC, 22 May 1895.

42 HWG to EŒS, 10 October 1892; 29 June 1895.

43 Georgina Chavasse to EŒS, 14 March 1895.

44 *The Minute*, 1 July 1895; Coghill Archive.

45 It was not unusual at that time for well-liked landlord family members to be keened: R.M. Salter-Townshend, interview with GL, October 2000.

46 Anna Selina Martin to EŒS, 8 December 1895.

47 EŒS to CFS, 3 April 1896.

48 EŒS to VFM, 14 June 1896.

49 The competition-winning drawing is in the Coghill Archive review scrapbook.

50 VFM to EŒS, undated fragment, published in Lewis 1989, pp 238–40.

51 Also VFM diary after her hunting accident in 1898: 'The wretched E slept on a couch in my room' to keep her fuelled with painkillers.

52 EŒS to CFS, 12 March 1897.

53 EŒS to VFM undated, published in Lewis 1989 pp 242–243.

54 EŒS to CFS, 21 March 1897.

55 *Wheeltracks*, pp 126–30. Also EŒS to VFM, 22 August 1897.

56 For example, see VFM's favourite photograph of EŒS, taken by HAC illustrated in Lewis 1985, p. 70, or VFM taken for *The Minute* interview, p. 75.

57 Georgina Chavasse to EŒS, 14 March 1898; Drishane Archive.

58 VFM to CFS, 13 January 1898.

59 The crucifix appears as a prop in the painting 'Retrospect'; it was rescued by Katharine Coghill from her eldest brother's bonfire when clearing out Glen B, and was subsequently given by her to GL.

60 *Wheeltracks*, p. 12. The Buddh Dictionary defines 'Brogueaneer' as 'One whose uncultivated accent offends the ear of the Buddh.'

61 EŒS to HAC, 13 January 1923.

62 False teeth were also referred to as 'Stores' as, according to the Buddh Dictionary, f. 62, many of the family bought theirs in the Army and Navy Stores.

63 EŒS to HAC, 6 July 1898.

64 Somerville and Ross, *Irish Memories*, p. 259.

65 Ibid., p. 262.

66 VFM to HAC, undated, but 1898.

67 EŒS to HAC, 29 September 1898.

68 In the library at the Castle, according to Rose Marie Salter Townshend, there used to be copies of Somerville and Ross books with identified characters on the flyleaves.

69 Jack Somerville to EŒS, 4 September 1894.

70 Maurice Healy, *The Old Munster Circuit*, pp 194–7.

71 TCD MS 3284, p. 6.

72 VFM to EŒS undated, and misdated by MPC.

73 Quoted in *Irish Memories*, p. 295. Not, so far, traced in their scrap books.

74 *An Irishman and His Family*, p. 279.

75 Somerville and Ross, *Irish Memories*, p. 268.

76 Ibid., pp 272–3.

77 VFM to Edith Dawson quoted in *Irish Memories*, p. 274.

CHAPTER SIX

1 EŒS to HAC, 12 January 1900.

2 Ibid.

3 EŒS to HAC, 16 February 1900.

4 On 14, 15 and 16 February 1900.

5 EŒS to HAC, undated, 1900.

6 Somerville and Ross, *Wheeltracks*, pp 131–2. There was only one other woman MFH in the British Isles at this time, and she was Welsh: Mrs T.H.R. Hughes of the Neuadd Fawr Hunt.

7 The Diary of VFM shows that she, who later set off on travels when Edith was house renovating, in this year came back from London on 14 January and left at the end of May for Ross. She did not reappear at CT until 17 February 1902.

8 A photograph was taken of Edith at Champex painting out of doors: illustration 15 of Lewis 1989.

9 VFM to EŒS, 8 August 1901: printed in Lewis, 1989, pp 251–3.

10 EŒS to VFM, undated, miscellaneous MPC No. alpha 1.

11 EŒS to HAC, 5 September 1901.

12 Enclosed in EŒS to VFM, 15 July 1901.

13 Described in Chapter II of *Notions in Garrison* (London, 1941).

14 EŒS Diary.

15 BTS to HAC, MS collection Faith Coghill Garson.

16 It is not known whether this was connected with her later tumour, which spread from the top of the spine. It may have been displaced discs from her fall. When travelling alone, and to save paying pennies to porters, she persisted in dragging trunks around on railway stations and 'putting her back out', to Edith's fury.

17 Strachey, John St Loe (1860–1927). Editor of the *Cornhill*, 1896; editor and proprietor of the *Spectator*, 1898–1925.

18 Not a Buddh word, perhaps common slang, but still known by K. Coghill in 1981.

19 Somerville and Ross, *Irish Memories*, pp 172–83 gives an account of him.

20 Weir, *Back Door to the Klondike*, pp 31–2.

21 Lady Gregory to VFM, 8 July 1914; R.M. Salter Townshend owns a photograph of Mrs de Burgh in the donkey-trap that Edith drew for Mrs Knox's conveyance; Mrs Townshend is described in *Irish Memories*, pp 71–2.

22 Wynne, *An Irishman and His Family* pp 278–9.

23 VFM Diary. This may be the photograph from EŒS's 1916 Diary illustrated in Lewis 1985, p. 124.

24 EŒS to HAC, 30 January and 3 February 1904.

25 Somerville and Ross, *Irish Memories*, pp 307–9.

26 EŒS Diary. Bridget is described in *Irish Memories*, pp 285–6, 'among horses, Bridget leads, the rest nowhere'.

27 Sir Bertram Windle, 1858–1929. President, Queen's College, Cork 1904–12. Cr. Kt. 1912; Professor of Cosmology and Anthropology at St Michael's College, Toronto.

28 The hall was a boon to the village; Egerton made a tennis court at the back of it. Because of its dust-bowl nature it was called the Gobi.

29 ECES to CFS, 8 August 1905.

30 VFM Diary.

31 VFM Diary.

32 ECES to HAC, 29 September 1905.

33 VFM Diary.

34 The new title, *Some Irish Yesterdays*, was to be published on 5 October.

35 VFM to ECES, 10 July 1906; printed in Lewis 1989, pp 277–9.

36 ECES to HAC 15 September 1906.

37 In *Irish Memories* there is a photograph by VFM facing p. 160.

38 ECES to CFS, 20 September 1906.

39 ECES Diary.

40 ECES to CFS, 6 June 1907.

41 ECES to VFM, 12 July 1907.

42 ECES to CFS, 10 October 1907.

43 *The Last Serjeant: The Memoirs of Serjeant A.M. Sullivan Q.C.* (London, 1952), opening of chapter I.

44 Thady's death was described in VFM to ECES, undated, 1895, printed in Lewis 1989, pp 234–5.

45 ECES to CFS, 25 June 1908.

46 ECES to HAC, 29 September 1908.

47 ECES to CFS, 26 June 1913.

48 Julia Lee to VFM, 7 February 1909.

49 ECES to CFS, 18 March 1909.

50 Somerville and Ross, *Irish Memories*, p. 310.

51 VFM Diary.

52 Beamish's pack is described in *Wheeltracks*, pp 116–122.

53 VFM Diary.

54 Ibid.

## CHAPTER SEVEN

1 ECES to CFS, 20 December 1909.

2 Ibid., 19 January 1910.

3 Foster, *Modern Ireland 1600–1972*, p. 409.

4 ECES Diary; M. Duffy, *A Thousand Capricious Chances: A History of the Methuen List, 1889–1989* (London, 1989), pp 43–44.

5 QUB Somerville and Ross Collection, No. 898.

6 VFM Diary.

7 ECES Diary.

8 Ibid.

9 VFM Diary.

10 VFM Diary.

11 ECES to HAC, 4 September 1910.

12 Ibid.

13 QUB Somerville and Ross Collection, Suffrage Speeches numbered 54 and 53 in the Coghill Archive MPC sequence.

14 ECES to CFS, 12 October 1910.

15 Ibid.

16 VFM Diary.

17 ECES to HAC, undated, 1910.

18 Ibid., 16 February 1911.

19 Somerville and Ross, *Dan Russel the Fox*, p. 147.

20 VFM to ECES, 23 June 1911; printed in Lewis 1989, pp 288–291.

21 ffolliott, *The Pooles of Mayfield*, p. 25.

22 VFM Diary, 13 September 1911.

23 Dan Russel the Fox, p. 25.

24 ECES to CFS, 15 January 1911.

25 ECES to CFS, 22 November 1911.

26 QUB Somerville and Ross Collection, Coghill Archive MPC Number 54.

27 Ibid. Number 58.

28 QUB Somerville and Ross Collection. Admiralty ledger 881, dated 1897. Coghill Archive MPC Number 27.

29 VFM Diary.

30 Ibid.

31 VFM to ECES, 20 March 1912. Printed in Lewis 1989, pp 295–6.

32 VFM to Rose Barton, TCD MS 2227.

33 VFM to ECES, 18 March 1912. Printed in Lewis 1989, pp 293–4.

34 VFM Diary.

35 Anne Gregory, *Me and Nu* (Gerrards Cross, 1970).

36 VFM Diary.

37 ECES to CFS, 25 March 1912.

38 Ibid., 4 June 1912.

39 Ibid.

40 ECES to HAC, 30 July 1912.

41 Ibid., 14 August 1912.

42 Charles Graves to VFM, QUB Somerville and Ross Collection. Sotheby's Catalogue No. 919.

43 St Loe Strachey to VFM. Ibid.

44 QUB Somerville and Ross Collection. Coghill Archive MPC No. 55.

45 Katharine Coghill recorded by BBC Radio 4 for their feature programme 'The Irish Cousins' in September 1985.

46 EŒS Diary.

47 EŒS to HAC, 23 August 1913.

48 Claude Chavasse interview with GL at Lemybrien, 19 March 1980.

49 EŒS to HAC, 23 August 1913.

50 The first creamery had been founded at Midleton by Penrose Fitzgerald, Lord Midleton's agent, in 1882.

51 VFM to Sir Horace Plunkett. Printed in the Sotheby's Catalogue No. 875.

52 Professor Macalister was the author of *Corpus Inscriptionum Insularum Celticarum* (Dublin, 1945).

53 Frank O'Connor, 'Somerville and Ross', *Irish Times*, 15 December 1945.

54 Somerville and Ross, *In Mr Knox's Country* (1915), concluding paragraph of chapter v.

55 EŒS to HAC, 31 May 1914.

56 VFM to HAC, 19 June 1914.

57 QUB Somerville and Ross Collection. Sotheby's Catalogue No. 898.

58 EŒS to HAC, undated, (June 1915).

59 TCD Somerville and Ross Pinker MSS 3331.

60 QUB Somerville and Ross Collection Sotheby's Catalogue No. 919.

61 EŒS to CFS, 6 September 1915.

62 Ibid., 9 October 1915.

63 2 December 1915.

64 Ibid., 8 December 1915.

65 Ibid., 7 December 1915.

66 EŒS to CFS, 10 December 1915.

67 EŒS to HAC, 20 December 1915.

68 Contessa Lovera interview with GL, Red House, 15 August 1980, and with K. Coghill, Cassington Interview D.

69 The Nightingale and Wilberforce quotations are written out on a loose leaf inserted in the EŒS 1916 Diary.

70 HAC to Alice Kinkead 28 December 1915.

71 Katherine Tynan Hinkson, *The New Witness*, 30 December, 1915.

72 EŒS to CFS, 6 January 1916.

73 EŒS Diary.

74 Robert Lynd, *Ireland a Nation* (London, 1919), p. 137.

75 QUB Somerville and Ross Collection. Sotheby's Catalogue No. 881.

76 *The Women of Royaumont* (East Linton 1997), p. 77.

77 EŒS to CFS, 2 February 1917.

78 Ibid., 4 June 1917.

79 EŒS to Pinker, 13 May 1917.

80 Ibid.

81 Ibid., 24 October 1917.

82 EŒS to HAC, 19 September 1918.

83 EŒS to MPC, 28 December 1918.

84 *The Smile and the Tear* (1933), p. 29.

85 EŒS Diary.

86 EŒS to HAC, 17 September 1919.

87 Christopher St John, *Ethel Smyth: a biography* (London, 1959), p. 196.

88 Ibid., p. 89.

89 Louise Collis, *Impetuous Heart: The Story of Ethel Smyth* (London, 1984), p. 160.

90 William Plomer, *At Home*, pp 142–3.

91 Louise Collis, *Impetuous Heart*, p. 154.

92 Amy Lowell, 'To Two Unknown Ladies', *North American Review*, June 1919.

93 EOES to Maurice Baring, 31 August 1945.

94 EOES to HAC, 1 December 1919.

CHAPTER EIGHT

1 EŒS to HAC, 21 November 1919.

2 Ibid.

3 *Wheeltracks*, pp 111–63 dwells on her lifetime with hunting hounds.

4 Ethel's father was General J.H. Smyth.

5 EŒS to HAC, 10 January 1920.

6 Collis, *Impetuous Heart*, p. 156.

7 EŒS to HAC, 24 January 1920.

8 Quoted by Collis in *Impetuous Heart*, p. 156.

9 Ethel Smyth to EŒS, 23 January 1920.

10 EŒS to J.E.M. Barlow, 28 January 1920.

11 EŒS to HAC, 27 January 1920.

12 Ethel Smyth, *Streaks of Life* (London, 1921), pp 112–18.

13 EŒS to HAC, 1 April 1920.

14 EŒS to J.E.M. Barlow, 20 April 1920.

15 Quoted by Collis in *Impetuous Heart*, p. 173.

16 Ethel Smyth to EŒS, 7 June 1920.

17 Ibid., 11 June 1920. Quoted in Collis, *Impetuous Heart*, p. 160.

18 Ethel Smyth to EŒS 7 June 1920. Virginia Woolf to Quentin Bell, quoted in Collis, *Impetuous Heart*, p. 180.

19 Ibid., 25 June 1920.

20 Ibid., 11 July 1920.

21 EŒS to HAC, 7 September 1920.

22 Ibid., 7 September 1920.

23 Ibid., 21 August 1920.

24 Ibid., 27 November 1920.

25 Ibid., 2 December 1920.

26 Charles Graves, 'Martin Ross', *National Review*, 71. p. 353.
27 Hilary Robinson, *Somerville and Ross: A Critical Appreciation* (Dublin, 1980), p. 164.
28 EŒS Diary.
29 Quoted by C. St John, *Ethel Smyth*, p. 200.
30 EŒS to HAC, undated but later marked March 1921.
31 Ibid., 6 March 1921.
32 Ibid., 1 March 1921.
33 ffolliott, *The Pooles of Mayfield*, p. 282.
34 Collis, *Impetuous Heart*, p. 168.
35 Somerville and Ross, *Happy Days*, p. 127.
36 EŒS to HAC, 17 September 1921.
37 Arthur Griffith, *The Resurrection of Hungary: A Parallel for Ireland* (Dublin, 1904).
38 EŒS Diary.
39 GBS to EŒS, 20 January 1922.
40 GBS to Hesketh Pearson, 13 September 1939. Quoted in Hesketh Pearson, *Bernard Shaw* (London, 1942), p. 440.
41 EŒS to HAC, 24 March 1922.
42 EŒS to GBS, 21 January 1922.
43 EŒS to HAC, 24 March 1922.
44 Ibid., 18 March 1922.
45 Bertram Windle to EŒS, 8 February 1922.
46 Somerville and Ross, *Notions in Garrison*, p. 56.
47 EŒS to HAC, 6 June 1922.
48 Ibid., 8 June 1922.
49 Ibid., 27 June 1922.
50 Ibid.
51 Ibid., 20 July 1922.
52 Ibid., 31 July 1922.
53 EŒS to BTS, 12 August 1922.
54 EŒS to ECP, 30 August 1922 (within HAC sequence).
55 EŒS to HAC, 30 September 1922.
56 It was later published by Robert Lynd, who was originally to have been the editor.
57 EŒS to HAC, 19 October 1922.
58 Diary EŒS.
59 Ibid., 6 February 1923.
60 EŒS Diary.
61 Collis, *Impetuous Heart*, p. 160.
62 EŒS to Ethel Smyth, 19 April 1923.
63 Wynne, *An Irishman and His Family*, p. 312.
64 EŒS to HAC, 16 December 1923.
65 Quoted in Collis, *Impetuous Heart*, p. 197.
66 EŒS Diary.
67 Quoted in Collis, *Ethel Smyth*, p. 203.
68 EŒS Diary.

69 Diaries of EŒS and HAC.
70 The design for the mosaic floor, adapted from a motif from the Book of Kells, may have been worked up from the facsimile volume donated to the Village Hall by Charles Loftus Townshend, ref. EŒS to HAC, 1 July 1913.
71 After a time with Heinemann she returned to Methuen in 1933: M. Duffy, *A Thousand Capricious Chances*, pp 120 and 139.
72 EŒS to HAC, 16 August 1925.
73 EŒS to HAC, 2 September 1925.
74 Jessica Douglas-Home, *The Life and Loves of Violet Gordon Woodhouse* (London, 1996), pp 205–6.
75 EŒS Diary.
76 Shane Leslie, *The Film of Memory* (London, 1938), p. 358.
77 Sir Horace Plunkett to EŒS, 1 December 1925.
78 Commissioned from Egans of Cork.
79 The Townshends were generous in legacies to the women of their family. Thomas Somerville of Drishane, High Sheriff 1863, m. Henrietta Augusta, eldest d. of Col. Richard Boyle Townshend. They had two children: Thomas, Edith's father, and Henrietta.
80 The BBC Archive no longer holds any of these recordings.
81 EŒS to HAC, 5 November 1928.
82 Somerville and Ross, *French Leave*, pp 15 and 23.
83 EŒS to HAC, 13 February 1928.
84 Charlotte Perkins Gilman, *Herland* (New York, 1915, reprint, London, 1979), pp 73–4.
85 EŒS Diary.
86 CFS to RCB, 2 April 1928.
87 The de Burghs of Kilfinnan Castle were related to the Townshends. Jane de Burgh was the grandmother of Rose Marie Salter Townshend.
88 EŒS to CFS, 11 October 1906.
89 EŒS Diary. Published anonymously as *Elizabeth and Her German Garden* (London, 1898) by Elizabeth von Arnim (1866–1941), who married Earl Russell in 1916.

CHAPTER NINE

1 EŒS Diary.
2 Quoted by Collis, *Impetuous Heart*, p. 180.

3  Sylvia Townshend Lovera to Gifford Lewis, 9 May 1981.

4  EŒS to Elizabeth Hudson, 26 April 1930. Coghill Archive, out of sequence.

5  Lady Russell had been overtaken by Virginia Woolf as it were in a horse race.

6  In BLGI Maria Bushe is given as the fifth of CKB's six daughters; she married the Rev. John Harris.

7  EŒS Diary.

8  J. Wills, *Lives of Illustrious Irishmen* (Dublin, 1840–7).

9  Although she did use it, *An Incorruptible Irishman* reveals nothing of its reliance on extra-mundane correspondence.

10  EŒS Diary.

11  EŒS to HAC, 27 February 1931.

12  EŒS Diary.

13  EŒS to GC. Quoted in Cummins 1952, pp 70–1.

14  EŒS to HAC, 28 March 1932.

15  EŒS Diary.

16  Coghill Archive typescript. HWG to EŒS.

17  EŒS Diary.

18  Ibid. This was not true, as she was shortly to discover in person from Frank O'Connor and others.

19  Sylvia Townshend Lovera to Gifford Lewis, 9 May 1981.

20  EŒS to HAC, 9 December 1932.

21  Ibid. Marked by K. Coghill 'December 1932'.

22  Foster, *Modern Ireland,* p. 549.

23  EŒS Diary.

24  Sir Oliver Lodge, F.R.S., published *The Survival of Man: A Study in Unrecognised Human Faculty,* 1908, which contains his scientific analysis of automatic writing.

25  EŒS to HAC, 6 March 1933.

26  Walter Starkie, *Raggle-Taggle: Adventures with a Fiddle in Hungary and Roumania* (London, 1933).

27  EŒS to CFS, 7 March 1933.

28  EŒS to Elizabeth Hudson, 26 March 1933.

29  EŒS Diary.

30  Ibid.

31  Written in the spring of 1890 and first published by *Blackwood's Magazine.*

32  EŒS to HAC, 22 June 1933.

33  Ibid.

34  EŒS Diary.

35  EŒS to HAC, 21 November 1933.

36  EŒS to Elizabeth Hudson, 7 December 1933.

37  EŒS Diary. Maurice Healy, *The Old Munster Circuit* (London, 1939).

38  Ibid.

39  The receipt survived, dated 27 February 1918. Illustrated in Lewis 1985, p. 228.

40  EŒS to HAC, 14 June 1934.

41  His collection was donated to TCD in 1951.

42  EŒS to HAC, 22 December 1934.

43  Eddy [Edmund] Aylmer died 28 March 1931. The Aylmer brothers lived at the end of their lives at their Welsh estate in North Wales, Farchynis, near Dolgellau.

44  EŒS to HAC, 12 and 29 January 1935.

45  EŒS Diary.

46  EŒS to HAC, 18 February 1935.

47  Published privately in 1934, and not for sale, by Peter Davies, the print run was mostly given away at Christmas 1934.

48  EŒS to HAC, 15 June 1935.

49  Ibid., 28 June 1935.

50  EŒS to Elizabeth Hudson, 28 November 1935.

51  EŒS to HAC, 23 January 1936.

52  Ibid., 18 January 1936.

53  Ibid., 1 February 1936.

54  Ibid., 7 February 1936.

55  Geraldine Cummins, *Dr E.Œ. Somerville,* p. 96.

56  EŒS to HAC, 22 March 1936.

57  Sylvia Townshend Lovera interviewed by GL at the Red House August 1980.

58  Quoted in Collis, *Ethel Smyth,* p. 198.

59  Joseph O'Neill, *Blood Dark Track* (London, 2000) ill. on p. 295.

60  HAC to K. Coghill, 25 March 1936.

61  EŒS to Elizabeth Hudson, 17 July 1936.

62  EŒS to HAC, 3 October 1936.

63  Ibid., 13 November 1936.

64  Ibid., 15 December 1936.

65  Ibid., 15 December 1936.

66  Ibid.

67  Ibid., 20 January 1937.

68  Ibid., 29 December 1936.

69  IMC Catalogue, p. 170. A Recollection of EŒS by Mrs Desmond Somerville.

70  Automatic scripts by Cummins and Somerville's letters to Cummins are now in QUB Special Collections.

71  EŒS Diary.

72  EŒS to Elizabeth Hudson, 17 September 1937.

73  Ruth Duffin to EŒS, 14 October 1937.

74  EŒS to Elizabeth Hudson, 16 October 1937.

75  EŒS to HAC, 15 December 1937.

76  Ibid., 13 January 1938.

77  Ibid.

78 Ibid., 12 January 1938.
79 Ibid. Undated but marked 'January 1938'.
80 Quoted by H. & M. Cecil, *Clever Hearts*, p. 270.
81 Sylvia Lovera and Claude Chavasse interviewed by GL in 1980.
82 EŒS to HAC undated but marked 'January 1938'.
83 Quoted by Cummins in *Dr E.Œ. Somerville*, p. 128.
84 EŒS to HAC, 14 June 1938.
85 Ibid.
86 Ibid., 24 June 1938.
87 Ibid.
88 Ibid., 2 July 1938.
89 Ibid., September 1938, out of sequence.
90 Somerville and Ross, *Sarah's Youth*, pp 266–7.
91 EŒS Diary.
92 EŒS to HAC, 17 June 1939.
93 Ibid., 24 June 1939.
94 EŒS Diary.
95 Sir Toby Coghill letter to GL, 5 May 1993.
96 MPC to Professor John Cronin, 27 September 1972.
97 EOES Diary.

CHAPTER TEN

1 Katharine Coghill interview C1 with GL at Cassington.
2 EŒS to E. Hudson, 28 February 1940.
3 Will of Thomas Cameron Fitzgerald Somerville, made at Drishane 30 April 1936. Proved 16 May 1942. NAI.
4 EŒS Diary.
5 EŒS to HAC, 5 September 1940.
6 Ibid., 9 September 1940.
7 EŒS Diary.
8 EŒS to HAC, 15 March 1941.
9 EŒS Diary.
10 Ibid.
11 EŒS to HAC, 21 March 1941.
12 Ibid.
13 Clodagh Somerville interview with GL, Oxford, 15 April 1983.
14 EŒS Diary.
15 EŒS to CFS, 18 November 1941.

16 Ibid.
17 Ibid., 25 November 1941.
18 Ibid., 8 December 1941.
19 Ibid., 18 December 1941.
20 Desmond Somerville to EŒS, 29 January 1942.
21 Desmond Somerville to EŒS, 30 January 1942.
22 Jack Somerville to EŒS, 25 February 1942.
23 EŒS to Maurice Baring, 3 April 1942.
24 TCD MS 7684/31. EŒS to Comte de Suzannet, 7 October 1943.
25 Claude Chavasse interview with GL at Lemybrien, 19 March 1980.
26 EŒS Diary, 25 May 1944, quoting Walter Savage Landor.
27 Ibid., 28 June 1944.
28 HAC Diary, 25 February 1945.
29 EŒS Diary, 6 May 1945.
30 Ibid., 8 May 1945.
31 MPC Memoir typescript Sourden.
32 EŒS to G. Cummins, 2 December 1945.
33 Typescript now in the collection of GL.
34 Sylvia Lovera interview with GL, Red House Top Flat, CT, August 1980.
35 IMC Catalogue B.12.a-c.
36 Account of burial by R.M. Salter-Townshend, interview October 2000.
37 Professor Crookshank in conversation with GL, October 1999.
38 Katharine Coghill interview with GL at Elsfield.
39 HAC to RCB, telegram 10 October 1949; letter 26 January 1950.
40 MPC to Ambrose Coghill, 14 March 1954.
41 Bridget O'Driscoll to Ambrose Coghill, 4 April 1954.
42 Katharine Coghill to Toby Coghill, 1 October 1976.
43 Nevill Coghill to MPC, 5 June 1966.
44 Katharine Coghill Johnston to GL, 14 July 1980.

CONCLUSION

1 Edith Somerville MWSL. speech in Cork, 23 September 1910.

# Select bibliography

## SOURCES

Four sequences of letters provide the most precise detail for this biography:

1. Edith Somerville/Martin Ross correspondence, New York Public Library.
2. Edith Somerville to Cameron Somerville, letters, Drishane House Papers.
3. Edith Somerville/Hildegarde, Lady Coghill correspondence, Coghill Papers, Sourden House.
4. Edith Somerville to Jack Somerville, letters, Queen's University, Belfast (QUB).

The copyright of all Somerville and Ross material is held by the current executor, the present Sir Patrick Coghill.

   The chronology depends on the sequence of diaries kept by Martin Ross and Edith Somerville (now held at QUB), used with the additional source of the annotated transcript of the diaries made by Violet Martin's niece, Muriel Currey, with her marginal notes (in the Coghill Papers) and those of Edith Somerville's niece Katharine 'K' Coghill (in the Coghill Papers). For the chronology of publication dates and the lapses between serialisation of writing and its emergence in book form, the source is the scrapbooks of Somerville and Ross (Coghill Papers). For the sources of material in quotation taken from conversation, QUB holds the literary notebooks. The Somerville and Ross material now held in Drishane House, where the original Coghill numbers have been overlaid by a meticulous new sequence made by Professor Otto Rauchbauer, was read in microfiche form in the National Library of Ireland with the kind permission of Christopher Somerville of Drishane.

   The biography also uses material from my letters from and interviews with relatives of Edith Somerville (dating from 1979 onwards): Mrs Douglas Weir (daughter of Rose Cameron Bingham, who loaned to me her mother's letters from Edith Somerville, now in UCC); the late Canon Claude Chavasse; Judith Chavasse; Faith Coghill Garson; the late Katharine Coghill Johnston; the late Sir Patrick Coghill; the late Sir Toby Coghill; Mrs Brian Somerville; Clodagh Somerville Kempson; the late Diana Somerville; the late Michael Somerville; the late Rose Marie Salter Townshend whose genealogical knowledge and careful notes on my manuscript were invaluable.

   The memoir by Ethel Penrose was loaned by Peter Cave Bigley; the Buddh Dictionary, without which many of the letters cannot be fully understood, is in the Coghill Papers that include the remainder of the Somerville and Ross papers left to her nephew and godson by Edith Somerville.

There are shorter sequences of letters that are important: Edith Somerville's letters to her mother and to her brother Boyle, among the Drishane House Papers, and Martin Ross's letters to Hildegarde, Lady Coghill, in the Coghill Papers. The partially destroyed sequence of letters between Ethel Smyth and Edith Somerville is at QUB.

Molly Keane discussed the writing partnership with me in conversation and letters, during our co-operation on a script for a television documentary, providing many insights.

## SELECTIVE BIBLIOGRAPHY

Alexander, W., *The First Ladies of Medicine* (Glasgow, 1987).

Benezit, E., *Dictionnaire des Peintres, Sculpteurs, Dessinateurs et Graveurs* (Paris, 1948).

Bew, P., *C.S. Parnell* (Dublin, 1980).

Bowen, E., *Bowenscourt* (London, 1942).

Campbell, J., *The Irish Impressionists* (Dublin, 1984).

Cecil, H and M., *Clever Hearts: Desmond and Molly MacCarthy* (London, 1990).

Collis, L., *Impetuous Heart: The Story of Ethel Smyth* (London, 1984).

Collis, M., *Somerville and Ross: A Biography* (London, 1968).

Crofton, E., *The Women of Royaumont* (East Linton, 1997).

Cronin, J., *Somerville and Ross* (Lewisburg, NJ, 1972).

Crookshank, A., and The Knight of Glin, *The Painters of Ireland c.1660–1920* (London, 1978).

Cummins, G., *Dr E.Œ Somerville: A Biography* (London, 1952).

Douglas-Home, J., *The Life and Loves of Violet Gordon Woodhouse* (London, 1996).

Duffy, M., *A Thousand Capricious Chances: A History of the Methuen List, 1889–1989* (London, 1989).

Faderman, L., *Surpassing the Love of Men: Romantic Friendship and Love between Women from the Renaissance to the Present* (London, 1985).

Fingall, D., *Seventy Years Young* (Dublin, 1991).

ffolliott, R., *The Pooles of Mayfield* (Dublin, 1958).

Foster, R.F., *Modern Ireland, 1600–1972* (London, 1988).

Griffith, A., *The Resurrection of Hungary: A Parallel for Ireland* (Dublin, 1904).

Gregory, A., *Me and Nu* (Gerrards Cross, 1970).

Healy, M., *The Old Munster Circuit: A Book of Memories and Traditions* (London, 1939).

Jenkins, R., *Gladstone* (London, 1995).

Kiberd, D., *Irish Classics* (London, 2001).

Lawlor, J., and W.H. Auden (eds), *To Nevill Coghill from Friends* (London, 1966).

Lecky, W.H., *Leaders of Public Opinion in Ireland* (London, 1912).

Leslie, S., *The Film of Memory* (London, 1938).

Lewis, G., *Somerville and Ross: The World of the Irish R.M.* (London, 1985).

Lewis, G. (ed.), *Selected Letters of Somerville and Ross* (London, 1989).

Lewis, G., *Eva Gore Booth and Esther Roper* (London, 1989).

Lewis, I.M., *Ecstatic Religion: A Study of Shamanism and Spirit Possession* (London, 1989).

Lynd, R., *Ireland a Nation* (London, 1919).

Lyons, F.S.L., *Ireland since the Famine* (London, 1973).

Maddox, B., *George's Ghosts* (London, 1999).

McLysaght, E., *The Surnames of Ireland* (Dublin, 1978).

O'Neill, J., *Blood Dark Track* (London, 2000).

Pearson, H., *Bernard Shaw* (London, 1942).

Perkins Gilman, C., *Herland* (London, 1979).

Pim, S., *The Wood and the Trees: A Biography of Augustine Henry* (Kilkenny, 1984).

Plumer, W., *At Home* (London, 1958).

Rauchbauer, O., *The Edith Œnone Somerville Archive in Drishane: A Catalogue and Evaluative Essay* (Dublin, 1995).

Robertson, N., *Crowned Harp* (Dublin, 1960).

Robinson, H., *Somerville and Ross: A Critical Appreciation* (Dublin, 1980)

Shaw, G.B., *Heartbreak House* (London, 1919).

Smyth, E., *Streaks of Life* (London, 1921).

Somerville, B., *The Chartmakers* (London, 1928).

—— *Commodore Anson's World Voyage* (London, 1934).

——*Will Mariner: A True Record of Adventure* (London, 1936).

Somerville, E., *Notes of the Horn: Hunting Verse* (London, 1934).

—— *The States through Irish Eyes* (London, 1930).

Somerville and Ross (all London imprints)

—— *An Irish Cousin* (1889).

—— *Naboth's Vineyard* (1891).

—— *Through Connemara in Governess Cart* (1892).

—— *In the Vine Country* (1893).

—— *The Real Charlotte* (1894).

—— *Beggars on Horseback* (1895).

—— *The Silver Fox* (1897).

—— *Some Experiences of an Irish RM* (1899).

—— *A Patrick's Day Hunt* (1902).

—— *All on the Irish Shore* (1903).

—— *Slipper's A.B.C. of Foxhunting* (1903).

—— *Some Irish Yesterdays* (1906).

—— *Further Experiences of an Irish RM* (1908).

—— *Dan Russel the Fox* (1911).

—— *The Story of the Discontented Little Elephant* (1912).

—— *In Mr Knox's Country* (1915).

Though Martin Ross died in 1915, Somerville continued to publish under both names:

—— *Irish Memories* (1917).

—— *Mount Music* (1919).

—— *Stray-Aways* (1920).

—— *An Enthusiast* (1921).

—— *Wheeltracks* London (1924).

—— *The Big House of Inver* (1925).

—— *French Leave* (1928).

—— *An Incorruptible Irishman* (1932).

—— *The Smile and the Tear* (1933).

—— *The Sweet Cry of Hounds* (1936).

—— *Sarah's Youth* (1938).

—— *Notions in Garrison* (1941).

—— *Happy Days* (1946).

—— *Maria, and Some Other Dogs* (1949).

St John, C., *Ethel Smyth: A Biography* (London, 1959).

Sullivan, A.M., *The Last Serjeant: The Memoirs of Serjeant A.M. Sullivan Q.C.* (London, 1952).

Thompson, D., *Woodbrook* (London, 1976).

Waldron, J., *Maamtrasna: The Murders and the Mystery* (Dublin, 1992).

Weir, J., *Back Door to the Klondyke* (Ontario, 1988).

Wills, J., *Lives of Illustrious Irishmen* (Dublin, 1840–7).

Wynne, M.M., *An Irishman and his Family: Lord Morris and Killanin* (London, 1937).

# *Index*

---

* The list that follows includes names of stories that are referred to in the text.

---

* The list that follows includes names of stories that are not referred to in the text.